Contents

iii

1993

THINKING CRITICALLY

Third Edition

John Chaffee, Ph.D.

Director, Critical Thinking and Reasoning Studies
LaGuardia Community College of the City University of New York

Houghton Mifflin Company   **Boston**

Dallas   Geneva, Illinois   Palo Alto   Princeton, New Jersey

For Jessie and Joshua

Acknowledgments

Cover artwork © 1990 M. C. Escher Heirs/Cordon Art-Baarn-Holland.
Line art drawn by Scot Graphics Center.

(Acknowledgments continued on page 584.)

Printed in the U.S.A.

ISBN: 0-395-43247-2
Library of Congress Catalog Number: 90-82999

BCDEFGHIJ-B-9987654321

Check List of Readings

Preface

Teaching a course in critical thinking is one of the most inspiring and rewarding experiences that a teacher can have. Because the thinking process is such an integral part of who we are as people, the prospect of expanding students' thinking implies expanding who they are as human beings — the perspective from which they view the world, the concepts and values they use to guide their choices, and the impact they have on the world as a result of those choices. Teaching people to become critical thinkers does not mean simply equipping them with certain intellectual tools; it involves their personal transformation and its commensurate impact on the quality of their lives and those around them. This is truly education at its most inspiring!

Thinking Critically, Third Edition, is designed to serve as a comprehensive introduction to the cognitive process while helping students develop the higher-order thinking abilities needed for academic study and career success. Based on a nationally recognized interdisciplinary program in critical and creative thinking established in 1979 at LaGuardia Community College and involving more than eight hundred students annually, *Thinking Critically* integrates various perspectives on the thinking process drawn from a variety of disciplines such as philosophy, cognitive psychology, linguistics, and the language arts (English, reading, and oral communication.)

Thinking Critically addresses a crucial need in higher education by introducing students to the rapidly emerging field of critical thinking and fostering sophisticated intellectual and language abilities. Students apply their evolving thinking abilities to a variety of subjects drawn from academic disciplines, contemporary issues, and their life experiences. *Thinking Critically* is based on the assumption, supported by research, that learning to think more effectively is a synthesizing process, knitting critical thinking abilities together with academic content and the fabric of students' experiences. Thinking learned in this way becomes a constitutive part of who students are.

With these considerations in mind, it should be clear that teaching a course in critical thinking involves embarking on high adventure, a journey that is full of unanticipated challenges and unexpected triumphs. I have written *Thinking Critically* to serve as an effective guide for this journey. In the final analysis, however, you must embark on the journey alone, relying on your experience, expertise, and critical thinking abilities to provide productive educational experiences for your students.

Features

This book has a number of distinctive characteristics that make it an effective tool for both instructors and students. *Thinking Critically*

- **teaches the fundamental thinking, reasoning, and language abilities that students need for academic success.** By focusing on the major thinking and language abilities needed in all disciplines, and by including a wide variety of readings, the text helps students perform more successfully in other courses.

- **presents foundational thinking, reasoning, and language abilities in a developmentally sequenced way.** The text begins with basic abilities and then carefully progresses to more sophisticated thinking and reasoning skills. Cognitive maps open each chapter to help students understand the thinking process as well as the interrelationship of ideas in that chapter.

- **engages students in the active process of thinking.** Interspersed exercises, discussion topics, readings, and writing assignments encourage active participation, stimulating students to critically examine their own and others' thinking and to sharpen and improve their abilities. *Thinking Critically* provides structured opportunities for students to develop their thinking processes in a progressive, reflective way.

- **provides context by continually relating critical thinking abilities to students' daily lives.** Once students learn to apply critical thinking skills to their own experience, they then apply these skills to more abstract, academic contexts. Additionally, by asking students to think critically about themselves and their experience, the text fosters their personal development as mature, responsible critical thinkers.

- **integrates the development of thinking abilities with the four language skills so crucial to success in college and careers: reading, writing, speaking, and listening.** The abundant writing assignments (short answer, paragraph, and essay), challenging readings, and discussion exercises serve to improve students' language skills.

New to the Third Edition

I have made significant changes in the third edition of *Thinking Critically*, which reflect my experiences in using the second edition, as well as the suggestions of many faculty who used the text in a variety of classes. In addition to rewriting many sections of the text, I have included these features in the new edition:

- **Additional readings.** Twenty-four new readings added to the many articles already present create a deeply diverse collection of perspectives on important, current themes. As with the previous editions, the readings are carefully integrated into the text, illustrating key concepts and stimulating students to develop their thinking abilities through critical reading and written analysis. New topics include biological patterns in addiction, euthanasia, college campus racism, social apathy, overpopulation and world hunger, the value of college education, femininity and masculinity, altruistic behavior, AIDS testing, and the psychological stages of dying.

- **New Thinking Activities.** Many new Thinking Activities, created for this edition, focus on contemporary topics such as the Tiananmen Square massacre and the disturbing rise in teenage suicide. Each Thinking Activity is carefully designed both to enlarge students' understanding of the world and to develop their critical thinking abilities through systematic exploration and reflection.

- **Expanded language sections.** The treatment of language has been expanded considerably: The previous Chapter Six, *Language,* is now two chapters: *Language as a System* (six) and *Language as a Tool* (seven). These chapters carefully explore the all-important relationship between language and thought and include newly created sections on word meaning, sentence meaning, language styles, slang, dialects, jargon, and cliches.

- **Illustrations.** The cognitive maps opening each chapter have been redesigned and redrawn to illustrate central ideas more graphically and dynamically. In addition, a variety of new illustrations have been added throughout the book to provoke thoughtful responses, present key concepts, and visually engage the reader.

- **Critical thinking videotape.** A one-hour critical thinking videotape, developed by the author, entitled "Thinking Towards Decisions" is designed to work in conjunction with Chapter Two, *Thinking Critically.* The tape uses a creative interweaving of a dramatic scenario, expert testimony, and a seminar group to develop students' critical thinking abilities.

Instructor's Resource Manual

Major work has produced a completely new *Instructor's Resource Manual* designed to help instructors tailor this book to their own courses. Part 1, "Using *Thinking Critically*," written by John Chaffee, contains an overview of the field of critical thinking as well as suggestions and exercises of interest to teachers using this text. Parts 2 and 3 — "*Thinking Critically* and Reading" and "*Think-*

ing Critically and Writing" — present assignments, useful suggestions, and syllabi for instructors using *Thinking Critically* in reading and writing courses. These materials were developed by Roberta Wright, Hill Junior College, Cecilia Macheski, La Guardia Community College, Leonard Vogt, La Guardia Community College, and Susan Huard, Manchester Community College, Connecticut. The *Manual* concludes with a bibliography.

Acknowledgments

Many people from a variety of disciplines have contributed to this book at various stages of its development. I would like to give special thanks to the following colleagues for their thorough scrutiny of the manuscript and their incisive and creative comments: Nancy Nager (Bank Street College), Thomas Fink (LaGuardia Community College), Janet Lieberman (LaGuardia Community College), Karsten Struhl (Adelphi University), Diane Ducat (LaGuardia Community College), Daniel Lynch (LaGuardia Community College), Susan Lowndes (Rockland Community College), and James Friel (SUNY at Farmingdale).

The following reviewers also provided detailed and systematic evaluations that were of great help in preparing the third edition:

Anatole Anton, *San Francisco State University*
Kathleen M. Bernstein, *Mohawk Valley Community College, New York*
Frances Bixler, *Southwest Missouri State University*
Ann S. Butler, *Elon College, North Carolina*
Stephen Coble, *Tennessee Technological University*
Sue Hackett, *Rio Hondo College, California*
Kathy Kemper, *Northwood Institute, Texas*
Jane M. Harmon, *Lakewood Community College, Minnesota*
Steve Jones, *Wake Technical College, North Carolina*
David B. Kellish, *Midlands Technical College, South Carolina*
Joanne Kurfiss, *Santa Clara University, California*
Ann Jared Lewald, *Tennessee Technological University*
Richard F. Malena, *Phoenix College, Arizona*
Patricia A. Malinowski, *Community College of the Finger Lakes, New York*
Joel Rudinow, *Sonoma State University, California*

I would like to express my special gratitude to Sandra Dickinson of LaGuardia Community College, who helped shape and develop the expanded materials on language in Chapter Six, *Language as a System*, and Chapter

Seven, *Language as a Tool*. Her expertise in linguistics and creative insights into the crucially significant relationship between language and thought provided the theoretical structure and much of the content for key sections in these chapters, including sections on word meaning, sentence meaning, and using language in social contexts. She also contributed the perceptive and engaging essay, "When Is a Kamoodgel Not a Kamoodgel?" in Chapter Six.

I would like to acknowledge my debt to Richard Paul, Director of the Center for Critical Thinking at Sonoma State University, who is a prime mover in the field of critical thinking. He has enriched and deepened my thinking through his generous friendship, his many articles, and the acclaimed Critical Thinking Conference, which he hosts each year. Similarly, my thanks go to Robert Swartz, founder of the Critical and Creative Thinking program at the University of Massachusetts, for freely sharing his significant work in the field and his personal counsel.

Special acknowledgment is given to Curtis Miles, Director of the Center for Reasoning Studies at Piedmont Technical College, who generously provided both materials and guidance when I first began working in the area of critical thinking. His pioneer work in problem solving provided the original basis for Chapter Three, *Solving Problems*. I am also indebted to Professor Eric Linder-mayer of Suffolk County Community College for his work in the area of concept development. His teaching materials provided a basis for key ideas in Chapter Eight, *Forming and Applying Concepts*.

I would also like to thank the following colleagues for their valuable contributions: Anita Ulesky (Suffolk Community College), Harriet Schenk (Caldwell College), Ana Maria Hernandez (LaGuardia Community College), Joan Richardson (LaGuardia Community College), Daniel Kurland (Johns Hopkins University), Mary Beth Early (LaGuardia Community College), Neil Rossman (LaGuardia Community College), Robert Millman (LaGuardia Community College), Gilbert Muller (LaGuardia Community College), and Norma Rowe (Minneapolis Community College).

My grateful acknowledgment is extended to the National Endowment for the Humanities for their generous support of the Critical Thinking and Reasoning Studies program at LaGuardia. In addition, I would like to offer my deepest gratitude to the faculty members who have participated so creatively in the program; to the administrators at LaGuardia for their steadfast support of the program's development; and to the countless students whose enthusiasm and commitment to learning are the soul of this text.

I have been privileged to work with very special people at Houghton Mifflin Company who have respected the purposes of this book while giving it the kind of wise and imaginative attention that every author hopes for.

Finally, I want to thank my wife, Heide, my children, Jessie and Joshua, and my parents, Charlotte and Hubert Chaffee, for their ongoing understanding and support.

Although this is a published book, it continues to be a work in progress. In this spirit, I invite you to share your experiences with the text by sending me your comments and suggestions. I hope that this book serves as an effective vehicle for your own creative and critical thinking resources. Address your letter to me % Marketing Services, College Division, Houghton Mifflin Company, One Beacon Street, Boston, MA 02108.

J. C.

Solving Problems
What is the problem?
What are the alternatives?
What are the advantages and disadvantages?
What is the solution?
How well is the solution working?

THINKING:
An active, purposeful,
organized process that we use
to make sense of the world.

Analyzing Issues
What is the issue?
What is the evidence?
What are the arguments?
What is the conclusion?

Working Toward Goals
How do goals function in our lives?
What is the appropriate goal?
What are the steps and strategies?

Thinking can be developed and improved by becoming aware of,
carefully examining, and practicing the thinking process.

THINKING IS THE EXTRAORDINARY PROCESS we use every waking moment to make sense of our world and our lives. Successful thinking enables us to solve the problems we are continually confronted with, to make intelligent decisions, and to achieve the goals that give our lives purpose and fulfillment. It is an activity that is crucial for living in a meaningful way.

This book is designed to help you understand the complex, incredible process of thinking. You might think of this text as a map to guide you in exploring the way your mind operates. This book is also founded on the conviction that we can *improve* our thinking abilities by carefully examining our thinking process and working systematically through challenging activities. Thinking is an active process, and we learn to do it better by becoming aware of and actually using the thought process, not simply by reading about it. By participating in the thinking activities contained in the text and applying these ideas to your own experiences, you will find that your thinking — and language — abilities are becoming sharper and more powerful.

In this chapter we will examine three areas of our lives in which we use the thinking process to understand our world and make informed decisions:

1. Solving problems
2. Working toward our goals
3. Analyzing issues

Solving Problems

My best friend is addicted to drugs, but he won't admit it. Jack always liked to drink, but I never thought too much about it. After all, a lot of people like to drink socially, get relaxed and have a good time. But over the last few years he's started using other drugs as well as alcohol, and it's ruining his life. He's stopped taking classes at the college and will soon lose his job if he doesn't change. Last week I told him that I was really worried about him, but he told me that he has no drug problem and that in any case it really isn't any of my business. I just don't know what to do. I've known Jack since we were in grammar school together and he's a wonderful

```
person. It's as if he's in the grip of some terrible force
and I'm powerless to help him.
```

In working through this problem, the student who wrote this description will have to think carefully and systematically in order to reach a solution. When we think effectively in situations like this, we usually ask ourselves a series of questions, although we may not be aware of the process that our minds are going through.

1. What is the *problem*?
2. What are the *alternatives*?
3. What are the *advantages* and/or *disadvantages* of each alternative?
4. What is the *solution*?
5. How well is the solution *working*?

Let's explore these questions further — and the thinking process that they represent — by applying them to the problem described here. Put yourself in the position of the student whose friend seems to have a serious drug problem.

What Is the Problem?

There are a variety of ways to define the problem facing this student. In the space provided, describe what you think is the problem.

_____

_____

_____

What Are the Alternatives?

In dealing with this problem, you have a wide variety of possible actions to consider before selecting the best choices. Identify some of the alternatives you might consider.

1. Speak to your friend in a candid and forceful way to convince him that he has a serious problem.

2. _____

3. _____

4. _____

What Are the Advantages and/or Disadvantages of Each Alternative?

For each of the alternatives you identified, evaluate the strengths and weaknesses so you can weigh your choices and decide on the best course of action.

1. Speak to your friend in a candid and forceful way to convince him that he has a serious problem.
   Advantage: He may respond to your direct emotional appeal, acknowledge that he has a problem, and seek help.
   Disadvantage: He may react angrily, further alienating you from him and making it more difficult for you to have any influence on him.

2. _____

   Advantage: _____

   Disadvantage: _____

3. _____

   Advantage: _____

   Disadvantage: _____

4. _____

   Advantage: _____

   Disadvantage: _____

What Is the Solution?

After evaluating the various alternatives, select what you think is the most effective alternative for solving the problem and describe the sequence of steps you would take to act on the alternative.

Alternative: _____

Steps:

1. _____

2. _____

3. _____

How Well Is the Solution Working?

The final step in the process is to review the solution and decide whether it is working well. If it is not, we must be able to modify our solution or perhaps choose an alternate solution we had disregarded earlier. Describe what results would inform you that the alternative you selected to pursue was working well or poorly.

_____

_____

_____

If you concluded that your alternative was working poorly, describe what your next action would be.

_____

_____

_____

In this situation, trying to figure out the best way to assist our friend recognize his problem and seek treatment leads to a series of decisions. This is what the thinking process is all about — trying to make sense of what is going on in our world and acting appropriately in response. When we solve problems effectively, our thinking process exhibits a coherent organization. It follows the general approach we have just explored.

1. What is the *problem*?
2. What are the *alternatives* available to me?
3. What are the *advantages* and/or *disadvantages* of each alternative?
4. What is the *solution*?
5. How well is the solution *working*?

If we can understand the way our mind operates when we are thinking effectively, then we can apply this understanding to improve our thinking in new, challenging situations. In Chapter Three, *Solving Problems*, we will explore a more sophisticated version of this problem-solving approach and will apply it to a variety of complex, difficult problems.

<u>THINKING ACTIVITY</u>

1.1   ▶ 1. Describe in specific detail an important problem you have solved recently.

2. Explain how you went about solving the problem. What were the steps, strategies, and approaches you used to understand the problem and make an informed decision?

3. Analyze the organization exhibited by your thinking process by completing the five-step problem-solving method we have been exploring.

4. Share your problem with other members of the class and have them try to analyze and solve it. Then explain the solution you arrived at. ◀

<u>THINKING ACTIVITY</u>

1.2   ▶ Solving problems effectively requires knowledge and expertise about the situation we are dealing with. For example, to solve a complex, challenging problem like addiction, we have to ask — and be able to answer — questions such as: What are the various causes of addiction and how do they interact with one another? What treatment options are available? What are the risks and benefits of different forms of intervention? The following article, which first appeared in the *New York Times*, addresses some of these important questions. Review the article and then answer the questions that follow it.

SCIENTISTS PINPOINT BRAIN IRREGULARITIES IN DRUG ADDICTS *by Daniel Goleman*

A radically new approach to fighting drug abuse is emerging from discoveries of brain irregularities that make certain people much quicker to become addicted than others, and much harder to cure.

For several years, scientists have suspected that at least some drug addicts suffer imbalances in brain chemistry that make them vulnerable to depression, anxiety or intense restlessness. For such people, addiction becomes a kind of self-medication in which drugs correct the chemical imbalance and bring a sort of relief.

Now researchers are beginning to identify the particular imbalances associated with addictions to particular drugs like cocaine, heroin or alcohol. Because scientists believe many of these imbalances are inherited, they are seeking to identify genetic markers and other evidence, such as behavioral signs, that indicate a person is vulnerable.

Eventually, scientists say, this research will result in an entirely new strategy for fighting drug addiction: early identification of those most prone to a specific addiction and specific treatments to correct the chemical imbalances implicated.

The new line of research is generating rising enthusiasm among Federal health officials. The Alcohol, Drug Abuse and Mental Health Administration increased its support for studies on the genetic and biological basis of alcoholism alone to $53.5 million in the fiscal year 1991, up from $41.7 million in 1989.

"We already can breed lab animals with these irregularities who selectively crave opiates or stimulants," said Dr. Frederick K. Goodwin, administrator of the agency. "There's a direct analog to humans."

No one can yet say precisely what portion of addicts have the biological patterns. Dr. Goodwin estimated that a third to half of those addicted to a given drug may have genetic susceptibilities to it.

The biological approach took a big step forward in April, when researchers reported the identification of a specific gene that may play a key role in some forms of alcoholism, as well as in other addictions. Of the alcoholics they studied, 77 percent had the gene. The discovery, announced by researchers at the University of Texas and the University of California at Los Angeles, is for a gene linked to the receptors for dopamine, a brain chemical involved in the sensation of pleasure.

Such discoveries, scientists say, herald biological markers that may one day make possible early identification of those most at risk of becoming addicted, allowing more effective prevention or treatment.

"My guiding hypothesis is that there are specific neurotransmitter irregularities for each addiction," said Dr. Kenneth Blum, director of the division of addictive diseases at the University of Texas Health Science Center in San Antonio, one of those who discovered the gene involved in alcoholism.

Some conditions that lead to addiction, like depression, can already be treated with medications. But some substances used to treat addicts, like methadone, are themselves addictive. Scientists are seeking to tailor new drugs that will correct the imbalances without causing other addictions.

However, many social scientists criticize the biological research, saying it is wrong to focus only on biology and ignore the social forces at play, especially among the urban poor.

"I object to seeing the vulnerability in the person rather than in their poverty," said Robert Jessor, a sociologist at the University of Colorado.

The greatest risk of drug abuse, he points out, is among children who come from impoverished, single-parent families in drug-ridden neighborhoods, with no strong counterbalance from church or school.

Other objections are legal and ethical. "I'd be very concerned about the issue of consent," said Leonard Rubenstein, director of the Mental Health Law Project in Washington, an advocacy group for the mentally ill. "Even if the scientific evidence turns out to be strong, people have the right to refuse being tested or given medications."

He said he also worried that people would be denied insurance, rejected for employment or otherwise stigmatized.

Some backers of the new approach acknowledge these problems but say that, given the huge social costs of addiction, the benefits outweigh the risks. They said biological vulnerabilities may help untangle the puzzle of why some people can experiment with powerful drugs like cocaine and never become addicted, while others become addicts almost overnight.

"For people who are biologically predisposed, the first drink or dose of the drug is immensely reinforcing, in a way others just don't experience it," said Ralph Tarter, a psychologist at the Western Psychiatric Institute and Clinic in Pittsburgh. "Many recovering drug abusers tell me, 'The moment I took my first drug, I felt normal for the first time.' It stabilizes them physiologically, at least in the short term."

Scientists still express some uncertainty on the specific biological details of these vulnerabilities. But from dozens of studies, prototypes are emerging of the brain chemical imbalance, temperament and life history that typifies those drawn to particular drugs.

Depression: First Confidence, Then Addiction

The woman was depressed and overweight as a teen-ager, until a friend gave her amphetamines. She started taking them regularly at 17 to lose weight; they also made her feel confident, even buoyant. She was 19 when her boyfriend offered her some cocaine. She became addicted within a week. By 25, she had an out-of-wedlock child, a chaotic life and a $5,000-a-week cocaine habit that she supported by helping distribute the drug. She was hospitalized twice for the deep depression that would come whenever she tried to stop taking cocaine.

But when Dr. Edward Khantzian, a psychiatrist at Harvard Medical

School, treated her with a small daily dose of the stimulant Ritalin she made a dramatic recovery. She has not had cocaine in eight years.

For Dr. Khantzian, a leading proponent of the "self medication" theory of drug abuse, such alternate drug treatments, which seem to treat the biological irregularities underlying the addiction, are a logical approach. Although Dr. Khantzian acknowledged that using Ritalin is controversial because it can be addictive, he said he believed it was effective in weaning his patient from cocaine because it acts on dopamine receptors.

Some kinds of depression are related to low levels of dopamine in the brain, and many antidepressants, like Ritalin, work by increasing dopamine levels. Cocaine and other stimulants do the same, though by a different biochemical route.

"We suspect that cocaine is a way certain people medicate themselves for depression," said Dr. Khantzian.

The depression-cocaine link has emerged in several studies. For example, research in 1986 with 30 consecutive patients admitted for treatment of cocaine addiction in a drug unit at Yale Medical School found that half suffered from pre-existing depression. And the heavier the cocaine habit, the deeper the depression.

Exhilaration: A Natural "High" Is Not Enough

He is a 26-year-old advertising executive whose therapist describes him as "naturally outgoing, energetic and hyped up." As a child he was the class clown; in high school his extroversion made him a popular class officer. In college he partied a lot. A few years out of college someone offered him cocaine at a party. He loved it: it made him intensely exhilarated, more chatty than ever. Over the next year he began needing increasingly large doses to get his high.

It was then that he turned to crack, the smokable, fast-acting form of cocaine. His first hit of crack, he said, "was like an orgasm." During the next three hours, he took crack eight times; within a day, all he could think of was getting more crack.

According to Dr. Roy King, a psychiatrist at Stanford Medical School who treated the advertising executive, such energetic, outgoing people often have unusually high levels of dopamine, in contrast to the depressed cocaine user, who has too little.

"If you're highly extroverted, even slightly manic, by temperament, cocaine augments your natural bent," said Dr. King. "For people who

are naturally bubbling with excitement, crack seems to intensify the normal biology of a state they seek: it's an exhilarating, exciting high."

In a 1989 study of 70 cocaine abusers, Dr. King found that those
who abused cocaine the most and longest, in all forms, were more
outgoing.

"Cocaine makes more dopamine available to the brain, and they already have higher levels of dopamine," Dr. King said. "Smaller
amounts of cocaine would have greater effects with them, making it
more rewarding than in most people. They become more readily addicted to it because they get more intense pleasure from a given dose.
That makes crack, the most intense form, especially appealing."

Anger: Trying to Escape His Pent-Up Rage

As a boy, he had been beaten by his father every week or so. His mother
was distant and insensitive. He grew up with a brooding resentment;
like his father, he was quick to become enraged. In his early 30's, he
grew deeply embittered after a series of relationships ended because of
his quick temper. A pharmacist now, he could get morphine on the sly
easily; more than anything else, he said, he liked its calming effects on
his bitter resentment and mounting rage.

The angry pharmacist, said Dr. Khantzian, is typical of more than 400
patients he has treated for narcotic addiction. Their histories reveal life-
long difficulty handling rage; opiates like heroin and morphine, they
say, help them feel normal and relaxed.

"They don't take opiates for pleasure, but to regulate emotions that
are out of control," said Dr. Khantzian. "Opiates are a powerful, anti-
rage, anti-aggression drug. It makes them feel normal."

Dr. Khantzian speculates that people who are in a chronic state of
agitation and anger suffer from a depletion of opioids, the neurotrans-
mitters that drugs like heroin imitate in the brain.

"They take to heroin or morphine because they're seeking opioids
from outside to feel calm again," said Dr. Khantzian.

About 15 percent of addicts "look strictly for heroin, not other drugs,"
said Dr. Kenneth Blum, a psychiatrist at the University of Texas Health
Science Center in San Antonio.

In his book "Alcohol and the Addictive Brain," to be published later
this year by Macmillan, Dr. Blum proposes that the "mu receptor," a
site for a form of morphine that occurs naturally in the human brain, is
defective in those addicted to opiates.

Anxiety: The Need for Poise Leads to the Bottle

Even as a child, he was always anxious. But in junior high, his anxiety increased, especially when he was around girls. In high school, he discovered that alcohol let him be glib, funny, charming. And he could get it easily, at home: his father was an alcoholic. By college, he was drinking to ready himself for any social encounter: he would sometimes drink before going to class or at lunch. In his mid-30's, working as an accountant, he drank throughout the day; it was having alcohol on his breath during I.R.S. audits that lost him his job and brought him to treatment.

Now that his underlying anxiety has been treated with behavior therapy, he has had no trouble staying sober the past year and a half.

Underlying the accountant's pattern of behavior is an imbalance in the brain's receptors for GABA, a neurotransmitter that regulates anxiety among other things, according to Dr. Howard Moss, a psychiatrist at the University of Pittsburgh who treated him. "Our data suggest that the less GABA activity, the more tense you feel," Dr. Moss said.

Sedatives, including alcohol, make cells with receptors for GABA less reactive, increasing the amount of GABA that is active in the brain, thus relieving tension.

In a new study, published in April in the journal Biological Psychiatry, Dr. Moss showed that sons of alcoholic fathers had lower levels of GABA and higher tension levels than men whose fathers were not alcoholic. But when they drank a glass of vodka, the GABA levels of the first group rose to levels equivalent to those of the other men and their tension declined.

"Those sons of alcoholics who are unusually anxious drink to ease their tension, which is due to a perturbation of GABA," said Dr. Moss. "Our hypothesis is that this GABA irregularity is a trait marker linked to a genetic vulnerability to alcoholism."

In Dr. Moss's and Dr. Khantzian's view, people with this pattern are also vulnerable to abusing sedatives other than alcohol, like tranquilizers.

Treatment: The Need to Find the Craving Early

The immediate implication is to treat addicts with corrective medications. "Many traditional treatments for alcoholism may be unsuccessful because they do not address the disturbances that predisposed the person to alcoholism in the first place," said Dr. Tarter of the Western Psychiatric Institute and Clinic in Pittsburgh.

"A combination of early detection and pharmaceutical intervention is the most sensible way to proceed," said Dr. Goodwin of the Alcohol, Drug Abuse and Mental Health Administration.

For some addictions, there may be a critical period in life, such as late adolescence and early adulthood, when the risk of addiction is highest. Offering a medication that corrects the vulnerability during those years is one potential treatment strategy. For instance, for those whose susceptibility to alcoholism is due to a level of serotonin that is too low, Dr. Goodwin said, "if they are protected by a drug that enhances and stabilizes serotonin during those years when they are most vulnerable to alcoholism, then later in life they may be able to drink socially with low risk." For the dopamine irregularities seen in cocaine addiction, medications now used as anticonvulsants might counter the craving for cocaine by blocking the dopamine center, he added.

Dr. Goodwin said there was a need for new medications designed to correct the exact irregularities being identified for each addiction. "We're launching a major medication development program to find drugs that react with the specific receptors to reduce craving," he said. "Eighty percent of those in therapy programs who leave too early do so because of craving." ■

1. Explain the new approach to fighting addiction described in this article.

2. In the article, a sociologist named Robert Jessor objects to an exclusively biological approach to addiction because it ignores the social forces at play, especially among the urban poor. He states: "I object to seeing the vulnerability in the person rather than in their poverty." Explain how social forces can influence people to become addicted. Use examples to illustrate your explanations.

3. Many psychologists and psychiatrists believe that addictive behavior is the result of emotional dysfunction, often originating in the person's family. From this perspective, the most effective approach to dealing with addiction is understanding how these addictive patterns became established, recognizing the emotional needs they are expressing, and then devising strategies to overcome them. Describe an experience with addictive behavior (drinking, smoking, overeating, gambling, etc.) that you or someone you know well has experienced, and explain how the addiction was overcome.

4. Some believe that to overcome addiction, people must first accept the responsibility for their situation and then exercise their freedom of choice to

change. Explain what role you think that free choice and responsibility play in breaking the cycle of addiction. ◄

Working Toward Goals

As we have just seen, thinking helps us make sense of the world by giving us the means to solve problems in a careful and organized way. Thinking also helps us make sense of the world by enabling us to identify *goals* in our lives and to plan ways to reach these goals.

How Do Goals Function?

Goals are those aims in life that we are striving to achieve. Consider the following activities:

• A person running for a bus
• A person trying to throw a ball through a metal hoop
• A student studying for an exam

In each of these activities, a person behaves in a certain way for a specific purpose, with a goal in mind. Most of our behavior has a purpose or purposes, a goal or goals, that we are trying to reach. We can begin to discover the goals of our actions by asking the question *why* of what we are doing or thinking.

Answer the following questions:

Why did you come to school today? _____

_____

This question may have stimulated any number of responses:

• Because I want to pass this class.
• Because I want to get my money's worth.
• Because I was curious about the topics to be discussed.

Whatever your response, it reveals at least some of your goals in attending class. We attempt to make sense of what people, including ourselves, are doing by figuring out the goal or purpose of the behavior, by asking the reason *why*.

- *Why* is that person running for a bus?
- *Why* is that person trying to throw a ball through a metal hoop?
- *Why* is that student studying for an exam?

In answering the question *why*, we often find that our answer leads us to ask *why* again:

- *Why* is that person trying to throw a ball through a metal hoop?
- Because he/she wants to score points.
- *Why* does he/she want to score points?

Asking *why* about our goal usually leads to additional *why* questions because a specific goal in our lives is part of larger goal patterns. For example, the person throwing the ball through the metal hoop is pursuing the goal of scoring points, which is part of the larger goal of winning the game, which is part of the larger goal of keeping the team in first place, and so on.

Of course, many of our actions are directed at achieving more than one goal. For example, in addition to the competitive aspects of playing basketball, the player might also be interested in getting exercise, having fun, and socializing with friends. Some of these more complex goal patterns might be expressed in the following diagram:

Because of the ways our goals are organized, one approach we can use to try to discover our goal patterns is to ask *why* we did something, then to ask *why* about the answer, and so on. Although this approach is reminiscent of the maddening *why* game played by children at grownups' expense, it can lead to some interesting results, as revealed in the following activity.

Using your response to the question "Why did you come to school today?" as a starting point, try to discover part of your goal patterns by asking a series of *why* questions. After each response, ask *why* again. Try to give thoughtful and specific answers.

Why did you come to school today? *Because:* _____

_____

Why do you want to _____

Because: _____

Why do you want to _____

Because: _____

As you may have found in completing the activity, this "child's game" begins to reveal the networks of goals that structure our experience and leads us to progressively more profound questions regarding our basic goals in life, such as "Why do I want to be successful?" These are complex issues that require thorough and ongoing exploration. A first step in this direction is to examine the way we work to achieve our goals, the "goal" of this section. As we saw in the section on solving problems, if we can understand the way our mind functions when we think effectively, then we can use this knowledge to improve our thinking abilities. This in turn will enable us to deal more effectively with new situations we encounter.

Goals play extremely important roles in our lives by organizing our thinking and giving our lives order and direction. Whether we are preparing food, preparing for an exam, or preparing for a career, goals suggest courses of action and influence our decisions. By performing these functions, goals help make life meaningful. They give us something to aim for and lead to a sense of accomplishment when we reach them, like the satisfaction you may have received by graduating from high school or entering college. It is our thinking abilities that enable us first to identify what our goals are and then to plan how to reach these goals.

THINKING ACTIVITY

1.3 ▶ 1. Describe an important goal you recently achieved.

2. Explain the reasoning process that led you to select this goal.

3. Identify the steps you had to take to achieve this goal in the order in which they were taken and estimate the amount of time each step took.

4. Describe how you felt when you achieved your goal. ◄

What Are the Appropriate Goals?

Thinking effectively plays a crucial role in helping to achieve our goals by enabling us to perform two distinct, thought-interrelated activities.

1. Identifying the appropriate goals

2. Devising effective plans and strategies to achieve our goals

Identifying our immediate or "short-term" goals tends to be a fairly simple procedure: activities for the day, plans for Saturday night, aims for the next few weeks. Identifying the appropriate "long-term" goals, however, is a much more complex and challenging process: career aims, plans for marriage and children, goals for personal development. Think, for example, about the people you know who have full-time jobs. How many of these people get up in the morning excited and looking forward to going to work that day? If it's a fairly low number, what do you think accounts for this fact? One explanation is that some of these people may not have been successful in identifying the most appropriate career goals for them, goals that reflect their interests and talents and reward them with a sense of fulfillment.

In many areas of life, in fact, people are often unaware of the most appropriate goals for themselves. For example, people often have goals that are not really their own but have been inherited from someone else. We may be studying for a certain line of work because that is what our parents want for us — not necessarily what we want for ourselves. Or maybe we want to get married because "everybody's getting married" — not necessarily because we want to. It is important for us to determine that our goals are our own goals, not someone else's.

Have you ever been in the position of pursuing someone else's goal? Consider the following student's passage, which describes this dilemma.

> The goal I inherited was to be a nurse. Since my mother was
> a nurse, she wanted me to be one. In fact, she wanted all
> of her daughters to be nurses. They had all tried it and
> didn't like it at all. She said I would be very happy but
> I tried and hated it. It's not that I don't like helping
> others, it's just that it's not for me. I was very con-
> fused and didn't know what to do. I finally spoke to her

```
and explained that being a nurse holds no future for
me -- I'm not happy in that field of work. She was hurt,
but better her than me for the rest of my life.
```

How do we identify the most appropriate long-term goals for ourselves? To begin with, we need to develop an in-depth understanding of ourselves: our talents, our interests, the things that stimulate us and bring us satisfaction. We also need to discover what our possibilities are, either through research or actual experience. Of course, appropriate goals do not necessarily remain the same throughout our lives. It is unlikely that the goals we had as eight-year-olds are the ones we have now. As we grow, change, and mature, it is natural for our goals to change and evolve as well. The key point is that we should keep examining our goals to make sure that they reflect our own thinking and current interests.

What Are the Steps to Take?

Research studies* have shown that high-achieving people are able to envision a detailed, three-dimensional picture of their future in which their goals and aspirations are clearly inscribed. In addition, they are able to construct a mental plan that includes the sequence of steps they will have to take, the amount of time each step will involve, and strategies for overcoming the obstacles they are likely to encounter. Such realistic and compelling concepts of the future enable these people to make sacrifices in the present to achieve their long-term goals. Of course, they may modify these goals as circumstances change and they acquire more information, but they retain a well-defined flexible plan that charts their life course.

On the other hand, research also reveals that people who are low achievers tend to live in the present and the past. Their concepts of the future are vague and ill defined: "I want to be happy," or "I want a high-paying job." This unclear concept of the future makes it difficult for them to identify the most appropriate goals for them, to devise effective strategies for achieving these goals, and to make the necessary sacrifices in the present that will ensure that the future becomes a reality.

Many of the topics, concepts, and abilities explored in this book will help you identify the goals most appropriate for you and will also assist you in

---

* See, for example: D. E. Freyre, "Future Orientation and High Academic Achievement in Inner-City College Students," Presented to the 94th Annual Convention of the American Psychological Association, August 19, 1986.

developing effective plans of action for successfully achieving the goals you have established.

1.4   ▶ Apply some of the insights we have been examining about working toward goals to a situation in your own life.

1. Describe as specifically as possible an important goal that you want to achieve in your life. Your goal can be academic, professional, or personal. For example, your goal might be to attain a certain grade point average for the term, to become a lawyer, or to quit smoking.

2. Explain the reasons that led you to select the goal that you did.

3. Explain why you believe that your goal is appropriate.

4. Identify both the major and minor steps you will have to take to achieve your goal. List your steps in the order they need to be taken and indicate how much time you think each step will take.

5. Identify the most important problem you have encountered (or you expect to encounter) in pursuing your goal, and analyze how you might approach solving the problem by using the method we developed in the last section, namely, by asking the following sequence of questions.

    a. What is the problem?

    b. What are the alternatives?

    c. What are the advantages and/or disadvantages of each alternative?

    d. What is the solution?

    e. How well is the solution working?

As an example, the following passage describes the professional goal of one student who is using her thinking abilities to achieve her aims. The problems the student faces in achieving her goal are analyzed following the passage.

> The most important goal in my life at this point is to be—
> come a registered professional nurse. I have been working
> as a licensed practical nurse in a city hospital for the
> past fifteen years. I have always enjoyed my work and al—
> ways looked forward to being there, but for the last three
> years changes by the administration have been making
> things difficult for the practical nurse. At one time we
> were allowed to be in charge of a unit if there were no

registered nurses on duty, we were allowed to administer IV medication and to assess patients' needs and follow through on that assessment. We were also allowed to count narcotics and to work in intensive care units. With these functions taken away from my job description I feel I am becoming stagnant, so I made the decision to go back to school and further my education.

LaGuardia's nursing program offered the courses I needed, and there was no waiting list to enter the pre-nursing program. This is my second quarter. I know it's not going to be easy because I have a full-time job and I need a full-time salary, so I never considered working part-time. I have taken the following steps to keep from becoming discouraged and to make sure I reach my goal. First, I set a time limit. I plan to be finished in two and a half to three years. Second, I plan to attend winter and summer quarters and, third, I plan to have my work sched-ule changed to work weekends and to give me more time dur-ing the week for my studies. Fourth, I will get tutoring when needed.

The most important problems I face are not having enough time for school and not being able to afford to work part-time.

Alternatives:

1. Work part-time
2. Go to school part-time
3. Seek financial help
4. Not go to school at all

Advantages:	*Disadvantages:*
1. Will not be as tired	1. Salary doesn't cover expenses
2. Pace a little slower	2. Will take much longer
3. Good for school expenses	3. Not enough for home needs
4. No headaches at all	4. Will remain in same situation at work

Solution:

Have my hours changed at work so I can go to school full-time and keep my full-time salary. Save my vacation time and use it for school; it will give me more time. ◄

In the following passage from his autobiography, Malcolm X, a civil rights activist and black Muslim leader who was assassinated in 1965, describes the steps he took in pursuit of a significant goal while serving time in prison. During his stay at Norfolk Prison Colony, Malcolm X began writing letters to former friends as well as to various government officials. His frustration in trying to express his ideas led him to a course of self-education.

From THE AUTOBIOGRAPHY OF MALCOLM X
by Malcolm X with Alex Haley

I became increasingly frustrated at not being able to express what I wanted to convey in letters that I wrote, especially those to Mr. Elijah Muhammad. In the street, I had been the most articulate hustler out there — I had commanded attention when I said something. But now, trying to write simple English, I not only wasn't articulate, I wasn't even functional. How would I sound writing in slang, the way I would *say* it, something such as, "Look, daddy, let me pull your coat about a cat, Elijah Muhammad —"

Many who today hear me somewhere in person, or on television, or those who read something I've said, will think I went to school far beyond the eighth grade. This impression is due entirely to my prison studies.

It had really begun back in the Charlestown Prison, when Bimbi first made me feel envy of his stock of knowledge. Bimbi had always taken charge of any conversation he was in, and I had tried to emulate him. But every book I picked up had few sentences which didn't contain anywhere from one to nearly all of the words that might as well have been in Chinese. When I just skipped those words, of course, I really ended up with little idea of what the book said. So I had come to the Norfolk Prison Colony still going through only book-reading motions. Pretty soon, I would have quit even these motions, unless I had received the motivation that I did.

I saw that the best thing I could do was get hold of a dictionary — to study, to learn some words. I was lucky enough to reason also that I should try to improve my penmanship. It was sad. I couldn't even write in a straight line. It was both ideas together that moved me to request a dictionary along with some tablets and pencils from the Norfolk Prison Colony school.

I spent two days just riffling uncertainly through the dictionary's pages. I'd never realized so many words existed! I didn't know *which* words I needed to learn. Finally, just to start some kind of action, I began copying.

In my slow, painstaking, ragged handwriting, I copied into my tablet everything printed on that first page, down to the punctuation marks.

I believe it took me a day. Then, aloud, I read back, to myself, everything I'd written on the tablet. Over and over, aloud, to myself, I read my own handwriting.

I woke up the next morning, thinking about those words — immensely proud to realize that not only had I written so much at one time, but I'd written words that I never knew were in the world. Moreover, with a little effort, I also could remember what many of these words meant. I reviewed the words whose meanings I didn't remember. Funny thing, from the dictionary first page right now, that "aardvark" springs to my mind. The dictionary had a picture of it, a long-tailed, long-eared, burrowing African mammal, which lives off termites caught by sticking out its tongue as an anteater does for ants.

I was so fascinated that I went on — I copied the dictionary's next page. And the same experience came when I studied that. With every succeeding page, I also learned of people and places and events from history. Actually the dictionary is like a miniature encyclopedia. Finally the dictionary's A section had filled a whole tablet — and I went on into the B's. That was the way I started copying what eventually became the entire dictionary. It went a lot faster after so much practice helped me to pick up handwriting speed. Between what I wrote in my tablet, and writing letters, during the rest of my time in prison I would guess I wrote a million words.

I suppose it was inevitable that as my word-base broadened, I could for the first time pick up a book and read and now begin to understand what the book was saying. Anyone who has read a great deal can imagine the new world that opened. Let me tell you something: from then until I left that prison, in every free moment I had, if I was not reading in the library, I was reading on my bunk. You couldn't have gotten me out of books with a wedge. Between Mr. Muhammad's teachings, my correspondence, my visitors — usually Ella and Reginald — and my reading of books, months passed without my even thinking about being imprisoned. In fact, up to then, I never had been so truly free in my life.

The Norfolk Prison Colony's library was in the school building. A variety of classes was taught there by instructors who came from such places as Harvard and Boston universities. The weekly debates between inmate teams were also held in the school building. You would be astonished to know how worked up convict debaters and audiences would get over subjects like "Should Babies Be Fed Milk?"

Available on the prison library's shelves were books on just about every general subject. Much of the big private collection that Parkhurst had willed to the prison was still in crates and boxes in the back of the library — thousands of old books. Some of them looked ancient: covers faded, old-time parchment-looking binding. Parkhurst, I've mentioned, seemed to have been principally interested in history and religion. He had the money and the special interest to have a lot of books that you wouldn't have in general circulation. Any college library would have been lucky to get that collection.

As you can imagine, especially in a prison where there was heavy emphasis on rehabilitation, an inmate was smiled upon if he demonstrated an unusually intense interest in books. There was a sizable number of well-read inmates, especially the popular debaters. Some were said by many to be practically walking encyclopedias. They were almost celebrities. No university would ask any student to devour literature as I did when this new world opened to me, of being able to read and *understand*.

I read more in my room than in the library itself. An inmate who was known to read a lot could check out more than the permitted maximum number of books. I preferred reading in the total isolation of my own room.

When I had progressed to really serious reading, every night at about ten P.M. I would be outraged with the "lights out." It always seemed to catch me right in the middle of something engrossing.

Fortunately, right outside my door was a corridor light that cast a glow into my room. The glow was enough to read by, once my eyes adjusted to it. So when "lights out" came, I would sit on the floor where I could continue reading in that glow.

At one-hour intervals the night guards paced past every room. Each time I heard the approaching footsteps, I jumped into bed and feigned sleep. And as soon as the guard passed, I got back out of bed onto the floor area of that light-glow, where I would read for another fifty-eight minutes — until the guard approached again. That went on until three or four every morning. Three or four hours of sleep a night was enough for me. Often in the years in the streets I had slept less than that. ■

This passage touches on a variety of important issues related to developing our thinking and language abilities. We can analyze some of the issues raised by answering the following questions:

1. As described in this passage, what is the overall goal that Malcolm X decides to pursue?

   _____

   _____

2. Malcolm X states that, although he was an articulate "street hustler," this ability was of little help in expressing his ideas in writing. Explain the differences between expressing your ideas verbally and in writing.

   _____

   _____

   _____

3. Malcolm X envied one of the other inmates, Bimbi, because his stock of knowledge enabled him to take charge of any conversation he was in. Explain why knowledge — and our ability to use it — leads to power in our dealings with others.

   _____

   _____

   _____

4. Malcolm X states about pursuing his studies in prison that "up to then, I never had been so truly free in my life." Explain what you think he means by this statement.

   _____

   _____

   _____

5. In addition to reading and studying, Malcolm X enjoyed exchanging and debating ideas with other inmates, and he states, "You would be astonished to know how worked up convict debaters and audiences would get over subjects like 'Should Babies Be Fed Milk?'" Why do you think the convicts became so interested in analyzing and exchanging these ideas?

   _____

_____

_____

_____

_____

_____

Analyzing Issues

We live in a complex world filled with challenging and often perplexing issues that we are expected to make sense of. For example, the media informs us every day of issues related to abortion, AIDS, animal experimentation, apartheid, arms control, budget priorities, child custody, crime and punishment, the death penalty, drugs, euthanasia, foreign policy, gender roles, genetic engineering, human rights, insider trading, conflict in the Middle East, nuclear energy, organ donation, moral values, pornography, individual rights, racism, religion and the state, reproductive technology, right to die, sex education, surrogate motherhood, and many others. Often these broad social issues intrude into our own personal lives, taking them from the level of abstract discussion into our immediate experience. As effective thinkers, we have an obligation to develop informed, intelligent opinions about these issues so that we can function as responsible citizens and also make appropriate decisions when confronted with these issues in our lives.

Almost everyone has opinions about these and other issues. Some opinions, however, are more informed and well supported than others. The Baltimore newspaperman H. L. Mencken once said: "To every complex question there's a simple answer — and it's wrong!" To make sense of complex issues, we need to bring to them a certain amount of background knowledge and an integrated set of thinking and language abilities. One of the central goals of this book is to help you develop the knowledge and sophisticated thinking and language abilities needed to analyze a range of complex issues.

What Is the Issue?

Many social issues are explored, analyzed, and evaluated through our judicial system. Imagine that you have been called for jury duty and subsequently impaneled on a jury that is asked to render a verdict on the following situation. (*Note:* This fictional case is based generally on an actual case that was tried in May 1990, in Minneapolis, Minnesota.)

On January 23, the defendant, Mary Barnett, left Chicago to visit her fiancé in San Francisco. She left her six-month-old daughter, Alison, unattended in the apartment. Seven days later, Mary Barnett returned home to discover that her baby had died of dehydration. She called the police and initially told them that she had left the child with a babysitter. She later stated that she knew she had left the baby behind, that she did not intend to come back and that she knew Alison would die in a day or two. She has been charged with the crime of second-degree murder: intentional murder without premeditation. If convicted, she could face up to eighteen years in jail.

As a member of the jury, your role is to hear and weigh the evidence, evaluate the credibility of the witnesses, analyze the arguments presented by the prosecution and defense, determine whether the law applies specifically to this situation, and render a verdict on the guilt or innocence of the defendant. To perform these tasks with clarity and fairness, you will have to use a variety of sophisticated thinking and language abilities. To begin with, describe your initial assessment of whether the defendant is innocent or guilty and explain your reasons for thinking so.

_____

_____

_____

_____

As part of the jury selection process, you are asked by the prosecutor and defense attorney whether you will be able to set aside your initial reactions or preconceptions to render an impartial verdict, issues this book deals with in Chapter Two, *Thinking Critically*. Identify in the space provided any ideas or feelings related to this case that might make it difficult for you to view it objectively. Are you a parent? Have you ever had any experiences related to the issues in this case? Do you have any preconceived views concerning individual responsibility in situations like this?

_____

_____

_____

14 8, 259

Now evaluate whether you will be able to go beyond your initial reactions to see the situation objectively, and explain how you intend to accomplish this.

_____

_____

_____

What Is the Evidence?

The evidence at judicial trials is presented through the testimony of witnesses called by the prosecution and the defense. As a juror, your job is to absorb the information being presented, evaluate its accuracy, and assess the reliability of the individuals giving the testimony. The following are excerpts of testimony from some of the witnesses at the trial. Witnesses for the prosecution are presented first, followed by witnesses for the defense.

Caroline Hospers: On the evening of January 30, I was in the hallway when Mary Barnett entered the building. She looked distraught and didn't have her baby Alison with her. A little while later the police arrived and I discovered that she had left poor little Alison all alone to die. I'm not surprised this happened. I always thought that Ms. Barnett was a disgrace — I mean, she didn't have a husband. In fact, she didn't even have a steady man after that sailor left for California. She had lots of wild parties in her apartment and that baby wasn't taken care of properly. Her garbage was always filled with empty whiskey and wine bottles. I'm sure that she went to California just to party and have a good time, and didn't give a damn about little Alison. She was thinking only of herself. It's obvious that she is entirely irresponsible and was not a fit mother.

Policeman A: We were called to the defendant's apartment at 11 P.M. on January 30 by the defendant, Mary Barnett. Upon entering the apartment, we found the defendant holding the deceased child in her arms. She was sobbing and was obviously extremely upset. She stated that she had left the deceased with a babysitter one week before when she went to California, and had just returned to discover the deceased alone in the apartment. When I asked defendant to explain in detail what had happened before she left, she stated: "I remember making airline reservations for my trip. Then I tried to find a babysitter, but I couldn't. I knew that I was leaving Alison alone and that I wouldn't be back for a while, but I had to get to California at all costs. I visited my mother and then left." An autopsy was later performed that determined that the deceased had died of dehydration several days earlier. There were no other marks or bruises on the deceased.

Dr. Parker: I am a professional psychiatrist who has been involved in many judicial hearings on whether a defendant is mentally competent to stand trial and I am familiar with these legal tests. At the request of the District Attorney's office, I interviewed the defendant four times during the last three months. Ms. Barnett is suffering from depression and anxiety, possibly induced by the guilt she feels for what she did. These symptoms can be controlled with proper medication. Based on my interview, I believe that Ms. Barnett is competent to stand trial. She understands the charges against her, the roles of her attorney, the prosecutor, judge and jury, and can participate in her defense. Further, I believe that she was mentally competent on January 23, when she left her child unattended. In my opinion she knew what she was doing and what the consequences of her actions would be. She was aware that she was leaving her child unattended and that the child would be in great danger. I think that she feels guilty for the decisions she made, and that this remorse accounts for her current emotional problems.

To be effective critical thinkers, we should not simply accept information as it is presented. We need to try to determine the accuracy of the information and evaluate the credibility of the people providing the information. Evaluate the credibility of the prosecution witnesses by identifying those factors that led you to believe their testimony and those factors that raised questions in your mind about the accuracy of the information presented.

Caroline Hospers: _____

_____

Policeman A: _____

_____

Dr. Parker: _____

_____

As a juror, performing these activities effectively involves using many of the higher-order thinking and language abilities explored in the chapters ahead, including Chapter Four, *Perceiving*; Chapter Five, *Believing and Knowing*; Chapter Six, *Language as a System*; and Chapter Ten, *Reporting, Inferring, Judging*. Based on the testimony you have heard up to this point, do you think the defendant is innocent or guilty of intentional murder without premeditation? Explain the reasons for your conclusion.

_____

_____

_____

Now let's review testimony from the witnesses for the defense.

Alice Jones: I have known the defendant, Mary Barnett, for over eight years. She is a very sweet and decent woman, and a wonderful mother. Being a single parent isn't easy, and Mary has done as good a job as she could. But shortly after Alison's birth Mary got depressed. Then her fiancé, Tim Stewart, was transferred to California. He's a Navy engine mechanic. She started drinking to overcome her depression, but this just made things worse. She began to feel trapped in her apartment with little help raising the baby and few contacts with her family or friends. As her depression deepened, she clung more closely to Tim, who as a result became more distant and put off their wedding, which caused her to feel increasingly anxious and desperate. She felt that she had to go to California to get things straightened out, and by the time she reached that point I think she had lost touch with reality. I honestly don't think she realized that she was leaving Alison unattended. She loved her so much.

Dr. Bloom: Although I have not been involved in judicial hearings of this type, Mary Barnett has been my patient, twice a week for the last four months, beginning two months after she returned from California and was arrested. In my professional opinion, she is mentally ill and not capable of standing trial. Further, she was clearly not aware of what she was doing when she left Alison unattended and should not be held responsible for her action. Ms. Barnett's problems began after the birth of Alison. She became caught in the grip of the medical condition known as postpartum depression, a syndrome that affects many women after the birth of their children, some more severely than others. Women feel a loss of purpose, a sense of hopelessness, and a deep depression. The extreme pressures of caring for an infant create additional anxiety.

When Ms. Barnett's fiancé left for California, she felt completely over-whelmed by her circumstances. She turned to alcohol to raise her spir-its, but this just exacerbated her condition. Depressed, desperate, anx-ious, and alcoholic, she lapsed into a serious neurotic state and became obsessed with the idea of reaching her fiancé in California. This single hope was the only thing she could focus on, and when she acted on it she was completely unaware that she was putting her daughter in dan-ger. Since the trial has begun, she has suffered two anxiety attacks, the more severe resulting in a near-catatonic state necessitating her hospi-talization for several days. This woman is emotionally disturbed. She needs professional help, not punishment.

Mary Barnett: I don't remember leaving Alison alone. I would never do that if I realized what I was doing. I don't remember saying any of the things that they said I said, about knowing I was leaving her. I have tried to put the pieces together through the entire investigation, and I just can't do it. I was anxious and I was real frightened. I didn't feel like I was in control and it felt like it was getting worse. The world was closing in on me, and I had nowhere to turn. I know that I had to get to Tim, in California, and that he would be able to fix everything. He was always the one I went to, because I trusted him. I must have as-sumed that someone was taking care of Alison, my sweet baby. When I was in California I knew something wasn't right, I just didn't know what it was.

Based on this new testimony, do you think that the defendant is innocent or guilty of intentional murder without premeditation? Have your views changed? Explain the reasons for your current conclusion.

_____

_____

_____

Evaluate the credibility of the defense witnesses by identifying those factors that led you to believe their testimony and those factors that raised questions in your mind about the accuracy of the information being presented.

Alice Jones: _____

_____

Dr. Bloom: _____

_____

Mary Barnett: _____

_____

What Are the Arguments?

After the various witnesses present their testimony through examination and
cross-examination questioning, the prosecution and defense then present
their final arguments and summation. The purpose of this phase of the trial
is to tie together — or raise doubts about — the evidence that has been presented in order to persuade the jury that the defendant is guilty or innocent.
Included here are excerpts from these final arguments.

Prosecution Arguments: Child abuse and neglect is a national tragedy.
Every day thousands of innocent children are neglected, abused, and
even killed. The parents responsible for these crimes are rarely brought
to justice because their victims are usually not able to speak in their
own behalf. In some sense, all of these abusers are emotionally disturbed, because it takes emotionally disturbed people to torture, maim,
and kill innocent children. But these people are also responsible for
their actions and they should be punished accordingly. They don't have
to hurt these children. No one is forcing them to hurt these children.
They can choose not to hurt these children. If they have emotional
problems, they can choose to seek professional help. Saying you hurt a
child because you have "emotional problems" is the worst kind of
excuse.

The defendant, Mary Barnett, claims that she left her child unattended, to die, because she has "emotional problems," and that she is
not responsible for what she did. This is absurd. Mary Barnett is a self-
centered, irresponsible, manipulative, deceitful mother, who abandoned her six-month-old daughter to die so that she could fly to San
Francisco to party all week with her fiancé. She was conscious, she was
thinking, she knew exactly what she was doing, and that's exactly what
she told the police when she returned from her little pleasure trip. Now
she claims that she can't remember making these admissions to the police, nor can she remember leaving little Alison alone to die. How
convenient!

You have heard testimony from her neighbor, Caroline Hospers, that she was considerably less than an ideal mother: a chronic drinker who liked to party rather than devoting herself to her child. You have also heard the testimony of Dr. Parker, who stated that Mary Barnett was aware of what she was doing on the fateful day in January and that any emotional disturbance is the result of her feelings of guilt over the terrible thing she did, and her fear of being punished for it.

Mary Barnett is guilty of murder, pure and simple, and it is imperative that you find her so. We need to let society know that it is no longer open season on our children.

After reviewing these arguments, describe those points you find most persuasive and those you find least persuasive.

Strongest Arguments: _____

_____

_____

_____

Weakest Arguments: _____

_____

_____

_____

Defense Arguments: The district attorney is certainly correct — child abuse *is* a national tragedy. Mary Barnett, however, is *not* a child abuser. You heard the police testify that the hospital found no marks, bruises, or other indications of an abused child. You also heard her friend, Alice Jones, testify that Mary was a kind and loving mother who adored her child. But if Mary Barnett was not a child abuser, then how could she have left her child unattended? Because she had snapped psychologically. The combination of postpartum depression, alcoholism, the pressures of being a single parent, and the loss of her fiancé were too much for her to bear. She simply broke under the weight of all that despair and took off blindly for California, hoping to find a way out of her personal hell. How could she leave Alison unattended? Because she was completely unaware that she was doing so. She had lost touch with reality and had no idea what was happening around her.

You have heard the in-depth testimony of Dr. Bloom, who has

explained to you the medical condition of postpartum depression and how this led to Mary's emotional breakdown. You are aware that Mary has had two severe anxiety attacks while this trial has taken place, one resulting in her hospitalization. And you have seen her desperate sobbing whenever her daughter Alison has been mentioned in testimony.

Alison Barnett is a victim. But she is not a victim of intentional malice from the mother who loves her. She is the victim of Mary's mental illness, of her emotional breakdown. And in this sense Mary is a victim also. In this enlightened society we should not punish someone who has fallen victim to mental illness. To do so would make us no better than those societies who used to torture and burn mentally ill people whom they thought were possessed by the devil. Mary needs treatment, not blind vengeance.

After reviewing the arguments presented by the defense, identify those points you find most persuasive and those you find least persuasive.

Strongest Arguments: _____

_____

_____

_____

Weakest Arguments: _____

_____

_____

_____

The process of analyzing and evaluating complex arguments like those presented by the prosecution and defense involves using a number of sophisticated thinking and language abilities we will be exploring in the chapters ahead, including Chapter Two, *Thinking Critically*; Chapter Seven, *Language as a Tool*; Chapter Eleven, *Constructing Arguments*; and Chapter Twelve, *Reasoning Critically*.

What Is the Verdict?

Following the final arguments and summations, the judge will sometimes give specific instructions to clarify the issues to be considered. In this case the judge reminds the jury that they must focus on the boundaries of the law and determine whether this case falls within these boundaries or outside them. The jury then retires to deliberate the case and render a verdict.

For a defendant to be found guilty of second-degree murder, the prosecution must prove that he or she intended to kill someone, made a conscious decision to do so at that moment (without premeditation), and was aware of the consequences of his or her actions.

In your discussion with the other jurors, you must determine whether the evidence indicates, *beyond a reasonable doubt,* that the defendant's conduct in this case meets these conditions. What does the qualification "beyond a reasonable doubt" mean? A principle like this is always difficult to define in specific terms, but in general the principle means that it would not make good sense for thoughtful men and women to conclude otherwise. The whole area of forming, defining, and applying concepts is a key dimension of thinking effectively and is examined in Chapter Eight, *Forming and Applying Concepts.*

Based on your analysis of the evidence and arguments presented in this case, describe what you think the verdict ought to be and explain your reasons for thinking so.

Verdict: Guilty _____ Not Guilty _____

Supporting Reasons:

1. _____

_____

2. _____

_____

3. _____

_____

4. _____

_____

A Working Definition of *Thinking*

The first line of this chapter stated, "Thinking is the extraordinary process we use every waking moment to make sense of our world and our lives."

Throughout this chapter we have been exploring the different ways our thinking enables us to make sense of the world by

- Solving problems
- Working toward our goals
- Analyzing issues

Of course, our thinking helps us make sense of the world in other ways as well. When we attend a concert, listen to a lecture, or try to understand someone's behavior, it is our thinking that enables us to figure out what is happening. In fact, these attempts to make sense of what is happening are going on all the time in our lives, and they represent the heart of the thinking process.

If we review the different ways of thinking we have been exploring in this chapter, we can reach several conclusions about thinking:

1. *Thinking is an **active** process.* Whether we are trying to solve a problem, reach a goal, or analyze an issue, we are actively using our minds to figure out the situation.
2. *Thinking is directed toward a **purpose.*** When we think, it is usually for a purpose — to solve a problem, reach a goal, or analyze an issue.
3. *Thinking is an **organized** process.* When we think effectively, there is usually an order or organization to our thinking. For each of the thinking activities we explored, we saw that there are certain steps or approaches to take that help us solve problems, reach goals, and analyze issues.

We can put together these conclusions about thinking explored in this chapter to form a working definition of the term.

Thinking   An active, purposeful, organized process that we use to make sense of our world.

At this point, our definition of thinking is too general; we need to *specify* more exactly what thinking involves. We will continue to define thinking as we work through this book.

Summary

Thinking develops with use over a lifetime, whether we are trying to decide what courses to take in school, which career to pursue, or simply how much to bet on a poker hand. By continuing to develop our thinking abilities, we become even better prepared to make sense of our world, to explore the choices available to us, and to make appropriate decisions.

We can improve our thinking in an organized and systematic way by following these three steps:

1. *Becoming aware of our thinking process.* We usually take thinking for granted and do not pay much attention to it. Developing our thinking means that we have to think about the way we think.

2. *Carefully examining our thinking process and the thinking process of others.* In this chapter we have explored various ways in which our thinking works. By focusing our attention on these (and other) thinking approaches and strategies, we can learn to think more effectively.

3. *Practicing our thinking abilities.* To improve our thinking, we actually have to think for ourselves, to explore and make sense of thinking situations by using our thinking abilities. Although it is important to read about thinking and learn how other people think, there is no substitute for actually doing it ourselves.

The ability to think for ourselves by carefully examining the way that we make sense of the world is one of the most satisfying aspects of being a mature human being. We will refer to this ability to think carefully about our thinking as the ability to *think critically.* Using our definition of *thinking* as a starting point, we can define *thinking critically* as follows.

> **Thinking Critically**   An active, purposeful, organized process we use to make sense of our world by carefully examining our thinking and the thinking of others, in order to clarify and improve our understanding.

We are able to think critically because of our natural human ability to *reflect* — to think back on what we are thinking, doing, or feeling. By carefully thinking back on our thinking, we are able to figure out the way our thinking operates and so learn to do it more effectively. In the following chapters we will be systematically exploring many dimensions of the way our minds work, providing the opportunity to deepen our understanding of the thinking process and stimulating us to become more effective thinkers.

CHAPTER 2

Thinking Critically

Thinking for
Ourselves

Carefully Exploring
Situations with
Questions

Viewing Situations
from Different
Perspectives

THINKING CRITICALLY:
Making sense of the world by
carefully examining the thinking
process to clarify and improve
our understanding.

Thinking
Actively

Discussing
Ideas in an
Organized Way

> ***Thinking Critically***   Making sense of our world by carefully examining the thinking process in order to clarify and improve our understanding.

WE HAVE ARRIVED at this definition of *thinking critically* through our exploration of the thinking process. Thinking is the way we make sense of the world; thinking critically is thinking *about* our thinking so that we can clarify and improve it. If we can understand the way our minds work when we solve problems, work toward our goals, and analyze complex issues then we can learn to think more effectively in these situations.

In this chapter we will explore ways to examine our thinking so that we can develop it to the fullest extent possible. That is, we will discover how we think critically.

The word *critical* comes from the Greek word for "critic" (*kritikos*), which means to question, to make sense of, to be able to analyze. It is by questioning, making sense of things and people, and analyzing that we examine our thinking and the thinking of others. These critical activities aid us in reaching the best possible conclusions and decisions.

The word *critical* is also related to the word *criticize,* which means to question and evaluate. Unfortunately, the ability to criticize is often only used destructively, to tear down someone else's thinking. Criticism, however, can also be *constructive* — analyzing for the purpose of developing a better understanding of what is going on. We will engage in constructive criticism as we develop our ability to think critically.

Critical thinking is not simply one way of thinking; it is a total approach to understanding how we make sense of a world that includes many parts. In this chapter we will explore the various activities that make up thinking critically, including the following:

• Thinking actively

• Carefully exploring situations with questions

• Thinking for ourselves

• Viewing situations from different perspectives

• Discussing ideas in an organized way

Thinking Actively

When we think critically, we are *actively* using our intelligence, knowledge, and abilities to deal effectively with life's situations. When we are thinking actively, we are:

- Getting involved in potentially useful projects and activities instead of remaining disengaged
- Taking initiative in making decisions on our own instead of waiting passively to be told what to think or do
- Following through on our commitments instead of giving up when we encounter difficulties
- Taking responsibility for the consequences of our decisions rather than unjustifiably blaming others or events "beyond our control"

When we are thinking actively, we are not just waiting for something to happen. We are engaged in the process of solving problems, achieving goals, and analyzing issues. Imagine, for example, that you are unsure of what career you want to commit your life to. Perhaps you just graduated from high school or perhaps you have been working in a job that is not sufficiently fulfilling or financially rewarding. A friend suggests that you not go to college until you get a clear idea of what you want to be. This way, the friend argues, you won't waste time and money studying in a field you might ultimately decide is not for you.

1. What are the disadvantages of following your friend's advice?

   a. _____

   b. _____

   c. _____

2. What are the advantages of enrolling in college even if you are not sure what you might ultimately want to do?

   a. _____

   b. _____

   c. _____

3. What are some steps you might take actively to explore and determine what career might be appropriate for you?

a. _____

b. _____

c. _____

d. _____

Thinking critically involves making a conscious effort to meet challenges and solve problems. When we react passively, we let events control us or permit others to do our thinking for us, behaviors that are not effective in the long run. To make an intelligent decision about our future careers, for example, we usually have to work actively to secure more information, try out various possibilities, speak with people who are experienced in our area of interest, and then critically reflect on all these factors. Thinking critically requires that we think actively — not react passively — to deal effectively with life's situations.

Influences on Our Thinking

As our minds grow and develop, we are exposed to influences that encourage us to think actively. We also, however, have many experiences that encourage us to think passively. For example, some analysts believe that when people, especially children, spend much of their time watching television they are being influenced to think passively, thus inhibiting their intellectual growth. Read carefully the following passage about television watching and think about whether you agree with the author's analysis.

THE EFFECTS OF WATCHING TELEVISION ON GORILLAS AND OTHERS

My four-year-old daughter has recently begun to appreciate jokes and riddles, although her understanding is not yet complete. Her latest effort goes something like this: "Why did the gorilla watch TV? Because he wanted to get dopey!" (followed by gales of laughter). This "joke" originated in my observation to her that, after watching several hours of television on Saturday morning, she usually becomes "dopey" — listless, unaware of anything going on around her, moody, and not interested in doing anything but watching more television. It doesn't matter much what show she is watching. What's important is only that she is *watching*. What is the power of this electronic box that will transform a lively, energetic, inquisitive little child into a hypnotized zombie in a matter of hours?

In the first place, watching television is an almost totally *passive* experience. We are being entertained, provided with images, characterizations, stories, and so on. Many other children's activities — like reading and playing imaginary games — require that children *create* images, producing a world of their own making. With television, we are not encouraged — or even normally permitted — to use our minds actively to create images, characters, or stories. That work has already been done for us. All we have to do is keep our eyes open and passively receive an experience that we have no control over.

Secondly, the television screen presents a world that in some ways is more fascinating and more visually intense than the world outside of television. Within the boundaries of the screen, we are usually offered an entire room, a complete landscape, a total panorama. If we were observing these scenes in real life, we would only be able to see a small part of them in a single glance. In addition, the action on television — unlike real life — is non-stop. The camera is constantly moving; the people and characters are always doing or saying something. Finally, the content of television shows and commercials has been carefully constructed to engage and hold our interest. All of these factors contribute to making television more visually entertaining than real life, and they also seem to have the effect of inducing a trancelike connection with the television that is difficult to break.

Thirdly, television is something that we have absolutely no control over, short of turning it on or off and switching the channels. We can't speed it up or slow it down. We can't ask questions, return to an earlier scene, or influence what we are experiencing. The television is immobile and can only be watched in a certain place at a certain time, sitting in furniture that is secured in place like movie seats. And unlike reading, which is composed of words that we ourselves can use for creative expression, the dynamic images of television are alien, completely beyond our power to produce. A television set is a controlling force, a technological god that demands the surrender of our imagination, our creative expression, and the control of our minds. It's no wonder that watching it can make gorillas — and others — a little dopey. ■

THINKING ACTIVITY

2.1   ▶ 1. Describe the main reasons the author provides to support his conclusion that watching too much television discourages active thinking, especially in children. Evaluate whether you think these reasons make good sense. If not, explain why.

2. Many people believe that watching television can stimulate *active* thinking. Describe the reasons someone might use to support this contrasting viewpoint.

3. Identify a specific *type* of television program (soap opera, situation comedy, game show, talk show) and analyze the ways that type of program encourages both active and passive thinking. Identify strategies that could be used for responding more actively to these programs. ◄

Listed here are some of the influences we experience in our lives along with space for you to add your own influences. As you read through the list, place an *A* next to those items you believe in general influence you to think *actively*, and a *P* next to those you consider to be generally *passive* influences.

Activities:	*People:*
Reading books	Family members
Writing	Friends
Taking drugs	Employers
Dancing	Advertisers
Drawing/painting	School/college teachers
Playing video games	Police officers
Playing sports	Religious leaders
Listening to music	Politicians
_____	_____
_____	_____

Of course, in many cases people and activities can act as both active and passive influences, depending on the specifics of situations and our individual responses. For example, consider employers. If we are performing a routine, repetitive job, like the summer the author spent in a peanut butter cracker factory hand-scooping 2,000 pounds of peanut butter a day, the very nature of the work tends to encourage passive, uncreative thinking (although it might also lead to creative daydreaming!). We are also influenced to think passively if our employer gives us detailed instructions for performing every task, instructions that permit no exception or deviation. On the other hand, when our employer gives us general areas of responsibility within which we are expected to make thoughtful and creative decisions, then we are being stimulated to think actively and independently.

These contrasting styles of supervision are mirrored in different approaches to raising children. Some parents encourage children to be active thinkers by teaching them to express themselves clearly, make independent decisions, look at different points of view, and choose what they think is right for themselves. Other parents influence their children to be passive thinkers by not letting them do things on their own. The parents give the children detailed instructions that they are expected to follow without question, make the important decisions for them, and are reluctant to give them significant responsibilities. Although often well intentioned, this sort of treatment can influence children to become passive, dependent thinkers who are not well adapted to making independent decisions and assuming responsibility for their lives.

THINKING ACTIVITY

2.2   ▶ Identify one important influence in your life that mostly stimulates you to think actively and another that encourages you to think passively. For each influence, write a passage that addresses the following points:

1. Explain why you believe that the influence has affected your thinking. Provide specific examples of how the influence affects you.

2. Analyze whether you think this influence affects everyone the same way or some people differently. Give two or three examples.

3. Describe strategies for becoming more intellectually active in interacting with these influences. ◀

Carefully Exploring Situations with Questions

As we have just seen, thinking critically involves actively using our thinking abilities to attack problems, meet challenges, and analyze issues. An important dimension of thinking actively is carefully exploring the situations we are involved in with relevant questions. In fact, the ability to ask appropriate and penetrating questions is one of the most powerful thinking tools we possess, although many of us do not make full use of it. Let's see how asking appropriate questions can help us understand our world and make informed decisions. Consider the following situation:

> Paul is a twenty-five-year-old college student who hopes to attend medical school. After graduating from high school, he went to work in his father's building supply business. Although he did well in the business, he ultimately decided that the business was his father's dream and that he had to pursue a dream of his own. This realization prompted him to enroll in college and take up a pre-med major.
>
> One night, while studying for his medical school entrance examinations, he receives a desperate phone call from his mother informing him that his father has had a heart attack and is in a coma. Paul returns home immediately and discovers that his father is still comatose and that his prognosis is unclear at this time. In addition, his mother is worried about their financial situation if the father remains ill, since the building supply business depends almost entirely on the father's overseeing operations, giving estimates, and making deals.

In the space provided, identify the important issues confronting Paul and his mother.

_____

_____

_____

_____

_____

When we are confronted with difficult situations like this, our first step should be to explore carefully their many interacting elements so that we can understand the overall situation, the alternatives we have, and the decisions we ought to make. To accomplish these goals, we have to ask the right questions.

Questions come in many different forms and are used for many different purposes. One way of classifying questions is in terms of the ways people organize and interpret information. For our purposes, we will be using a classification system that involves six categories of questions:

1. Fact   4. Synthesis

2. Interpretation   5. Evaluation

3. Analysis   6. Application

   Using this classification system as a guide, we can develop an approach to formulating questions that will help us explore complex situations like the one just described. Of course, these various types of questions are closely interrelated; an effective thinker is able to use them flexibly and in a harmonious relation to one another.

1. *Questions of Fact.* Questions of fact seek to determine the basic information of a situation: who, what, when, where, how. These questions seek information that is relatively straightforward and objective, though as we will see in Chapter Four, *Perceiving*, and Chapter Five, *Believing and Knowing*, this objectivity is not always easy to achieve. The scenario we are dealing with has several dimensions that need to be carefully explored, and factual questions are a good place to begin. For each dimension of the scenario described, identify the key questions that need to be addressed.

The Father's Medical Condition:

1. How much time elapsed after the heart attack before medical help arrived?

2. _____

3. _____

4. _____

The Family's Financial Situation:

1. What is the operational structure of the business?

2. _____

3. _____

4. _____

The Son's Academic Situation:

1. What is involved in taking a leave of absence from school?

2. _____

3. _____

4. _____

2. *Questions of Interpretation.* Questions of interpretation seek to discover relationships between facts and ideas. Examples of such relationships, which are explored in greater detail in Chapter Nine, *Relating and Organizing,* include the following:

- *Chronological relationships:* relating things in time sequence
- *Process relationships:* relating aspects of growth, development, or change
- *Comparison relationships:* relating things in terms of their similar features
- *Contrast relationships:* relating things in terms of their different features
- *Causal relationships:* relating events in terms of the way some event(s) are responsible for bringing about other event(s)

As a part of our unfolding scenario, imagine that we seek the opinions of two different doctors, who give us the following opinions regarding the father's condition and prognosis:

> *Doctor A (geriatric medicine):* What we know about this patient is that 24 hours ago he suffered a heart attack and for a period of 3 to 8 minutes was deprived of oxygen to the brain. In situations like this, depending on what neurologic signs are present during the first 24 to 48 hours, there is a 90 percent chance of brain function return. The longer out in time you go, the less the chances of recovery. There are exceptions, however. I recently had the case of a seventy-five-year-old man who was admitted in a similar condition. He had to be kept alive with heart and lung life-support systems and showed no neurologic improvement for over six weeks. But he gradually began to improve and after six months walked out of the hospital pretty much neurologically intact. This illustrates the old maxim, "Where there's life there's hope." If we err, we must err on the side of life.

> *Dr. B (neurologist):* I reviewed the patient's profile, and when you have a situation like this — cardiorespiratory arrest, anoxia, coma, brainstem reflex — the outlook is grim. The possibilities are as follows: He may become brain dead if the cerebrum swells, and then we can pronounce him dead; he may remain in a persistent vegetative state, in which the odds of recovery are 1 in 10,000; he may become severely incapacitated and be a burden on the family and society; he may develop some

limited capacities to function; or he may recover entirely, although this is extremely unlikely. We'll have to monitor him and see.

Let's explore the relationships between these two medical opinions by first identifying some *factual* questions we might ask and then developing some *interpretative* questions:

Factual Questions:

1. What is the patient's current medical condition?

2. _____

3. _____

4. _____

Interpretative Questions:

CHRONOLOGY

1. _____

2. _____

PROCESS

1. What does Dr. A think are possible patterns of development for the father?

2. _____

COMPARE/CONTRAST

1. What are the similarities in the two doctors' views about the patient's current medical condition?

2. _____

3. _____

4. _____

CAUSAL

1. What are the effects of anoxia (deprivation of oxygen to the brain)?

2. _____

3. _____

4. _____

GENERAL INTERPRETATION

1. What might be the relationship between each doctor's medical specialty and his or her medical prognosis of the patient?

2. _____

3. *Questions of Analysis.* Questions of analysis seek to separate an entire process or situation into its component parts and understand the relation of these parts to the whole. These questions attempt to classify various elements, outline component structures, articulate various possibilities, and clarify the reasoning being presented — thinking processes we will be examining in Chapter Eight, *Forming and Applying Concepts.* Let's explore these questions by carefully examining the financial aspects of our developing scenario as presented by two financial experts.

> *Financial Expert A:* This is a healthy, family-owned building supply business that shows a net operating profit of $200,000 annually, $100,000 of which the family has lived on comfortably and the other $100,000 of which has been reinvested into the business. The father is the mainstay of the business, overseeing all operations, making all the important decisions, and personally making the large sales to contractors. I think the family should sell the business as soon as possible for the following reasons. First, the son's dream is to go to medical school. If he returns to help out with the business, he may never be able to pursue his dream. Second, this is the best time to sell. The business has a strong track record and the family can realize the greatest profit. Third, if the son comes in to run the business, it may deteriorate and lose value. The family should sell the business.

> *Financial Expert B:* I think that this is the worst time to sell the business for the following reasons. First, I don't think we can conclude that the son wants to go to medical school more than he wants to run the business. The problem may be that the father never really listened to the son's ideas or let him make important decisions. Second, because the father is seriously ill, the family would be at a negotiating disadvantage and may not be able to get the best possible price. Third, instead of deteriorating, the business may grow and flourish under the son's fresh, creative leadership. The family should keep the business.

Factual Questions:

1. _____

2. _____

3. _____

Interpretative Questions:

1. _____

2. _____

3. _____

Analytical Questions:

OUTLINE STRUCTURES

1. What is the organizational structure of the family business?

2. _____

3. _____

ARTICULATE POSSIBILITIES

1. What are possible options for the son?

2. _____

3. _____

CLARIFY REASONING

1. What are the reasons that the family should sell the business?

2. _____

3. _____

4. *Questions of Synthesis.* Questions of synthesis have as their goal combining ideas to form a new whole or come to a conclusion, making inferences about future events, creating solutions, and designing plans of action. These are processes dealt with in such chapters as Chapter Nine, *Relating and Organizing* and Chapter Ten, *Reporting, Inferring, and Judging.* Let's identify some synthesizing questions we might use to carefully explore our dramatic scenario.

Combining Ideas to Come to a Conclusion:

1. Based on everything we have learned about the father's medical condition, what decisions should we make about his care?

2. _____

3. _____

Making Inferences About Future Events:

1. How will the son feel if he postpones his plans for medical school in order to help out with the family business?

2. _____

3. _____

Designing Plans of Action:

1. In what ways might the business be restructured to function effectively?

2. _____

3. _____

5. *Questions of Evaluation.* The aim of evaluation questions is to help us make informed judgments and decisions by determining the relative value, truth, or reliability of things. The process of evaluation involves identifying the criteria or standards we are using and then determining to what extent the things in common meet those standards. This is the approach that informed critical thinkers use, whether they are deciding what courses to take, which alternatives to pursue in solving a problem, or what to believe about a serious issue (processes we will examine in more detail in Chapter Eleven, *Constructing Arguments,* and Chapter Twelve, *Reasoning Critically.* Let's explore how questions of evaluation might help us make sense of moral issues in our dramatic scenario.

> The father's condition has remained unchanged for six months. The odds of recovery at this point are extremely small — approximately 1 in 10,000. He is still on a respirator and feeding tube, and his medical care is a continuing drain on the family resources. The mother and son are trying to decide whether they should ask the hospital to remove him from the life-support systems, letting him die. Here are two contrasting views on their dilemma.

Lawyer from the Society for the Right to Die: This family is faced with a very twentieth-century problem, because medical technology has developed to the point where people in a comatose state can be kept alive for years or even decades with artificial life-support systems, whereas in the past they would have simply died a natural death. It is ethically appropriate for the family to question whether these treatments are providing any benefit to the patient and try to determine what the patient would have wanted if he could speak for himself. As the people who knew him best, the family should have the right to determine whether artificial life-support systems should be continued.

Lawyer Who Is Also a Catholic Priest: No person has the right to determine when someone else's life should end — that can only be determined by God. Life is a gift, an endowment, and we must seek to preserve it in any way we can. Simply because someone is comatose does not give us the right to conclude that their life is not worth living. If we withdraw a feeding tube from such a patient, then we are guilty of starving that person to death. Such an action would also set a dangerous precedent, as society might then take a more active role in ending the lives of people they consider "unqualified." The family should not have the legal right to make this determination.

Evaluative Questions:

CRITERIA

1. What are the criteria for determining when someone has ceased "living" in a normal sense?

2. _____

3. _____

JUDGMENT

1. If the family believes that the father would not want to exist in this way, what decision should they make about withdrawing life-support systems?

2. _____

3. _____

6. *Questions of Application.* The aim of application questions is to help us take the knowledge or concepts we have gained in one situation and apply them to other situations. In this section we have used different categories of ques-

tions to make sense of a complex decision-making situation. Learning to ask these questions can also give us the means to make sense of other complex decision-making situations, such as the one described in Thinking Activity 2.3.

THINKING ACTIVITY

2.3 ▶ Review the following decision-making situation (based on an incident that happened in Springfield, Missouri, in 1989), and then critically examine it by posing questions from each of the six categories we have considered in this section:

1. Fact   4. Synthesis
2. Interpretation 5. Evaluation
3. Analysis   6. Application

Imagine that you are a member of a student group at your college that has decided to stage the controversial play, *The Normal Heart,* by Larry Kramer. The play is based on the lives of real people and dramatizes their experiences in the early stages of the AIDS epidemic. It focuses on their efforts to publicize the horrific nature of this disease and to secure funding from a reluctant federal government to find a cure. The play is considered controversial because of its exclusive focus on the AIDS subject, its explicit homosexual themes, and the large amount of profanity contained in the script. After lengthy discussion, however, your student group has decided that the educational and moral benefits of the play render it a valuable contribution to the life of the college.

While the play is in rehearsal, a local politician seizes it as an issue and mounts a political and public relations campaign against it. She distributes selected excerpts of the play to the newspapers, religious groups, and civic organizations. She also introduces a bill in the state legislature to withdraw state funding for the college if the play is performed. The play creates a firestorm of controversy, replete with local and national news reports, editorials, and impassioned speeches for and against it. Everyone associated with the play is subjected to verbal harassment, threats, crank phone calls, and hate mail. The firestorm explodes when the house of one of the key spokespersons for the play is burned to the ground. The director and actors go into hiding for their safety, rehearsing in secret and moving from hotel to hotel.

Your student group has just convened to decide what course of action to take. Analyze the situation using the six types of questions listed above and then conclude with your decision and the reasons that support your decision. ◀

Thinking for Ourselves

Answer the following questions, based on what you believe to be true.

	Yes	No	Not Sure

1. Is the earth flat?
2. Is there a God?
3. Is abortion wrong?
4. Is democracy the best form of government?
5. Should men be the breadwinners and women the homemakers?

Our responses to these questions reveal aspects of the way our minds work. How did we arrive at these conclusions? Our views on these and many other issues probably had their beginnings with our families, especially our parents. When we are young, we are very dependent on our parents and we are influenced by the way they see the world. As we grow up, we learn how to think, feel, and behave in various situations. In addition to our parents, our "teachers" include our brothers and sisters, friends, religious leaders, schoolteachers, books, television, and so on. Most of what we learn we absorb without even being aware of it. Many of our ideas about the issues raised in the questions above were most likely shaped by the experiences we had growing up.

As a result of our ongoing experiences, however, our minds — and our thinking — continue to mature. Instead of simply accepting the views of others, we gradually develop the ability to examine this thinking and to decide whether it makes sense to us and whether we should accept it. As we think through such ideas, we use this standard to make our decision: Are there good reasons or evidence that support this thinking? If there are good reasons, we can actively decide to adopt these ideas. If they do not make sense, we can modify or reject them.

Of course, we do not *always* examine our own thinking or the thinking of others so carefully. In fact, we very often continue to believe the same ideas we were brought up with, without ever examining and deciding for ourselves what to think. Or we often blindly reject the beliefs we have been brought up with, without really examining them.

How do we know when we have examined and adopted ideas ourselves instead of simply borrowing them from others? One indication of having thought through our ideas is being able to explain *why* we believe them. Such explanations involve telling how we arrived at these views and giving the reasons and evidence that support them.

For each of the views you expressed at the beginning of this section, explain how you arrived at it and give the reasons and evidence that you believe support it.

1. *Example:* Is the earth flat?
   Explanation: I was taught by my parents and in school that the earth was round.

   Reasons/Evidence:

   a. *Authorities:* My parents and teachers taught me this.

   b. *References:* I read about this in science textbooks.

   c. *Factual evidence:* I have seen photographs taken from outer space that show the earth as a globe.

   d. *Personal experience:* When I flew across the country, I could see the horizon line changing.

2. Is there a God?

   Explanation: _____

   _____

   Reasons/Evidence:

   a. *Authorities:* _____

   b. *References:* _____

   c. *Factual evidence:* _____

   d. *Personal experience:* _____

3. Is abortion wrong?

   Explanation: _____

   _____

Reasons/Evidence:

a. *Authorities:* _____

b. *References:* _____

c. *Factual evidence:* _____

d. *Personal experience:* _____

4. Is democracy the best form of government?

Explanation: _____

Reasons/Evidence:

a. *Authorities:* _____

b. *References:* _____

c. *Factual evidence:* _____

d. *Personal experience:* _____

5. Should men be the breadwinners and women the homemakers?

Explanation: _____

_____

Reasons/Evidence:

a. *Authorities:* _____

b. *References:* _____

c. *Factual evidence:* _____

d. *Personal experience:* _____

Of course, not all reasons and evidence are equally strong or accurate. For example, before the fifteenth century the common belief that the earth was flat was supported by the following reasons and evidence:

- *Authorities:* Educational and religious authorities taught people that the earth was flat.
- *References:* The written opinions of scientific experts supported belief in a flat earth.
- *Factual evidence:* No person had ever circumnavigated the earth.
- *Personal experience:* From a normal vantage point, the earth *looks* flat.

Many considerations go into evaluating the strengths and accuracy of reasons and evidence, and we will be exploring these areas in this and future chapters, including Chapter Five, *Believing and Knowing*; Chapter Eleven, *Constructing Arguments*; and Chapter Twelve, *Reasoning Critically.* For the present time, let's examine some basic questions that critical thinkers automatically consider when evaluating reasons and evidence.

THINKING ACTIVITY

2.4 ▶ Evaluate the strengths and accuracy of the reasons and evidence you identified to support your beliefs on the five issues by addressing questions such as the following:

- *Authorities:* Are the authorities knowledgeable in this area? Are they reliable? Have they ever given inaccurate information? Do other authorities disagree with them?

- *References:* What are the credentials of the authors? Are there other authors that disagree with their opinions? On what reasons and evidence do the authors base their opinions?

- *Factual evidence:* What is the source and foundation of the evidence? Can the evidence be interpreted differently? Does the evidence support the conclusion?

- *Personal experience:* What were the circumstances under which the experiences took place? Were distortions or mistakes in perception possible? Have other people had either similar or conflicting experiences? Are there other explanations for the experience? ◀

The opposite of thinking for ourselves is when we simply accept the thinking of others without examining or questioning it. Imagine that a friend assures you that a course you are planning to take is very difficult. Although the thinking of your friend may be accurate, it still makes sense for you to investigate the evidence for that particular view yourself. For example, consider the following situation. Explain how you would respond to the ideas that are being suggested to you, and then give the reasons that support your views.

One of your professors always wears blue jeans and sneakers to class. He says that the clothes you wear have nothing to do with how intelligent or how capable you are or the quality of your work. Other people should judge you on *who* you are, not on the clothes you wear. Your supervisor at work, however, has just informed you that you have been dressing too casually. How do you respond?

Response: _____

Reasons that support your response: _____

_____

Thinking for ourselves doesn't always mean doing exactly what we want to; it may mean becoming aware of the social guidelines and expectations of a given situation and then making an informed decision about what is in our best interests. In this situation, even though we may have a legal right to choose whatever clothes we want at the workplace, if our choice doesn't conform to the employer's guidelines or "norms," then we may suffer unpleasant consequences as a result. In other words, thinking for ourselves often involves balancing our view of things against those of others; integrating ourselves into social structures without sacrificing our independence or personal autonomy.

Learning to become independent, critical thinkers is a complex, ongoing process, which involves all the abilities we have been examining in this chapter to this point:

• Thinking actively

• Carefully exploring situations with questions

• Thinking for ourselves

As we confront the many decisions we have to make in our lives, we should try to gather all the relevant information, review our priorities, and then carefully weigh all the factors before arriving at a final decision. One helpful strategy for exploring thinking situations is the one we have been practicing: *Identify* the important questions that need to be answered and then try to *answer* these questions.

THINKING ACTIVITY

2.5   ▶   In the following reading selection, Peter Rondinone describes the personal challenges he encountered in attending college and working toward his goals. The story of his struggle to succeed traces his evolution from a socially dependent, largely uncritical thinker to a person who was actively pursuing his objectives, carefully exploring his situation with relevant questions, and becoming an autonomous, critical thinker. After carefully reading the selection, complete the activities that follow it. ◀

OPEN ADMISSIONS AND THE INWARD "I"
by Peter J. Rondinone

The fact is, I didn't learn much in high school. I spent my time on the front steps of the building smoking grass with the dudes from the dean's squad. For kicks we'd grab a freshman, tell him we were undercover cops, handcuff him to a banister, and take his money. Then we'd go to the back of the building, cop some "downs," and nod away the day behind the steps in the lobby. The classrooms were overcrowded anyhow, and the teachers knew it. They also knew where to find me when they wanted to make weird deals: If I agreed to read a book and do an oral report, they'd pass me. So I did it and graduated with a "general" diploma. I was a New York City public school kid.

I hung out on a Bronx streetcorner with a group of guys who called themselves "The Davidson Boys" and sang songs like "Daddy-lo-lo." Everything we did could be summed up with the word "snap." That's a "snap." She's a "snap." We had a "snap." Friday nights we'd paint ourselves green and run through the streets swinging baseball bats. Or we'd get into a little rap in the park. It was all very perilous. Even though I'd seen a friend stabbed for wearing the wrong colors and another blown away with a shotgun for "messin'" with some dude's woman, I was too young to realize that my life too might be headed toward a violent end.

Then one night I swallowed a dozen Tuminols and downed two quarts of beer at a bar in Manhattan. I passed out in the gutter. I puked and rolled under a parked car. Two girlfriends found me and carried me home. My overprotective brother answered the door. When he saw me — eyes rolling toward the back of my skull like rubber — he pushed me down a flight of stairs. My skull hit the edge of a marble step with a thud. The girls screamed. My parents came to the door and there I was: a high school graduate, a failure, curled in a ball in a pool of blood.

The next day I woke up with dried blood on my face. I had no idea what had happened. My sister told me. I couldn't believe it. Crying, my mother confirmed the story. I had almost died! That scared hell out of me. I knew I had to do something. I didn't know what. But pills and violence didn't promise much of a future.

I went back to a high school counselor for advice. He suggested I go to college.

I wasn't aware of it, but it seems that in May 1969 a group of dissident students from the black and Puerto Rican communities took over the south campus of the City College of New York (CCNY). They demanded that the Board of Higher Education and the City of New York adopt an open-admission policy that would make it possible for anybody to go to CCNY without the existing requirements: SATs and a high school average of 85. This demand was justified on the premise that college had always been for the privileged few and excluded minorities. As it turned out, in the fall of 1970 the City University's 18 campuses admitted massive numbers of students — 15,000 — with high school averages below 85. By 1972, I was one of them.

On the day I received my letter of acceptance, I waited until dinner to tell my folks. I was proud.

"Check out where I'm going," I said. I passed the letter to my father. He looked at it.

"You jerk!" he said. "You wanna sell ties?" My mother grabbed the letter.

"God," she said. "Why don't you go to work already? Like other people."

"Later for that," I said. "You should be proud."

At the time, of course, I didn't understand where my parents were coming from. They were immigrants. They believed college was for rich kids, not the ones who dropped downs and sang songs on streetcorners. . . .

Anyhow, I wasn't about to listen to my parents and go to work; for a dude like me, this was a big deal. So I left the dinner table and went to tell my friends about my decision.

The Davidson Boys hung out in a rented storefront. They were sitting around the pool table on milk boxes and broken pinball machines, spare tires and dead batteries. I made my announcement. They stood up and circled me like I was the star of a cockfight. Sucio stepped to the table with a can of beer in one hand and a pool stick in the other.

"Wha' you think you gonna get out of college?" he said.

"I don't know, but I bet it beats this," I said. I shoved one of the pool balls across the table. That was a mistake. The others banged their sticks on the wood floor and chanted, "Oooh-ooh — snap, snap." Sucio put his beer on the table.

"Bull!" he yelled. "I wash dishes with college dudes. You're like us — nuttin', man." He pointed the stick at my nose.

Silence.

I couldn't respond. If I let the crowd know I thought their gig was uncool, that I wanted out of the club, they would have taken it personally. And they would have taken me outside and kicked my ass. So I lowered my head. "Aw, hell, gimme a hit of beer," I said, as if it were all a joke. But I left the corner and didn't go back.

I spent that summer alone, reading books like *How to Succeed in College* and *30 Days to a More Powerful Vocabulary.* My vocabulary was limited to a few choice phrases like, "Move over, Rover, and let Petey take over." When my friends did call for me I hid behind the curtains. I knew that if I was going to make it, I'd have to push these guys out of my consciousness as if I were doing the breaststroke in a sea of logs. I had work to do, and people were time consuming. As it happened, all my heavy preparations didn't amount to much.

On the day of the placement exams I went paranoid. Somehow I got the idea that my admission to college was some ugly practical joke that I wasn't prepared for. So I copped some downs and took the test nodding. The words floated on the page like flies on a crock of cream.

That made freshman year difficult. The administration had placed me in all three remedial programs: basic writing, college skills, and math. I was shocked. I had always thought of myself as smart. I was the only one in the neighborhood who read books. So I gave up the pills and pushed aside another log.

The night before the first day of school, my brother walked into my room and threw a briefcase on my desk. "Good luck, Joe College," he said. He smacked me in the back of the head. Surprised, I went to bed early.

I arrived on campus ahead of time with a map in my pocket. I wanted enough time, in case I got lost, to get to my first class. But after wandering around the corridors of one building for what seemed like a long time and hearing the sounds of classes in session, the scrape of chalk and muted discussions, I suddenly wondered if I was in the right place. So I stopped a student and pointed to a dot on my map.

"Look." He pointed to the dot. "Now look." He pointed to an inscription on the front of the building. I was in the right place. "Can't you read?" he said. Then he joined some friends. As he walked off I heard someone say, "What do you expect from open admissions?"

I had no idea that there were a lot of students who resented people like me, who felt I was jeopardizing standards, destroying their institution. I had no idea. I just wanted to go to class.

In Basic Writing I the instructor, Regina Sackmary, chalked her name in bold letters on the blackboard. I sat in the front row and reviewed my *How to Succeed* lessons: Sit in front/don't let eyes wander to cracks on ceilings/take notes on a legal pad/make note of all unfamiliar words and books/listen for key phrases like "remember this," they are a professor's signals. The other students held pens over pads in anticipation. Like me, they didn't know what to expect. We were public school kids from lousy neighborhoods and we knew that some of us didn't have a chance; but we were ready to work hard.

Before class we had rapped about our reasons for going to college. Some said they wanted to be the first in the history of their families to have a college education — they said their parents never went to college because they couldn't afford it, or because their parents' parents were too poor — and they said open admissions and free tuition ($65 per semester) was a chance to change that history. Others said they wanted to be educated so they could return to their neighborhoods to help "the people"; they were the idealists. Some foreigners said they wanted to return to their own countries and start schools. And I said I wanted to escape the boredom and the pain I had known as a kid on the streets. But none of them said they expected a job. Or if they did they were reminded that there were no jobs.

Ms. Sackmary told us that Basic Writing I was part of a three-part program. Part one would instruct us in the fundamentals of composition: sentence structure, grammar, and paragraphing; part two, the outline and essay; and part three, the term paper. She also explained that we weren't in basic writing because there was something wrong with us — we just needed to learn the basics, she said. Somehow I didn't believe her. After class I went to her office. She gave me a quick test. I couldn't write a coherent sentence or construct a paragraph. So we made an agreement: I'd write an essay a day in addition to my regular classwork. Also, I'd do a few term papers. She had this idea that learning to write was like learning to play a musical instrument — it takes practice, everyday practice.

In math I was in this remedial program for algebra, geometry, and trigonometry. But unlike high school math, which I thought was devised to boggle the mind for the sake of boggling, in this course I found I could make a connection between different mathematical principles and my life. For instance, there were certain basics I had to learn — call them 1, 2, and 3 — and unless they added up to 6 I'd probably be a failure. I also got a sense of how math related to the world at large:

Unless the sum of the parts of a society equaled the whole there would be chaos. And these insights jammed my head and made me feel like a kid on a ferris wheel looking at the world for the first time. Everything amazed me!

Like biology. In high school I associated this science with stabbing pins in the hearts of frogs for fun. Or getting high snorting small doses of the chloroform used for experiments on fruit flies. But in college biology I began to learn and appreciate not only how my own life processes functioned but how there were thousands of other life processes I'd never known existed. And this gave me a sense of power, because I could deal with questions like, Why do plants grow? not as I had before, with a simple spill of words: "'Cause of the sun, man." I could actually explain that there was a plant cycle and cycles within the plant cycle. You know how the saying goes — a little knowledge is dangerous. Well, the more I learned the more I ran my mouth off, especially with people who didn't know as much as I did.

I remember the day Ms. Sackmary tossed Sartre's *No Exit* in my lap and said, "Find the existential motif." I didn't know what to look for. What was she talking about? I never studied philosophy. I turned to the table of contents, but there was nothing under E. So I went to the library and after much research I discovered the notion of the absurd. I couldn't believe it. I told as many people as I could. I told them they were absurd, their lives were absurd, everything was absurd. I became obsessed with existentialism. I read Kafka, Camus, Dostoevski, and others in my spare time. Then one day I found a line in a book that I believed summed up my unusual admittance to the college and my determination to work hard. I pasted it to the headboard of my bed. It said: "Everything is possible."

To deal with the heavy workload from all my classes, I needed a study schedule, so I referred to my *How to Succeed* book. I gave myself an hour for lunch and reserved the rest of the time between classes and evenings for homework and research. All this left me very little time for friendships. But I stuck to my schedule and by the middle of the first year I was getting straight A's. Nothing else mattered. Not even my family.

One night my sister pulled me from my desk by the collar. She sat me on the edge of the bed. "Mom and Dad bust their ass to keep you in school. They feed you. Give you a roof. And this is how you pay them back?" She was referring to my habit of locking myself in my room.

"What am I supposed to do?" I said.

"Little things. Like take down the garbage."

"Come on. Mom and Dad need me for that?"

"You know Dad has arthritis. His feet hurt. You want *him* to take it down?" My sister can be melodramatic.

"Let Mom do it," I said. "Or do her feet hurt too?"

"You bastard," she said. "You selfish bastard. The only thing you care about is your books."

She was right. I *was* selfish. But she couldn't understand that in many ways college had become a substitute for my family because what I needed I couldn't get at home. Nobody's fault. She cried.

When I entered my second year my family began to ask, "What do you want to do?" And I got one of those cards from the registrar that has to be filled out in a week or you're dropped from classes. It asked me to declare my major. I had to make a quick decision. So I checked off BS degree, dentistry, though I didn't enroll in a single science course.

One course I did take that semester was The Writer and the City. The professor, Ross Alexander, asked the class to keep a daily journal. He said it should be as creative as possible and reflect some aspect of city life. So I wrote about different experiences I had with my friends. For example, I wrote "Miracle on 183rd Street" about the night "Raunchy" Rick jumped a guy in the park and took his portable radio. When the guy tried to fight back Rick slapped him in the face with the radio; then, using the batteries that spilled out, he pounded this guy in the head until the blood began to puddle on the ground. Those of us on the side-lines dragged Rick away. Ross attached notes to my papers that said things like: "You really have a great hit of talent and ought to take courses in creative writing and sharpen your craft! Hang on to it all for dear life."

In my junior year I forgot dentistry and registered as a creative writing major. I also joined a college newspaper, *The Campus*. Though I knew nothing about journalism, I was advised that writing news was a good way to learn the business. And as Ross once pointed out to me, "As a writer you will need an audience."

I was given my first assignment. I collected piles of quotes and facts and scattered the mess on a desk. I remember typing the story under deadline pressure with one finger while the editors watched me struggle, probably thinking back to their own first stories. When I finished, they passed the copy around. The editor-in-chief looked at it at last and said, "This isn't even English." Yet, they turned it over to a rewrite man and the story appeared with my by-line. Seeing my name in print was like seeing it in lights — flashbulbs popped in my head and I walked into the school cafeteria that day expecting to be recognized by everyone. My mother informed the relatives: "My son is a writer!"

Six months later I quit *The Campus.* A course in New Journalism had made me realize that reporting can be creative. For the first time I read writers like Tom Wolfe and Hunter S. Thompson, and my own news stories began to turn into first-person accounts that read like short stories. *The Campus* refused to publish my stuff, so I joined the *Observation Post*, the only paper on campus that printed first-person material. I wanted to get published.

My first *Post* feature article (a first-person news story on a proposed beer hall at CCNY) was published on the front page. The staff was impressed enough to elect me assistant features editor. However, what they didn't know was that the article had been completely rewritten by the features editor. And the features editor had faith in me, so he never told. He did my share of the work and I kept the title. As he put it: "You'll learn by hanging around and watching. You show talent. You might even get published professionally in 25 years!" Another thing they didn't know — I still hadn't passed my basic English proficiency exam. . . .

God, those early days were painful. Professors would tear up my papers the day they were due and tell me to start over again, with a piece of advice — "Try to say what you really mean." Papers I had spent weeks writing. And I knew I lacked the basic college skills; I was a man reporting to work without his tools. So I smiled when I didn't understand. But sometimes it showed and I paid the price: A professor once told me the only reason I'd pass his course was that I had a nice smile. Yes, those were painful days.

And there were nights I was alone with piles of notebooks and textbooks. I wanted to throw the whole mess out the window; I wanted to give up. Nights the sounds of my friends singing on the corner drifted into my room like a fog over a graveyard and I was afraid I would be swept away. And nights I was filled with questions but the answers were like moon shadows on my curtains: I could see them but I could not grasp them.

Yet I had learned a vital lesson from these countless hours of work in isolation: My whole experience from the day I received my letter of acceptance enabled me to understand how in high school my sense of self-importance came from being one of the boys, a member of the pack, while in college the opposite was true. In order to survive, I had to curb my herd instinct.

Nobody, nobody could give me what I needed to overcome my sense of inadequacy. That was a struggle I had to work at on my own. It could never be a group project. In the end, though people could point out what I had to learn and where to learn it, I was always the one who did the work; and what I learned I earned. And that made me feel as good as being one of the boys. In short, college taught me to appreciate the importance of being alone. I found it was the only way I could get any serious work done.

But those days of trial and uncertainty are over, and the open-admission policy has been eliminated. Anybody who enters the City University's senior colleges must now have an 80 percent high school average. And I am one of those fortunate individuals who in a unique period of American education was given a chance to attend college. But I wonder what will happen to those people who can learn but whose potential doesn't show in their high school average; who might get into street crime if not given a chance to do something constructive? I wonder, because if it weren't for open admissions, the likelihood is I would still be swinging baseball bats on the streets on Friday nights. ■

1. Rondinone's educational experiences led him to the insight that literacy — learning to read, write, and speak articulately — could liberate him from his past limitations and propel him to a future of his own creation. Review the passage by Malcolm X on pages 20–22 and compare the two writers' opinions of the importance of literacy in overcoming obstacles and achieving goals.

2. Besides helping him achieve literacy, Rondinone's educational experiences stimulated his intellectual development and understanding of himself and the world around him. While he was in high school, his mind was set in fixed ruts, limited in perspective, and dominated by the thinking of his friends. In college he began to break out of these fixed patterns and think in new ways, finally arriving at the conclusions that "Everything is possible," and "In order to survive, I had to curb my herd instinct." Describe this evolution in his ways of thinking about the world, identifying the insights he achieved and explaining what experiences led him to these insights.

3. Describe an important decision you have made. In your description, try to reconstruct all the questions that you raised and the issues that your mind

weighed and balanced. After reexamining your decision making, explain whether you find that you would change any part of the final decision. Which part? How would you change it? ◄

Viewing Situations from Different Perspectives

While it is important to think for ourselves, others may have good ideas from which we can learn and benefit. A critical thinker is a person who is willing to listen to and examine carefully other views and new ideas. Nobody has all the answers. Our beliefs represent only one viewpoint or perspective on the problem we are trying to solve or the situation we are trying to understand. In addition to our viewpoint, there may be *other* viewpoints that are equally important and need to be taken into consideration if we are to develop a more complete understanding of the situation.

As children we understand the world from only our own point of view. As we grow, we come into contact with people with different viewpoints and begin to realize that our viewpoint is often inadequate, that we are frequently mistaken, and that our perspective is only one of many. If we are going to learn and develop, we must try to understand and appreciate the viewpoints of others.

THINKING ACTIVITY

2.6   ► Imagine that you have been employed at a new job for the past six months. Although you enjoy the challenge of your responsibilities and you are performing well, you find that you simply cannot complete all your work during office hours. To keep up, you have to work late, take work home, and even work occasionally on weekends. When you explain this to your employer, she says that although she is sorry that the job interferes with your personal life, it has to be done. She suggests that you view this as an investment in your future and that you try to work more efficiently. She reminds you that there are many people who would be happy to have your position.

1. Describe another way to approach your employer, and include some of the reasons that might support your point of view.

2. Now describe this situation from your employer's standpoint, identifying reasons that might support her views.

3. Can you think of any additional steps that you and your employer might take to help resolve this situation? ◀

For most of the important issues and problems in our lives, one viewpoint is simply not adequate to give a full and satisfactory understanding. Thus, to increase and deepen our knowledge, we must seek *other perspectives* on the situations we are trying to understand. We can sometimes accomplish this by using our imagination to visualize other viewpoints. Usually, however, we need to seek actively (and *listen* to) the viewpoints of others. It is often very difficult for us to see things from points of view other than our own, and if we are not careful we can make the very serious mistake of thinking that the way we see things is the way things really are. As well as identifying with perspectives other than our own, we also have to work to understand the *reasons* that support these alternate viewpoints. This approach deepens our understanding of the issues and also stimulates us to evaluate critically our beliefs.

THINKING ACTIVITY

2.7   ▶ Describe a belief of yours that you feel very strongly about. Then explain the reasons or experiences that led you to this belief.

Next, describe a point of view that is *different* from your belief. Identify some of the reasons that someone might hold this belief. ◀

Being open to new ideas and different viewpoints means being *flexible* enough to change or modify our ideas in the light of new information or better insight. Each of us has a tendency to cling to the beliefs we have been brought up with and the conclusions we have arrived at. If we are going to continue to grow and develop as thinkers, however, we have to be willing to change or modify our beliefs when evidence suggests that we should. For example, imagine that you have been brought up with certain views concerning an ethnic group — black, white, Hispanic, Asian, Native American, or any other. As you mature and your experience increases, you may find that the evidence of your experience conflicts with the views you have been raised with. As critical thinkers, we have to be *open* to receiving this new evidence and *flexible* enough to change and modify our ideas on the basis of it. For example, some people are against the possibility of a woman being elected president.

1. What do you think might be the reasons for their opposition?

_____

_____

2. Do you think that their reasons make sense? Explain why or why not.

_____

_____

In contrast to open and flexible thinking, *un*critical thinking tends to be one sided and close minded. People who think this way are convinced that they alone see things as they really are and that everyone who disagrees with them is wrong. The words we use to describe this type of person include "dogmatic," "subjective," and "egocentric." It is very difficult for such people to step outside their own viewpoint in order to see things from other people's perspectives. Part of being an educated person is being able to think in an open-minded and flexible way.

Supporting Diverse Perspectives with Reasons and Evidence

When we are thinking critically, what we think makes sense and we can give good reasons to back up our ideas. As we have seen and will continue to see throughout this book, it is not enough simply to take a position on an issue or make a claim; we have to *back up our views* with other information that we feel supports our position. In other words, there is an important distinction and relationship between *what* we believe and *why* we believe it.

If someone questions *why* we see an issue the way we do, we usually respond by giving reasons or arguments that we feel support our belief. For example, take the question of whether to attend college. What are some of the reasons you might offer to support your decision to enroll in school?

1. It will sharpen my ability to think clearly, solve problems, and make intelligent decisions.

2. _____

3. _____

4. _____

5. _____

6. _____

Although all the reasons you just gave for attending college support your decision, some are obviously more important to you than others. In any case, even though going to college may be the right thing for you to do, this decision does not mean that it is the right thing for everyone to do. In order for us really to appreciate this fact, to see both sides of the issue, we have to put ourselves in the position of others and try to see things from their points of view. What are some of the reasons or arguments someone might give for *not* attending school?

1. _____

2. _____

3. _____

4. _____

5. _____

The responses you just gave demonstrate that, if we are interested in seeing all sides of an issue, we have to be able to give supporting reasons and evidence not just for *our* views, but for the views of *others* as well. Seeing all sides of an issue thus combines these two critical thinking abilities:

• Viewing issues from different perspectives
• Supporting diverse viewpoints with reasons and evidence

Combining these two abilities enables us not only to understand other views about an issue, but also to understand *why* these views are held. Consider the issue of whether seat-belt use should be mandatory. As we try to make sense of this issue, we should attempt to identify not just the reasons that support our views, but also the reasons that support other views. The following are reasons that support each view of this issue.

Issue:

Seat-belt use should be mandatory.	Seat-belt use should not be mandatory.
Supporting Reasons:	*Supporting Reasons:*
1. Studies show that seat belts save lives and reduce injury in accidents.	1. Many people feel that seat belts may trap them in a burning vehicle.

Now see if you can identify additional supporting reasons for each of these views on making use of seat belts mandatory.

Supporting Reasons: *Supporting Reasons:*

2. _____   2. _____

   _____   _____

3. _____   3. _____

   _____   _____

4. _____   4. _____

   _____   _____

THINKING ACTIVITY

2.8 ▶ For each of the following issues, identify reasons that support each side of the issue.

Issue:

1. Multiple-choice and true/false exams should be given in college-level courses.
   Multiple-choice and true/false exams should not be given in college-level courses.

Issue:

2. It is better to live in a society that minimizes the role of government in the lives of its citizens.
   It is better to live in a society in which the government plays a major role in the lives of its citizens.

Issue:

3. The best way to deal with crime is to give long prison sentences.
   Long prison sentences will not reduce crime.

Issue:

4. When a couple divorces, the children should choose the parent with whom they wish to live.
   When a couple divorces, the court should decide all custody issues regarding the children. ◀

THINKING ACTIVITY

2.9 ▶ Working to see different perspectives is crucial in helping us get a more complete understanding of the ideas being expressed in the passages we are reading. Read each of the following passages and then do the following:

1. Identify the main idea of the passage.
2. List the reasons that support the main idea.
3. Develop another view of the main issue.
4. List the reasons that support the other view.

More than at any other time in history, America is plagued by the influence of cults, exclusive groups that present themselves as religions devoted to the worship of a single individual. Initially, most Americans were not terribly concerned with the growth of cults, but then in 1979 more than nine hundred cult members were senselessly slaughtered in the steamy jungles of a small South American country called Guyana. The reason for the slaughter was little more than the wild, paranoid fear of the leader, the Reverend Jim Jones, who called himself father and savior. Since that time, evidence has increased that another cult leader, the Reverend Sun Myung Moon, has amassed a large personal fortune from the purses of his followers, male and female "Moonies," who talk of bliss while peddling pins and emblems preaching the gospel of Moon. Cults, with their hypnotic rituals and their promises of ecstasy, are a threat to American youth, and it is time to implement laws that would allow for a thorough restriction of their movements.

The truth is, deer are a long way from being an endangered species. They survive in a human-dominated environment almost as well as the Norway rat, partly because humans obligingly kill off the deer's predators. In a classic experiment some years ago in the Kaibab Forest in Arizona, local hunters prevailed on government rangers to eliminate the entire cougar population so that humans would be the only deer predators. Humans turned out to be less efficient than the cougar. In a few years the forest was populated by thousands of bony deer starving to death; all vegetation within their reach had been gnawed down to bare wood. At great expense, the government had to trap cougars elsewhere and bring them into the Kaibab.

In contrast to traditional assumptions, it appears that nonunion shops have better benefits than those with unions. During the last month, the Rand Corporation of Boston has surveyed fifteen different industrial companies in North and South Carolina. In ten of the fifteen cases, workers who were not unionized actually had better employee benefits than those who were members of a union. Although their wages were slightly lower, nonunionized workers had better health care and more than the average number of paid sick days. Unions are no longer necessary the way they were twenty or thirty years ago.

If we want auto safety but continue to believe in auto profits, sales, styling, and annual obsolescence, there will be no serious accomplishments. The moment we put safety ahead of these other values, something will happen. If we want better municipal hospitals but are unwilling to disturb the level of spending for defense, for highways, for household appliances, hospital service will not improve. If we want peace but still believe that countries with differing ideologies are threats to one another, we will not get peace. What is confusing is that up to now, while we have wanted such things as conservation, auto safety, hospital care, and peace, we have tried wanting them without changing consciousness, that is, while continuing to accept those underlying values that stand in the way of what we want. The machine can be controlled at the "consumer" level only by people who change their whole value system, their whole world view, their whole way of life. One cannot favor saving our wildlife and wear a fur coat.

Most wicked deeds are done because the doer proposes some good to himself. The liar lies to gain some end; the swindler and thief want things which, if honestly got, might be good in themselves. Even the murderer may be removing an impediment to normal desires or gaining possession of something which his victim keeps from him. None of these people usually does evil for evil's sake. They are selfish or unscrupulous, but their deeds are not gratuitously evil. The killer for sport has no such comprehensible motive. He prefers death to life, darkness to light. He gets nothing except the satisfaction of saying, "Something which wanted to live is dead. There is that much less vitality, consciousness, and, perhaps, joy in the universe. I am the Spirit that Denies." When a human wantonly destroys one of humankind's own works we call him Vandal. When he wantonly destroys one of the works of God we call him Sportsman. ◄

Discussing Ideas in an Organized Way

As we have just seen, exploring different sides of situations and issues helps us come to a clearer understanding of what is taking place. This is the way in which thinking develops. To promote the development of our thinking, we have to be open to the viewpoints of others and be willing to listen and exchange ideas with them. This process of give-and-take, of advancing our views and considering those of others, is known as *discussion*. When we participate in a discussion, we are not simply talking; we are exchanging and exploring our ideas in an organized way.

Unfortunately, our conversations with other people about important topics are too often not productive exchanges, but often degenerate into name calling, shouting matches, or worse. Consider the following dialogue.

> *Person A:* I have a friend who just found out she's pregnant and is trying to decide whether she should have an abortion or have the baby. What do you think?
>
> *Person B:* Well, I think that having an abortion is murder. Your friend doesn't want to be a murderer, does she?
>
> *Person A:* How can you call her a murderer? An abortion is a medical operation.
>
> *Person B:* Abortion *is* murder. It's killing another human being, and your friend doesn't have the right to do that.
>
> *Person A:* Well, you don't have the right to tell her what to do — it's her body and her decision. Nobody should be forced to have a child that is not wanted.
>
> *Person B:* Nobody has the right to commit murder — that's the law.
>
> *Person A:* But abortion isn't murder.
>
> *Person B:* Yes, it is.
>
> *Person A:* No, it isn't.
>
> *Person B:* Good-by! I can't talk to anyone who defends murderers.
>
> *Person A:* And I can't talk to anyone who tries to tell other people how to run their lives.

How would you evaluate the level of communication — or noncommunication — taking place in this exchange? What are the reasons?

_____

_____

_____

_____

If we examine the dynamics of this dialogue, we can see that the two people here are not really:

- Listening to each other
- Supporting their views with reasons and evidence
- Responding to the points being made
- Asking — and trying to answer — important questions
- Trying to increase their understanding rather than simply winning the argument

In short, the people in this exchange are not *discussing* their views, they are simply *expressing* them and trying to influence the other person into agreeing. Contrast this first dialogue with the following one. Although it begins the same way, it quickly takes a much different direction.

Person A: I have a friend who just found that she's pregnant and is trying to decide whether she should have an abortion or have the baby. What do you think?

Person B: Well, I think that having an abortion is murder. Your friend doesn't want to be a murderer, does she?

Person A: Of course she doesn't want to be a murderer! But why do you believe that having an abortion is the same thing as murder?

Person B: Because murder is when we kill another human being, and when you have an abortion, you are killing another human being.

Person A: But is a fetus a human being yet? It certainly is when it is born. But what about before it's born, while it's still in the mother's womb? Is it a person then?

Person B: I think it is. Simply because the fetus hasn't been born doesn't mean that it isn't a person. Remember, sometimes babies are born prematurely, in their eighth or even seventh month of development. And they go on to have happy and useful lives.

Person A: I can see why you think that a fetus in the *last stages* of development — the seventh, eighth, or ninth month — is a person. After all, it can survive outside the womb with special help at the hospital. But what about at the *beginning* of development? Human life begins when an egg is fertilized by a sperm. Do you believe that the fertilized egg is a person?

Person B: Let me think about that for a minute. No, I don't think that a fertilized egg is a person, although many people do. I think that a fertilized egg has the *potential* to become a person — but it isn't a person yet.

Person A: Then at what point in its development do you think a fetus *does* become a person?

Person B: That's a good question, one that I haven't really thought about. I guess you could say that a fetus becomes a person when it begins to look like a person, with a head, hands, feet, and so on. Or you might say that a fetus becomes a person when all of its organs are formed — liver, kidneys, lungs, and so on. Or you might say that it becomes a person when its heart begins to start beating, or when its brain is fully developed. Or you might say that its life begins when it can survive outside the mother. I guess determining when the fetus becomes a person all depends on the *standard* that you use.

Person A: I see what you're saying! Since the development of human life is a continuous process that begins with a fertilized egg and ends with a baby, deciding when the fetus becomes a person depends on at what point in the process of development you decide to draw the line. But *how* do you decide where to draw the line?

Person B: That's a good place to begin another discussion. But right now I have to leave for class. See you later.

How would you contrast the level of communication taking place in this dialogue with that in the first dialogue? What are the reasons?

_____

_____

_____

Naturally, our discussions in life are not always quite this organized and direct. Nevertheless, this second dialogue does provide a good model for what can take place in our everyday lives when we carefully explore an issue or a situation with someone else. Let us take a closer look at this discussion process.

Listening Carefully

Review the second dialogue and notice how each person in the discussion *listens carefully* to what the other person is saying and then tries to comment directly on what has just been said. When we are working hard at listening to others, we are trying to understand the point they are making and the reasons for it. This enables us to imagine ourselves in their position and see things as they see them. Listening in this way often suggests to us new ideas and different ways of viewing the situation that might never have occurred to us. An effective dialogue in this sense is like a game of tennis — you hit the ball to me, I return the ball back to you, you return my return, and so on. The "ball" the discussants keep hitting back and forth is the subject they are gradually analyzing and exploring.

When we have trouble discussing a subject with others, it is often because one or more of the people involved is not really listening, as the first dialogue illustrated. When this happens to us, we are so concerned about expressing our ideas and convincing others that our ideas are right that we do not make much of an effort to understand what they are trying to say. In this case, the discussion usually moves in unproductive directions.

Supporting Views with Reasons and Evidence

As we have seen, critical thinkers strive to support their points of view with evidence and reasons, developing an in-depth understanding of the evidence and reasons that support other viewpoints. Review the second dialogue and identify some of the reasons used by the participants to support their points of view. For example, Person B expresses the view that "abortion is murder" and supports this view with the reasoning that "murder is killing another human being"; if a fetus is a human being, removing it from the womb prematurely is the same thing as murder.

1. *Viewpoint:* _____

   Supporting Reason: _____

2. *Viewpoint:* _____

   Supporting Reason: _____

3. *Viewpoint:* _____

   Supporting Reason: _____

Responding to the Points Being Made

When people engage in effective dialogue, they listen carefully to the people speaking and then respond directly to the points being made instead of simply trying to make their own points. In the second dialogue, Person A responds to Person B's view that "abortion is murder" with the question, "But is a fetus a human being yet?" When we respond directly to other people's views, and they to ours, we extend and deepen our explorations into the issues being discussed. Although people involved in the discussion may not ultimately agree, they should develop more insightful understanding of the important issues and a greater appreciation of other viewpoints. Examine the sample dialogue and notice how each person keeps responding to what the other is saying, creating an ongoing interactive development.

Asking Questions

Asking questions is one of the driving forces in our discussions with others. We explore a subject by raising important questions and then trying to answer them together. This questioning process gradually reveals the various reasons and evidence that support each of the different viewpoints involved. For example, although the two dialogues earlier begin the same way, the second dialogue moves in a completely different direction from the first when Person A poses the question: "But why do you believe that having an abortion is the same thing as murder?" Asking this question directs the discussion toward a mutual exploration of the issues and away from angry confrontation. Identify some of the other key questions that are posed in the dialogue.

1. _____

2. _____

3. _____

4. _____

A guide to the various types of questions that can be posed in exploring issues and situations begins on page 44 of this chapter.

Increasing Understanding

When we discuss subjects with others, we often begin by disagreeing with them. In fact, this is one of the chief reasons that we have discussions. In an effective discussion, however, our main purpose should be to develop our understanding — not to prove ourselves right at any cost. If we are determined to prove ourselves right at any cost, then we are likely not to be open to the ideas of others and to viewpoints that differ from our own.

Imagine that, instead of ending, the second dialogue had continued for a while. In the space provided, create responses that expand the exploration of the ideas being examined. Be sure to keep the following discussion guidelines in mind as you continue the dialogue.

- When we discuss, we have to listen to each other.
- When we discuss, we keep asking — and trying to answer — important questions.
- When we discuss, our main purpose is to develop a further understanding of the subject we are discussing, not to prove that we are right and the other person wrong.

> *Person A:* I see what you're saying! Since the development of human life is a continuous process that begins with a fertilized egg and ends with a baby, deciding when the fetus becomes a person depends on at what point in the process of development you decide to draw the line. But *how* do you decide where to draw the line?

> *Person B:* _____
>
> _____
>
> *Person A:* _____
>
> _____
>
> *Person B:* _____
>
> _____

THINKING ACTIVITY

2.10 ▶ Read the following dialogue exploring the issue of capital punishment written by a student and then continue the discussion, creating an additional three or four responses for each person.

> *Person A:* I heard on the news yesterday that a group of prisoners in Virginia took some hostages in one floor of the prison in protest for the death sentence of one of their inmates who was going to be executed last night. Nine persons were injured in the revolt.

> *Person B:* Why was the man sentenced to die in the electric chair?

> *Person A:* Because he had killed a pregnant woman and her five-year-old daughter a few years ago.

> *Person B:* Do you believe in the death penalty?

Person A: Well, crime has been on the rise year after year. There has to be a way to regulate the increase, and capital punishment is one way.

Person B: It is true that crime has been on the rise, but to take such an option as capital punishment would make us less civilized and desperate. Capital punishment was used in the past with no positive results.

Person A: It may seem desperate to bring back capital punishment. What do you suggest instead?

Person B: I think there should be longer prison terms and less plea bargaining. Also, social programs should be available to help prisoners who finish their terms adapt to civilian life.

Person A: That sounds great, but you are talking about a great increase in the budget in correction and social programs. Why not just kill them and save the money?

Person B: Killing them is the easy way out. And if we kill them, that would make us just as bad as the criminals. What gives us the right to take a life?

Person A: Suppose someone kills, serves his prison sentence, and then kills again. What then?

Now continue the dialogue. ◀

THINKING ACTIVITY

2.11 ▶ Select an important social issue and write a dialogue that analyzes the issue from two different perspectives. As you write your dialogue, keep in mind the qualities of effective discussion: listening carefully to each other and trying to comment directly on what has been said: asking and trying to answer important questions about the subject; and trying to develop a fuller understanding of the subject and not simply trying to prove ourselves right.

After completing your dialogue, read it to the class (with a classmate as a partner). Analyze the class's dialogues by using the criteria for effective discussions that we have examined. ◀

In this chapter we have discovered that critical thinking is not just one way of thinking — it is a total approach to the way we make sense of the world, and it involves an integrated set of thinking abilities and attitudes that include the following:

- Actively using our intelligence, knowledge, and skills to question, explore, and deal effectively with ourselves, others, and life's situations

- Carefully exploring situations by asking — and trying to answer — relevant questions

- Thinking for ourselves by carefully examining various ideas and arriving at our own thoughtful conclusions

- Viewing situations from different perspectives to develop an in-depth, comprehensive understanding

- Discussing ideas with others to exchange and explore ideas in an organized way

THINKING ACTIVITY

2.12 ▶ One useful strategy for developing our critical thinking abilities is to contrast the views of authors who discuss different sides of the same issue. The three reading selections that follow argue different viewpoints on the issue of euthanasia (mercy killing). Apply the skills we have been developing in this chapter by thinking critically about the ideas in the reading selections and then answering the questions that follow.

LIFE SENTENCE: INDIVIDUAL AUTONOMY, MEDICAL TECHNOLOGY, AND THE "COMMON GOOD"
by Howard Moody

Elizabeth Bouvia, a 28-year-old California woman, suffers from severe cerebral palsy; she is quadriplegic — physically helpless and wholly unable to care for herself, totally dependent on others for all her needs. She can only lie flat on her back for the rest of her life, for she also suffers from degenerative arthritis and is in continuous pain.

Our society, using the medical establishment as our surrogate, has condemned Elizabeth Bouvia to life even though this intelligent, if despairing, young woman wants to die. The hospital in which she is a patient, practicing defensive medicine out of fear of liability, denies her the right to refuse treatment on the grounds that it will result in her death.

Elizabeth Bouvia exposes the underside of the miracle of modern medical technology. Her predicament threatens our "happy ending" culture which wants to believe that every problem has a solution, every question an answer, and that the admission of complexity and ambiguity are ways of avoiding progress. She makes it impossible to ignore the fact that the same technologies that make human life more bearable and bodily suffering less formidable can also keep alive severely brain-damaged children, the comatose, and others like Bouvia who endure extreme degrees of pain. Her decision to die and her inability to have that decision honored lay bare our society's attitudes and values about not only modern medical technology but also our most fundamental beliefs about death and life.

Who Shall Say?

The petitioner for Elizabeth Bouvia in the Court of Appeals in the State of California stated what I believe to be the only morally defensible position:

> Who shall say what the minimum amount of available life must be? Does it matter if it be 15 to 20 years, 15 to 20 months or 15 to 20 days, if such life has been physically destroyed and its quality, dignity and purpose gone? As in all matters, lines must be drawn at some point, somewhere, but the decision must ultimately belong to the one whose life is at issue.
>
> Here Elizabeth Bouvia's decision to forego medical treatment or life support through mechanical means belongs to her. It is not a medical decision for physicians to make. Neither is it a legal question whose soundness is to be resolved by lawyers and judges. It is not a conditional right subject to approval by ethics committees or courts of law. It is a moral and philosophical decision that, being a competent adult, is hers alone.

But Elizabeth Bouvia does not have the right to make that decision. The medical experts and attendants testify that if she is force-fed, she could live 15 or 20 more years in that demoralizing and debilitating condition. The "right-to-lifers" believe she has a duty to endure. The concern about there being no foul play or breaching of medical ethics is legitimate. So too is resistance to the unending pain inflicted on her body and mind until death comes to end her artificially prolonged life. Bouvia's passive acceptance of death is no longer sufficient. Our technology has negated that alternative and forced her to endure a highly invasive therapeutic prolongation of her life against her will. In other words, society is protecting her from the death she prefers to her interminable pain.

The person in our society best protected from death is the one that society has condemned to die. Death row inmates are under meticulous surveillance lest they take their own lives before the appointed hour — namely that time when the state has decided they shall die. Ironically, Bouvia also has no right to end her wretched existence until the state is ready. Only when her body finally revolts against all the new technologies of medicine will the state allow her to die.

If you are a hospital chaplain or Bouvia's pastor, what do you say to her or do for her in her utterly helpless and powerless position? How will you honor her integrity in the face of this massive resistance pitted against her weak will? The only theology germane to her case will be that which is born in and of her pain.

Ancient Beliefs

Many, of course, believe that it is wrong for an individual to commit suicide or at least that the individual decision to terminate life cannot be aided or abetted by the larger community (the public). Such beliefs are as old as the ancient Greeks and continue to influence contemporary medical ethics.

". . . [W]e must not participate or assist in taking life, for that would violate what we as a civic community stand for," says Francis I. Kane in a Hastings Center Report ("Keeping Elizabeth Bouvia Alive for the Public Good," December 1985). "Ironically in demanding her individual autonomy, Elizabeth Bouvia has forced us to reaffirm the common good. In demanding that we help destroy her life, she has led us to profess, not just abstractly, the value of this individual life."

But what is the value of this individual life, and who shall make that determination? Society's harsh moralism against the right of a person to terminate his or her own life makes it difficult to draw any distinctions concerning the reason for such decisions. So of course does the medical professional's (society's surrogate) inordinate preoccupation with prolonging life no matter the quality or the circumstances.

If the Constitution of this nation defends any freedom, it is the fundamental "right to privacy." And in a number of Superior Court cases, a person of adult years and in sound mind has the right to determine whether or not to submit to lawful medical treatment. It follows that such a patient has the right to refuse any medical treatment, even that which may prolong or save her life. This basic right to privacy informed the Presidential Commission for the Study of Ethical Problems in Medicine in its conclusion:

> The voluntary choice of a competent and informed patient should determine whether or not life sustaining therapy will be undertaken, just as such choices provide the basis for other decisions about medical treatment . . . Health care professionals serve patients best by maintaining a presumption in favor of sustaining life while recognizing that competent patients are entitled to choose to forego any treatments including those that sustain life (*Deciding to Forego Life Sustaining Treatment*, U.S. Govt. Printing Office).

This right to privacy might enhance an individual's ability to choose life or death. Clearly this has not been the case for Bouvia. Why this is so is related to our society's view of death. Death is thoroughly institutionalized and medicalized. The Enemy or the Grim Reaper, not a welcome Friend, death is deemed unnatural, and its delay, however briefly, seen as the triumph of human achievement over the limitations of nature.

This medical warfare against death is highly dramatized in media events of artificial organ transplants and the heart of a baboon in the body of a newborn baby. A medical and scientific hubris promises a seemingly unending and miraculous control of the life process, foretelling the time when death is a curable disease and immortality a medical commodity.

A "few setbacks" occur. The plague of AIDS is killing off our young people at alarming rates. But this is but a momentary setback to inevitable progress; AIDS will be conquered like all the diseases before it. Listen to the language of "right-to-lifers." In their fanatical semantics God is no longer ultimate but life is the ultimate. And if life becomes God, then the death of a life is deicide. A fetus must not be allowed to die no matter what pain, sorrow, or suffering may result from the consequence of its birth. Likewise, a brain-dead 80-year-old must be kept alive no matter the pain and expense to family and society.

The same logic leads to the refusal to let Elizabeth Bouvia die. That decree does not come from overzealous fundamentalists but from a secular court of law deciding on the values that this society stands for. The absolutizing of life can occur whether one is religious or not.

But surely, the absolute deification of life is an idolatry for the followers of a Master who said "Greater love hath no man than he who lays down his life for a friend" or "she who loses life will find it." For people of faith, life is meaningful and precious (sometimes), but not the only value in this world. Something more important can cause us to lay it on the line. Or we may lay it down when it becomes unbearably painful and meaningless.

In our faith, death and life go together. Death may be irrational to the mind's grasp and irreconcilable to the spirit's longing, but it is natural to the body's functioning. When we say death and life go together, we mean that death is written into our bodies — these bodies are the time-keepers of our lives. A symbol of our finitude and creatureliness, death is also an integral part of our human existence.

In Stanley Keleman's book *Living Your Dying,* he writes, "Our bodies know about dying and at some point in our lives are irrefutably, absolutely and totally committed to it with the lived experience of the genetic code." Death is inscribed into the birth of our bodies. We die to uterine life when we are born into the world, and our dying begins with that birth. But very quickly our minds deny what our bodies know, and in that repression or denial of the idea of our death grows fear, dread, and anxiety. For a society which values eternal youth and deifies life, thinking and talking about death — not as a morbid distraction from the joy of living, but as part of that living, just like illness and disease — is hard but necessary.

Death Not an End

Death with its mystery and unknown quality sometimes repels us, or scares us with its foreboding. Yet we still affirm that some part of us is unafraid of death; something sometimes is elevated and confirmed by death, something we cherish in the face of death, something we sometimes choose even though it means our death. I find it very hard to name, but I know that only in the presence of death are some things made believable.

Those of us believers, conservative and liberal, who loudly proclaim in our faith that life not death has the last word ought to be able to affirm the wish of an Elizabeth Bouvia. We ought to question seriously the use of a technology that, at incredible cost, might prolong life for a few more weeks or months, when the pain is intolerable or existence is a drugged semiconsciousness. Furthermore, people of faith who declare their belief in the resurrection and another reality that is the promise of God ought, more than most, to know that death is not the last word. Therefore, to grasp one more week or month or year even at unbearable pain and often excessive cost is a kind of act of ultimate distrust in God. The cynic in me conjectures that if Christians really believed in life after death, we could save the billions of dollars in health care spent in the last six months of life, trying to rob death of a few more days, weeks, or months.

We need to resist the very real temptation to idolize life while at the same time we value and affirm life as a precious gift of creation. Not life as some kind of intellectual abstraction but life as a contextual reality where body, mind, and spirit are functioning so as to make it desirable, even with its disabilities and suffering.

The sole determiner of that life's quality and meaning is the one whose life it is. In an earlier time when death gave us no options and came earlier, individuals had no choice. With the advance of medical technology and the institutionalization of death, that choice is as valuable as life itself. That choice in modern society may be the ultimate test of our freedom, and to be able to say *no* to life is only possible if we have control of our lives. That control is meaningless if finally the state, through its medical surrogates, decides the time of death.

The right to die is as integral a part of our human freedoms as the right to live, and that right should not be hampered by the state's threat to impose penal sanctions on those medical personnel who might be disposed to lend assistance in ending an unbearable life. The medical profession freed from the threat of governmental or legal reprisal would, very likely, have no difficulty in accommodating an individual in Elizabeth's Bouvia's situation.

Editor's note: Elizabeth Bouvia has been transferred to a nursing home and has accepted life sustaining treatment. She dropped her suit against the hospital which denied her request to withdraw treatment. ■

COURT'S HIDEOUS DECISION MAKES LIFE THE ULTIMATE ABSURDITY *by Frank Morriss*

A Colorado district judge has ruled that a person has a "right to die," and that no one may interfere with that choice. The implications of Judge Charles Buss' ruling are frightening and hideous, and since in the case at hand there was no appeal, the ruling will stand as precedent law until and if it is overruled.

Hector Rodas, 35, has been paralyzed for many months as a result of drug abuse. He cannot speak or swallow, but it is claimed he can communicate by eye or finger movement. A message he began delivering many months ago, it is said, asked that injected nutrition via tubes being given at Hilltop Rehabilitation Hospital, Grand Junction, be discontinued so he could die. The hospital refused this request, claiming it would be liable under suicide or homicide statutes, and questioned Rodas' competence owing to his condition.

In defending his decision on television, Judge Buss insisted that life belongs to the individual and may be terminated at choice. In his opinion, the judge wrote that unwanted treatment such as was being given to Rodas amounted to "an on-going battery" imposed on him. Thus, forced feeding becomes a "battery."

If this is the case, then certainly seizing a person about to jump from a bridge or a building ledge becomes a "battery" if the jumper chooses to discontinue living. Doctors, who are pledged to do all possible to sustain life and prevent death, become guilty of battery if they act to revive someone who has overdosed on drugs in order to kill themselves.

Society is ordered by Judge Buss to become the abetter of self-chosen death, even if by being prohibited from interfering. It is only a small step to demanding that society become the active cooperator in suicide, even though in the Rodas case, Judge Buss by fiat declared the action neither suicide nor murder. Judges, however, do not have the miraculous power to change the nature of an act by renaming it.

Since I have only media reports on this case, I don't know if the judge was able to cite just from where the "right to die" is derived. Of course, the U.S. Supreme Court gave him the example of fabricating a deadly "right" when it held in *Roe v. Wade* that a woman has the "right" to kill her unborn child, and by fiat declared such action by her and her physician not homicide or murder.

Rodas' physician, Larry Cobb, was reported to have refused to take part in the discontinuation of the nutritional sustenance via tubes of his patient's life. The hospital's attorney said that another physician had agreed to step in and act as Rodas' "physician" in the process of neglect that will lead to his death.

The Rodas decision was reinforced by Dr. Frederick R. Abrams, said to be "a nationally recognized medical ethicist," principally I suppose by his association with the Center for Applied Biomedical Ethics at Rose Medical Center, Denver. Dr. Abrams called the "right to die" a "legitimate upholding of personal autonomy."

Were we really given life as an absolute possession, which we may discard as we may throw away any gift? This speaks of the existential idea that life is absurd. But only if life is an absolute possession, to be honored or trashed, can the "right to die" be recognized, as Dr. Abrams' logic recognizes.

The very purpose of life then becomes subject to individual opinion. Autonomy installs each individual as the master of his own life and for his own purposes.

If the autonomous individual sees happiness as his purpose in living, then unhappiness becomes the excuse for the "right to die." If he sees success as his purpose in living, then failure becomes such an excuse. If education and advancement are his purposes, then failure in school or in career becomes an excuse to exercise the "right to die."

What are we going to tell our youth in the face of the Judge Buss decision and the reasoning of Dr. Abrams? We can only say, we think there are things to live for, but if you prefer to die we can't interfere. If, as Dr. Abrams says, Rodas was trapped in a paralyzed body, I might say in his ethic of the autonomous individual we are all trapped in a paralyzed vision of humanity. We are trapped in the evil idea that man is supreme — his own end and purpose, his own measure of the value of any and all things.

It is a terrible situation, as indeed the history of modern society shows, particularly the history of the effect of the philosophy of atheistic existentialism.

If we aren't the property of God, then we are the playthings of chance, or worse, of the Devil. If we are really autonomous to the point of having a right to choose death, then life as a gift we did not ask to be given and did not have the chance to refuse indeed is absurd — as the radical existentialists have said all along.

Hell is the proper home of the fully autonomous individual. It is the place where those who choose to be "on their own" have that wish fulfilled. Heaven is the place for those who concluded life was given to them not by blind fortune, but by a living God. Heaven is the reason *for* life and the end *of* life. You don't get there by concluding that life is given you for your own purposes, rather than God's. Heaven is the reward for accepting life on God's terms and using it on those terms. If that insults your individual autonomy and your "right to die," don't blame God for your missing that reward. ■

MORTAL CHOICES *by Ruth Macklin*

Few would argue against the proposition that modern medicine has brought untold benefits to millions of people. Most would agree that cures for diseases, relief from pain and suffering, and the ability to prolong life are advances for which we can be grateful. But for some patients the burdens of modern medical treatment outweigh the benefits, with the result that an increasing number are now claiming the "right to die."

If the "right to die" seems like an odd sort of right, it is easy to see why. Our society not only opposes suicide, but it spends a considerable amount of money and effort on prevention. It appears to be inconsistent, then, to denounce suicide on the one hand, and yet to proclaim that there exists a "right to die." But the inconsistency is only apparent, as can be shown by first identifying clear, undisputed cases of suicidal behavior, and then comparing these cases with the circumstances in which patients and their families seek to exercise the newly recognized "right to die."

Ann B., a seventy-year-old woman, was admitted against her wishes to the psychiatric ward at City Hospital. She was found by a housekeeper in her apartment, playing with a knife at her wrists. The housekeeper called the emergency medical service, and Ann B. was whisked by ambulance to the psychiatric emergency room, where a psychiatrist evaluated her and found her to be "dangerous to self," meaning "suicidal." The psychiatrist also made a diagnosis of depression. Once she was admitted, Ann B. revealed that she had made a suicide pact with her sister, who had recently fallen ill and was a patient in another unit at City Hospital. The two sisters had had little contact with the outside world and, it appears, had led a somewhat eccentric life in isolation from anyone but each other. Ann B.'s actions with the knife, along with her disclosure of the pact with her sister, make this a clear, undisputed case of genuinely suicidal behavior.

Soon after her admission Ann B. developed a fever and was found to have pneumonia. She said she wanted to die and had to be restrained to keep her in the hospital bed. From that point on, her medical condition deteriorated: a catheter, or thin tube, had to be inserted into her bladder because she was retaining her urine; her respiratory status declined, and a breathing tube was placed; she developed skin infections over her whole body, as well as localized bedsores; and she became incontinent, unable to control her bowel functions. Although the patient had been mentally alert and oriented when she was admitted to the hospital, by this time her mental status had changed. She became lethargic and unresponsive. She lay in bed all day staring at the ceiling. Caregivers rarely found her in any other position. They wondered: Is this patient mentally capable of making decisions on her own behalf? Does her suicidal behavior suggest that she suffers from diminished autonomy, thus opening the way for justified paternalism on the part of her caregivers? Or, on the other hand, does the onset of multiple medical problems change the picture, so that now Ann B. has a rational reason to refuse life-prolonging medical treatments?

Psychiatrists consider depression to be both a life-threatening condition and a "treatable illness." The incidence of suicide attempts among depressed persons is high, and so clinicians in psychiatry and other medical specialties consider it their obligation to treat depression. They tend to dismiss refusals of treatment made by such patients. By definition, it is claimed, a diagnosis of depression means the patient has a bleak outlook on life, decision-making is impaired, and paternalistic behavior toward the patient is warranted. If the depression can be cured, the patient's outlook will improve and he will most likely cease to refuse life-prolonging medical therapies. This reasoning demonstrates the need to distinguish between refusals of medical treatment that stem from suicidal wishes and those that emanate from patients' rational judgments about their own quality of life.

Patients can be kept alive hooked up to respirators, dialysis machines, and other devices that keep their vital organs functioning; terminally ill cancer patients suffering intractable pain are given chemotherapy, blood transfusions, radiation, and other treatments to prolong their lives by a few weeks or months; severely demented elderly patients must often have a tube inserted through the nose and esophagus to the stomach, in order to receive medicines and food. To equate the right to die with suicide would be to fail to recognize that such treatments can sometimes make continued life an excessive burden. Many patients on life supports, who are not depressed, judge the quality of their own life to be so poor that they do not want it prolonged further by artificial means. And those patients whose depression results from learning their diagnosis of terminal illness may wish to die sooner rather than later. Such a wish might then be entirely rational.

Suicidologists have devised the category of "rational" or "logical" suicide to apply to such cases. This approach recognizes a distinction, one that has ethical implications, between suicidal wishes or actual attempts to end one's life that are a consequence of mental illness or emotional disorder and those that arise from a miserable quality of life or a hopeless prognosis. To mark these distinctions, better than the simple phrase "the right to die" are two alternative descriptions: "the right to die a natural death" and "the right to die with dignity."

Hospitalized patients have come up against two formidable barriers in seeking to have treatments withdrawn or withheld. The first is the unwillingness of physicians to allow their patients to forgo therapies that could preserve their lives. Doctors are dedicated to curing disease and to prolonging life. They have traditionally seen it as their duty to pursue these goals, even in the face of refusals by patients who are fully competent to decide about their own treatments. The second barrier has been the law, which until quite recently stood behind physicians in their reluctance to allow patients to refuse treatments when the likely result would be death.

Now, however, much has changed, because of some leading court decisions as well as more assertive actions by patients and their families. Physicians are acknowledging, alongside their obligation to preserve and prolong life, another equally valid goal of medical practice: to relieve suffering. As in any practice having multiple goals, these two noble aims of medicine may sometimes conflict. Even when a life could be prolonged, a physician might question the wisdom of continuing treatment. . . .

The legal developments surrounding patients' rights to refuse life-sustaining treatments are not without their moral problems. Although the trend in living-will statutes suggests that formerly competent patients can now have their wishes honored once they are no longer able to decide for themselves, what about individuals who have never stated what they would want done medically when they are no longer capable of making decisions? Is it morally acceptable for others to make decisions for them? And if so, who should those others be: Doctors? Family members? Judges? Hospital ethics committees? Is there an objective basis for making such decisions? And is there a danger in allowing any person to decide for another based on "quality-of-life" considerations?

In the years since courts were first brought into cases involving termination of life supports, there has been a gradual progression from greater to lesser moral certainty. Early cases dealt with removal of respirators from patients in permanent coma, or withdrawing treatment from patients who had clearly stated their wishes about life prolongation. The final court case to consider here is one in which these features were absent, and in which several important precedents were set. In January 1985, nine years after the [Karen Ann] Quinlan case was decided, the New Jersey Supreme Court permitted the withdrawal of life supports from a nursing-home patient who was not comatose. The patient had no written living will, the "treatment" in question was food and fluids rather than a respirator or other high-technology device, and the life-sustaining measures had to be withdrawn rather than simply withheld.

Claire Conroy was an eighty-four-year-old nursing-home resident who suffered from serious and irreversible physical and mental impairments, including arteriosclerotic heart disease, hypertension, and diabetes. Her condition eventually reached a point where she could not speak and could not swallow enough food and water to sustain herself. She was fed and medicated through a nasogastric tube inserted through her nose and extending down into her stomach. She was incontinent. She could, though, move to a minor extent, and occasionally smiled and moaned in response to stimuli. The patient's nephew, her guardian, sought court permission to remove his incompetent aunt's feeding tube. This request was opposed by the patient's court-appointed guardian, known as guardian *ad litem* (a guardian appointed solely for the purpose of making specific decisions during a limited time period). The patient's own physician stated that he did not think it would be acceptable medical practice to remove the tube and that he was in favor of keeping it in place. Ms. Conroy's nephew, based on his knowledge of his aunt's attitudes, said that if she had been competent, she would never have permitted the nasogastric tube to be inserted in the first place.

Ms. Conroy was a Roman Catholic. A Catholic priest testified in the case that acceptable church teaching could be found in a document entitled "Declaration of Euthanasia" published by the Vatican Congregation for the Doctrine of the Faith, dated June 26, 1980. The test that this document used required a weighing of the burdens and benefits to the patient of remaining alive with the aid of extraordinary life-sustaining medical treatment. The priest said that life-sustaining procedures could be withdrawn if they were extraordinary, which he defined to embrace "all procedures, operations or other interventions which are excessively expensive, burdensome or inconvenient or which offer no hope of benefit to a patient." The priest concluded that the use of the nasogastric tube was extraordinary, and that removal of the tube would be ethical and moral, even though the ensuing period until Ms. Conroy's death would be painful. . . .

Situations involving great ethical and legal uncertainty are those in which a patient is no longer competent, had never clearly stated any preferences while still competent about what sorts of medical treatment should be administered or withheld, but had provided some bit of evidence through attitudes or behavior during prior illnesses. Even more troubling are situations in which no evidence whatsoever is available about what the patient would have wanted. The standard in such cases should be the "best interest" of the patient. But that is precisely the problem: Is there any objective way of determining what is in the best interest of someone lacking the mental capacity to decide about continued life?

The court in the Conroy case tackled this problem head-on. It did not want to rule out the possibility of terminating life-sustaining treatment for persons who had never clearly expressed any desires but who are now suffering a prolonged and painful death. Judge Schreiber, who wrote the opinion in the Conroy case, articulated two best-interest tests for determining when life-sustaining treatment may be withheld, tests that supplement the "subjective test" (what the patient would have wanted).

The two standards are a "limited-objective" test and a "pure-objective" test.

> Under the "limited-objective" test, life-sustaining treatment may be withheld or withdrawn from a patient in Claire Conroy's situation when there is some trustworthy evidence that the patient would have refused treatment, and the decision-maker is satisfied that it is clear that the burdens of the patient's continued life with the treatment outweigh the benefits of that life for him.

The pure-objective test is similar to the limited-objective test but omits the element requiring evidence of the patient's prior wishes. Thus,

> the net burdens of the patient's life with the treatment should clearly and markedly outweigh the benefits that the patient derives from life.

These two tests — limited-objective and pure-objective — constitute a bold step in interpreting the vague notion of "best interest," and the Conroy decision sets an important legal precedent. This is not to say that it will always be an easy matter to apply the tests. The court's wording makes it appear that determining a patient's objective best interest is a matter of arithmetic calculation: the net burdens of his prolonged life (the pain and suffering of his life with the treatment less the amount and duration of pain that the patient would likely experience if the treatment were withdrawn) markedly outweigh any physical pleasure, emotional enjoyment, or intellectual satisfaction that the patient may still be able to derive from life. Yet even if this cannot be accomplished by means of simple calculations, it is a step forward in trying to explicate the notion of "best interest" as it applies to incompetent patients.

It is widely agreed — but with objections voiced by some — that decisions to forgo life-sustaining treatment should not be based on assessments of the personal worth or social utility of another's life, or the value of that life to others. A morally acceptable reason to withdraw or withhold life supports exists when continued life would not be a benefit to the patient. This description clearly fits patients who are irreversibly comatose. With perhaps less certainty it also applies to patients on life supports who have deteriorated mentally to the point where they can no longer recognize their loved ones, cannot experience any pleasure, and can engage in no human relationships. Although safeguards should always be in place for the protection of patients, sound moral principles support the view that it is sometimes permissible to forgo life-sustaining treatments. ■

1. The author of the first article, Howard Moody, states that "the right to die is as integral a part of our human freedoms as the right to live." Explain what Moody means by this statement and identify the reasons he gives to support this view.

2. According to Frank Morriss, the author of the second article, "There is little to live for in a culture and society that talks about death and dying as a 'right.'" Explain what Morriss means by this statement and identify the reasons he gives to support this view.

3. In the view of Ruth Macklin, the author of the third article, "Sound moral principles support the view that it is sometimes permissible to forgo life-sustaining treatments." Explain the circumstances in which Macklin believes these actions are morally permissible and the reasons that she gives to support this position.

4. The patient in the scenario that we explored in this chapter, Paul's father, is in a comatose state, being kept alive with a ventilator and feeding tube. How would we apply the standard of the "limited-objective" test, described in the Ruth Macklin article, to determine what action we should take regarding the patient.

5. There is an important distinction between "passive euthanasia," which refers to the withdrawal of life-sustaining medical equipment, and "active euthanasia," in which an action is taken to end a person's life who is not on life-sustaining equipment. Identify some of the potential abuses that might occur if society enacts laws legitimizing each of these different forms

of euthanasia (as is already beginning to happen), and describe strategies that might be used to avoid these abuses. ◀

Summary

Becoming a critical thinker is a life-long process. Developing the sophisticated thinking abilities needed to understand the complex world we live in and make informed decisions requires ongoing analysis, reflection, and practice. The five qualities of critical thinking that we have identified in this chapter represent signposts in our journey to become mature critical thinkers:

• Thinking actively
• Carefully exploring situations with questions
• Thinking for ourselves
• Viewing situations from different perspectives
• Discussing ideas in an organized way

These critical thinking qualities are a combination of cognitive abilities, basic attitudes, and thinking strategies that enable us to clarify and improve our understanding of the world. By carefully examining the process and products of our thinking — and the thinking of others — we develop insight into the thinking process and learn to do it better. Becoming critical thinkers does not simply involve mastering certain thinking abilities, however; it affects the entire way that we view the world and live our lives. For example, the process of striving to understand other points of view in a situation changes the way we think, feel, and behave. It catapults us out of our own limited way of viewing things, helps us understand others' viewpoints, and broadens our understanding. All of these factors contribute to our becoming sophisticated thinkers and mature human beings.

Critical thinkers are better equipped to deal with the difficult challenges that life poses: to solve problems, to establish and achieve goals, and to make sense of complex issues. The foundation of thinking abilities and critical attitudes introduced in this chapter will be reinforced and elaborated in the chapters ahead, as we continue to explore our remarkable thinking and language processes.

CHAPTER 3

Solving Problems

AN ORGANIZED APPROACH TO SOLVING PROBLEMS

Step One: What Is the Problem?

What do I know about the situation?
What results am I aiming for?
How can I define the problem?

Step Five: How Well Is the Solution Working?

What is my evaluation?
What adjustments are necessary?

Step Two: What Are the Alternatives?

What are the boundaries?
What are possible alternatives?

Step Four: What Is the Solution?

Which alternative(s) will I pursue?
What steps can I take?

Step Three: What Are the Advantages and/or Disadvantages of Each Alternative?

What are the advantages?
What are the disadvantages?
What additional information do I need?

IMAGINE YOURSELF in the following situation. What would your next move be, and what are your reasons for it?

> You are a single parent with one four-year-old child. You have a job as a check-out cashier at a local supermarket. The job just barely pays the bills for you and your child, and you find the job tedious and boring. You have just completed your first semester of school, which you enjoyed immensely. You're hoping that a college education will lead to a career that is financially secure and personally satisfying. Although you're enjoying school, you're physically exhausted and depressed. There just doesn't seem to be enough time in a day for school, your job, and your child. What do you do?

Throughout our lives, we are continually solving problems. Every day each one of us has to solve the relatively minor problem of what to wear. To make a decision, we have to gather certain information — what clothes are clean and available, what is the weather report, what activities do we have planned? Putting all these factors together, we make our choice.

Simple problems like choosing what to wear do not require a systematic or complex analysis. We can solve them with just a little effort and concentration. But the difficult and complicated problems in life are a different story.

When we first approach a difficult problem, it often seems a confused tangle of information, feelings, alternatives, opinions, considerations, and risks. The problem of the single parent just described is a complicated situation that does not seem to offer a single simple solution. Without the benefit of a systematic approach, our thoughts might wander through the tangle of issues like this:

> I want to stay in school . . . but I can't afford to lose my job . . . and I'm not spending enough time with my child — will she stop loving me? . . . but if I don't stay in school, what kind of future do I have? . . . I've got to earn enough to pay the bills, that's most important . . . but if I don't get an education, I'll never get out of the rut I'm in.

Very often when we are faced with difficult problems like this, we simply do not know where to begin in trying to solve them. Every issue is connected to many others. Frustrated by not knowing where to take the first step, we often give up trying to understand the problem. Instead, we may:

1. *Act impulsively*, without thought or consideration (e.g., "I'll just quit school — it's too much work").

2. *Do what someone else suggests* without seriously evaluating the suggestion (e.g., "Tell me what I should do — I'm tired of thinking about this").

3. *Do nothing* as we wait for events to make the decision for us (e.g., "I'll just wait and see what happens before doing anything").

Unfortunately, none of these approaches is likely to succeed in the long run, and they can gradually reduce our confidence in dealing with complex problems.

An alternative to these reactions is to subject the problem to a careful, organized examination. In Chapter One, *Thinking,* we saw that solving problems is one of the important ways our thinking process helps us make sense of the world. We discovered that by carefully exploring our thinking process we could identify the key steps in solving problems and then apply this understanding to new problem situations. The key steps we discovered were:

1. What is the *problem*?
2. What are the *alternatives*?
3. What are the *advantages* and/or *disadvantages* of each alternative?
4. What is the *solution*?
5. How *well* is the solution *working*?

In Chapter Two, *Thinking Critically,* we found that, if we carefully examine our own thinking and the thinking of others, we can clarify and improve our understanding of the world. This is the purpose of critical thinking, and in this chapter we will be thinking critically about the way we solve problems. As we gradually increase our understanding of the thinking involved in solving problems, we will be developing at the same time our ability to solve effectively the complex problems in our lives, such as the problem of the single parent we have been considering here.

The five steps to solving problems that we identified in Chapter One will form the core of our approach. By integrating the critical thinking abilities we explored in Chapter Two, we will further develop this basic approach to thinking through problems. The result of our efforts will be an organized method of analyzing problems that will enable us to work through the complexities of problem situations and help us arrive at thoughtful conclusions. Before we examine the steps that make up the critical problem-solving approach, however, we need to look more deeply at the nature of problems and the response they generate in us.

Accepting the Problem

To solve a problem, we must be willing to admit that a problem exists and we must also be willing to involve ourselves actively in doing something about it. The truth is, we can only solve problems effectively if we are genuinely interested in making sense of them. This means that we must accept responsibility for the problem, actively work toward a solution, and then commit ourselves to action. If we are unwilling — or unable — to think critically by taking an active role in figuring things out and then *acting* on our conclusions, then many of the problems in our lives will simply remain unsolved.

There are two distinct dimensions to accepting problems or challenges: (1) *acknowledging* that the problem exists, and (2) *committing* ourselves to trying to solve the problem. Sometimes we have difficulty in recognizing that there *is* a problem, unless it is pointed out to us. Other times we may actively *resist* acknowledging a problem, even when it is pointed out to us. The person who confidently states, "I don't really have any problems," sometimes has very serious problems — but is simply unwilling to acknowledge them.

On the other hand, mere acknowledgment is not enough to solve a problem. Once we have identified a problem, we must commit ourselves to trying to solve it. Successful problem solvers are highly motivated and willing to persevere through the many challenges and frustrations of the problem-solving process. This willingness to persevere is an important factor in preparing to solve a problem.

How do we find the motivation and commitment that ready us to enter the problem-solving process? There are no simple answers to this question, but a number of strategies may be useful to us:

1. *List the benefits:* Making a detailed list of the benefits we will derive from successfully dealing with the problem is a good place to begin. Such a process helps us clarify why we might want to tackle the problem; motivates us to get started; and serves as a source of encouragement to us when we encounter difficulties or lose momentum.

2. *Formalize our acceptance:* When we formalize our acceptance of a problem, we are "going on record," either by preparing a signed declaration or by signing a "contract" with someone else. This formal commitment serves as an explicit statement of our original intentions that we can refer to if our resolve weakens.

3. *Accept responsibility for our lives:* Robert F. Kennedy, the former presidential candidate who was assassinated in 1968, once said, "Some people see things as they are, and ask, 'Why?' I see things as they could be, and ask, 'Why not?'" Each one of us has the potential to control the direction of our lives, but to do so we must accept our freedom to choose and the responsibility that goes with it. As we saw in the last chapter, critical thinkers actively work to take charge of their lives rather than letting themselves be passively controlled by external forces.

4. *Create a "worst case" scenario:* Some problems persist because we are able to ignore their possible implications. When we use this strategy, we remind ourselves, as graphically as possible, of the potentially disastrous consequences of our actions. For example, using vivid color photographs and research conclusions, we can remind ourselves that excessive smoking, drinking, or eating can lead to myriad health problems and social and psychological difficulties as well as an early and untimely demise.

5. *Identify the constraints:* If we are having difficulty accepting a problem, it is usually because something is holding us back. For example, we might be concerned about the amount of time and effort involved; we might be reluctant to confront the underlying issues the problem represents; we might be worried about finding out unpleasant things about ourselves or others; or we might be inhibited by other problems in our lives, such as a tendency to procrastinate. Whatever the constraints, using this strategy involves identifying and describing all of the factors that are preventing us from attacking the problem, and then addressing these factors one at a time.

Challenging and complex problems rarely solve themselves. To be successful, we must have both the courage to acknowledge these problems and the determination to work through the steps of the problem-solving process.

The Problem-Solving Process

Although we will be using an organized method for working through difficult problems and arriving at thoughtful conclusions, the fact is that our minds do not always work in such a logical, step-by-step fashion. Effective problem solvers typically pass through all the steps we will be examining, but they don't always do so in the sequence we will be describing. Instead, the best problem solvers have an integrated and flexible approach to the process in which they deploy a repertoire of problem-solving strategies as needed. Sometimes exploring the various alternatives helps them go back and redefine the original problem; equally, seeking to implement the solution can often suggest new alternatives.

The key point is that although the problem-solving steps are presented in a logical sequence here, we are not locked into following these steps in a mechanical and unimaginative fashion. At the same time, in learning a problem-solving method like this it is generally not wise to skip steps, because each step deals with an important aspect of the problem. As we become more proficient in using the method, we will find that we can apply its concepts and strategies to problem solving in an increasingly flexible and natural fashion, just as learning the basics of an activity like driving a car gradually gives way to a more organic and integrated performance of the skills involved.

Here is an outline of the method we will be using, an approach built around the five key steps we explored in Chapter One:

1. Step One: What is the problem?
   a. What do I know about the situation?
   b. What are the results I am aiming for in this situation?
   c. How can I define the problem?
2. Step Two: What are the alternatives?
   a. What are the boundaries of the problem situation?
   b. What alternatives are possible within these boundaries?
3. Step Three: What are the advantages and/or disadvantages of each alternative?
   a. What are the advantages of each alternative?
   b. What are the disadvantages of each alternative?
   c. What additional information do I need to evaluate each alternative?
4. Step Four: What is the solution?
   a. Which alternative(s) will I pursue?
   b. What steps can I take to act on the alternative(s) chosen?

5. Step Five: How well is my solution working?

    a. What is my evaluation?

    b. What adjustments are necessary?

Step One: What Is the Problem?

The first step in solving problems is to determine exactly what the central issues of the problem are. If we do not clearly understand what the problem really is, then our chances of solving it are considerably reduced. We may spend our time trying to solve the wrong problem. For example, consider the different formulations of the following problems. How might these formulations lead us in different directions in trying to solve the problem?

"I'm too short."	vs.	"I feel short."
"School is boring."	vs.	"I feel bored in school."
"I'm a failure."	vs.	"I just failed an exam."

In each of these cases a very general conclusion (left column) has been replaced by a more specific characterization of the problem (right column). The general conclusions ("I'm a failure") do not suggest productive ways of resolving the difficulties. They are too absolute, too all encompassing. On the other hand, the more specific descriptions of the problem situation ("I just failed an exam") *do* permit us to attack the problems with useful strategies. In short, the way we define a problem determines not only *how* we will go about solving it, but whether we feel that the problem can be solved at all. Consider the following problem situation that confronted a student.

> The problem that I solved recently dealt with my nine-year-old son Damon. He is a very bright child in the fourth grade who has a reading score of 8.3 and a math score of 7.3. The problem was that he got bored very quickly when the class moved at a slow pace. He started to clown around, fought with other children, and left the room when he got too bored. I went constantly to the

school and met with the teachers to discuss Damon's behavior.

The teachers suggested that Damon had an emotional
problem and asked me to have him tested. I took him to be
tested, but instead of finding an emotional problem, they
found that he was academically way above average. Unfortunately, his school doesn't have a placement for gifted
children in his grade. Despite this result, the principal
and his teachers continued to maintain that Damon was
emotionally disturbed. I knew that Damon was capable of
doing the work and so did his teacher. He just needed a
different learning environment.

I solved the problem by going to my district office to
discuss what was going on. We came to the conclusion that
Damon needed to be placed in a class that specializes in
gifted children. He will be tested again, and if he meets
the requirements, he will be eligible for admission and
financial support to a private school where he can get the
kind of work he needs.

In reflecting on this situation, think about how different "definitions" of the
problem lead to two contrasting analyses (and hence two entirely different
courses of action):

• Damon's problem is that he is emotionally disturbed.

• Damon's problem is that he is academically gifted and gets bored in class.

As this example shows, correct identification of a problem is essential if we
are going to be able to perform a successful analysis and reach an appropriate
conclusion. If we misidentify the problem, we can find ourselves pursuing
an unproductive and even destructive course of action.

Let us return to the problem of the single parent (page 95) and see if we
can answer the question, "What is the problem?" (*Note:* As you work through
this problem-solving approach, apply the steps and strategies to an unsolved
problem(s) in your own life. You will have an opportunity to write up your
analysis when you complete Thinking Activity 3.1 on page 118.) Three additional questions arise when we consider this basic question:

1. What do I know about the situation?

2. What results am I aiming for?

3. How can I state the problem clearly?

What Do I Know about the Situation?

Solving a problem begins with determining what information we *know* to be the case and what information we *think* might be the case. We need to have a clear idea of the details of our beginning circumstances to explore the problem successfully. Sometimes a situation may appear to be a problem when it really isn't, simply because our information isn't accurate. For example, we might be convinced that someone we are attracted to doesn't reciprocate our interest. If this belief is inaccurate, however, then our "problem" doesn't really exist.

We can identify and organize what we know about the problem situation by using *key questions.* In Chapter Two, we examined six types of questions that can be used to explore situations and issues systematically: *fact, interpretation, analysis, synthesis, evaluation, application.* By asking — and trying to answer — questions of fact, we are establishing a sound foundation for the exploration of our problem. Answer the following questions of fact — who, what, where, when, how, why — about the problem at the beginning of the chapter.

1. *Who* are the people involved in this situation? _____

   Who will benefit from solving this problem? _____

   Who can help me solve this problem? _____

2. *What* are the various parts or dimensions of the problem? _____

   _____

   What are our strengths and resources for solving this problem? _____

   _____

   What additional information do we need to solve this problem? _____

   _____

3. *Where* can we find people or additional information to help us solve the problem? _____

4. *When* did the problem begin? _____

   When should the problem be resolved? _____

5. *How* did the problem develop or come into being? _____

   _____

6. *Why* is solving this problem important to me? _____

_____

   Why is this problem difficult to solve? _____

_____

7. *Additional questions:* _____

_____

_____

_____

What Results Am I Aiming For in This Situation?

The second part of answering the question, "What is the problem?" consists of identifying the specific *results* or objectives we are trying to achieve. The results are those aims that will eliminate the problem if we are able to attain them. Whereas the first part of Step One oriented us in terms of the history of the problem and the current situation, this part encourages us to look ahead to the future. In this respect, it is similar to the process of establishing and working toward our goals that we examined in Chapter One. To identify our results, we need to ask ourselves the question: "What are the objectives that, once achieved, will have the effect of solving our problem?" For instance, one of the results or objectives in the sample problem might be gaining a college education. Describe additional results the parent might be trying to achieve in this situation.

1. _____

2. _____

3. _____

4. _____

How Can I Define the Problem?

After exploring what we know about the problem and the results we are aiming to achieve, we need to wind up Step One by defining the problem as clearly and specifically as possible. Defining the problem is a crucial task in the entire problem-solving process because this definition will determine the direction of our analysis, as we saw in the story of Damon on pages 100–101. To define the problem, we need to identify its central issue(s). Sometimes defining the problem is relatively straightforward, such as: "Trying to find enough time to exercise." Often, however, identifying the central issue of a problem is a much more complex process. For example, the statement "My problem is relating to other people" suggests a complicated situation with many interacting variables that resists simple definition. In fact, we may only begin to develop a clear idea of the problem as we engage in the process of trying to solve it. We might begin by believing that our problem is, say, not having the *ability* to succeed and end by concluding that the problem is really a *fear* of success. As we will see, the same insights apply to nonpersonal problems as well. For example, the problem of high school dropouts might initially be defined in terms of problems in the school system, whereas later formulations may identify drug use or social pressure as the core of the problem.

Although there are no simple formulas for defining challenging problems, we can pursue several strategies in identifying the central issue most effectively:

1. *View the problem from different perspectives:* As we saw in Chapter Two, perspective-taking is a key ingredient of thinking critically, and it can help us zero in on many problems as well. For example, when we describe how various individuals might view a given problem — such as the high school dropout rate — the essential ingredients of the problem begin to emerge. In our sample single parent problem, how would you describe the following perspectives?

Parent's perspective: _____

_____

Child's perspective: _____

_____

College counselor's perspective: _____

_____

2. *Identify component problems:* Larger problems are often composed of component problems. To define the larger problem, it is often necessary to identify and describe the subproblems that make it up. For example, poor performance at school might be the result of a number of factors like ineffective study habits, inefficient time management, and preoccupation with a per-

sonal problem. Defining, and dealing effectively with, the larger problem means defining and dealing with the subproblems first. Identify possible subproblems in our sample problem:

Subproblem a: _____

Subproblem b: _____

Subproblem c: _____

3. *State the problem clearly and specifically:* A third defining strategy is to state the problem as clearly and specifically as possible, based on our examination of the problem's objectives. This sort of clear and specific description of the problem is an important step in solving it. For if we state the problem in very *general* terms, we won't have a clear idea of how best to proceed in dealing with it. But if we can describe our problem in more *specific* terms, then our description will begin to suggest actions we can take to solve the problem. Examine the differences between the statements of the following problem:

General: "My problem is money."

More specific: "My problem is budgeting my money so that I won't always run out near the end of the month."

Most specific: "My problem is developing the habit and the discipline to budget my money so that I won't always run out near the end of the month."

Review your analysis of our sample problem and then state the problem as clearly and specifically as possible. _____

_____

_____

Step Two: What Are the Alternatives?

Once we have identified our problem clearly and specifically, our next move is to examine each of the possible actions that might help us solve the problem. Before we list the alternatives, however, it makes sense to determine first which actions are possible and which are impossible. We can do this by exploring the *boundaries* of the problem situation.

What Are the Boundaries of the Problem Situation?

Boundaries are the limits in the problem situation that we simply cannot change. They are a part of the problem, and they must be accepted and dealt with. For example, in our sample situation, the fact that a day has only 24 hours must be accepted as part of the problem situation. There is no point in developing alternatives that ignore this fact. At the same time, we must be careful not to identify as boundaries circumstances that can actually be changed. For instance, we might assume that our problem must be solved in our current geographical location without realizing that relocating to another area — perhaps closer to relatives or friends — is one of our options. Identify additional boundaries that might be a part of our sample situation and some of the questions we would want to answer regarding the boundary.

Time limitations: How much time do I need for each of my basic activities — work, school, child, travel, and sleep? What is the best way to budget this time?

_____ : _____

_____ : _____

_____ : _____

_____ : _____

What Alternatives Are Possible Within These Boundaries?

After we have established a general idea of the boundaries of the problem situation, we can proceed to identify the possible courses of action that can take place within these boundaries. Of course, identifying all the possible alternatives is not always easy; in fact, it may be part of our problem. Often we do not see a way out of a problem because our thinking is set in certain ruts, fixed in certain perspectives. We are blind to other approaches, either because we reject them before seriously considering them ("That will never work!") or because they simply do not occur to us. We can use several strategies to overcome these obstacles:

1. *Discuss the problem with other people:* Discussing possible alternatives with others uses a number of the aspects of critical thinking we explored in Chap-

ter Two. As we saw then, thinking critically involves being open to seeing situations from different viewpoints and discussing our ideas with others in an organized way. Both of these abilities are important in solving problems. As critical thinkers we live — and solve problems — in a community, not simply by ourselves. Other people can often suggest possible alternatives that we haven't thought of, in part because they are outside the situation and thus have a more objective perspective, and in part because they naturally view the world differently than we do, based on their past experiences and their personalities. In addition, discussions are often creative experiences that generate ideas the participants would not have come up with on their own. The dynamics of these interactions often lead to products that are greater than the individual "sum" of those involved.

2. *Brainstorm ideas:* Brainstorming, a method introduced by Alex Osborn, builds on the strengths of working with other people to generate ideas and solve problems. In a typical brainstorming session, a group of people work together to generate as many ideas as possible in a specific period of time. As ideas are produced, they are not judged or evaluated, as this tends to inhibit the free flow of ideas and discourages people from making suggestions. Evaluation is deferred until a later stage. People are encouraged to build on to the ideas of others, since the most creative ideas are often generated through the constructive interplay of various minds. A useful visual adjunct to brainstorming is creating mind maps, a process described in Chapter Nine, *Relating and Organizing.*

3. *Change your location:* Our perspectives on a problem are often tied into the circumstances in which the problem exists. For example, a problem we may be having in school is tied into our daily experiences and habitual reactions to these experiences. Sometimes what we need is a fresh perspective, getting away from the problem situation so that we can view it with more clarity and in a different light.

Using these strategies, as well as your own reflections, identify as many alternatives to help solve our sample problem that you can think of. (Continue additional ideas on a separate sheet of paper.)

1. Take fewer courses.

2. _____

3. _____

4. _____

5. _____

Step Three: What Are the Advantages and/or Disadvantages of Each Alternative?

Once we have identified the various alternatives, our next step is to *evaluate* them, using the kinds of evaluation questions we examined in Chapter Two. Each possible course of action has certain advantages in the sense that if we select that alternative there will be some positive results. At the same time, each of the possible courses of action has disadvantages as well, in the sense that if we select that alternative there may be a cost involved or a risk of some negative results. It is important to examine the potential advantages and/or disadvantages in order to determine how helpful each course of action would be in solving the problem.

What Are the Advantages of Each Alternative?

The alternative we listed in Step Two for the sample problem ("Take fewer courses") might include the following advantages:

Alternatives: *Advantages:*

1. Take fewer courses   This would remove some of the immediate time pressures I am experiencing while still allowing me to prepare for the future. I would have more time to focus on the courses that I am taking and greater opportunity to be with my child.

Identify the advantages of each of the alternatives that you listed in Step Two. Be sure that your responses are thoughtful and specific.

Alternatives: *Advantages:*

2. _____   _____

   _____   _____

3. _____   _____

4. _____   _____

5. _____   _____

What Are the Disadvantages of Each Alternative?

We also need to consider the disadvantages of each alternative. The alternative we listed for the sample problem might include the following disadvantages:

Alternatives: *Disadvantages:*

1. Take fewer courses   It would take me much longer to complete my schooling, thus delaying my progress to my goals. Also, I might lose interest or motivation and drop out before completing school because the process was taking so long. Being a part-time student might threaten my eligibility for financial aid.

Now identify the disadvantages of each of the alternatives that you listed above. Be sure that your responses are thoughtful and specific.

Alternatives: *Disadvantages:*

2. _____   _____

   _____   _____

   _____   _____

   _____   _____

3. _____   _____

   _____   _____

   _____   _____

   _____   _____

4. _____   _____

   _____   _____

   _____   _____

   _____   _____

5. _____   _____

   _____   _____

   _____   _____

   _____   _____

What Additional Information Do I Need to Evaluate Each Alternative?

The next part of Step Three consists in determining what we must know (information needed) to best evaluate and compare the alternatives. For each alternative there are questions that must be answered if we are to establish which alternatives make sense and which do not. In addition, we need to figure out where best to get this information (*sources*).

One useful way to identify the information we need is to ask ourselves the question, *"What if* I select this alternative?" For instance, one alternative in our sample problem was "taking fewer courses." When we ask ourselves the question, *"What if* I take fewer courses?" we are trying to predict what will occur if we select this course of action. To make these predictions, we must answer certain questions and find the information to answer them.

- How long will it take me to complete my schooling?
- How long can I continue in school without losing interest and dropping out?
- Will I threaten my eligibility for financial aid if I become a part-time student?

The information — and the sources for it — that must be located for the first alternative in our sample problem might include the following:

Alternative:

Information Needed and Sources:

1. Taking fewer courses

Information: How long will it take me to complete my schooling? How long can I continue in school without losing interest and dropping out? Will I threaten my eligibility for financial aid if I become a part-time student?

Sources: Myself, other part-time students, school counselors, financial aid office.

Identify the information needed and the sources of this information for each of the alternatives that you identified on page 107. Be sure that your responses are thoughtful and specific.

Alternatives:

Information Needed and Sources:

2. _____   *Information:* _____

_____   _____

_____   _____

_____

Sources: _____

_____

_____

3. _____   *Information:* _____

_____   _____

_____   _____

_____   _____

                           Sources: _____

                           _____

                           _____

4. _____   *Information:* _____

_____   _____

_____   _____

_____   _____

                           Sources: _____

                           _____

                           _____

5. _____   *Information:* _____

_____   _____

_____   _____

_____   _____

                           Sources: _____

                           _____

                           _____

_____

Step Four: What Is the Solution?

The purpose of Steps One, Two, and Three is to analyze our problem in a systematic and detailed fashion — to work through the problem in order to become thoroughly familiar with it and the possible solutions to it. After breaking down the problem in this way, our final step should be to try to put the pieces back together — that is, to decide on a thoughtful course of action based on our increased understanding. Even though this sort of problem analysis does not guarantee finding a specific solution to the problem, it should *deepen our understanding* of exactly what the problem is about. And in locating and evaluating our alternatives, it should give us some very good ideas about the general direction we should move in and the immediate steps we should take.

What Alternative(s) Will I Pursue?

There is no simple formula or recipe to tell us which alternatives to select. As we work through the different courses of action that are possible, we may find that we can immediately rule some out. For example, in our sample problem we may know with certainty that we do not want to take fewer courses (alternative 1). However, it may not be so simple to select which of the other alternatives we wish to pursue. How do we decide?

The decisions we make usually depend on what we believe to be most important to us. These beliefs regarding what is most important to us are known as *values*. Our values are the starting points of our actions and strongly influence our decisions. For example, if we value staying alive (as most of us do), then we will make many decisions each day that express this value — eating proper meals, not walking in front of moving traffic, and so on.

Our values help us set *priorities* in life — that is, decide what aspects of our lives are most important to us. We might decide that for the present going to school is more important than having an active social life. In this case, going to school is a higher priority than having an active social life. Unfortunately, our values are not always consistent with each other — we may have to choose *either* to go to school *or* to have an active social life. Both activities may be important to us; they are simply not compatible with each other. Very often the *conflicts* between our values constitute the problem. Let's examine some strategies for selecting alternatives that might help us solve our problem:

1. *Evaluate and compare alternatives:* Although each alternative may have certain advantages and disadvantages, not all advantages are equally desirable or potentially effective. For example, giving up the child for adoption would certainly solve some aspects of our sample problem, but its obvious disadvantages would rule out this solution for most people. Thus it makes sense

to try to evaluate and rank the various alternatives, based on how effective they are likely to be and how they match up with our value system. A good place to begin is the "Results" stage in Step One. Examine each of the alternatives and evaluate how well it will contribute to achieving the results we are aiming for in the situation. We may want to rank the alternatives or develop our own rating system to assess their relative effectiveness.

After evaluating the alternatives in terms of their anticipated *effectiveness*, the next step is to evaluate them in terms of their *desirability*, based on our needs, interests, and value systems. Again, we can use either a ranking or a rating system to assess their relative desirability. After completing these two separate evaluations, we can then select the alternative(s) that seem most appropriate. Review the alternatives you identified in the sample problem and then rank or rate them according to their potential effectiveness and desirability, assuming this problem was your own.

2. *Synthesize a new alternative:* After reviewing and evaluating the alternatives we generated, we may develop a new alternative that combines the best qualities of several options while avoiding the disadvantages some of them have if chosen exclusively. In our sample problem, we might combine taking fewer courses during the academic year with attending school during the summer session so that progress toward our degree won't be impeded. Examine the alternatives you identified and develop a new option that combines the best elements of several of them.

3. *Try out each alternative — in your imagination:* Focus on each alternative and try to imagine, as concretely as possible, what it would be like if you actually selected it. Visualize what impact your choice would have on your problem and what the implications would be for your life as a whole. By trying out the alternative in our imaginations, we can sometimes avoid unpleasant results or unexpected consequences. As a variation of this strategy, we can sometimes test alternatives on a very limited basis in a practice situation. For example, if we are trying to overcome our fear of speaking in groups, we can practice various speaking techniques with our friends or family until we find an approach we are comfortable with.

After trying out these strategies on our sample problem, select the alternative you think would be most effective and desirable from your standpoint.

Alternative: _____

_____

What Steps Can I Take to Act on the Alternative(s) Chosen?

Once we have decided on the correct alternative(s) to pursue, our next move is to plan the steps we will have to take to put it in action. This is the same process of working toward our goals that we explored in Chapter One. Planning the specific steps we will take is extremely important. Although thinking carefully about our problem is necessary, it is not enough if we hope to solve the problem. We have to *take action*, and planning specific steps is where we begin. In our sample problem, for example, imagine that one of the alternatives we have selected is "Find additional sources of income that will enable me to work part time, go to school full time, and spend more time with my child." The specific steps we would want to take might include the following:

1. Contact the financial aid office at the school to see what aid is available and what I have to do to apply for it.

2. Contact some of the local banks to see what sort of student loans are available.

3. Talk to my parents about the problem to determine what assistance they might be willing and able to offer.

4. Contact the other parent of my child to see if he or she is willing to contribute to the child's support. (If not, consider whether legal action makes sense.)

5. Talk with other students who are attending school part-time, to share their experiences.

Identify the steps you would have to take in pursuing the alternative(s) you identified on page 107.

1. _____

_____

2. _____

_____

3. _____

_____

4. _____

_____

5. _____

_____

Of course, plans do not implement themselves. Once we know what actions we have to take, we need to commit ourselves to taking the necessary steps. This is where many people stumble in the problem-solving process, paralyzed by inertia or fear. Sometimes, to overcome these blocks and inhibitions, we need to reexamine our original acceptance of the problem, perhaps making use of some of the strategies we explored on pages 97–98. Once we get started, the rewards of actively attacking our problem are often enough incentive to keep us focused and motivated.

Step Five: How Well Is the Solution Working?

As we work toward reaching a reasonable and informed conclusion, we should not fall into the trap of thinking that there is only one "right" decision and that all is lost if we do not figure out what it is and carry it out. We should remind ourselves that any analysis of problem situations, no matter how careful and systematic, is ultimately limited. We simply cannot anticipate or predict everything that is going to happen in the future. As a result, every decision we make is provisional, in the sense that our ongoing experience will inform us if our decisions are working out or if they need to be changed and modified. As we saw in Chapter Two, this is precisely the attitude of the critical thinker — someone who is *receptive* to new ideas and experiences and *flexible* enough to change or modify beliefs based on new information. Critical thinking is not a compulsion to find the "right" answer or make the "correct" decision; it is an ongoing process of exploration and discovery.

What Is My Evaluation?

In many cases the relative effectiveness of our efforts will be apparent. In other cases it will be helpful to pursue a more systematic evaluation, along the lines suggested in the following strategies.

1. *Compare the results with the goals:* The essence of evaluation is comparing the results of our efforts with the initial goals we are trying to achieve. For example, the goals of our sample problem are embodied in the results we specified on page 103. Compare the anticipated results of the alternative(s)

you selected. To what extent will your choice meet these goals? Are there goals that are not likely to be met by your alternative(s)? Which ones? Could they be addressed by other alternatives? Asking these and other questions will help you clarify the success of your efforts, and provide a foundation for future decisions.

2. *Get other perspectives:* As we have seen throughout the problem-solving process, getting the opinions of others is a productive strategy at virtually every stage, and this is certainly true for evaluation. Other people can often provide perspectives that are both different and more objective than ours. Naturally, the evaluations of others are not always better or more accurate than our own, but even when they are not, reflecting on these different views usually deepens our understanding of the situation. It is not always easy to receive the evaluations of others, but open-mindedness to outside opinions is a very valuable attitude to cultivate, for it will stimulate and guide us to produce our best efforts.

To receive specific, practical feedback from others, we need to ask specific, practical questions that will elicit this information. General questions ("What do you think of this?") typically result in overly general, unhelpful responses ("It sounds O.K. to me"). Be focused in soliciting feedback, and remember: We do have the right to ask people to be *constructive* in their comments, providing suggestions for improvement rather than flatly expressing what they think is wrong.

What Adjustments Are Necessary?

As a result of our review, we may discover that the alternative we selected is not feasible or is not leading to satisfactory results. For example, in our sample problem, we may find that it is impossible to find additional sources of income so that we can work part time instead of full time. In that case, we simply have to go back and review the other alternatives to identify another possible course of action. At other times we may find that the alternative we selected is working out fairly well but still requires some adjustments as we continue to work toward our desired outcomes. In fact, this is a typical situation that we should expect to occur. Even when things initially appear to be working reasonably well, an active thinker continues to ask questions such as "What might I have overlooked?" and "How could I have done this differently?" Of course, asking — and trying to answer — questions like this is even more essential if solutions are hard to come by (as they usually are in real-world problems) and if we are to retain the flexibility and optimism we need to tackle a new option.

THINKING ACTIVITY

3.1   ▶ Select a problem from your own life. It should be one that you are currently grappling with and have not yet been able to solve. After selecting the problem you want to work on, use the five-step problem-solving method we have explored in the chapter to guide your analysis. Discuss your problem with other class members to generate fresh perspectives and unusual alternatives that might not have occurred to you. Using your own paper, write your analysis in outline style, giving specific responses to the questions in each step of the problem-solving method. Although you might not reach a "guaranteed" solution to your problem, you should deepen your understanding of the problem and develop a concrete plan of action that will help you move in the right direction. Implement your plan of action and then monitor the results. The problem-solving outline we developed in this chapter is as follows:

1. Step One: What is the problem?
    a. What do I know about the situation?
    b. What are the results I am aiming for in this situation?
    c. How can I define the problem?
2. Step Two: What are the alternatives?
    a. What are the boundaries of the problem situation?
    b. What alternatives are possible within these boundaries?
3. Step Three: What are the advantages and/or disadvantages of each alternative?
    a. What are the advantages of each alternative?
    b. What are the disadvantages of each alternative?
    c. What additional information do I need to evaluate each alternative?
4. Step Four: What is the solution?
    a. Which alternative(s) will I pursue?
    b. What steps can I take to act on the alternative(s) chosen?
5. Step Five: How well is the solution working?
    a. What is my evaluation?
    b. What adjustments are necessary? ◀

THINKING ACTIVITY

3.2 ▶ Analyze the following problems using the problem-solving approach presented in this chapter. Follow the guidelines established in Thinking Activity 3.1.

Problem 1   *Background Information*

The most important unsolved problem that exists for me is the inability to make that crucial decision of what to major in. I want to be secure with respect to both money and happiness when I make a career for myself, and I don't want to make a mistake in choosing a field of study.

I want to make this decision before beginning the next semester so that I can start immediately in my career. I've been thinking about managerial studies. However, I often wonder if I have the capacity to make executive decisions when I can't even decide on what I want to do with my life.

Problem 2   *Background Information*

One of my problems is my difficulty in taking tests. It's not that I don't study. What happens is that when I get the test I become nervous and my mind goes blank. For example, in my social science class, the teacher told the class on Tuesday that there would be a test on Thursday. That afternoon I went home and began studying for the test. By Thursday I knew most of the work, but when the test was handed out, I got nervous and my mind went blank. For a long time I just stared at the test, and I ended up failing it.

Problem 3   *Background Information*

My problem is "the weed." I have been smoking cigarettes for over five years. At first I did it because I liked the image and most of my friends were smoking as well. Gradually, I got hooked. It's such a part of my life now, I don't know if I can quit. Having a cup of coffee, studying, talking to people — it just seems natural to have a cigarette in my hand. I know there are a lot of good reasons for me to stop. I've even tried a few times, but I always ended up bumming cigarettes from friends and then giving up entirely. I don't want my health to go up in smoke, but I don't know what to do.

Problem 4   *Background Information*

One of the serious problems in my life is learning English as a second language. It is not so easy to learn a second language, especially when you live in an environment where only your native language is spoken.

When I came to this country three years ago, I could speak almost no English. I have learned a lot, but my lack of fluency is getting in the way of my studies and my social relationships. ◀

Solving Nonpersonal Problems

The problems we have analyzed up until this point are "personal" problems in the sense that they represent individual challenges encountered by us as we live our lives. Problems are not only of a personal nature, however. We also face problems as members of a community, society, and the world. As with personal problems, we need to approach these kinds of problems in an organized and thoughtful way in order to explore the issues, develop a clear understanding, and decide on an informed plan of action. For example, racism and prejudice directed toward blacks, Hispanics, Asians, Jews, homosexuals, and other minority groups seems to be on the rise at many college campuses. There has been an increase of overt racial incidents at colleges and universities during the past several years, a particularly disturbing situation given the lofty egalitarian ideals of higher education. Experts from different fields have offered a variety of explanations to account for this behavior. In the space provided, describe why you believe these racial and ethnic incidents are occurring with increasing frequency.

_____

_____

_____

_____

_____

Making sense of a complex, challenging situation like this is not a simple process. Although the problem-solving method we have been using in this chapter is a powerful approach, its successful application depends on having sufficient information about the situation we are trying to solve. As a result, it is often necessary for us to research articles and other sources of information to develop informed opinions about the problem we are investigating.

THINKING ACTIVITY

3.3 ▶ Identify an important national or international problem that needs to be solved. Locate two or more articles that provide background information and analysis of the problem. Using these articles as a resource, analyze the problem using the problem-solving method developed in this chapter. ◀

THINKING ACTIVITY

3.4 ▶ The final section of this chapter includes three articles dealing with significant social problems in our lives today. The first, "Young Hate," by David Shenk, examines the problem of racism on college campuses. This information provides a foundation from which we can construct a thoughtful analysis of this troubling problem and perhaps develop some productive solutions. The next, "Profiles of Today's Youth: They Couldn't Care Less," by Michael Oreskes, similarly provides background information regarding young people's apathy toward larger social issues. The final article, "Looking Ahead: More Mouths, Less Food," addresses the problem of world hunger and overpopulation.

After reading each article, identify and analyze the problem being discussed using the problem-solving method developed in this chapter.

YOUNG HATE *by David Shenk*

Death to gays. Here is the relevant sequence of events: On Monday night Jerry Mattioli leads a candlelight vigil for lesbian and gay rights. *Gays are trash.* On Tuesday his name is in the school paper and he can hear whispers and feel more, colder stares than usual. On Wednesday morning a walking bridge in the middle of the Michigan State campus is found to be covered with violent epithets warning campus homosexuals to *be afraid, very afraid,* promising to *abolish faggots from existence,* and including messages specifically directed at Mattioli. Beginning Friday morning fifteen of the perpetrators, all known to Mattioli by name and face, are rounded up and quietly disciplined by the university. *Go home faggots.* On Friday afternoon Mattioli is asked by university officials to leave campus for the weekend, for his own safety. He does, and a few hours later receives a phone call from a friend who tells him that his dormitory room has been torched. MSU's second annual "Cross Cultural Week" is over.

"Everything was ruined," Mattioli says. "What wasn't burned was ruined by smoke and heat and by the water. On Saturday I sat with the fire investigator all day, and we went through the room, literally ash by ash . . . The answering machine had melted. The receiver of the telephone on the wall had stretched to about three feet long. That's how intense the heat was."

"Good News!" says Peter Jennings. A recent *Washington Post*/ABC News poll shows that integration is up and racial tension is down in America, as compared with eight years ago. Of course, in any trend there are fluctuations, exceptions. At the University of Massachusetts at Amherst, an estimated two thousand whites chase twenty blacks in a clash after a 1986 World Series game, race riots break out in Miami in 1988 and in Virginia Beach in 1989; and on college campuses across the country, our nation's young elite experience an entire decade's aberration from the poll's findings: incidents of ethnic, religious, and gender-related harassment surge throughout the eighties.

Greatest hits include Randy Bowman, a black student at the University of Texas, having to respectfully decline a request by two young men wearing Ronald Reagan masks and wielding a pistsol to exit his eighth-floor dorm room through the window; homemade T-shirts, *Thank God for AIDS* and *Aryan by the Grace of God*, among others, worn proudly on campus; Jewish student centers shot at, stoned, and defaced at Memphis State, University of Kansas, Rutgers (*Six million, why not*), and elsewhere; the black chairperson of United Minorities Council at U Penn getting a dose of hi-tech hate via answering machine: *We're going to lynch you, nigger shit. We are going to lynch you.*

The big picture is less graphic, but just as dreadful: reports of campus harassment have increased as much as 400 percent since 1985. Dropout rates for black students in predominantly white colleges are as much as five times higher than white dropout rates at the same schools and black dropout rates at black schools. The Anti-Defamation League reports a sixfold increase in anti-Semitic episodes on campuses between 1985 and 1988. Meanwhile, Howard J. Ehrlich of the National Institute Against Prejudice and Violence reminds us that "up to 80 percent of harassed students don't report the harassment." Clearly, the barrage of news reports reveals only the tip of a thoroughly sour iceberg.

Colleges have responded to incidents of intolerance — and the subsequent demands of minority rights groups — with the mandatory ethnic culture classes and restrictions on verbal harassment. But what price tranquility? Libertarian and conservative student groups, faculty, and political advisors lash out over limitations on free speech and the improper embrace of liberal political agendas. "Progressive academic administrations," writes University of Pennsylvania professor Alan Charles Kors in the *Wall Street Journal*, "are determined to enlighten their morally benighted students and protect the community from political sin."

Kors and kind bristle at the language of compromise being attached to official university policy. The preamble to the University of Michigan's new policy on discriminatory behavior read, in part, "Because there is tension between freedom of speech, the right of individuals to be free from injury caused by discrimination, and the University's duty to protect the educational process . . . it may be necessary to have varying standards depending on the locus of regulated conduct." The policy tried to "strike a balance" by applying different sets of restrictions to academic centers, open areas, and living quarters, but in so doing, hit a wall. Before the policy could go into effect, it was struck down in a Michigan court as being too vague. At least a dozen schools in the process of formulating their own policies scurried in retreat as buoyant free-speech advocates went on the offensive. Tufts University president Jean Mayer voluntarily dismissed his school's "Freedom of Speech versus Freedom from Harassment" policy after a particularly inventive demonstration by late-night protestors, who used chalk, tape, and poster board to divide the campus into designated free speech, limited speech, and non–free speech zones. "We're not working for a right to offensive speech," says admitted chalker Andrew Zappia, co-editor of the conservative campus paper, *The Primary Source*. "This is about protecting free speech, in general, and allowing the community to set its own standards about what is appropriate . . .

"The purpose of the Tufts policy was to prosecute people for what the university described as 'gray area' — meaning unintentional — harassment." Zappia gives a hypothetical example: "I'm a Catholic living in a dorm, and I put up a poster in my room [consistent with my faith] saying that homosexuality is bad. If I have a gay roommate or one who doesn't agree with me, he could have me prosecuted, not because I hung it there to offend him, but because it's gray area harassment . . . The policy was well intended, but it was dangerously vague. They used words like *stigmatizing, offensive, harassing* — words that are very difficult to define."

Detroit lawyer Walter B. Connolly, Jr. disagrees. He insists that it's quite proper for schools to act to protect the victims of discrimination as long as the restrictions stay out of the classroom. "Defamation, child pornography, fighting words, inappropriate comments on the radio — there are all sorts of areas where the First Amendment isn't the preeminent burning omnipotence in the sky . . . Whenever you have competing interests of a federal statute [and] the Constitution, you end up balancing."

If you want to see a liberal who follows this issue flinch, whisper into his or her ear the name Shelby Steele. Liberals don't like Steele, an English professor at California's San Jose State; they try to dismiss him as having no professional experience in the study of racial discrimination. But he's heavily into the subject, and his analyses are both lucid and disturbing. Steele doesn't favor restrictions on speech, largely because they don't deal with what he sees as the problem. "You don't gain very much by trying to legislate the problem away, curtailing everyone's rights in the process," he says. In a forum in which almost everyone roars against a shadowy, usually nameless contingent of racist thugs, Steele deviates, choosing instead to accuse the accusers. He blames not the racists, but the weak-kneed liberal administrators and power-hunger victims' advocates for the mess on campuses today.

"Racial tension on campus is the result more of racial equality than inequality," says Steele. "On campuses today, as throughout society, blacks enjoy equality under the law — a profound social advancement. . . . What has emerged in recent years . . . in a sense as a result of progress . . . is a *politics of difference,* a troubling, volatile politics in which each group justifies itself, its sense of worth and its pursuit of power, through difference alone." On nearly every campus, says Steele, groups representing blacks, Hispanics, Asians, gays, women, Jews, and any combinations therein solicit special resources. Asked for — often demanded, in intense demonstrations — are funds for African-American (Hispanic . . .) cultural centers, separate (face it, segregated) housing, ethnic studies programs, and even individual academic incentives — at Penn State, minority students are given $275 per semester if they earn a C average, twice that if they do better than 2.75.

These entitlements, however, do not just appear *deus ex machina.* Part two of Steele's thesis addresses what he calls the "capitulation" of campus presidents. To avoid feelings of guilt stemming from past discrimination against minority groups, Steele says, "[campus administrators have] tended to go along with whatever blacks put on the table, rather than work with them to assess their real needs. . . . Administrators would never give white students a theme house where they could be 'more comfortable with people of their own kind,' yet more and more universities are doing this for black students." Steele sees white frustration as the inevitable result.

"White students are not invited to the negotiating table from which they see blacks and others walk away with concessions," he says. "The presumption is that they do not deserve to be there, because they are white. So they can only be defensive, and the less mature among them will be aggressive."

Course, some folks see it another way. The students fighting for minority rights aren't wicked political corruptors, but champions of a cause far too long suppressed by the white male hegemony. Responsive administrators are engaged not in capitulation, but in progress. And one shouldn't look for the cause of this mess on any campus, because he doesn't live on one. His address used to be the White House, but then he moved to 666 St. Cloud Road. Ronald Reagan, come on down.

Dr. Manning Marble, University of Colorado: "The shattering assault against the economic, social, and political status of the black American community as a whole [is symbolized by] the Reagan Administration in the 1980s. The Civil Rights Commission was gutted; affirmative action became a 'dead letter'; social welfare, health care, employment training, and educational loans were all severely reduced. This had a disproportionately more negative impact upon black youth."

The "perception is already widespread that the society at large is more permissive toward discriminatory attitudes and behaviors, and less committed to equal opportunity and affirmative action," concluded a 1988 conference at Northern Illinois University. John Wiener, writing in *The Nation,* attacks long-standing institutions of bigotry, asserting, for example, that "racism is endemic to the fraternity subculture," and praises the efforts of some schools to double the number of minority faculty and increase minority fellowships. On behalf of progressives across the land, Wiener writes off Shelby Steele as someone who is content to "blame the victim."

So the machine has melted, the phone has stretched to where it is useless. This is how intense the heat is. Liberals, who largely control the administration, faculty, and students' rights groups of leading academic institutions, have, with virtually no intensive intellectual debate, inculcated schools with their answers to the problem of bigotry. Conservatives, with a long history of insensitivity to minority concerns, have been all but shut out of the debate, and now want back in. Their intensive pursuit of the true nature of bigotry and the proper response to it — working to assess the "real needs" of campuses rather than simply bowing to pressure — deserves to be embraced by all concerned parties, and probably would have been by now but for two small items: a) Reagan, their fearless leader, clearly *was* insensitive to ethnic/feminist concerns (even Steele agrees with this); and b) some of the more coherent conservative pundits *still* show a blatant apathy to the problems of big-otry in this country. This has been sufficient ammunition for liberals who are continually looking for an excuse to keep conservatives out of the dialogue. So now we have clashes rather than debates: on how much one can say, on how much one should have to hear. Two negatives: one side wants to crack down on expression, the other on awareness. The machine has melted, and it's going to take some consensus to build a new one. Intellectual provincialism will have to end before young hate ever will.

A Month in the Life of Campus Bigotry

April 1.

Vandals spray-paint "Jewhaters will pay" and other slogans on the office walls of *The Michigan Daily* (University of Michigan) in response to edi-torials condemning Israel for policies regarding the Palestinians. Pro-Israeli and pro-Palestinian shanties defaced; one is burned.

U of M: Fliers circulated over the weekend announce "White Pride Month."

Southern Connecticut State University reportedly suspends five frater-nity officers after racial brawl.

April 2.

Several gay men of the University of Connecticut are taunted by two students, who yell "faggot" at them.

April 3.

The University of Michigan faculty meet to discuss a proposal to require students to take a course on ethnicity and racism.

April 4.

Students at the University of California at Santa Barbara suspend hun-ger strike after university agrees to negotiate on demands for minority faculty hiring and the changed status of certain required courses.

April 5.

The NCAA releases results of survey on black student athletes, report-ing that 51 percent of black football and basketball players at predomi-nantly white schools express feelings of being different; 51 percent re-port feelings of racial isolation; 33 percent report having experienced at least six incidents of individual racial discrimination.

The *New York Times* prints three op-ed pieces by students on the subject of racial tension on campus.

Charges filed against a former student of Penn State for racial harass-ment of a black woman.

April 6.

University of Michigan: Hundreds of law students wear arm bands, boycott classes to protest lack of women and minority professors.

Michigan State University announces broad plan for increasing number of minority students, faculty, and staff, the appointment of a senior advisor for minority affairs; and the expansion of multicultural conferences. "It's not our responsibility just to mirror society or respond to mandates," President John DiBioggio tells reporters, "but to set the tone."

April 7.

Wayne State University (Detroit, Michigan) student newspaper runs retraction of cartoon considered offensive following protest earlier in the week.

Controversy develops at the State University of New York at Stony Brook, where a white woman charges popular black basketball player with rape. Player denies charges. Charges are dismissed. Protests of racism and sexual assault commence.

April 12.

Twelve-day sit-in begins at Wayne State University (Michigan) over conditions for black students on campus.

April 14.

Racial brawl at Arizona State.

April 20.

Demonstrations at several universities across the country (Harvard, Duke, Wayne State, Wooster College, Penn State, etc.) for improvements in black student life.

Separate escort service for blacks started at Penn State out of distrust of the regular service.

April 21.

200-student sit-in ends at Arizona State University when administrators agree to all thirteen demands.

April 24.

Proposed tuition increase at City Universities of New York turns into racial controversy.

April 25.

After eighteen months in office, Robert Collin, Florida Atlantic University's first black dean, reveals he has filed a federal discrimination complaint against the school.

Two leaders of Columbia University's Gay and Lesbian Alliance receive death threat. "Dear Jeff, I will kill you butt fucking faggots. Death to CGLA!"

April 26.
A black Smith College (Massachusetts) student finds note slipped under door. ". . . African monkey do you want some bananas? Go back to the jungle . . ."

"I don't think we should have to constantly relive our ancestors' mistakes," white student at University of North Carolina at Greensboro tells reporter. "I didn't oppress anybody. Blacks are now equal. You don't see any racial problems anymore."

White Student Union is reported to have been formed at Temple University in Philadelphia, "City of Brotherly Love."

April 28.
Note found in Brown University (Rhode Island) dorm. "Once upon a time, Brown was a place where a white man could go to class without having to look at little black faces, or little yellow faces or little brown faces, except when he went to take his meals. Things have been going downhill since the kitchen help moved into the classroom. Keep white supremecy [sic] alive!!! Join the Brown chapter of the KKK today." Note is part of series that began in the middle of the month with "Die Homos." University officials beef up security, hold forum.

April 29.
Controversy reported over proposed ban on verbal harassment at Arizona State.

April 30.
Anti-apartheid shanty at University of Maryland, Baltimore County, is defaced. Signs read "Apartheid now" and "Trump Plaza."

University of California at Berkeley: Resolution is passed requiring ethnic studies course for all students.

University of Connecticut: Code is revised to provide specific penalties for acts of racial intolerance. ■

PROFILES OF TODAY'S YOUTH:
THEY COULDN'T CARE LESS *by Michael Oreskes*

COLUMBUS, Ohio, June 27 — John Karras, 28 years old, was in a card shop the other day as the radio, which provides the soundtrack for his generation, offered a report on the dead and missing in the floods that had just flashed throughout southeastern Ohio.

The cashier, a man a bit younger than Mr. Karras, looked up at the radio and said: "I wish they'd stop talking about it. I'm sick of hearing about it."

Mr. Karras, a doctoral student in education at Ohio State, recalled this incident to illustrate what he sees as a "pervasive" attitude among the members of his generation toward the larger world: the typical young person doesn't want to hear about it "unless it's knocking on my door."

Studies Find Indifference

The findings of two national studies concur. The studies, one released today and the other late last year, paint a portrait of a generation of young adults, from 18 to 29 years of age, who are indifferent toward public affairs. It is a generation that, as the Times Mirror Center for the People and the Press put it in a report released today, "knows less, cares less, votes less and is less critical of its leaders and institutions than young people in the past."

Caught in the backwash of the baby boom, whose culture and attitudes still dominate American discourse, members of the "baby bust" seem almost to be rebelling against rebellion. Anyone who was hoping that the energy of this new generation would snap the nation out of its political lethargy, as young people helped awaken the nation from the quiescent 1950's, will probably be disappointed.

"My teacher told me: 'Always question authority,'" said Paul Grugin, 22, one of two dozen young people interviewed this week by The New York Times in this midsize city in the middle of the country. "You can question authority, but you can burden authority. Let them authoritate."

The indifference of this generation — to politics, to government, even to news about the outside world — is beginning to affect American politics and society, the reports suggest, helping to explain such seemingly disparate trends as the decline in voting, the rise of tabloid television and the effectiveness of negative advertising.

While apathy and alienation have become a national plague, the disengagement seems to run deeper among young Americans, those 18 to 29, setting them clearly apart from earlier generations.

No one has yet offered a full explanation for why this should be so. The lack of mobilizing issues is a part of the answer, as are the decline of the family and the rise of television.

Young people themselves mention the weakness of their civics education, and they talk incessantly of stress — their preoccupation with getting jobs or grades and their concern about personal threats like AIDS and drugs. "There are a lot more pressures on them than there were on us," said 48-year-old Ron Zeller, who talked about the differences along with his 22-year-old daughter, Susan, and his 18-year-old son, John.

The study by Times Mirror, a public opinion research center supported by Times Mirror Co., looked at 50 years of public opinion data and concluded, "Over most of the past five decades, younger members of the public have been at least as well informed as older people. In 1990 that is no longer the case."

This concern was echoed in a second report, prepared last year by People for the American Way, a liberal lobby and research organization, which concluded that there is "a citizenship crisis" in which "America's youth are alarmingly ill-prepared to keep democracy alive in the 1990's and beyond."

Susan Zeller, 22, who is about to enter Case Western law school, agreed. "I don't think many people my age group are very concerned," she said. "They're only concerned about issues that affect them. When the drinking age went up, quite a few people were upset."

The decline in voting is one illustration of how what seems to be a general problem is, in fact, most heavily concentrated among the young. Surveys by the census bureau show that since 1972 almost all of the decline in voting has been among those under 45, and that the sharpest drop is among those between 18 and 25. Among the elderly, voting has risen, according to the census bureau surveys.

Older people, more settled than the young, have always participated more in elections. But the gap has widened substantially. In 1972, half of those between 18 and 24 said they voted, as did 71 percent of those 45 to 64, a gap of 21 percentage points. In 1988, 36 percent of the 18- to 24-year-olds and 68 percent of the 45- to 64-year-olds said they voted, a gap of 32 percentage points.

Avoiding Controversy

Shonda Wolfe, 24, who has waited tables since dropping out of college, said she had voted only once, when she was 18 and still living at home. "I guess my mom was there to push me," she said.

Now, she said, she does not pay much attention to politics or the news. "I try to avoid it — all the controversy," she said. "It just doesn't interest me at this point in my life. I'd rather be outside doing something, taking a walk."

Young people have always had to worry about getting started in life, beginning a career and a family. But this young generation, for whom Vietnam is a history lesson and Watergate a blurry childhood memory, seems to have adopted the cynicism of parents and older siblings without going through the activism and disappointments that produced that cynicism.

Not one of the young people interviewed in Columbus, at the Street Scene Restaurant and the Short North Tavern, had a good word to say about politics or politicians. But unlike older people, who often express anger about news about sloth or corruption in government, these young people seem simply to be reporting it as a well-known fact. "Most politicians are liars," said Deborah Roberts, a 29-year-old secretary.

Flawed View of Citizenship

People for the American Way, in its report, noted that young people seemed to have a half-formed understanding of citizenship, stressing rights but ignoring responsibilities.

When asked to define citizenship, Shonda Wolfe said it meant the right not to be harassed by the police. She cited as an intrusion on her rights the security guards' insistence at a concert that she and her boyfriend stop turning on their cigarette lighters.

Nancy Radcliffe-Spurgeon, 24, a student at Ohio State, said she thought that many of the attitudes of her generation were based on feeling safe. "It's easy to isolate yourself when you think things are going pretty well for you, so you don't rock the boat."

Occasionally, someone in the interviews would mention voting. None of the young people, when asked about citizenship, included in their definition of good citizenship running for office, attending a community board meeting, studying an issue, signing a petition, writing a letter to the governor, or going to a rally.

These young people are aware that some of their attitudes are a product of different times. Young people protesting the war in Vietnam were also engaged by an issue that affected them, but one that the rest of the country also accepted as being of central importance. "When people your age were our age, there was a lot more strife," Jeff Brodeur, a 22-year-old senior at Ohio State, told a 36-year-old visitor.

Interest in Some Issues

Certain issues do get their attention, almost always involving government interference in personal freedoms. They generally favor access to abortion, and a few of the young people were upset by efforts to cut off Federal funds for art work deemed obscene.

Their concern about the arts was not surprising because in the interviews the young people showed that their main contact with the larger world was through culture. Mr. Brodeur, for example, said he first became aware of apartheid in South Africa through the song "Biko," written by Peter Gabriel about Steve Biko, a prominent antiapartheid leader in South Africa of the 1970's.

But Mr. Brodeur's research seems more the exception than the rule. Andrew Kohut, director of surveys for Times Mirror, said there was a new generation gap, in which those under 30 were separated by their lack of knowledge and interest from those over 30.

People in their 30's and 40's are disenchanted with the world, but remain aware, said Mr. Kohut. But those under 30, he said, "are not so much disillusioned as disinterested."

The Times Mirror analysis was based on its own public opinion polling as well as comparisons with polling conducted by other organizations over the past 50 years.

Deborah Roberts, the secretary, says she still reads a newspaper, sort of. "There's more bad news on the front page," she said, explaining why she skips over it. "I like to go to the local news; it's the fun news."

Attitudes Affect News Media

Attitudes like this are having a considerable effect on the news media, Mr. Kohut said. The number of people who read newspapers is declining, in general, but that number has plunged among the young. And not simply because they have turned to television, according to surveys. Viewing of traditional television news by the young is also shown to be down, although they do watch the new types of shows that concentrate on scandal and celebrity.

"The generation gap in news and information is playing out in politics in very significant ways," Mr. Kohut added.

"The 30-second commercial spot is a particularly appropriate medium for the MTV generation," he continued.

"At the conclusion of the 1988 campaign, Times Mirror's research showed that young voters, who began the campaign knowing less than older voters, were every bit as likely to recall advertised political themes such as pollution in Boston Harbor, Willie Horton and the flag.

"Sound bites and symbolism, the principal fuel of modern political campaigns, are well suited to young voters who know less and have limited interest in politics and public policy. Their limited appetites and aptitudes are shaping the practice of politics and the nature of our democracy." ■

LOOKING AHEAD: MORE MOUTHS, LESS FOOD

"The world's farmers are finding it more difficult to keep up with growth in population."

This modest statement in *State of the World 1990,* by Worldwatch Institute (Norton), is an omen of tragedy.

The International Foundation for the Survival and Development of Humanity reports: "The uncontrolled growth of the world's population, projected to reach at least 10 billion people by 2050, exacerbates the full range of environmental problems: it increases pressure on forests, water, soils and fisheries; increases the use of nonrenewable resources and the generation of waste; favors the adoption of technologies of production that can increase output in the short term without regard to their environmental costs; and strains the capacity of institutions to plan and manage. The shortage of arable land for food production, insufficient supplies of energy and the spread of malnutrition and disease will worsen as population increases."

These facts are well known to presidents, prime ministers and other political leaders. But they tend to look the other way because the answers often are unpopular.

State of the World describes what is happening today in Africa, where "the combination of record population growth and widespread land degradation is reducing grain production per person. A drop of 20 percent from the peak in 1967 has converted the continent into a grain importer, fueled the region's mounting external debt, and left millions of Africans hungry and physically weakened, drained of their vitality and productivity." What is happening in Africa is "a nightmare scenario," according to the World Bank.

To add to Africa's troubles, the giant desert is spreading ever southward because trees are being cut for firewood.

The current world population of 5.2 billion "will increase this decade by nearly one billion, the fastest population growth in history, threatening to erase the gains that many countries have struggled to achieve," according to a UN report in the *Los Angeles Times.* "In 1990 alone, 90 million to 100 million people, or about the combined population of the Philippines and South Korea, will be added to the world. The decade's growth of one billion will add the equivalent of an extra China to the world's population. . . . By and large, the biggest increases will happen in the poorest countries, those by definition least equipped to meet the needs of the new arrivals and invest in their future."

A Few Answers

The experts suggest four steps to avert serious famine and suffering in this decade:

- Address and change conditions that bring on high birthrates. World-watch Institute says that "social [and economic] conditions underlying high fertility" include "the low status of women, illiteracy and low wages."

  The Institute for Food & Development Policy points out: "Living at the economic margin, many poor parents perceive their children's labor as necessary to augment meager family income. By working in the fields and around the home, children also free up adults and older siblings to earn outside income."

  On the island of Java, children care for chickens and ducks at seven years old, tend goats and cattle at nine, and are sent out to work for wages at 12. In parts of India, 12-year-old girls work up to 10 hours a day picking tea. In Manila, children collect and sell scrap from dumps. "Bangkok and São Paulo are both notorious for child prostitutes, many of whom are the sole support of their families."

  Many governments and even population-control groups "appear unwilling to address the roots of these problems that lie largely in the economic and political order." Radical reforms inevitably bring tough opposition from those who cling to the status quo. President François Mitterrand, of France, is one political leader demanding reform. He told the *National Geographic:* "There is madness in not striving to reduce the gap between rich and poor. The gap is more dangerous than nuclear bombs. When people do not have enough to eat — and this will soon be the case in eight out of ten human beings — their revolt can prove impossible to check."

- Boost the status of women in the Third World, so that they will have more control over the number of children they bear. *Population Briefing Paper* reports: "The world's poorest women are not merely poor, they live on the edge of subsistence. They are economically dependent and vulnerable, politically and legally powerless. As wives and mothers, they are caught in a life cycle that begins with early marriage and too often ends with death in childbirth. They work longer hours and sometimes work harder than men, but their work is typically unpaid and undervalued."

Many Third World women would like to have only as many children as they know they can feed and care for. But women have a subservient role in many developing countries. The Institute for Food & Development Policy speaks of the "disproportionate powerlessness of women. Excluded from many decisions that determine their role in the family, as well as in the society at large, many women have little opportunity for pursuits outside the home. Perpetual motherhood becomes the only 'choice.'"

A doctor in a Mexican clinic reports that many women want to avoid or delay pregnancy. "When a wife wants to [try] to limit the number of mouths to feed in the family, the husband will become angry and even beat her. He thinks it is unacceptable that she is making a decision of her own. She is challenging his authority, his power over her — and thus the very nature of his virility." (*Message from the Village*, by Perdita Huston)

In many Third World areas, girls marry early: The average age of marriage is 11.6 years in Bangladesh; 15.3 in Pakistan and 15.7 in Sierra Leone. An Indian parent says, "Society will condemn us if our daughters are not married by the age of 15."

• Undertake a program to teach families about birth control. Make it "part of a package which includes other types of investments in human resources," a UN official suggests.

• Provide women with birth control devices and methods. Women are more likely than men to practice birth control.

The U.S. has a compelling interest in world population problems. The *Christian Science Monitor* reports: "The population explosion could put tremendous immigration pressure on the U.S."

Burgeoning populations in Latin America are forcing thousands of refugees north. "For example, Mexico City, which had about eight million people in 1970, is projected to surge to 21 million residents by the year 2000. São Paulo, with about six million in 1970, could have 23 million in 2000. . . . In the future, the U.S. is expected to continue to be a major destination for millions of immigrants" from Latin America and Asia. "During the 10-year period 1985–1994, the Federal Government estimates that there will be nearly three million legal immigrants from Asia and over 2.5 million from Latin America and the Caribbean."

"Famine and War"

In the Middle East, population growth coupled with a water shortage could lead to serious conflict. The *Christian Science Monitor* reports: "Water resources, historically in short supply, are on the verge of being overwhelmed by runaway population growth. Famine and war" would be the inevitable results.

The *Monitor* states: "Population growth . . . has stretched available resources to the breaking point in the region's three main river basins — the Nile, the Jordan and the Tigris-Euphrates. Unless population growth rates, now averaging three percent in the Middle East, are curbed, excess population will wipe out all the projected gains in water development and conservation within 30 years."

An Egyptian diplomat says, "The politics of the Middle East after 2000 will be a struggle over water." A Syrian official adds, "No region on Earth is as vulnerable to war because of conflicts over water between neighboring states."

Example: Jordan, Syria and Israel compete for the water of the Jordan River. A river-sharing agreement promoted by the Eisenhower Administration in 1953 has broken down. The *Monitor* says, "Israel and Syria are taking more than their share. . . . A scheme to avert a disaster in Jordan, building a dam on the Yarmuk River to hold back water, has been delayed by objections from Israel."

Water scarcity appears "in a number of [world] areas where irrigation is critical to farming, often accounting for 80 percent or more of water consumption. Many of these regions also are experiencing rapid population growth and urbanization — setting the stage for heated competition between cities and farms. In much of northern and eastern Africa, increasing human numbers are on a collision course with scarce water resources." (*State of the World 1990*)

One answer is to desalinize sea water. This is being done to a limited degree in Saudi Arabia and Israel, but the price is prohibitive at present.

Looking for Food

Feeding the increasing numbers of people who inhabit the Earth is another pressing problem.

Lester R. Brown, the learned president of Worldwatch Institute, writes: "Facing the '90s, the world's farmers are looking at an annual growth in world population projected to reach 91 million, up roughly from 70 million in 1970. If farmers had unlimited soil and water resources, they could easily meet these staggering increases in demand, but the reality is that they begin the decade with a cropland base that is no longer expanding and a scarcity of fresh water and no major new technologies to help . . ." (*Washington Post*)

Throughout the world, we have been using up the soil and water with little thought to the future. In the U.S., for example, an estimated 11 million hectares of cropland is losing topsoil so rapidly that Congress has called for conversion to grassland or forest before it turns to wasteland. Twenty-four billion tons of topsoil a year are being lost to overuse of land in major food-producing areas.

Brown states: "Future improvement in the world food situation depends heavily on reversing land degradation and braking population growth. Without a massive reordering of priorities that will restore soils and slow the population growth that is already outstripping food production in Africa and Latin America, food scarcity and higher food prices may well dominate the '90s.

"Deteriorating diets in both Africa and Latin America during the '80s, a worldwide fall in per capita grain production since 1984, and the rise in world wheat and rice prices may be early signs of the trouble that lies ahead."

Spread of Birth Control

Many governments, alarmed by the crisis posed by food shortages, now advocate birth control. The Institute for Food & Development Policy states: "In at least a dozen countries, mainly in Asia, a variety of incentives and disincentives are now used to induce people to undergo sterilization or to use contraceptives.

"Incentives are usually material. They range from payments to the individual, family, or family-planning clinic to awards of small farm animals, clothes and even food. Disincentives tend to be financial: tax differentials (higher taxes after a certain number of children), employment policies, or limitations on social services, such as health or education."

In India, for example, during an "emergency" in 1976–77, stern measures were taken to hold down the birthrate. In some states, parents with three or more children who failed to become sterilized were denied loans, land for housing and free medical treatment at government hospitals. Those who agree to sterilization today are paid an amount equal to 10 to 12 days' wages. In Bangladesh, both men and women are given clothing and paid a sum equal to two weeks' earnings for sterilization. In a very poor area of northeast Thailand, those who agree to birth control are given money and technical help in farming and raising animals. In Indonesia, the government offers towns that meet fertility targets such benefits as road repairs and a water supply system.

Sterilization is the most popular birth control method in some Third World areas, for it is final. In India, 90 percent of the couples practicing contraception have been sterilized, according to "The Missing Piece of the Population Puzzle," a study by the Institute for Food & Development Policy. In Puerto Rico, a government campaign using radio and TV urged women to get "la oparacion." In 1965, one-third of all married women had been sterilized, two-fifths before the age of 25.

Use of the Pill

The birth control pill has been particularly popular in the U.S. In an article in *Science*, chemist Carl Djerassi points out: "By the end of that decade [the '60s], the cumulative decisions of nearly 10 million American women had made the pill the most popular method of birth control [because of] the privacy it offered a woman."

Use of the pill has decreased recently because of fears of side effects. However, "the consensus now is that for healthy young women, the pill is the most effective contraceptive method and probably one of the safest. Women in their middle thirties or older were thought to be at increased risk in terms of cardiovascular complications, [but] the most recent . . . evidence concerning low-dose pills suggests that such risk applies only to heavy smokers."

In other parts of the world, the IUD is widely used. "In China, at least 35 million women are estimated to be wearing an IUD developed in the 1960s, thus making it the most prevalent contraceptive in that country." (*Science*)

Still another birth control option is RU486, the French pill, that World Development Forum says has been "tested and recognized as a safe, effective and simple means of terminating early pregnancy." The pill works by blocking the normal action of progesterone, thus preventing the fertilized egg from attaching itself to the uterine wall.

The world is teeming with ideas for holding down the birthrate, but in the meantime, food and water supplies in some areas are being critically diminished by the rise in population. ■ ◄

Summary

The famous newspaperman H. L. Mencken once said, "To every complex question there is a simple answer — and it's wrong!" We have seen in this chapter that complex problems do not admit simple solutions, whether they concern personal problems in our lives or larger social problems like racial prejudice or world hunger. We have also seen that by working through these complex problems thoughtfully and systematically, however, we can achieve a deeper understanding of their many interacting elements, as well as develop and implement strategies for solving them.

Becoming an effective problem-solver does not merely involve applying a problem-solving method in a mechanical fashion, any more than becoming a mature critical thinker involves mastering a set of thinking skills, Rather, solving problems, like thinking critically, reflects a total approach to making sense of experience. When we think like problem-solvers, we approach the world in a distinctive way. Instead of avoiding difficult problems, we have the courage to meet them head-on and the determination to work through them. Instead of acting impulsively or relying exclusively on the advice of others, we are able to make sense of complex problems in an organized way and develop practical solutions and initiatives.

A sophisticated problem-solver employs all of the critical thinking abilities that we have examined so far and those we will explore in the chapters ahead. And while we might agree with H. L. Mencken's evaluation of simple answers to complex questions, we might endorse a rephrased version: "To many complex questions there are complex answers — and these are worth pursuing!"

Organizing
sensations into a
design or pattern.

Selecting
sensations to pay
attention to.

Interpreting
what this pattern or
event means.

PERCEIVING:
Actively selecting, organizing,
and interpreting what is
experienced by our senses.

Experiences shape our
perceptions.

We construct beliefs based
on our perceptions.

We view the world through
our own unique "lenses,"
which shape and influence
our perceptions.

We construct
knowledge based on
our beliefs.

Thinking Critically involves understanding how "lenses"
influence perceptions, beliefs, and knowledge.

THINKING IS THE WAY we make sense of the world. By thinking in an active, purposeful, and organized way, we are able to understand what is happening in our experience — to solve problems, work toward our goals, make sense of information, and understand other people. Our experience of the world is presented to us by means of our *senses:* sight, hearing, smell, touch, and taste. These senses are our bridges to the world, making us aware of what occurs outside us, and the process of becoming aware of our world through our senses is known as *perceiving.*

In this chapter we will examine the way our perceiving process operates and how it relates to our ability to think effectively. In particular, we will discover the way each of us shapes personal experience by actively selecting, organizing, and interpreting the sensations provided by the senses. In a way, each of us views the world through a pair of individual "spectacles," which reflect our past experiences and unique personalities. As critical thinkers, we want to become aware of the nature of our own "spectacles" to help eliminate any bias or distortion they may be causing. We also want to become aware of the "spectacles" of others so that we can better understand how and why they view things the way they do.

At almost every waking moment of our lives, our senses are being bombarded by a tremendous number of stimuli: images to see, noises to hear, odors to smell, textures to feel, and flavors to taste. The experience of all these sensations happening at once creates what the nineteenth-century American philosopher William James called "a bloomin' buzzin' confusion." Yet for us, the world usually seems much more orderly and understandable. Why is this so?

In the first place, our sense equipment can receive sensations only within certain limited ranges. For example, there are many sounds and smells that animals can detect but we cannot because their sense organs have broader ranges in these areas than ours do.

A second reason we can handle this sensory bombardment is that from the stimulation available to us we *select* only a small amount on which to focus our attention. To demonstrate this, try the following exercise. Concentrate on what you can see, ignoring your other senses for the moment. Focus on sensations that you were not previously aware of. Then answer the first question in the space provided. Concentrate on each of your other senses in turn, following the same procedure.

1. What can you *see*? (For example, the shape of the letters on the page, the design of the clothing on your arm.)

   _____

   _____

2. What can you *hear*? (For example, the hum of the air circulator, the rustling of a page.)

_____

_____

3. What can you *feel*? (For example, the pressure of the clothes against your skin, the texture of the page on your fingers.)

_____

_____

4. What can you *smell*? (For example, the perfume or cologne someone is wearing, the odor of stale cigarette smoke.)

_____

_____

5. What can you *taste*? (For example, the aftereffects of your last meal.)

_____

_____

Compare your responses with those of the other students in the class. Do your classmates perceive sensations that are different from the ones you perceived? If so, how do you explain these differences?

By practicing this simple exercise, we learn that for every sensation that we focus our attention on there are countless sensations that we are simply ignoring. If we were aware of *everything* that is happening at every moment, we would be completely overwhelmed. By selecting certain sensations, we are able to make sense of our world in a relatively orderly way. The activity of using our senses to experience and make sense of our world is known as *perceiving*.

> *Perceiving*   Being directly aware of our world based on what is experienced through our senses.

Actively Selecting, Organizing, and Interpreting Sensations

It is tempting to think that our senses simply record what is happening out in the world, as if we were human cameras or tape recorders. We are not, however, simply passive receivers of information, "containers" into which sense experience is poured. Instead, we are *active participants* who are always trying to understand the sensations we are encountering. As we perceive our world, our experience is the result of combining the sensations we are having with the way we understand these sensations. For example, examine the following collection of markings. What do you see?

If all you see is a collection of black spots, try looking again. After a while, you will probably perceive a familiar animal. (If you're still having trouble, turn the page.)

From this example we can see that when we perceive the world we are doing more than simply recording what our senses experience. Besides experiencing sensations, we are also actively making sense of these sensations. That is why this collection of black spots suddenly became the figure of an animal — because we were able actively to organize these spots into a pattern we recognized. Or think about the times you were able to look up at the white, billowy clouds in the sky and see different figures and designs. The figures you were perceiving were not actually in the clouds but were the result

of your giving a meaningful form to the shapes and colors you were experiencing.

The same is true for virtually everything we experience. Our perceptions of the world result from combining the information provided by our senses with the way we actively make sense of this information. And since making sense of information is what we are doing when we are thinking, we can see that perceiving our world involves using our minds in an active way. Of course, we are usually not aware that we are using our minds to interpret the sensations we are experiencing. We simply see the animal or the figures in the clouds as if they were really there.

When we actively perceive the sensations we are experiencing, we are usually engaged in three distinct activities:

1. *Selecting* certain sensations to pay attention to

2. *Organizing* these sensations into a design or pattern

3. *Interpreting* what this design or pattern means to us

In the case of the figure on page 143 we were able to perceive an animal because we *selected* certain of the markings to concentrate on, *organized* these markings into a pattern, and *interpreted* this pattern as representing a familiar animal.

Of course, when we perceive, these three operations of selecting, organizing, and interpreting are usually performed quickly, automatically, and often at the same time. Also, we are normally unaware that we are performing these operations, they are so rapid and automatic. In this chapter we try to slow down this normally automatic process of perceiving so that we can understand how the process works.

Let us explore more examples that illustrate how we actively select, organize, and interpret our perceptions of the world. Carefully examine the next figure. Do you see both the young woman and the old woman? If you do, try switching back and forth between the two images. As you switch back and forth, notice how for each image you are:

- *Selecting* certain lines, shapes, and shadings to focus your attention on.

- *Organizing* these lines, shapes, and shadings into different patterns.

- *Interpreting* these patterns as representing things that you are able to recognize — a hat, a nose, a chin.

Now perform a similar analysis on the figure at the bottom of page 145, the drawing of the bird/rabbit. (Additional detail is provided in the two smaller drawings to help you see both the bird and the rabbit.)

Another way for us to become aware of our active participation in perceiving our world is to consider how we see objects. Examine the following illustration. Do you perceive different-sized people, or the same-sized people at different distances?

When we see someone who is far away, we usually do not perceive a tiny person. Instead, we perceive a normal-sized person who is far away from us. Our experience in the world has enabled us to discover that the farther things are from us, the smaller they look. The moon in the night sky appears about the size of a quarter, yet we perceive it as being considerably larger. As we look down a long stretch of railroad tracks or gaze up at a tall building, the boundary lines seem to come together. Even though these images are what our eyes "see," however, we do not usually perceive the tracks meeting or the building coming to a point. Instead, our minds actively organize and interpret a world composed of constant shapes and sizes, even though the images we actually see usually vary, depending on how far we are from them and the angle from which we are looking at them.

THINKING ACTIVITY

4.1 ▶ Examine carefully the engraving pictured on the next page, entitled "Satire on False Perspective," completed by William Hogarth in 1754. In this engraving, the artist has changed many of the clues we use to perceive a world of constant shapes and sizes, thus creating some unusual effects. By analyzing how the artist has created these unusual perspectives, we gain insight into the way our minds actively take fragmentary information and transform it into the predictable, three-dimensional world that is so familiar to us.

1. Identify which elements of the picture are different from the way we normally perceive things in the world.

   a. The man in the foreground is fishing in water that is in the background.

   b. _____

   _____

Whoever makes a DESIGN, *without the Knowledge of* PERSPECTIVE, *will be liable to such Absurdities as are shewn in this* Frontispiece.

All rights reserved. The Metropolitan Museum of Art. Gift of Sarah Lazarus, 1891. (91.1.33)

c. _____

_____

d. _____

_____

2. For each alteration of normal perception you have identified, explain how
   the artist created a perception that is different from the way our minds
   usually organize and interpret the world.

   a. The fishing pole seems to extend into the background of the picture
      because the artist did not reduce its size.

   b. _____

   _____

   c. _____

   _____

   d. _____

   _____ ◄

So far, we have been exploring how our minds actively participate in the
way we perceive the world. By combining the sensations we are receiving
with the way our minds select, organize, and interpret these sensations, we
perceive a world of things that is stable and familiar, a world that usually
makes sense to us.

At the beginning of the chapter we defined perceiving as "being directly
aware of our world based on what is experienced through our senses." Based
on what we have discovered so far, we can now make this definition somewhat more specific:

> *Perceiving*   Actively selecting, organizing, and interpreting what
> is experienced by our senses.

The process of perceiving takes place at a variety of different levels. At the
most basic level, the concept of "perceiving" refers to the selection, organization, and interpretation of sensations: for example, being able to perceive
the various objects in our experience, like a basketball. However, we also
perceive larger patterns of meaning at more complex levels, as in watching
the action of a group of people engaged in a basketball game. Although these
are very different contexts, both engage us in the process of actively selecting,

organizing, and interpreting what is experienced by our senses — in other words, "perceiving."

People's Perceptions Differ

Our *active* participation in perceiving our world is something we are not usually aware of. We normally assume that what we are perceiving is what is actually taking place. Only when we find that our perception of the same event differs from the perceptions of others we are forced to examine the manner in which we are selecting, organizing, and interpreting the events in our world. For example, consider the contrasting perceptions of the various characters in the following cartoon. How do you think each individual arrived at his or her (or its) perception?

THINKING ACTIVITY

4.2 ▶ Carefully examine the picture of the boy sitting at the desk. What do you
think is happening in this picture?

   1. Describe as specifically as possible what you perceive is taking place in the
      picture.

      _____

      _____

   2. Describe what you think will take place next.

      _____

      _____

   3. Identify the details of the picture that led you to your perceptions.

      a. _____

      b. _____

      c. _____

   4. Compare your perceptions with the perceptions of other students in the
      class. List several perceptions that differ from yours.

      a. _____

b. _____

c. _____ ◀

In most cases, people in a group will have a variety of perceptions about what is taking place in the picture in Thinking Activity 4.2. Some will see the boy as frustrated because the work is too difficult. Others will see him concentrating on what has to be done. Still others may see him as annoyed because he is being forced to do something he does not want to do. In each case, the perception depends on how the person is actively using his or her mind to organize and interpret what is taking place. Since the situation pictured is by its nature somewhat puzzling, different people perceive it in different ways.

Thinking Activity 4.3 reveals another example of how people's perceptions can differ.

THINKING ACTIVITY
_____

4.3 ▶ Closely examine the photograph.

Courtesy of Frankel Gallery, San Francisco and © The Estate of Gary Winogrand.

1. Describe as specifically as possible what you think is taking place in the photograph.

   _____

   _____

2. Now describe what you think will take place next.

   _____

   _____

3. Identify the details of the picture that led you to your perceptions.

   a. _____

   b. _____

   c. _____

4. Compare your perceptions with the perceptions of other students in the class. List several perceptions that differ from yours.

   a. _____

   b. _____

   c. _____ ◀

Viewing the World Through "Spectacles"

To understand how various people can be exposed to the same stimuli or events and yet have different perceptions, it helps to imagine that each of us views the world through our own pair of spectacles (or contact lenses, if you prefer). Of course, we are not usually aware of the spectacles we are wearing. Instead, our spectacles act as *filters* that select and shape what we perceive without our realizing it.

This image of "spectacles" helps explain why people can be exposed to the same stimuli or events and yet perceive different things. It is because people are wearing *different spectacles* that influence what they are perceiving.

For example, in "The Investigation" on page 149, each witness is giving what he or she (or it!) believes is an accurate description of the man in the center, unaware that their descriptions are being influenced by who they are and the way that they see things. When members of your class had different perceptions of the boy at the desk in Thinking Activity 4.2 and of the photograph in Thinking Activity 4.3, their different perceptions were the result of the different spectacles through which each views the world.

To understand the way people perceive the world, we have to understand their individual spectacles, which influence how they actively select, organize, and interpret the events in their experience. A diagram of the process might look like this:

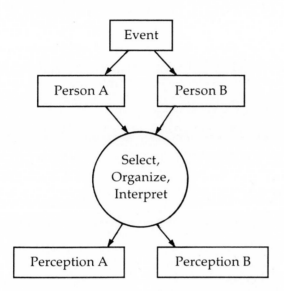

THINKING ACTIVITY
_____

4.4   ▶ Consider the following pairs of statements. In each of these cases, both people are being exposed to the same basic *stimulus* or *event*, yet each has a totally different *perception* of the experience. In the space provided, explain how you think the various perceptions might have developed.

1. a. That chili was much too spicy to eat.

   Explanation: _____

   _____

   b. That chili needed more hot peppers and chili powder to spice it up a little.

   Explanation: _____

   _____

2. a. People who wear lots of make-up and jewelry are very sophisticated.

    Explanation: _____

    _____

    b. People who wear lots of make-up and jewelry are ostentatious and overdressed.

    Explanation: _____

    _____

3. a. The drinking age should be twenty-one, because younger people are not mature and responsible enough to handle the effects of alcohol.

    Explanation: _____

    _____

    b. The drinking age should be eighteen, because if you're mature and responsible enough to vote and serve in the armed forces, then you're mature and responsible enough to drink alcohol.

    Explanation: _____

    _____

4. a. Increasing the speed limit to 65 mph is an intelligent decision that supports individual rights.

    Explanation: _____

    _____

    b. Increasing the speed limit to 65 mph will waste both gas and lives.

    Explanation: _____

    _____

5. a. It is appropriate for children in public school to have a time for prayer because this country was founded on a belief in God.

    Explanation: _____

    _____

    b. It is inappropriate for children in public school to have a time for prayer because this violates the Constitution's separation of church and state.

    Explanation: _____

    _____ ◀

To become effective critical thinkers, we have to become aware of the spectacles that we — and others — are wearing. These spectacles aid us in actively selecting, organizing, and interpreting the sensations in our experience. If we are unaware of the nature of our own spectacles, we can often mistake our own perceptions for objective truth without bothering to examine either the facts or others' perceptions on a given issue.

Selecting Perceptions

We spend much of the time experiencing the world in a very general way, not aware of many of the details of the events that are taking place. Police officers encounter this problem when they ask witnesses for a description of the people involved in a crime. Most witnesses can provide only the broadest descriptions — "medium height, average weight, dark clothes," and so forth. To communicate to others the specific details of our experience, we first have to develop the habit of becoming aware of these details. For example, try to draw a picture of the face of a push-button phone, complete with numbers and letters. Then compare your drawing with an actual phone. Did you have any difficulty? Why? (Consider all the times you have looked at the buttons on a phone.) Similarly, examine the drawings of the pennies. See if you can select the correct rendering of the U.S. penny from the collection of drawings people did from memory.

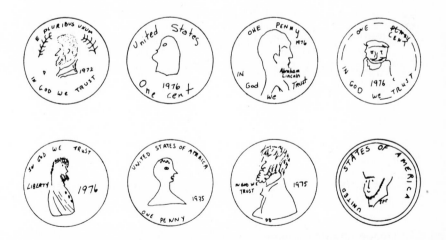

We tend to select perceptions about subjects that have been called to our attention for some reason. For example, while driving, someone might point out a vanity license plate (HOTSHOT) or an amusing bumper sticker.

Suddenly, we start seeing other license plates or bumper stickers because we have had our attention focused on that type of perception. At the age of three, the author's daughter suddenly became aware of beards. On entering a subway car, she would ask in a penetrating voice, "Any beards here?" and then proceed to count them out loud. In doing this, she naturally focused my attention — as well as the attention of many of the other passengers — on beards.

As another aspect of our "perceiving" spectacles, we tend to notice what we need, desire, or find of interest. When we go shopping, we focus on the items we are looking for. Walking down the street, we tend to notice certain kinds of people or events while completely ignoring others. Even watching a movie or reading a book, we tend to concentrate on and remember the elements we find of interest. Another person can perform *exactly* the same actions — shop at the same store, walk down the same street with us, read the same book, or go to the same movie — and yet see and remember entirely different things. In other words, what we see and do not see depends largely on our interests, needs, and desires.

Consider the following lists of perceptions compiled by two people taking a walk together. What are the different needs and interests reflected in the two lists?

Person A:

1. Antique store with quilt
2. Fire engine with siren blaring
3. Boutique with cable sweaters and wool plaid skirt
4. Woman charging $3 to analyze handwriting
5. Jewelry store with bracelets on sale
6. Strange man asking for $1 for coffee
7. Dance classes in second floor studio
8. Leather store featuring belts made while you wait
9. Variety store with Halloween costumes in window
10. Cat sleeping in store window

Person B:

1. Three teenage boys talking loudly
2. Hook and ladder on way to fire
3. Woman driving BMW motorcycle
4. Ray's Famous Pizza
5. Elderly man pushing grocery cart
6. Woman at card table offering handwriting analysis
7. Szechuan restaurant
8. Young man carrying large radio
9. Panhandler — unshaven, shabby clothes, bloated stomach
10. Mercedes stretch limousine
11. Messenger on bicycle weaving through traffic

The way we are feeling — our mood or emotional state — can also affect the perceptions we select. Imagine that you are at home alone or camping out in the woods and you begin to feel uneasy. Suddenly, you may begin to hear suspicious noises that you are certain come from an ax-wielding murderer or a ferocious beast. (The makers of horror films know exactly how to focus our attention on certain details — like a creaking door — in order to frighten us.) Or think back on the times when you have felt cranky, perhaps because you did not get enough sleep or were under pressure, and recall how you behaved. When we are in a bad mood, we often seem ready to focus our attention on every potential insult or criticism by others — and ready to respond the same way.

We also tend to select stimuli that are very familiar or very unfamiliar to us. Imagine that you are in a public place — in a restaurant or at a party — surrounded by the conversations of other people. These conversations are simply "noise" to you until you hear something familiar — your first name perhaps, or a subject that interests you. Suddenly you find yourself tuning into that conversation. The sound of something familiar made you select it from all the others to listen to. The process is something like flipping the radio dial and stopping when you hear a recognizable song.

Although we tend to focus on what is familiar to us, we are normally not aware that we are doing so. In fact, we often take for granted what is familiar to us — the taste of chili or eggs, the street that we live on, our family or friends — and normally do not think about our perception of it. But when something happens that makes the familiar seem strange and unfamiliar, we become aware of our perceptions and start to evaluate them.

To sum up, we actively select our perceptions, based on what has been called to our attention, our needs or interests, our mood or feelings, and what seems familiar or unfamiliar. The way we select our perceptions is an important factor in shaping the spectacles through which we view the world.

Organizing Perceptions

Not only do we actively *select* certain perceptions, we also actively *organize* these perceptions into meaningful relationships and patterns. Consider the following series of lines:

Do you perceive them as individual lines or did you group them into pairs? We seem naturally to try to organize our perceptions to create order and meaning. Consider the items pictured here.

In the following space, try to organize the pieces into patterns that are probably more familiar to you.

As we perceive the world, we naturally try to order and organize what we are experiencing into patterns and relationships that make sense to us. And when we are able to do so, the completed whole means more to us than the sum of the individual parts.

We are continually organizing our world in this way at virtually every waking moment. We do not live in a world of isolated sounds, patches of color, random odors, and individual textures. Instead, we live in a world of objects and people, language and music — a world in which all these individual stimuli are woven together. We are able to perceive this world of complex experiences because we are able to organize the individual stimuli we are receiving into relationships that have meaning to us.

The way we organize our experience is an important part of the spectacles through which we perceive the world. Think back on the examples we considered earlier in the chapter. You were able to perceive objects, human expressions, and potential human action because of your ability to organize the lines, shapes, and shadings into meaningful patterns. We also organize events in our world into a variety of complex relationships, as we will explore in Chapter Nine, *Relating and Organizing*.

Interpreting Perceptions

Besides selecting and organizing our perceptions, we also actively *interpret* what we perceive. When we interpret, we are figuring out what something means. For example, imagine that you are a parent of a baby and that you are having a party at your house. Suddenly, through all the sounds of people talking, you hear your baby cry. As you actively *select* this perception to focus your attention on and *organize* the sounds into a recognizable human cry, you also attempt to *interpret* what the crying means. Is your baby startled by the noise of the party? Frightened? Hungry? Wet? Frustrated? Lonely? By trying to interpret your perception, you are attempting to determine exactly what meaning is being expressed by the crying.

One of the elements that influence our interpretations of what we are perceiving is the *context*, or overall situation, within which the perception is occurring. Examine the center figure in the group of figures pictured here. What do you see?

When most people view the center figure as part of the horizontal line, they perceive the letter *B*, whereas if they view it as part of the vertical line, they perceive the number 13. In each case, our interpretation of the figure depends on the context within which it is occurring. The same is true for most of our perceptions; our interpretation of the perception is related to the overall situation within which it is taking place. For example, imagine that you see a man running down the street. Your interpretation of his action will depend on the specific context. For example, is there a bus waiting at the corner? Is a police officer running behind him? Is he wearing a jogging suit?

We are continually trying to interpret what we perceive, whether it is a design, someone's behavior, or a social situation. Like the example of a baby crying, most of the perceptions we experience can be interpreted in more than one way. When a situation has more than one possible interpretation, we say that the situation is ambiguous. The more ambiguous a situation is, the greater the number of possible meanings or interpretations it has.

Let us think again about the pictures we examined in Thinking Activities 4.2 and 4.3. In each instance, your description of what was happening — and what was about to happen — was based on your interpretation of the situation. Other members of the class may have given different descriptions of what was occurring because they interpreted the situation differently. Since these two pictures are by their nature puzzling and ambiguous, no one interpretation is necessarily more correct than the other interpretations. Instead, each interpretation simply reveals the spectacles through which this person views the world. Of course, we may feel that some interpretations make more sense than others, based on the details and the relationships that we perceive in the situation. Let's explore some of the ways our interpretations of our perceptions reveal the spectacles through which we are viewing the event.

As we saw in the last section, our interests and desires influence the perceptions we select to focus our attention on. Our interests and desires, however, can also affect our interpretation of what we are perceiving. Watching your team play baseball, for example, you may really believe that the opposing runner was "out by a mile" — even though the replay may show otherwise. Or imagine that you are giving a speech to the class and that you are being evaluated by two people — someone who likes you and someone who does not. Do you believe that different perceptions of your performance may result? Describe how each of the following people might perceive your performance.

1. Yourself

2. A friend of yours

3. Someone who does not like you

Similarly, the way we are feeling can influence our interpretations of what we are experiencing. When we feel happy and optimistic, the world often seems friendly and the future full of possibilities, and we interpret the problems we encounter as challenges to be overcome. On the other hand, when we are depressed or unhappy, we may perceive our world entirely differently. The future can appear full of problems that are trying to overcome us. In both cases the outer circumstances may be very similar; it is our own interpretation of the world through our spectacles that varies so completely.

Our perceptions of the world are dramatically influenced by our past experiences: the way we were brought up, the relationships we have had, and the training and education we have undergone. For example, imagine that an accident between a car and a tractor trailer has just taken place. Notice how the event might be perceived differently based on the interests and the past experience of the individuals involved.

Police Officer: Who was coming down the main road with the right of way? Why didn't both of you slow down at the intersection? Didn't you see that the streets were icy? Give me your licenses and registrations.

Tow Truck Operator: These tractor trailers don't have very much control on the ice. If he did stop before the intersection, it still wouldn't give him enough time to make a full stop. The truck has suffered only minor damage, but the car is totally disabled. It will definitely have to be towed.

Doctor: Is anybody seriously hurt? Is anything broken? Are you experiencing any head or neck pains? Why don't you just lie down and relax while I look you over. Help is on the way.

A Friend of the Victim: I thought that he had better sense than to drive on icy roads. I just hope that he's all right. I'd better call his parents to let them know what happened. I know they won't care about the car — just let him be all right.

What we perceive also depends on our past experience in terms of how "educated" our eyes are. Take the case of two people who are watching a football game. One person, who has very little understanding of football, sees merely a bunch of grown men hitting each other for no apparent reason. The other person, who loves football, sees complex play patterns, daring coaching strategies, effective blocking and tackling techniques, and zone defenses with "seams" that the receivers are trying to "split." Both have their eyes focused on the same event, but they are perceiving two entirely different situations. The perceptions differ because each person is actively selecting, organizing, and interpreting the available stimuli in different ways. The same is true of any situation in which we are perceiving something about which we have special knowledge or expertise. The following are examples:

- A builder examining the construction of a new house
- A music lover attending a concert
- A naturalist experiencing the outdoors
- A cook tasting a dish just prepared
- A lawyer examining a contract
- An art lover visiting a museum

Think about a special area of interest or expertise that you have and how your perceptions of that area differ from those who don't share your knowledge. Ask other class members about their areas of expertise. Notice how their

perceptions of that area differ from your own because of their greater knowledge and experience.

In all these cases, the perceptions of the knowledgeable person differ substantially from the perceptions of a person who lacks knowledge of that area.
Of course, we do not have to be an expert to have more fully developed
perceptions. It is a matter of degree. In general, the more understanding we
have of a particular area, the more detailed and complete our perceptions can
be of all matters related to it.

THINKING ACTIVITY

4.5   ▶ Let's examine a situation in which a number of different people had somewhat different perceptions about an event they were describing. The first
chapter of this book contains a passage by Malcolm X (pages 20–22) written
when he was just beginning his life's work. A few years later, this work came
to a tragic end with his assassination at a meeting in Harlem. The following
are four different accounts of what took place on that day. As you read
through the various accounts, pay particular attention to the different perceptions each one presents of this event. After you have completed reading the
accounts, analyze some of the differences in these perceptions by answering
the questions that follow.

FOUR ACCOUNTS OF THE ASSASSINATION OF
MALCOLM X

The New York Times (February 22, 1965)

Malcolm X, the 39-year-old leader of a militant Black Nationalist movement, was shot to death yesterday afternoon at a rally of his followers
in a ballroom in Washington Heights. The bearded Negro extremist had
said only a few words of greeting when a fusillade rang out. The bullets
knocked him over backwards.

A 22-year-old Negro, Thomas Hagan, was charged with the killing.
The police rescued him from the ballroom crowd after he had been shot
and beaten.

Pandemonium broke out among the 400 Negroes in the Audubon
Ballroom at 160th street and Broadway. As men, women and children
ducked under tables and flattened themselves on the floor, more shots
were fired. The police said seven bullets struck Malcolm. Three other
Negroes were shot. Witnesses reported that as many as 30 shots had
been fired. About two hours later the police said the shooting had apparently been a result of a feud between followers of Malcom and mem-

bers of the extremist group he broke with last year, the Black Muslims. . . .

Life *(March 5, 1965)*

His life oozing out through a half dozen or more gunshot wounds in his chest, Malcolm X, once the shrillest voice of black supremacy, lay dying on the stage of a Manhattan auditorium. Moments before, he had stepped up to the lectern and 400 of the faithful had settled down expectantly to hear the sort of speech for which he was famous — flaying the hated white man. Then a scuffle broke out in the hall and Malcolm's bodyguards bolted from his side to break it up — only to discover that they had been faked out. At least two men with pistols rose from the audience and pumped bullets into the speaker, while a third cut loose at close range with both barrels of a sawed-off shotgun. In the confusion the pistol man got away. The shotgunner lunged through the crowd and out the door, but not before the guards came to their wits and shot him in the leg. Outside he was swiftly overtaken by other supporters of Malcolm and very likely would have been stomped to death if the police hadn't saved him. Most shocking of all to the residents of Harlem was the fact that Malcolm had been killed not by "whitey" but by members of his own race.

The New York Post *(February 22, 1965)*

They came early to the Audubon Ballroom, perhaps drawn by the expectation that Malcolm X would name the men who firebombed his home last Sunday . . . I sat at the left in the 12th row and, as we waited, the man next to me spoke of Malcolm and his followers: "Malcolm is our only hope . . . You can depend on him to tell it like it is and to give Whitey hell.". . .

There was a prolonged ovation as Malcolm walked to the rostrum . . . Malcolm looked up and said "A salaam aleikum (Peace be unto you)" and the audience replied "We aleikum salaam (And unto you, peace)."

Bespectacled and dapper in a dark suit, sandy hair glinting in the light, Malcolm said: "Brothers and sisters . . ." He was interrupted by two men in the center of the ballroom, . . . who rose and, arguing with each other, moved forward. Then there was a scuffle at the back of the room . . . I heard Malcolm X say his last words: "Now, brothers, break it up," he said softly. "Be cool, be calm."

Then all hell broke loose. There was a muffled sound of shots and Malcolm, blood on his face and chest, fell limply back over the chairs behind him. The two men who had approached him ran to the exit on my side of the room, shooting wildly behind them as they ran. . . . I heard people screaming, "Don't let them kill him." "Kill those bastards." . . . At an exit I saw some of Malcolm's men beating with all their strength on two men. . . . I saw a half dozen of Malcolm's followers bending over his inert body on the stage. Their clothes stained with their leader's blood. . . .

Four policemen took the stretcher and carried Malcolm through the crowd and some of the women came out of their shock . . . and one said: ". . . I hope he doesn't die, but I don't think he's going to make it.". . .

Associated Press *(February 22, 1965)*

A week after being bombed out of his Queens home, Black Nationalist leader Malcolm X was shot to death shortly after 3 P.M. yesterday at a Washington Heights rally of 400 of his devoted followers. Early today, police brass ordered a homicide charge placed against a 22-year-old man they rescued from a savage beating by Malcolm X supporters after the shooting. The suspect, Thomas Hagan, had been shot in the left leg by one of Malcolm's bodyguards as, police said, Hagan and another assassin fled when pandemonium erupted. Two other men were wounded in the wild burst of firing from at least three weapons. The firearms were a .38, a .45 automatic and a sawed-off shotgun. Hagan allegedly shot Malcolm X with the shotgun, a double barrelled sawed-off weapon on which the stock also had been shortened, possibly to facilitate concealment. Cops charged Reuben Frances, of 871 E. 179th St., Bronx, with felonious assault in the shooting of Hagan, and with Sullivan Law violation — possession of the .45. Police recovered the shotgun and the .45.

1. What details of the events has each writer *selected* to focus on?

2. How has each writer *organized* the details that have been selected? Remember that most newspapers present what they consider the most important information first and the least important information last.

3. How does each writer *interpret* Malcolm X, his followers, the gunmen, and the significance of the assassination?

4. What kind of *language* has been used to describe the event? ◄

THINKING ACTIVITY

4.6   ▶ In the spring of 1989, a vigorous pro-democracy movement erupted in Beijing, the capital of China. Protesting the authoritarian control of the Communist regime, thousands of students staged demonstrations, engaged in hunger strikes, and organized marches involving hundreds of thousands of people. The geographical heart of these activities was the historic Tiananmen Square, taken over by the demonstrators who had erected a symbolic "Statue of Liberty." On June 4, 1989, the fledgling pro-democracy movement came to a bloody end when the Chinese army entered Tiananmen Square and seized control of it. The following are various accounts of this event from different sources. After you have completed reading the accounts, analyze their different perspectives by answering the concluding questions.

SEVEN ACCOUNTS OF EVENTS AT TIANANMEN SQUARE, 1989

The New York Times *(June 4, 1989)*

Tens of thousands of Chinese troops retook the center of the capital from pro-democracy protestors early this morning, killing scores of students and workers and wounding hundreds more as they fired submachine guns at crowds of people who tried to resist. Troops marched along the main roads surrounding central Tiananmen Square, sometimes firing in the air and sometimes firing directly at crowds who refused to move. Reports on the number of dead were sketchy. Students said, however, that at least 500 people may have been killed in the crackdown. Most of the dead had been shot, but some had been run over by personnel carriers that forced their way through the protesters' barricades.

A report on the state-run radio put the death toll in the thousands and denounced the Government for the violence, the Associated Press reported. But the station later changed announcers and broadcast another report supporting the governing Communist party. The official news programs this morning reported that the People's Liberation Army had crushed a "counter-revolutionary rebellion." They said that more than 1,000 police officers and troops had been injured and some killed, and that civilians had been killed, but did not give details.

Deng Xiaoping, *chairman of the Central Military Commission, as reported in* Beijing Review *(July 10–16, 1989)*

The main difficulty in handling this matter lay in that we had never experienced such a situation before, in which a small minority of bad people mixed with so many young students and onlookers. Actually, what we faced was not just some ordinary people who were misguided, but also a rebellious clique and a large number of the dregs of society. The key point is that they wanted to overthrow our state and the Party. They had two main slogans: to overthrow the Communist Party and

topple the socialist system. Their goal was to establish a bourgeois republic entirely dependent on the West.

During the course of quelling the rebellion, many comrades of ours
were injured or even sacrificed their lives. Some of their weapons were
also taken from them by the rioters. Why? Because bad people mingled
with the good, which made it difficult for us to take the firm measures
that were necessary. Handling this matter amounted to a severe political
test for our army, and what happened shows that our People's Liberation Army passed muster. If tanks were used to roll over people, this
would have created a confusion between right and wrong among the
people nationwide. That is why I have to thank the PLA officers and
men for using this approach to handle the rebellion. The PLA losses
were great, but this enabled us to win the support of the people and
made those who can't tell right from wrong change their viewpoint.
They can see what kind of people the PLA are, whether there was blood-
shed at Tiananmen, and who were those that shed blood.

This shows that the people's army is truly a Great Wall of iron and
steel of the Party and country. This shows that no matter how heavy
the losses we suffer and no matter how generations change, this army
of ours is forever an army under the leadership of the Party, forever the
defender of the country, forever the defender of socialism, forever
the defender of the public interest, and they are the most beloved of the
people. At the same time, we should never forget how cruel our enemies are. For them we should not have an iota of forgiveness.

The *New York Times*, June 4, 1989

Changan Avenue, or the Avenue of Eternal Peace, Beijing's main east-
west thoroughfare, echoed with screams this morning as young people
carried the bodies of their friends away from the front lines. The dead
or seriously wounded were heaped on the backs of bicycles or tricycle
rickshaws and supported by friends who rushed through the crowds,
sometimes sobbing as they ran.

The avenue was lit by the glow of several trucks and two armed personnel carriers that students and workers set afire, and bullets
swooshed overhead or glanced off buildings. The air crackled almost
constantly with gunfire and tear gas grenades.

Students and workers tried to resist the crackdown, and destroyed at
least 16 trucks and 2 armored personnel carriers. Scores of students and
workers ran alongside the personnel carriers, hurling concrete blocks
and wooden staves into the treads until they ground to a halt. They then

threw firebombs at one until it caught fire, and set the other alight after first covering it with blankets soaked in gasoline.

The drivers escaped the flames, but were beaten by students. A young American man, who could not be immediately identified, was also beaten by the crowd after he tried to intervene and protect one of the drivers.

Clutching iron pipes and stones, groups of students periodically advanced toward the soldiers. Some threw bricks and firebombs at the lines of soldiers, apparently wounding many of them.

Many of those killed were throwing bricks at the soldiers, but others were simply watching passively or standing at barricades when soldiers fired directly at them.

It was unclear whether the violence would mark the extinction of the seven-week-old democracy movement, or would prompt a new phase in the uprising, like a general strike. The violence in the capital ended a period of remarkable restraint by both sides, and seemed certain to arouse new bitterness and antagonism among both ordinary people and Communist Party officials for the Government of Prime Minister Li Peng.

"Our Government is already done with," said a young worker who held a rock in his hand, as he gazed at the army forces across Tiananmen Square. "Nothing can show more clearly that it does not represent the people."

Another young man, an art student, was nearly incoherent with grief and anger as he watched the body of student being carted away, his head blown away by bullets.

"Maybe we'll fail today," he said. "Maybe we'll fail tomorrow. But someday we'll succeed. It's a historical inevitablity."

Official Chinese Government Accounts

"Comrades, thanks for your hard work. We hope you will continue with your fine efforts to safeguard security in the capital."

Prime Minister Li Peng (addressing a group of
soldiers after the Tiananmen Square event)

"It never happened that soldiers fired directly at the people."

General Li Zhiyun

"The People's Liberation Army crushed a counter-revolutionary rebellion. More than 1,000 police officers and troops were injured and killed, and some civilians were killed."

Official Chinese News Program

"At most 300 people were killed in the operation, many of them soldiers."

Yuan Mu, official Government spokesman

"Not a single student was killed in Tiananmen Square."

Chinese Army Commander

"My government has stated that a mob led by a small number of people prevented the normal conduct of the affairs of state. There was, I regret to say, loss of life on both sides. I wonder whether any other government confronting such an unprecedented challenge would have handled the situation any better than mine did."

Han Xu, Chinese Ambassador to the United States

The New York Times *(June 5, 1989)*

It was clear that at least 300 people had been killed since the troops first opened fire shortly after midnight on Sunday morning but the toll may be much higher. Word-of-mouth estimates continued to soar, some reaching far into the thousands. . . . The student organization that coordinated the long protests continued to function and announced today that 2,600 students were believed to have been killed. Several doctors said that, based on their discussions with ambulance drivers and colleagues who had been on Tiananmen Square, they estimated that at least 2,000 had died. Soldiers also beat and bayoneted students and workers after daybreak on Sunday, witnesses said, usually after some provocation but sometimes entirely at random. "I saw a young woman tell the soldiers that they are the people's army, and that they mustn't hurt the people," a young doctor said after returning from one clash Sunday. "Then the soldier shot her, and ran up and bayoneted her."

Xiao Bin *(eyewitness account immediately after the event)*

Tanks and armored personnel carriers rolled over students, squashing them into jam, and the soldiers shot at them and hit them with clubs. When students fainted, the troops killed them. After they died, the troops fired one more bullet into them. They also used bayonets. They were too cruel. I never saw such things before.

Xiao Bin *(account after being taken into custody by Chinese authorities)*

I never saw anything. I apologize for bringing great harm to the party and the country.

1. Identify what details of the event each person has *selected* to focus on.

2. Describe how each person *organized* the details that have been selected.

3. Explain how each person *interprets* the protestors, the Chinese army, and the significance of the Tiananmen Square event.

4. Describe the kind of *language* that has been used by each person to describe the event.

5. Explain how the identity and circumstances of each person influenced his or her perception of the event. ◀

THINKING ACTIVITY
4.7 ▶ Locate three different newspaper or magazine accounts of an important event — a court decision, a crime, and a political demonstration are possible topics. Analyze the perceptual "spectacles" of each of the writers by answering the questions in Thinking Activity 4.5. ◀

Experiences Shape Our Perceptions

Our ways of viewing the world are developed over a long period of time through the experiences we have and our thinking about these experiences.

As we think critically about our perceptions, we learn more from our experiences and about how we make sense of the world. Our perceptions may be strengthened by this understanding, or they may be changed by this understanding. In the following reading selection, Roberto Acuna describes changes in his perceptions of his world. This section is taken from the book *Working: People Talk About What They Do All Day and How They Feel About What They Do* by Studs Terkel. Terkel traveled throughout the United States interviewing people from a wide range of occupations, including farmers, steelworkers, corporate executives, and prostitutes. In his narrative, Roberto Acuna describes how he became an organizer for the United Farm Workers of America. At the beginning of his narrative, Acuna says, "The things I saw shaped my life." After reading his story, ask yourself, "Did 'things' shape Acuna's life? Or did Acuna shape and reshape the things he saw into his life?"

MIGRANT WORKER *by Roberto Acuna*

I walked out of the fields two years ago. I saw the need to change the California feudal system, to change the lives of farm workers, to make these huge corporations feel they're not above anybody. I am thirty-four years old and I try to organize for the United Farm Workers of America.

His hands are calloused and each of his thumbnails is singularly cut. "If you're picking lettuce, the thumbnails fall off 'cause they're banged on the box. Your hands get swollen. You can't slow down because the foreman sees you're so many boxes behind and you'd better get on. But people would help each other. If you're feeling bad that day, somebody who's feeling pretty good would help. Any people that are suffering have to stick together, whether they like it or not, whether they be black, brown, or pink."

According to Mom, I was born on a cotton sack out in the fields, 'cause she had no money to go to the hospital. When I was a child, we used to migrate from California to Arizona and back and forth. The things I saw shaped my life. I remember when we used to go out and pick carrots and onions, the whole family. We tried to scratch a livin' out of the ground. I saw my parents cry out in despair, even though we had the whole family working. At the time, they were paying sixty-two and a half cents an hour. The average income must have been fifteen hundred dollars, maybe two thousand.*

This was supplemented by child labor. During those years, the grow-ers used to have a Pick-Your-Harvest Week. They would get all the mi-grant kids out of school and have 'em out there pickin' the crops at peak harvest time. A child was off that week and when he went back to school, he got a little gold star. They would make it seem like something civic to do.

We'd pick everything: lettuce, carrots, onions, cucumbers, cauli-flower, broccoli, tomatoes — all the salads you could make out of veg-etables, we picked 'em. Citrus fruits, watermelons — you name it. We'd be in Salinas about four months. From there we'd go down into the Imperial Valley. From there we'd go to picking citrus. It was like a cycle. We'd follow the seasons.

After my dad died, my mom would come home and she'd go into her tent and I would go into ours. We'd roughhouse and everything and then we'd go into the tent where Mom was sleeping and I'd see her

---

* "Today, because of our struggles, the pay is up to two dollars an hour. Yet we know that is not enough."

crying. When I asked her why she was crying she never gave me an answer. All she said was things would get better. She retired a beaten old lady with a lot of dignity. That day she thought would be better never came for her.

"One time, my mom was in bad need of money, so she got a part-time evening job in a restaurant. I'd be helping her. All the growers would come in and they'd be laughing, making nasty remarks, and make passes at her. I used to go out there and kick 'em and my mom told me to leave 'em alone, she could handle 'em. But they would embarrass her and she would cry.

"My mom was a very proud woman. She brought us up without any help from nobody. She kept the family strong. They say that a family that prays together stays together. I say that a family that works together stays together — because of the suffering. . . ."

I'd go barefoot to school. The bad thing was they used to laugh at us, the Anglo kids. They would laugh because we'd bring tortillas and frijoles to lunch. They would have their nice little compact lunch boxes with cold milk in their thermos and they'd laugh at us because all we had was dried tortillas. Not only would they laugh at us, but the kids would pick fights. My older brother used to do most of the fighting for us and he'd come home with black eyes all the time.

"I wanted to be accepted. It must have been in sixth grade. It was just before the Fourth of July. They were trying out students for this patriotic play. I wanted to do Abe Lincoln, so I learned the Gettysburg Address inside and out. I'd be out in the fields pickin' the crops and I'd be memorizin'. I was the only one who didn't have to read the part, 'cause I learned it. The part was given to a girl who was a grower's daughter. She had to read it out of a book, but they said she had better diction. I was very disappointed. I quit about eighth grade.

"Any time anybody'd talk to me about politics, about civil rights, I would ignore it. It's a very degrading thing because you can't express yourself. They wanted us to speak English in the school classes. We'd put out a real effort. I would get into a lot of fights because I spoke Spanish and they couldn't understand it. I was punished. I was kept after school for not speaking English."

We used to have our own tents on the truck. Most migrants would live in the tents that were already there in the fields, put up by the company. We got one for ourselves, secondhand, but it was ours. Anglos used to laugh at us. "Here comes the carnival," they'd say. We couldn't keep our clothes clean, we couldn't keep nothing clean, because we'd go by the dirt roads and the dust. We'd stay outside the town.

I never did want to go to town because it was a very bad thing for me. We used to go to the small stores, even though we got clipped more. If we went to the other stores, they would laugh at us. They would always point at us with a finger. We'd go to town maybe every two weeks to get what we needed. Everybody would walk in a bunch. We were afraid. (Laughs.) We sang to keep our spirits up. We joked about our poverty. This one guy would say, "When I get to be rich, I'm gonna marry an Anglo woman, so I can be accepted into society." The other guy would say, "When I get rich I'm gonna marry a Mexican woman, so I can go to that Anglo society of yours and see them hang you for marrying an Anglo." Our world was around the fields.

I started picking crops when I was eight. I couldn't do much, but every little bit counts. Every time I would get behind on my chores, I would get a carrot thrown at me by my parents. I would daydream: If I were a millionaire, I would buy all these ranches and give them back to the people. I would picture my mom living in one area all the time and being admired by all the people in the community. All of a sudden I'd be rudely awakened by a broken carrot in my back. That would bust your whole dream apart and you'd work for a while and come back to daydreaming.

We used to work early, about four o'clock in the morning. We'd pick the harvest until about six. Then we'd run home and get into our supposedly clean clothes and run all the way to school because we'd be late. By the time we got to school, we'd be all tuckered out. Around maybe eleven o'clock, we'd be dozing off. Our teachers would send notes to the house telling Mom that we were inattentive. The only thing I'd make fairly good grades on was spelling. I couldn't do anything else. Many times we never did our homework, because we were out in the fields. The teachers couldn't understand that. I would get whacked there also.

School would end maybe four o'clock. We'd rush home again, change clothes, go back to work until seven, seven thirty at night. That's not counting the weekends. On Saturday and Sunday, we'd be there from four thirty in the morning until about seven thirty in the evening. This is where we made the money, those two days. We all worked.

I would carry boxes for my mom to pack the carrots in. I would pull the carrots out and she would sort them into different sizes. I would get water for her to drink. When you're picking tomatoes, the boxes are heavy. They weigh about thirty pounds. They're dropped very hard on the trucks so they have to be sturdy.

The hardest work would be thinning and hoeing with a short-handled hoe. The fields would be about a half mile long. You would be bending and stooping all day. Sometimes you would have hard ground and by the time you got home, your hands would be full of calluses. And you'd have a backache. Sometimes I wouldn't have dinner or anything. I'd just go home and fall asleep and wake up just in time to go out to the fields again. . . .

The grower would keep the families apart, hoping they'd fight against each other. He'd have three or four camps and he'd have the people over here pitted against the people over there. For jobs. He'd give the best crops to the people he thought were the fastest workers. This way he kept us going harder and harder, competing.

When I was sixteen, I had my first taste as a foreman. Handling braceros, aliens, that came from Mexico to work. They'd bring these people to work over here and then send them back to Mexico after the season was over. My job was to make sure they did a good job and pushin' 'em even harder. I was a company man, yes. My parents needed money and I wanted to make sure they were proud of me. A foreman is recognized. I was very naïve. Even though I was pushing the workers, I knew their problems. They didn't know how to write, so I would write letters home for them. I would take 'em to town, buy their clothes, outside of the company stores. They paid me $1.10 an hour. The farm workers' wage was raised to eighty-two and a half cents. But even the braceros were making more money than me, because they were working piecework. I asked for more money. The manager said, "If you don't like it you can quit." I quit and joined the Marine Corps.

"I joined the Marine Corps at seventeen. I was very mixed up. I wanted to become a first-class citizen. I wanted to be accepted and I was very proud of my uniform. My mom didn't want to sign the papers, but she knew I had to better myself and maybe I'd get an education in the services.

"I did many jobs. I took a civil service exam and was very proud when I passed. Most of the others were college kids. There were only three Chicanos in the group of sixty. I got a job as a correctional officer in a state prison. I quit after eight months because I couldn't take the misery I saw. They wanted me to use a rubber hose on some of the prisoners — mostly Chicanos and blacks. I couldn't do it. They called me chicken-livered because I didn't want to hit nobody. They constantly harassed me after that. I didn't quit because I was afraid of them but because they were trying to make me into a mean man. I couldn't see it. This was Soledad State Prison."

I began to see how everything was so wrong. When growers can have an intricate watering system to irrigate their crops but they can't have running water inside the houses of workers. Veterinarians tend to the needs of domestic animals but they can't have medical care for the workers. They can have land subsidies for the growers but they can't have adequate unemployment compensation for the workers. They treat him like a farm implement. In fact, they treat their implements better and their domestic animals better. They have heat and insulated barns for the animals but the workers live in beat-up shacks with no heat at all.

Illness in the fields is 120 percent higher than the average rate for industry. It's mostly back trouble, rheumatism and arthritis, because of the damp weather and the cold. Stoop labor is very hard on a person. Tuberculosis is high. And now because of the pesticides, we have many respiratory diseases.

The University of California at Davis has government experiments with pesticides and chemicals. To get a bigger crop each year. They haven't any regard as to what safety precautions are needed. In 1964 or '65, an airplane was spraying these chemicals on the fields. Spraying rigs they're called. Flying low, the wheels got tangled on the fence wire. The pilot got up, dusted himself off, and got a drink of water. He died of convulsions. The ambulance attendants got violently sick because of the pesticides he had on his person. A little girl was playing around a sprayer. She stuck her tongue on it. She died instantly.

These pesticides affect the farm worker through the lungs. He breathes it in. He gets no compensation. All they do is say he's sick. They don't investigate the cause.

There were times when I felt I couldn't take it any more. It was 105 in the shade and I'd see endless rows of lettuce and I felt my back hurting . . . I felt the frustration of not being able to get out of the fields. I was getting ready to jump any foreman who looked at me cross-eyed. But until two years ago, my world was still very small.

I would read all these things in the papers about Cesar Chavez and I would denounce him because I still had that thing about becoming a first-class patriotic citizen. In Mexicali they would pass out leaflets and I would throw 'em away. I never participated. The grape boycott didn't affect me much because I was in lettuce. It wasn't until Chavez came to Salinas, where I was working in the fields, that I saw what a beautiful man he was. I went to this rally, I still intended to stay with the company. But something — I don't know — I was close to the workers. They couldn't speak English and wanted me to be their spokesman in favor of going on strike. I don't know — I just got caught up with it all, the beautiful feeling of solidarity.

You'd see the people on the picket lines at four in the morning, at the camp fires, heating up beans and coffee and tortillas. It gave me a sense of belonging. These were my own people and they wanted change. I knew this is what I was looking for. I just didn't know it before.

My mom had always wanted me to better myself. I wanted to better myself because of her. Now when the strikes started, I told her I was going to join the union and the whole movement. I told her I was going to work without pay. She said she was proud of me. (His eyes glisten. A long, long pause.) See, I told her I wanted to be with my people. If I were a company man, nobody would like me any more. I had to belong to somebody and this was it right here. She said, "I pushed you in your early years to try to better yourself and get a social position. But I see that's not the answer. I know I'll be proud of you."

All kinds of people are farm workers, not just Chicanos. Filipinos started the strike. We have Puerto Ricans and Appalachians too, Arabs, some Japanese, some Chinese. At one time they used us against each other. But now they can't and they're scared, the growers. They can organize conglomerates. Yet when we try organization to better our lives, they are afraid. Suffering people never dreamed it could be different. Cesar Chavez tells them this and they grasp the idea — and this is what scares the growers.

Now the machines are coming in. It takes skill to operate them. But anybody can be taught. We feel migrant workers should be given the chance. They got one for grapes. They got one for lettuce. They have cotton machines that took jobs away from thousands of farm workers. The people wind up in the ghettos of the city, their culture, their families, their unity destroyed.

We're trying to stipulate it in our contract that the company will not use any machinery without the consent of the farm workers. So we can make sure the people being replaced by the machines will know how to operate the machines.

Working in the fields is not in itself a degrading job. It's hard, but if you're given regular hours, better pay, decent housing, unemployment and medical compensation, pension plans — we have a very relaxed way of living. But the growers don't recognize us as persons. That's the worst thing, the way they treat you. Like we have no brains. Now we see they have no brains. They have only a wallet in their head. The more you squeeze it, the more they cry out.

If we had proper compensation we wouldn't have to be working seventeen hours a day and following the crops. We could stay in one area and it would give us roots. Being a migrant, it tears the family apart. You get in debt. You leave the area penniless. The children are the ones hurt the most. They go to school three months in one place and then on to another. No sooner do they make friends, they are uprooted again. Right here, your childhood is taken away. So when they grow up, they're looking for this childhood they have lost.

If people could see — in the winter, ice on the fields. We'd be on our knees all day long. We'd build fires and warm up real fast and go back onto the ice. We'd be picking watermelons in 105 degrees all day long. When people have melons or cucumber or carrots or lettuce, they don't know how they got on their table and the consequences to the people who picked it. If I had enough money, I would take busloads of people out to the fields and into the labor camps. Then they'd know how that fine salad got on their table. ■

After reflecting critically on his experiences, Roberto Acuna changed the course of his life and became a union organizer for the United Farm Workers of America. This process of changing his perceptions based on his experiences resulted in a new and clearer understanding of his life.

For Acuna, the process of coming to a new awareness based on his perceptions was complex. As a migrant worker, he was an oppressed member of a system that dominated and exploited him. He tried to escape from this domination while staying within the system by becoming a foreman, a Marine, and a prison guard. His goal was to become socially accepted, "a first-class citizen." However, his experiences conflicted with this belief in social acceptability. As a foreman, he found that "My job was to make sure they did a good job and pushin' 'em even harder. I was a company man, yes." While he was working as a prison guard, he explains, "I quit after eight months because I couldn't take the misery I saw. They wanted me to use a rubber hose on some of the prisoners — mostly Chicanos and blacks."

Acuna's critical thinking about these experiences led him to perceive that he was becoming a part of the system of oppression that he himself had suffered under and that he despised for its inhumane treatment of people. His encounter with Cesar Chavez led him to the deeper perception that, instead of trying to become part of the system, he should try to change it. While acting as a spokesperson for striking workers, he says, "I don't know — I just got caught up with it all, the beautiful feeling of solidarity. . . . It gave me a sense of belonging. These were my own people and they wanted change. I knew this is what I was looking for. I just didn't know it before."

Acuna's story illustrates the main purpose of our ongoing attempts to think critically about the way our experiences shape our perceptions. By engaging in this process, we are continually trying to develop a clearer and more complete understanding of what is taking place so that we can make the most effective decisions in our lives.

Because our perceptions are based on our experiences, they often change and evolve based on new experiences. Analyzing Roberto Acuna's personal odyssey will illustrate how experiences can shape and reshape our perceptions.

1. *Initial Perceptions*

   a. What were Acuna's initial perceptions of being a migrant worker?

   b. What were his initial perceptions of his future goals?

   c. What were his initial perceptions of the growers?

   d. What were his initial perceptions of his fellow migrant workers?

Acuna states that "The things I saw shaped my life." What were the experiences that shaped his initial perceptions?

2. *Experiences That Shaped His Initial Perceptions*

   a. What experiences shaped his initial perceptions about being a migrant worker?

   b. What experiences shaped his initial perceptions of his future goals?

   c. What experiences shaped his initial perceptions of the growers?

   d. What experiences shaped his initial perceptions of his fellow migrant workers?

Acuna used his perceptions to make sense of his situation and then acted on the basis of his perceptions. He became a foreman, working for the growers; he joined the Marines; and he became a correctional officer. After taking these actions, however, Acuna began to find out that his initial perceptions of his life and goals did not seem to be working effectively in explaining his experiences. He states that "I began to see how everything was so wrong." Explain how the following experiences influenced him to doubt and raise questions of his initial perceptions:

3. *Experiences That Raised Doubts and Questions About His Initial Perceptions*

    a. How did becoming a foreman raise doubts about his initial perceptions?

    b. How did becoming a correctional officer raise doubts about his initial perceptions?

    c. How did meeting Cesar Chavez raise doubts about his initial perceptions?

As Acuna questioned the accuracy of his initial perceptions, he began to form revised perceptions of his life and future. Describe the new perceptions he formed as a result of having these experiences and thinking critically about them.

4. *Revised Perceptions He Formed About His Situation*

    a. What were Acuna's revised perceptions of being a migrant worker?

    b. What were his revised perceptions of his future goals?

    c. What were his revised perceptions of the growers?

    d. What were his revised perceptions of his fellow migrant workers?

THINKING ACTIVITY

4.8   ▶ Think of an experience that has shaped your life. Write an essay describing the experience and the ways it changed your life and the way that you perceive the world. Before writing, analyze your experience by answering the following questions.

1. What were your *initial* perceptions about the situation? As you began the experience that you will describe, you brought into the situation certain perceptions about the experience and the people involved.

2. What previous experiences had you undergone? Identify some of the influences that helped to shape these perceptions. Describe the actions that you either took or thought about taking.

3. As you became involved in the situation, what experiences in the situation influenced you to question or doubt your initial perceptions?

4. In what new ways did you view the situation that would better explain what was taking place? Identify the revised perceptions that you began to form about the experience.

A Shaping Experience

As long as I can remember, I have seen telethons and other programs on television asking for money to help stop sickness and diseases. I never had any interest in these programs, however, and when I read about the same subjects — serious diseases, transplants, surgery — I was equally uninterested.

My little brother, Jason, has always had very bad kidneys, and when he was eight years old he needed a kidney transplant. I had never realized how serious the matter was, so his condition didn't have any real effect on me. However, after seeing the mental suffering of my mother and the physical suffering of my little brother, I began to feel the pain as well. Despite this, I ignored the situation as much as I could. I turned my social life into my whole life and tried to forget about my family. I did this to save myself from suffering. But something, somewhere, would always remind me of the telethons, the programs, and the articles dealing with the suffering of others.

Even though I ignored Jason and his problems, he idolized and emulated me, a fact I hated because the person he wanted to be only cared about himself. And Jason's problems grew even worse. Several weeks after the transplant, his body rejected his new kidney. The doctors gave him more powerful drugs to help his body accept the kidney, but the drugs caused other problems. His left lung collapsed and he had several heart failures. The rest of the family suffered along with him. My mother had breakdowns and my brothers and sisters couldn't study or work. Yet I would carry on trouble—free, happiness in my voice, always with my friends.

At Christmas following his operation Jason was still in the hospital, and we all went to see him. I don't remember a place on his face or arms that didn't have tubes stuck in it. He could only whisper and could not see who was in the room. My mother asked him, ''Jason, what do you want for Christmas?'' He answered, ''I want to be just like my favorite brother, Kevin,'' and then he fell back into a deep sleep.

That night changed me as a person. Since then I have become very caring and considerate. I now feel and understand the suffering of others, and I am always trying to help other people. I contribute money to organizations such as UNICEF and CARE and to other programs that help people. My family has become the most important thing in my life, and a day doesn't go by without me and my brother spending time together. My new perception of life is to

```
help and care for all that I can, and this makes me happier
than when I didn't have any concern for others. Now I ap-
preciate and take advantage of having such a wonderful
brother instead of trying to ignore the voice inside of
me which was angry, panicky, and full of fear of losing
him at any time. ◄
```

Thinking Critically About Perceptions

So far, we have emphasized the great extent to which we actively participate in what we perceive by selecting, organizing, and interpreting. We have suggested that each of us views the world through our own unique spectacles. This means that no two of us perceive the world in exactly the same way.

Because we actively participate in selecting, organizing, and interpreting the sensations we experience, however, our perceptions are often incomplete, inaccurate, or subjective. To complicate the situation even more, our own limitations in perceiving are not the only ones that can cause us problems. Other people often purposefully create perceptions and *mis*perceptions. An advertiser who wants to sell a product may try to create the impression that our life will be changed if we use this product. Or a person who wants to discredit someone else may spread untrue rumors about her, in order to influence others' perceptions of her.

The only way we can correct the mistakes, distortions, and incompleteness of our perceptions is to *become aware* of this normally unconscious process by which we perceive and make sense of our world. By becoming aware of this process, we can think critically about what is going on and then correct our mistakes and distortions. In other words, we can use our critical thinking abilities to create a clearer and more informed idea of what is taking place. Perception alone cannot be totally relied on, and if we remain unaware of how it operates and of our active role in it, then we will be unable to exert any control over it. And in that case, we will be convinced that the way *we see* the world is the way the world *is*, even when our perceptions are mistaken, distorted, or incomplete.

The first step in critically examining our perceptions is to be willing to *ask questions* about what we are perceiving. As long as we believe that the way we see things is the only way to see them, we will be unable to recognize when our perceptions are distorted or inaccurate. For instance, if we are certain that our interpretation of the boy at the computer in Thinking Activity

4.2 or the photograph of a social scene in Thinking Activity 4.3 is the only correct one, then we will not be likely to try and see other possible interpretations. But if we are willing to question our perception ("What are some other possible interpretations?"), then we will open the way to more fully developing our perception of what is taking place.

Besides asking questions, we have to try to become aware of the personal factors our spectacles bring to our perceptions. As we have seen, each of us brings to every situation a whole collection of expectations, interests, fears, and hopes that can influence what we are perceiving. Consider the following situations:

> You've been fishing all day without a nibble. Suddenly you get a strike! You reel it in, but just as you're about to pull the fish into the boat, it frees itself from the hook and swims away. When you get back home later that night, your friends ask you: "How large was the fish that got away?"

> The teacher asks you to evaluate the performance of a classmate who is giving a report to the class. You don't like this other student because he acts as if he's superior to the rest of the students in the class. How do you evaluate his report?

> You are asked to estimate the size of an audience attending an event that your organization has sponsored. How many people are there?

In each of these cases, you can imagine that your perceptions might be influenced by certain hopes, fears, or prejudices that you brought to the situation, causing your observations to become distorted or inaccurate. Although we usually cannot eliminate the personal feelings that are influencing our perceptions, we can become aware of them and try to control them. For instance, if we are asked to evaluate a group of people, one of whom is a good friend, we should try to keep these personal feelings in mind when making our judgment in order to make our perceptions as accurate as possible.

When we explored the different aspects of critical thinking in Chapter Two, we emphasized the importance of seeing things from different perspectives. One of the best ways to do so is by communicating with others and engaging in *dialogue* with them. This means exchanging and critically examining ideas in an open and organized way. Similarly, dialogue is one of the main ways that we check out our perceptions — by asking others what their perceptions are and then comparing and contrasting these with our own. This is exactly what you did when you discussed the different possible interpretations of the boy with the trumpet and the photograph of a social scene. By exchanging your perceptions with the perceptions of other class members, you developed a more complete sense of how these different events could be viewed, as well as the reasons that support these different perspectives.

Looking for reasons that support various perceptions also involves trying to discover any independent proof or evidence regarding the perception. When evidence is available in the form of records, photographs, videotapes, or experimental results, this will certainly help us evaluate the accuracy of our perceptions. For example, consider the situation we mentioned before:

> You are asked to estimate the size of an audience attending an event that your organization has sponsored. How many people are there?

What are some of the independent forms of evidence you could look for in trying to verify your perception?

1. _____

2. _____

3. _____

Thinking critically about our perceptions means trying to avoid developing impulsive or superficial perceptions that we are unwilling to change. As we saw in Chapter Two, a critical thinker is *thoughtful* in approaching the world and *open* to modifying his or her views in the light of new information or better insight. Consider the following perceptions:

- Women are very emotional.
- Politicians are corrupt.
- Teen-agers are wild and irresponsible.
- Movie stars are self-centered.
- People who are good athletes are usually poor students.

These types of general perceptions are known as *stereotypes* because they express a belief about an entire group of people without recognizing the individual differences between members of the group. For instance, it is probably accurate to say that there are *some* politicians who are corrupt, but this is not the same thing as saying that all, or even most, politicians are corrupt. Stereotypes affect our perception of the world because they encourage us to form an inaccurate and superficial idea of a whole group of people ("All cops are brutal"). When we meet someone who falls into this group, we automatically perceive that person as having these stereotyped qualities ("This person is a cop and so he's brutal"). Even if we find that this person does not fit our stereotyped perception ("This cop is not brutal"), this sort of superficial and unthoughtful labeling does not encourage us to change our perception of the group as a whole. Instead, it encourages us to overlook the conflicting information in favor of our stereotyped perception ("All cops are brutal — except for this one"). On the other hand, when we are perceiving in a thoughtful fashion, we try to see what a person is like as an individual, instead of trying to fit him or her into a pre-existing category.

THINKING ACTIVITY

4.9 ▶ The news accounts of the assassination of Malcolm X and the autobiographical narrative of Roberto Acuna are filled with examples of stereotypes — fixed ways of perceiving which unfairly and inaccurately characterize an entire group of people. Review these passages and then write an essay following the instructions below.

1. Identify the group that is being stereotyped and list the characteristics that compose the stereotype.

2. For each stereotype, explain why the characterization of the group is unfair and inaccurate.

3. For each stereotype, explain how the characterization of the group is used for destructive purposes. ◀

THINKING ACTIVITY

4.10 ▶ 1. Describe an incident in which you were perceived as a stereotype because of your age, ethnic or religious background, employment, accent, or place of residence.

2. Describe how it felt to be stereotyped in this way.

3. Explain what you think are the best ways to overcome stereotypes such as these. ◀

Summary

As our minds develop through the experiences we have and our reflection on these experiences, our perceptions of the world should continue to develop as well. By thinking critically about our perceptions, by seeking to view our world from perspectives other than our own and to understand the reasons that support these perspectives, our understanding of the world should become increasingly accurate and complete. We can view our efforts to think critically about what we are perceiving as a problem-solving process, as we continually attempt to interpret our experiences.

As we have seen in this chapter, much of our knowledge of the world begins in perceiving. But to develop knowledge and understanding, we must make use of our thinking abilities in order to examine this experience critically. Increased understanding of the way the world operates thus increases the accuracy and completeness of our perceptions and leads us to informed beliefs about what is happening. In the next chapter we will be exploring further how we develop our informed beliefs and knowledge of the world by combining our perceiving with critical thinking.

CHAPTER 5

Believing and Knowing

BELIEFS:
Interpretations, evaluations, conclusions, and predictions about the world that we endorse as true.

Beliefs based on indirect experience (oral or written sources of information).

Beliefs based on direct experience.

How reliable is the information?

How reliable is the source of information?

DEVELOPING KNOWLEDGE
by thinking critically about our beliefs.

Are the beliefs compelling and coherent explanations?

Are the beliefs based on reliable sources?

Are the beliefs consistent with other beliefs/knowledge?

Are the beliefs accurate predictions?

Are the beliefs supported by reasons and evidence?

IT SEEMS TO BE a natural human impulse to try to understand the world we live in. This is the overall goal of thinking, which we have defined as the mental process by which we make sense of the world. As we saw in the last chapter, perceiving is an important part of this process of making sense because it is the way we actively select, organize, and interpret our sense experience. As we also discovered, however, our perceptions, taken by themselves, do not provide a reliable, sound foundation for our understanding of the world. Our perceptions are often incomplete, distorted, and inaccurate. They are shaped and influenced by our perceiving "spectacles," which reflect our own individual personalities, experiences, biases, assumptions, and ways of viewing things. To clarify and validate our perceptions, we must critically examine and evaluate these perceptions.

Thinking critically about our perceptions results in the formation of our beliefs and ultimately the construction of our knowledge about the world. The beliefs we form about the world help us explain why the world is the way it is and how we ought to behave. For example, consider the following statements and answer "Yes," "No," or "Not sure" to each.

1. Humans need to eat to stay alive.

2. Smoking marijuana is a harmless good time.

3. Every human life is valuable.

4. Developing our minds is as important as taking care of our bodies.

5. People should care about other people, not just themselves.

Our responses to these statements reflect certain beliefs we have, and these beliefs help us explain why the world is the way it is and how we ought to behave. In this chapter we will see that beliefs are the main tools we use to make sense of the world and guide our actions. The total collection of our beliefs represent our view of the world, our philosophy of life.

What exactly are "beliefs"? If we examine the concept closely, we can see that beliefs represent an interpretation, evaluation, conclusion, or prediction about the nature of the world. For example, the statement, "I believe that the whale in the book *Moby Dick* by Herman Melville symbolizes a primal, natural force that men are trying to destroy," represents an *interpretation* of that novel. To say, "I believe that watching soap operas is unhealthy because they focus almost exclusively on the seamy, evil side of human life," expresses an *evaluation* of soap operas. The statement, "I believe that one of the main reasons two out of three people in the world go to bed hungry each night is that industrially advanced nations like the United States have not done a satisfactory job of sharing their knowledge," expresses a *conclusion* about the problem of world hunger. To say, "If drastic environmental measures are not undertaken to slow the global warming trend, then I believe that the polar ice caps will melt and the earth will be flooded," is to make a *prediction* about events that will occur in the future.

Besides expressing an interpretation, evaluation, conclusion, or prediction about the world, beliefs also express an *endorsement* that the views being advanced are true. In the preceding statements the speakers are not simply expressing interpretations, evaluations, conclusions, and predictions; they are also indicating that they believe these views are *true*. In other words, the speakers are saying that they have adopted these beliefs as their own because they are convinced that they represent accurate viewpoints based on some sort of evidence. This "endorsement" by the speaker is a necessary dimension of beliefs, and we assume it to be the case even if the speaker doesn't directly say, "I believe." For example, the statement, "Astrological predictions are meaningless because there is no persuasive reason to believe that the position of the stars has any effect on human affairs," expresses a belief even though it doesn't specifically include the words "I believe."

> *Beliefs*   Interpretations, evaluations, conclusions, predictions about the world that we endorse as true.

In the space provided, describe beliefs you have in each of these categories (interpretation, evaluation, conclusion, prediction) and then explain the reason(s) you have for endorsing the beliefs.

1. **(Interpretation)** I believe that _____

   _____

   Supporting Reason(s): _____

   _____

2. **(Evaluation)** I believe that _____

   _____

   Supporting Reason(s): _____

   _____

3. **(Conclusion)** I believe that _____

   _____

   Supporting Reason(s): _____

   _____

4. **(Prediction)** I believe that _____

_____

Supporting Reason(s): _____

_____

Believing and Perceiving

The relationship between the activities of believing and perceiving is complex and interactive. On one hand, our perceptual encounters with the world form the foundation of many of our beliefs about it. On the other hand, our beliefs about the world shape and influence our perceptions of it. Let's explore this interactive relationship by examining a variety of beliefs, including:

1. *Interpretations* ("Poetry enables humans to communicate deep, complex emotions and ideas that resist simple expression.")

2. *Evaluations* ("Children today spend too much time watching television and too little time reading.")

3. *Conclusions* ("An effective college education provides not only mastery of information and skills, but also evolving insight and maturing judgment.")

4. *Predictions* ("With the shrinking and integration of the global community, there will be an increasing need in the future for Americans to speak a second language.")

These beliefs, for people who endorse them, are likely to be based in large measure on a variety of perceptual experiences: events that people have seen and heard. The perceptual experiences by themselves, however, do not result in beliefs — they are simply experiences. For them to become beliefs, we must *think about* our perceptual experiences and then organize them into a belief structure. This thinking process of constructing beliefs is known as *cognition*, and it forms the basis of our understanding of the world. In the space provided, describe some of the perceptual experiences that might have led to the construction of the beliefs just described:

1. Perceptual experiences: _____

_____

2. Perceptual experiences: _____

_____

3. Perceptual experiences: _____

_____

4. Perceptual experiences: _____

_____

As we noted, our perceptual experiences not only contribute to the formation of our beliefs, the beliefs we have formed also have a powerful influence on the perceptions we *select* to focus on, how we *organize* these perceptions, and the manner in which we *interpret* them. For example, if we are reading a magazine and come across a poem, our perceptual responses to the poem are likely to be affected by our beliefs about poetry. These beliefs may influence whether we select the poem as something to read, the manner in which we organize and relate the poem to other aspects of our experience, and our interpretation of the poem's meaning. This interactive relationship holds true for most beliefs. Assume that you endorse the four beliefs listed earlier and describe how holding these beliefs could influence a perceptual experience you might have.

1. Perceptual experience: _____

_____

2. Perceptual experience: _____

_____

3. Perceptual experience: _____

_____

4. Perceptual experience: _____

_____

The belief systems we have developed to understand and explain our world help us correct inaccurate perceptions. When we watch a magician perform seemingly impossible tricks, our beliefs about the way the world operates inform us that what we are seeing is really a misperception, an illusion. In this context, we expect to be tricked, and our question is naturally, "How did he or she do that?" Potential problems arise, however, in those situations where it is not apparent that our perceptions are providing us with inaccurate information, and we use these experiences to form mistaken beliefs. For example, we may view advertisements linking youthful, attractive, fun-loving people with smoking cigarettes and form the apparently inaccurate belief that smoking cigarettes is an integral part of being youthful, attractive and fun loving. As critical thinkers, we have a responsibility to monitor and evaluate continually both aspects of this interactive process — our beliefs and our perceptions — so that we can develop the most informed perspective on the world.

THINKING ACTIVITY

5.1 ▶ Describe an experience of a perception you had that later turned out to be false, based on subsequent experiences or reflection. Address the following questions:

1. What qualities of the perception led you to believe it to be true?

2. How did this perceptual experience influence your beliefs about the world?

3. Describe the process that led you to the conclusion that the perception was false. ◀

Believing and Knowing

We have seen that beliefs are a major tool that helps us explain how and why the world is the way it is and guides us in making effective decisions. As we form and re-form our beliefs, based on our experiences and our thinking about these experiences, we usually try to develop beliefs that are as accurate as possible. The more accurate our beliefs are, the better able we are to understand what is taking place and to predict what will occur in the future.

The beliefs we form vary tremendously in accuracy. For example, how accurate do you think the following beliefs are?

1. I believe that there is a very large man who lives on the moon.

2. I believe that there is life on other planets.

3. I believe that a college education will lead me to a satisfying and well-paying job.

4. I believe that there is life on this planet.

In considering these beliefs, you probably came to the conclusion that belief 1 was not accurate at all, belief 2 was possible but far from being certain, belief 3 was likely but not guaranteed to be accurate, and belief 4 was definitely accurate.

The idea of *knowing* is one of the ways humans have developed to distinguish beliefs supported by strong reasons or evidence (such as belief that there is life on earth) from beliefs for which there is less support (such as beliefs that there is life on other planets and that college will lead to a job) or from beliefs disproved by reasons or evidence to the contrary (such as belief in the man in the moon). Let's try replacing the word *believe* with the word *know* in the preceding statements:

1. I *know* that there is a very large man who lives on the moon.
2. I *know* that there is life on other planets.
3. I *know* that a college education will lead me to a satisfying and well-paying job.
4. I *know* that there is life on this planet.

The only statement in which it makes sense to use the word *know* is the fourth one, because we have conclusive evidence that this belief is accurate. In the case of sentence 1, we would say that this person is seriously mistaken. In the case of sentence 2, we might say that, although life on other planets is a possibility, there is no conclusive evidence (at present) that supports this view. In the case of sentence 3, we might say that, although for many people a college education leads to a satisfying and good-paying job, this is not always the case. As a result, we cannot say we *know* this belief (or belief 2) is accurate. Another way of expressing the difference between "believing" and "knowing" is by means of the following saying:

You can *believe* what is not so, but you cannot *know* what is not so.

THINKING ACTIVITY

5.2 ▶ State whether you think that each of the following beliefs is:

- *Completely accurate* (so that you would say, "I know this is the case")
- *Generally accurate* but not completely accurate (so that you would say, "This is often, but not always, the case")
- *Generally not accurate,* but sometimes accurate (so that you would say, "This is usually *not* the case, but is sometimes true")
- *Definitely not accurate* (so that you would say, "I know that this is *not* the case")

After determining the *degree of accuracy* in this way, explain *why* you have selected your answer.

- *Example:* I believe that if you study hard you will achieve good grades.
- *Degree of accuracy:* Generally, but not completely, accurate.
- *Explanation:* Although many people who study hard achieve good grades, this is not always true. Sometimes people have difficulty understanding the work in a certain subject no matter how hard they study. And sometimes they just don't know how to study effectively. In other cases, the student may lack adequate background of experience for a certain subject area (for example, English may be a second language), or there might be a personality conflict with the instructor.

1. I believe that essay exams are more difficult than multiple-choice exams.

   Degree of accuracy: _____

   Explanation: _____

   _____

2. I believe that longer prison sentences will discourage people from committing crimes.

   Degree of accuracy: _____

   Explanation: _____

   _____

3. I believe that there are more people on the earth today than there were one hundred years ago.

   Degree of accuracy: _____

   Explanation: _____

   _____

4. I believe that your astrological sign determines your basic personality traits.

   Degree of accuracy: _____

   Explanation: _____

   _____

5. I believe that you will never get rich by playing the lottery.

Degree of accuracy: _____

Explanation: _____

_____

6. *Your example of a belief:* _____

_____

    Degree of accuracy: _____

    Explanation: _____

_____

7. *Your example of a belief:* _____

_____

    Degree of accuracy: _____

    Explanation: _____

_____ ◀

When someone indicates that he or she thinks a belief is completely accurate by saying, *"I know,"* our response is often *"How* do you know?" If the person cannot give us a satisfactory answer to this question, we are likely to say something like, "If you can't explain how you know it, then you don't *really* know it — you're just saying it." In other words, when we say that "we know" something, we mean at least two different things.

1. I think this belief is completely accurate.
2. I can explain to you the reasons or evidence that support this belief.

If either of these standards is not met, we would usually say that the person does not really "know."

We work at evaluating the accuracy of our beliefs by examining the reasons or evidence that support them (known as the *justification* for the beliefs). Looked at in this way, our beliefs form a *range* as pictured below.

Beliefs that we know *are:*	*Beliefs that we are* not sure *are:*	*Beliefs that we* know *are:*
inaccurate	accurate	accurate
unjustified	justified	justified

Just as temperature is a scale that varies from cold to hot with many degrees in between, so our beliefs can be thought of as forming a rough scale based on their accuracy and justification. As we learn more about the world and ourselves, we try to form beliefs that are increasingly accurate and justified.

Of course, determining the accuracy and justification of our beliefs is a challenging business. We generally use a number of different questions to explore and evaluate our beliefs, including the following:

- How well do our beliefs *explain* what is taking place?
- How do these beliefs *relate to other beliefs* we have about the world?
- How well do these beliefs enable us to *predict* what will happen in the future?
- How well do the *reasons or evidence* support our beliefs?
- How *reliable is the information* on which our beliefs are based?

The key point is that as critical thinkers we should continually try to form and re-form our beliefs so that we can make sense of the world in increasingly effective ways. Even when we find that we maintain certain beliefs over a long period of time, we should discover that our explorations result in a deeper and fuller understanding of these beliefs.

THINKING ACTIVITY
_____

5.3   ▶ In Chapter Two, *Thinking Critically*, we examined the process that led us to the conclusion that the earth is round, not flat. In the following article, "Is the Earth Round or Flat?" by the author and astrophysicist Alan Lightman, analyzes this process and provides a clear analysis of the difference between "believing" and "knowing." Read the article and answer the questions that follow.

IS THE EARTH ROUND OR FLAT? *by Alan Lightman*

I propose that there are few of us who have personally verified that the Earth is round. The suggestive globe in the den or the Apollo photographs don't count. These are secondhand pieces of evidence that might be thrown out entirely in court. When you think about it, most of us simply believe what we hear. Round or flat, whatever. It's not a life-or-death matter, unless you happen to live near the edge.

A few years ago I suddenly realized, to my dismay, that I didn't know with certainty if the Earth were round or flat. I have scientific colleagues, geodesists they are called, whose sole business is determining the detailed shape of the Earth by fitting mathematical formulae to someone else's measurements of the precise locations of test stations on the Earth's surface. And I don't think those people really know either.

Aristotle is the first person in recorded history to have given proof that the Earth is round. He used several different arguments, most likely because he wanted to convince others as well as himself. A lot of people believed everything Aristotle said for 19 centuries.

His first proof was that the shadow of the Earth during a lunar eclipse is always curved, a segment of a circle. If the Earth were any shape but spherical, the shadow it casts, in some orientations, would not be circular. (That the normal phases of the moon are crescent-shaped reveals the moon is round.) I find this argument wonderfully appealing. It is simple and direct. What's more, an inquisitive and untrusting person can knock off the experiment alone, without special equipment. From any given spot on the Earth, a lunar eclipse can be seen about once a year. You simply have to look up on the right night and carefully observe what's happening. I've never done it.

Aristotle's second proof was that stars rise and set sooner for people in the East than in the West. If the Earth were flat from east to west, stars would rise as soon for Occidentals as for Orientals. With a little scribbling on a piece of paper, you can see that these observations imply a round Earth, regardless of whether it is the Earth that spins around or the stars that revolve around the Earth. Finally, northbound travelers observe previously invisible stars appearing above the northern horizon, showing the Earth is curved from north to south. Of course, you do have to accept the reports of a number of friends in different places or be willing to do some traveling.

Aristotle's last argument was purely theoretical and even philosophical. If the Earth had been formed from smaller pieces at some time in the past (or *could* have been so formed), its pieces would fall toward a common center, thus making a sphere. Furthermore, a sphere is clearly the most perfect solid shape. Interestingly, Aristotle placed as much emphasis on this last argument as on the first two. Those days, before the modern "scientific method," observational check wasn't required for investigating reality.

Assuming for the moment that the Earth is round, the first person who measured its circumference accurately was another Greek, Eratosthenes (276–195 B.C.). Eratosthenes noted that on the first day of summer, sunlight struck the bottom of a vertical well in Syene, Egypt, indicating the sun was directly overhead. At the same time in Alexandria, 5,000 stadia distant, the sun made an angle with the vertical equal to $\frac{1}{50}$ of a circle. (A stadium equaled about a tenth of a mile.) Since the sun is so far away, its rays arrive almost in parallel. If you draw a circle with two radii extending from the center outward through the perimeter (where they become local verticals), you'll see that a sun ray coming in parallel to one of the radii (at Syene) makes an angle with the other (at Alexandria) equal to the angle between the two radii. Therefore Eratosthenes concluded that the full circumference of the Earth is $50 \times 5,000$ stadia, or about 25,000 miles. This calculation is within one percent of the best modern value.

For at least 600 years educated people have believed the Earth is round. At nearly any medieval university, the quadrivium was standard fare, consisting of arithmetic, geometry, music, and astronomy. The astronomy portion was based on the *Tractatus de Sphaera,* a popular textbook first published at Ferrara, Italy, in 1472 and written by a 13th-century, Oxford-educated astronomer and mathematician, Johannes de Sacrobosco. The *Sphaera* proves its astronomical assertions, in part, by a set of diagrams with movable parts, a graphical demonstration of Aristotle's second method of proof. The round Earth, being the obvious center of the universe, provides a fixed pivot for the assembly. The cutout figures of the sun, the moon, and the stars revolve about the Earth.

By the year 1500, 24 editions of the *Sphaera* had appeared. There is no question that many people *believed* the Earth was round. I wonder how many *knew* this. You would think that Columbus and Magellan might have wanted to ascertain the facts for themselves before waving goodbye.

To protect my honor as a scientist, someone who is supposed to take nothing for granted, I set out with my wife on a sailing voyage in the Greek islands. I reasoned that at sea I would be able to calmly observe landmasses disappear over the curve of the Earth and thus convince myself, firsthand, that the Earth is round.

Greece seemed a particularly satisfying place to conduct my experiment. I could sense those great ancient thinkers looking on approvingly, and the layout of the place is perfect. Hydra rises about 2,000 feet above sea level. If the Earth has a radius of 4,000 miles, as they say, then Hydra should sink down to the horizon at a distance of about 50 miles, somewhat less than the distance we were to sail from Hydra to Kea. The theory was sound and comfortable. At the very least, I thought, we would have a pleasant vacation.

As it turned out, that was all we got. Every single day was hazy. Islands faded from view at a distance of only eight miles, when the land was still a couple of degrees above the horizon. I learned how much water vapor was in the air but nothing about the curvature of the Earth.

I suspect that there are quite a few items we take on faith, even important things, even things we could verify without much trouble. Is the gas we exhale the same as the gas we inhale? (Do we indeed burn oxygen in our metabolism, as they say?) What is our blood made of? (Does it indeed have red and white "cells"?) These questions could be answered with a balloon, a candle, and a microscope.

When we finally do the experiment, we relish the knowledge. At one time or another, we have all learned something for ourselves, from the ground floor up, taking no one's word for it. There is a special satisfaction and joy in being able to tell somebody something you have pieced together from scratch, something you really know. I think that exhilaration is a big reason why people do science.

Someday soon, I'm going to catch the Earth's shadow in a lunar eclipse, or go to sea in clear air, and find out for sure if the Earth is round or flat. Actually, the Earth is reported to flatten at the poles, because it rotates. But that's another story. ■

1. Explain why Lightman states that although he always *believed* that the earth was round, "A few years ago I suddenly realized, to my dismay, that I didn't know with certainty if the Earth were round or flat."

2. In your own words, explain how you could prove to someone else that the Earth is round.

3. Describe a scientific fact that you believe but do not "know," in Lightman's sense. Explain how you might prove this to someone else. ◄

Knowledge and Truth

Most people in our culture are socialized to believe that knowledge and truth are absolute and unchanging. One major goal of our social institutions, including family, school system, and religion, is to transfer to us the knowledge that has been developed over the ages. Under this model, the role of learners is to absorb this information passively, like sponges. As we have seen in this text, however, achieving knowledge and truth is a much more complicated process than this. Instead of simply relying on the testimony of authorities like parents, teachers, textbooks and religious leaders, critical thinkers have a responsibility to engage *actively* in the learning process and participate in developing their own understanding of the world.

The need for this active approach to knowing is underscored by the fact that authorities often disagree about the true nature of a given situation or the best course of action. It is not uncommon, for example, for doctors to disagree about a diagnosis; for economists to differ on the state of the economy; for researchers to present contrasting views on the best approach to curing cancer; for psychiatrists to disagree on whether a convicted felon is a menace to society or a harmless victim of social forces; and for religions to present conflicting approaches to achieving eternal life.

What do we do when experts disagree? As critical thinkers, we must analyze and evaluate all the available information, develop our own well-reasoned beliefs, and recognize when we don't have sufficient information to arrive at well-reasoned beliefs. We must realize that these beliefs may evolve over time as we gain information or improve our insight.

Although there are compelling reasons to view knowledge and truth in this way, many people resist it. Either they take refuge in a belief in the absolute, unchanging nature of knowledge and truth, as presented by the appropriate authorities, or they conclude that there is no such thing as knowledge or truth and that trying to seek either is a futile enterprise. In this latter view of the world, known as *relativism,* all beliefs are considered as "relative" to the person or context in which they arise. For the relativist, all opinions are equal in validity to all others; we are never in a position to say with confidence that one view is right and another view is wrong.

Although a relativistic view is appropriate in some areas of experience — for example, in many matters of taste (such as fashion, as shown in the photographs of the three women) — in many other areas it is not. Although it is often difficult to achieve, knowledge, in the form of well-supported beliefs, does exist. Some beliefs *are* better than others, not because an authority has proclaimed them so but because they meet the following criteria. The beliefs:

- Provide compelling and coherent *explanations.*
- Are consistent with *other well-supported beliefs* we have about the world.
- Provide accurate *predictions* about what events will take place.
- Are supported by substantive *reasons and evidence* derived from *reliable sources.*
- Are *"falsifiable,"* meaning that they state conditions — tests — under which the beliefs could be disproved, and they *pass* those tests.

Left: Culver Pictures. Middle: The Bettman Archive. Right: UPI/Bettman Newsphotos.

A critical thinker sees knowledge and truth as goals that we are striving to achieve, processes that we are all actively involved in as we construct our understanding of the world. Developing accurate knowledge about the world is often a challenging process of exploration and analysis in which our understanding grows and evolves over a period of time. In Chapter Four, *Perceiving,* we examined four contrasting media accounts of the assassination of Malcolm X. All four authors, we found, viewed the event through their own perceiving spectacles, which shaped and influenced the information they selected, the way they organized it, their interpretations of the individuals involved, and the language they chose to describe it. Despite the differences in these accounts, we *know* that an actual sequence of events occurred on that February day in 1965. The challenge for us is to try to figure out what actually happened by investigating different accounts, evaluating the reliability of the accounts, and putting together a coherent picture of what took place.

This is the process of achieving knowledge and truth that occurs in every area of human inquiry — a process of exploration, critical analysis, and evolving understanding.

THINKING ACTIVITY

5.4 ▶ Read the following passages, which purport to give factual reports about the events that were observed at the Battle of Lexington during the American Revolution.* After analyzing these accounts, construct your own version of what you believe took place on that day. Include such information as the size of the two forces, the sequence of events (for example, who fired the first shot?), and the manner in which the two groups conducted themselves (were they honorable? brave?). Use these questions to guide your analysis of the varying accounts:

• Does the account provide a convincing description of what took place?

• What reasons and evidence support the account?

• How reliable is the source? What are the author's perceiving lenses which might influence his account?

• Is the account consistent with other reliable descriptions of this event?

Here is some background information to aid you in your analysis:

• *Account 1* is drawn from a mainstream American history textbook.

• *Account 2* is taken from a British history textbook, written by a former prime minister of England.

• *Account 3* comes from a colonist who participated in this event with the American forces. He gave the account thirty years after the battle to qualify for a military pension.

• *Account 4* comes from a British soldier who participated in the event. He gave the account in a deposition while he was a prisoner of war, captured by the American forces.

FOUR ACCOUNTS OF THE BATTLE OF LEXINGTON

In April 1775, General Gage, the military governor of Massachusetts, sent out a body of troops to take possession of military stores at Concord, a short distance from Boston. At Lexington, a handful of "embattled farmers," who had been tipped off by Paul Revere, barred the way. The "rebels" were ordered to disperse. They stood their ground. The English fired a volley of shots that killed eight patriots. It was not long before the swift-riding Paul Revere spread the news of this new atrocity

---

* This exercise was developed by Kevin O'Reilly, creator of the Critical Thinking in History Project in Boston, Massachusetts.

to the neighboring colonies. The patriots of all of New England, although still a handful, were now ready to fight the English. Even in faraway North Carolina, patriots organized to resist them.

Samuel Steinberg, *The United States: Story of a Free People*

At five o'clock in the morning the local militia of Lexingon, seventy strong, formed up on the village green. As the sun rose the head of the British column, with three officers riding in front, came into view. The leading officer, brandishing his sword, shouted, "Disperse, you rebels, immediately!"

The militia commander ordered his men to disperse. The colonial committees were very anxious not to fire the first shot, and there were strict orders not to provoke open conflict with the British regulars. But in the confusion someone fired. A volley was returned. The ranks of the militia were thinned and there was a general *melee*. Brushing aside the survivors, the British column marched on to Concord.

Winston Churchill, *History of the English Speaking Peoples*

The British troops approached us rapidly in platoons, with a General officer on horse-back at their head. The officer came up to within about two rods of the centre of the company, where I stood. — The first platoon being about three rods distant. They there halted. The officer then swung his sword, and said, "Lay down your arms, you damn'd rebels, or you are all dead men — fire." Some guns were fired by the British at us from the first platoon, but no person was killed or hurt, being probably charged only with powder. Just at this time, Captain Parker ordered every man to take care of himself. The company immediately dispersed; and while the company was dispersing and leaping over the wall, the second platoon of the British fired, and killed some of our men. There was not a gun fired by any of Captain Parker's company within my knowledge.

Sylvanus Wood, *Deposition*

I, John Bateman, belonging to the Fifty-Second Regiment, commanded by Colonel Jones, on Wednesday morning on the nineteenth day of April instant, was in the party marching to Concord, being at Lexington, in the County of Middlesex; being nigh the meeting-house in said Lexington, there was a small party of men gathered together in that place when our Troops marched by, and I testify and declare, that I heard the word of command given to the Troops to fire, and some of said Troops did fire, and I saw one of said small party lay dead on the ground nigh said meeting-house, and I testify that I never heard any of the inhabitants so much as fire one gun on said Troops.

John Bateman Testimony ◀

Beliefs Based on Direct Experience

As we attempt to make sense of the world, our thinking abilities give us the means to:

1. Ask questions about our experience.
2. Work toward forming beliefs that will enable us to answer these questions and make useful decisions.

When we ask questions, it means that we are not simply content to take things for granted. Asking questions encourages us to try to form more accurate beliefs to explain what is taking place. By questioning our experience, we are better able to understand the situation we are in and to take effective control.

Let us explore how these activities of asking questions and forming beliefs enable us to make sense of our world. Read carefully the following passage, in which a student, whom we will call Maria, describes her experiences with the "system."

> A few years ago my oldest son went to a party. On his way home (about 11 p.m.) he was accosted by three individuals who tried to take his belongings. Seeing guns, my son's first reaction was to run away, which he did. While running he was shot. His wounds left him paralyzed from his neck down. As he lay in the intensive care unit of the hospital, I started to receive threatening phone calls telling us that "if we identify them to the police, they will finish the work."
>
> At this time I reported the phone calls to both the police and the telephone company. I was irritated by the way the police handled the whole situation. I was told that there was no reason why the city should pay for having a police officer protect my son and was asked what he was

```
doing in the streets at this time. (The time was 11 p.m.,
and my son was almost eighteen years old.) Finally I was
told there was nothing that could be done. In my anger, I
called the mayor's office, the senator's office, and the
councilman. Also, I immediately wrote a letter to the
police commissioner regarding the whole situation and
mailed it special delivery, registered, for proof in case
the matter became worse. In less than a few hours, there
was an officer at my son's bedside making sure that noth-
ing further happened to him.
     I learned that although there are many laws to protect
citizens, if citizens don't fight for their rights these
laws will never be exercised. My opinion of the "sys-
tem" changed after this experience. I believe that I
shouldn't have had to go through so much red tape in order
to have my legal rights. I feel that, if you don't take a
stand, there is no one who will go out of the way to in-
struct you or to help out. I was never informed at the po-
lice headquarters about what to do and how to go about
doing it. I was left standing without any hope at all. I
feel sorry for those persons who are ignorant about how
you can make the system work for you.
```

Throughout this experience, Maria's initial beliefs influenced her decisions. Before her son got shot, she had formed certain beliefs about the law, the police, and the legal system as a whole. What were these initial beliefs?

1. Initial beliefs about the situation
   a. What were Maria's initial beliefs about *the law*?

      The law exists to protect the citizens.
   b. What were her initial beliefs about *the police*?

      _____

   c. What were her initial beliefs about *the system*?

      _____

After her son was shot, Maria tried to make sense of the situation in terms of her initial beliefs and then acted on the basis of these beliefs. What actions did she take once she received phone calls threatening to "finish the work" if she identified the culprits to the police?

2. Actions based on her initial beliefs

    a. _____

    b. _____

Once she took these actions, Maria began to discover that her initial beliefs did not seem to explain what was happening. Her experiences with the police department forced her to have doubts and ask questions about her beliefs concerning the law, the police, and the system. What were the police's reactions to Maria's request that her son be protected from further harm?

3. Experiences that raised doubts and questions about her initial beliefs

    a. _____

    b. _____

    c. _____

As Maria came to doubt the accuracy of her initial beliefs, she began to form new beliefs to explain what was happening in this situation. What were the new beliefs she formed about the law, the police, and the system?

4. Revised beliefs that she formed about the situation

    a. What were Maria's revised beliefs about *the law*?

        _____

    b. What were her revised beliefs about *the police*?

        _____

    c. What were her revised beliefs about *the system*?

        _____

After Maria took action based on her revised beliefs, she was naturally anxious to discover whether these actions would lead to more satisfactory results than those produced by her initial beliefs. What response did she receive to these actions?

5. Response to actions based on her revised beliefs

    a. _____

The response Maria received seemed to support her revised beliefs about the law, the police, and the system. These revised beliefs helped her to understand and control the situation in a way her initial beliefs had not, leading her to the following conclusion:

> I learned that although there are many laws to protect citizens, if citizens don't fight for their rights these laws will never be exercised.

After reflecting critically on her experiences, Maria was convinced that the revised beliefs she had formed to explain her situation and guide her actions were more accurate than her initial beliefs. As a result, she advises those who find themselves in similar circumstances to "take a stand" and "make the system work" for them. In giving this advice, Maria uses her newly formed beliefs to predict what will happen in similar encounters with the system.

Maria's story illustrates the process by which we form and re-form our beliefs, a process that often follows the following sequence:

1. We *form* beliefs to explain what is taking place. (These initial beliefs are often based on our past experiences.)

2. We *test* these beliefs by acting on the basis of them.

3. We *revise* (or re-form) these beliefs if our actions do not result in our desired goals.

4. We *retest* these revised beliefs by acting on the basis of them.

As we actively participate in this ongoing process of forming and re-forming beliefs, we are using our critical thinking abilities to identify and critically examine our beliefs by asking the following questions:

• How effectively do our beliefs *explain* what is taking place?

• How effectively do our beliefs *guide our actions* so that we can reach our carefully considered goals?

• How effectively do our beliefs help us *predict* what will happen in similar situations that occur in the future?

This process of critical exploration enables us to develop a greater understanding of various situations in our experience and also gives us the means to exert more effective control in these situations.

THINKING ACTIVITY

5.5 ▶ Examine the process of forming and re-forming beliefs by reading the following interview, which Studs Terkel conducted with C. P. Ellis. Ellis, who was fifty-three years old when the interview took place, was once president (Exalted Cyclops) of the Durham, North Carolina, chapter of the Ku Klux Klan. Answer the questions that follow.

WHY I QUIT THE KLAN *by C. P. Ellis*

All my life, I had work, never a day without work, worked all the overtime I could get and still could not survive financially. I began to see there's something wrong with this country. I worked my butt off and just never seemed to break even. I had some real great ideas about this nation. They say to abide by the law, go to church, do right and live for the Lord, and everything'll work out. But it didn't work out. It just kept gettin worse and worse. . . .

Tryin to come out of that hole, I just couldn't do it. I really began to get bitter. I didn't know who to blame. I tried to find somebody. Hatin America is hard to do because you can't see it to hate it. You gotta have somethin to look at to hate. The natural person for me to hate would be black people, because my father before me was a member of the Klan. . . .

So I began to admire the Klan. . . . To be part of somethin. . . . The first night I went with the fellas . . . I was led into a large meeting room, and this was the time of my life! It was thrilling. Here's a guy who's worked all his life and struggled all his life to be something, and here's the moment to be something. I will never forget it. Four robed Klansmen led me into the hall. The lights were dim and the only thing you could see was an illuminated cross. . . . After I had taken my oath, there was loud applause goin throughout the buildin, musta been at least four hundred people. For this one little ol person. It was a thrilling moment for C. P. Ellis. . . .

The majority of [the Klansmen] are low-income whites, people who really don't have a part in something. They have been shut out as well as blacks. Some are not very well educated either. Just like myself. We had a lot of support from doctors and lawyers and police officers.

Maybe they've had bitter experiences in this life and they had to hate somebody. So the natural person to hate would be the black person. He's beginnin to come up, he's beginnin to . . . start votin and run for political office. Here are white people who are supposed to be superior to them, and we're shut out. . . . Shut out. Deep down inside, we want to be part of this great society. Nobody listens, so we join these groups. . . .

We would go to the city council meetings, and the blacks would be there and we'd be there. It was a confrontation every time. . . . We began to make some inroads with the city councilmen and county commissioners. They began to call us friend. Call us at night on the telephone: "C. P., glad you came to that meeting last night." They didn't want integration either, but they did it secretively, in order to get elected. They couldn't stand up openly and say it, but they were glad somebody was sayin it. We visited some of the city leaders in their homes and talked to em privately. It wasn't long before councilmen would call me up: "The blacks are comin up tonight and makin outrageous demands. How about some of you people showin up and have a little balance?". . .

We'd load up our cars and we'd fill up half the council chambers, and the blacks the other half. During these times, I carried weapons to the meetings, outside my belt. We'd go there armed. We would wind up just hollerin and fussin at each other. What happened? As a result of our fightin one another, the city council still had their way. They didn't want to give up control to the blacks nor the Klan. They were usin us.

I began to realize this later down the road. One day I was walkin downtown and a certain city council member saw me comin. I expected him to shake my hand because he was talkin to me at night on the telephone. I had been in his home and visited with him. He crossed the street [to avoid me]. . . . I began to think, somethin's wrong here. Most of em are merchants or maybe an attorney, an insurance agent, people like that. As long as they kept low-income whites and low-income blacks fightin, they're gonna maintain control. I began to get that feelin after I was ignored in public. I thought: . . . you're not gonna use me any more. That's when I began to do some real serious thinkin.

The same thing is happening in this country today. People are being used by those in control, those who have all the wealth. I'm not espousing communism. We got the greatest system of government in the world. But those who have it simply don't want those who don't have it to have any part of it. Black and white. When it comes to money, the green, the other colors make no difference.

I spent a lot of sleepless nights. I still didn't like blacks. I didn't want to associate with them. Blacks, Jews or Catholics. My father said: "Don't have anything to do with em." I didn't until I met a black person and talked with him, eyeball to eyeball, and met a Jewish person and talked to him, eyeball to eyeball. I found they're people just like me. They cried, they cussed, they prayed, they had desires. Just like myself.

Thank God, I got to the point where I can look past labels. But at that time, my mind was closed.

I remember one Monday night Klan meeting. I said something was wrong. Our city fathers were using us. And I didn't like to be used. The reactions of the others was not too pleasant: "Let's just keep fightin them niggers."

I'd go home at night and I'd have to wrestle with myself. I'd look at a black person walkin down the street, and the guy'd have ragged shoes or his clothes would be worn. That began to do something to me inside. I went through this for about six months. I felt I just had to get out of the Klan. But I wouldn't get out. . . .

[Ellis was invited, as a Klansman, to join a committee of people from all walks of life to make recommendations on how to solve racial problems in the school system. He very reluctantly accepted. After a few stormy meetings, he was elected co-chair of the committee, along with Ann Atwater, a black woman who for years had been leading local efforts for civil rights.]

A Klansman and a militant black woman, co-chairman of the school committee. It was impossible. How could I work with her? But it was in our hands. We had to make it a success. This give me another sense of belongin, a sense of pride. This helped the inferiority feeling I had. A man who has stood up publicly and said he despised black people, all of a sudden he was willin to work with em. Here's a chance for a low-income white man to be somethin. In spite of all my hatred for blacks and Jews and liberals, I accepted the job. Her and I began to reluctantly work together. She had as many problems workin with me as I had workin with her.

One night, I called her: "Ann, you and I should have a lot of differences and we got em now. But there's something laid out here before us, and if it's gonna be a success, you and I are gonna have to make it one. Can we lay aside some of these feelins?" She said: "I'm willing if you are." I said: "Let's do it."

My old friends would call me at night: "C. P., what the hell is wrong with you? You're sellin out the white race." This begin to make me have guilt feelins. Am I doin right? Am I doin wrong? Here I am all of a sudden makin an about-face and tryin to deal with my feelins, my heart. My mind was beginnin to open up. I was beginnin to see what was right and what was wrong. I don't want the kids to fight forever. . . .

One day, Ann and I went back to the school and we sat down. We began to talk and just reflect. . . . I begin to see, here we are, two people from the far ends of the fence, havin identical problems, except hers bein black and me bein white. . . . The amazing thing about it, her and I, up to that point, has cussed each other, bawled each other, we hated each other. Up to that point, we didn't know each other. We didn't know we had things in common. . . .

The whole world was openin up, and I was learning new truths that I had never learned before. I was beginning to look at a black person, shake hands with him, and see him as a human bein. I hadn't got rid of all this stuff. I've still got a little bit of it. But somethin was happenin to me. . . .

I come to work one mornin and some guys says: "We need a union." At this time I wasn't pro-union. My daddy was anti-labor too. We're not gettin paid much, we're havin to work seven days in a row. We're all starvin to death. . . . I didn't know nothin about organizin unions, but I knew how to organize people, stir people up. That's how I got to be business agent for the union.

When I began to organize, I began to see far deeper. I begin to see people again bein used. Blacks against whites. . . . There are two things management wants to keep: all the money and all the say-so. They don't want none of these poor workin folks to have none of that. I begin to see management fightin me with everythin they had. Hire anti-union law firms, badmouth unions. The people were makin $1.95 an hour, barely able to get through weekends. . . .

It makes you feel good to go into a plant and . . . see black people and white people join hands to defeat the racist issues [union-busters] use against people. . . .

I tell people there's a tremendous possibility in this country to stop wars, the battles, the struggles, the fights between people. People say: "That's an impossible dream. You sound like Martin Luther King." An ex-Klansman who sounds like Martin Luther King. I don't think it's an impossible dream. It's happened in my life. It's happened in other people's lives in America. . . .

. . . They say the older you get, the harder it is for you to change. That's not necessarily true. Since I changed, I've set down and listened to tapes of Martin Luther King. I listen to it and tears come to my eyes cause I know what he's sayin now. I know what's happenin. ■

1. What were C. P. Ellis's most important *initial beliefs*? From where did his stereotypes originate?

2. What were some of the *experiences* that helped form these initial beliefs?

3. What *actions* did he take based on these initial beliefs?

4. What *experiences* raised doubts and questions about his initial beliefs? Why was he able to say: "Thank God, I got to the point where I can look past labels. . . . I was beginning to look at a black person, shake hands with him, and see him as a human being."

5. What *revised beliefs* did he form to better make sense of his experiences? ◀

THINKING ACTIVITY

5.6   ▶   1. Interview another person about a belief he or she once held but no longer holds. Ask that person the following questions. (*Note:* Try asking the questions in the course of a conversation you have with the person rather than confronting him or her with an intimidating series of formal questions. Most people like to be asked about their beliefs and are very cooperative.)

   a. What is the belief?

   b. On what evidence did you hold that belief? (Was it based on personal perception or oral or written sources? What were they?)

   c. What caused you to change the belief?

   d. What were your feelings or attitudes when you found that changing the belief was necessary?

   e. How do you feel now about changing the belief?

   Next, write a summary of the interview. Begin by describing the person and explaining your relationship to him or her. Then give his or her answers to the questions. Be as detailed as possible.

2. Describe your reaction to the other person's experience. What did you learn about perception and belief from his or her experience? ◀

We can now see that two aspects of the way we make sense of the world, perceiving and believing, continually influence each other. On one hand, the experiences we perceive influence what we come to believe. Thus, for example, the fact that C. P. Ellis's friends and family insulted and disparaged blacks, Jews, and Catholics led him to form racist beliefs about these groups. On the other hand, our beliefs influence the way we perceive things; that is, they influence the perceptual spectacles we use to view the world. Thus the racist beliefs that C. P. Ellis had formed were reflected in his perceptual stereotypes of blacks, Jews, and Catholics.

Fortunately, beliefs do not stand still in the minds of critical thinkers. We continue to form and re-form our beliefs, based in part on what we are experiencing and how we think about what we are experiencing. For C. P. Ellis, the experience of meeting and working with people from other ethnic groups broke down his perceptual stereotypes of them, for he discovered: "I found they're people just like me. They cried, they cussed, they prayed, they had desires. Just like myself."

Beliefs Based on Indirect Experience

Until now, we have been exploring the way we form and revise beliefs based on our direct experiences. Yet no matter how much we have experienced in our life, the fact is that no one person's direct experiences are enough to establish an adequate set of accurate beliefs. Each of us is only one person. We can only be in one place at one time — and with a limited amount of time at that. As a result, we depend on the direct experience of *other people* to provide us with beliefs and also to act as foundations for those beliefs. For example, does China exist? How do you know? Have you ever been there and seen it with your own eyes? Probably not, although in all likelihood you still believe in the existence of China and its over 1 billion inhabitants. Or consider the following questions. How would you go about explaining the reasons or evidence for your beliefs?

1. Were you really born on the day that you have been told you were?
2. Do germs really exist?
3. Do you have a brain in your head?
4. Does outer space extend infinitely in all directions?

In all probability, your responses to these questions reveal beliefs that are based on reasons or evidence beyond your direct experience. Of all the beliefs each one of us has, few are actually based on our direct experience. Instead, virtually *all* are founded on the experiences of others, who then communicated to us these beliefs and the evidence for them in some shape or form.

Of course, some people claim they do not really believe anything unless they have personally experienced it. They say, "Seeing is believing," "The proof of the pudding is in the eating," or "Show me" (the famous slogan of the state of Missouri). A little critical reflection, however, should convince us that these people are simply being unrealistic and unreasonable. It would be impossible for us to make most of the choices or decisions we do without depending on beliefs based on the experiences and knowledge of others. For instance, if I step out into moving traffic, will I really get hurt? Do guns really kill? Do I really have to eat to survive?

As we reach beyond our personal experience to form and revise beliefs, we find that the information provided by other people is available in two basic forms:

• Writings

• Spoken testimony

Of course, we should not accept the beliefs of others without question. It is crucial that we use all our critical thinking abilities to examine what others suggest we believe. In critically examining the beliefs of others, we should pursue the same goals of accuracy and completeness that we seek when examining beliefs based on our personal experience. As a result, we are interested in the reasons or evidence that support the information others are presenting. When we ask directions from others, we try to evaluate how accurate the information is by examining the reasons or evidence that seem to support the information being given.

When we depend on information provided by others, however, there is a further question to be asked: How *reliable* is the person providing the information? For instance, what sort of people do you look for if you need to ask directions? *Why* do you look for these particular types of people? In most cases, when we need to ask directions, we try to locate someone who we think will be reliable — in other words, a person who we believe will give us accurate information.

During the remainder of this chapter, we will explore the various ways we depend on others to form and revise our beliefs. In each case we will try to evaluate the information being presented by asking the following questions:

1. How reliable is the *information*?
2. How reliable is the *source* of the information?

How Reliable Are the Information and the Source?

One of the main goals of our thinking is to make sense of information. Much of the information we are exposed to is from advertisers seeking to sell their products. Review the following advertisement taken from a popular magazine and then evaluate the information presented by answering the questions that follow it:

> This is the new Nissan Stanza GL. A family car that seats 5 with room to spare. Room that includes luxuries like 6-speaker stereo with cassette, power windows and door locks, and plush upholstery. Now you're talking major value.
>
> And when a family sedan has Nissan technology going for it, you get even more than room and luxuries. You also get performance. Performance from a semi-combustion engine with two spark plugs per cylinder, fed by electronic fuel-injection. Go ahead, step on it, and feel your Stanza come to life.
>
> Another nice thing about owning a Nissan Stanza, you don't have to feel guilty every time you step on the gas. Because Stanza's highly developed Nissan engine is as gas efficient as it is responsive.
>
> So before you buy your family's next car, compare its specifications to that of a new Stanza. Stanza thrives on comparison. After all, Stanza has Nissan technology behind it. And that takes it way beyond transportation; all the way to Major Motion.

1. How reliable is the information?
   a. What are the main ideas being presented?

   _____

   b. What reasons or evidence support the information?

   _____

   c. Is the information accurate? Is there anything you believe to be false? Is there anything that you believe has been left out?

   _____

2. How reliable is the source of the information?
   a. What is the source of the information?

   _____

   b. What are the interests or purposes of the source of this information?

   _____

   c. How have the interests and purposes of the source of the information influenced the information selected for inclusion?

   _____

d. How have these interests and purposes influenced the way this information is presented?

_____

In trying to answer question 2, it is helpful to recall again one of the key lessons we learned in Chapter Four, _Perceiving_: each of us views the world through our own unique "spectacles," which influence the way we select, organize, and interpret our perceptions. When we examined the different accounts of the Battle of Lexington in Thinking Activity 5.5, we saw that the various reports reflected the different interests and purposes of those reporting the event. As a result, if we are to evaluate effectively the accuracy and completeness of information, we have to try to understand the "spectacles" of the people who are presenting the information. These spectacles, and the individual needs and interests they represent, influence the information that the source has decided to include as well as the manner in which this information is presented.

Another insight we discovered in examining the various accounts of the Battle of Lexington was that our evaluation of the accuracy of the information and the reliability of each source was aided by comparing the different accounts. Since each account reflects the individual spectacles of the source, comparing different accounts helps us to identify the different interests and purposes involved. For example, examine carefully this description of the Nissan Stanza GL from _Consumer Reports_, a magazine that tests various consumer products and then reports its findings.

- _On the road._ The 2-liter Four started quickly and ran well. The 5-speed manual transmission shifted easily. This front-wheel drive model handled very well. Excellent brakes.

- _Comfort and convenience._ Very comfortable individual front seats. Short on driver leg room. Comfortable rear seat for two, fairly comfortable for three. Moderate noise level. Choppy ride on poor roads, satisfactory on expressways. Excellent climate-control system, controls, displays.

- _Major options._ Automatic transmission, $350. Air-conditioner, $650.

- _Fuel economy._ Mpg with 5-speed manual transmission: city, 23; expressway, 45. Gallons used in 15,000 miles, 465. Cruising range, 485 miles.

- _Predicted reliability._ Much better than average.

Analyze the information being presented here by answering the following questions.

1. How reliable is the information?

    a. What are the main ideas being presented?

    _____

    b. What reasons or evidence support the information?

    _____

    c. Is the information accurate? Is there anything you believe to be false? Is there anything that you believe has been left out?

    _____

2. How reliable is the source of the information?

    a. What is the source of the information?

    _____

    b. What are the interests or purposes of the source of this information?

    _____

    c. How have the interests and purposes of the source of the information influenced the information selected for inclusion?

    _____

    d. How have these interests and purposes influenced the way this information is presented?

    _____

After analyzing the information presented in various accounts, the next step is to compare the accounts with one another. For example, how do these two descriptions of the Nissan Stanza GL compare in terms of the information provided and the way that this information is presented?

THINKING ACTIVITY

5.7 ▶ Locate two different passages concerning the same topic and then analyze each passage using the questions we have developed. For example, you might choose two different reviews of a movie, a play, a book, an art exhibit, or a concert, or two different passages analyzing a topic of current interest such as nuclear power or American foreign policy.

1. How reliable is the information?

    a. What are the main ideas being presented?

b. What are the reasons or evidence that support the information being presented?

c. Is the information accurate? Is there anything you believe to be false? Is there anything that you believe has been left out?

2. How reliable is the source of the information?

a. What is the source of the information?

b. What are the interests or purposes of the source of this information?

c. How have the interests and purposes of the source of the information influenced the information selected for inclusion?

d. How have these interests and purposes influenced the way this information is presented?

3. How do these accounts compare in terms of the information provided and the way this information is presented? ◄

Your responses to the questions on page 215 probably indicate that you were more likely to believe the accuracy of the information provided by *Consumer Reports* than you were the information given in the Nissan advertisement. Sometimes, however, the reliability of the source of information is not immediately clear. In those cases, we usually employ a variety of standards or criteria in evaluating the reliability of the sources of information. Let us examine some of the most frequently used criteria for evaluating the reliability of sources. These criteria are useful for evaluating both written and spoken testimony.

1. Was the source of the information able to make accurate observations?

2. What do we know about the past reliability of the source of the information?

3. How knowledgeable or experienced is the source of the information?

Let us explore these different criteria in more detail.

Was the source of the information able to make accurate observations? Imagine that you are serving as a juror at a trial in which two youths are accused of mugging an elderly person and stealing her social security check. During the trial the victim gives the following account of the experience:

I was walking into the lobby of my building at about six o'clock. It was beginning to get dark. Suddenly these two young men rushed in behind me and tried to grab my pocketbook. However, my bag was wrapped around my arm, and I just didn't want to let go of it. They pushed me around, yelling at me to let go of the bag. They finally pulled the bag loose and went running out of the building. I saw them pretty well while we were fighting, and I'm sure that the two boys sitting over there are the ones who robbed me.

In evaluating the accuracy of this information, we have to try to determine how reliable the source of the information is. In doing this, we might ask ourselves whether the person attacked was in a good position to make accurate observations. In the case of this person's testimony, what questions could you ask in order to evaluate the accuracy of the testimony?

1. How sharp is the person's eyesight? (Does she wear glasses? Were the glasses knocked off in the struggle?)

2. _____

3. _____

4. _____

5. _____

When trying to determine the accuracy of testimony, we should try to use the same standards we would apply to ourselves if we were in a similar situation. Was there enough light to see clearly? Did the excitement of the situation influence my perceptions? Were my senses operating at full capacity?

Often the questions we ask regarding someone's initial testimony lead us to locate additional information. Imagine that you were the police detective assigned to the case just described. Identify some of the ways you might look for additional information to supplement the victim's testimony.

1. Interview other witnesses who might have seen the robbers.

2. _____

3. _____

4. _____

5. _____

As we work toward evaluating the reliability of the source of the information, it is helpful to locate whatever additional sources of information are available. For instance, if we can locate others who can identify the muggers or if we find stolen items in their possession, this will serve as evidence to support the testimony given by the witness.

Finally, accurate observations depend on more than how well our senses are functioning. Accurate observations also depend on how well we understand the personal factors (our "spectacles") we or someone else brings to a situation. These personal feelings, expectations, and interests often influence what we are perceiving without our being aware of it. Once we become aware of these influencing factors, we can attempt to make allowances for them in order to get a more accurate view of what is taking place. Thinking Activity 5.8 involves a situation in which such personal factors could influence the accuracy of information.

THINKING ACTIVITY

5.8   ▶ Your friends have sponsored an antiracism rally on your college campus. The campus police estimate the crowd to be 250, while your friends who organized the rally claim it was more than 500.

1. Describe how you would go about determining the reliability of your friends' information by speaking to them. What questions could you ask them to help clarify the situation?

   a. _____

   b. _____

   c. _____

2. Describe how you could go about locating additional information to gain a more accurate understanding of the situation.

   a. _____

   b. _____

   c. _____ ◀

What do we know about the past reliability of the source of the information? As we work at evaluating the reliability of information sources, it is useful to consider how accurate and reliable their information has been in the past. If someone we know has consistently given us sound information over a period of time, we gradually develop confidence in the accuracy of that person's reports. Police officers and newspaper reporters must continually evaluate the reliability of information sources. Over time, people in these professions establish information sources who have consistently provided reliable information. For instance, according to *Washington Post* reporters Bob Woodward and Carl Bernstein, much of the Watergate investigation was based on the information provided by one key source, whom they named "Deep Throat."

Of course, this works the other way as well. When people consistently give us *in*accurate or *in*complete information, we gradually lose confidence in their reliability and the reliability of their information.

Nevertheless, few people are either completely reliable or completely unreliable in the information they offer. You probably realize that your own reliability tends to vary, depending on the situation, the type of information you are providing, and the person you are giving the information to. Thus, in trying to evaluate the information offered by others, we have to explore each of these different factors before arriving at a provisional conclusion, which may then be revised in the light of additional information.

THINKING ACTIVITY

5.9 ▶ A local politician comes to your school to campaign for votes. She assures you that she fully supports higher education.

1. Describe how you would go about determining the reliability of the politician's information by speaking to her. What questions could you ask her to help clarify the situation?

   a. _____

   b. _____

   c. _____

2. Describe how you could go about locating additional information to gain a more accurate understanding of this situation.

   a. _____

   b. _____

   c. _____ ◀

How knowledgeable or experienced is the source of the information? A third step in evaluating information from other sources is to determine how knowledgeable or experienced the person is in that particular area. When we seek information from others, we try to locate people who we believe will have a special understanding of the area in which we are interested. When asking directions, we look for a policeman, a cab driver, or a resident. When seeking information in school, we try to find a school employee or another student who may be experienced in that area. When our car begins making strange noises, we search for someone who has knowledge of car engines. In each case, we try to identify a source of information who has special experience or understanding of a particular area because we believe that this person will be reliable in giving us accurate information.

Of course, there is no guarantee that, even when we carefully select knowledgeable sources, the information will be accurate. Cab drivers do sometimes give the wrong directions; school personnel do occasionally dispense the wrong information; and people experienced with cars cannot always figure out the problem the first time. By seeking people who are experienced or knowledgeable rather than those who are not, however, we increase our chances of gaining accurate information.

Suppose you are interested in finding out more information about the career you are planning to go into. Identify some of the people you would select to gain further information and explain why you have selected them.

1. *Source of information:* _____

   Reasons for selection: _____

   _____

2. *Source of information:* _____

   Reasons for selection: _____

   _____

3. *Source of information:* _____

   Reasons for selection: _____

   _____

In seeking information from others whom we believe to be experienced or knowledgeable, it is important to distinguish between the opinions of "average" sources, such as ourselves, and the opinions of experts. Experts are people who have specialized knowledge in a particular area, based on special training and experience. If you are experiencing chest pains and your friend (who is not a doctor or nurse) tells you, "Don't worry, I've had a lot of experience with this sort of thing — it's probably just gas," you may decide to seek the opinion of an expert to confirm your friend's diagnosis. (After all, you don't want to find out the hard way that your friend was mistaken.)

Who qualifies as an expert? Someone with professional expertise as certified by the appropriate standards qualifies as an expert. For instance, you do not want someone working on your teeth just because he or she has always enjoyed playing with drills or is fascinated with teeth. Instead, you insist on someone who has graduated from dental college and been professionally certified.

It is also useful to find out how up to date the expert's credentials are. Much knowledge has changed in medicine, dentistry, and automobile mechanics in the last twenty years. If practitioners have not been keeping abreast of these changes, they will have gradually lost their expertise, even though they may have an appropriate diploma. Identify two experts whose information and services you rely on. Then explain how you could go about discovering how up to date and effective their expertise is.

1. *Expert:* _____

   Explanation: _____

   _____

2. *Expert:* _____

   Explanation: _____

   _____

We should also make sure that the experts are giving us information and opinions in their field of expertise. It is certainly all right for someone like John Madden to give his views on beer, but we should remember that he is speaking as another human being (and one who has been paid a large sum of money and told exactly what to say), not as a scientific expert. This is exactly the type of mistaken perception encouraged by advertisers to sell their products. Ray Charles and Michael J. Fox are extremely talented in their respective fields, but what specialized knowledge do they have of the soft drinks they are advertising?

THINKING ACTIVITY

5.10 ▶ Identify two "experts" in television or magazine advertising who are giving testimony *outside* their field of expertise. Explain why you think each was chosen for the particular product he or she is endorsing and whether you trust such expertise in evaluating the product. ◄

Finally, we should not accept expert opinion without question or critical examination, even if the experts meet all the criteria that we have been exploring. Just because a mechanic assures us that we need a new transmission for $900 does not mean that we should accept that opinion at face value. Or simply because one doctor assures us that surgery is required for our ailment does not mean that we should not investigate further. In both cases, seeking a second (or even third) expert opinion makes a lot of sense.

THINKING ACTIVITY
_____

5.11 ▶ The two historical accounts of the Vietnam war that follow, from Kevin O'Reilly's *Critical Thinking in American History*, were written for the purpose of presenting two contrasting views of this event. In each passage, the information is presented in a way that seems authoritative and factual and the main ideas are based on outside references. It would be natural to conclude that the information presented in *either* passage is accurate. A critical descriptive analysis of each passage, however, shows that it is influenced by the interests and purposes of the sources of the information. These interests and purposes form the point of view of each purported author, the spectacles or frame of reference through which each views the war in Vietnam, American foreign policy, and the world as a whole. After reviewing the two passages, answer the questions that follow in order to analyze the reliability of the information and to develop your own beliefs about the issues discussed.

TWO HISTORICAL ACCOUNTS OF THE VIETNAM WAR
by Kevin O'Reilly

Historian A

The Vietnam War is a chapter of American history which many Americans would like to forget. The tragedy is that American involvement could have been avoided from the beginning. But American leaders, driven by fear of Communist expansion, committed ever increasing American men and resources to a war which really was not in the country's national interest.

It is important to remember that the Vietnam War was basically a struggle for independence. The Vietminh (Vietnamese who fought for independence) fought the Japanese, the French, and then the United States, to achieve nationhood. American leaders even supported the Vietminh struggle at first. During World War II the Vietminh and the American military worked together against the Japanese.[1] After World War II the French moved back into Vietnam to retake control of their former colony. A war broke out between the Vietminh and the French. American leaders, remembering our own struggle for independence against the British, refused to aid the French.

However, by 1950 America switched away from this sensible policy. The "fall" of China to Communism, the Korean War, and the anti-Communist charges by Senator Joseph McCarthy made American leaders paranoid of Communists.[2] The French argument that the Vietminh were Communists was now more convincing. By 1954 America was supplying 80 percent of the cost of the War for the French.[3]

The War went badly for the French, nevertheless. They were defeated in the major battle of Dien Bien Phu in May, 1954. They soon negotiated a peace settlement at Geneva with the Vietminh. In the Geneva Peace Conference the country was *temporarily* divided. The French forces were to withdraw south of the 17th parallel and the Vietminh were to withdraw north of the line. The agreement further stated that there would be an election within two years to reunify the country.[4] Everyone agreed that the leader of the independence movement, Ho Chi Minh, would win that election.[5] He was the symbol of Vietnamese independence,

Historian A Footnotes (All are quotes from the sources given.)

[1] Bernard Fall (Historian), *The Two Viet Nams* (1964), pp. 100–101.

[2] Statement by President Truman linking aid to Vietnam with United States intervention in the Korean War. *Department of State Bulletin*. July 3, 1950, p. 5. State Department Policy Statement on Indochina. September 27, 1948: "We have not urged the French to negotiate with Ho Chi Minh, even though he probably is supported by a considerable majority of the Vietnamese people, because of his record as a Communist. . . ."

[3] *New York Times*, April 7, 1954.

[4] Geneva Agreements, 1954, paragraph 7.

[5] CIA National Intelligence Estimate, August 3, 1954: "If the scheduled national elections are held in July 1956, and if the Viet Minh does not prejudice its political prospects, the Viet Minh will almost certainly win." Dwight David Eisenhower, *Mandate for Change* (1963), p. 372: "I have never talked or corresponded with a person knowledgeable in Indochinese affairs who did not agree that had elections been held as of the time of the fighting, possibly 80 percent of the population would have voted for the Communist Ho Chi Minh. . . ."

just as George Washington represented American independence from England.

At this point the United States could have stayed out of the situation and Vietnam would have become an independent Communist nation under Ho Chi Minh in 1956. But the United States decided to intervene to stop the Vietminh.

First the United States made a military alliance called SEATO. According to the Geneva Conference neither part of Vietnam could be part of an alliance. So the United States had "the free territory under the jurisdiction of Vietnam" added as a territory to be defended by the alliance.[6] The regroupment zone in the southern part of Vietnam, which was not a country, and which did not participate in the SEATO talks, was made an honorary member of a military alliance!

Second, the United States gave its backing to Ngo Dinh Diem, to build him up as leader of a separate South Vietnamese government. Diem, who had been living in New Jersey up to 1954,[7] was viewed favorably by the United States since he also opposed the elections scheduled for 1956. In 1955 Diem, backed by American aid and in clear violation of the Geneva Agreement declared that South Vietnam was a country and stated that the nationwide elections would not be held.

Diem was an oppressive ruler who created problems for himself by his foolish policies. First he said that anyone who was or had been a Communist or had associated with Communists could be thrown into jail. The problem was that anyone who had opposed French rule had associated with Communists in the Vietminh. Any freedom lover could now be thrown into jail! South Vietnam was a police state.[8]

Second, Diem started a land reform program which "reduced" rents. The problem with this was that the peasants in Vietminh-controlled areas now owned their land; the landlords had fled to the cities. The

[6] *Southeast Asia Collective Defense Treaty, Southeast Asia Treaty Organization*, Department of State Publication 6305 (1956). See especially "Protocol to the Southeast Asia Collective Defense Treaty."

[7] George Kahin and John Lewis (Historians), *The United States in Vietnam* (1976), p. 66.

[8] P. J. Honey, "The Problem of Democracy in Vietnam," *The World Today*, Vol. 16, No. 2, February 1960, p. 73. On the basis of talks with former inmates of Diem's prison camps he stated: "The majority of detainees are neither Communist nor pro-Communist." William Henderson, "South Viet Nam Finds Itself," *Foreign Affairs*, Vol. 35, No. 2, January 1957, pp. 285–288: "South Viet Nam is today a quasi-police state characterized by arbitrary arrests and imprisonment. . . ."

land reform program actually put many landlords back into control.[9] The South Vietnamese people hated these two policies.

Needless to say, war again broke out, this time between the Vietcong (South Vietnamese who fought for independence) and Diem's authoritarian government. In 1960 the North Vietnamese began sending large amounts of aid to the Vietcong in the struggle for Vietnamese independence. The United States also stepped up its military aid to the South Vietnamese Government. And President Kennedy began sending American "advisors" to help the South Vietnamese military.

By 1964 the United States could still have disengaged from Vietnam. The number of troops there was small (about 16,000) and few Americans had been killed. But President Johnson could not stand to see Vietnam become Communist. In the Gulf of Tonkin Resolution (1964) Congress agreed to let the president use "whatever means necessary" to stop Communist aggression in Vietnam. American troops could now fight. In 1965 large numbers of American troops were committed to the War. By 1968 over 500,000 American troops were in Vietnam. President Johnson also increased the amount of bombing. By the end of the War the United States had dropped over 6 million tons of bombs on Indochina (Vietnam, Laos, and Cambodia), over 4 million of which fell on South Vietnam.[10] This is three times as much tonnage as was dropped by the United States in all of World War II.

What did all these troops and bombings accomplish? Basically, it led to the destruction of Vietnamese society. Large numbers of innocent civilians were killed by American soldiers.[11] The My Lai Massacre was unusual because of the large number of civilians killed, but the killing of civilians by American soldiers was not unusual. American generals emphasized the number of enemy killed (called body count), rather than capture of territory. Officers were under pressure to get a high body count. This led to such expressions as, "If he's Vietnamese and he's

---

[9] John D. Montgomery, *The Politics of Foreign Aid* (1962), p. 124: ". . . The Vietnamese government, not wishing to disturb the strong landowning classes, resisted the proposed transfers of land (to the peasants) and the sharper rent controls (lower than 25 percent)."

[10] Raphael Lattauer and Norman Uphoff, editors, *The Air War in Indochina* (1972), Graph 11, Figure 1-1, "Annual Tonnage of Aerial Munitions, 1965–1971."

[11] U.S. Senate, *U.S. Policy with Respect to Mainland China*, 89th Congress, 2nd Session (1966), P. 349. Also Kahin and Lewis, *The United States in Vietnam*, p. 239; the ratio of civilian to Vietcong casualties (was) reported as high as 2 to 1. . . .

dead, he's Vietcong," and to the counting of bodies on the battlefield several times by different American troops (for example, three dead bodies would lead to a count of three dead by the infantry, three by the artillery, and three by the Air Force).

Vietnamese civilians were also killed by bombing. There is no possible way from an airplane to separate civilians from guerrillas (which the Vietcong were), so large numbers of civilians had to be killed by the bombing. Each of the civilians killed had relatives who might then join the Vietcong out of hatred for the Americans.

American firepower destroyed Vietnamese society and basically guaranteed we would lose the War. American generals did what they thought was best — use American weapons to defeat the enemy militarily. The problem was that the Vietnam War was a struggle for the hearts and minds of the Vietnamese peasants. You can't win people over to your side by destroying their villages and killing their relatives. Our firepower continually created more enemies.

Another way the United States could have disentangled from Vietnam was through a negotiated settlement among the Vietcong, the South Vietnamese Government, and the Buddhists. The Americans told the South Vietnamese not to negotiate.[12]

No wonder American soldiers didn't know what they were fighting for. There was no good reason why we were fighting — we never should have become involved in Vietnam from the beginning. Having continually lied to the American people about the War, the Johnson Administration was embarrassed by the unusual strength of the Vietcong in the Tet Offensive in 1968.[13] The Administration had said that the enemy was too weak to attack. American citizens wondered if government statements were truthful, and began to protest in large numbers against the War. The continuous protests gradually brought about an end to the insanity of American involvement in the War by 1973.

The United States consciously became involved in a war in which it had no business. It tried to fight the political war by military firepower. But American firepower only made more Vietnamese join the guerrilla side. We could not win as long as most South Vietnamese supported the

[12] *New York Times*, November 10, 1964: ". . . a negotiated settlement and neutralization of Vietnam are not to be ruled out." President Johnson's New Year's message to the government of South Vietnam, *New York Times*, January 1 and 2, 1964: "Neutralization of South Vietnam would only be another name for a Communist take-over."

[13] *New York Times*, December 27, 1967 and February 13, 1968.

Vietcong. In the end the American people forced the end of the useless killing of this needless War.

Historian B

The Vietnam War was a frustrating conflict for the United States. American soldiers won every battle yet the Communists won the War. This frustration has led to a number of misinterpretations about this tragic event.

Some historians blame the United States for almost every evil that took place during the War. The United States, they argue, had no legitimate reason for getting involved in the conflict from the beginning. Once we were involved we incorrectly fought the War militarily and destroyed Vietnamese society with our bombing and other firepower. This viewpoint is wrong on every count.

It is important to recognize that the United States had legitimate national interests in Vietnam. Our enemies were Communists (Ho Chi Minh had been a long-time member of the international Communist movement), and the Korean War showed that Communists were not afraid to try to take over other nations by force. Our aid to the French would help contain Communism.

After the French were defeated at Dien Bien Phu in 1954 they negotiated the Geneva Agreement with the Vietminh Communists. Some historians argue that the Vietminh were cheated out of a legitimate victory by American and South Vietnamese violations of the Geneva Agreement. But the Agreement itself was not signed and not even adopted by a formal vote. The nationwide election scheduled for 1956, which Ho Chi Minh would supposedly have won by a landslide, was not taken seriously by any country at the Conference.[1] Why would the Agreement allow people to escape from one zone (the North) to the other (the South) when the two zones would be reunified in 700 days? South Vietnam said it would not agree to the elections if the elections jeopardized its independence.[2] Moreover, Communists never hold free

---

Historian B Footnotes (All are quotes from the sources given.)

[1] Guenter Lewy (Historian), *America in Vietnam* (1978), p. 8.

[2] Summarized from a statement by the South Vietnamese delegate to the Geneva Conference. *Documents on American Foreign Relations,* Council of Foreign Relations (1955), pp. 315–316.

elections, so the whole idea was a sham. As John F. Kennedy stated in 1956:

> Neither the United States nor Free Vietnam was a party to that agreement (on elections) — and neither the United States nor Free Vietnam is ever going to be a party to an election obviously stacked and subverted in advance, urged on us by those (the Communists) who have already broken their own pledges under the agreement they now seek to enforce.[3]

So Ngo Dinh Diem, South Vietnam's new leader, was indeed justified in declaring South Vietnam a separate nation and in saying that he would not allow the 1956 election to be held in South Vietnam. The majority of the people in South Vietnam wanted independence from North Vietnam.

When the elections were not held North Vietnam now began to use force to take over South Vietnam. Some people have argued that the War in South Vietnam was fought by the Vietcong (or National Liberation Front) which was independent of Vietnam. In fact, however, North Vietnam controlled the War in South Vietnam from the start. The North Vietnamese created the NLF as a cover for their own role in the War, to prevent the charge that they had invaded South Vietnam. North Vietnamese defectors found it humorous that Americans believed Communist propaganda.[4]

With the introduction in 1965 of large numbers of American troops the tide turned in favor of the South Vietnamese Government. But the effectiveness of American soldiers on the battlefield was undermined by the strategy, or rather lack of strategy, by American civilian leaders. For what several presidents, but especially President Johnson, did was fail to resolve to fight to win the War. War is a serious matter. It requires the undivided attention of the president, the Congress, and the citi-

---

[3] Speech to Friends of Vietnam in Hans J. Morgenthau (Historian), "The 1951 Geneva Conference: An Assessment." *America's Stake in Vietnam* (1956), p. 13.

[4] Jeffrey Race, *War Comes to Long An: Revolutionary Conflict in a Vietnamese Province* (1972), pp. 107 and 122. Race interviewed two Communist defectors: "They both commented humorously that the (Communist) Party (of North Vietnam) had apparently been more successful than was expected in concealing its role (in the war in South Vietnam)." Another defector said: "The Central Committee could hardly permit the International Control Commission to say that there was an invasion from the North, so it was necessary to have some name (the National Liberation Front) . . . to clothe these forces with some political organization."

zenry. The president, in particular, has the duty to define the aims of the war, fix a strategy for success, and clarify to the American people why they and their sons should be willing to sacrifice. President Johnson never confronted the American people with the reality of this choice.[5]

Johnson was concerned about domestic politics, especially his Great Society program. Consequently, he sent in enough troops to avoid losing the War but not enough to win it. The Joint Chiefs of Staff protested but Johnson wasn't listening. He had put civilian strategists in charge of the War. Their psychological strategy was to "calibrate" American bombing — increase it a little to get the North Vietnamese to negotiate. The gradual increases in American bombing missions reduced their effectiveness by allowing the North Vietnamese to adjust gradually.

Despite these limitations on the American military, there were several points at which the United States and South Vietnam were close to winning the war. In 1968 the Vietcong tried an all-out attack in the Tet Offensive. They were thoroughly defeated and effectively eliminated as a fighting force.[6] Without the Vietcong, the guerrilla war withered. Thus, the North Vietnamese Army had to fight large-scale battles against the better-armed Americans and South Vietnamese. The advantage on the battlefield swung clearly to the United States' side. However, many Americans at home withdrew their support for the War after the Tet Offensive. No one had told them why they were making such sacrifices in Vietnam. With no overall goals or strategy for the War, Americans could not see why we should keep fighting. The American people forced Johnson to start withdrawing troops precisely when our military leaders were saying that more troops and an offensive strategy would bring us victory.

Again in 1972 the Communists made a desperate gamble when they invaded South Vietnam in the Easter Offensive. They were thrown back by the South Vietnamese Army (most American troops were out of

---

[5] Former Secretary of State Dean Rusk stated in 1976: "We never made any effort to create a war psychology in the United States during the Vietnam affair. We didn't have military parades through cities. . . ."

[6] *Conduct of the War in Vietnam.* A report commissioned in 1971 by the U.S. Army Deputy Chief of Staff for Military Operations, Reference Document I (Summary of the document — not a direct quote): The number of attacks by enemy battalions or larger forces dropped from 16 per month in the first half of 1968 to less than 5 per month in the second half of 1968. See also S. Robert Thompson, *Peace Is Not at Hand* (1974), Chapter 5.

Vietnam by 1972) with losses of over 130,000 men.[7] So the North Vietnamese switched strategy. They decided to win at the negotiating table what they had failed to win on the battlefield. The Nixon Administration could have decided on a tough policy in order to achieve victory. However, by this time, seven years after the introduction of large numbers of American troops, support for the War had vanished. Our leaders had to negotiate. Henry Kissinger won the Nobel Peace Prize for negotiating the 1973 Paris Peace Agreement, but it was a sellout of South Vietnam. The North Vietnamese were allowed to keep their army in South Vietnam while the United States forces were withdrawn. Meanwhile, the Communists agreed to return American prisoners of war (POWs).[8] The Communists used the breather provided by the agreement to build up their army for the final attack in 1975 in which they took over South Vietnam.

It is curious that American reporters criticized the American military for committing atrocities in Vietnam while dismissing the barbarity of the Communists. There should be no mistaking the nature of warfare — it is brutal. The American soldiers were heavily armed and made lavish use of their firepower. Occasionally, some soldiers committed crimes, but they were tried in military courts. American bombing was extremely heavy. However, most of the tonnage was dropped in the lightly populated jungle, so few civilians were killed.

The Communists, meanwhile, used systematic terror to control the population. From the start, the North Vietnamese Government was as totalitarian and oppressive as any government in the world. North Vietnamese people had almost no rights. People who opposed the Communists or their programs were executed. At least 50,000 (estimates go as high as 500,000) North Vietnamese died in the Communist land "reform" program alone.[9] Over 1 million people escaped from North Vietnam after 1954 to get away from Communist oppression.

The Vietcong also used terror and executions (several thousand per year) to intimidate the population of South Vietnam. The American media seemed to pay scant attention to the Vietcong atrocity in Dak San, where the Communists used flamethrowers to burn the residents to death. There was very little in the American press about the mass grave

---

[7] Thompson, *Peace*, Chapter 6.

[8] Douglas Pike, "The Other Side." *The Wilson Quarterly*, Vol. VII, No. 3, Summer, 1983, p. 121.

[9] Bernard Fall, *The Two Viet Nams: A Political and Military Analysis* (1967), p. 156.

of 5,700 civilians killed at Hue by the Vietcong in the 1968 Tet Offensive. In captured documents the Vietcong gloated over the executions, lamenting only that they couldn't have killed more people.[10]

Some observers believe that the United States lost the War because we fought it militarily. The real struggle was for the allegiance of the South Vietnamese people. The more people we bombed, they argue, the more enemy guerrillas we created. This argument is refuted by the fact that South Vietnam was defeated by a conventional military invasion, not by a guerrilla takeover. Winning hearts and minds had less to do with victory in Vietnam than tanks and artillery.

In short, in the Vietnam War the United States was trying to protect the independence of a free people from an invasion by a determined and brutal enemy. The American military did its job admirably — winning every battle. What was missing was a decision by our civilian leaders to focus the national will and determination on the fight. We needed to make the choice as a nation on whether the sacrifice was worth it. Instead President Johnson tried to fight the war secretly, with no national debate. As time wore on Americans lost interest in what they saw as a needless meatgrinder chewing up our young men and resources. They had no clear idea of why the country was fighting. In the end our determined enemy simply outlasted us. The tragedy is not that America fought in Vietnam. Rather, the tragedy is that we fought the War without the determination to fight it to victory. ■

1. How does *each* account answer the following questions?

    a. What were the reasons the United States became involved in Vietnam?

    b. Should the United States have been involved in Vietnam? Why or why not?

    c. Why did the United States lose the war?

2. What are the main ideas and information that both accounts *agree* on?

3. What are the main ideas and information that the accounts *disagree* on?

4. What is some of the important *evidence* used in each account to support the author's beliefs?

5. After reviewing and analyzing these passages, what are *your* conclusions

---

[10] Robert F. Turner, *Vietnamese Communism: Its Origins and Development* (1975), p. 254: "A captured Vietcong document stated that at Hue the Communists: '. . . eliminated 1,892 administrative personnel, 38 policeman, 790 tyrants.'"

about questions 1a, 1b, and 1c? Explain the reasons you arrived at these conclusions.

6. What additional information do you need to answer 1a, 1b, and 1c conclusively? ◄

THINKING ACTIVITY

5.12 ▶ As we saw with the various accounts of the Battle of Lexington on pages 200–202, the perspectives of individual participants are often quite different from the perspectives of historians trying to provide general, integrated accounts. We have just reviewed and analyzed two contrasting historical accounts of the Vietnam War. The following is an exchange of correspondence between Lyndon B. Johnson, then President of the United States, and Ho Chi Minh, President of the Democratic Republic of Vietnam. The exchange took place three years after the U.S. Congress passed the Gulf of Tonkin Resolution, which authorized President Johnson to "use whatever means necessary" to stop the communist aggression in Vietnam, and one year before the devastating Tet Offensive by the North Vietnamese, which catalyzed the antiwar movement in the United States. After reading the two letters, answer the questions that follow.

On 8 February 1967 President Johnson secretly sends this letter to Ho Chi Minh.

His Excellency
Ho Chi Minh
President
Democratic Republic of Vietnam

Dear Mr. President:

I am writing to you in the hope that the conflict in Vietnam can be brought to an end. That conflict has already taken a heavy toll — in lives lost, in wounds inflicted, in property destroyed, and in simple human misery. If we fail to find a just and peaceful solution, history will judge us harshly.

Therefore, I believe that we both have a heavy obligation to seek earnestly the path to peace. It is in response to that obligation that I am writing directly to you.

We have tried over the past several years, in a variety of ways and through a number of channels, to convey to you and your colleagues our desire to achieve a peaceful settlement. For whatever reasons, these efforts have not achieved any results.

It may be that our thoughts and yours, our attitudes and yours, have been distorted or misinterpreted as they passed through these various channels. Certainly that is always a danger in indirect communication.

There is one way to overcome this problem and to move forward in the search for a peaceful settlement. That is for us to arrange for direct talks between trusted representatives in a secure setting and away from the glare of publicity. Such talks should not be used as a propaganda exercise but should be a serious effort to find a workable and mutually acceptable solution.

In the past two weeks, I have noted public statements by representatives of your government suggesting that you would be prepared to enter into direct bilateral talks with representatives of the US Government, provided that we ceased "unconditionally" and permanently our bombing operations against your country and all military actions against it. In the last day, serious and responsible parties have assured us indirectly that this is in fact your proposal.

Let me frankly state that I see two great difficulties with this proposal. In view of your public position, such action on our part would inevitably produce worldwide speculation that discussions were under way and would impair the privacy and secrecy of those discussions. Secondly, there would inevitably be grave concern on our part whether your government would make use of such action by us to improve its military position.

With these problems in mind, I am prepared to move even further towards an ending of hostilities than your Government has proposed in either public statements or through private diplomatic channels. I am prepared to order a cessation of bombing against your country and the stopping of further augmentation of US forces in South Viet-Nam as soon as I am assured that infiltration into South Viet-Nam by land and by sea has stopped. These acts of restraint on both sides would, I believe, make it possible for us to conduct serious and private discussions leading toward an early peace.

I make this proposal to you now with a specific sense of urgency arising from the imminent New Year holidays in Viet-Nam. If you are able to accept this proposal I see no reason why it could not take effect at the end of the New Year, or Tet, holidays. The proposal I have made would be greatly strengthened if your military authorities and those of the

Government of South Viet-Nam could promptly negotiate an extension of the Tet truce.

As to the site of the bilateral discussions I propose, there are several possibilities. We could, for example, have our representatives meet in Moscow where contacts have already occurred. They could meet in some other country such as Burma. You may have other arrangements or sites in mind, and I would try to meet your suggestions.

The important thing is to end a conflict that has brought burdens to both our peoples, and above all to the people of South Viet-Nam. If you have any thoughts about the actions I propose, it would be most important that I receive them as soon as possible.

Sincerely,
Lyndon B. Johnson

A few days later Ho Chi Minh replies.

Your Excellency:

On 10 February 1967, I received your message. This is my reply.

Vietnam is thousands of miles away from the United States. The Vietnamese people have never done any harm to the United States. But contrary to the pledges made by its representative at the 1954 Geneva conference, the U.S. Government has ceaselessly intervened in Vietnam; it has unleashed and intensified the war of aggression in South Vietnam with a view to prolonging the partition of Vietnam and turning South Vietnam into a neocolony and a military base of the United States. For over two years now, the U.S. Government has with its air and naval forces carried the war to the Democratic Republic of Vietnam, an independent and sovereign country.

The U.S. Government has committed war crimes, crimes against peace and against mankind. In South Vietnam, half a million U.S. and satellite troops have resorted to the most inhuman weapons and the most barbarous methods of warfare, such as napalm, toxic chemicals and gases, to massacre our compatriots, destroy crops and raze villages to the ground.

In North Vietnam, thousands of U.S. aircraft have dropped hundreds of thousands of tons of bombs, destroying towns, villages, factories, roads, bridges, dikes, dams, and even churches, pagodas, hospitals, schools. In your message, you apparently deplored the sufferings and destructions in Vietnam. May I ask you: Who has perpetrated these monstrous crimes? It is the U.S. and satellite troops. The U.S. Government is entirely responsible for the extremely serious situation in Vietnam.

The U.S. war of aggression against the Vietnamese people constitutes a challenge to the countries of the Socialist camp, a threat to the national independence movement and a serious danger to peace in Asia and the world.

The Vietnamese people deeply love independence, freedom and peace. But in the face of the U.S. aggression, they have risen up, united as one man. Fearless of sacrifices and hardships, they are determined to carry on their resistance until they have won genuine independence and freedom and true peace. Our just cause enjoys strong sympathy and support from the peoples of the whole world, including broad sections of the American people.

The U.S. Government has unleashed the war of aggression in Vietnam. It must cease this aggression. That is the only way to the restoration of peace. The U.S. Government must stop definitively and unconditionally its bombing raids and all other acts of war against the Democratic Republic of Vietnam, withdraw from South Vietnam all U.S. and satellite troops, and let the Vietnamese people settle themselves their own affairs. Such (is the basic) content of the four-point stand of the Government of the D. R. V., which embodies the essential principles and provisions of the 1954 Geneva agreements on Vietnam. It is the basis of a correct political solution to the Vietnam problem.

In your message, you suggested direct talks between the D. R. V. and United States. If the U.S. Government really wants these talks, it must first of all stop unconditionally its bombing raids and all other acts of war against the D. R. V. It is only after the unconditional cessation of the U.S. bombing raids and all other acts of war against the D. R. V. that the D. R. V. and the United States would enter into talks and discuss questions concerning the two sides.

The Vietnamese people will never submit to force, they will never accept talks under the threat of bombs.

Our cause is absolutely just. It is to be hoped that the U.S. Government will act in accordance with reason.

Ho Chi Minh ■

1. Explain how each president defines the situation in Vietnam, which leads to contrasting analyses and conflicting conclusions.

2. Describe the ways in which these letters bring a deeper and enriched perspective to our understanding of the Vietnam conflict.

3. Compare the perspectives presented by Lyndon Johnson and Ho Chi Minh with the perspectives presented by Historian A and Historian B in the previous Thinking Activity.

4. Explain the ways that examining these two letters has changed or modified your perspective on the Vietnam War. ◄

Summary

In this chapter we have explored the way we form and revise our beliefs. The purpose of this ongoing process of forming and revising beliefs is to develop a clear understanding of what is taking place so that we can make the most effective decisions in our lives. Our ability to think critically about our beliefs guides us in asking the questions necessary to explore, evaluate, and develop our beliefs.

We use both direct and indirect experience to form and re-form our beliefs. Our indirect experiences are based on outside sources of information, both spoken and written. To evaluate critically these outside sources of information, we have to ask the following questions:

- How reliable is the *information*? (How accurate and justified?)
- How reliable is the *source* of the information?

By thinking critically about the process by which we form and revise our beliefs about the world, we are able to develop our understanding insightfully and creatively.

CHAPTER 6

Language as a System

SENTENCE MEANING

Semantic Meaning

Pragmatic Meaning

WORD SENSE

Perceptual Meaning

Syntactic Meaning

LANGUAGE: A system of symbols for thinking and communicating.

UP TO THIS POINT in the book, we have been exploring the various ways we use our thinking abilities to make sense of the world: solving problems, working toward our goals, analyzing issues, perceiving, forming beliefs, and gaining knowledge. In all these cases, we have found that by *thinking critically* about the different ways in which we are trying to make sense of the world ("thinking about our thinking") we can sharpen and improve our thinking abilities. Through the process of critically examining the way we solve problems, work toward our goals, analyze issues, perceive, and form beliefs, we learn to perform these activities more effectively.

Throughout this process, language is the tool we have been using to understand and develop our thinking. We have been:

- Learning about the thinking of others through *reading.*

- Expressing our own thinking through *writing.*

- Exchanging ideas with others by *speaking* and *listening.*

We could not be developing our thinking in all these ways without the ability to use language. As we will see in the pages ahead, if we lacked the ability to use language, we would not even be able to *think* in any meaningful sense. In this chapter we focus our attention on language as a means of creating and communicating our thoughts. As we develop our skill in using language, we will improve at the same time our ability to think and make sense of the world.

Communicating with Others

Imagine a world without language. Imagine that you suddenly lost your ability to speak, to write, to read. Imagine that your only means of expression were grunts, shrieks, and gestures. And finally, imagine that you soon discovered that *everyone* in the world had also lost the ability to use language. What do you think such a world would be like?

As this exercise of the imagination illustrates, language forms the bedrock of our relations with others. It is the means we have to communicate our thoughts, feelings, and experiences to others, and they to us. This mutual sharing draws us together and leads to our forming relationships. Consider the social groups in your school, your neighborhood, or your community. Notice how language plays a central role in bringing people together into groups and in maintaining these groups.

A loss of language would both limit the complexity of our individual relationships with others and drastically affect the entire way we live in society. The experience would be somewhat like moving to a foreign country where the language was totally unfamiliar. We would probably experience continual frustration in communicating with others and might even feel a sense of hopelessness in trying to function effectively within the society.

Virtually all the achievements of our civilization are based on our ability to communicate with one another. Without communication, the social cooperation necessary for our culture would break down, and our society would soon become very primitive indeed.

Read the following story of the Tower of Babel, from the biblical book of Genesis, and then answer the questions after the passage.

> Hitherto, the world had only one way of speech, only one language. And now, as men travelled westwards, they found a plain in the land of Sennaar, and made themselves a home there; Here we can make bricks, they said to one another, baked with fire; and they built, not in stone, but in brick, with pitch for their mortar. It would be well, they said, to build ourselves a city, and a tower in it with a top that reaches to heaven; we will make ourselves a great people, instead of scattering over the wide face of earth. But now God came down to look at the city, with its tower, which Adam's children were building; and he said, Here is a people all one, with a tongue common to all; this is but the beginning of their undertakings, and what is to prevent them carrying out all they design? It would be well to go down and throw confusion into the speech they use there, so that they will not be able to understand each other. Thus God broke up their common home, and scattered them over the earth, and the building of the city came to an end. That is why it was called Babel, Confusion, because it was there that God confused the whole world's speech, and scattered them far away, over the wide face of earth.

1. Explain why you think that the people in the story were unable to continue working on the city and the tower they were building.

   _____

   _____

2. Imagine that you were the head builder of this project. Describe what steps you could take to enable work to continue, and explain why you would take each step.

   a. *Step:* _____

Explanation: _____

_____

b. *Step:* _____

   Explanation: _____

   _____

3. This story seems to symbolize the splintering of the human family into different races and cultures, each with its own language, customs, and ways of thinking about the world.

   a. Why does sharing a language serve to bind people together?

      _____

      _____

   b. Why does speaking different languages create such deep divisions between groups of people?

      _____

      _____

   Language is the framework that makes all our social activities and relationships possible. In the rest of this chapter we will explore how language can accomplish this task.

The Symbolic Nature of Language

As human beings, we are able to share our thoughts and feelings with each other because of our ability to *symbolize,* or let one thing represent something else. Words are the most common symbols we use in our daily life. Although words are only sounds or written marks that have no meaning in and of themselves, they stand for objects, ideas, and other aspects of human experience. For example, the word *sailboat* is a symbol that represents a water-going vessel with sails that is propelled by the wind. When we speak or write *sailboat,* we are able to communicate the sort of thing we are thinking about. Of course, if other people are to understand what we are referring to when we use this symbol, they must first agree that this symbol (*sailboat*) does in fact represent that wind-propelled vessel that floats on the water. If others do not agree with us on what this symbol represents, then we will not be able to communicate what we would like to. Naturally, we could always take others to the object we have in mind and point it out to them, but using a symbol instead is much more convenient.

Language symbols (or words) can take two forms; they can be spoken sounds or written markings.* The symbol *sailboat* can be either written down or spoken aloud. Either way it will communicate the sort of thing we are referring to, providing that others share our understanding of what the symbol means.

Since using language is so natural to us, we rarely stop to realize that our language is really a system of spoken sounds and written markings that we use to represent various aspects of our experience. These sounds and markings enable us to communicate our thoughts and feelings to others, based on a shared understanding of what the sounds and markings symbolize.

Consider the following list of markings. What do you think they symbolize?

- *Segelboot* (German)
- *barco velero* (Spanish)
- *bateau à voiles* (French)
- *barco de vela* (Italian)

These markings are actually the symbols used in languages other than English to represent the same object we have referred to with the symbol *sailboat*. To understand what these other symbols mean, we would first have to develop an understanding of what each symbol represents in that language.

> *Language* A system of symbols for thinking and communicating.

In certain respects, language is like a set of symbolic building blocks. The basic blocks are sounds, which may be symbolized by letters:

Letters — A T C Q Y N, etc. — symbolize sounds

* A unique language case is posed by American Sign Language (ASL). Traditionally viewed as little more than a crude and broken form of English, ASL is now regarded by linguists as a full-fledged language, capable of conveying abstract thoughts. ASL evolved separately from English and possesses its own grammar and syntax; it employs specific facial expressions as part of its grammar and expresses meaning through a creative and organized use of space.

Sounds form the phonetic foundation of a language, and this explains why different languages have such distinctly different "sounds." Try having members of the class who speak other languages speak a word or a few sentences in the language. Listen to how the sound of each language differs from the others. When humans are infants, they are able to make all the sounds of all languages. As they are continually exposed to the specific group of sounds of their society's language, they gradually concentrate on making only those sounds while discarding or never developing others.

Sounds combine to form larger sets of blocks called words. Words are used to represent the various aspects of our world of experience, including — as the poem goes — "shoes and ships and sealing wax, of cabbages and kings."

Words — *love, students, learning* — symbolize $\left\{\begin{array}{l}\text{objects}\\\text{thoughts}\\\text{feelings}\\\text{actions}\\\text{concepts}\end{array}\right.$

When we read, hear, or think about a word, it usually elicits in us a variety of ideas and feelings. Describe the ideas or feelings that the following words arouse in you:

College education: _____

_____

Happiness: _____

_____

Freedom: _____

_____

Creative: _____

_____

Love: _____

_____

The combination of all the ideas and feelings that a word arouses in our minds comprises the "meaning" of that word to us. For instance, the ideas and feelings that you just listed reflect the meaning that each of those words has for you as an individual. And although the meanings that these words have for you is likely similar in many respects to the meanings they have for other people, there are also many differences. Consider the different meanings these words have for the two people in the following dialogue:

A: For me, a *college education* represents the most direct path to my dreams. It's the only way I can develop the knowledge and abilities required for my career.

B: I can't agree with you. I pursued a *college education* for a while, but it didn't work out. I found that most of my courses consisted of large classes with professors lecturing about subjects that had little relation to my life. The value of a college education is overblown. I know many people with college degrees who have not been able to find rewarding careers.

A: Don't you see? An important part of achieving *happiness* is learning about things you aren't familiar with, expanding your horizons about the world, developing new interests. That's what college can give you.

B: I have enough interests. As far as I'm concerned, *happiness* consists of having the opportunity to do the things that I enjoy doing with the people I enjoy doing them with. For me, happiness is *freedom*!

A: *Freedom* to do what? Freedom is only meaningful when you have worthwhile options to select and the wisdom to select the right ones. And a college education can help provide you both!

B: That sounds very idealistic, but it's also naive. Many of the college graduates I have met are neither wise nor happy. In order to be truly happy, you have to be involved in *creative* activities. Every day should be a surprise, something different to look forward to. Many careers pay well, but they don't provide creative opportunities.

A: Being *creative* means doing things you *love*. When you really love something you're doing, you are naturally creative. For example, I love to draw and paint, and this provides a creative outlet for me. I don't need to be creative at work — I have enough creative opportunities outside of work.

B: You're wrong! *Creativity* doesn't simply mean being artistic. We should strive to be creative in every part of our lives, keep looking for new possibilities and unique experiences. And I think that you are misusing the word *love*. We can only really love things that are alive, like people and pets.

> *A:* That's a very weird idea of *love* you have. As far as I'm concerned, love is a word that expresses a strong positive emotion that can be directed towards objects ("I love my car"), activities ("I love to dance"), or people. I don't see what's so complicated about that.
>
> *B:* To be able to *love* in any meaningful sense, the object of your love has to be able to respond to you, so that the two of you can develop a relationship together. When was the last time that your car responded to your love for it?
>
> *A:* Very funny. I guess that we just have different ideas about the word *love* — as well as the words *happiness*, *freedom*, and *creative*.

As this dialogue suggests, words are not simple entities with one clear meaning that everyone agrees on. Instead, most words are complex, multidimensional carriers of meaning; their exact meaning often varies from person to person. These differences in meaning can lead to disagreements and confusion as illustrated in the previous dialogue. To clarify our understanding about the way words function in our language and our thinking, we have to examine the way words serve as vehicles to express meaning.

For each of us, words arouse in our consciousness a variety of ideas, feelings, and experiences. Taken together, these ideas, feelings, and experiences express the total meaning of the words for the individual person. If we examine words carefully, we can see that the *total* meaning of words is actually composed of four distinct types of meaning.

- Semantic meaning
- Perceptual meaning
- Syntactic meaning
- Pragmatic meaning

We acquire language by realizing that a person can *mean* a thought, concept, action, or feeling by putting words together and by speaking or writing them in specific situations or contexts. That is, language extends relationships between our own consciousness and the world around us. The four types of meaning just mentioned express these relationships. Let us examine each of them in turn.

Semantic Meaning

The *semantic meaning* of a word expresses the relationship between a linguistic event (speaking or writing) and a nonlinguistic event.

Linguistic Event:		*Nonlinguistic Event:*
Saying "chair"	*relates to*	an object we sit in.
Saying "mustache"	*relates to*	hair growth on upper lip.
Saying "college education"	*relates to*	the experience of earning an academic degree through postsecondary study.

In the space provided, identify the nonlinguistic events (ideas, feelings, objects) that the following linguistic events relate to:

1. Saying "happiness" relates to _____

_____

2. Saying "freedom" relates to _____

_____

3. Saying "creative" relates to _____

_____

4. Saying "love" relates to _____

_____

5. Saying "_____ " relates to _____

_____

The semantic meaning of a word expresses the general properties of the word, and these properties determine how the word is used within its language system. How do we discover the general properties that determine word usage? Besides examining our own knowledge of the meaning and use of words, we can also check dictionary definitions. Dictionary definitions tend to focus on the general properties that determine word usage. Here, for example, are some definitions for the words we have been considering according to one dictionary, *The American Heritage Dictionary of the English Language*:

- *Chair:* A piece of furniture consisting of a seat, legs, and back, and often arms, designed to accommodate one person.
- *Mustache:* The hair growing on the upper lip, especially when it is cultivated and groomed.

Using a fairly large dictionary as a resource, look up and complete dictionary definitions for the following words:

College education: _____

_____

Happiness: _____

_____

Freedom: _____

_____

Creative: _____

_____

Love: _____

_____

_____: _____

_____

   Notice that each word's dictionary definition describes many (though often not all) of the general properties that determine how the word is used in the English language. These general properties that determine a word's usage constitute the semantic meaning of the word. For example, by explaining to someone the general properties of the word *chair* ("a piece of furniture consisting of a seat, legs, and back, and often arms, designed to accommodate one person"), we are indicating how the word is used in the system of language we call English, and in so doing we are communicating much of the semantic meaning of the word.

   To understand clearly the semantic meaning of a word, we often need to go beyond defining its general properties to identifying examples of the word that embody those properties. If you are sitting in a chair or can see one from where you are, examine its design: Does it embody all the properties identified in the definition? (Sometimes unusual examples embody most, but not all, of the properties of a dictionary definition — for example, a "beanbag chair" lacks legs and arms.) If we are trying to communicate the semantic meaning of a word to someone, it is generally useful to provide both the general properties of the word as well as examples which embody the general properties.

For each of the words listed, describe a specific example from your experience that embodies the general properties of the word as suggested by the dictionary definitions you located:

1. *College education:* _____

2. *Happiness:* _____

3. *Freedom:* _____

4. *Creative:* _____

5. *Love:* _____

6. _____: _____

In Chapter Eight, *Forming and Applying Concepts,* we will examine in much more detail the way in which language and thinking work together to enable us to create and express meaning through the interrelationship of symbols, examples, and general properties.

THINKING ACTIVITY

6.1   ▶ In the sentences that follow, describe the semantic meaning of each of the underlined words as it is used in the sentence and then provide an example that illustrates that semantic meaning.

1. A *college education* is currently necessary for many careers that formerly required high school preparation.

   Semantic meaning: _____

   Example: _____

2. The utilitarian ethical system is based on the principle that the right course of action is that which brings the greatest *happiness* to the greatest number of people.

   Semantic meaning: _____

   Example: _____

3. The laws of this country attempt to balance the *freedom* of the individual with the rights of society as a whole.

   Semantic meaning: _____

   Example: _____

4. "We are all part of things, we are all part of *creation*, all kings, all poets, all musicians, we have only to open up, to discover what is already there." (Henry Miller)

   Semantic meaning: _____

   Example: _____

5. "If music be the food of *love*, play on." (William Shakespeare)

   Semantic meaning: _____

   Example: _____

6. (Compose a sentence and underline a key word.)

   _____

   Semantic meaning: _____

   Example: _____ ◄

Perceptual Meaning

The total meaning of a word also includes its perceptual meaning. The *perceptual meaning* of a word expresses the relationship between a linguistic event and an individual's consciousness. For each of us, words elicit unique and personal thoughts and feelings based on previous experiences and past associations.

Linguistic Event:		*Individual's Consciousness:*
Saying "chair"	*relates to*	comfortable chair in the living room / small fourth grade classroom chair / cozy chair at the kitchen table.
Saying "mustache"	*relates to*	father's large handlebar mustache / brother's amusing peach fuzz / Hitler's frightening brush mustache.

Perceptual meaning also includes an individual's positive and negative responses to the word. When you read or hear the word *book*, for example, what positive or negative feelings does it arouse in you? What about the word *textbook? Mystery book? Comic book? Cookbook?* In each case, the word probably elicited distinct feelings in your mind, both positive and negative. These feelings contribute to the meaning each word has for you.

Think about the words we considered earlier and describe what personal perceptions, experiences, associations, and feelings they evoke in your mind.

1. *College education:* _____

   _____

2. *Happiness:* _____

   _____

3. *Freedom:* _____

   _____

4. *Creative:* _____

   _____

5. *Love:* _____

   _____

6. _____: _____

   _____

Syntactic Meaning

A third component of a word's total meaning is its syntactic meaning. The *syntactic meaning* of a word defines its relation to other words in the sentence. Syntactic relationships extend among all the parts of the sentence that are spoken or written, or which will be spoken or written. The syntactic meaning defines three relationships among linguistic events:

- Content: linguistic events that express the major message of the sentence
- Description: linguistic events that elaborate or modify the major message of the sentence
- Connection: linguistic events that join the major message of the sentence

For example, in the sentence: "The two novice hikers crossed the ledge cautiously," *hikers* and *crossed* represent the content, or major message, of the sentence. *Two* and *novice* define a descriptive relationship to *hikers*, and *cautiously* defines a descriptive relationship to *crossed*. At first, we may think that this sort of relationship among words involves nothing more than semantic meaning. The following sentence, however, clearly demonstrates the importance of syntactic meaning in language: "Invisible fog rumbles in on lizard legs." Although *fog* does not *rumble*, and it is not *invisible*, and the concept of moving on *lizard legs* instinctively seem incompatible with *rumbling*, still the sentence "makes sense" at some level of meaning — namely, at the syntactic level. One reason it does is that, in this sentence, we still have three basic content words — *fog, rumbles,* and *legs* — and we also have two descriptive words, namely *invisible* and *lizard.*

The third major syntactic relationship is that of connection. We use connective words to join ideas, thoughts, or feelings being expressed. For example, we could connect content meaning to either of our two sentences in the following fashion:

• "The two novice hikers crossed the ledge cautiously *after* one of them slipped."

• "Invisible fog rumbles in on lizard legs, *but* acid rain doesn't."

When we add content words such as *one slipped* and *rain doesn't,* we join the ideas, thoughts, or feelings they represent to the earlier expressed ideas, thoughts, or feelings (*hikers crossed* and *fog rumbles*) using connective words like *after* and *but,* as in the previous sentences.

THINKING ACTIVITY

6.2   ▶ In the space provided, give descriptive words that add to or change the ideas or feelings that the following content words relate to.

    1. _____ college education

    2. _____ happiness

    3. _____ freedom

    4. _____ creation

    5. _____ love

Now provide connective words that join the ideas or feelings represented by the following content and descriptive word relationships.

1. College _____ employment are both valuable life experiences.

2. The miser's soul shriveled as his body aged, _____ wealth, _____ happiness became his goal.

3. The revolutionaries held freedom _____ all else.

4. Anything may be beautiful _____ it is our own creation.

5. Two great gifts are love _____ joy.

Express two alternative thoughts in each of the following pairs of sentences by using different content, descriptive, and connective words to complete them.

1a. A college education is important _____

1b. A college education is important _____

2a. Happiness is a result _____

2b. Happiness is a result _____

3a. Freedom _____ is not allowed in some societies.

3b. Freedom _____ is not allowed in some societies.

4a. _____ a creative _____ .

4b. _____ a creative _____ .

5a. _____ love makes people _____ .

5b. _____ love makes people _____ . ◄

The second reason that "invisible fog rumbles in on lizard legs" makes sense at the syntactic level of meaning is that the words of that sentence obey the *syntax*, or order, of English. Most speakers of English would have trouble making sense of "Invisible rumbles legs lizard on fog in" — or "Barks big endlessly dog brown the," for that matter. Because of syntactic meaning, each word in the sentence derives part of its total meaning from its combination with the other words in that sentence in order to express and join ideas, thoughts, and feelings. Look at the following sentences and explain the difference in meaning between each pair of sentences:

1a. The process of achieving an *education at college* changes a person's future possibilities.

1b. The process of achieving a *college education* changes a person's future possibilities.

2a. She felt *happiness* for her long-lost brother.

2b. She felt the *happiness* of her long-lost brother.

3a. The most important thing to me is *freedom* from the things that restrict my choices.

3b. The most important thing to me is *freedom* to make my choices without restrictions.

4a. Michelangelo's painting of the Sistene Chapel represents his *creative* genius.

4b. The Sistene Chapel represents the *creative* genius of Michelangelo's greatest painting.

5a. I *love* the person I have been involved with for the past year.

5b. I am in *love* with the person I have been involved with for the past year.

Pragmatic Meaning

The fourth element that contributes to the total meaning of a word is its pragmatic meaning. The *pragmatic meaning* of a word involves the person who is speaking and the situation in which the word is spoken. For example, the sentence "That student likes to borrow books from the library" allows a number of pragmatic interpretations:

1. Was the speaker outside looking at *that student* carrying books out of the library?

2. Did the speaker have this information because he or she was a classmate of *that student* and didn't see him/her carrying books?

3. Was the speaker in the library watching *that student* check the books out?

The correct interpretation or meaning of the sentence depends on what was actually taking place in the situation — in other words, its pragmatic meaning.

THINKING ACTIVITY

6.3   ▶ For each of the sentences we have been considering, describe a possible pragmatic field in terms of the person speaking and the situation in which it is being spoken.

1. A college education is currently necessary for many careers that formerly required high school preparation.

Person speaking: _____

Situation: _____

2. The utilitarian ethical system is based on the principle that the right course of action is that which brings the greatest *happiness* to the greatest number of people.

   Person speaking: _____

   Situation: _____

3. The laws of this country attempt to balance the *freedom* of the individual with the rights of society as a whole.

   Person speaking: _____

   Situation: _____

4. "We are all part of things, we are all part of *creation,* all kings, all poets, all musicians, we have only to open up, to discover what is already there." (Henry Miller)

   Person speaking: _____

   Situation: _____

5. "If music be the food of *love,* play on." (William Shakespeare)

   Person speaking: _____

   Situation: _____

6. _____

   Person speaking: _____

   Situation: _____

After completing the activity, compare your answers with those of your classmates. In what ways are the answers similar or different? Analyze the way different pragmatic contexts (persons speaking and situations) affect the meanings of the italicized words. ◄

   The four meanings we just examined — semantic, perceptual, syntactical, pragmatic — create the total meaning of a word. That is to say, all the dimensions of any word — all the relationships that connect linguistic events with nonlinguistic events, our consciousness, other linguistic events, and situations in the world — make up the *meaning* we assign to a word. Let's examine these various aspects of word meaning in the following activity.

THINKING ACTIVITY
_____

6.4   ▶ The following pieces elaborate the meanings of the key words we have been examining in this section:

Education

Happiness

Freedom

Creative

Love

After each piece, write a one-page analysis examining the meaning that the author is investing in the key word. Each analysis should discuss the different dimensions of the word's meaning: semantic, perceptual, syntactic, and pragmatic.

HOW TO MAKE PEOPLE SMALLER THAN THEY ARE
by Norman Cousins

Three months ago in this space we wrote about the costly retreat from the humanities on all the levels of American education. Since that time, we have had occasion to visit a number of campuses and have been troubled to find that the general situation is even more serious than we had thought. It has become apparent to us that one of the biggest problems confronting American education today is the increasing vocationalization of our colleges and universities. Throughout the country, schools are under pressure to become job-training centers and employment agencies.

The pressure comes mainly from two sources. One is the growing determination of many citizens to reduce taxes — understandable and even commendable in itself, but irrational and irresponsible when connected to the reduction or dismantling of vital public services. The second source of pressure comes from parents and students who tend to scorn courses of study that do not teach people how to become attractive to employers in a rapidly tightening job market.

It is absurd to believe that the development of skills does not also require the systematic development of the human mind. Education is being measured more by the size of the benefits the individual can extract from society than by the extent to which the individual can come into possession of his or her full powers. The result is that the life-giving juices are in danger of being drained out of education.

Emphasis on "practicalities" is being characterized by the subordination of words to numbers. History is seen not as essential experience to be transmitted to new generations, but as abstractions that carry dank odors. Art is regarded as something that calls for indulgence or patronage and that has no place among the practical realities. Political science is viewed more as a specialized subject for people who want to go into politics than as an opportunity for citizens to develop a knowledgeable relationship with the systems by which human societies are governed. Finally, literature and philosophy are assigned the role of add-ons — intellectual adornments that have nothing to do with "genuine" education.

Instead of trying to shrink the liberal arts, the American people ought to be putting pressure on colleges and universities to increase the ratio of the humanities to the sciences. Most serious studies of medical-school curricula in recent years have called attention to the stark gaps in the liberal education of medical students. The experts agree that the schools shouldn't leave it up to students to close those gaps.

The irony of the emphasis being placed on careers is that nothing is more valuable for anyone who has had a professional or vocational education than to be able to deal with abstractions or complexities, or to feel comfortable with subtleties of thought or language, or to think sequentially. The doctor who knows only disease is at a disadvantage alongside the doctor who knows at least as much about people as he does about pathological organisms. The lawyer who argues in court from a narrow legal base is no match for the lawyer who can connect legal precedents to historical experience and who employs wide-ranging intellectual resources. The business executive whose competence in general management is bolstered by an artistic ability to deal with people is of prime value to his company. For the technologist, the engineering of consent can be just as important as the engineering of moving parts. In all these respects, the liberal arts have much to offer. Just in terms of career preparation, therefore, a student is shortchanging himself by shortcutting the humanities.

But even if it could be demonstrated that the humanities contribute nothing directly to a job, they would still be an essential part of the educational equipment of any person who wants to come to terms with life. The humanities would be expendable only if human beings didn't have to make decisions that affect their lives and the lives of others; if the human past never existed or had nothing to tell us about the present; if thought processes were irrelevant to the achievement of purpose; if creativity was beyond the human mind and had nothing to do with the joy of living; if human relationships were random aspects of life; if human beings never had to cope with panic or pain, or if they never had to anticipate the connection between cause and effect; if all the mysteries of mind and nature were fully plumbed; and if no special demands arose from the accident of being born a human being instead of a hen or a hog.

Finally, there would be good reason to eliminate the humanities if a free society were not absolutely dependent on a functioning citizenry. If the main purpose of a university is job training, then the underlying philosophy of our government has little meaning. The debates that went into the making of American society concerned not just institutions or governing principles but the capacity of humans to sustain those institutions. Whatever the disagreements were over other issues at the American Constitutional Convention, the fundamental question sensed by everyone, a question that lay over the entire assembly, was whether the people themselves would understand what it meant to hold the ultimate power of society, and whether they had enough of a sense of history and destiny to know where they had been and where they ought to be going.

Jefferson was prouder of having been the founder of the University of Virginia than of having been President of the United States. He knew that the educated and developed mind was the best assurance that a political system could be made to work — a system based on the informed consent of the governed. If this idea fails, then all the saved tax dollars in the world will not be enough to prevent the nation from turning on itself. ■

EPICURUS TO MENOECEUS *by Epicurus (Ancient Greek philosopher)*

Let no one when young delay to study philosophy, nor when he is old grow weary of his study. For no one can come too early or too late to secure the health of his soul. And the man who says that the age for philosophy has either not yet come or has gone by is like the man who says that the age for happiness is not yet come to him, or has passed away. Wherefore both when young and old a man must study philosophy, that as he grows old he may be young in blessings through the grateful recollection of what has been, and that in youth he may be old as well, since he will know no fear of what is to come. We must then mediate on the things that make our happiness, seeing that when that is with us we have all, but when it is absent we do all to win it. ■

I HAVE A DREAM *by Martin Luther King, Jr.*

Five score years ago, a great American, in whose symbolic shadow we stand, signed the Emancipation Proclamation. This momentous decree came as a great beacon light of hope to millions of Negro slaves who had been seared in the flames of withering injustice. It came as a joyous daybreak to end the long night of captivity.

But one hundred years later, we must face the tragic fact that the Negro is still not free. One hundred years later, the life of the Negro is still sadly crippled by the manacles of segregation and the chains of discrimination. One hundred years later, the Negro lives on a lonely island of poverty in the midst of a vast ocean of material prosperity. One hundred years later, the Negro is still languishing in the corners of American society and finds himself an exile in his own land. So we have come here today to dramatize an appalling condition.

In a sense we have come to our nation's capital to cash a check. When the architects of our republic wrote the magnificent words of the Constitution and the Declaration of Independence, they were signing a promissory note to which every American was to fall heir. This note was a promise that all men would be guaranteed the unalienable rights of life, liberty, and the pursuit of happiness.

It is obvious today that America has defaulted on this promissory note insofar as her citizens of color are concerned. Instead of honoring this sacred obligation, America has given the Negro people a bad check; a check which has come back marked "insufficient funds." But we refuse to believe that the bank of justice is bankrupt. We refuse to believe that there are insufficient funds in the great vaults of opportunity of this nation. So we have come to cash this check — a check that will give us upon demand the riches of freedom and the security of justice. We have also come to this hallowed spot to remind America of the fierce urgency of *now*. This is no time to engage in the luxury of cooling off or to take the tranquilizing drugs of gradualism. *Now* is the time to make real the promises of Democracy. *Now* is the time to rise from the dark and desolate valley of segregation to the sunlit path of racial justice. *Now* is the time to open the doors of opportunity to all of God's children. *Now* is the time to lift our nation from the quicksands of racial injustice to the solid rock of brotherhood.

It would be fatal for the nation to overlook the urgency of the moment and to underestimate the determination of the Negro. This sweltering summer of the Negro's legitimate discontent will not pass until there is an invigorating autumn of freedom and equality. 1963 is not an end, but a beginning. Those who hope that the Negro needed to blow off steam and will now be content will have a rude awakening if the nation returns to business as usual. There will be neither rest nor tranquillity in America until the Negro is granted his citizenship rights. The whirlwinds of revolt will continue to shake the foundations of our nation until the bright day of justice emerges.

But there is something that I must say to my people who stand on the warm threshold which leads into the palace of justice. In the process of gaining our rightful place we must not be guilty of wrongful deeds. Let us not seek to satisfy our thirst for freedom by drinking from the cup of bitterness and hatred. We must forever conduct our struggle on the high plane of dignity and discipline. We must not allow our creative protest to degenerate into physical violence. Again and again we must rise to the majestic heights of meeting physical force with soul force. The marvelous new militancy which has engulfed the Negro community must not lead us to a distrust of all white people, for many of our white brothers, as evidenced by their presence here today, have come to realize that their destiny is tied up with our destiny and their freedom is inextricably bound to our freedom. We cannot walk alone.

And as we walk, we must make the pledge that we shall march ahead. We cannot turn back. There are those who are asking the devotees of civil rights, "When will you be satisfied?" We can never be satisfied as long as the Negro is the victim of the unspeakable horrors of police brutality. We can never be satisfied as long as our bodies, heavy with the fatigue of travel, cannot gain lodging in the motels of the highways and the hotels of the cities. We cannot be satisfied as long as the Negro's basic mobility is from a smaller ghetto to a larger one. We can never be satisfied as long as a Negro in Mississippi cannot vote and a Negro in New York believes he has nothing for which to vote. No, no, we are not satisfied, and we will not be satisfied until justice rolls down like waters and righteousness like a mighty stream.

I am not unmindful that some of you have come here out of great trials and tribulations. Some of you have come fresh from narrow jail cells. Some of you have come from areas where your quest for freedom left you battered by the storms of persecution and staggered by the winds of police brutality. You have been the veterans of creative suffering. Continue to work with the faith that unearned suffering is redemptive.

Go back to Mississippi, go back to Alabama, go back to South Carolina, go back to Georgia, go back to Louisiana, go back to the slums and ghettos of our northern cities, knowing that somehow this situation can and will be changed. Let us not wallow in the valley of despair.

I say to you today, my friends, that in spite of the difficulties and frustrations of the moment I still have a dream. It is a dream deeply rooted in the American dream.

I have a dream that one day this nation will rise up and live out the true meaning of its creed: "We hold these truths to be self-evident; that all men are created equal."

I have a dream that one day on the red hills of Georgia the sons of former slaves and the sons of former slaveowners will be able to sit down together at the table of brotherhood.

I have a dream that one day even the state of Mississippi, a desert state sweltering with the heat of injustice and oppression, will be transformed into an oasis of freedom and justice.

I have a dream that my four little children will one day live in a nation where they will not be judged by the color of their skin but by the content of their character.

I have a dream today.

I have a dream that one day the state of Alabama, whose governor's lips are presently dripping with the words of interposition and nullification, will be transformed into a situation where little black boys and black girls will be able to join hands with little white boys and white girls and walk together as sisters and brothers.

I have a dream today.

I have a dream that one day every valley shall be exalted, every hill and mountain shall be made low, the rough places will be made plain, and the crooked places will be made straight, and the glory of the Lord shall be revealed, and all flesh shall see it together.

This is our hope. This is the faith with which I return to the South. With this faith we will be able to hew out of the mountain of despair a stone of hope. With this faith we will be able to transform the jangling discords of our nation into a beautiful symphony of brotherhood. With this faith we will be able to work together, to pray together, to struggle together, to go to jail together, to stand up for freedom together, knowing that we will be free one day.

This will be the day when all of God's children will be able to sing with new meaning

> My country, 'tis of thee,
> Sweet land of liberty,
>   Of thee I sing:
> Land where my fathers died,
> Land of the pilgrims' pride,
> From every mountain-side
>   Let freedom ring.

And if America is to be a great nation this must become true. So let freedom ring from the prodigious hilltops of New Hampshire. Let freedom ring from the mighty mountains of New York. Let freedom ring from the heightening Alleghenies of Pennsylvania!

Let freedom ring from the snowcapped Rockies of Colorado!

Let freedom ring from the curvaceous peaks of California!

But not only that; let freedom ring from Stone Mountain of Georgia!

Let freedom ring from Lookout Mountain of Tennessee!

Let freedom ring from every hill and molehill of Mississippi. From every mountainside, let freedom ring.

When we let freedom ring, when we let it ring from every village and every hamlet, from every state and every city, we will be able to speed up that day when all of God's children, black men and white men, Jews and Gentiles, Protestants and Catholics, will be able to join hands and sing in the words of the old Negro spiritual, "Free at last! free at last! thank God almighty, we are free at last!" ■

CREATIVITY *by Michelle Austin*

Creativity is an energizing force: powerful, generative, productive. Sadly, for the most part, its potential remains unused, as men and women circle the periphery of its domain. The author Kahlil Gibran writes: "For the self is a sea, boundless and measureless," and for many of us that sea remains largely undiscovered. Creativity is a treasure that if nurtured can become a harvest of possibilities and riches.

Why is creativity important? Very simply, creativity brings fulfillment and enrichment to every dimension of our lives. A creative disposition sees difficulties not as problems but as challenges to be met. The intuitive thinker draws upon the combined resources of insight, illumination, imagination and an inner strength. He puts ideas and strategies into effect, while developing a sense of competency and control over his environment. Creativity fosters limitless opportunities because it draws upon the power of discovery and invention.

Creativity's realm is in the vast uncharted portions of the mind. What we call full consciousness is a very narrow thing, and creativity springs from the unknown and unconscious depths of our being. In the words of Gibran: "Vague and nebulous is the beginning of all things." Creativity always begins with a question and we must abandon preconceived ideas and expectations. But while the phenomenon of creativity involves innovating, developing, playing and speculating, there must ultimately be a point of synthesis. Ideas in flight are of little use; a convergence and application gives substance to our visions.

Fostering our creative gifts is a lifelong project. The Buddhists use the term "mindfulness" to describe the creative state of being. Mindfulness involves developing an openness to ideas, suggestions and even once discarded thoughts. The goal is to increase our sensitivity and awareness to the mystery and beauty of life. We must adopt a playful attitude, a willingness to fool around with ideas, with the understanding that many of these fanciful notions will not be relevant or practical. But some will, and these creative insights can lead to profound and wondrous discoveries. At the same time, cultivating a creative attitude stretches our imaginations and makes our lives vibrant and unique.

Worry and mental striving create anxiety that clogs rather than stimulates the flow of ideas. It is impossible to impose one's will with brute force on the chaos. We must be gentle with ourselves, harmonize rather than try to conquer, and in the words of Albert Einstein, "The solution will present itself quietly and say 'Here I am.'" And while we need critical evaluation to provide direction and focus for our creative efforts, a premature and excessive critical judgment suppresses, overpowers and smothers creative spontaneity. This "voice of judgment" shrinks our creative reservoir and undermines our courage to take creative risks.

The author Napoleon Hill has stated, "Whatever the mind can conceive and believe, it can achieve." Similarly, if we approach our lives with a mindful sense of discovery and invention, we can continually create ourselves in ways that we can only imagine. In such lives, there are no predetermined outcomes, only creativity searching for seeds of progress. Over two thousand years ago the Greek philosopher Heraclitus gave eloquent voice to this crucial insight when he said: "If you do not expect the unexpected you will not find it, for it is not to be reached by search or trail." ■

SONNET 116 *by William Shakespeare*

Let me not to the marriage of true minds
Admit impediments. Love is not love
Which alters when it alteration finds,
Or bends with the remover to remove.
O, no! it is an ever-fixed mark
That looks on tempests and is never shaken;
It is the star to every wand'ring bark,
Whose worth's unknown, although his height be taken.
Love's not Time's fool, though rosy lips and cheeks
Within his bending sickle's compass come;
Love alters not with his brief hours and weeks,
But bears it out even to the edge of doom.
    If this be error and upon me proved,
    I never writ, nor no man ever loved. ■ ◄

Naming and Describing

To develop our ability to use language effectively to communicate our thoughts, feelings, and experiences, we have to understand how language functions. The first step in this process is to become familiar with the details of the experience we are trying to represent. This means that we must be *open and sensitive* to what we are experiencing. For example, if we fall asleep at a concert or don't pay attention at a lecture we are attending, then our symbolic representations of these experiences will be of little use.

Symbolizing our experiences effectively involves *understanding* what we are experiencing. If we lack knowledge of the elements and the context of the experience — whether it is wine, art, or hockey — then our symbolic description will be much less effective than it might have been if we had this understanding.

Finally, representing our experiences effectively also requires *facility with the language symbols* we are using to describe our experiences. We need a large enough vocabulary, as well as knowledge of how to put these words together, to describe all the various details and aspects of the experience. If we are to symbolize our experiences effectively, so that others can share them, we must:

1. Be *open and sensitive* to what we are experiencing.
2. Have an *understanding* of what we are experiencing.
3. Possess a *facility with language* to represent what we are experiencing.

Representing our thoughts, feelings, and experiences begins with trying to identify these thoughts, feelings, and experiences by giving them names. Our thinking abilities develop as we learn to symbolize our world in increasingly precise and distinct ways. When a baby cries "Mama" or "Dada," that one word is being used to represent one of a number of experiences: "I'm hungry," "I'm wet," "I'm lonely," and so on. As children develop, their ability to use more specific symbols for their experience also develops as they learn to distinguish each of these experiences by giving them different names. Our ability to symbolize thoughts, feelings, and objects in our experience by giving them descriptive names thus enables us to:

- *Identify* the various things in our experience.
- *Distinguish* these things from one another.
- *Describe* these things to others who share an understanding of our symbols.

Imagine that you have in front of you a large bowl containing a wide variety of different fruits. You are able to identify the various fruits (plum, apple, orange, cherry, banana, etc.) because you have given them names. Identifying these fruits means that you can distinguish them from one another and that you can recognize various types of fruits if you see them again. Finally, if a friend asks, "What are you eating?" you are able to describe what you are eating by giving the name that symbolizes it ("I'm eating a kumquat").

THINKING ACTIVITY

6.5 ▶ Naming is therefore the thinking process that enables us to organize our world. If we could not give various things in our experience different names, our world would be very chaotic, for we would not be able to identify or distinguish the various aspects of it. A vivid illustration of the power of naming can be found in the life of Helen Keller, a woman who was unable to see or hear from birth. In the following passages, the first written by her teacher, Anne Sullivan, and the second written by Helen Keller, we can see how learning to name things in her experience became the key that transformed her world from one of confusion to one of order and intelligibility. As you read these two accounts of this turning point in Helen's life, compare the similarities and differences between them.

LEARNING TO NAME *by Anne Sullivan*

I must write you a line this morning because something very important has happened. Helen has taken the second great step in her education. She has learned that everything has a name, and that the manual alphabet is the key to everything she wants to know.

In a previous letter I think I wrote that "mug" and "milk" had given Helen more trouble than all the rest. She confused the nouns with the verb "drink." She didn't know the word for "drink" but went through the pantomime of drinking whenever she spelled "mug" or "milk." This morning, while she was washing, she wanted to know the name for "water." When she wants to know the name of anything, she points to it and pats my hand. I spelled "w-a-t-e-r" and thought no more about it until after breakfast. Then it occurred to me that with the help of this new word I might succeed in straightening out the "mug-milk" difficulty. We went out to the pump-house and I made Helen hold her mug under the spout while I pumped. As the cold water gushed forth, filling the mug I spelled "w-a-t-e-r" in Helen's free hand. The word coming so close upon the sensation of cold water rushing over her hand seemed to startle her. She dropped the mug and stood as one transfixed. A new light came into her face. She spelled "water" several times. Then she dropped on the ground and asked for its name and pointed to the pump and the trellis, and suddenly turning round she asked for my name. I spelled "Teacher." Just then the nurse brought Helen's little sister into the pump-house, and Helen spelled "baby" and pointed to the nurse. All the way back to the house she was highly excited, and learned the name of every object she touched, so that in a few hours she had added thirty new words to her vocabulary. Here are some of them: Door, open, shut, give, go, come, and a great many more.

P.S. — I didn't finish my letter in time to get it posted last night; so I shall add a line. Helen got up this morning like a radiant fairy. She has flitted from object to object, asking the name of everything and kissing me for very gladness. Last night when I got in bed, she stole into my arms of her own accord and kissed me for the first time, and I thought my heart would burst, so full was it of joy. ■

THE STORY OF MY LIFE *by Helen Keller*

She brought me my hat and I knew I was going out into the warm sunshine. This thought, if a wordless sensation may be called a thought, made me hop and skip with pleasure.

We walked down the path to the well-house, attracted by the fragrance of the honeysuckle with which it was covered. Some one was drawing water and my teacher placed my hand under the spout. As the cool stream gushed over my hand she spelled into the other the word *water,* first slowly, then rapidly. I stood still, my whole attention fixed upon the motion of her fingers. Suddenly I felt a misty consciousness as of something forgotten — a thrill of returning thought; and somehow the mystery of language was revealed to me. I knew then that w-a-t-e-r meant the wonderful cool something that was flowing over my hand. That living word awakened my soul, gave it light, hope, joy, set it free! There were barriers still, it is true, but barriers that in time could be swept away.

I left the well-house eager to learn. Everything had a name, and each name gave birth to a new thought. As we returned to the house every object which I touched seemed to quiver with life. That was because I saw everything with the strange, new sight that had come to me. ■ ◄

Helen was unable to distinguish "mug," "milk," and "drink" as different aspects of her experience because she had not yet developed the idea that "everything has a name, and that the manual alphabet is the key to everything she wants to know." Helen came to this critical insight when she realized that the substance she was washing with in the morning ("water") was the same substance coming out of the pump ("water") and that she could identify both of these substances, now and in the future, by *giving them a name* ("water").

Clarity and Precision in Naming   Naming is the way that we identify things in the world, make distinctions among them, and describe them to others. Additionally, as we will see in the chapters ahead, naming is also the way that we *relate* things to one another. For example, using the name *apple* enables us to recognize and group together all the various kinds of apples in the world. At the same time, our more precise names for apples (such as MacIntosh, Delicious, Northern Spy, etc.) give us the means to distinguish the various kinds of apples contained in this larger group of "apples."

As another example, list all the different types of ice and snow that you can think of.

1. _____   4. _____   7. _____

2. _____   5. _____   8. _____

3. _____   6. _____   9. _____

Your ability to give descriptive names for ice and snow probably depends on what part of the country you live in (people in southern climates don't see a lot of ice and snow) and what your outdoor interests are (do you enjoy skiing?). Each different kind of ice and snow you are able to identify represents a distinction you are able to make in the world. Even people who live in northern climates will probably be able to identify only nine or ten different kinds of ice and snow.

One of the most striking examples of the power of naming in helping us identify and distinguish things in the world was discovered by the anthropologist Benjamin Lee Whorf. While studying the language of the Eskimos, he found that it included seventy-six different names for ice and snow. Each name described a distinct kind of ice and snow condition.

If you examine the names for ice and snow that you just listed, you will find that each of the words you identified represents a distinction you make in describing and understanding the world. "Slush" describes a much different condition than hard "glare ice." We must make these distinctions to understand what is going on in the world (is it snowing or sleeting?) and to make intelligent decisions based on this understanding. If we are driving a car, knowing whether we are driving on slush or glare ice will dramatically affect the decisions we make, such as how fast to drive, how much time to allow for braking, and even whether we should be driving at all.

Thus the names we have for ice and snow represent our understanding of this area of experience. Although these names are probably adequate for our needs and purposes, the knowledge they represent is general indeed compared with the highly detailed understanding of the Eskimos. For the Eskimos, almost every aspect of life (housing, travel, hunting, and fishing) depends on understanding the *exact* nature of ice and snow. Their detailed knowledge of this area of experience is expressed by using names to symbolize all the distinctions being made.

In most cases, our ability to develop a detailed understanding of an area of experience depends on our needs and interests. As we saw when exploring the perceiving process, the precision of our perceptions is based on our knowledge of the territory we are experiencing. For example, a person with musical expertise is able to make many distinctions about a given piece of music because of his or her interest and background in this area.

THINKING ACTIVITY

6.6 ▶ Select an area of experience in which you have a special interest and knowledge — plants, cars, music, sewing, food, sports, etc. Within that area of expertise, list some of the distinctive words that are a part of this experience. For example, your list could be of *things* (say, different types of spices or flours used in cooking), *techniques* or *strategies* (types of pitches used in baseball or shots in basketball), or *conditions* (road conditions for driving, soil or sun conditions for gardening).

Using the names or distinctive words you have identified, write a passage that describes this particular area of experience.

After completing your descriptive passage, share it with other members of your class so that they can experience your detailed understanding of this area of experience.

As a sample, a list of distinctive words and a piece about types of woodworking joints is included here.

WOODWORKING JOINTS

butt	rabbet	edge
miter	mortise and tenon	tongue and groove
lap	dovetail	finger
dado	halved-together	lock

At the heart of woodworking is the question: How do you join two pieces of wood together? In fact, this is the reason why cabinetmaking was traditionally known as the art of "joinery."

The simplest way to attach two pieces of wood is simply to nail or screw the edge of one board to another. This is known as a *butt joint*, from the word "abut." Though this is a simple joint, it is not a very strong joint because it depends entirely on the nail or screw to hold the two pieces together.

The *miter joint*, used in most picture frames, is like a butt joint except that the two edges which are to be joined are cut at an angle (usually 45 degrees) which together form a 90 degree corner.

Although it sounds like a cartoon character, the *dado joint* is in reality a strong, effective joint found in many bookshelves. It is formed by cutting a channel across one of the pieces to be joined into which the other board fits snugly.

To understand the *tongue and groove joint*, imagine sticking your tongue into a small opening — and then having it glued in place! Because of its unusual strength, this joint is used extensively in the construction of furniture (particularly chairs) that will receive a lot of active use over its lifetime.

The *dovetail joint*, cut in the shape of a dove's tail, is formed by fitting together two interlocking sets of "tails" in the same way that you interlock your fingers together. It is one of the strongest edge joints, and for this reason is used in making desk and bureau drawers because of the constant pulling and pushing these joints will receive.

In summary, joining two pieces of wood is not simply a matter of nailing them together — it is an art which has been developed over the last seven thousand years. In each case, the particular wood joint selected should reflect the specific purposes for which the joint will be used. ■ ◄

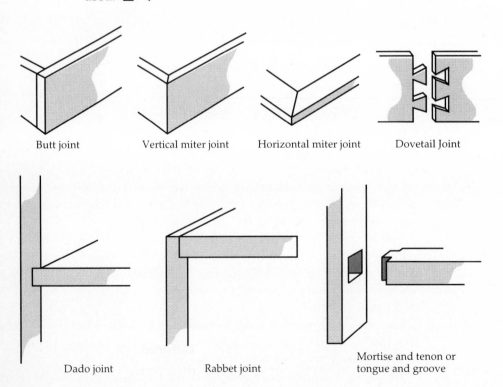

Butt joint   Vertical miter joint   Horizontal miter joint   Dovetail Joint

Dado joint   Rabbet joint   Mortise and tenon or tongue and groove

Sentence Meaning

It is said that the word is the basic element of language, and we have just discussed the importance of word meaning to language. Word meaning is important to our ability to organize experience and express concepts. But we rarely use single words alone. "Oh!" or "Help!" may be exceptions, but when we use even those words alone the pragmatic meaning (or situation) is usually unmistakable. That is why we could argue that the *sentence*, not the word, is the basic unit of speech.

When we relate concepts and ideas to each other, and when we speak or write about events, we use sentences that may be combined in a variety of structural combinations, or in other words, "grammatical constructions." We may have learned to think of *grammar* as "how we should speak or write." In this view, known as *prescriptive grammar*, "grammar" is an artificial mechanism that prescribes speakers' and writers' use of language. Prescriptive grammar tells us, for example, not to use double negatives like "don't have no" and not to end sentences with prepositions, as in, "Russian is the language the letter was written in." But people *do* use language in these ways, and they do it very naturally. Prescriptive grammar, then, really represents the "accepted" use of language.

In contrast to prescriptive grammar, *descriptive* grammar describes the nature of language and the way language functions. In other words, descriptive grammar reflects the structure of natural language. Because language and thinking are so closely related, the knowledge about language that descriptive grammar provides is essentially related to the structure of thinking. As a result, the process of becoming a sophisticated thinker is integrally involved in the process of mastering the complex structure of language.

Sentence Units: Verb Phrases and Noun Phrases

Natural language sentences (designated with the abbreviation *S*) are made up of *sentence units* (*SU*) that can be arranged in a variety of patterns. The sentences may:

- Stand alone (in *simple sentence* construction).
- Combine in a linear fashion (in *coordinate* construction).
- Combine hierarchically (in *subordinate* construction).

Each sentence unit is made up of two basic structural units: *verb phrases* (*VP*) and *noun phrases* (*NP*). We can represent this structure with the following diagram:

SU [NP   VP] ,

I   swim

Verb phrases consist of the verb, the representative of action or existence. For example, the verb phrase in the simple sentence unit "I swim" is "swim." The verb phrase also includes all the words that help describe or clarify the meaning represented by the verb. That means that in the simple sentence unit, "I swim in the summer," the verb phrase includes the group of words "in the summer" along with the verb "swim."

SU [NP   VP   ]

I   swim in the summer

Underline the verb phrase in the following sentences:

1. They ate beans for dinner.
2. A tall tree grew in the forest.
3. (Compose a sentence of your own and underline the verb phrase.)

———————————————————————————————

Noun phrases consist of the noun, the representative of people and objects. Noun phrases also include all the words that describe or add to the meaning of the noun. In the simple sentence unit, "I swim," then, the NP includes only "I." The same is true for the simple sentence unit, "I swim in the summer." If we add the group of words, "My friend and" to make the simple sentence unit, "My friend and I swim in the summer," then the NP becomes, "My friend and I."

SU [NP   VP   ]

My friend and I   swim in the summer

Underline the noun phrases in the previous two simple sentence units and in the simple sentence unit you composed as well.

1. They ate beans for dinner.

2. A tall tree grew in the forest.

3. _____

Simple Sentences

We mentioned that sentence units, made up of noun phrases and verb phrases, combine in three major constructions, or forms: *simple, coordinate,* or *subordinate*. The sentence forms we use when we speak or write reflect the connections of our thoughts, and these connections are influenced by the contexts in which they occur. These sentence forms also influence the connections of the thoughts of our listeners and readers. As an example, in the course of our discussion, the following situation narrated by a traveler will be explained from three perspectives. These perspectives illustrate the varying relationships of simple, coordinate, and subordinate sentence forms with patterns of thinking. Here is the first version:

> It was Memorial Day 1990 and a lovely time to take a leisurely trip up the coast. I looked forward to the relaxing prospect of browsing around the lazy town and maybe catching an old time parade. As I drove along the scenic route, dividing my attention between the gentle curves of the road and the spectacular view to my right, I came upon a police car blocking the road. The officer standing outside his vehicle flagged me off the road.
>
> "Stop right here. No traffic's goin' through," he told me.
> "I just want to get into town."
> "Then park ya' car over there." (He pointed.) "Walk right down that street. Take ya' first right. Then take a left. You'll be standin' in Dock Square."
> "Okay."
> "Wait a minute, ma'am. Let me see ya' handbag."
> "What?"
> "Well, he's givin' a speech in the square in just about an hour. We've got to check everything." (He smiled.) "Hurry up now. You'll miss the whole thing."

In this account, the officer's "explanation" consists of *simple* sentences, with the exception of "We've got to check everything." The simple sentence contains only one *sentence unit*; that is, one noun phrase and one verb phrase. Examples of the officer's sentence forms are:

SU [NP   VP   ]
         Well, he   's givin' a speech in the square in just about an hour

SU [NP   VP   ]
         No traffic   's goin' through

Remember that both the noun phrase and the verb phrase may contain a number of words (and phrases) that enhance the meaning of the noun — as in "your first *right*" — or the verb — as in, "*givin'* a speech in the square." Underline the noun phrases and circle the verb phrases in the following sentences from the officer's dialogue.

1. You'll miss the whole thing.

2. Walk right down that street.

3. You'll be standin' in Dock Square.

THINKING ACTIVITY
_____

6.7   ▶ Reread the traveler's interaction with the officer. Explain how using simple sentences influence the thoughts and actions that are being expressed. ◀

THINKING ACTIVITY
_____

6.8   ▶ Think about a situation in which you were trying to figure out what was going on and someone was giving you an explanation. Recreate the explanation using only simple sentence construction. ◀

Coordinate and Subordinate Sentences

Language is rich and complex. Usually sophisticated thinkers don't speak or write only in simple sentences, they use more complex types of sentences as well. Although language and thinking are distinct processes, they are closely and inextricably intertwined at an early stage of human development. As a result, complexity of language goes hand in hand with complexity of thought. That is, complex language encourages complex thinking, and thinking in complex ways gives rise to complex language structures. Combining sentences in complex and varied ways encourages thinking that joins and juxtaposes thoughts and ideas from various perspectives.

Coordinate sentences and *subordinate sentences* are the two types of complex sentence structures that the English language uses, and they are common in both our speech and writing. Coordinate sentences and subordinate sentences both include more than one sentence unit (SU), composed of a noun phrase (NP) and verb phrase (VP). The difference between these two major sentence types is the way in which the sentence units are connected to each other.

Coordinate sentences   In *coordinate sentences*, neither sentence unit is more important or carries more weight in terms of the meaning of the whole sentence. In a *subordinate sentence*, one of the sentence units can always stand on its own with respect to the meaning of the sentence while the others depend on it to make the meaning of the entire sentence complete. These relationships are illustrated in the diagram:

- Coordinate sentence = S [[SU] [SU]]
- Subordinate sentence = S [SU [[SU]]]

Let's see how *coordinate sentence* construction works in the continuing narrative of our traveler's situation.

> My mouth opened to question the officer further, but he had already addressed another driver. So I made my way on foot. It was only a minute before I approached what seemed to me a native — also on foot.
>
> "What's going on?"
> "Memorial Day ceremonies. There's a parade and we'll hear a speech. Same as usual. We're awful proud to have George doin' the honors this year. All those important folks in Washington, and he comes down here and he's just like one of us. And he's movin' all the time he's here — golfin', fishin', joggin'. But you better get movin' yourself or you won't see anything."

The explanation by the local resident was comprised largely of *coordinate sentences* such as "There's a parade and we'll hear a speech." Coordinate sentences are made up of at least two sentence units (SU), each with a noun phrase (NP) and a verb phrase (VP). This example can be diagrammed:

```
S [SU [NP        VP       ]   SU [NP        VP        ] ]
There         's a parade          we        'll hear a speech
```

Now underline the sentence units in the sentences spoken by the local resident:

1. All those important folks in Washington, and he comes down here and he's just like one of us.

2. And he's movin' all the time he's here — golfin', fishin', joggin'. But you better get movin' yourself or you won't see anything.

Just as in the case of the simple sentence, the degree of description in the noun phrase or in the verb phrase has nothing to do with making a sentence coordinate. A sentence is a coordinate sentence if it contains two or more sentence units that carry the same weight in the meaning of the entire sentence. "The ship rolled to its side and then it sank" is a coordinate sentence; so is, "The giant passenger ship with hundreds on board rolled to its side, and then it sank" and "The ship rolled slowly, laboriously, to its side, and then it sank with a mighty splash."

THINKING ACTIVITY
─────────────────────

6.9   ▶ Rewrite the "explanation" you wrote in simple sentences in Thinking Activity 6.8 using coordinate sentences. How does using coordinate sentences influence your interpretation of the situation? Compare the relationship between the ideas in the simple sentence explanation to that of the explanation you wrote in coordinate sentences. ◀

Coordinate sentence construction is often used to express a number of important thinking patterns, which we will be examining in Chapter Nine, *Relating and Organizing*:

• *Chronological* thinking patterns: relating events in time sequence

• *Process* thinking patterns: relating aspects of the growth, development, or change of an act, event, or object

• *Comparative* thinking patterns: relating things in the same general category in terms of their similarities and dissimilarities

• *Analogical* thinking patterns: relating things belonging to different categories in terms of each other to increase our understanding of them

The following chart describes some of the language-thinking links between these syntactic patterns and thinking patterns:

Syntactic Patterns:	Language-Thinking Links (Connectors):	Thinking Patterns:
Sentence coordination	and, or, but, nor, either, neither, like, as, -er, more, similar to	Chronological, process Comparative, analogical

Subordinate sentences   In *subordinate sentences*, two or more sentence units are joined in hierarchical relationships: That is, one sentence is considered to be more important to the meaning being expressed than the other sentence unit. One of the sentence units always carries the main idea or meaning of the sentence, whereas the other sentence units add to or modify that meaning, as illustrated in the diagram:

$$\text{Subordinate sentences} = S \left[\; SU \left[\; [SU] \; \right] \right]$$

When we *subordinate* sentence units, we are relating ideas so closely that they rely on each other to express the full meaning of the sentence — the entire meaning that the speaker or writer wants to convey. When we use *subordinate* sentences, we reveal the relationships of our thoughts to each other in a specific way, just as we do with *simple* sentences and *coordinate* sentences. In other words, our syntax reflects and influences our thinking processes.

Let's examine the final explanation of the roadblock situation given our traveler — this time in *subordinate* sentence form.

> — George? Then it clicked. This was Kennebunkport, the location of the President's summer house. He must have come for the weekend and agreed to participate in the town's Memorial Day ceremonies. Although I could only catch a glimpse of George Bush through the crowd, I could recognize my situation in the article in the next day's local newspaper.

Residents and Tourists Cram K'port for Memorial

When media hype hit Kennebunkport during George Bush's first presidential summer at Walker's Point, it drew even more vacationers than usual to a town that has catered to tourists since the turn of the century. Kennebunkport police officer William Redman noted that traffic this weekend suggests that this summer will bring an equally large number of tourists coming to gawk at Bush.

Monday morning, authorities blocked off roads so that no one would know which route Bush was taking to Dock Square, where he was scheduled to deliver the annual Memorial Day address. Increased concern with security required all those who wanted to observe the holiday in town to have their handbags and packages examined after parking their cars outside the commercial area. Despite minor inconvenience, all went smoothly, and townfolk and visitors alike seemed to appreciate Presidential participation in a long-standing local tradition.

A sentence like "Increased concern with security required all those who wanted to observe the holiday in town to have their handbags and packages examined after parking their cars outside the commercial area" is subordinate. This is because the sentence is composed of sentence units that, although dependent on each other to express the full meaning of the sentence, are unequal in importance. This structure is illustrated in the following diagram of the sentence:

Increased concern with security required all those	*Main sentence unit*
who wanted to observe the holiday in town	*Subordinate sentence unit*
to have their handbags and packages examined	*Main sentence unit*
after parking their cars outside the commercial area	*Subordinate sentence unit*

As the diagram indicates, this single sentence contains several sentence units, all of which connect to the idea that people were having their handbags and packages examined. Connections among sentence units in subordinate sentences often reflect a number of important thinking concepts.

• *Time* concepts: relating things in time sequence
• *Condition* concepts: relating events when the occurrence of one event depends on the occurrence of another event
• *Causal* concepts: relating events in terms of the way some event(s) are responsible for bringing about other event(s)

In the sentence we are examining, for example, the sentence unit "who wanted to observe the holiday in town" reflects a *condition* on "having their handbags and packages examined"; whereas the sentence unit "after parking their cars outside the commercial area" reflects an element of *time* related to "having their handbags and packages examined." If the sentence had read, "People going into town had to have their handbags and packages examined because police were concerned about security," the sentence unit beginning "because" would have reflected an element of *cause*. The following chart demonstrates the language-thinking links between subordinate linguistic forms and thinking patterns that we will explore in Chapter Nine, *Relating and Organizing.*

Syntactic Patterns:	Language-Thinking Links (connectors):	Thinking Patterns:
S Subordination *Time*	when, until, after, before, since	Chronological, process
S Subordination *Condition*	when, until, unless, if	Comparative, analogical
S Subordination *Cause*	because, so, so that, since	Causal

Sentence subordination is particularly important because whenever we change a *connector* (language-thinking link) or change the order of a sentence unit, the focus of meaning and thinking expressed by the sentence also changes. For example, in the sentence, "When media hype hit Kennebunkport during George Bush's first presidential summer at Walker's Point, it drew even more vacationers than usual to a town that has catered to tourists since the turn of the century," the focus is on the effect of "media hype." Notice how the focus changes if we reconstruct the sentence subordination: "Media hype drew even more vacationers than usual to a town that has catered to tourists since the turn of the century, when it hit Kennebunkport during George Bush's first presidential summer at Walker's Point."

THINKING ACTIVITY

6.10 ▶ Rewrite the "explanation" you previously wrote in simple sentences and coordinate sentences in Thinking Activities 6.8 and 6.9, this time using only subordinate sentences. ◀

THINKING ACTIVITY

6.11 ▶ Review the "explanations" you wrote in simple, coordinate, and subordinate form and analyze them by answering the following questions:

1. How do the various syntactic forms influence the thoughts and actions you expressed?

2. What thinking patterns are linked to each of the different accounts?

3. Describe possible contexts and audiences for which you might use each "explanation."

Review the three accounts of the Kennebunkport traveler and analyze them by answering these same questions. ◄

It is clear from our explorations that a very close relationship exists between language on one hand and thinking and thinking patterns on the other. We have just examined some of the interrelationships between syntactic patterns and thinking patterns. Earlier in the chapter we discussed the connection between types of word meaning and the ideas, feelings, and experiences being expressed. Besides syntax and word choice, vocal signals such as emphasis, pausing, and inflection offer strong support to meaning. Even a single word like "Oh!" can be spoken to suggest a number of meanings. The same is true of simple sentences. For example, the question: "Where is the waiter?" asked in a restaurant, can convey a variety of thoughts depending on the emphasis that the speaker places on the individual words and his or her inflection of the question. In coordinate and subordinate sentences, emphasis, pausing, and inflection signals help clarify meaning and make it precise, and in this way vocal attributes contribute to linking syntactic and thinking patterns. These links complete the holistic process of thought and language connection.

Using Language Effectively

To develop our ability to use language effectively to communicate our thoughts, feelings, and experiences, we have to understand how language functions when it is used well. We do this without conscious thought by reading widely. By reading much good writing, we get a "feel" for how language can be used effectively. We can get more specific ideas by analyzing the work of highly regarded writers, who use semantic and syntactical meanings accurately. They also often use many action verbs, concrete nouns, and vivid adjectives to communicate effectively. By doing so, they appeal to our senses and help us understand clearly what is being communicated. Good writers may also vary sentence length to keep the reader's attention and create a variety of sentence styles to enrich meaning. An equally important strategy is for us to write ourselves and then have others evaluate our writing and give us suggestions for improving it. We will be using both of these strategies in the pages that follow.

THINKING ACTIVITY

6.12 ▶ The following selection — an ongoing narrative that the author separates into three episodes, one about a place, one about an experience, and one about a person — is from *Blue Highways*, a book written by a young man of Native American heritage named William Least Heat Moon. After losing his teaching job at a university and separating from his wife, he decided to explore America. He outfitted his van (named "Ghost Dancing") and drove around the country using back roads (represented on the maps by blue lines) rather than superhighways. During his travels, he saw fascinating sights, met intriguing people, and developed some significant insights about himself.

These passages use language to communicate aspects of Moon's experience. Read each passage carefully and then answer the questions that follow.

From BLUE HIGHWAYS *by William Least Heat Moon*

A Place

Two Steller's jaybirds stirred an argy-bargy in the ponderosa. They shook their big beaks, squawked and hopped and swept down the sunlight toward Ghost Dancing and swooshed back into the pines. They didn't shut up until I left some orts from breakfast; then they dropped from the branches like ripe fruit, nabbed a gobful, and took off for the tops of the hundred-foot trees. The chipmunks got in on it too, letting loose a high peal of rodent chatter, picking up their share, spinning the bread like pinwheels, chewing fast.

It was May Day, and the warm air filled with the scent of pine and blooming manzanita. To the west I heard water over rock as Hat Creek came down from the snows of Lassen. I took towel and soap and walked through a field of volcanic ejections and broken chunks of lava to the stream bouncing off boulders and slicing over bedrock; below one cascade, a pool the color of glacier ice circled the effervescence. On the bank at an upright stone with a basin-shaped concavity filled with rainwater,

I bent to drink, then washed my face. Why not bathe from head to toe? I went down with rainwater and lathered up.

An Experience

Now, I am not unacquainted with mountain streams; a plunge into Hat Creek would be an experiment in deep-cold thermodynamics. I knew that, so I jumped in with bravado. It didn't help. Light violently flashed in my head. The water was worse than I thought possible. I came out, eyes the size of biscuits, metabolism running amuck and setting fire to the icy flesh. I buffed dry.

Then I began to feel good, the way the old Navajos must have felt after a traditional sweat bath and roll in the snow. I dressed and sat down to watch Hat Creek. A pair of dippers flew in and began feeding. Robin-like birds with stub tails and large, astonished eyes, dippers feed in a way best described as insane. With two or three deep kneebends (hence their name) as if working up nerve, they hopped into the water and walked upstream, completely immersed, strolling and pecking along the bottom. Then they broke from the water, dark eyes gasping. I liked Hat Creek. It was reward enough for last night.

Another Person

Back at Ghost Dancing, I saw a camper had pulled up. On the rear end, by the strapped-on aluminum chairs, was something like "The Wandering Watkins." Time to go. I kneeled to check a tire. A smally furry white thing darted from behind the wheel, and I flinched. Because of it, the journey would change.

"Harmless as a stuffed toy." The voice came from the other end of the leash the dog was on. "He's nearly blind and can't hear much better. Down just to the nose now." The man, with polished cowboy boots and a part measured out in the white hair, had a face so gullied even the Soil Conservation Commission couldn't have reclaimed it. But his eyes seemed lighted from within.

"Are you Mr. Watkins?" I asked.

"What's left of him. The pup's what's left of Bill. He's a Pekingese. Chinese dog. In dog years, he's even older than I am, and I respect him for that. We're two old men. What's your name?"

"Same as the dog's."

"I wanted to give him a Chinese name, but old what's-her-face over there in the camper wouldn't have it. Claimed she couldn't pronounce

Chinese names. I says, 'You can't say Lee?' She says, 'You going to name a dog Lee?' 'No,' I says, 'but what do you think about White Fong?' Now, she's not a reader unless it's a beauty parlor magazine with a Kennedy or Hepburn woman on the cover, so she never understood the name. You've read your Jack London, I hope. She says, 'When I was a girl we had a horse called William, but that name's too big for that itty-bitty dog. Just call him Bill.' That was that. She's a woman of German descent and a decided person. But when old Bill and I are out on our own, I call him White Fong."

Watkins had worked in a sawmill for thirty years, then retired to Redding; now he spent time in his camper, sometimes in the company of Mrs. Watkins.

"I'd stay on the road, but what's-her-face won't have it."

As we talked, Mrs. What's-her-face periodically thrust her head from the camper to call instructions to Watkins or White Fong. A finger-wagging woman, full of injunctions for man and beast. Whenever she called, I watched her, Watkins watched me, and the dog watched him. Each time he would say, "Well, boys, there you have it. Straight from the back of the horse."

"You mind if I swear?" I said I didn't. "The old biddy's in there with her Morning Special — sugar doughnut, boysenberry jam, and a shot of Canadian Club in her coffee. In this beauty she sits inside with her letters.

"What kind of work you in?" he asked.

That question again. "I'm out of work," I said to simplify.

"A man's never out of work if he's worth a damn. It's just sometimes he doesn't get paid. I've gone unpaid my share and I've pulled my share of pay. But that's got nothing to do with working. A man's work is doing what he's supposed to do, and that's why he needs a catastrophe now and again to show him a bad turn isn't the end, because a bad stroke never stops a good man's work. Let me show you my philosophy of life." From his pressed Levi's he took a billfold and handed me a limp business card. "Easy. It's very old."

The card advertised a cafe in Merced when telephone numbers were four digits. In quotation marks was a motto: "Good Home Cooked Meals."

"'Good Home Cooked Meals' is your philosophy?"

"Turn it over, peckerwood."

Imprinted on the back in tiny, faded letters was this:

> I've been bawled out, balled up, held up, held down, hung up, bulldozed, blackjacked, walked on, cheated, squeezed and mooched; stuck for war tax, excess profits tax, sales tax, dog tax, and syntax, Liberty Bonds, baby bonds, and the bonds of matrimony, Red Cross, Blue Cross, and the double cross; I've worked like hell, worked others like hell, have got drunk and got others drunk, lost all I had, and now because I won't spend or lend what little I earn, beg, borrow or steal, I've been cussed, discussed, boycotted, talked to, talked about, lied to, lied about, worked over, pushed under, robbed, and damned near ruined. The only reason I'm sticking around now is to see
> WHAT THE HELL IS NEXT.

"I like it," I said.

"Any man's true work is to get his boots on each morning. Curiosity gets it done about as well as anything else." ■

1. How effectively does the selection share the thoughts, feelings, or experiences of the author? The following questions may help you evaluate your understanding of what is being communicated. For the passage about a place, ask yourself, "How well can I visualize the place that is being described?" For the description of an experience, ask, "How well can I imagine what it might be like to undergo a similar experience?" Finally, after reading the passage about a person, ask, "How well do I get a sense of what this person is like?"

2. If the selection is effective, why? Which words made this writing effective? Why? ◄

THINKING ACTIVITY

6.13 ▶ After rereading the passages from *Blue Highways*, create your own descriptions of:

1. A *place* you are familiar with.

2. An important *experience* you have had.

3. A *person* whom you know.

These passages do not have to be related to each other, though they may be, if you wish. As you write your passages, try to use language to communicate as effectively as possible the thoughts, feelings, and experiences you are trying to share. The following is a passage written by a student. As you read it, evaluate how successful she is in communicating her thoughts and feelings about this experience.

An Experience

The most important experience that I've ever had was leaving home to go live in a group home. I was nine years old on the day I was leaving. I knew why I was going, but I still didn't really understand what good my leaving home was going to do.

It was 12:00 p.m. and there was a knock at the door. I looked through the peephole, and I saw a tall, Caucasian woman. My heart started to race; I knew she was here to take me away from everything I had ever known and loved. I looked at my mother and she said, ''What are you waiting for? Open the door.'' When I opened the door, Miss Gold smiled at me and said, ''Good morning.'' She and my mother spoke for a while while I got my suitcases from my room. I came out of the room, and asked her if she was ready. I didn't want to spend too much time saying goodbye, because I knew that after more than three minutes of this I'd break down in tears. I was supposed to be strong and brave and leave with a smile; so I did.

I got into the car and I said nothing to Miss Gold during the ride to the Bronx.

It felt as though I was starting a new life all over again. I was to live in a place where I had never lived before. I was to live with girls I had never met in my life. I was to be taken care of by people whom I didn't know and, worst of all, by people who didn't know me. In a way, I had to forget the lifestyle I was living and start a new one, but I was never going to forget the fact that I had to be strong and brave and always with a smile.

I lived there for three years. I learned a lot from this experience. I learned how to deal with strangers. I learned to appreciate a family, family life, and all the things that go along with it. Most of all I learned a lot about myself and how to deal with certain feelings that I had. Ever since then I've been the kind of person who keeps a lot of thoughts to myself. I've learned to deal with a lot of problems myself.

```
     All in all, I feel it was a good experience for me. I've
matured much faster than I would have if I didn't expe-
rience this, and this helps me with a lot of people and
things I deal with now. When I look back at this experi-
ence, I say to myself, ''If you made it through that,
Kathy, you can make it through almost anything.'' ◄
```

THINKING ACTIVITY

6.14   ►   The following essay, written by the linguist Sandra Dickinson, ties together
many of this chapter's major themes regarding the nature of language and its
relation to thought. After reading the essay, complete the questions that
follow.

WHEN IS A KAMOODGEL NOT A KAMOODGEL?
by Sandra Dickinson

"Which came first — the chicken or the egg?" As a child, do you remember the moment when this seemingly innocuous question suddenly became transformed into a most delightful and baffling riddle? "If the
chicken came first, then there was no egg it could hatch from! But if the
egg came first, then there was no chicken to lay the egg!" Our lives are
full of mind-twisting questions that resist our efforts at clear, precise
analysis: "What happens when an irresistible force meets an immovable
object?" "What is the relation between my mind and my body?" "How
do I know that the color 'red' that I see is the same as the color 'red' that
you see?" "Is my personality determined by my genetic history or my
environmental experiences?" "If God created the universe, then who
created God?" "If God didn't create the universe, then how did everything get here?"

When we reflect on the twin phenomena of language and thought,
we immediately find ourselves entrapped in a thicket of vexing questions and baffling riddles. For example, consider the following question:
"In developing our understanding of the world around us, which comes
first — the word or the idea?" The question of the relation between
language and thought expresses a riddle that embraces a basic mystery
of human nature. It is the question of how language, often cited as the
single phenomenon most clearly separating humans from animals, relates to thinking, the highest and noblest attribute of humans.

Let us try to dramatize this conundrum. Write your first name in the space provided: _____ . Now consider this question: How did you come to realize that these sounds symbolized *you*, your "self"? Did the experience of people consistently referring to you by this *word* gradually lead you to develop an *idea* or *thought* of "who" you are, your "self"? Or did you first develop an *idea* or *thought* of your "self" that then gradually became associated with this *word*? Which came first, the word or the idea, language or thought?

This same issue can be dramatized in the following scenario. Imagine that a friend excitedly describes the strange animal she encountered while vacationing in Australia. Walking along an isolated stream, she came upon an animal that she has decided to name a "kamoodgel," in honor of the small Scandinavian village where her family comes from. "What does it look like?" you ask. "It's hard to believe that you've actually discovered a new species!" She responds: "I first saw it swimming in the water towards the bank. It's large and hairy, and it has a broad, flat tail and webbed feet." You laugh. Easily retrieving what you believe is the correct word/idea, you state condescendingly: "It's only a beaver! You saw a beaver! I'm afraid that won't get you on the cover of *Natural History*!" "That's what I thought at first, too," your friend replies. "But when it reached the bank, it walked over to a nest containing several large eggs, and it carefully *sat* on them like a chicken!" Shaken, you vainly search your mental file for the correct word/idea. Beavers don't lay eggs! "And that's not all," your friend continues. "It didn't have a regular mouth or nose — it had a *bill*, like a duck!" Thoroughly confused, with no ready word or idea to attach to this strange creature, you begin to wonder if there will be room for *two* people and the creature on the cover of *Natural History*. And then, somewhere in the subterranean depths of your mind, a small bubble is released, a bubble formed years ago in the dim memories of your sixth-grade biology class. As it rises slowly towards the surface of your consciousness, its shape gradually becomes more defined, until the word and idea burst simultaneously in your mind and out your mouth: "It's a *platypus*!"

As both of these examples suggest, language and thought are typically so intertwined as often to be indistinguishable from each other. But let us return to our earlier question: Which comes first, the word or the idea, language or thought? The dilemma posed by the relationship between language and thought has preoccupied philosophers, linguists, writers, and psychologists for centuries. For example, many thinkers have tried to explain our development of language and thought in terms of teaching and experience. Following in the tradition of seventeenth-century English philosopher John Locke, this perspective assumes that the human mind enters life as a blank slate (*tabula rasa*) that is gradually inscribed through teaching and experience. This school of thought was termed *Empiricism* because of its emphasis on empirical experience in the development of human understanding. The main difficulty with this view is that although teaching and experience certainly have a significant impact on the development of language and thought, teaching and experience simply cannot account for the speed and complexity with which thought and language are developed by children. It seems clear that the human mind enters life with certain inborn ("innate") capacities to develop language and thought.

In contrast to John Locke, the eighteenth-century French philosopher René Descartes believed that the important elements of thought and language are "innate," existing in the human mind independently of experience. Beginning with a point of absolute certainty, his famous *cogito ergo sum* ("I think, therefore I am"), Descartes believed that we could, through rational reflection, deduce all of the important principles of human thought and reason. Many philosophers and linguists have followed in this *Rationalist* tradition (so termed because of its emphasis of reflective reason over empirical experience), including the modern linguist, Noam Chomsky. Chomsky proposed the existence of innate, universal language abilities possessed by virtually all people in all cultures. Critics of this view, however, have argued that it tends to ignore the extremely significant role that experience plays in the development of language and thought.

Immanuel Kant, an eighteenth-century German philosopher, brought an integrating perspective to the way we develop language and thought, combining both the Empiricist and the Rationlist viewpoints. He believed that even though some basic thought and language structures are innate, they must be used in conjunction with our experience in order to produce knowledge and ability. He summed up this position with the statement: "Percepts [*perceptions*] without concepts are blind; concepts without percepts are empty."

The ideas of the twentieth-century linguist Edward Sapir on the relation of language and thought follow in this Kantian tradition. Sapir examines the question through literature, describing language as a prepared "road" or "groove" for thinking. In his view of the language-thought relationship, thought is implicit in the forms of language and, reciprocally, language builds thought. Instead of regarding language as merely a means of labeling and expressing thought, he believes that the product (thought) grows with the instrument (language). In literature, for example, language is a subtle skeleton providing form for thought that becomes evident only when the regular form is changed. Languages, according to Sapir, are "invisible garments that drape themselves about our spirit and give a predetermined form to all its symbolic expression." (1921:221)

As a medium for symbolic expression we know as literature, Sapir says that language goes unnoticed until the artist transgresses the law of his medium. Only then do we realize that there is a medium to obey. Certainly the use of language in the two following stanzas of the poem by e e cummings draws attention to the form of the thought expressed:

> o by the by
> has anybody seen
> little you — i
> who stood on a green
> hill and threw   5
> his wish at blue
>
> with a swoop and a dart
> out flew his wish
> (it dived like a fish
> but it climbed like a dream)   10
> throbbing like a heart
> singing like a flame

In this poem e e cummings "transgresses" not only the conventions of written language, such as punctuation and capitalization that signal language units, but, more in accord with Sapir's remarks, the laws of language itself. For example, he violates syntax, using adjectives such as "blue" in line 6 as a noun. cummings also rearranges the semantic features of some words: "wish" given animation in line 8 is an example. cummings, however, is a master transgressor, as he knows that other breaks of form such as exchanging nouns and verbs — an example would be the transformation of line 11 to "hearting like a throb" — would not draw attention to his thoughts and feelings but would rather obscure them. He recognizes that thinking and language — even in literature — intertwine within certain boundaries.

The modern American linguist Noam Chomsky outlined these boundaries in his theory on language — a theory very much concerned with the language and thought question in the Rationalist tradition. His theory defines language as a unique aspect of knowing — in some ways separate from all other faculties of mind. In his view, human beings are predetermined to acquire language much in the same way they are predetermined to walk upright. Just as humans display variation in gait and style of walking within the boundaries of upright motor patterns, human languages display variety of sound combinations and grammar within the boundaries of certain linguistic universals.

Chomsky's theory proposes that all human languages have linguistic universals such as relationships between Subjects (dogs, for example) and Predicates (bark, for example) in the sentence "Dogs bark." His theory also identifies major syntactic categories such as Noun Phrase (the big brown dog) and Verb Phrase (barks all night in the yard) in the sentence "The big brown dog barks all night in the yard." In addition, Chomsky's theory identifies ways of making sounds (like lip closure in the sound "p") and basic language categories such as "animate" and "inanimate," as linguistic universals.

Like Descartes, Chomsky bases his approach to the language-thinking problem entirely on the concept of innate "competence," the *capacity* to use language, rather than on the actual *use* of that capacity, as Sapir did. The use of language Chomsky calls "performance." Although performance constitutes the only real-world evidence of competence, Chomsky contends that an individual's linguistic performance is clouded by "imperfections" such as slips of the tongue, "We were beaten (eaten) by mosquitoes"; malapropisms, "I was told to see the choreographer (coordinator)"; and memory lapses, "I uh, uh, forgot what I was going to say!"

Those who disagree with Chomsky's theory, on the other hand, contend that it doesn't make sense to separate "competence" from "performance," arguing that if you can't say it, then you don't really "know" it. They claim that theory should be demonstrated through behavior and that Chomsky's universals should be testable by linguistic experiments.

These concerns have led many people to a view that integrates competence and performance, capacity and use, in the tradition of Kant. This point of view, that language is a mental process integral to cognition (knowing) and that both language and cognition are reflected in human behavior, spawned a new field of study now known as "psycholinguistics" because of its dual emphasis on mental processes ("psycho") and language ("linguistics"). Psycholinguists' interest in the language and thinking questions tends to focus on performance as opposed to competence; but they approach the problem from the point of view of processes, particularly the process of development.

Psycholinguists in the Western world began initially to examine earlier research done by Soviet psychologists on the relationships between language and thought. Most known among these Soviets are Lev Vygotsky and his pupil A. R. Luria. Both Vygotsky and Luria take the view that language and thought are inextricably linked. It is a link that forms in childhood and continues thereafter. Vygotsky states this view explicitly: "Thought and speech have different roots, merging only at a certain moment in ontogenesis, after which these two functions develop together under reciprocal influence." (1934:xxxi)

Solving the riddle of the relationship between language and thought constitutes one of the major questions in the work of both these scientists. In attempting to unravel this relation, they sometimes focus on thinking and sometimes on language. According to their view, an individual's intellectual development is comprised of processes. One early process in the child's development of thinking is the formation of "chains of ideas." An example is three-year-old Jonathan who, having watched several objects being removed from a bag, responded to the questions, "Which things go together?" by saying, "boy and girl." When he was asked "Why?" he answered, "because they belong in the bag," chaining these ideas together by physical proximity rather than more abstract connections like shared properties (for instance, "They both represent people").

This earlier level of thinking creates a basis for later generalizations and concepts. But sophisticated concepts presuppose more than unification. To form a concept it is also necessary to abstract, to single out elements and view these elements apart from the concrete situation in which they are imbedded. An older child might, for example, group the boy and girl together because, "They're going to be the brother and sister in my playhouse after snack time." In concept formation it is equally important to unite and to separate; to analyze elements and synthesize them, and then to organize them in a hierarchical system of relations.

Vygotsky and Luria point out that language is involved in these thinking processes from the beginning. By naming objects, and so defining their connections and relations (to the world), the adult creates new forms of the reflection of reality in the child, incomparably deeper than what he would have formed from individual experience. This process of transmitting knowledge helps in forming concepts. The word distinguishes necessary features among objects and relates the perceived object to a definite category: for example, relating the girl doll to the category of "sister."

At the same time, behind words there is the independent grammar of thought, the syntax of word meanings. The simplest utterance, far from reflecting a constant, rigid correspondence between sound and meaning, is really a process. When a two-year-old says excitedly, "car!" he may mean he sees a car, he wants a car, he wants to ride in a car, or another action related to cars. The child's thought, because it is initially amorphous, must find expression in a single word. As his thoughts become more differentiated, the child is less likely to express them in single words, but constructs a composite whole such as, "I want to play with the blue car." Conversely, Vygotsky and Luria contend that progress in speech helps the child's thoughts progress as well, to become increasingly complex and precise. This complexity and precision is expressed in thought through conceptual clarity and logical relationships, and is expressed in language through word use and syntax (grammar).

As thinking and language develop to maturity, the combination of words in a sentence enables humans not only to indicate an object and include it in a system of relationships, but also to formulate and express thoughts. The existence of language and its complex logico-grammatical structures enable humans to derive conclusions on the basis of logical arguments. The mystery is that these logical arguments are far removed from the "reasons" that objects belong together offered by Jonathan and others of his classmates who asserted, for example, that "the spoon goes with the washcloth because they belong"; or even the more sophisticated, "the boy and girl belong together because they wanna kiss." The logico-grammatical relationships and organization of thinking expressed in language such as "because," "if," "as soon as," "in order to," and "before" are all evident in a college student's thinking, as his statement of a problem and his proposed solution demonstrates:

> I have a problem with money *because* I'm an impulsive spender. I need to resolve this problem *because* I'm always out of money at a time of need. First, I'm going to start a personal ledger and put my money into the bank *as soon as* I get it. Second, I must stop buying on impulse. Third, I will take a few days to decide *if* I'm going to purchase something I want. *In order to* do this I must weigh pros against cons in buying an item. Last, but not least, I'm going to check my budget *before* I finally purchase anything.

Despite our increased understanding regarding the nature of language and thought, however, the profound philosophical questions remain. How do you get from amorphous thoughts and simple words to complex, logical thinking and complex arrangements of sentences? What is the relation between thought and language, and which comes first? When is a kamoodgel not a kamoodgel? (When it's a platypus?)

Historical and developmental study have left the nature of the relationships between language and thinking a glorious riddle. Even in light of centuries of questions and investigation, says Vygotsky, "As soon as we start approaching these relations, the most complex and grand panorama opens before our eyes. Its intricate architectonics surpasses the richest imagination of research schemas." (1934:218) His conclusion, Vygotsky believes, can be elaborated only by one of the great masters of thinking and language in modern history, the Russian novelist Leo Tolstoy: "The relations of word to thought, and the creation of new concepts is a complex, delicate, and enigmatic process unfolding in our soul." ■

References

Primary

cummings, e e *100 selected poems*. Grove Press, Inc., New York, 1923.
Sapir, Edward. *Language*. Harcourt Brace Jovanovich, New York, 1921.
Vygotsky, Lev. *Thought and Language* (1934). A. Kozulin, ed. and trans. The MIT Press, Cambridge, Mass., 1986.

Secondary

Luria, A. R. *Language and Cognition*. John Wiley and Sons, New York, 1982.
Luria, A. R., and Yudovich, F. *Speech and the Development of Mental Processes in the Child*. Penguin Books, Baltimore, 1971.
Piatelli-Palmarini, M. (ed.) *Language and Learning*. Harvard University Press, Cambridge, Mass., 1980.

1. Explain why the author believes that the relation between language and thought presents a complex and problematic dilemma.

2. Reflect on the mental process you used in conceiving and writing your answer to the first question. What role did your thinking play? What role did your use of language play? Describe how your thinking and language interacted with one another.

3. a. Compose a description of something you think is beautiful. Make the description as precise and vivid as possible.

   b. Read your description to a classmate and have that person draw a picture of it.

   c. Ignoring variation and artistic talent, explain the degree to which your classmate's drawing reflects your thoughts about what you had in mind.

   d. Explain how this activity embodies the relation between language and thought. ◄

Summary

Every time we use language we send a message about our thinking. We have just examined in some detail the creature we call *language*. We have seen that it is composed of small cells, or units, pieces of sound that combine to form larger units called *words*. In exploring words, we noted that they themselves are not simple. Rather, words relate to each other (*syntactically*); to objects, feelings, actions, and thoughts in the world (*semantically*); to each person's individual associations and consciousness (*perceptually*); and to the situation in which they are used (*pragmatically*).

When they combine into groups (noun phrases and verb phrases) allowed by the rules of the language to create sentences, the creature grows by leaps and bounds. Three types of sentence structure (simple, coordinate, and subordinate) not only provide multiple ways of expressing the same ideas, thoughts, and feelings, but also help to structure those thoughts, weaving into them nuances of focus and the nature of their relationships. In turn, our patterns of thinking breathe life into language, giving both processes power. We use this power in a variety of ways. Language is a tool — powered by patterns of thinking. We will examine uses of language in the next chapter.

CHAPTER 7

Language as a Tool

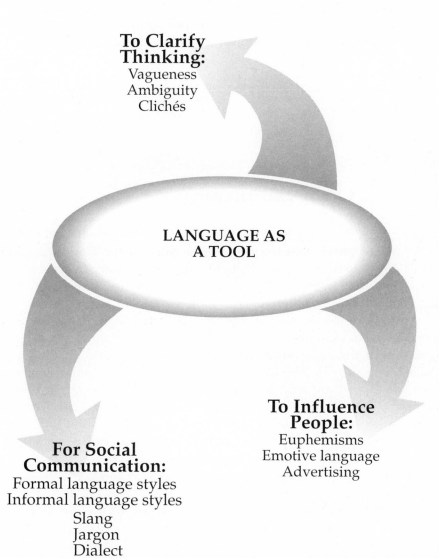

**To Clarify
Thinking:**
Vagueness
Ambiguity
Clichés

**LANGUAGE AS
A TOOL**

**For Social
Communication:**
Formal language styles
Informal language styles
Slang
Jargon
Dialect

**To Influence
People:**
Euphemisms
Emotive language
Advertising

IN THE LAST CHAPTER we explored language as a system: its symbolic structure, the "meaning" of individual words, the way language names and describes our experience, the syntactic relationships among words that enable us to create meaning, and the way all of these language abilities are put together so that we can effectively communicate our thoughts and feelings. In this chapter we will explore some of the important ways we use language as a tool in the normal course of our lives, including the following:

1. To clarify our thinking
2. To identify social groups and communicate within different social contexts
3. To influence others

Using Language to Clarify Our Thinking

Throughout this book, we have found that thinking is the organized and purposeful mental *process* that we use to make sense of the world. Language, with its power to represent our thoughts, feelings, and experiences symbolically, is the most important tool our thinking process has. Although research shows that thinking and communicating are two distinct processes, these two processes are so closely related that they are often difficult to separate or distinguish.* For example, when we write or speak, we are not simply making sounds or writing symbols; we are using language to communicate our thinking by conveying ideas, sharing feelings, and describing experiences. When we read, we are actively using our minds to comprehend the thinking of others. At the same time, the process of using language generates ideas, and the language we (or others) use shapes and influences our thinking. In short, the development and use of our thinking abilities is closely tied to the development and use of our language abilities — and vice versa.

Working together, thinking and communicating in language enable us to identify, represent, and give form to our thoughts, feelings, and experiences. By representing our thoughts, feelings, and experiences, we can share them with others who use the same language system. The key to effective thinking and communication, however, lies in using language clearly and precisely, a vital requirement if other people are going to be able to understand the

---

* Seminal works on this topic are *Thought and Language*, by Lev Vygotsky, and *Cognitive Development: Its Cultural and Social Foundation*, by A. R. Luria.

thoughts we are trying to communicate. At the same time, using language clearly and precisely leads in turn to clear and precise thinking.

Language is a social phenomenon. As children, we internalize language from our social surroundings and develop it through our relations with other people. As we develop our language abilities through these social interactions, our thinking capacities expand as well. Others help advance our thinking, and as we become literate our interactions with them shape our thinking. These social relationships also act as important vehicles for fostering precise thinking and language use: by talking to others and being responded to, by writing and discovering how others understand (or misunderstand) the ideas.

Because language and thinking are so closely related, how well we perform one process is directly related to how well we perform the other. In most cases, when we are thinking clearly, we are able to express our ideas clearly in language. For instance, develop a clear and precise thought about a subject you are familiar with and express this thought in language, using the space provided.

_____

_____

_____

On the other hand, if we are *not* able to develop a clear and precise idea of what we are thinking about, then we have great difficulty in expressing our thinking in language. When this happens, we usually say something like this:

"I know what I want to say, but I just can't find the right words."

Of course, when this happens, we usually *don't* "know" exactly what we want to say — if we did, we would say it! When we have unclear thoughts, it is usually because we lack a clear understanding of the situation or we do not know the right language to give form to these thoughts. When our thoughts are truly clear and precise, this means that we know the words to give form to these thoughts and so are able to express them in language. One of the great benefits of critically examining and revising our writing is that we are able to develop the language that expresses our thinking more clearly.

Not only does unclear thinking contribute to unclear language expression; unclear language contributes to unclear thinking. For example, read the following passage from William Shakespeare's *As You Like It*, Act 5, scene i. Here language is being used in a confusing way for the purpose of confusing our thinking. Examine the passage carefully and then describe as clearly as you can the thinking that the author is trying to express:

> Therefore, you clown, abandon — which is in the vulgar, leave — the society — which in the boorish is company — of this female — which in the common is woman; which together is, abandon the society of this female, or, clown, thou perishest; or, to thy better understanding, diest; or, to wit, I kill thee, make thee away, translate thy life into death.

Write your interpretation:

_____

_____

_____

_____

The relationship between thinking and language is *interactive*; both processes are continually influencing each other in many ways. This is particularly true in the case of language, as the writer George Orwell examines in the following passage from his essay, "Politics and the English Language":

> A man may take to drink because he feels himself to be a failure, and then fail all the more completely because he drinks. It is rather the same thing that is happening to the English language. It becomes ugly and inaccurate because our thoughts are foolish, but the slovenliness of our language makes it easier for us to have foolish thoughts. The point is that the process is reversible. Modern English, especially written English, is full of bad habits which spread by imitation and which can be avoided if one is willing to take the necessary trouble. If one gets rid of these habits one can think more clearly.

Just as the drunk falls into a vicious circle that keeps getting worse, the same is true of the relation between language and thinking. When our use of language is sloppy — that is, vague, general, indistinct, imprecise, foolish, inaccurate, and so on — it leads to thinking of the same sort. Of course, the reverse is also true. Clear and precise language leads to clear and precise thinking:

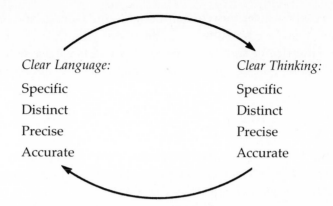

Clear Language: *Clear Thinking:*

Specific   Specific

Distinct   Distinct

Precise   Precise

Accurate   Accurate

If we are to develop our ability to think clearly, we have to pay a great deal of attention to developing our command of language.

Drawing by M. Stevens; © 1985 The New Yorker Magazine, Inc.

Language gives form to our thoughts and feelings and enables us to express them, and our thinking also affects our language. That is, as our thinking becomes clearer and more precise, the words we use will also become clearer and more precise. And as our language use improves, so too will our thinking.

THINKING ACTIVITY

7.1   ▶ In the following article, the columnist Tom Wicker analyzes what he sees as President Bush's lack of precision in language and thought. After reading the article, complete the questions that follow.

LIKE TOO BAD, YEAH *by Tom Wicker*

Asked at a news conference about his refusal to support a ban on semi-automatic rifles, President Bush promised to take "a hard look." Beyond that, he said little and said it badly:

"But I also want to have — be the President that protects the rights of, of people to, to have arms. And that — so you don't go so far that the legitimate rights on some legislation are, are, you know, impinged on."

It was discouraging enough to hear the President expressing banalities ("I am in the mode of being deeply concerned and would like to be a part of finding a national answer") on one of the deadliest problems Americans face; or reaching for political advantage ("I'd like to find a way to be supportive of the police who are out there on the line all the time") when he has been unwilling even to endorse a ban on "cop-killer" bullets.

But could he not express himself at least in, like, maybe, you know, sixth- or seventh-grade English, rather than speaking as if he were Dan Quayle trying to explain the Holocaust?

Here is more Bushspeak, concerning Middle East policy:

"Now we want to see that there's some follow on there. So the policy is set, I campaigned on what the policy is. . . . So the principles are there and I think we're, you know, we've got to, now, flesh that out and figure out what we do specifically."

Does that "figure out what we do specifically" remind you of an earlier Bush puzzlement? Perhaps his not having "sorted out" what the penalties should be for women who engage in what he had called, in a debate with Michael Dukakis, the crime of abortion?

Mr. Bush also has a way of saying nothing at numbing length — this, for example, on whether or not his support for former President Reagan's Strategic Defense Initiative was "conditional" on a 90-day review (my boldfacing of his clichés):

"I'm not ruling anything in or not. I have stated my **support for the principle** of S.D.I. I have not favored what some would call premature deployment, but **on the other hand** I will be very interested in seeing what this **overall review comes up with.** And I'm not going to close **any doors** or open any in regards to this or any other systems. We're going to have to **make some tough choices** on defense. I'm aware of that and **so let's wait and see** what the review produces."

Read carefully — and how else could you read him? — the President may be saying that he might favor "premature deployment" if the "overall review" "comes up with" such a proposal. You betcha.

On his way to Japan, at a stopover in Alaska, Mr. Bush was in good form. Asked at a news conference if he would present "new initiatives" in Tokyo, he replied, or something:

"We're ready to roll, yeah."

Let them figure that one out at the K.G.B. If, however, "yeah" meant that Mr. Bush indeed was ready with "new initiatives," he was confounding his national security adviser, Brent Scowcroft. General Scowcroft had said in a pre-departure briefing that "the substance will not be extensive" in the President's talks with other leaders.

Mr. Bush has learned one Presidential lesson well — when in doubt, point to the press. He was asked last week if there was "nothing you can do about the murder capital of the United States [Washington, D.C.] as the No. 1 resident?"

"Well," the President ventured, "we need the help of all the press to do something about it." Then, boldly, pursuing the subject, he evoked the ghost of Willie Horton: "The answer is the criminal — do more with the criminal."

Most Americans talk about as Mr. Bush has been talking. Almost everyone lapses into clichés, leaves sentences hanging in the confidence that listeners will understand, adds meaning to utterance with eyebrows and hands, and relies on, like, you know, the vernacular and slang. But George Bush is not "most Americans." He is the President of the United States and needs to speak as well as look like a President.

For one thing, he should set a needed example, in precision of speech as well as clarity of thought, neither of which distinguishes his constituency nor many of his predecessors. Mr. Bush will find, moreover, that

Americans may be briefly charmed by a President who talks as they do, but that the charm will wear off; remember Jimmy Carter's sweater. Finally, a President can't afford to be imprecise, in speech *or* thought, when his every word is weighed in the capitals of the world.

Andover, where are you when we need you? Eli Yale, speak to your favored son. ■

1. a. Describe three examples that Wicker cites as imprecise language use by President Bush.

    b. In each case, explain how the imprecise language might contribute to imprecise thinking, and vice versa.

    c. Rewrite the examples to make them more clear and specific.

2. a. Explain what Wicker means by the statement, "A President can't afford to be imprecise, in speech *or* thought, when his every word is weighed in the capitals of the world."

    b. Create a scenario in which a president's use of imprecise language could lead to an international disaster.

3. a. Describe an experience you had in which imprecise language led to a misunderstanding and explain how more precise communication would have avoided the problem. ◄

Vague Language

Although our ability to name and identify gives us the power to describe the world in a precise way, we often do not use words that are precise. Instead, we make many of our descriptions of the world using words that are very imprecise and general. Such general and nonspecific words we call *vague* words. Consider the following sentences:

• I had a *nice* time yesterday.

• That is an *interesting* book.

• She is an *old* person.

In each of these cases, the italicized word is vague because it does not give a precise description of the thought, feeling, or experience that the writer or speaker is trying to communicate. A word (or group of words) is vague if its meaning is not clear and distinct. That is, vagueness occurs when a word is used to represent an area of experience in such a way that the area is not clearly defined.

Let us examine the last sentence in the list: "She is an old person." At what age do you think that a person becomes "old"? The word "old" is vague because it does not seem to have one clear meaning. If you compare your idea of an old person with the ideas of other members of your class, you will probably find considerable variation. For instance, when we are children, the age of twenty-one seems old, and we can hardly wait to get there. People who are twenty-one traditionally do not trust those over thirty years old because of their advanced age and possible senility. When we become thirty, forty-five seems old, and when we turn forty-five, sixty becomes old, and so on. To an anthropologist, an "old" person might be one who lived 10,000 years ago. The problem with the word "old" is simply that its meaning is not clear and distinct.

> **Vague Word**   A word that lacks a clear and distinct meaning.

Most words of general measurement — *short, tall, big, small, heavy, light,* and so on — are vague. The exact meanings of these words depend on the specific situation in which they are used and on the particular perspective of the person using them. For example, give specific definitions for the following words in italics by filling in the blanks. Then compare your responses with those of other members of the class. Can you account for the differences in meaning?

1. A *middle-aged* person is one who is _____ years old.

2. A *tall* person is one who is _____ feet _____ inches tall.

3. It's *cold* outside when the temperature is _____ degrees.

4. A person is *wealthy* when _____ .

Although the vagueness of general measurement terms can lead to confusion, other forms of vagueness are more widespread and often more problematic. Terms such as *nice* and *interesting,* for example, are imprecise and unclear. Vagueness of this sort permeates every level of human discourse, undermines clear thinking, and is extremely difficult to combat. To use language clearly and precisely, we must develop an understanding of the way language functions and commit ourselves to breaking the entrenched habits of vague expression.

Avoiding Vague Words   Let us continue our examination of vagueness — and how to avoid it — by examining the following opinion of a movie. As you read through the passage, circle all the vague, general words that do not express a clear meaning.

Born on the Fourth of July

Born on the Fourth of July is a terrific movie about the
Vietnam war. It shows the experiences of a soldier who
loses his legs in battle, then comes home and becomes a
war protester. The movie is very exciting, has an interesting plot, and is definitely not for the squeamish. The
main characters — especially Tom Cruise — are very good.
I liked this movie a lot.

Because of the vague language in this passage, it expresses only general approval — it does not explain in exact or precise terms what the experience
was like. Thus the writer of the passage is not successful in communicating
the experience.

Sloppy language does a poor job of describing thoughts and feelings, and
when we use it, we are unable to communicate to others our recollection of
the experience in any direct or complete way. Strong writers have the gift of
symbolizing their experiences so clearly that we can actually relive those experiences with them. We can identify with them, sharing the same thoughts,
feelings, and perceptions that they had when they underwent (or imagined)
the experience. Consider how effectively the passages written by William
Least Heat Moon on pages 279–282 in Chapter Six communicate the thoughts,
feelings, and experiences of the author.

Clarifying Vague Language   One useful strategy for clarifying vague language
often used by journalists is to ask and try to answer the following questions:
Who? What? Where? When? How? Why? Let us see how this strategy applies to
the movie vaguely described above.

- *Who* were the people involved in the movie? (actors, director, producer,
  characters portrayed, etc.)
- *What* took place in the movie? (setting, events, plot development, etc.)
- *Where* does the movie take place? (physical location, cultural setting, etc.)
- *When* do the events in the movie take place? (historical situation)
- *How* does the film portray its events? (How do the actcors create their char-
  acters? How does the director use film techniques to accomplish his or her
  goals?)
- *Why* do I have this opinion of the film? (What are the reasons that I formed
  that opinion?)

Now use these questions to examine a review of this same film by a professional movie reviewer.

THINKING ACTIVITY

7.2   ▶ Read the review and then analyze it by answering the questions that follow.

DAYS OF RAGE *by David Denby*

Ron Kovic, the decorated Vietnam vet who was wounded in combat — paralyzed, at the age of 21, from the chest down — is not the kind of man to spare others his suffering. Condemned to his wheelchair, miserable over acts he had committed in the war, he lost faith not only in the conflict but in mother, country, and God — everything. From *Born on the Fourth of July* (opening December 20), the pulverizing epic movie Oliver Stone has made out of Kovic's account of his life, we can see that Kovic (Tom Cruise) was as hard on himself as on everyone else. The movie takes him down to the depths of degradation, and then part of the way back. All through it, he wails and howls, like a figure in a Greek tragedy crying out to the gods.

He shares some other things with those heroes — courage and a driving need to face disaster openly. His conviction that what matters to him should matter to other people as well can seem, at times, like righteous showing-off. It can also seem like inspiration. *Born on the Fourth of July* is a relentless but often powerful and heartbreaking piece of work, dominated by Tom Cruise's impassioned performance. His Ron Kovic is not a natural winner like other Cruise characters but a clenched, patriotic, working-class boy — a "Yankee-Doodle dandy" who has to fight for every bit of intellectual and moral clarity he gets.

Cruise has dropped his confident smile, his American-eagle look. In the past, he has seemed callow, a failing he disguised with cockiness. But Ron Kovic, who believed everything his parents and his country told him, was himself callow, and when Cruise shrieks in dismay he sounds right. His work may lack the precision, the sense of proportion, the feeling for climax that a great actor would bring to suffering, but he does, undeniably, have power. Raging against helplessness, he gives a brave and vulnerable performance that many people, I think, will find harrowing — not just young men but women and Cruise's natural audience, teenage girls, who may be shocked and moved as Cruise picks fights in bars and throws himself drunkenly on girls and screams at his religious and priggish mother about his limp penis.

Oliver Stone has become as unrelenting as Kovic. From his earlier films (*Salvador, Platoon, Wall Street, Talk Radio*), we understood that he was enraged by the softness of American mythmaking — the lies, the evasions, the Reaganite media scam that turned greed into public virtue and the disaster of Vietnam into an illusion of noble endeavor undermined by weakhearted liberals. But *Platoon* was almost consoling in comparison with *Born on the Fourth of July.*

Stone and Kovic have consciously created an anti-myth. Born on July 4, 1946, Kovic is raised in a large family in Massapequa, Long Island. At first, Stone makes everything exemplary, almost dreamy in its sunshiny Americanness: a slow-motion homer in a baseball game; a pretty girl kissing Kovic. But he also plants intimations that Kovic can fail: Kovic trains for and then fights hard in a championship wrestling match, which (in a startling reversal of movie convention) he loses. Uneasiness creeps in.

From the beginning, Kovic is primed with patriotism, war, and God. His mother (Caroline Kava) enters the family dining room in the early sixties saying things like "Those Communists have to be stopped." Stone makes every line, every moment, part of Kovic's conditioning, as if the boy had no secret life, no *self.* Trying to show us the perfect American hero-dummy (Mom's victim), Stone holds the movie in too tight a grip. The war scenes, set along a sparkling river rather than in the usual lush jungle, are a frenzied horror of confusion and panic. Recovering from his wounds in a Bronx V.A. hospital, Kovic encounters a new horror, the decrepitude of urban America. Rats roam the squalid wards. The nurses and aides — urban blacks, alien to Kovic — are alternately cheerful and callously indifferent; one aide, caring only for the civil-rights struggle, lectures the half-dead Kovic on the futility of the war. Stone, a liberal, demonstrates almost Purple Heart courage himself in putting this painful stuff on the screen.

Obsessed with making sexual contact with a girl, Kovic turns against his mother. It's Mom, socializing America's youth with patriotic drivel while trying to subdue their sexual drives, who gets the most shocking abuse in the movie. Escaping from home, Kovic heads for a vacation village in Mexico that caters to crippled men, and he finds solace with a beautiful whore. For a while, the savagery breaks free into a bitter joyousness. Willem Dafoe, in magnificent voice, shows up as a Vietnam vet who's in even worse shape than Kovic. In a hilarious scene, the two men in their wheelchairs fight in the middle of the Mexican desert. They could be figures out of Samuel Beckett — Zed and Zero, lunging at an empty universe. Kovic, hitting bottom, pulls himself together and heads home.

Through most of the movie, Stone directs as if he were in as much pain as his impotent hero — as if he didn't have an obligation as an artist to shape his anger and then turn it loose when it counts most. Mistakenly, he tries to blow us away in every scene. Watching the movie is like being held in the grip of a brilliant monomaniac. In scene after scene, Stone jams the camera right up against people's faces, as if he were grabbing them by the lapels; or he gets cinematographer Robert Richardson to jerk the camera from one place to another in a rough, heart-stopping blur.

What Stone wants, of course, is not only to re-create Kovic's experiences from the inside but to bring us closer to mess and suffering — the blood and puke and disorder — so we can't escape into consoling "aesthetic" responses. Sometimes, I admit, the power of the movie is overwhelming. After Kovic's unit has accidentally wiped out a Vietnamese family in a chaotic battle, Kovic accidentally kills an American Marine as well. A pious Catholic boy, he wants to confess the act to his commanding officer, but the officer won't listen to him (and therefore won't absolve him), and the close-ups of the two men sweating in the officer's tent are anguishing. Later, back home, an anti-war protester along with other vets, Kovic enters the 1972 Republican National Convention in Miami, and from his point of view, as he looks up, the outraged faces, swollen under their straw boaters, look obscene in their contempt for him.

But there's a problem in staying so close to Kovic's anger: His personal torments, rather than any reasoned political arguments, appear to be what turned him against the war. The movie seems out of balance. A young man's loss of potency is equated with the country's loss of honor.

Stone, better than anyone before him, has caught the combined nightmarish and exhilarating quality of the 1966–1972 period, a time when many young people, mesmerized by the government's lies about the war, wanted to waste themselves, wanted to become filthy and obscene as a way of bearing witness, in their own bodies, to the truth. Truth is all-important to Oliver Stone. At a noisy Fourth of July parade, the *pop-pop-pop* of firecrackers makes the World War II veterans flinch. Yet there's a damaging literal-mindedness in Stone's work. He's often overexplicit. He doesn't trust us to get his point, and although he has the instincts and the courage to tackle major themes, he doesn't really trust his art either. Someday, he may discover that art can be a way to truth rather than an escape from it. ■

According to the review:

1. *Who* were the people involved with the movie?
2. *What* took place in the movie?
3. *Where* does the movie take place?
4. *When* do the events in the movie take place?
5. *How* does the film portray its events?
6. *Why* did the reviewer form this particular opinion about the film? ◀

Virtually all of us use vague language extensively in our day-to-day conversations. In many cases, it is natural that our immediate reaction to an experience would be fairly general ("That's nice," "She's interesting," etc.). If we are truly concerned with sharp thinking and meaningful communication, however, we should follow up these initial general reactions with a more precise clarification of what we really mean.

• I think that she is a nice person *because* . . .
• I think that he is a good teacher *because* . . .
• I think that this is an interesting class *because* . . .

Vagueness is always a matter of degree. In fact, we can think of our descriptive/informative use of language as falling somewhere on a scale between extreme generality and extreme specificity. For example, the following statements move from the general to the specific.

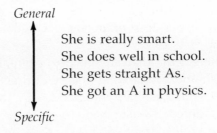

General

She is really smart.
She does well in school.
She gets straight As.
She got an A in physics.

Specific

Although different situations require various degrees of specificity, we should work at becoming increasingly precise in our use of language. For example, examine the following response to the assignment, "Describe what you think about the school you are attending." Circle the vague words.

I really like it a lot. It's a very good school. The people are nice and the teachers are interesting. There are a lot of different things to do, and students have a good time doing them. Some of the courses are pretty hard, but if you study enough, you should do all right.

Notice how general the passage is. The writer says, for example, that "the people are nice," but gives no concrete and specific descriptions of *why* he thinks the people are nice. The writer would have been more specific if he had used statements such as the following:

- "Everyone says hello."
- "The students introduced themselves to me in class."
- "I always feel welcome in the student lounge."
- "The teachers take a special interest in each student."

Although these statements are more precise than saying, "The people are nice," they can also be made more specific. To illustrate this, create more specific descriptions for each of these statements:

"Everyone says hello."

_____

"The students introduced themselves to me in class."

_____

"I always feel welcome in the student lounge."

_____

"The teachers take a special interest in each student."

_____

Ambiguous Language

Ambiguity is another obstacle that can interfere with clear expression of our thoughts and feelings. We have noted that words are used to represent various areas of experience. We sometimes make the mistake of thinking that each word stands for one distinct area of experience — an object, thought, or feeling. In fact, a word may represent various areas of experience and so have a number of different meanings. When a word has more than one distinct meaning and we are not sure which meaning is being intended, then we say that the word is *ambiguous*. For example, the word *rich* can mean having lots of money (like a millionaire), or it can mean having lots of sugar and calories (like chocolate cream pie). Thus *rich* is a potentially ambiguous word.

> ***Ambiguous Word***   A word with more than one meaning that is open to different interpretations.

How do we know to which of its multiple meanings an ambiguous word is referring? Usually we can tell by *how* the word is used — the situation, or context, in which it is employed. When someone asks you if you are "rich," you can be pretty certain that that person is *not* asking if you are full of sugar and calories. As an example, give at least two meanings for the following potentially ambiguous words. Then, list two additional words that are potentially ambiguous and give the various meanings.

1. *Exercise:* _____

2. *Critical:* _____

3. *Major:* _____

4. *Firm:* _____

5. *Fast:* _____

6. *Free:* _____

7. *Bar:* _____

8. *Battery:* _____

9. *Heavy:* _____

10. *Cool:* _____

11. _____

12. _____

Groups of words can also be ambiguous. If someone tells us, "I hope you get what you deserve!" we may not be sure if the speaker is wishing us well or ill unless the context of the remark makes clear his or her intention.

Actions and situations can be ambiguous as well. An action or situation is considered to be ambiguous if it can be given more than one possible interpretation. For example, suppose someone you know suddenly gives you a hard slap on the back, or a casual friend gives you a passionate good-night kiss. In each of these situations, you may be uncertain about what is being expressed and therefore unsure of how to interpret the meaning of the action.

In such cases, we usually rely on our beliefs to resolve the ambiguity, a matter that we discussesd in Chapter Five.

In all cases of ambiguous human behavior, whether verbal or nonverbal, the same principle applies: We have to carefully examine the relevant aspects of the situation to arrive at the most accurate and complete interpretation.

Think of an ambiguous experience from your own life, in which you initially were not sure of the "correct" interpretation of what was taking place. How did you figure out which of the several possible interpretations was the most accurate explanation?

Even groups of words in context can be ambiguous. Write two meanings for each of the following sentences.

1. The woman wiped the glasses.

   _____

   _____

2. He fed her dog biscuits.

   _____

   _____

3. The duck is ready to eat.

   _____

   _____

4. Flying planes can be dangerous.

   _____

   _____

5. The shooting of the hunter disturbed him.

   _____

   _____

When words are used in unique or unexpected ways, we need the ability to think about the nature of language. That is, we must not only know the double meanings of words, but we must also understand the relationships among words in the language, as we explored in Chapter Six, *Language as a System*. We must know, for example, to interpret sentence 2, that although the word *dog* usually represents content (as a noun), in a sentence where it is ordered next to another noun such as: *food, dish, collar*, it is used as a descriptive word (as an adjective). To see two interpretations of the word *shooting* in sentence 5, we need to know that *shooting* may function as either of the two types of content word. It may take the role of a noun or of a verb.

Sentence ambiguity forms the basis of some kinds of humor — riddles in particular. Here is an example.

Q: What did the short tree say to the tall tree?

A: I'm stumped.

Sentence ambiguity also works as a tool to influence people's thinking, as in the advertisement for Ford Tempo cars: "Designed to move you."

THINKING ACTIVITY

7.3   ▶ Using language imprecisely can lead to miscommunication, sometimes with disastrous results. For example, on January 29, 1990, an Avianca Airlines flight from Colombia, South America, to New York City ran out of fuel and crashed, killing seventy-three persons. After circling Kennedy Airport for 45 minutes, the plane ran out of fuel before it could land, apparently the result of imprecise communication between the plane's pilot and the air traffic controllers. Read the following excerpts from the *New York Times* account of the incident on January 30, 1990, and then answer the questions that follow.

AN ACCOUNT OF AVIANCA FLIGHT 52

The Federal Aviation Administration today defended the controllers who guided a Colombian jetliner toward Kennedy International Airport, releasing the first verbatim transcripts of communications in the hour before the jet crashed. The officials suggested that the plane's pilot should have used more precise language, such as the word "emergency," in telling controllers how seriously they were short of fuel. They made the statements a day after Federal investigators said that regional controllers never told local controllers the plane was short of fuel and had asked for priority clearance to land.

The transcripts show that the crew of Avianca Flight 52 told regional controllers about 45 minutes before the plane crashed that "we would run out of fuel" if the plane was redirected to Boston instead of being given priority to land at Kennedy. The crew said it would be willing to continue in its holding pattern 40 miles south of Kennedy for "about five minutes — that's all we can do" before the plane would have to move onward to Kennedy. But the regional controllers who gave that message to the local controllers who were to guide the plane on its final descent to Kennedy did not tell them that there was a problem with fuel supplies on the jet or that the plane had requested priority handling, the transcripts recorded by the F.A.A. confirmed.

Taken by itself, the information that the plane could circle for just five more minutes would not make the immediate danger of the plane clear to the local controllers. Without being told that the plane did not have enough fuel to reach Boston or that its crew had asked for priority clearance, the local controllers might have assumed that it had reached a point where it could still land with adequate reserves of fuel still on board.

Despite the apparent lapse in communications among controllers, an F.A.A. spokesman said they acted properly because the plane's crew had not explicitly declared a fuel emergency. An emergency would require immediate clearance to land.

R. Steve Bell, president of the National Air Traffic Controllers Association, called the safety board's statements during its inquiry "highly misleading and premature." . . . Mr. Bell, in a statement issued today, said the pilots of the plane should have made known to controllers the extent of their problem in order to obtain immediate clearance to land the plane. "The Avianca pilot never declared a 'fuel emergency' or 'minimum fuel,' both of which would have triggered an emergency response by controllers," he said. "Stating that you are low on fuel does not imply an immediate problem. In addition, this information would not necessarily be transmitted when one controller hands off to another."

Chronology of final minutes of Flight 52:

8:00 P.M.: Forty miles south of Kennedy, Avianca Flight 52 is delayed for 46 minutes, after earlier delays of 16 minutes over Norfolk, Va., and 27 minutes farther north.

8:46 P.M.: The plane's crew tells regional air controllers in Islip, L.I., that they have a low-fuel problem. Regional controllers immediately release the plane from its holding pattern, passing it to local controllers in Garden City, L.I.

9:24 P.M.: First landing attempt at Kennedy is aborted and jet circles. Pilot twice tells Kennedy tower that he is low on fuel.

9:32 P.M.: Pilot tells tower while circling: "Two engines lost"; he also says that he is very short on fuel.

9:35 P.M.: The plane crashes. ■

1. If the pilot of the airplane was alive (all crew died in the crash), how do you think he would analyze the cause of the crash?

2. How do the air traffic controllers and the FAA analyze the cause of the crash?

3. How do you analyze the cause of the crash? What reasons led you to that conclusion?

4. Describe a situation that you were involved in, or that you heard about, in which a misunderstanding resulted from an ambiguous use of language. ◀

Clichés

Clichés are worn-out and overused expressions that supposedly contain some common-sense truth or insight — for example, the sayings "A stitch in time saves nine" or "Never too late to mend." Their very overfamiliarity makes them vague and ambiguous, thus contributing to unclear and imprecise thinking. Each society tends to accumulate such phrases and sayings over time, and because they are often clever, catchy, and seemingly appropriate, people tend to use them frequently.

> ***Cliché***   Worn-out and overused expressions that supposedly contain some common-sense truth or insight.

Clichés may seem harmless, but they can actually encourage poor thinking habits. For example, someone might reason, "Better late than never," to justify never completing anything on time. Clichés can also encourage us to *oversimplify* a problem or situation. Instead of exerting our critical thinking abilities to analyze a problem thoughtfully, using clichés to describe a situation makes it easy to gloss over its complexities and fine points. And instead of making the most intelligent decisions based on this critical analysis, we end up making thoughtless and impulsive decisions (for example: "Even though I don't know what I want to do with my life, I am going to choose this career, because 'He who hesitates is lost!'"). It is generally more productive to base our decisions on careful thought and analysis of the specific situation, not on popular sayings or catchwords, no matter how clever they may be.

Another misuse of clichés occurs when people use them to justify actions they have already taken for entirely different reasons (for example: "Don't blame me for insulting you — remember, 'Honesty is the best policy!'"). Instead of accepting the responsibility for our decisions, we sometimes seem to be blaming our decisions on the "wisdom of the ages," passed down in these sayings.

Taken by themselves, clichés don't really help us understand situations, nor do they help us prove or disprove anything. In fact, they are so vague and ambiguous that they can be used to prove (or disprove) virtually anything. The best way to see this is to take a cliché and think of an example of a situation when the cliché doesn't apply. For example, it may make sense to eat dinner "better late than never" — but what about catching a plane? Or submitting an application after the filing deadline has expired?

This sort of example used to disprove a general statement is called a *counterexample*. Sometimes clichés themselves provide their own "counterexamples" by contradicting each other. For example:

- Absence makes the heart grow fonder.
- Out of sight, out of mind.

- Haste makes waste.
- Don't put off 'till tomorrow what you can do today.

Thus, although each cliché may possess a "grain of truth" (the situations in which it applies), it also possesses at least one "grain of *un*truth" (the situations in which it doesn't apply).

How do we know whether or not a cliché applies to a given situation? By thinking critically. We have to examine the situation, analyze the issues and then come to a conclusion based on our understanding. The trouble with clichés is that using them uncritically often represents superficial, unquestioning, or impulsive thinking.

Therefore, if we use clichés at all, we should probably restrict our use of them to the task of *summarizing* our careful analysis of a situation, not as a *guide* to making our decisions. No collection of clichés is a satisfactory substitute for critical, thoughtful, and reflective thinking. If we understand enough to know whether the cliché applies to a situation, then we know enough not to need it.

THINKING ACTIVITY

7.4   ▶ For each cliché listed, explain a "grain of truth" *and* a "grain of *un*truth."

1.a. Better safe than sorry. _____

_____

b. Nothing ventured, nothing gained. _____

_____

2.a. Two heads are better than one. _____

_____

b. Too many cooks spoil the soup. _____

_____

3.a. An eye for an eye, a tooth for a tooth. _____

_____

b. Good hearts forgive, great hearts forget. _____

_____

4.a. Don't change horses in midstream. _____

_____

b. It's time for a change. _____

_____

5.a. Idle hands are the devil's workshop. _____

_____

b. Too much work and not enough play makes Jack a dull boy. _____

_____

6.a. What's good for the goose is good for the gander. _____

_____

b. Two wrongs don't make a right. _____

_____

7.a. Money is the root of all evil. _____

_____

b. Poverty breeds anger. _____

_____

8.a. Seeing is believing. _____

_____

b. Believe nothing you hear, and half of what you see. _____

_____

9.a. _____

b. _____

10.a. _____

b. _____ ◀

Using Language in Social Contexts

Language is always used in a context. That is, we always speak or write with a person or group of people in mind. The group may include friends, co-workers, strangers, or only ourselves! We also always use language in a particular situation. We may converse with our friends, meet with our boss, or carry out a business transaction at the bank or supermarket.

Language Styles

In each of these cases, we use the *language style* that is appropriate to the social situation. For example, describe how you usually greet the following people when you see them:

A good friend: _____

A teacher: _____

A parent: _____

An employer: _____

A waiter/waitress: _____

When greeting a friend, we are likely to say something like, "Hey, Richard, how ya been!" or "Hi, Sue, good to see ya." When greeting our employer, however, or even a coworker, something more like, "Good morning, Mrs. Jones," or "Hello, Dan, how are you this morning?" is in order. The reason for this variation is that the two social contexts, personal friendship and the workplace, are very different and call for different language responses. In a working environment, no matter how frequently we interact with coworkers or employers, our language style tends to be more formal and less abbreviated than it is in personal friendships. Conversely, the more familiar we are with someone, the better we know him or her, the more abbreviated our *style* of language will be in that context. The language we use with someone is more abbreviated when we share a variety of ideas, opinions, and experiences with that person. The language style identifies this shared thinking and consequently *restricts* the group of people who can communicate within this context.

We all belong to social groups in which we use styles that separate "insiders" from "outsiders." When we use an abbreviated style of language with our friend, we are identifying that person as a friend and sending a social message that says, "I know you pretty well, and I can assume many common perspectives between us." On the other hand, when we are speaking to someone at the office in a more elaborate language style, we are sending a different social message, namely, "I know you within a particular context (this workplace), and I can assume only certain common perspectives between us."

In this way we use language to identify the social context in which we are using it and define the relationship between the people communicating. Language styles vary from *informal*, in which we abbreviate not only sentence structure but also the sounds that form words — as in "ya" in the examples — to increasingly *formal*, in which we use more complex sentence structure as well as complete words in terms of sound patterns.

THINKING ACTIVITY

7.5   ▶ 1. Write a conversation you would be likely to carry on with a classmate about a problem you might have had in class.

2. Now rewrite the conversation as if you were explaining the problem to your professor.

3. Finally, rewrite the conversation as if you were explaining the problem to a family member.

4. Compare the similarities and differences between these conversations in terms of their language styles: formality, word choice, sentence construction, and sound patterns. ◀

As we learned in Chapter Six, language always has a pragmatic meaning. When the pragmatic meanings of words change, their syntactic and perceptual meanings may change, too. Sometimes they change only slightly. For example, the words we use and the way we put them together when we are talking to the bank teller might be less "friendly" than when we are talking with our coworkers, but the basic system of linguistic relationships — including semantic and syntactic meanings — would probably be about the same. That is, only our *style* of speech might be a little different, but semantic and syntactic relationships would be similar.

Slang

Read the following dialogue.

> *Girl 1:* "Hey, did you see that new guy? He's gnarly. I mean, like really radical."
>
> *Girl 2:* "All the guys in my class are barfo. Geeks or skids or wastoids. Let's blow this clambake. I have to powerdrill."

Rewrite the dialogue in your own style on the lines provided.

_____

_____

_____

_____

How would you describe the style of the original dialogue? How would you describe the style of your version of the dialogue? The linguist Shoshana Hoose writes:

> As any teen will tell you, keeping up with the latest slang takes a lot of work. New phrases sweep into town faster than greased lightning, and they are gone just as quickly. Last year's "hoser" is this year's "dweeb" (both meaning somewhat of a "nerd"). Some slang consists of everyday words that have taken on a new, hip meaning. "Mega" for instance, was used mainly by astronomers and mathematicians until teens adopted it as a way of describing anything great, cool, and unbelievable. Others are words, such as *gag* that seem to have naturally evolved from one meaning (to throw up) to another (a person or thing that is gross to the point of making one want to throw up). And then there are words that

come from movies, popular music, and the media. "Rambo," the macho movie character who singlehandedly defeats whole armies, has come to mean a muscular, tough, adventurous boy who wears combat boots and fatigues.

As linguists have long known, cultures create the most words for the things that preoccupy them the most. We saw in an earlier chapter that Eskimos have more than seventy-six words for *ice* and *snow*, and Hawaiians can choose from scores of variations on the word *water*. Most teenage slang falls into one or two categories: words meaning "cool" and words meaning "out of it." A person who is really out of it could be described as a *nerd*, a *goober*, a *geek*, a *tade*, or a *pinhead*, to name just a few possibilities.

THINKING ACTIVITY

7.6   ▶ Review the slang terms and definitions in the following glossary. How do your terms match up? For each term, list a word that you use or have heard of to mean the same thing.

Word:	Your Word:	Meaning:
babe	_____	a good-looking guy
barfo	_____	gross, disgusting
burnout	_____	someone who hangs out, smokes, drinks, or takes drugs
gnarly	_____	really cool, weird, strange, funky, totally awesome
mongo	_____	really big; cool
posers	_____	showoffs
wastoids	_____	druggies, delinquents, losers
beat	_____	stupid, out of date, a drag
nada	_____	no good
power	_____	to study
powerdrill	_____	to study intensely

If your meanings did not match those in the glossary or if you did not recognize some of the words in the glossary, what do you think was the main reason?

_____

_____

_____

Slang is a restrictive style of language that limits its speakers to a particular group. As Hoose points out, age is usually the determining factor in using slang. But there are special forms of slang that are not determined by age; rather, they are determined by profession or interest group. Let's look at this other type of language style.

Jargon

Jargon is made up of words, expressions, and technical terms that are intelligible to professional circles or interest groups but not to the general public. Consider the following interchanges:

1. *A:* Breaker 1-9. Com'on Little Frog.
   B: Roger and back to you Charley.
   A: We got to back down, we got a Smokey ahead.
   B: I can't afford to feed the bears this week. Better stay at 5-5 now.
   A: That's a big 10-4.
   B: I'm gonna cut the coax now.

2. OK Al, number six takes two eggs, wreck 'em, with a whiskey down and an Adam and Eve on a raft. Don't forget the Jack Tommy, express to California.

3. Please take further notice, that pursuant to and in accordance with Article II, Paragraph Second and Fifteen of the aforesaid Proprietary Lease Agreement, you are obligated to reimburse Lessor for any expense Lessor incurs including legal fees in instituting any action or proceeding due to a default of your obligations as contained in the Proprietary Lease Agreement.

Word meaning in these interchanges is shared by (1) CB operators; (2) restaurant/diner cooks; and (3) attorneys. Most of the rest of us would be confused listening to these forms of English, or in other words, these types of *jargon* — even if we speak English fluently!

Dialects

Within the boundaries of geographical regions and ethnic groups, the form of a language used may be so different from the usual (or standard) in terms

of its sound patterns, vocabulary, and sentence structure that it either is no-
ticeably different or cannot be understood by people outside the specific regional or ethnic group. In this case, we are no longer talking about variations
in language *style*, we are talking instead about distinct *dialects*. Consider these
sentences from three different dialects of English:

Dialect A: Dats allabunch of byoks at de license bureau.
He fell out de rig and broke his leg boon.

Dialect B: My teacher she said I passed on the skin of my teeth. My sisters
and them up there talkin' 'bout I should stayed back.

Dialect C: I went out to the garden to pick the last of them Kentucky Wonder pole beans of mine, and do you know, there on the grass was just a
little mite of frost.

Probably you can recognize these sentences as English, but you may not recognize all of the words, sentence structures, and sound patterns that these
speakers used.

Dialects differ from language styles in being generally restricted to geographical and/or ethnic groups. They also vary from the standard language
to a greater degree than language styles do. Dialects vary not only in words
but also in sound patterns and in syntax. In the following four examples of
dialect, how do the sound patterns, vocabulary, and sentence structure differ
from that of standard English?

1. We left here about four in the mornin' and went up off Boon Island, outside Boon Island about five miles and set these trawls all baited, see. . . .
We tried to go into York Harbor which was nearer, and quarter into the
wind like. But we never made it. We come back awful early that afternoon
and couldn't find the entrance to the harbor, so we turned round and went
back out to sea again, cause it was the only chance we had. Stayed round
those rocks and we'd be lost.

2. Ah don lak to fly in dem big jat arrowpleen. Dey had a bad wreck on de
hairline. Tie loose de boat!

3. I can skate better than Lois and I be only eight. If you be goin' real fast,
hold it. You be goin' too fast, well, you don't be in the ring. You be outside
if you be goin' too fast. That man he a clip you up. I think they call him
Sonny. He real tall.

4. *A:* Mornin' Alf, 'ow're yer goin?
B: Not bad, me ol' mate, not bad. Ow's yerself?
A: Oh, same as usual, can't complain.
B: 'Ow much are yer Herberts then?

A: To you me ol' son, an Alan Whicker for a bag.

B: Gawdelpus! An Alan Whicker! Yer goin' orf yer head. That's too dear. I'll give yer ten bob, not a penny more.

A: Alrigh mate — let's not have a bull and cow — gimme the bees and honey and take yer bag of Herberts.

B: Cheers! An give me regards to yer carving knife.

Can you interpret the meaning conveyed by these passages? What words or syntactic forms contributed to your difficulty in interpreting the meaning? If you speak a dialect of your language as well as the standard dialect, write one or two sentences in that dialect on the lines provided.

_____

_____

_____

How does your dialect vary from the standard in terms of words and syntactic forms?

The Social Boundaries of Language

As we have seen in the last two chapters, a language is a system of communication, by sounds and markings, among given groups of people. Within each language community, members' thinking patterns are defined in many respects by the specific patterns of meaning that language imposes. Smaller groups within language communities display distinctive language patterns. When there are some differences from the norm, mainly in vocabulary and length of sentences, we say the speakers are using a specific *language style.* When the form of the language spoken by these smaller groups shows many differences from the "usual" or "regular" form in words and sentence structure, we call this language form a *dialect.* Both language styles and dialects place boundaries on communication. The most obvious are social; they identify people as belonging to a particular group.

We cannot, however, overlook the tie between language and thinking. That is, we cannot ignore the way in which our thoughts about a social situation determine the variety of language we use. The connection between language and thought turns language into a powerful social force that separates us as well as binds us together. The language that we use and the way we use it serve as important clues to our social identity. For example, dialect identifies our geographical area or group; slang marks our age group and subculture;

jargon often identifies our occupation; and accent typically suggests the place we grew up and our socioeconomic class. These dimensions of language are important influences in shaping our response to others. Sometimes they can trigger stereotypes we hold about someone's interests, social class, intelligence, personal attributes, and so on. The ability to think critically gives us the insight and the intellectual ability to distinguish people's language use from their individual qualities, to correct inaccurate beliefs about people and avoid stereotypical responses in the future.

THINKING ACTIVITY

7.7 ▶ 1. Interview someone who speaks a dialect different than standard English. Transcribe several paragraphs of his or her language, spelling the words the way they sound.

2. Analyze the dialect by comparing it with standard English in terms of vocabulary, sentence structure, and sound patterns. ◀

THINKING ACTIVITY

7.8 ▶ 1. Describe examples, drawn from individuals in your personal experience, of each of the following: dialect, accent, jargon, slang.

2. Describe your immediate responses to the examples you just provided. For example, what is your immediate response to someone speaking in each of the dialects on pages 320–321? To someone with a British accent? To someone speaking "computerese"? To someone speaking a slang that you don't understand?

3. Analyze the responses you just described. How did they get formed? Do they represent an accurate understanding of the person or a stereotyped belief?

4. Identify strategies for using critical thinking abilities to overcome inaccurate and inappropriate responses to others based on their language usage. ◀

Using Language to Influence

The intimate relationship between language and thinking makes it natural that people use language to influence the thinking of others. As we have seen, within the boundaries of social groups people use a given language style or dialect to emphasize shared information and experience. Not only does this sharing socially identify the members of the group, it also provides a base for them to influence each other's thinking. The expression, "Now you're speaking my language!" illustrates this point. Some people make a profession of using language to influence people's thinking. In other words, many individuals and groups are interested in influencing — and sometimes controlling — our thoughts, our feelings, and (as a result) our behavior. To avoid being unconsciously manipulated by these efforts, we must have an understanding and awareness of how language functions. Such an understanding will help us distinguish actual arguments, information, and reasons from techniques of persuasion that others use to try to get us to accept their viewpoint without critical thought. Three types of language are often used to promote the uncritical acceptance of viewpoints:

- Euphemistic language
- Emotive language
- Advertising language

By developing insight into these language strategies, we will strengthen our abilities to function as critical thinkers.

Euphemistic Language

The term *euphemism* derives from a Greek word meaning "to speak with good words," and involves substituting a more pleasant, less objectionable way of saying something for a blunt or more direct way. For example, an entire collection of euphemisms exists to disguise the unpleasantness of death: "passed away," "went to his or her reward," "departed this life," "blew out the candle," and "kicked the bucket."

Why do people use euphemisms? Probably to help smooth out the "rough edges" of life, to make the unbearable bearable and the offensive inoffensive. Sometimes people use them to make their occupations seem more important. For example, a garbage collector may be called a "sanitation engineer," a traveling salesman a "field representative," and a police officer a "law enforcement official."

Euphemisms can become dangerous when they are used to create misperceptions of important issues. For example, an alcoholic may describe himself or herself as a "social drinker," thus avoiding the problem and the help he or she needs. Or a politician may indicate that one of his or her other statements was "somewhat at variance with the truth" — meaning that he or she lied. Even more serious examples would include describing rotting slums as "substandard housing," making the deplorable conditions appear reasonable and the need for action less important. One of the most devastating examples of the destructive power of euphemisms was Nazi Germany's characterization of the slaughter of over 12 million men, women, and children by such innocuous phrases as the "final solution" and the "purification of the race."

George Orwell, the author of the futuristic novel *1984*, describes how governments often employ euphemisms to disguise and justify wrongful policies in the following passage taken from his classic essay "Politics and the English Language."

> In our time, political speech and writing are largely the defense of the indefensible. Things like the continuance of British rule in India, the Russian purges and deportations, the dropping of the atom bombs on Japan, can indeed be defended, but only by arguments which are too brutal for most people to face, and which do not square with the professed aims of political parties. Thus political language has to consist largely of euphemism, question-begging and sheer cloudy vagueness. Defenseless villages are bombarded from the air, the inhabitants driven out into the countryside, the cattle machine-gunned, the huts set on fire with incendiary bullets: this is called *pacification*. Millions of peasants are robbed of their farms and sent trudging along the roads with no more than they can carry: this is called *transfer of population* or *rectification of frontiers*. People are imprisoned for years without trial, or shot in the back of the neck or sent to die of scurvy in Arctic lumber camps: this is called *elimination of unreliable elements*. Such phraseology is needed if one wants to name things without calling up mental pictures of them.

THINKING ACTIVITY

7.9   ▶ Select an important social problem, such as drug use, crime, poverty, juvenile delinquency, support for wars in other countries, racism, unethical or illegal behavior in government, and so on. Identify several euphemisms used to describe the problem and explain how the euphemisms can lead to dangerous misperceptions. ◀

Emotive Language

What is your *immediate* reaction to the following words?

sexy	peaceful	disgusting	God
filthy	mouth-watering	bloodthirsty	whore
adorable	Nazi	Communist	

Most of these words probably stimulate certain feelings in you. In fact, this ability to evoke feelings in people accounts for the extraordinary power of language.

Making sense of the way that language can influence our thinking and behavior means understanding the emotional dimension of language. Special words (like those just given) are used to stand for the emotive areas of our experience. These emotive words symbolize the whole range of human feelings, from powerful emotions ("I adore you!") to the subtlest of feeling, as revealed in this passage spoken by Chief Seattle in 1855, responding to a U.S. government proposal to buy his tribe's land and place the tribe on a reservation:

> Every part of this soil is sacred in the estimation of my people. Every hillside, every valley, every plain and grove, has been hallowed by some sad or happy event in days long vanished. . . . The very dust upon which you now stand responds more lovingly to their footsteps than to yours, because it is rich with the blood of our ancestors and our bare feet are conscious of the sympathetic touch. . . . And when the last red man shall have perished, and the memory of my tribe shall have become a myth among the white men, these shores will swarm with the invisible dead of my tribe. . . . At night when the streets of your cities and villages are silent and you think them deserted, they will throng with the returning hosts that once filled and still love this beautiful land. The white man will never be alone. Let him be just and deal kindly with my people, for the dead are not powerless. Dead, did I say? There is no death, only a change of worlds.

Emotive language often plays a double role — it not only symbolizes and expresses our feelings but also arouses or *evokes* feelings in others. When we say "I love you" to someone, we usually are not simply expressing our feelings toward the person — we also hope to inspire similar feelings in that person toward us. Even when we are communicating factual information (which we will explore more fully in Chapter Ten, *Reporting, Inferring, Judging*), we make use of the emotive influence of language to interest other people in what we are saying. For example, compare the factually more objective account by the *New York Times* (pages 162–163) of Malcolm X's assassination with the more emotive/action account by *Life* magazine (page 163). Which account do you find more engaging? Why?

Although an emotive statement may be an *accurate* description of how we feel, it is *not* the same as a factual statement, because it is true only for ourselves — not for others. For instance, even though we may feel that a movie is tasteless and repulsive, someone else may find it exciting and hilarious. By describing our feelings about the movie, we are giving our personal evaluation, which often differs from the personal evaluation of others (consider the case of conflicting reviews of the same movie). A factual statement, on the other hand, is a statement with which all "rational" people will agree, providing that suitable evidence for its truth is available (for example, the fact that mass transit uses less energy than automobiles).

In some ways, symbolizing our emotions is more difficult than representing factual information about the world. Expressing our feelings toward a person we know well often seems considerably more challenging than describing facts about the person.

When emotive words are used in larger groups (such as sentences, paragraphs, compositions, poems, plays, novels, and so on) they become even more powerful. The pamphlets of Thomas Paine helped inspire American patriots in the Revolutionary War, and Abraham Lincoln's Gettysburg Address has endured as an expression of our most cherished values. On the other hand, it was the impassioned oratory of Adolf Hitler that helped influence the German people before and during World War II.

One way to think about the meaning and power of emotive words is to see them on a scale or continuum, from mild to strong. For example:

Overweight/Plump   Fat   Obese

The thinker Bertrand Russell used this feature of emotive words to show how we perceive the same trait in various people:

• I am firm.

• You are stubborn.

• He/she is pigheaded.

We usually tend to perceive ourselves favorably ("I am firm"). I am speaking to you face to face, so I view you only somewhat less favorably ("You are stubborn"). But since a third person is not present, we can use stronger emotive language ("He/she is pigheaded").

Try this technique with three other emotive words:

1. I am _____   You are _____   He/she is _____

2. I am _____   You are _____   He/she is _____

3. I am _____   You are _____   He/she is _____

Finally, emotive words can be used to confuse opinions with facts, a situation that commonly occurs when we combine emotive uses of language with informative uses. Although people may appear to be giving *factual* information, they actually may be adding personal evaluations that are not factual. These opinions are often emotional, biased, unfounded, or inflammatory. Consider the following statement: "New York City is a filthy and dangerous pigpen — only idiots would want to live there." Although the speaker is pretending to give factual information, he or she is really using emotive language to advance an opinion. But emotive uses of language are not always negative. The statement, "She's the most generous, wise, honest, and warm friend that a person could have" also illustrates the confusion of the emotive and the informative uses of language, except that in this case the feelings are positive.

The presence of emotive words is usually a sign that a personal opinion or evaluation rather than a fact is being stated. Speakers occasionally do identify their opinions as opinions with such phrases as "In my opinion . . ." or "I feel that . . ." Often, however, speakers do *not* identify their opinions as opinions because they *want* us to treat their judgments as *facts*. In these cases the combination of the informative use of language with the emotive use can be misleading and even dangerous.

THINKING ACTIVITY

7.10 ▶ Give examples of emotive language in the following passages and explain how it is used by the writer to influence people's thoughts and feelings.

> I draw the line in the dust and toss the gauntlet before the heel of tyranny, and I say segregation now, segregation tomorrow, segregation forever.
>
> Governor George C. Wallace, 1963

> We dare not forget today that we are heirs of that first revolution. Let the word go forth from this time and place, to friend and foe alike, that the torch has been passed to a new generation of Americans — born in this century, tempered by war, disciplined by a hard and bitter peace, proud of our ancient heritage — and unwilling to witness or permit the slow undoing of those human rights to which this nation has always been committed, and to which we are committed today at home and around the world.
>
> President John F. Kennedy, Inaugural Address, 1961

Every criminal, every gambler, every thug, every libertine, every girl ruiner, every home wrecker, every wife beater, every dope peddler, every moonshiner, every crooked politician, every pagan Papist priest, every shyster lawyer, every white slaver, every brothel madam, every Rome controlled newspaper, every black spider — is fighting the Klan. Think it over. Which side are you on?

From a Ku Klux Klan circular

We need another and a wiser and perhaps a more mystical concept of animals. Remote from universal nature, and living by complicated artifice, man in civilization surveys the creature through the glass of his knowledge and sees thereby a feather magnified and the whole image in distortion. We patronize them for their incompleteness, for their tragic fate of having taken form so far below ourselves. And therein we err, and greatly err. For the animal shall not be measured by man. In a world older and more complete than ours they move finished and complete, gifted with extensions of the senses we have lost or never attained, living by voices we shall never hear. They are not brethren, they are not underlings; they are other nations, caught with ourselves in the net of life and time, fellow prisoners of the splendour and travail of the earth.

Henry Beston, The Outermost House

Wherefore, O judges, be of good cheer about death, and know of a certainty, that no evil can happen to a good man, either in life or after death. He and his are not neglected by the gods; nor has my own approaching end happened by mere chance. But I see clearly that the time had arrived when it was better for me to die and be released from trouble; wherefore the oracle gave no sign. For which reason, also, I am not angry with my condemners, or with my accusers; they have done me no harm, although they did not mean to do me any good; and for this I may gently blame them.

Still I have a favor to ask of them. When my sons are grown up, I would ask you, O my friends, to punish them; and I would have you trouble them, as I have troubled you, if they seem to care about riches, or anything, more than about virtue; or if they pretend to be something when they are really nothing — then reprove them, as I have reproved you, for not caring about that for which they ought to care, and thinking that they are something when they are really nothing. And if you do this, both I and my sons will have received justice at your hands.

The hour of departure has arrived, and we go our ways — I to die, and you to live. Which is better God only knows.

Plato (describing the final moments
of Socrates's life), The Apology ◄

The Language of Advertising

Advertisers have nearly made a science out of using language to influence people's perceptions, beliefs, and actions. Most advertisements blend visual images and written messages to influence us to buy the products. One basic advertising strategy is to associate positive or negative thoughts and emotions with the product or service being sold. If the strategy succeeds, we are likely to recall these associations (although we are not always conscious of this) when we see the product on our next shopping trip and buy it as a result of the associations. Many people buy products not because they are of better quality than another, but because of associations that have absolutely *nothing* to do with the products. Here are some products and some of the associations for which their advertisers aim:

Product Name:	*Associations:*
Coca-Cola	"Adds life" — young, attractive people having lots of fun
Marlboro cigarettes	"Marlboro Country" — macho, strong, ruggedly handsome, independent cowboy riding on the range
Wisk detergent	"No more ring-around-the-collar" — average person saved by the detergent from social embarrassment and humiliation
Sanka decaffeinated coffee	Actor Robert Young, former star of *Father Knows Best* and *Marcus Welby, M.D.*, "prescribes" Sanka for people who are nervous, anxious, and irritable in various stressful situations — several weeks later, people are "cured" of their tension and anxiety

Modern advertising thus appeals to fundamental human *fears* and *desires*, offering *magic potions* and *sacred objects* that will help us avoid the things we dread (aging, dependence, and personal embarrassment, etc.) and gain the things we want (youth and beauty, independence, social grace, personal comfort, etc.). It appeals to our cultural values: dependability, tradition, excellence, sexual attractiveness, and pleasure. In these strategies advertisers are often no different than the "snake-oil" salesmen of a century ago who "guaranteed" relief from "all human ills and maladies."

THINKING ACTIVITY

7.11 ▶ Identify five products and explain what associations probably led to the selection of their names (such as LUV's Diapers, Ivory Snow Soap, and Lip-Quencher Lipstick). ◀

Emotive language often combines with visual imagery to present what we might think of as extremes in ideas and feelings. These extremes appear in the language of advertising, and their purpose is definitely to influence people. At their least influential, advertisements catch our attention by playing with words, making use of their multiple meanings or focusing on specific semantic features. Look at the following newspaper advertisements. Which words in the text have more than one meaning? What differing semantic meanings allow the plays on the words?

THE FALL Of $19.89 a sq. yard

TAKE COVER! DOWN COMFORTER $99.99 OVERNIGHT SENSATIONS

THINKING ACTIVITY

7.12 ▶ Here is the text of three advertisements. Explain what positive emotions or cultural values probably contributed to their creation.

1. Revlon Fashion Tech Pencils: With pencils this creamy, it's easy to draw attention.

2.   *TOYOTA 4 RUNNER*

   No other 4-wheel drive opens up so many avenues.

   And certainly no other 4-door vehicle lets you travel down them with so much confidence. After all, 4Runner has been ranked highest in customer satisfaction in its segment for four straight years. And now, with the most technologically advanced engine in its class — a 3.0 liter, 150-hp V6 — and shift-on-the-move 4WDemand, the 1990 4Runner 4WD SR5 V6 is even better equipped to carry you and your family away. Up a snowy mountain pass. Or down to the corner store. Because where you go is your concern. Getting you back is ours.

   Toyota, I love what you do for me.

3.   *A FORCE*

   It's what you are when you discard all the nonessentials, everything that isn't you.
   GAP CLASSICS, to be reckoned with. Individuals of style.
   GAP

◀

7.13 ▶ The following article, written by a professional advertising writer, explores the various language strategies advertisers use to shape our thinking and influence our behavior. Read the article carefully and then analyze its ideas by answering the questions that follow.

From THE LANGUAGE OF ADVERTISING *by Charles O'Neill*

One night in 1964, a copywriter named Shirley Polykoff was pacing around her office, thinking about Clairol's new hair coloring, Nice 'n Easy. The interesting, "saleable" thing about Nice 'n Easy — important to Clairol, to the advertising agency, and (at least potentially) to the haircolor-consuming public — was its basic difference from other hair colorings. Until the day Clairol put Nice 'n Easy on the market, a woman who wanted to dye her hair had to put the dye onto every strand. Coloring the older, longer hairs, sometimes meant missing the roots. The result was an interesting, but somewhat less than fashionable, horizontal-striped look. New Nice 'n Easy, however, could be shampooed right through the hair, producing what Miss Polykoff calls that "beautiful, even, natural-looking color."

But that night in 1964, Shirley Polykoff's problem was to translate the product feature into a benefit consumers could feel; she had to translate the even-coloring idea into a memorable, potent, and attractive advertisement. So there she paced, searching for a way to motivate people into running out and buying Nice 'n Easy. She looked down at the rug, and, as she remembers it, this is what happened:

> My mind wandered back to those early days when George and I used to meet each other after work and I'd spend the afternoon anticipating the rush of joy when I'd first glimpse him coming down the block. We'd be flying toward each other, but, compared to our eagerness to bridge the distance, it was like wading through molasses.
>
> Though the street was crowded, we were alone, the people in our path merely obstacles to cut around. On about the fourth time we met this way, he lifted me off my feet with a hug of sheer happiness. We were both a little breathless and as we stood there grinning at each other he said, "You know, you look pretty good from afar."
>
> "And from near?"
>
> "Even better."*

* Shirley Polykoff, *Does She . . . or Doesn't She?* (Garden City, N.J.: Doubleday, 1975).

To anyone but Shirley Polykoff, that brief romantic reverie would probably have been nothing more than a pleasant distraction, but way back in her mind, she was still thinking about Nice 'n Easy.

> As I sat there recalling those delicious days, the campaign for Nice 'n Easy shampoo-in hair color unfolded like a dream. And, as if in a dream, the man and woman in the commercial would float toward each other in slow motion across fields or through crowds with arms outstretched in anticipation. Though the message would have to express to the consumer that the color results would be even enough to pass closest inspection, it would have to capture the romance of the visual. And that is how I hit on the line, *The closer he gets . . . the better you look! With Nice 'n Easy, it's hair color so natural, the closer he gets the better you look!**

Clairol found the concept appealing, and Nice 'n Easy sales proved that Polykoff had indeed touched something deep in the psyche of the public. The campaign had immediate, lasting impact: across America, women who had feared that tell-tale, horizontal-striped, less-than-convincing look changed their minds and bought Nice 'n Easy. In the media/advertising business, as elsewhere, imitation is the best form of flattery. Suddenly, everybody who made television commercials and movies wanted to show slim, long-haired girls running in slow motion across sun-lit fields.

Through a carefully chosen combination of visual images and spoken words, one small group of human beings had caused a larger group to take a specific, desired course of action. When Polykoff hammered out "The closer he gets . . . the better you look! With Nice 'n Easy, it's hair color so natural, the closer he gets the better you look!" on the typewriter, she set in motion a sequence of events that changed the buying habits of hundreds of thousands (or perhaps millions) of people. People who had previously bought other brands of hair-color products now switched to Nice 'n Easy; others who had never thought much about coloring their hair now felt an impulse to do so. Creating that impulse — the impulse to *buy* — is the reason for advertising. The final test of any advertisement (for hair color, automobiles, detergents, cereals, life insurance, or pantyhose) is simply the degree to which it creates the impulse.

What creates the impulse? The strategy may call for printed ads in

* Ibid.

magazines, thirty-second spots on national television, handbills distributed on Main Street, tee shirts, or town criers. Whatever the strategy, advertisements derive their power from a purposeful, directed combination of two elements: visual images and words. The precise balance of words and pictures is determined by the creative concept and the medium used; but that balance of images and words makes up the language of advertising.

Every member of our society soon learns that advertising language is "different" from other languages. Most children would be unable to explain how "With Nice 'n Easy, it's color so natural, the closer he gets the better you look!" differed from ordinary language; but they *would* be able to tell you, "It sounds like an ad." Advertising language *is* different from most of the other languages we use in our everyday life. Its differences exist because when Polykoff or one of her colleagues sits down to write an ad, she is attempting to change our behavior . . . to motivate us . . . to *sell* us something.

Over the years, the texture of advertising language has frequently changed. Styles and creative concepts come and go. But there are at least four distinct characteristics general to the language of advertising, characteristics that make it different from other languages.

- The language of advertising is edited and purposeful, when most other language transactions are "elliptical."
- The language of advertising is rich and arresting; it is specifically intended to attract and hold our attention.
- The language of advertising involves us; in effect, *we* complete the advertising message.
- The language of advertising holds no secrets from us; it is a simple language.

Edited and Purposeful

One way to develop quickly a feeling for a basic difference between advertising language and other languages is to make a transcription of a television talk show.* An examination of the transcript shows first that the conversation skipped from one topic to another, even though the guests and the host were attempting to discuss a specific subject. Sec-

---

* The dialog on a television talk show provides a good example of free-form, unstructured speech. A better example is a transcript of casual conversation about an innocuous topic like the weather.

ondly, the conversation was rife with repetitive comments. After all, informal, conversational language transactions are not ordinarily intended to meet specific objectives. Advertising language cannot afford to be so desultory. It *does* have a specific purpose — to sell us something.

In *Future Shock*, Alvin Toffler draws a distinction between normal, "coded" messages and "engineered" messages. As an example of an "uncoded" message, Toffler writes about a random, unstructured experience:

> A man walks along a street and notices a leaf whipped along a sidewalk by the wind. He perceives this event through his sensory apparatus. He hears a rustling sound. He sees movement and greenness. He feels the wind. From these sensory perceptions he somehow forms a mental image. We can refer to these sensory signals as a message. But the message is not, in any ordinary sense of the term, man-made. It was not designed by anyone to communicate anything, and the man's understanding of it does not depend directly on a social code — a set of agreed-upon signs and definitions.*

The talk show conversation, however, *is* coded; the guests' ability to exchange information with their host, our ability to understand it depends, as Toffler puts it, upon social conventions.

Beyond the coded and uncoded messages there is another kind — the engineered message — a variation of the coded message. The language of advertising is a language of finely engineered, ruthlessly purposive messages. By Toffler's calculation,† the average adult American is assaulted by at least 560 advertising messages a day. Not one of these messages would reach us, to attract and hold our attention, if it were uncoded or completely unstructured. Similarly, even if they happened to attract us for a fleeting moment, coded but "unengineered" messages (that is, a group of talk show guests chatting about Nice 'n Easy) would quickly lose our attention. But when a slim girl runs through the field in slow motion and a voice says, "The closer he gets, the better you look!" women looking for a hair color product pay attention, because the message has been carefully engineered, carefully compressed. Advertising's messages have a clear purpose; they are intended to trigger a *specific* response.

---

* Alvin Toffler, *Future Shock* (New York: Random House, 1970), p. 146.
† Ibid., p. 149.

Rich and Arresting

No advertisement, no matter how carefully engineered and packed with information, has even a remote chance of succeeding unless it attracts our attention in the first place. Of the 560 advertising messages waiting for us each day, very few (Toffler estimates 76)* will actually obtain our conscious attention. The remaining 484 are screened out. The people who design and write ads recognize that this screening process takes place; they anticipate and accept it as a basic premise of their business. Nonetheless, they expend a great deal of energy to guarantee that *their* ads are among the few that penetrate the defenses and distraction which surround us. The classic, all-time favorite device used to penetrate the barrier is sex. The archetypal sex ad is simply headlined "SEX," with the text running something like this: "Now that we've got your attention. ... ." Whether it takes the sex approach or another, every successful advertisement contains a "hitch": a word or image intended to bring us into the ad. The hitch is usually one or a set of strong visuals (photos or illustrations with emotional value) or a disarming, unexpected — even incongruous — set of words:

"My chickens eat better than you do."	*(Perdue Chickens)*
"Are soufflés your downfall?"	*(Better Homes and Gardens)*
"Introducing the ultimate concept in air freight. Men that fly."	*(Emery Air Freight)*
"Look deep into our ryes."	*(Wigler's bakery products)*
"There is no such thing as a xerox."	*(Xerox)*
"Me. 4 U"	*(The State of Maine)*
"If gas pains persist, try Volkswagen."	*(Volkswagen)*
"Volvo. Ideally situated between the sublime and the ridiculous."	*(Volvo)*

The point is that people do not watch television or read magazines in order to see ads — the ads have to earn the right to be seen, read, and heard. Jerry Della Femina, a man who earns a good living in the advertising business, sums up the problem:

* Ibid.

There are a lot of copywriters who get mixed up and think they're
Faulkner or Hemingway. They sit there and they mold and they play
and when it's over they've written something that's absolutely beautiful but they forgot one thing. It's within the confines of a page. . . .
What kills most copywriters is that people don't buy *Life* magazine to
read their ads. People don't buy *Gourmet* to read their ad for Bombay
Gin. People are buying *Gourmet* to read the recipes, and the ads are
just an intrusion on people's time. That is why our job is to get more
attention than anything else.*

Participation

We have seen that the language of advertising is carefully engineered;
we have seen that it uses various devices to get our attention. Clairol
has us watching the girl running across a field in slow motion . . . Frank
Perdue has us looking at a photo of his chickens at a dining table . . .
Volkswagen has us thinking about our gas pains . . . Marlboro has us
looking at the muscular man on a sleek horse. Now that they have our
attention, what will they do next? They present information intended
to show us that the product they are offering for sale fills a need and,
in filling this need, is different from its competitors. At this point, the
name of the process is "product placement." On the night she developed the Nice 'n Easy campaign, Polykoff's problem was to express the
differences between the Clairol product and its competitors. Nice 'n
Easy *was* different. Its feature was that it could be shampooed through
the hair. To the consumer, the benefit was that it did not cause tell-tale
streaks. Once our attention has been obtained, it is the copywriter's responsibility to express such product differences (when they exist) to ex-
ploit and intensify them.

What happens when product differences *do not* exist? Then the writer
must glamorize the superficial differences (for example, differences of
color, packaging, or other qualities with no direct connection to the
product's basic function) or else *create* differences in the consumer's
mind. At this point the language of advertising becomes more abstract,
more difficult to define and analyze. It is also at this stage — the stage
at which an image is fixed in the consumer's mind — that advertising
becomes powerful, because now we, the consumers, are brought directly into the process. While the ad still attempted to attract us, the
action took place mostly in the ad, in the words and visual images. But

---

* Jerry Della Femina, *From Those Wonderful Folks Who Brought You Pearl Harbor* (New
York: Simon and Schuster, 1970), p. 118.

when we read an ad or watch one on television, we become more deeply involved. In effect, the action takes place in *us*. Because our minds are triggered, our individual fears and aspirations, our little quirks and insecurities, are superimposed on that tightly engineered, attractively packaged message. Polykoff did not create the consumers' need to feel attractive "up close." The drive to feel attractive was already there; she merely exploited and intensified it.

So the language of advertising is different from other languages because it holds a brightly-lit mirror up to us. Once we have been brought into an ad — once that blonde Noxzema girl starts purring, "Take it off . . . take it all off!" — we become participants in an ad.

This process is especially significant in ads for products that do not differ significantly from their competitors. Take the case of the Noxzema commercial: basically, shaving cream is made of soap filled with water and air, and perhaps a little perfume. Millions of men get up every morning and apply it to their faces. How can one shaving cream differ from another? Most are based on the same chemical formula. Yet once we have been attracted by the Noxzema girl, our feelings about shaving cream take on emotional connotation. The commercial is consciously designed to build, in our minds, an association between the girl and the product. We are subtly led to think that if we use the shaving cream, the girl will be available to us — or at least associated with us in some manner. Even if we make a conscious effort to reject that association, we will remember her, and the Noxzema messages we see in the future will probably trigger a pleasant memory. In other words, the ad leaves us favorably disposed to the product.

Symbols have become important elements in the language of advertising, not so much because they carry meanings of their own but because we bring a meaning to them: we charge them with significance. Symbols are efficient, compact vehicles for the communication of an advertising message. As Toffler says, "Today, advertising men, in a deliberate attempt to cram more messages into the individual's mind within a given moment of time, make increasing use of the symbolic techniques of the arts. Consider the 'tiger' that is allegedly put into one's tank. Here a single word transmits to the audience a distinct visual image that has been associated since childhood with power, speed, and force."* The

* Toffler, *Future Shock,* p. 149.

language of advertising is different from other languages because we participate in it; in fact, we — not the words we read on the magazine page or the pictures unreeling before us on the television screen — charge the ads with most of their power.

Simplicity

Clip a story out of a typical article in the publication you read most frequently. Calculate the number of words in an average sentence. Count the number of words of three or more syllables in a typical one-hundred-word passage, neglecting words that are capitalized, combinations of two simple words, or verb forms made into three-syllable words by the addition of -ed or -es. Add the two factors (the average number of words per sentence and the number of three-syllable words per hundred words), then multiply the result by .4. According to Robert Gunning, if the resulting number is seven, there is a good chance that you are an avid reader of *True Confessions.** He developed this equation, the "Fog Index," to determine the comparative ease with which any given piece of written communication can be read. With this equation, the first passages of this essay measure somewhere between *Reader's Digest* and *Time.*

Now consider the complete text of a typical cigarette advertisement:

> I demand two things from my cigarette. I want a cigarette with low tar and nicotine. But, I also want taste. That's why I smoke Winston Lights. I get a lighter cigarette, but I still get real taste. And real pleasure. Only one cigarette gives me that: Winston Lights.

The average sentence in this ad runs seven words. "Cigarette" and "nicotine" are three-syllable words, with "cigarette" appearing four times, "nicotine," once. The ad is exactly fifty words long, so the average number of three-syllable words per hundred is fourteen.

$$
\begin{array}{rl}
7 & \text{words per sentence} \\
+\;\;14 & \text{three-syllable words/hundred} \\
\hline
21 & \\
\times\;\;.4 & \\
\hline
8.4 & \text{Fog Index}
\end{array}
$$

---

* Curtis D. MacDougall, *Interpretive Reporting* (New York: Macmillan, 1968), p. 94.

According to Gunning's scale, this particular ad is written at about the eighth grade level*; a little harder to read than a typical passage in *Ladies' Home Journal*, but easier than *Reader's Digest*, and a few points harder than *True Confessions*. The level of the Winston Lights ad is representative of the ads regularly found in most mass circulation, consumer magazines. Of course, the Fog Index does not evaluate the visual aspect of an ad. The headline "I demand two things from my cigarette" works with the picture (that of an attractive woman) to create consumer interest. The text reinforces the image. It is unlikely that many consumers actually take the trouble to read the entire text.

Since three-syllable words are harder to read than one- or two-syllable words, and since simple ideas are more easily transferred from one human being to another than complex ideas, advertising copy tends to use simpler language all the time. Toffler speculates: "If the [English] language had the same number of words in Shakespeare's time as it does today, at least 200,000 words — perhaps several times that many — have dropped out and been replaced in the intervening four centuries. . . . The high turnover rate reflects changes in things, processes, and qualities in the environment from the world of consumer products and technology."† It is no accident that the first terms Toffler uses to illustrate his point ("fast-back," "wash-and-wear," and "flashcube") were invented not by engineers, journalists, or marketing managers but by advertising copywriters.

The language of advertising is simple language; in the engineering process, difficult words (which could be used in other forms of communication to lend color or fine shades of meaning) are edited out and replaced by simple words not open to misinterpretation. ■

1. O'Neill states that the language of advertising has the following characteristics:

- Edited and purposeful
- Rich and arresting
- Participatory
- Simple

Locate what you consider to be an effective advertisement and analyze its use of language in terms of these characteristics.

---

* Ibid., p. 95.
† Toffler, *Future Shock*, p. 151.

2. Select a product that you are familiar with and compose an advertisement following the guidelines listed above. Try to make your advertisement as influential as possible. ◄

THINKING ACTIVITY

7.14 ▶ Critically evaluate the issue of whether advertising is damaging to our language, our thinking, or our culture. Be sure to develop arguments on both sides of the issue and reach an informed conclusion. ◄

THINKING ACTIVITY

7.15 ▶ Examine the next three advertisements. Analyze them by answering the questions that follow.

1. Describe your subjective response to each ad — what are your first impressions and emotional reactions? What does the ad *do* for you? How do you look at it? Do you focus on the images or begin to read the text? Do you read it carefully or skim over it? What parts attract your attention most? Do you find yourself staring at a certain portion of it?

2. Analyze the way the ads are designed to create the responses that you described in the first question.

   a. What is the major theme of each ad?

   b. What words and phrases in the ad express that idea? Identify the action verbs, concrete nouns, and vivid adjectives.

   c. What images in each ad express its major theme? Why were these images selected?

3. To what audience does each ad appeal? What assumptions does each ad make about the tastes, habits, hopes, weaknesses, and fears of its audience? ◄

The eagle has landed.

In Oklahoma and Mississippi. Georgia and Alabama. Where few bald eagle nests have produced young in the last 50 years. Using precious eggs and dedicated effort, the Sutton Avian Research Center is successfully raising eaglets from fuzzy to fierce. And releasing them into the habitats bald eagles used to call home. Phillips Petroleum supports this unique program to re-establish our endangered national symbol.

After all, if Man can land an Eagle on the moon, he can surely keep them landing on the earth.

Phillips 66

For more information, contact the George Miksch Sutton Avian Research Center, Inc., P.O. Box 2007, Bartlesville, OK 74005, (918) 336-7778.

Courtesy of Phillips Petroleum Company.

Sometimes what it takes to put a life back together is a hammer and nails.

In Lima, Ohio, a woman drives home a nail. And drives home a new skill. Another tears down an old wall. And tears down old defeatism.

These women are rehabilitating a neighborhood. And at the same time, they are rehabilitating themselves. They are inmates at the nearby Marysville prison who are contributing to a neighborhood revitalization project funded, in part, by General Dynamics.

They learn to replace drywall, fixtures, cabinetry, stairways, porches, siding, roofing, and more.

For the community, the result is very high quality, affordable family housing.

For prisoners turned productive, the result is new confidence, new job skills, and a new chance at life.

GENERAL DYNAMICS
A Strong Company For A Strong Country

Courtesy of General Dynamics.

342

Sweat. It's the only way to run an American business. It's the only way we know to run an airline.

Northwest is doing more than ever to help you run your business. If you've flown with us lately, you've noticed. We're getting you where you need to go, on time. We're setting standards of comfort and efficiency. From ticketing to baggage handling, we're racing ahead of the competition. It takes a lot of effort to stay on the fast track, but finishing first is the only place we want to be. For reservations, call your travel agent or Northwest at 1-800-225-2525.

NORTHWEST AIRLINES

Courtesy of Northwest Airlines.

Summary

The themes of these two chapters on language reveal the essential role of language in developing sophisticated thinking abilities. The goal of clear, effective thinking and communication — avoiding ambiguity and vagueness — is accomplished through the joint efforts of thought and language. Learning to use the appropriate language style, depending on the social context in which we are operating, requires both critical judgment and flexible expertise with various language forms. Critically evaluating the pervasive attempts of advertisers and others to bypass our critical faculties and influence our thinking involves insight into the way language and thought create and express meaning.

Its link with thinking makes language so powerful a tool that we not only rely on it as a vehicle for expressing our thoughts and feelings and for influencing others, we use language to provide a structure for learning. Like a choreographer who creates a dance, language shapes and forms our thoughts. It organizes them. It relates one idea to the other so that their combinations, many and varied, can be reported with strength and vitality, creating meaning that no one idea could convey alone. Used expertly, language *expresses* our thinking in a way that clearly evokes the images, feelings, and ideas that we as speakers and writers want to present. It also *communicates* our thinking in such a way that others can comprehend our meaning, making in turn appropriate inferences and judgments and thereby expanding their own thinking. We will be examining these further relationships between language and thought in the next chapters.

CHAPTER 8

Forming and Applying Concepts

CONCEPTS:
General ideas that we use to identify
and organize our experience.

Properties

The
**Structure
of Concepts**

Symbol   **Referents**

**Forming
Concepts:**
An interactive process
of generalizing and
interpreting.

**Applying
Concepts:**
Meeting the concept's
necessary requirements.

**Defining
Concepts:**
Identifying
necessary
requirements and
providing examples.

WE BEGAN OUR EXPLORATION of the thinking process in Chapter One by defining it as an active, purposeful, organized process we use to make sense of the world. Each succeeding chapter has helped us clarify the nature of this thinking process and the way it operates. In Chapter Six, *Language as a System,* we discovered that this process of making sense of the world depends in large measure on our ability to represent our thoughts, feelings, and experiences with language symbols. In using language, we are able to:

- *Identify* (or name) our experiences. ("That's a panda bear!")
- *Distinguish* these experiences from one another. ("A panda bear is much larger than a koala bear.")
- *Describe* these experiences to others who share an understanding of our language. ("Panda bears are large, furry, vegetarian mammals with distinctive black and white markings and adorable faces.")
- *Relate* these experiences to other experiences or ideas. ("Panda bears are revered in their native China as symbols of fertility and are objects of universal affection.")

Many of the language symbols we use — such as "panda bear" and "koala bear" — represent *concepts* that we have formed. We can define concepts as follows:

> *Concepts*   General ideas that we use to identify and organize our experience.

In this chapter we will explore concepts. We will discover what they are and the way we form and apply them, as well as strategies we can use to improve our mastery of them. Because concepts play such an essential role in the thinking process, improving our ability to use them will necessarily sharpen our thinking process as well.

One of the main goals of thinking critically is to develop informed, well-supported beliefs about the world that will enhance our understanding of it and enable us to make intelligent decisions based on this understanding. Every aspect of this complex process of making sense of the world involves forming and applying concepts. Whether we are carefully examining our perceptions, developing and critically evaluating beliefs, or constructing knowledge of the world, we are involved in the process of *conceptualizing*, forming and applying concepts.

As a result, learning to master concepts will help you in every area of your life: academic, career, and personal. In college study, each academic discipline or subject is composed of many different concepts that are used to organize experience, give explanations, and solve problems. Here is a sampling of college-level concepts: entropy, subtext, *Gemeinschaft*, cell, metaphysics, relativity, unconscious, transformational grammar, aesthetic, minor key, interface, health, quantum mechanics, schizophrenia. To make sense of how disciplines function, we need to understand what the concepts of that discipline mean, how to apply them, and the way they relate to other concepts. We also need to learn the methods of investigation, patterns of thought, and forms of reasoning that various disciplines use to form larger *conceptual structures*, subjects that we will explore in the remaining chapters of the text.

Using language effectively in academic studies also involves mastering and using concepts. For example, when we read textbooks or listen to lectures and take notes, we are required to grasp the key concepts and follow them as they are developed and supported. When we write papers or homework assignments, we are usually expected to focus on certain concepts, develop a thesis around them, present the thesis (itself a concept!) with carefully argued points, and back it up with specific examples. Many course examinations involve applying key concepts we have learned to new sets of circumstances.

Regardless of their specific knowledge content, all careers require conceptual abilities, whether we are trying to apply a legal principle, develop a promotional theme, or devise a new computer program. Similarly, expertise in forming and applying concepts helps us make sense of our personal lives, understand ourselves and others, and make informed decisions. In short, we might agree with the Greek philosopher Aristotle, who once said that the intelligent person is a "master of concepts."

What Are Concepts?

Our world is filled with concepts. A large number of the words we use to represent our experience express concepts we have formed. *Sportscar, person, education, computer, sport, elated,* and *thinking* are only a few examples of concepts. Consider the sorts of things that most people in our culture wear on their feet. The word we use to identify and describe these sorts of things — "shoes" — expresses a concept or general idea we have formed. This concept represents *all* the different sorts of shoes people actually wear, including the specific things we are wearing on our feet at this moment. In this respect, concepts are different from names that refer to a specific individual, such as *Ping-Ping*. The name *Ping-Ping* is not a general idea. Instead, it represents a specific panda bear. Concepts, on the other hand, describe a general type of thing — such as "shoes" or "panda bears" — that may represent many specific items or individuals.

As we previously noted, many of our language symbols represent concepts. These concepts enable us to

- *Identify* the various things in our experience as "kinds" of things.
- *Distinguish* these kinds of things from other kinds of things.
- *Describe* these kinds of things to others who share an understanding of our symbols.
- *Relate* these kinds of things to other kinds of things.

Consider the concept of "sports." When we see other people engaged in a sports activity we are able to recognize and *identify* the kind of sport they are playing, such as baseball. At the same time, the concepts we have formed enable us to *distinguish* this sport from other types of sports, such as soccer, shot putting, squash, and swimming sidestroke. Each of these names identifies another type of sport expressing another concept we have formed. Concepts also enable us to *describe* the sport that is being played by listing the properties or features that make up the concept. For example, the sport of baseball usually involves playing with nine people on each team on a field the shape of a slice of pie. The goal of the team on offense is to hit a ball thrown by the opposing "pitcher" and run to each of four bases while the team on defense tries to catch the ball in the air or throw the ball to a base before the runner — and so on. Let us examine how this process works by studying the diagram on page 349, which identifies and shows some of the relationships among various sports. Replace the question marks with concepts you think are appropriate. Then select three of the types of sports identified in the diagram (including two that you identified) and describe some of the properties that distinguish them from each other.

Example: Badminton: Played with two or four players, the object of this sport is to prevent the shuttlecock ("birdie") from landing on your side of the net by hitting it over the net with a racket.

1. *Sport:* _____

   Properties: _____

   _____

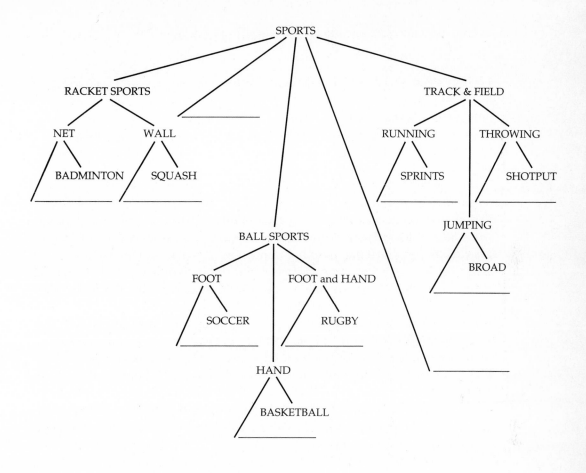

2. *Sport:* _____

   Properties: _____

   _____

3. *Sport:* _____

   Properties: _____

   _____

How do we use concepts to organize and make sense of experience? Let's look at an example. Think back to the first day of classes. For most students, this is a time to evaluate their courses by trying to determine which concepts apply.

• Will this course be interesting? Useful? A lot of work?

- Is the teacher stimulating? Demanding? Entertaining?
- Are the students friendly? Intelligent? Conscientious?

Each of these words or phrases represents a concept we are attempting to apply so that we can understand what is occurring at the moment and also anticipate what the course will be like in the future.

To take another example, imagine that you are a physician and that one of your patients comes to you complaining of shortness of breath and occasional pain in his left arm. After he describes his symptoms, you would ask a number of questions, examine him, and perhaps administer some tests. Your ability to identify the underlying problem would depend on your knowledge of various human diseases. Each disease is identified and described by a different concept. Identifying these various diseases means that you can distinguish different concepts and that you know in what situations to apply a given concept correctly. In addition, when the patient asks, "What's wrong with me, doctor?" you are able to describe the concept (for example, heart disease) and explain how it is related to his symptoms.

As our thinking abilities develop, we gradually form concepts that enable us to symbolize our world in increasingly precise ways. Fortunately for us, modern medicine has developed (and is continuing to develop) remarkably precise concepts to describe and explain the diseases that afflict us. In the patient's case, we may conclude that the problem is heart disease. Of course, there are many different kinds of heart disease, represented by different concepts, and success in treating the patient will depend on figuring out exactly which type of disease is involved.

The Structure of Concepts

Concepts are general ideas we use to identify, distinguish, and relate the various aspects of our experience. Concepts allow us to organize our world into patterns that make sense to us. This is the process by which we discover and create meaning in our lives.

In their role as organizers of experience, concepts act to group aspects of our experience based on their similarity to one another. Consider the thing that you usually write with: a pen. The concept "pen" represents a type of object that we use for writing. But look around the classroom at all other instruments people are using to write. We use the concept "pen" to identify these things as well, even though they may look very different from the one you are using.

Thus the concept "pen" not only helps us make distinctions in our experience by indicating how pens differ from pencils, crayons, or magic markers, but it also helps us determine which items are similar enough to each other to be called pens. When we put items into a group with a single description — like "pen" — we are focusing on the *similarities* between the items:

- They use ink.
- They are used for writing.
- They are held with a hand.

But we are ignoring the *differences* among them, such as color, size, brand, and so forth.

Being able to see and name the similarities between certain things in our experience is the way we form concepts and is crucial for making sense of our world. If we were not able to do this, then everything in the world would be different, with its own individual name. Just imagine having to give a different name to every pen in the world.

Concepts therefore fulfill two important jobs for us:

1. Concepts represent/express how various things in our experience are *similar* to each other, enabling us to place things in groups on the basis of certain similarities between them. These groups give us the means to identify each thing as a kind of thing — "That's a kind of pen."
2. Concepts represent/express how things in our experience are *different* from each other, enabling us to make distinctions.

The process by which we group things based on their similarities is known as *classifying*. Classifying is a natural human activity that is going on all of the time. In most cases, however, we are not conscious that we are classifying something in a particular sort of way; we do so automatically. The process of classifying is one of the main ways that we order, organize, and make sense of our world. Because no two things or experiences are exactly alike, our ability to classify things into various groups is what enables us to recognize things in our experience. When we perceive a pen, we recognize it as a *kind of thing* we have seen before. Even though we may not have seen this particular pen, we recognize that it belongs to a group of things that we are familiar with.

For each of the following concepts, identify properties shared by the members of the classification.

1. Tables: _____

2. Dances: _____

3. Human beings: _____

Identify two concepts from your experience and describe the common properties shared by the members of the classification.

4. _____: _____

5. _____: _____

The best way to understand the structure of concepts is to visualize them by means of a model:

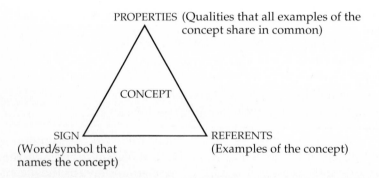

PROPERTIES (Qualities that all examples of the concept share in common)

CONCEPT

SIGN
(Word/symbol that names the concept)

REFERENTS
(Examples of the concept)

The *sign* is the word or symbol used to name or designate the concept; the word *triangle*, for example, is a sign. The *referents* represent all the various examples of the concept; the three-sided figure we are using as our model is an example of the concept *triangle*. The *properties* of the concept are the features that all things named by the word or sign share in common; all examples of the concept *triangle* share the characteristics of being a polygon and having three sides. These are the properties that we refer to when we *define* concepts; thus, "A triangle is a three-sided polygon."

Let's take another example. Suppose we wanted to explore the structure of the concept *automobile*. The *sign* that names the concept is the word *automobile* or the symbol 🚗 . *Referents* of the concept include the 1954 MG "TF" currently residing in the garage as well as the Dodge Ramcharger parked in front of the house. The *properties* that all things named by the sign *automobile* include are wheels, a chassis, an engine, seats for passengers, and so on. The following is a specific model of the concept *automobile*:

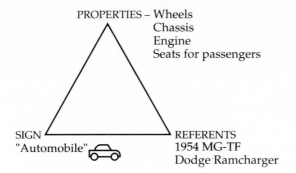

THINKING ACTIVITY

8.1   ▶ Using the model we have developed, diagram the structure of the concepts
       we considered on page 352 (tables, dances, human beings) as well as the two
       concepts you identified. ◀

Forming Concepts

Throughout our lives we are engaged in the process of forming — and applying — concepts to organize our experience, make sense of what is happening
at the moment, and anticipate what may happen in the future. We form concepts by the interactive process of *generalizing* (focusing on the common properties shared by a group of things) and *interpreting* (finding examples of the
concept). The common properties form the necessary requirements that must
be met in order to apply the concept to our experience. If we examine the
diagram of concepts in the last section, we can see that the process of forming
concepts involves moving back and forth between the *referents* (examples) of
the concept and the *properties* (common features) shared by all examples of the
concept. Let's explore further the way this interactive process of forming concepts operates.

Consider the following sample conversation between two people trying to
form and clarify the concept "city."

A: What is your idea of a "city"?

B: Well, I guess that it's a place where different people live together —
    like Chicago.

A: Is our neighborhood a city? After all, it's a place where different people live together.

B: No. A neighborhood may be *part* of a city, but a city usually has many different neighborhoods in it, like Miami.

A: What about North Salem — is that a city? After all, it contains various neighborhoods in which different people live together.

B: I don't think North Salem is a city; it's too small. I think that North Salem is only a town or maybe only a village. A city needs to have *a lot* of people living there — like New York.

A: Then what about Monroe County — is *that* a city? It's got neighborhoods and lots of different people living together.

B: I'm afraid not. A county is usually much larger than a city. In fact, some counties contain more than one city. I think that a city needs to be concentrated in a smaller area. And I think that it needs a lot of rather large buildings, businesses, sidewalks, traffic, and so on — like Los Angeles.

A: What about Boston? Is that a city? I believe that it has all the qualities that you mentioned.

B: *Now* you've got it!

As we review this dialogue, we can see that *forming* the concept "city" works hand in hand with *applying* the concept to different examples. When two or more things work together in this way, we say that they interact. In this case, there are two parts of this interactive process.

Generalizing and Interpreting

We form concepts by *generalizing,* by focusing on the similarities between different things. In the dialogue just given, the things from which generalizations are being made are the cities — Chicago, Miami, New York, and Los Angeles. By focusing on the similarities among these cities, the two people in the dialogue develop a list of properties the cities share, including

• Different people living together.
• Various neighborhoods.
• A lot of people residing there.
• Being larger than a town.

- Being concentrated in a limited area.
- Containing a lot of buildings, sidewalks, businesses, traffic, and so on.

These common properties act as the *requirements* that an area must meet to be considered a city.

We apply concepts by *interpreting*, by looking for different examples of the concept and seeing if they meet the requirements of the concept we are developing. In the conversation, one of the participants attempts to apply the concept "city" to the following examples:

- North Salem
- A neighborhood
- Monroe County
- Boston

Each of the proposed examples suggests the development of new requirements for the concept, which helps to clarify how the concept can be applied. Applying a concept to different possible examples thus becomes the way that we develop and gradually sharpen our idea of the concept. Even when a proposed example turns out *not* to be an example of the concept, our understanding of the concept is often clarified. For example, although the proposed example "North Salem" in the dialogue turns out not to be an example of the concept "city" (it shares the properties of containing various neighborhoods in which different people live together, but it is too small in size), examining it as a possible example helps clarify the concept "city" and suggests other examples.

The process of developing concepts involves a constant back-and-forth movement between these two activities:

> *Generalizing* Focusing on certain basic similarities between things to develop the requirements for the concept.
>
> *Interpreting* Looking for different things to apply the concept to, in order to determine if they "meet the requirements" of the concept we are developing.

As the back-and-forth movement progresses, we gradually develop a specific list of requirements that something must have to be considered an example of the concept. As we develop a more specific list of requirements, we are at the same time giving ourselves a clearer idea of how it is defined. We are also developing a collection of examples that embody the qualities of the concept and demonstrate in what situations the concept applies.

<u>THINKING ACTIVITY</u>

8.2   ▶ Select a type of music with which you are familiar (e.g., pop music) and write a dialogue similar to the one just examined. In the course of the dialogue, be sure to include

1. Examples that you are generalizing from (e.g., soul, rock).
2. General properties shared by various types of this music (e.g., pop's main audience is younger people).
3. Examples to which you are trying to apply the developing concept (e.g., is "salsa" or "reggae" pop music?).

Analyze the dialogue that you created in the same way that we analyzed the earlier one, by answering the following questions:

1. What examples of music did you use to generalize from?
2. What are the common properties or requirements of the music style that you selected?
3. What are some of the examples that you tried to apply the concept to? Did the concept apply? Why or why not?

Now focus on the list of features shared by all examples of the music style you selected. This list constitutes the *requirements* that must be met for something to qualify as an example of the concept. Are there other common properties/requirements you can think of? Compare your list with the lists of other classmates. Add to your list any requirements you may have overlooked. ◀

As we move back and forth between the general concept we are developing and the specific examples of it, our idea of the concept gradually becomes sharper and more detailed. This ongoing, back-and-forth movement (generalizing and interpreting) gradually refines and clarifies our concept, while also generating and developing examples of it. As we indicated, this back-and-forth process is an *interactive* process, as shown by the following diagram:

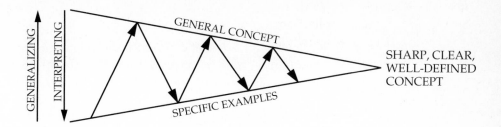

Forming concepts involves performing both of these operations (generalizing and interpreting) together, because

1. You cannot form a concept unless you know how it might apply. If you have absolutely *no idea* what "pop music" or "city" might be examples of, then you cannot begin to form the concept, even in vague or general terms.

2. You cannot gather up examples of the concept unless you know what they might be examples of. Until you begin to develop some idea of what the concepts "city" or "pop music" might be (based on certain similarities between various things), you will not know where to look for examples of the concept (or how to evaluate them).

This interactive process is the way that we usually form all concepts, particularly the complicated ones. In school, much of your education is focused on carefully forming and exploring key concepts such as "democracy," "dynamic equilibrium," and "personality." This book has also focused on certain key concepts, such as:

• Thinking critically

• Solving problems

• Perceiving

• Believing

• Knowing

• Language

In each case, we have carefully explored these concepts through the interactive process of *generalizing* the properties/requirements of the concept and *interpreting* the concept by examining examples to which the concept applies.

8.3   ▶ Review the following articles by Michael Norman and by Susan Brownmiller, which attempt to develop and describe two of the most confusing concepts in our culture: "masculinity" and "femininity." After reading the articles and thinking about the ideas discussed by the authors, answer the questions that follow.

STANDING HIS GROUND *by Michael Norman*

I have bruised a knuckle and bloodied another man's nose, but I am not, by most measures, a fighter. The last time I broke the peace was more than a decade ago in a small restaurant on the west slope of the Rocky Mountains in Colorado. My stepfather had encountered an old nemesis. Words were exchanged and the distance between the two narrowed. I stepped in to play the peacemaker and ended up throwing the first punch. For the record, my target, a towering 230-pound horseman, easily absorbed the blow and then dispatched the gnat in front of him.

The years since have been filled with discretion — I preach it, embrace it and hide behind it. I am now the careful watchman who keeps his eye on the red line and reroutes pressure before it has a chance to blow. Sometimes, I backslide and turn a domestic misdemeanor into a capital case or toss the cat out of the house without bothering to see where he lands. But I do not punch holes in the plaster or call my antagonists to the woodshed. The Furies may gather, but the storm always stays safely out to sea. And yet, lately, I have been struggling with this forced equanimity. The messenger of reason, the advocate of accord, once again has the urge to throw the first punch — in spirit at least.

All of this began rather quietly, a deep stirring that would come and go and never take form, an old instinct, perhaps, trying to reassert itself. I was angry, restless, combative, but I could not say why. It was a mystery of sorts. I was what I was expected to be, the very model of a modern man, a partner instead of a husband, a proponent of peace over action, thin-skinned rather than thick, a willow instead of a stone. And yet there was something about this posture that did not fit my frame. Then, an acquaintance, a gentle man who spent his Peace Corps days among the villagers of Nepal, suddenly acted out of character. He got into an argument with a local brute in a neighborhood tavern and instead of walking away from trouble, stood his ground. It was, he said, a senseless confrontation, but he had no regrets, and it made me think of Joey.

Joey, the bully of the sixth grade, used to roam the hallways picking victims at random and slugging them on the arm. When he rounded a corner, we scattered or practiced a crude form of mysticism and tried to think ourselves invisible in the face of the beast. Since I was slow and an inept mystic, my mother kept on hand an adequate supply of Ben Gay to ease the bruises and swelling.

One day, a boy named Tony told the marauder that he had had enough and an epic duel was scheduled in the playground after school. Tony had been taking boxing lessons on the sly. He had developed a stinging left jab and when the appointed hour arrived, he delivered it in the name of every bruised shoulder in the school.

The meek pack of which Tony was once a part took courage from his example and several weeks later when a boy at my bus stop sent me sprawling, I returned the favor.

There were only a few challenges after that. On the way up, a Joey would occasionally round the corner. But in the circles I traveled, he was the exception rather than the rule. In the Marine Corps in Vietnam, we were consumed by a much larger kind of warfare. In college, faculty infighting and bullying aside, violence was considered anti-intellectual. And in the newsrooms where I have practiced my trade, reporters generally have been satisfied with pounding a keyboard instead of their editors.

And then came Colorado and the battle of the west slope. For years, I was embarrassed by the affair. I could have walked away and dragged my stepfather with me. As it was, we almost ended up in jail. I had provoked a common brawl, a pointless, self-destructive exercise. The rationalist had committed the most irrational of acts. It was not a matter of family or honor, hollow excuses. I had simply succumbed to instinct, and I deeply regretted it. But not any longer. Now I see virtue in that vulgar display of macho. It disqualifies me from the most popular male club — the brotherhood of nurturers, fraternity sensitivus.

From analyst's couch to tavern booth, their message is the same: The male animus is out of fashion. The man of the hour is supposed to be gentle, thoughtful, endearing and compassionate, a wife to his woman, a mother to his son, an androgynous figure with the self-knowledge of a hermaphrodite. He takes his lumps on the psyche, not the chin, and bleeds with emotion. Yes, in the morning, he still puts on a three-piece suit, but his foulard, the finishing touch, is a crying towel.

He is so ridden with guilt, so pained about the sexist sins of his kind, he bites at his own flanks. Not only does he say that he dislikes being a man, but broadly proclaims that the whole idea of manhood in America is pitiful.

He wants to free himself from the social conditioning of the past, to cast off the yoke of traditional male roles and rise above the banality of rituals learned at boot camp or on the practice field. If science could provide it, he would swallow an antidote of testosterone, something to stop all this antediluvian thumping and bashing.

And he has gone too far. Yes, the male code needs reform. Our rules and our proscriptions have trapped us in a kind of perpetual adolescence. Why else would a full-grown rationalist think he could get even with Joey by taking a poke at another bully 25 years later in a bar in Colorado? No doubt there is something pitiful about that.

But the fashion for reform, the drive to emasculate macho, has produced a kind of numbing androgyny and has so blurred the lines of gender that I often find myself wanting to emulate some of the women I know — bold, aggressive, vigorous role models.

It sometimes seems that the only exclusively male trait left is the impulse to throw a punch, the last male watermark, so to speak, that is clear and readable. Perhaps that is why the former Peace Corps volunteer jumped into a brawl and why I suspect that the new man — the model of sensitivity, the nurturer — goes quietly through the day with a clenched fist behind his back. ■

FEMININITY *by Susan Brownmiller*

We had a game in our house called "setting the table" and I was Mother's helper. Forks to the left of the plate, knives and spoons to the right. Placing the cutlery neatly, as I recall, was one of my first duties, and the event was alive with meaning. When a knife or a fork dropped on the floor, that meant a man was unexpectedly coming to dinner. A falling spoon announced the surprise arrival of a female guest. No matter that these visitors never arrived on cue, I had learned a rule of gender identification. Men were straight-edged, sharply pronged and formidable, women were softly curved and held the food in a rounded well. It made perfect sense, like the division of pink and blue that I saw in babies, an orderly way of viewing the world. Daddy, who was gone all day at work and who loved to putter at home with his pipe, tobacco and tool chest, was knife and fork. Mommy and Grandma, with their ample proportions and pots and pans, were grownup soup spoons, large and capacious. And I was a teaspoon, small and slender, easy to hold and just right for pudding, my favorite dessert.

Being good at what was expected of me was one of my earliest projects, for not only was I rewarded, as most children are, for doing things right, but excellence gave pride and stability to my childhood existence. Girls were different from boys, and the expression of that difference seemed mine to make clear. Did my loving, anxious mother, who dressed me in white organdy pinafores and Mary Janes and who cried hot tears when I got them dirty, give me my first instruction? Of course. Did my doting aunts and uncles with their gifts of pretty dolls and miniature tea sets add to my education? Of course. But even without the appropriate toys and clothes, lessons in the art of being feminine lay all around me and I absorbed them all: the fairy tales that were read to me at night, the brightly colored advertisements I pored over in magazines before I learned to decipher the words, the movies I saw, the comic books I hoarded, the radio soap operas I happily followed whenever I had to stay in bed with a cold. I loved being a little girl, or rather I loved being a fairy princess, for that was who I thought I was.

As I passed through a stormy adolescence to a stormy maturity, femininity increasingly became an exasperation, a brilliant, subtle esthetic that was bafflingly inconsistent at the same time that it was minutely, demandingly concrete, a rigid code of appearance and behavior defined by do's and don't-do's that went against my rebellious grain. Femininity was a challenge thrown down to the female sex, a challenge no proud, self-respecting young woman could afford to ignore, particularly one with enormous ambition that she nursed in secret, alternately feeding or starving its inchoate life in tremendous confusion.

"Don't lose your femininity" and "Isn't it remarkable how she manages to retain her femininity?" had terrifying implications. They spoke of a bottom-line failure so irreversible that nothing else mattered. The pinball machine had registered "tilt," the game had been called. Disqualification was marked on the forehead of a woman whose femininity was lost. No records would be entered in her name, for she had destroyed her birthright in her wretched, ungainly effort to imitate a man. She walked in limbo, this hapless creature, and it occurred to me that one day I might see her when I looked in the mirror. If the danger was so palpable that warning notices were freely posted, wasn't it possible that the small bundle of resentments I carried around in secret might spill out and place the mark on my own forehead? Whatever quarrels with femininity I had I kept to myself; whatever handicaps femininity imposed, they were mine to deal with alone, for there was no women's movement to ask the tough questions, or to brazenly disregard the rules.

Femininity, in essence, is a romantic sentiment, a nostalgic tradition of imposed limitations. Even as it hurries forward in the 1980s, putting on lipstick and high heels to appear well dressed, it trips on the ruffled petticoats and hoopskirts of an era gone by. Invariably and necessarily, femininity is something that women had more of in the past, not only in the historic past of prior generations, but in each woman's personal past as well — in the virginal innocence that is replaced by knowledge, in the dewy cheek that is coarsened by age, in the "inherent nature" that a woman seems to misplace so forgetfully whenever she steps out of bounds. Why should this be so? The XX chromosomal message has not been scrambled, the estrogen-dominated hormonal balance is generally as biology intended, the reproductive organs, whatever use one has made of them, are usually in place, the breasts of whatever size are most often where they should be. But clearly, biological femaleness is not enough.

Femininity always demands more. It must constantly reassure its audience by a willing demonstration of difference, even when one does not exist in nature, or it must seize and embrace a natural variation and compose a rhapsodic symphony upon the notes. Suppose one doesn't care to, has other things on her mind, is clumsy or tone-deaf despite the best instruction and training? To fail at the feminine difference is to appear not to care about men, and to risk the loss of their attention and approval. To be insufficiently feminine is viewed as a failure in core sexual identity, or as a failure to care sufficiently about oneself, for a woman found wanting will be appraised (and will appraise herself) as mannish or neutered or simply unattractive, as men have defined these terms.

We are talking, admittedly, about an exquisite esthetic. Enormous pleasure can be extracted from feminine pursuits as a creative outlet or purely as relaxation; indeed, indulgence for the sake of fun, or art, or attention, is among femininity's great joys. But the chief attraction (and the central paradox, as well) is the competitive edge that femininity seems to promise in the unending struggle to survive, and perhaps to triumph. The world smiles favorably on the feminine woman: it extends little courtesies and minor privilege. Yet the nature of this competitive edge is ironic, at best, for one works at femininity by accepting restrictions, by limiting one's sights, by choosing an indirect route, by scattering concentration and not giving one's all as a man would to his own, certifiably masculine, interests. It does not require a great leap of imagination for a woman to understand the feminine principle as a grand collection of compromises, large and small, that she simply must make in order to render herself a successful woman. If she has difficulty in satisfying femininity's demands, if its illusions go against her grain, or if she is criticized for her shortcomings and imperfections, the more she will see femininity as a desperate strategy of appeasement, a strategy she may not have the wish or the courage to abandon, for failure looms in either direction.

It is fashionable in some quarters to describe the feminine and masculine principles as polar ends of the human continuum, and to sagely profess that both polarities exist in all people. Sun and moon, yin and yang, soft and hard, active and passive, etcetera, may indeed be opposites, but a linear continuum does not illuminate the problem. (Femininity, in all its contrivances, is a very active endeavor.) What, then, is the basic distinction? The masculine principle is better understood as a driving ethos of superiority designed to inspire straightforward, confident success, while the feminine principle is composed of vulnerability, the need for protection, the formalities of compliance and the avoidance of conflict — in short, an appeal of dependence and good will that gives the masculine principle its romantic validity and its admiring applause.

Femininity pleases men because it makes them appear more masculine by contrast; and, in truth, conferring an extra portion of unearned gender distinction on men, an unchallenged space in which to breathe freely and feel stronger, wiser, more competent, is femininity's special gift. One could say that masculinity is often an effort to please women, but masculinity is known to please by displays of mastery and competence while femininity pleases by suggesting that these concerns, except in small matters, are beyond its intent. Whimsy, unpredictability and patterns of thinking and behavior that are dominated by emotion, such as tearful expressions of sentiment and fear, are thought to be feminine precisely because they lie outside the established route to success.

If in the beginnings of history the feminine woman was defined by her physical dependency, her inability for reasons of reproductive biology to triumph over the forces of nature that were the tests of masculine strength and power, today she reflects both an economic and emotional dependency that is still considered "natural," romantic and attractive. After an unsettling fifteen years in which many basic assumptions about the sexes were challenged, the economic disparity did not disappear.

Large numbers of women — those with small children, those left high and dry after a mid-life divorce — need financial support. But even those who earn their own living share a universal need for connectedness (call it love, if you wish). As unprecedented numbers of men abandon their sexual interest in women, others, sensing opportunity, choose to demonstrate their interest through variety and a change in partners. A sociological fact of the 1980s is that female competition for two scarce resources — men and jobs — is especially fierce.

So it is not surprising that we are currently witnessing a renewed interest in femininity and an unabashed indulgence in feminine pursuits. Femininity serves to reassure men that women need them and care about them enormously. By incorporating the decorative and the frivolous into its definition of style, femininity functions as an effective antidote to the unrelieved seriousness, the pressure of making one's way in a harsh, difficult world. In its mandate to avoid direct confrontation and to smooth over the fissures of conflict, femininity operates as a value system of niceness, a code of thoughtfulness and sensitivity that in modern society is sadly in short supply.

There is no reason to deny that indulgence in the art of feminine illusion can be reassuring to a woman, if she happens to be good at it. As sexuality undergoes some dizzying revisions, evidence that one is a woman "at heart" (the inquisitor's question) is not without worth. Since an answer of sorts may be furnished by piling on additional documentation, affirmation can arise from such identifiable but trivial feminine activities as buying a new eyeliner, experimenting with the latest shade of nail color, or bursting into tears at the outcome of a popular romance novel. Is there anything destructive in this? Time and cost factors, a deflection of energy and an absorption in fakery spring quickly to mind, and they need to be balanced, as in a ledger book, against the affirming advantage. ■

1. According to Michael Norman, what are the *properties* of the concept "masculinity"? What are some *examples* of this concept?

2. Explain whether you agree with the conceptual properties he has identified. What properties of the concept "masculinity" do you think should be included that Norman has not addressed? For each property you identify, give at least one example.

3. According to Susan Brownmiller, what are the *properties* of the concept "femininity"? What are some *examples* of this concept?

4. Explain whether you agree with the conceptual properties she has identified. What properties of the concept of "femininity" do you think should be included that Brownmiller has not addressed? Give at least one example of each property you identify.

5. Some people feel that the concepts "masculinity" and "femininity" were formed by earlier cultures, are outdated in our current culture, and should be revised. Other people believe that these concepts reflect basic qualities of the human species, just like the sexual differences in other species, and should not be excessively tampered with.

   a. Explain where Michael Norman stands on this issue in terms of the concept of "masculinity" and describe the reasons he gives to support his position.

   b. Explain where Susan Brownmiller stands on this issue in terms of the concept of "femininity" and describe the reasons she gives to support her position.

   c. Explain where you stand on this issue in terms of both the concepts "masculinity" and "femininity," and describe the reasons that support your position. ◀

Applying Concepts

Making sense of our experience means finding the right concept to explain what is going on. To determine whether the concept we have selected fits the situation, we have to determine whether the requirements that form the concept are being met. For example, the original television series "Superman" used to begin with the words:

> Look — up in the sky! It's a bird! It's a plane! No! It's *Superman!*

To figure out which concept applies to the situation (so that we can figure out what is going on), we have to

1. Be aware of the properties/requirements that form the boundaries of the concept.

2. Determine whether the experience meets those requirements, for only if it does can we apply the concept to it.

In the previous example, what are some of the requirements for using the concepts being identified?

1. *Bird:* _____

2. *Plane:* _____

3. *Superman:* _____

If we have the requirements of the concept clearly in mind, we can proceed to figure out which of these requirements are met by the experience — whether it is a bird, a plane, or the "man of steel" himself. This is the way we apply concepts, which is one of the most important ways we figure out what is going on in our experience.

In determining exactly what the requirements of the concept are, we can ask ourselves the question:

> Would something still be an example of this concept, if it did not meet this requirement?

If the answer to this question is "no" — that is, something would *not* be an example of this concept if it did not meet this requirement — then we can say that the requirement is a necessary part of the concept.

Consider the concept "dog." Which of the following descriptions are requirements of the concept that must be met to say that something is an example of the concept "dog"?

1. Is an animal

2. Normally has four legs and a tail

3. Barks

4. Bites the postman

It is clear that descriptions 1 and 2 are requirements that must be met to apply the concept "dog," because if we apply our "test" question, "Would something be an example of this concept if it did not meet this requirement?" we can say that something would not be an example of the concept "dog" if it did not fit the first two descriptions: if it was not an animal and did not normally have four legs and a tail.

This does not seem to be the case, however, with descriptions 3 and 4. If we ask ourselves the same test question, we can see that something might still be an example of the concept "dog" *even if* it did not bark or bite the postman. This is because even though *many* dogs *do* in fact bark and bite, these are *not* necessary requirements for being a dog.

Of course, there may be other things that meet these requirements but are not dogs. For example, a cat is an animal (description 1) that normally has four legs and a tail (description 2). What this means is that the requirements of a concept only tell us what something *must* have to be an example of the concept. As a result, we often have to identify additional requirements that will define the concept more sharply. This point is clearly illustrated as children form concepts. Not identifying a sufficient number of the concept's requirements leads to such misconceptions as "All four-legged animals are doggies," or "All yellow-colored metal is gold."

This is why it is so important for us to have a very clear idea of the greatest possible number of specific requirements of each concept. These requirements determine when the concept can be applied and indicate those things that qualify as examples of it. When we are able to identify *all* of the requirements of the concept, we say that these requirements are both necessary *and* sufficient for applying the concept.

What are some additional requirements of the concept "dog" that would help us differentiate it from the concept "cat"?

_____

_____

THINKING ACTIVITY

8.4 ▶ For each concept listed, give at least three descriptions that are necessary requirements for the concept to apply to a situation. Then share your responses with the other members of your class and see if they agree with the requirements you have identified. If they do not agree, ask them to explain why the requirement is not an essential part of the concept.

1. *Friend*

   a. _____

   b. _____

   c. _____

2. *Music*

   a. _____

   b. _____

   c. _____

3. *Successful*

   a. _____

   b. _____

   c. _____

4. *Religion*

   a. _____

   b. _____

   c. _____

5. *Freedom*

   a. _____

   b. _____

   c. _____

6. _____

   a. _____

   b. _____

   c. _____ ◄

We have just seen that finding the right concept to best explain what is taking place in a situation involves both

1. Being aware of the properties/requirements that determine when the concept can be applied.
2. Determining whether the experience meets those requirements, for if it does, we can then apply the concept to it.

As a result, information plays a central role in the way that we develop, select, and apply concepts to our experience. In fact, our lives are a continual process of receiving and evaluating information to determine whether it *supports* or *conflicts with* the concepts we have adopted to understand a situation.

For example, as we try to size up a course on the first day of class, we form our initial concepts based on information we have already received.

• What have I heard about the course?

- What is the reputation of the instructor?
- What do I know about the other students?

As the course progresses, we gather further information from our actual experiences in the class. This information may support our initial concepts, or it may conflict with these initial concepts. If the information we receive supports these concepts, we tend to maintain them ("Yes, I can see that this is going to be a difficult course"). On the other hand, when the information we receive conflicts with these concepts, we tend to find new concepts to explain the situation ("No, I can see that I was wrong — this course isn't going to be as difficult as I thought at first"). A diagram of this process might look something like that shown below.

We see in this example that, if we get new information that does not fit into the picture we had of what was going on, we may change the picture based on that new information. We look for a different concept to understand what has happened. Using the new concept, we look for more information to find out whether the new concept applies. On the other hand, when things go smoothly, the new information we are getting fits into our picture of the situation formed by the concepts we have adopted. This encourages us to keep these concepts until new conflicting information suggests they are not giving us an accurate or adequate explanation of the situation.

Experience: Attending the first day of class
$\downarrow$
   leads to
$\downarrow$
Applying a concept to explain the situation: This course will be very difficult and I might not do very well.
$\downarrow$
   leads to
$\downarrow$
Looking for information to support or conflict with our concept.
$\swarrow \quad \searrow$

Supporting Information:	*Conflicting Information:*
The teacher is very demanding.	I find that I am able to keep up with the work.
	$\downarrow$
There are lots of writing assignments.	leads to
	$\downarrow$

The reading is challenging.

Forming a new concept to explain the situation: This course is difficult, but I will be able to handle the work and do well.

↓

action

THINKING ACTIVITY

8.5 ▶ Identify an initial concept you had about an event in your life (a new job, attending college, etc.) that changed as a result of your experiences. After identifying your initial concept, describe the experiences that led you to change or modify the concept and then explain the new concept you formed to explain the situation. Your response should therefore include the following steps:

1. Initial concept.
2. New information provided by additional experiences.
3. New concept formed to explain the situation. ◀

As critical thinkers, we should spend our lives in a continual process of conceptual clarification as we seek to evaluate our present situation and our future needs by forming and applying the most appropriate concepts. Those who develop this conceptual facility will best be able to make sense of their experience, meet the challenges and solve the problems that they encounter, understand themselves, and exert meaningful control over their lives.

Sometimes we resist changing or modifying concepts we already have, even when the information we are receiving suggests that we should. For instance, most of us share a common visual concept of the world. When we're presented with an inverted version of this concept, as illustrated in the figure on page 371, this new representation may appear unfamiliar and inaccurate because our initial concept is so deeply rooted. To take another example, the stereotyped beliefs that we examined in Chapter Five, *Believing and Knowing*, are based on inappropriate concepts that are resistant to change, even in the face of experiences or information that contradict these concepts. Similarly, virtually all of us subscribe to a variety of misconceptions about the world — such as superstitions — that we hold on to, even when confronted with information that seems to conflict with our concept. In dealing with incorrect beliefs that are so deeply rooted and resistant to change, we must use our critical thinking abilities with extraordinary commitment and determination if we are to change and modify them appropriately.

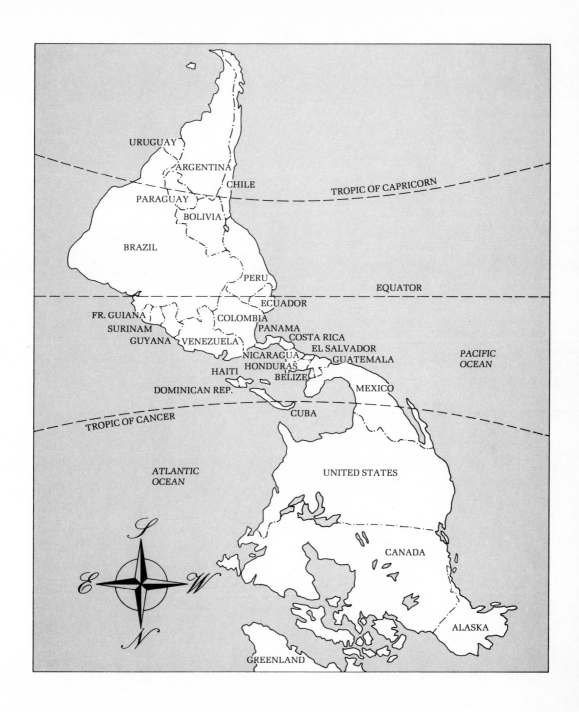

URUGUAY

ARGENTINA

CHILE

PARAGUAY

BOLIVIA

BRAZIL

PERU

TROPIC OF CAPRICORN

EQUATOR

ECUADOR

FR. GUIANA

COLOMBIA

SURINAM

PANAMA

COSTA RICA

GUYANA

VENEZUELA

EL SALVADOR

NICARAGUA

GUATEMALA

HAITI

HONDURAS

BELIZE

DOMINICAN REP.

MEXICO

CUBA

TROPIC OF CANCER

PACIFIC
OCEAN

ATLANTIC
OCEAN

UNITED STATES

CANADA

ALASKA

GREENLAND

8.6   ▶ Describe a misconception in your own life that has remained resistant to
change, even when challenged with conflicting experiences and contradictory
information. The misconception might involve superstitions, beliefs in the
occult (for example, astrology), adages like "love at first sight," or stereotyped
beliefs of a group of people because of their age, race, sex, nationality, appearance (dress, hairstyle, makeup). After describing the misconception, explain why it has been resistant to change and then identify strategies you can
use to help make the appropriate revisions of the concept. ◀

Classifying

When we apply a concept to an object, idea or experience, we are in effect
classifying the object, idea, or experience by placing it into the group of things
defined by the properties/requirements of the concept. The individual objects, ideas, or experiences belong to no particular class, however, until we
classify them. In fact, the same things can often be classified in many different
ways. For example, if someone handed you a tomato and asked: "Which class
does this tomato belong in, fruit or vegetable?" how would you respond? The
fact is, a tomato can be classified as *both* a fruit and a vegetable, depending
on our purposes. Interestingly enough, the government tried at one point to
have tomato catsup classified as a vegetable for the school lunch program so
that it would not have to provide a regular vegetable as part of a balanced
meal.

Let us consider another example. Imagine that you are walking on undeveloped land with some other people when you come across an area of soggy
ground with long grass and rotting trees. One person in your group surveys
the parcel and announces: "That's a smelly marsh. All it does is breed mosquitoes. It ought to be covered with landfill and built on, so that we can use
it productively." Another member of your group disagrees with the classification "smelly marsh," stating: "This is a wetland of great ecological value.
There are many plants and animals that need this area and other areas like it
to survive. Wetland areas also help prevent the rivers from flooding by ab-
sorbing excess water during heavy rains." Which person is right? Should the
wet area be classified as a "smelly marsh" or a "valuable wetland"? Actually,
the wet area can be classified both ways. The classification that we select
depends on our needs and our interests. Someone active in construction and
land development may tend to view the parcel through perceptual spectacles
that reflect his or her interests and experience and classify it accordingly. On

THE TREE, as seen by...

the planner...   the parks department...   the publisher...

the highways department...   the developer...   the landscape architect.

400 LUXURY HOMES
TO BE ERECTED
ON THIS SITE

the other hand, someone involved in preserving our natural resources will tend to view the same parcel through different spectacles and place it in a different category. To take another example, the diagram in the figure above illustrates how a tree might be "seen" from a variety of perspectives, depending on the interest and experience of those involved.

These examples illustrate that the way we classify reflects and influences the way we see the world, the way we think about the world, and the way we behave in the world. This is true for virtually all the classifications we make. Consider the race horse Secretariat, who won the Triple Crown in 1973 and was one of the most famous race horses that ever lived. Which classification should Secretariat be placed into?

- A magnificent thoroughbred
- A substantial investment
- An animal ill equipped for farming
- A large horse (seventeen hands high)
- A descendant of Bold Ruler

- A valuable stud horse
- A candidate for the glue factory

As individuals, we classify many of the things in our experience differently because of our individual needs, interests, and values. For instance, smoking marijuana might be classified by some as "use of a dangerous drug" and by others as a "harmless good time." Some view large cars as "gas guzzlers"; others see the same cars as "safer, more comfortable vehicles." Some people categorize the latest music as "meaningless noise," while others think of it as "creative expression." And so on. The way we classify aspects of our experience reflects the kind of individuals we are and the way we think and feel about the world.

We also place people into various classifications. The specific classifications we select depend on who we are and how we see the world. Similarly, each of us is placed into a variety of classifications by different people. For example, here are some of the classifications into which certain people placed me:

Classification:	People Who Classify Me:
First-born son	My parents
Taxpayer	Internal Revenue Service
Tickler	My daughter
Egg on a toasted roll	Cook at the restaurant where I pick up my breakfast every morning

List some of the different ways that you can be classified, and identify the people who would classify you that way.

Classification:	People Who Classify You:
_____	_____
_____	_____
_____	_____

Finally, besides classifying the same thing or event in a variety of different ways, we can classify most *collections* of things in various ways. For example, consider the different ways the members of your class can be classified. You could group them according to their majors, their ages, their food preferences, and so on. The specific categories you would use depend on the purposes of your classification. If you were trying to organize career counseling, then classifying according to majors makes sense. On the other hand, if you were trying to plan the menu for a class party, then food preferences would be the natural category for classification.

Not only do we continually classify things and people into various groups based on the common properties we choose to focus on, we also classify ideas, feelings, actions, and experiences. Explain, for instance, why the killing of another person might be classified in different ways, depending on the circumstances.

Classification:	*Circumstance:*	*Example:*
1. Manslaughter	Killing someone accidentally	Driving while intoxicated
2. Self-defense	_____	_____
3. Premeditated murder	_____	_____
4. Mercy killing	_____	_____
5. Diminished capacity murder (insanity plea)	_____	_____

Each of these classifications represents a separate legal concept, with its own properties and referents (examples). Of course, even when we understand clearly what the concept means, the complexity of the circumstances often makes it difficult to determine which concept applies. For example, in Chapter One, Thinking, we considered a court case that raised complex and disturbing issues. In circumstances like these, trying to identify the appropriate concepts and then to determine which of the further concepts, "guilty" or "innocent," also applies, is a challenging process. This is true of many of life's complex situations: We must work hard at identifying the appropriate concepts to apply to the situations we are trying to make sense of and then be prepared to change or modify these concepts based on new information or better insight.

THINKING ACTIVITY

8.7 ▶ The following essay by Desmond Morris offers a unique analysis of the concept "altruism" and the way this concept can be applied. Read the article carefully and answer the questions that follow.

ALTRUISTIC BEHAVIOR *by Desmond Morris*

Altruism is the performance of an unselfish act. As a pattern of behavior this act must have two properties: it must benefit someone else, and it must do so to the disadvantage of the benefactor. It is not merely a matter of being helpful, it is helpfulness at a cost to yourself.

This simple definition conceals a difficult biological problem. If I harm myself to help you, then I am increasing your chances of success relative to mine. In broad evolutionary terms, if I do this, your offspring (or potential offspring) will have better prospects than mine. Because I have been altruistic, your genetic line will stand a better chance of survival than mine. Over a period of time, my unselfish line will die out and your selfish line will survive. So altruism will not be a viable proposition in evolutionary terms.

Since human beings are animals whose ancestors have won the long struggle for survival during their evolutionary history, they cannot be genetically programmed to display true altruism. Evolution theory suggests that they must, like all other animals, be entirely selfish in their actions, even when they appear to be at their most self-sacrificing and philanthropic.

This is the biological, evolutionary argument and it is completely convincing as far as it goes, but it does not seem to explain many of mankind's "finer moments." If a man sees a burning house and inside it his small daughter, an old friend, a complete stranger, or even a screaming kitten, he may, without pausing to think, rush headlong into the building and be badly burned in a desperate attempt to save a life. How can actions of this sort be described as selfish? The fact is that they can, but it requires a special definition of the term "self."

When you think of your "self," you probably think of your living body, complete, as it is at this moment. But biologically it is more correct to think of yourself as merely a temporary housing, a disposable container, for your genes. Your genes — the genetic material that you inherited from your parents and which you will pass on to your children — are in a sense immortal. Our bodies are merely the carriers which they use to transport themselves from one generation to the next. It is they, not we, who are the basic units of evolution. We are only their guardians, protecting them from destruction as best we can, for the brief span of our lives.

Religion pictures man as having an immortal soul which leaves his body at death and floats off to heaven (or hell, as the case may be), but the more useful image is to visualize a man's immortal soul as sperm-shaped and a woman's as egg-shaped, and to think of them as leaving the body during the breeding process rather than at death. Following this line of thought through, there is, of course, an afterlife, but it is not in some mysterious "other world"; it is right here in the heaven (or hell) of the nursery and the playground, where our genes continue their immortal journey down the tunnel of time, re-housed now in the brand-new flesh-containers we call children.

So, genetically speaking, our children are us — or, rather, half of us, since our mate has a half share of the genes of each child. This makes our devoted and apparently selfless parental care nothing more than *genetic self-care*. The man who risks death to save his small daughter from a fire is in reality saving his own genes in their new body-package. And in saving his genes, his act becomes biologically selfish, rather than altruistic.

But supposing the man leaping into the fire is trying to save, not his daughter, but an old friend? How can this be selfish? The answer here lies in the ancient history of mankind. For more than a million years, man was a simple tribal being, living in small groups where everyone knew everyone else and everyone was closely genetically related to everyone else. Despite a certain amount of out-breeding, the chances were that every member of your own tribe was a relative of some kind, even if a rather remote one. A certain degree of altruism was therefore appropriate where all the other members of your tribe were concerned. You would be helping copies of your own genes, and although you might not respond so intensely to their calls for help as you would do with your own children, you would nevertheless give them a degree of help, again on a basis of genetic selfishness.

This is not, of course, a calculated process. It operates unconsciously and is based on an emotion we call "love." Our love for our children is what we say we are obeying when we act "selflessly" for them, and our love of our fellow-men is what we feel when we come to the aid of our friends. These are inborn tendencies and when we are faced with calls for help we feel ourselves obeying these deep-seated urges unquestioningly and unanalytically. It is only because we see ourselves as "persons" rather than as "gene machines" that we think of these acts of love as unselfish rather than selfish.

So far, so good, but what about the man who rushes headlong into the fire to save a complete stranger? The stranger is probably *not* genetically related to the man who helps him, so this act must surely be truly unselfish and altruistic? The answer is Yes, but only by accident. The accident is caused by the rapid growth of human populations in the last few thousand years. Previously, for millions of years, man was tribal and any inborn urge to help his fellow-men would have meant automatically that he was helping gene-sharing relatives, even if only remote ones. There was no need for this urge to be selective, because there were no strangers around to create problems. But with the urban explosion, man rapidly found himself in huge communities, surrounded by strangers, and with no time for his genetic constitution to alter to fit the startlingly new circumstances. So his altruism inevitably spread to include all his new fellow-citizens, even though many of them may have been genetically quite unrelated to him.

Politicians, exploiting this ancient urge, were easily able to spread the aid-system even further, to a national level called patriotism, so that men would go and die for their country as if it were their ancient tribe or their family.

The man who leaps into the fire to save a small kitten is a special case. To many people, animals are child-substitutes and receive the same care and love as real children. The kitten-saver is explicable as a man who is going to the aid of his symbolic child. This process of symbolizing, of seeing one thing as a metaphorical equivalent of another, is a powerful tendency of the human animal and it accounts for a great deal of the spread of helpfulness across the human environment.

In particular it explains the phenomenon of dying for a cause. This always gives the appearance of the ultimate in altruistic behavior, but a careful examination of the nature of each cause reveals that there is some basic symbolism at work. A nun who gives her life for Christ is already technically a "bride" of Christ and looks upon all people as the "children" of God. Her symbolism has brought the whole of humanity into her "family circle" and her altruism is for her symbolic family, which to her can become as real as other people's natural families.

In this manner it is possible to explain the biological bases for man's seemingly altruistic behavior. This is in no way intended to belittle such activities, but merely to point out that the more usual, alternative explanations are not necessary. For example, it is often stated that man is fundamentally wicked and that his kind acts are largely the result of the teachings of moralists, philosophers, and priests; that if he is left to his own devices he will become increasingly savage, violent, and cruel. The confidence trick involved here is that if we accept this viewpoint we will attribute all society's good qualities to the brilliant work of these great teachers. The biological truth appears to be rather different. Since selfishness is genetic rather than personal, we will have a natural tendency to help our blood relatives and hence our whole tribe. Since our tribes have swollen into nations, our helpfulness becomes stretched further and further, aided and abetted by our tendency towards accepting symbolic substitutes for the real thing. Altogether this means that we are now, by nature, a remarkably helpful species. If there are break-downs in this helpfulness, they are probably due, not to our "savage nature" reasserting itself, but to the unbearable tensions under which people so often find themselves in the strained and over-crowded world of today.

It would be a mistake, nevertheless, to overstate man's angelic helpfulness. He is also intensely competitive. But under normal circumstances these rival tendencies balance each other out, and this balance accounts for a great deal of human intercourse, in the form of *transactional behavior*. This is behavior of the "I'll-scratch-your-back-if-you'll-scratch-mine" type. We do deals with one another. My actions help you, but they are not altruistic because they also help me at the same time. This cooperative behavior is perhaps the dominant feature of day-to-day social interaction. It is the basis of trade and commerce and it explains why such activities do not become more ruthless. If the competitive element were not tempered by the basic urge to help one another, business practices would rapidly become much more savage and brutal than they are, even today.

An important extension of this two-way cooperative behavior is embodied in the phrase: "one good turn now deserves another later." This is delayed, or nonspecific cooperation. I give help to you now, even though you cannot help me in return. I do this daily to many people I meet. One day I will need help and then, as part of a "long-term deal," they will return my help. I do not keep a check on what I am owed or by whom. Indeed, the person who finally helps me may not be one of the ones I have helped. But a whole network of social debts will have built up in a community and, as there is a great division of labor and skills in our species today, such a system will be beneficial to all the members of the society. This has been called "reciprocal altruism." But once again it is not true altruism because sooner or later, one way or another, I will be rewarded for my acts of helpfulness.

Anticipation of a delayed reward of this kind is often the hidden motive for a great deal of what is claimed to be purely altruistic behavior. Many countries hand out official awards to their citizens for "services to the community," but frequently these services have been deliberately undertaken in the anticipation that they are award-worthy. Comparatively few public honors ever come as a surprise. And many other "good works" are undertaken with later social (or heavenly) rewards in mind. This does not necessarily make the "works" any less good, of course, it merely explains the motives involved.

The following table sums up the relationship between competitiveness and helpfulness, and their intermediates:

1. Self-assertive behavior	Helps me	Harms you	Mild competitiveness to full criminality
2. Self-indulgent behavior	Helps me	No effect on you	The private, nonsocial pleasures
3. Cooperative behavior	Helps me	Helps you	Transaction, trade, barter and negotiation
4. Courteous behavior	No effect on me	Helps you	Kindness and generosity
5. "Altruistic" behavior	Harms me	Helps you	Loving devotion, philanthropy, self-sacrifice and patriotism ■

1. According to Desmond Morris, what are the *properties* of the concept of "altruism"? What are some *examples* of this concept?

2. Describe several actions to which you think the concept "altruism" applies.

3. Morris contends that, biologically, the concept of our "self" can best be understood as a temporary housing, a disposable container, for our genes. Do you agree with his view of this concept? Why or why not?

4. What does Morris believe is the basic motivation for altruistic behavior? Do you agree with his analysis? Why or why not? If you think that altruistic behavior has other motivations — such as moral obligation or selfless concern for others — describe what these motivations are and explain why they seem more reasonable to you.

5. Describe an altruistic action that you engaged in and explain what you think your motivations were. Based on this experience, compare and contrast your analysis of the concept "altruism" with the concept that Morris identifies. ◄

Defining Concepts

When we define a concept, we usually identify the necessary properties/requirements that determine when the concept can be applied. In fact, the word *definition* is derived from the Latin word meaning "boundary" because that is exactly what a definition does: It gives the boundaries of the territory in our experience that can be described by the concept. For example, a definition of the concept "horse" might include the following requirements:

1. Large strong animal
2. Four legs with solid hoofs
3. Flowing mane and tail
4. Domesticated long ago for drawing or carrying loads, carrying riders, etc.

By understanding the requirements of the concept "horse," we understand what conditions must be met in order for something to qualify as an example of the concept. This lets us know in what situations we can apply the concept: to the animals running around the racetrack, the animals pulling wagons and carriages, the animals being ridden on the range, and so on. In addition, understanding the requirements lets us know to which things the concept can be applied. No matter how much a zebra looks like a horse, we won't apply the concept "horse" to it if we really understand the definition of the concept involved.

Definitions also often make strategic use of *examples* of the concept being defined. Consider the following definition by Ambrose Bierce.

> *An edible:* Good to eat and wholesome to digest, as a worm to a toad, a toad to a snake, a snake to a pig, a pig to a man, and a man to a worm.

Contrast this definition with the one illustrated in the following passage from Charles Dickens's *Hard Times:*

> "Bitzer" said Thomas Gradgrind. "Your definition of a horse." "Quadruped. Graminivorous. Forty teeth, namely twenty-four grinders, four eye teeth, and twelve incisive. Sheds coat in the spring; in marshy countries shed hoofs, too. Hoofs hard, but requiring to be shod with iron. Age known by marks in mouth." That (and much more) Bitzer. "Now girl number twenty," said Mr. Gradgrind, "you know what a horse is."

Although Bitzer has certainly done an admirable job of listing some of the necessary properties/requirements of the concept "horse," it is unlikely that "girl number twenty" has any better idea of what a horse is than she had before because the definition relies exclusively on a technical listing of the properties characterizing the concept "horse" without giving any examples that might illustrate the concept more completely. Definitions like this that rely exclusively on a technical description of the concept's properties are often not very helpful unless we already know what the concept means. A more concrete way of communicating the concept "horse" would be to point out various animals that qualify as horses and other animals that do not. You could also explain why they do not. (For example, "That can't be a horse because it has two humps and its legs are too long and skinny.")

Although examples do not take the place of a clearly understood definition, they are often very useful in clarifying, supplementing, and expanding such a definition. If someone asked you, "What is a horse?" and you replied by giving examples of different kinds of horses (thoroughbred racing horses, plow horses for farming, quarter-horses for cowboys, hunter horses for fox hunting, circus horses), you certainly would be communicating a good portion of the meaning of "horse." Giving examples of a concept complements and clarifies the necessary requirements for the correct use of that concept.

THINKING ACTIVITY

8.8   ▶ For each of the following concepts

a. Give a "dictionary" definition that describes the properties/necessary requirements of the concept.
b. Describe ways you could supplement and expand this definition.

Example: Smile

a. A facial expression characterized by an upward curving of the corners of the mouth and indicating pleasure, amusement, or derision.
b. Smiling at someone or drawing a picture of a smiling face.

1. *Ambivalent*

   a. _____

   b. _____

2. *Intelligent*

   a. _____

   b. _____

3. *Art*

    a. _____

    b. _____

4. *Thinking*

    a. _____

    b. _____

5. *Work*

    a. _____

    b. _____

6. *Create*

    a. _____

    b. _____ ◀

Giving an effective definition of a concept thus means both

1. Identifying the general qualities of the concept, which determine when it can be correctly applied.

2. Using significant examples to demonstrate actual applications of the concept — that is, examples that embody the general qualities of the concept.

The process of providing definitions of concepts is thus the same process we use to develop concepts. Of course, this process is often difficult and complex, and people don't always agree on how concepts should be defined. For example, consider the concepts "masculinity" and "femininity" that we explored earlier through the articles by Susan Brownmiller and Michael Norman. Notice how although areas of overlap exist between each author's definitions, there are also significant differences in the defining properties and examples that they identify.

THINKING ACTIVITY

8.9   ▶ Much of our education involves learning to understand, apply, and define the key concepts that make up each field of study. By developing our ability to form and apply concepts, we are better able to extract from assigned readings and lectures the concepts needed to understand the discipline we are studying. After reading this passage from a psychology textbook, examine the concepts being discussed by answering the questions that follow.

From CREATIVE THINKING AND CRITICAL THINKING
by Gardner Lindzey, Calvin S. Hall, and Richard F. Thompson

Creative thinking is thinking that results in the discovery of a new or improved solution to a problem. *Critical thinking* is the examination and testing of suggested solutions to see whether they will work. Creative thinking leads to the birth of new ideas, while critical thinking tests ideas for flaws and defects. Both are necessary for effective problem-solving, yet they are sometimes incompatible — creative thinking can interfere with critical thinking, and vice versa. To think creatively we must let our thoughts run free. The more spontaneous the process, the more ideas will be born and the greater the probability that an effective solution will be found. A steady stream of ideas furnishes the raw material. Then critical judgment selects and refines the best ideas, picking the most effective solution out of the available possibilities. Although we must engage in the two types of thinking separately, we need both for efficient problem-solving. . . .

Inhibitions to Creative Thinking

Conformity — the desire to be like everyone else — is the foremost barrier to creative thinking. People are afraid to express new ideas because they think they will make fools of themselves and be ridiculed. This feeling may date back to childhood, when their spontaneous and imaginative ideas may have been laughed at by parents or older people. During adolescence, conformity is reinforced because young people are afraid to be different from their peers. Then, too, history teaches us that innovators often are laughed at and even persecuted.

Censorship — especially self-imposed censorship — is a second significant barrier to creativity. External censorship of ideas, the thought control of modern dictatorships, is dramatic and newsworthy, but internal censorship is more effective and dependable. External censorship merely prevents public distribution of proscribed thoughts; the thoughts may still be expressed privately. But people who are frightened by their thoughts tend to react passively rather than think of creative solutions to their problems. Sometimes they even repress those thoughts, so they are not aware they exist. Freud called this internalized censor the *superego*. . . .

A third barrier to creative thinking is the *rigid education* still commonly imposed upon children. Regimentation, memorization, and drill may help instill the accepted knowledge of the day, but these classroom methods cannot teach students how to solve new problems or how to improve upon conventional solutions to old problems.

On the other hand, the progressive movement in education often has been criticized on the ground that its emphasis on creative thinking also encourages intellectual sloppiness and an inability to master basic skills and facts. . . .

A fourth barrier to creative thinking is the great *desire to find an answer quickly.* Such a strong motivation often narrows one's consciousness and encourages the acceptance of early, inadequate solutions. People tend to do their best creative thinking when they are released from the demands and responsibilities of everyday living. Inventors, scientists, artists, writers, and executives often do their most creative thinking when they are not distracted by routine work. The value of a vacation is not that it enables people to work better on their return but rather that it permits new ideas to be born during the vacation.

Daydreamers often are criticized for wasting time. Yet without daydreams, society's progress would be considerably slower, since daydreaming often leads to the discovery of original ideas. This is not to suggest that all daydreaming or leisurely contemplation results in valid and workable ideas — far from it. But somewhere, among the thousands of ideas conceived, one useful idea will appear. Finding this one idea without having to produce a thousand poor ones would achieve a vast saving in creative thinking. But such a saving seems unlikely, especially since creative thinking is generally enjoyable whether its results are useful or not.

Critical Thinking

Creative thinking must be followed by critical thinking if we want to sort out and refine those ideas that are potentially useful. Critical thinking is essentially an idea-testing operation. Will it work? What is wrong with it? How can it be improved? These are questions to be answered by a critical examination of newly hatched ideas. You may be highly creative, but if you cannot determine which ideas are practical and reasonable, your creativity will not lead to many fruitful consequences. In order to make such distinctions, you must maintain some distance and detachment, so that you can appraise your own ideas objectively.

Critical thinking requires some criteria by which to judge the practicality of the ideas. For example, if a community wants to do something about crime, it must decide what limitations are to be imposed upon the measures that are suggested. One limitation is the amount of money available; many proposals for curbing crime cost more than the community is willing or able to pay. Critical thinking must always take such realities into account.

What barriers stand in the path of critical thinking? One is the *fear of being aggressive and destructive*. We learn as children not to be critical, not to differ with what someone else says, especially an older person. To criticize is to be discourteous.

A closely related barrier is the *fear of retaliation*. If I criticize your ideas, you may turn about and criticize mine. This often involves yet another barrier, the *overevaluation* of one's own ideas. We like what we have created, and often we are reluctant to let others take apart our creation. By and large, those who are least secure hang on most tenaciously to their original ideas.

Finally, we should note again that if too much emphasis is placed upon being creative, the critical faculty may remain undeveloped. In their zeal to stimulate creativity in their pupils, teachers often are reluctant to be critical. One unintended result is that their students do not learn to think critically. This is unfortunate, since for most people life requires a balance between creative and critical thinking.

Critical Attitudes   There is an important distinction between critical thinking and a *critical attitude*. Critical thinking tries to arrive at a valid and practical solution to a problem. However much it may reject and discard, its final goal is constructive. A critical attitude, on the other hand, is destructive in intent. A person with a critical attitude tends to criticize solely for the sake of criticizing. Such an attitude is emotional rather than cognitive. ■

The authors of this passage discuss two main concepts — "creative thinking" and "critical thinking."

1. Describe the authors' basic definitions of each of these concepts.

    Creative thinking: _____

    _____

    Critical thinking: _____

    _____

2. Describe the factors the authors believe help and hinder the development of these two distinct ways of thinking.

Creative thinking: _____

_____

Critical thinking: _____

_____

3. Explain how the authors' concept of creative thinking is similar to or different from their concept of critical thinking.

Similarities: _____

_____

Differences: _____

_____

4. Explain how the authors' concept of critical thinking is similar to and different from the concept of critical thinking developed in Chapter Two of this text.

Similarities: _____

_____

Differences: _____

_____ ◄

THINKING ACTIVITY
_____

8.10 ► Identify a concept you are learning in another course — for example, you might choose "rhythm" or "melody" if you are taking a music class, or "cell" or "photosynthesis" if you are taking a biology or botany class. Define the concept by listing the requirements that form its boundaries and by providing examples. Pay special attention to the way defining a concept involves the interactive processes of generalizing and interpreting. ◄

THINKING ACTIVITY
_____

8.11 ► Review the ideas we have explored in this chapter by analyzing the concept "responsibility." "Responsibility" is a complex idea that has an entire network of meaning. The word comes from the Latin word *respondere*, which means "to pledge or promise."

Generalizing:

1. Describe two important responsibilities you have in your life.
2. Did these responsibilities originate with yourself or with others? Explain.
3. In reflecting on these responsibilities, identify the qualities they embody that lead you to think of them as "responsibilities."

When we encounter responsibilities in our lives, we can either accept them and act on them, or we can resist them and refuse to act on them. The manner in which we react to our responsibilities helps determine whether we are seen as being "responsible" or being "irresponsible."

4. Describe a person in your life who you think is very responsible.
5. Describe a person in your life who you think is very irresponsible.
6. In reflecting on these individuals, identify the qualities they embody that lead you to think of them as "responsible" and "irresponsible."

Interpreting:

Consider the following situations. In each case, describe what you consider to be examples of responsible behavior and irresponsible behavior. Be sure to explain the reasons for your answer.

7. You are a member of a group of three students who are assigned the task of writing a report on a certain topic. Your life is very hectic and in addition you find the topic dull. What is your response?
8. You are employed at a job in which you observe your supervisor and other employees engaged in activities that break the company rules. You are afraid that if you "blow the whistle" you might lose your job. What is your response?
9. Describe a situation of your own to illustrate these concepts, and describe examples of responsible and irresponsible behavior in response to it.
10. Describe an area in which you think the government has a responsibility to its citizens and explain the reasons why.

Defining:

Using these activities of generalizing and interpreting as a foundation, give definitions of each of the following concepts by listing the qualities that make up the boundaries of the concept and identifying the key examples that embody and illustrate the qualities of the concept.

11. Responsible

12. Irresponsible ◄

THINKING ACTIVITY

8.12 ► In the following article, "Suicide Solution," the columnist Anna Quindlen analyzes how the concept of "responsibility" is used — and misused — in our culture. After reading the article, answer the questions that follow.

SUICIDE SOLUTION *by Anna Quindlen*

It was two days before Christmas when Jay Vance blew the bottom of his face off with a shotgun still slippery with his best friend's blood. He went second. Ray Belknap went first. Ray died and Jay lived, and people said that when you looked at Jay's face afterward it was hard to tell which of them got the worst of the deal. "He just had no luck," Ray's mother would later say of her son to a writer from Rolling Stone, which was a considerable understatement.

Jay and Ray are both dead now. They might be only two of an endless number of American teen-agers in concert T-shirts who drop out of school and live from album to album and beer to beer, except for two things. The first was that they decided to kill themselves as 1985 drew to a close.

The second is that their parents decided to blame it on rock-and-roll.

When it was first filed in Nevada, the lawsuit brought by the families of Jay Vance and Ray Belknap against the members of the English band Judas Priest and their record company was said to be heavy metal on trial. I would love to convict heavy metal of almost anything — I would rather be locked in a room with 100 accordion players than listen to Metallica — but music has little to do with this litigation. It is a sad attempt by grieving grown-ups to say, in a public forum, what their lost boys had been saying privately for years: someone's to blame for my failures, but it can't be me.

The product liability suit, which sought $6.2 million in damages, contended that the boys were "mesmerized" by subliminal suicide messages on a Judas Priest album. The most famous subliminal before this case came to trial was the section of a Beatles song that fans believed

hinted at the death of Paul McCartney. The enormous interest that surrounded this seems terribly silly now, when Paul McCartney, far from
being dead, has become the oldest living cute boy in the world.

There is nothing silly about the Judas Priest case, only something infinitely sad. Ray Belknap was 18. His parents split up before he was
born. His mother has been married four times. Her last husband beat
Ray with a belt and, according to police, once threatened her with a gun
while Ray watched. Like Jay Vance, Ray had a police record and had
quit high school after two years. Like Jay, he liked guns and beer and
used marijuana, hallucinogens and cocaine.

Jay Vance, who died three years after the suicide attempt, his face a
reconstructed Halloween mask, had had a comparable coming of age.
His mother was 17 when he was born. When he was a child, she beat
him often. As he got older, he beat her back. Once, checking himself
into a detox center, he was asked "What is your favorite leisure time
activity?" He answered "Doing drugs." Jay is said to have consumed
two six-packs of beer a day. There's a suicide note if I ever heard one.

It is difficult to understand how anyone could blame covert musical
mumbling for what happened to these boys. On paper they had little to
live for. But the truth is that their lives were not unlike the lives of many
kids who live for their stereos and their beer buzz, who open the door
to the corridor of the next 40 years and see a future as empty and trun-
cated as a closet. "Get a life," they say to one another. In the responsibility department, no one is home.

They are legion. Young men kill someone for a handful of coins, then
are remorseless, even casual: hey, man, things happen. And their parents nab the culprit: it was the city, the cops, the system, the crowd, the
music. Anyone but him. Anyone but me. There's a new product on the
market I call Parent In A Can. You can wipe a piece of paper on something in your kid's room and then spray the paper with this chemical.
Cocaine traces, and the paper will turn turquoise. Marijuana, reddish
brown. So easy to use — and no messy heart-to-heart talks, no constant
parental presence. Only $44.95 plus $5 shipping and handling to do in
a minute what you should have been doing for years.

In the Judas Priest lawsuit, it's easy to see how kids get the idea that
they are not responsible for their actions. They inherit it. Heavy metal
music is filled with violence, but Jay and Ray got plenty of that even
with the stereo unplugged. The trial judge ruled that the band was not
responsible for the suicides, but the families are pressing ahead with an
appeal, looking for absolution for the horrible deaths of their sons.

Heavy metal made them do it — not the revolving fathers, the beatings, the alcohol, the drugs, a failure of will or of nurturing. Someone's to blame. Someone else. Always someone else. ■

1. Describe Quindlen's definition of the concept "responsibility" by listing the qualities that make up the boundaries of the concept for her and identifying the key examples she uses to illustrate the qualities of the concept.

2. Compare Quindlen's definition of the concept "responsibility" with the definition that you developed in Thinking Activity 8.11.

3. Consider the issues in the Judas Priest court case.

   a. Do you think that music can influence people to commit suicide or engage in illegal activities? Explain the reasons for your conclusion.

   b. If you think that music *can* influence people in these ways, explain whether you believe that the people who make the music should be held legally responsible for its effects.

4. Teen-age depression and suicide is a significant and tragic national problem.

   a. Explain what you believe are the major factors responsible for this problem.

   b. Describe what you think are effective strategies for solving this problem. ◄

Summary

In the same way that words are the vocabulary of language, concepts are the vocabulary of thought. Concepts are general ideas that we use to bring order and intelligibility to our experience. As organizers of our experience, concepts work in conjunction with language to identify, describe, distinguish, and relate all the various aspects of our world. They give us the means to understand our world and make informed decisions, to think critically and act intelligently.

To become sophisticated thinkers, we must develop expertise in the conceptualizing process, improving our ability to both *form* concepts, through the interactive process of generalizing and interpreting, and *apply* concepts, by matching their necessary requirements to potential examples. This complex conceptualizing process is going on all the time in our minds, enabling us to think in a distinctly human way.

By understanding the conceptualizing process, we can more fully appreciate the integral relationship between language and thought that we have been exploring in these last three chapters, the way in which these two processes work as one to create meaning and understanding. In the same way that words are combined according to the rules of language to produce an infinite variety of linguistic expression, so concepts are related according to the patterns of thought to create the infinite dimensions of thinking.

The remaining chapters of this text will focus on the rules and patterns of thought that determine the way concepts are combined and organized in complex relationships to produce the highest, most sophisticated levels of human thinking.

CHAPTER 9

Relating and Organizing

RELATING AND ORGANIZING: Using thinking patterns to make sense of the world.

MIND MAPS: Symbolize concepts and their relationships.

USING LANGUAGE: Reading, writing, speaking, and listening.

THINKING

Chronological and Process Relationships

Comparative and Analogical Relationships

Causal Relationships

THROUGHOUT THIS BOOK we have been considering and experiencing the insight that each one of us is a "creator." Each of us is actively shaping — as well as discovering — the world we live in. Our world does not exist as a finished product, waiting for us to perceive it, think about it, and describe it with words and pictures. Instead, we are *active participants* in composing the world that seems so familiar to us.

The goal of this composing process is to organize our world into meaningful patterns that will help us figure out what is going on and what we ought to do. Composing our world involves all the activities that we have been exploring, including

perceiving	symbolizing	interpreting
believing	describing	conceptualizing
knowing	classifying	defining
solving problems	generalizing	analyzing

Although we are usually unaware that we are performing these activities, our ability to think critically gives us the means to examine the different ways by which we are making sense of the world so that we can develop and sharpen our understanding. As we actively discover and compose various patterns, what we are really doing is exploring the ways in which different aspects of our experience *relate* to each other.

Ideas, things, and events in the world can be related and organized in a variety of ways. For example, different individuals might take the same furniture and decorations in the same space and arrange them in many different ways, reflecting each person's needs, ways of thinking, and aesthetic preferences. Or, to take another example, a class of students may develop ideas and write essays about the same subject and create widely differing results.

All these ways of relating and organizing reflect basic thinking patterns that we rely on constantly when we think, act, or use language. These basic thinking patterns are an essential part of our process of composing and making sense of the world. We will discuss three basic ways of relating and organizing in this chapter.

1. *Chronological and process relationships*
   - Chronological — relating events in time sequence
   - Process — relating aspects of the growth, development, or change of an act, event, or object

2. *Comparative and analogical relationships*

- Comparative — relating things in the same general category in terms of their similarities and dissimilarities
- Analogical — relating things belonging to different categories in terms of each other to increase our understanding of them

3. *Causal relationships*

- Causal — relating events in terms of the way some event(s) are responsible for bringing about other event(s)

These basic thinking patterns (and others besides) play an active role in the way we perceive, shape, and organize our world to make it understandable to us. The specific patterns we use to organize our ideas in thinking, writing, and speaking depend on the subject we are exploring, the goals we are aiming for, the type of writing or speaking we are doing, and the audience who will be reading or listening to our work. In most cases, we will use a variety of basic patterns in thinking, writing, and speaking to organize and relate the ideas we are considering.

Creating Mind Maps for Thinking and Using Language

Suppose someone handed you a pencil and a piece of paper with the request, "Please draw me a detailed map that shows how to get to where you live from where we are now." Draw such a map on a separate sheet of paper.

Maps, like the one you just drew, are really groups of symbols organized in certain relationships. In creating your visual map, you tried both to represent *and* to organize various aspects of your experience into a pattern that made sense to you and to others. As you constructed your map, you probably traveled the route home "in your mind," trying to recall the correct turns, street names, buildings, and so on. You then symbolized these experiences and organized the symbols into a meaningful pattern — your map.

We can see, therefore, that the activity of making maps draws on two skills needed for making sense of our world:

1. Representing our experience with symbols.
2. Organizing and relating these symbols into various patterns to gain an increased understanding of our experience.

Creating maps is thus a way to represent and organize experience so that we can make sense of it, and it is a strategy we can apply to many different areas of our world. For example, we can create maps of our minds — "mind maps" that express the patterns of our thinking processes.

A *mind map* is a visual presentation of the various ways ideas can be related to one another. For example, each chapter in this book opens with a diagram — what we will call a "mind map" — that visually summarizes the chapter's basic concepts as well as the way these concepts are related to each other. These maps are a reference guide that reveals basic themes and chapter organization.

Because they clearly articulate various patterns of thought, mind maps are effective tools for helping us understand complex bodies of information, either through reading or through listening. For example, consider the first paragraph from the essay "Our Two-Sided Brain."

> One of the most intriguing areas of scientific and educational exploration concerns the manner in which our brain processes information. It has been known for a long time that the brain is divided into two seemingly identical halves, usually termed the left hemisphere and the right hemisphere. Until recently, it was assumed that these two hemispheres were similar in the way that they operated. However, a variety of current research has shown conclusively that each hemisphere has a distinct "personality," processing information in its own unique way.

How would you represent the ideas and their relationships presented in this passage? Take a piece of paper and pencil and develop at least one mind map. This diagram illustrates one possible rendering:

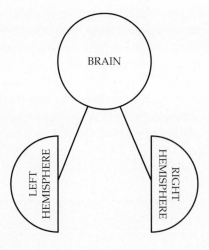

Now review the next paragraph of the essay, which focuses in on the qualities of the brain's left hemisphere.

> The left hemisphere exhibits those qualities that we normally associate with higher intellectual activities. For example, the left hemisphere functions analytically, tending to break things and processes down into component parts, like taking apart an automobile engine in order to diagnose the problem. The left hemisphere is also the seat of most of our verbal activity, decoding and encoding the bulk of our language, mathematical symbols, and musical notations. Finally, the left hemisphere tends to process information in a linear, sequential way, one step at a time. This is consistent with the verbal capacities which it exhibits, since language is spoken/heard/read one word at a time, and the meaning of the words depends in large measure on the order in which the words are placed. In short, the left hemisphere is similar to a modern, digital computer in that its individual operations unfold in an orderly, logical sequence.

Expand the mind map you developed for the first paragraph of the essay to include this additional information. Your ideas should be either written on lines connected to other lines, or within shapes connected by lines, to express clearly the relationship between the various ideas. Print the ideas in capital letters so that they can be easily read and referred to. Here is a sample of how the first mind map on page 396 might be elaborated to integrate this new information. Complete the information that has been omitted.

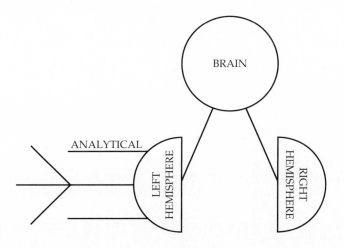

Now review the next paragraph of the essay, which describes the qualities of the right hemisphere and compares these qualities to those of the left hemisphere.

> The right hemisphere operates in a much different fashion. Instead of analyzing things and processes into component parts, it seeks to synthesize by organizing parts into patterns and wholes — like arranging individual flowers into a floral arrangement. The right hemisphere normally has much less to do with verbal activity. Instead, it is much more visually oriented, focusing on shapes, arrangements, and images. It also processes information based on what we personally experience with all of our senses (including touch). So, for example, while the left hemisphere might enable us to remember people by their name, the right hemisphere might enable us to recognize them by their face or the feel of their handshake. Finally, rather than processing information in a linear, sequential fashion, the right hemisphere tends to organize information into patterns and relationships which are experienced as a whole. For instance, in listening to music, the right hemisphere focuses on the overall melody rather than the individual notes, or on the pattern of play on the chessboard rather than the individual pieces. While we compared the linear functioning of the left hemisphere to a digital computer, we might compare the functioning of the right hemisphere to a kaleidoscope, as it continually works to organize information into meaningful shapes and patterns.

Using the mind map you created for the first two paragraphs of the essay as a starting point, expand your map by including this new information. In composing your map, be sure to represent the relationships between the various qualities of the two hemispheres. Complete the missing information in the spaces provided on this sample final map on page 399.

The final paragraph of the essay moves into a new direction, relating the information we have been reading (and thinking about) to education. Read this paragraph and then incorporate the ideas it presents into the mind map you have created for the essay.

> The modern research into how our brain functions has significant implications for human learning. Much of our education is structured for left hemisphere thinking — analytical, verbal, logical, and sequential. Yet much of our understanding about the world is based on the activities of the right hemisphere — synthesizing, visual, experiential, and pattern-seeking. If education is to become as effective as it can be, it must introduce teaching methods that address the right hemisphere as well as the left hemisphere.

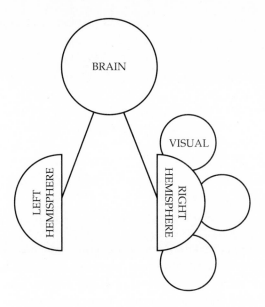

Clearly, creating mind maps can be a useful strategy in helping us understand complex written information. This versatile tool, however, is not limited to reading; it has other language uses as well — for example, organizing and interpreting spoken information. When people read and hear language, they normally do not try to interpret one word at a time, unless they are beginning to learn a new language. Instead, when we read and listen we typically group words together in "chunks" of meaning, trying to make sense of the *entire* meaning the words express. For instance, when you read the last two sentences, did you try to understand them one word at a time, or did you try to make sense of the complete ideas being expressed? In all likelihood, you tried to interpret the overall meaning being expressed, including the relationships among the various ideas.

The same is true when we speak. Although we pronounce the words one at a time, they form part of an entire meaning and network of relationships we are trying to express. Again, examine your thinking process as you attempt to explain an idea to someone. Are you thinking one word at a time, or do you find there is a complex process of examining, sorting, and relating the various words to express the meaning you are trying to communicate? Probably the latter.

Based on these considerations, we can see that a mapping approach offers some clear advantages in organizing the information you receive from oral communication. For instance, when you as a student take notes of what a teacher is speaking about, you may find that you try to copy down sentences and quotes the teacher has said. When you return to study these notes, you may find the notes are not adequate because they do not include the various relationships among the ideas expressed. Using a mapping approach to note taking will help provide you with the means for identifying the key ideas and their relationships.

Mapping is also an effective aid in preparing for oral presentations. By organizing the information we want to present in this way, we have all the key ideas and their relationships in a single whole. Probably the greatest fear of people making oral presentations is that they will "get stuck" or lose their train of thought. If you have a clear map of the main ideas and their relationships either in your mind or in notes, the chances of this sort of "freeze-up" are considerably reduced.

One of the advantages of using maps is that, once you have constructed them, you can place the ideas in whatever order you may need by simply numbering them or circling them in different colors. As a result, a map not only represents all the key ideas and their relationships simultaneously, it can also be used to construct more traditional outlines or speaking notes.

Maps for Writing

Along with reading, listening, and speaking, mapping is useful for writing. First, the organization grows naturally, reflecting the way our mind naturally makes associations and organizes information. Second, the organization can be easily revised on the basis of new information and our developing understanding of how this information should be organized. Third, we can express a range of relationships among the various ideas. And instead of being identified once and then forgotten, each idea remains an active part of the overall pattern, suggesting new possible relationships. Fourth, we do not have to decide initially on a beginning, subpoints, subsubpoints, and so on; we can do this after our pattern is complete, saving time and frustration. Let's explore how mind mapping can be used in the writing process through the following activity.

Review the last paragraph of the essay "Our Two-Sided Brain" on page 398. The author's point is that effective education must involve teaching methods that make use of learning activities associated with the functions of the right hemisphere. In other words, whereas traditional education places emphasis on left hemisphere activities (analytical, verbal, logical, and sequential), the most effective education will also include right hemisphere activities (synthesizing, visual, experiential, and pattern seeking). Let's explore this idea further.

A useful first step to any writing project is *brainstorming,* an activity in which, working individually or with a group of people, we write down as many ideas as we can think of related to a given theme. The goal is to produce as many ideas as possible in a specified period of time. While you are engaged in this idea-generating process, it is important to relax, let your mind run free, build on the ideas of others, and refrain from censoring or evaluating any ideas produced, no matter how marginal they seem at first. Working by yourself or with other class members, brainstorm as many examples of right hemisphere learning activities as you can think of in a 5-minute period. Some initial ideas to get you started are:

View films and video	Use diagrams
Go on field trips	Engage in role playing
Design group activities	Integrate music into lesson
Use meditation to increase concentration	Identify patterns in content

After completing your brainstorming list, create a mind map that begins to organize the ideas you have developed. Start with the main idea ("Right Hemisphere Learning Activities") in the center and then develop branches that present your ideas as well as the relationships between these ideas. As you do this, new ideas are likely to occur to you, for the act of creating mind maps also often generates ideas. In working on your map, try to relax your mind as much as possible, letting the ideas and associations flow freely. As you complete your map, look for possible connections among different branches. This strategy often suggests relationships you might not have thought of before. See sample beginning of such a map on page 402.

Once your map is more or less complete, you have laid the foundation for your writing assignment, described in the following thinking activity.

THINKING ACTIVITY

9.1   ▶ Review your map and select the ideas and relationships you want to include and how you want to organize this information. You may want to use an outline to represent this organization. Once you have made an outline, you can begin to express your ideas using full sentences and paragraphs. Use the following format to structure your assignment.

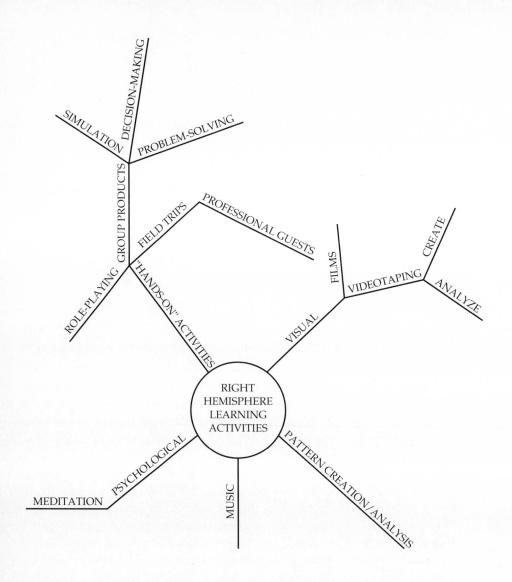

What is your point?   (Explain the concept of right-hemisphere learning
                          activities.)

Prove it to me!   (Give examples of these learning activities and explain
                          why you think these would be useful.)

So what!   (Conclude your paper with a closing summary.)

After writing the first draft of your paper, review it carefully to see if you can explain your ideas more clearly or provide additional examples to illustrate your points. ◀

Chronological and Process Relationships

Chronological and process patterns of thinking organize events or ideas in terms of their occurrence in time, though the two patterns tend to differ in focus or emphasis. The *chronological* pattern of thinking organizes something into a series of events in the sequence in which they occurred. For example, when we describe an experience we have had in the order it occurred, we are describing it chronologically. On the other hand, the *process* mode of thinking organizes an activity into a series of steps necessary for reaching a certain goal. Here the focus is on describing aspects of the growth, development, or change of something, as we might do when explaining how to prepare our favorite dish or perform a new dance.

Chronological Relationships

The simplest examples of chronological descriptions are logs or diaries, in which people record things that occurred at given points in time. The oldest and most universal form of chronological expression is the *narrative,* a way of thinking and communicating in which someone tells a story about experiences he or she has had. (Of course, the person telling the story can be a *fictional* character, created by a writer who is using a narrative form.) Every human culture has used narratives to pass on values and traditions from one generation to the next, exemplified by such enduring works as the *Odyssey* and the Bible. The word *narrative* is derived from the Latin word for "to know." Narrators are people who "know" what happened because they were there to experience it firsthand (or spoke to people who were there) and who share this experience with us.

One of America's great storytellers, Mark Twain, once said that a good story has to accomplish something and arrive somewhere. In other words, if a story is to be effective in engaging the interest of the audience, it has to have a purpose. The purpose may be to provide more information on a subject, to illustrate an idea, to lead us to a particular way of thinking, or merely to entertain us. An effective story does not merely record the complex, random, and often unrelated events of life. Instead, it has focus and purpose, possesses an ordered structure (a *plot*), and expresses a meaningful point of view.

THINKING ACTIVITY

9.2   ▶ Review the following narrative by Maria Muñiz, which uses chronological examples of thinking and expression, and then answer the questions that follow.

BACK, BUT NOT HOME *by Maria Muñiz*

With all the talk about resuming diplomatic relations with Cuba, and with the increasing number of Cuban exiles returning to visit friends and relatives, I am constantly being asked, "Would you ever go back?" In turn, I have asked myself, "Is there any reason for me to go?" I have had to think long and hard before finding my answer. Yes.

I came to the United States with my parents when I was almost five years old. We left behind grandparents, aunts, uncles and several cousins. I grew up in a very middle-class neighborhood in Brooklyn. With one exception, all my friends were Americans. Outside of my family, I do not know many Cubans. I often feel awkward visiting relatives in Miami because it is such a different world. The way of life in Cuban Miami seems very strange to me and I am accused of being too "Americanized." Yet, although I am now an American citizen, whenever anyone has asked me my nationality, I have always and unhesitatingly replied, "Cuban."

Outside American, inside Cuban.

I recently had a conversation with a man who generally sympathizes with the Castro regime. We talked of Cuban politics and although the discussion was very casual, I felt an old anger welling inside. After 16 years of living an "American" life, I am still unable to view the revolution with detachment or objectivity. I cannot interpret its results in social, political or economic terms. Too many memories stand in my way.

And as I listened to this man talk of the Cuban situation, I began to remember how as a little girl I would wake up crying because I had dreamed of my aunts and grandmothers and I missed them. I remembered my mother's trembling voice and the sad look on her face whenever she spoke to her mother over the phone. I thought of the many letters and photographs that somehow were always lost in transit. And as the conversation continued, I began to remember how difficult it often was to grow up Latina in an American world.

It meant going to kindergarten knowing little English. I'd been in this country only a few months and although I understood a good deal of what was said to me, I could not express myself very well. On the first day of school I remember one little girl's saying to the teacher: "But how can we play with her? She's so stupid she can't even talk!" I felt so helpless because inside I was crying, "Don't you know I can understand everything you're saying?" But I did not have words for my thoughts and my inability to communicate terrified me.

As I grew a little older, Latina meant being automatically relegated to the slowest reading classes in school. By now my English was fluent, but the teachers would always assume I was somewhat illiterate or slow. I recall one teacher's amazement at discovering I could read and write just as well as her American pupils. Her incredulity astounded me. As a child, I began to realize that Latina would always mean proving I was as good as the others. As I grew older, it became a matter of pride to prove I was better than the others.

As an adult I have come to terms with these memories and they don't hurt as much. I don't look or sound very Cuban. I don't speak with an accent and my English is far better than my Spanish. I am beginning my career and look forward to the many possibilities ahead of me.

But a persistent little voice is constantly saying, "There's something missing. It's not enough." And this is why when I am now asked, "Do you want to go back?" I say "yes" with conviction.

I do not say to Cubans, "It is time to lay aside the hurt and forgive and forget." It is impossible to forget an event that has altered and scarred all our lives so profoundly. But I find I am beginning to care less and less about politics. And I am beginning to remember and care more about the child (and how many others like her) who left her grandma behind. I have to return to Cuba one day because I want to know that little girl better.

When I try to review my life during the past 16 years, I almost feel as if I've walked into a theater right in the middle of a movie. And I'm afraid I won't fully understand or enjoy the rest of the movie unless I can see and understand the beginning. And for me, the beginning is Cuba. I don't want to go "home" again; the life and home we all left behind are long gone. My home is here and I am happy. But I need to talk to my family still in Cuba.

Like all immigrants, my family and I have had to build a new life from almost nothing. It was often difficult, but I believe the struggle made us strong. Most of my memories are good ones.

But I want to preserve and renew my cultural heritage. I want to keep "la Cubana" within me alive. I want to return because the journey back will also mean a journey within. Only then will I see the missing piece. ■

1. Because chronological thinking patterns represent a sequence of events in time, they can be visually represented with mind maps structured like the following diagram. Using this form as a guide, create a mind map that expresses the key events in the author's life and their relationship to one another.

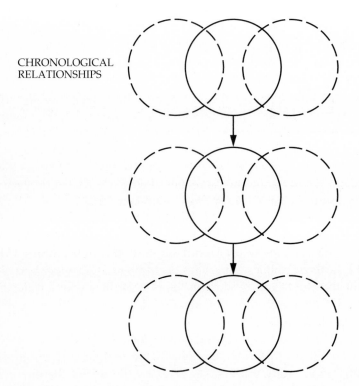

CHRONOLOGICAL
RELATIONSHIPS

2. Explain the purpose(s) you think the narrator is trying to achieve in writing this essay.

3. Identify the key points the author makes in trying to achieve her purpose(s). ◄

THINKING ACTIVITY

9.3 ▶ This text includes a number of narratives, including:

- Malcolm X (pages 20–22)
- Peter Rondinone (pages 57–64)
- Roberto Acuna (pages 169–176)

Read or reread those narratives identified by your teacher and analyze what you think are the most important purposes the authors try to achieve and what meaning or insights they try to communicate. ◀

THINKING ACTIVITY

9.4 ▶ Using a mind map that you created as a guide, write a narrative describing an event or experience that had special significance in your life. After completing your narrative, explain what you think is the most important point(s) that you are trying to share with your audience. Read your narrative to the other members of the class and then discuss it with them, comparing the meaning you intended with the meaning they derived. ◀

Process Relationships

A second type of time-ordered thinking pattern is the process relationship, which focuses on relating aspects of the growth, development, or change of an act, event, or object. From birth onward, we are involved with processes in every facet of our lives. The processes we are involved with can be classified in various ways: natural (e.g., growing physically), mechanical (e.g., assembling a bicycle), physical (e.g., learning a sport), mental (e.g., developing our thinking), creative (e.g., making a sculpture), and so on.

We use process relationships to describe aspects of the growth, development, or change of an act, event, or object by performing a *process analysis*, which involves two basic steps. The first step is to divide the process or activity we are analyzing into parts or stages. The second step is to explain the movement of the process through these parts or stages from beginning to end. The stages we have identified should be separate and distinct and should involve no repetition or significant omissions.

In performing a process analysis, we are typically trying to achieve one or both of two goals. The first goal is to give people step-by-step instruction in how to perform an activity, such as taking a photograph, changing a tire, or writing an essay. The second goal is simply to give information about a process, not to teach someone how to perform it. For example, your biology teacher might explain the process of photosynthesis to help you understand how green plants function, not to teach you how to go about transforming sunlight into chlorophyll!

THINKING ACTIVITY

9.5   ▶ Review the following passages, which are examples of the process analysis pattern of thinking. For each passage:

1. Identify the purpose of the passage.

2. Describe the main stages in the process identified by the author.

3. List questions you still have about how the process operates.

> Jacketing was a sleight-of-hand I watched with wonder each time, and I have discovered that my father was admired among sheepmen up and down the valley for his skill at it: *He was just pretty catty at that, the way he could get that ewe to take on a new lamb every time.* Put simply, jacketing was a ruse played on a ewe whose lamb had died. A substitute lamb quickly would be singled out, most likely from a set of twins. Sizing up the tottering newcomer, Dad would skin the dead lamb, and into the tiny pelt carefully snip four leg holes and a head hole. Then the stand-in lamb would have the skin fitted onto it like a snug jacket on a poodle. The next step of disguise was to cut out the dead lamb's liver and smear it several times across the jacket of pelt. In its borrowed and bedaubed skin, the new baby lamb then was presented to the ewe. She would sniff the baby impostor endlessly, distrustful but pulled by the blood-smell of her own. When in a few days she made up her dim sheep's mind to accept the lamb, Dad snipped away the jacket and recited his victory: *Mother him like hell now, don't ye? See what a helluva dandy lamb I got for ye, old sister? Who says I couldn't jacket day onto night if I wanted to, now-I-ask-ye?*
>
> Ivan Doig, *This House of Sky*

> If you are inexperienced in relaxation techniques, begin by sitting in a comfortable chair with your feet on the floor and your hands resting easily in your lap. Close your eyes and breathe evenly, deeply, and gently. As you exhale each breath let your body become more relaxed. Starting with one hand direct your attention to one part of your body at a time. Close your fist and tighten the muscles of your forearm. Feel the sensation of tension in your muscles. Relax your hand and let your forearm and hand become completely limp. Direct all your attention to the

sensation of relaxation as you continue to let all tension leave your hand and arm. Continue this practice once or several times each day, relaxing your other hand and arm, your legs, back, abdomen, chest, neck, face, and scalp. When you have this mastered and can relax completely, turn your thoughts to scenes of natural tranquility from your past. Stay with your inner self as long as you wish, whether thinking of nothing or visualizing only the loveliest of images. Often you will become completely unaware of your surroundings. When you open your eyes you will find yourself refreshed in mind and body.

Laurence J. Peter, *The Peter Prescription* ◀

THINKING ACTIVITY

9.6 ▶ One of the occasions when we are most acutely aware of process analysis is when we are learning a new activity for the first time, such as preparing formula for an infant or installing a new oil filter in a car. Identify such an occasion in your own life and then complete the activities on page 410.

PROCESS
RELATIONSHIPS

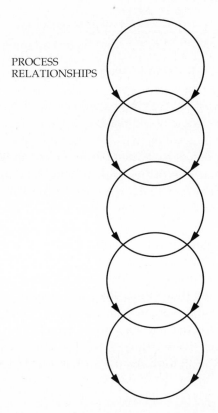

1. Create a mind map of the process, similar in form to the diagram on page 409.

2. Describe the steps or stages in the process.

3. Write a passage explaining how the steps or stages fit together in an overall sequence.

4. Describe any special problems you had to solve and the manner in which you went about solving them.

5. Describe the feelings you experienced in learning this process. ◀

THINKING ACTIVITY

9.7   ▶ The following essay by the psychologist Daniel Goleman focuses on the process of dying. He describes how the work of Dr. Elisabeth Kübler-Ross has helped change social attitudes towards dying and reviews her formulation of the psychological stages people typically go through once they know they are soon to die. After reading the article, answer the questions that follow.

WE ARE BREAKING THE SILENCE ABOUT DEATH*
by Daniel Goleman

Psychiatrist Elisabeth Kübler-Ross and I were to meet and fly together to Colorado Springs, where she was to give a workshop for nurses, doctors and volunteers who work with dying patients. Our flight was soon to board, but there was no sign of Kübler-Ross. Then she appeared, bustling down the corridor, a small, wiry woman carrying two huge shoulder-bags. After the briefest exchange of amenities, she explained that she was concerned that one of her patients might be late for the flight. The patient was to be one of 12 dying people at the seminar. They would teach those who work with the dying by sharing their private fears and hopes.

At the last minute her patient, an emaciated but smiling woman, showed up at the gate. Kübler-Ross and I had planned to talk on the plane, but instead she spent the entire flight giving her patient emergency oxygen. Later I learned that Kübler-Ross had met her patient the week before. She saw that the woman had only a few more weeks or months to live, and learned that she had never traveled far from her hometown. So, on the spur of the moment, Kübler-Ross invited her to come along as her guest. She should, the doctor felt, live her remaining days fully.

*Reprinted with Permission from Psychology Today Magazine. Copyright © 1976 (PT Partners, L.P.).

Kübler-Ross began her work with the dying in the mid '60s when she decided to interview a dying patient for a medical-school seminar she was teaching. She searched the school's 600-bed hospital, asking the staff on each ward if there were any dying patients. On every ward she got the same answer: No. Yet on any given day in a hospital that size, many patients are near death. When she then went back and asked about specific patients, their doctors reluctantly admitted that they were terminally ill.

Medical schools in those days avoided the topic of death and dying. Medical staffs treated the physical problems of their dying patients but, more often than not, ignored the fact of approaching death. Virtually no one, the doctor included, was comfortable with the fact of death. It was taboo, best kept out of sight and out of mind.

Once a patient died, he vanished. One of Kübler-Ross's students realized that in all her months as a hospital resident she could hardly recall seeing a dead person. In part she chose to avoid them, but there was also "the remarkable disappearing act that occurs as the body is cleverly whisked out of sight . . ."

In the decade since Kübler-Ross first gave her seminar on dying, the taboo has weakened. Death is in vogue as a topic of books, seminars, scholarly articles, and classes at every level from college down to elementary school. There are two professional journals devoted to the study of death, dozens of volunteer groups working with the dying, and one or two medical facilities geared solely to helping people die with dignity.

There is no single cause for this change, but Elisabeth Kübler-Ross has done more to further it than any other person. Through her 1969 best seller *On Death and Dying*, her seminars for physicians, clergy, and others who work with dying people, and her public talks, Kübler-Ross has alerted us to a new way of handling dying.

Kübler-Ross is Chairman of the National Advisory Council to Hospice in New Haven, Connecticut, which leads the way in humane care of the dying. Modeled on a similar center in London, New Haven Hospice puts Kübler-Ross's advice into practice with a team on call around-the-clock to help people die in their own homes rather than in a strange hospital. Hospice has plans for building a center for dying patients. In contrast to policy at most hospitals, family members will be encouraged to join the medical staff in caring for their dying relatives. Visiting hours will be unlimited, and patients' children and even pets will be free to visit.

Kübler-Ross's natural openness toward the dying reflects her experience as a child in rural Switzerland. In her community, she saw death confronted with honesty and dignity. She also has the authority of one whose medical practice has been limited for the last decade to dying patients and their families; lately, her practice has been restricted to dying children. Her public life as an author and a lecturer allows her a rare luxury in her medical work; she charges no one for her services.

Kübler-Ross's career has been unusually humanitarian from the start. Before entering medical school in Switzerland, she worked at the close of the Second World War in eastern Europe, helping the survivors of bombed-out cities and death camps. After becoming a psychiatrist, she gravitated to treating chronic schizophrenics, and then to work with retarded children, whose mental slowness was compounded by being deaf, dumb or blind.

From the thousands of hours she has spent with patients facing death, Kübler-Ross has charted the psychological stages people typically go through once they know they are soon to die. Though any single person need not go through the entire progression, most everyone facing death experiences at least one of these stages. The usual progression is from denial of death through rage, bargaining, depression, and finally, acceptance.

These reactions are not restricted to dying, but can occur with a loss of any kind. We all experience them to some degree in the ordinary course of life changes. Every change is a loss, every beginning an end. In the words of the Tibetan poet Milarepa, "All worldly pursuits end in sorrow, acquisition in dispersion, buildings in destruction, meetings in separation, birth in death."

A person's first reaction to the news that he has a terminal disease is most often denial. The refusal to accept the fact that one is soon to die cushions death's impact. It gives a person time to come to grips with the loss of everything that has mattered to him.

Psychoanalysts recognize that at the unconscious level, a person does not believe he will die. From this refusal to believe in one's own death springs the hope that, despite a life-threatening illness, one will not die. This hope can take many forms: that the diagnosis is wrong, that the illness is curable, that a miracle treatment will turn up. As denial fades into a partial acceptance, the person's concern shifts from the hope of longer life to the wish that his or her family will be well and his affairs taken care of after his death.

Denial too often typifies the hospital staff's reaction to a patient who faces death. Doctors and nurses see themselves as healers; a dying patient threatens this role. Further, a person who cannot contemplate his own death, even if he is a physician, feels discomfort with someone who is dying. For this reason hospital staffs often enclose the dying patient in a cocoon of medical details that keeps death under wraps.

Sociologists Barney Glaser and Anselm Strauss studied the mutual pretense that often exists when patient and staff know the patient is dying. A staff member and a terminal patient might safely talk about his disease, they found, so long as they skirt its fatal significance. But they were most comfortable when they stuck to safe topics like movies and fashions — anything, in short, that signifies life going on as usual.

This is a fragile pretense, but not one that either party can easily break. Glaser and Strauss found that a patient would sometimes send cues to the staff that he wanted to talk about dying, but the nurses and doctors would decide not to talk openly with him because they feared he would go to pieces. The patient would openly make a remark acknowledging his death, but the doctor or nurse would ignore him. Then, out of tact or empathy for the embarrassment or distress he caused, the patient would resume his silence. In this case, it is the staff's uneasiness that maintains the pretense, not the patient's.

In the reverse instance, a doctor may give the patient an opening to talk about dying, and have the patient ignore it. Kübler-Ross urges hospital staff members to let the patient know that they are available to talk about dying, but not to force the subject on the patient. When he no longer needs to deny his death, the patient will seek out a staff member and open the topic.

When the family knows a patient is dying and keeps the secret from him, they create a barrier that prevents both patient and family from preparing for the death. The dying patient usually sees through a make-believe, smiling mask. Genuine emotions are much easier on the patient, allowing relatives to share his feelings. When his family can be open about the seriousness of the illness, there is time to talk and cry together and to take care of important matters under less emotional pressure.

A student nurse hospitalized for a fatal illness wrote to her professional colleagues in a nursing journal: "You slip in and out of my room, give me medications and check my blood pressure. Is it because I am a student nurse myself that I sense your fright? If only we could be honest, both admit our fears, touch one another. Then it might not be so hard to die — in a hospital — with friends close by."

Denial becomes increasingly hard as the patient's health deteriorates. Although mutual pretense avoids embarrassment and emotional strains, it sacrifices valuable time in which the dying patient and his family could take care of unfinished emotional and practical matters, like unsettled arguments or unwritten wills, that death will forestall forever.

Kübler-Ross feels that a period of denial is useful if it gives the patient and his family time to find a way to deal with the stark truth of death. But when denial persists until the person dies, the survivors' grief is needlessly prolonged by the guilts and regrets. Often patients near death say they wished they had been told they were dying sooner so that they could have prepared themselves and their families.

A few rare patients, though, need to cling to denial because the reality is too much to bear. When those closest to the person offer no love or comfort, as when children of the dying patient blame the parent for deserting them, the patient may deny the inevitable to the very end. But this is rare; of 500 patients, Kübler-Ross found only four who refused to the last to admit that they were dying.

Once a dying patient accepts the invitation to talk about his death, Kübler-Ross tries to help him recognize any unfinished business that needs his attention. Straightforward truth helps the dying person fully live the time left. She tries to elicit their hidden hopes and needs, then find someone who can fulfill these needs.

Physical pain sometimes prevents a dying patient from making the best use of his remaining days. When his pain is overwhelming, he either becomes preoccupied with it or dependent on painkillers that leave him groggy. Kübler-Ross controls pain with Brompton's mixture. This old-time formula of morphine, cocaine, alcohol, syrup, and chloroform water dulls the patient's pain without dimming his alertness.

When a patient stops denying his impending death, the feelings that most often well up are rage and anger. The question, "Why me?" is asked with bitterness. The patient aims his resentment at whoever is handy, be it staff, friends or family. Healthy people remind the patient that he will die while they live. The unfairness of it all arouses his rage. He may be rude, uncooperative, or downright hostile. For example, when a nurse was late with his pain medication, the patient snapped, "Why are you late? You don't care if I suffer. Your coffee break is more important to you than my pain."

As the rage abates the patient may start to bargain with God or fate, trying to arrange a temporary truce. The question switches from "Why me?" to "Why now?" He hopes for more time to finish things, to put his house in order, to arrange for his family's future needs, to make a will. The bargain with God takes the form of the patient promising to be good or to do something in exchange for another week, month, or year of life.

With full acceptance of his approaching death, a person often becomes depressed. Dying brings him a sense of hopelessness, helplessness and isolation. He mourns past losses, and regrets things left undone or wrongs he's committed. One of Kübler-Ross's patients, for example, regretted that when his daughter was small and needed him, he was on the road making money to provide a good home. Now that he was dying, he wanted to spend every moment he could with her, but she was grown and had her own friends. He felt it was too late. At this stage the dying person starts to mourn his own death, the loss of all the people and things he has found meaningful, the plans and hopes never to be fulfilled. Kübler-Ross calls this kind of depression a "preparatory grief." It allows a person to get ready for his death by letting go of his attachments to life.

During this preparatory grief, the patient may stop seeing family and friends, and become withdrawn and silent. His outer detachment matches the inner renouncement of what once mattered to him. Family members sometimes misinterpret his detachment as a rejection. Kübler-Ross helps them to see that the patient is beginning to accept his death. Hence, he needs much less contact with family and friends.

After this preparatory mourning, the dying person can reach a peaceful acceptance. He is no longer concerned with the prolongation of his life. He has made peace with those he loves, settled his affairs, relinquished his unfinished dreams. He may feel an inner calm, and become mellow in outlook. He can take things as they come, including the progress of his illness. People bring him pleasure, but he no longer speaks of plans for the future. His focus becomes the simple joys of everyday life; he enjoys today without waiting for tomorrow. At this stage, the person is ready to live his remaining days fully and die well.

The story of a modern Zen master's death shows this frame of mind. As the master lay dying, one of his students brought him a special cake, of which he had always been fond. With a wan smile the master slowly ate a piece of the cake. As he grew weaker still, his students leaned close and asked if he had any final words for them. "Yes," he said, as they leaned forward eagerly, "My, but this cake is delicious."

What the dying teach us, says Kübler-Ross, is how to live. In summing up what she has learned from her dying patients, she likes to recite a poem by Richard Allen that goes:

. . . as you face your death,
it is only the love
you have given
and received
which will count . . .
if you have loved well
then it will have been worth it . . .
but if you have not
death will always come too soon
and be too terrible to face. ■

1. Create a mind map that illustrates the psychological stages most people undergo during the process of dying, according to Dr. Kübler-Ross.

2. Drawing on your own experiences with people you know who have died, analyze whether you believe that the stages Dr. Kübler-Ross has identified are accurate descriptions of the dying process.

3. Imagine that you just found out that you had six months left to live.

   a. Create a mind map that illustrates the psychological stages that you think you would go through.

   b. Using this map as a guide, write a passage that explains your thoughts on this subject.

   c. The author of this article, Daniel Goleman, gives the example of a dying man whose main regret was that he had never spent enough time with his daughter and now wanted to spend every minute with her. Describe how you would live the last six months of your life.

   d. Explain why thinking and writing about dying, a topic we usually try to avoid, can have a productive impact on our lives. ◀

Comparative and Analogical Relationships

Both comparative and analogical patterns of thinking focus on the similarities and/or dissimilarities among different objects, events, or ideas. Comparative modes of thinking relate things in the *same* general category in terms of their similarities and differences. For example, when we shop for something important, like a car, we generally engage in a process of organized *comparing* (evaluating similarities and differences) as we examine the various makes and models. On the other hand, analogical modes of thinking relate things in entirely *different* categories in terms of their similarities. For example, on our shopping expedition for a car, we might say of a used car badly in need of repair: "That car is a real lemon." Obviously cars and lemons are in different categories, but the analogy brings out some similarities between the two (a sense of "sourness" or "bitterness").

Comparative Relationships

Think of an item you shopped for and bought in the past month. It might have been an article of clothing, a good book or a new record, a radio, and so on. List the item you selected, noting as much specific information about it as you can remember — brand, color, size, cost, and so on. (The Levi's jeans information is included as an example.)

Item Purchased: Levi's jeans, size 31 × 31, blue, straight cut, $24.00

Item Purchased: _____

When you went shopping, you probably spent a fair amount of time examining other items of the same type, things that you looked at but *did not buy.* List one of these competing items below:

Item Not Purchased: _____

As you made your decision to purchase the item you did, you probably compared the various brands before making your selection. In the space below, list some of the factors you took into consideration in comparing the different items. For example:

Item Purchased:	*Comparative Factors:*	*Item Not Purchased:*
Levi's jeans	Brand	Guess! jeans
$24.00	Price	$34.00
Straight cut	Style	Designer cut
Regular denim	Material	Stretch denim
_____	_____	_____
_____	_____	_____
_____	_____	_____

We compare in this way all the time, usually without even realizing it. Whenever we select an item on a menu or in a store, or a seat in a theater or on a bus, we are automatically looking for similarities and differences among the various items from which we are selecting, and these similarities and differences guide us in making our decision.

Of course, we do not always engage in a systematic process of comparison. In many cases, the selections and decisions we make seem to be unconscious. This may be so because we have already performed an organized comparison some time in the past and already know what we want and why we want it (e.g., "I always choose an aisle seat so I don't have to climb over people").

Sometimes, however, we make decisions impulsively, without any thought or comparative examination. Maybe someone told us to, maybe we were influenced by the commercial we saw, or maybe we simply said, "What the heck, let's take a chance." Sometimes these impulsive decisions work out for us, but often they do not because they are simply a result of rolling the dice. On the other hand, when we engage in a critical and comparative examination, we gain information that can help us make intelligent decisions.

Standards for Comparison   Naturally, not all of the factors we use in comparing are equally important in our decision making. In any comparison, some similarities and differences outweigh others. How do we determine which factors are more important than others, and which information is more relevant than other information? Unfortunately, there is no simple formula for answering these questions. For example, review the lists you completed previously and place a check next to the factors that played an important part in your decision. These factors represent the comparative information you found to be most important and relevant and probably reflect your needs and purposes. If you are on a limited budget, price differences may play a key role in your decision. If money is no object, your decision may have been based solely on the quality of the item or on some other consideration.

Even though there is no hard and fast way to determine which areas of comparison are most important, it does help us to become *aware* of the factors that are influencing our perceptions and decisions. These areas of comparison represent the standards we use to come to conclusions, and a critical and reflective examination of them can help us sharpen, clarify, and improve our standards.

When making comparisons, there are pitfalls we should try to avoid:

1. *Incomplete comparisons.* This difficulty arises when we focus on too few points of comparison. For example, in looking for a competent surgeon to operate on us, we might decide to focus only on the fee that each doctor

charges. Even though this may be an important area for comparative analysis, we would be foolish to overlook other areas of comparison, such as medical training, experience, recommendations, and success rates.

2. *Selective comparisons.* This problem occurs when we take a one-sided view of a comparative situation — when we concentrate on the points favoring one side of the things being compared but overlook the points favoring the other side. For example, in selecting a dependable friend to perform a favor for you, you may focus on Bob because he is your best friend and you have known him the longest but overlook that he let you down the last few times you asked him to do something for you.

THINKING ACTIVITY

9.8 ▶ Review the following passages, which use comparative patterns of thinking to organize the ideas being presented. For each passage:

1. Identify the key ideas being compared.

2. Analyze the points of similarity and dissimilarity between the ideas being presented by using a mind map like the diagram on page 420.

3. Describe the conclusions the passage leads you to.

> The difference between an American cookbook and a French one is that the former is very accurate and the second exceedingly vague. American recipes look like doctors' prescriptions. Perfect cooking seems to depend on perfect dosage. You are told to take a teaspoon of this and a tablespoon of that, then to stir them together until thoroughly blended. A French recipe seldom tells you how many ounces of butter to use to make *crepes suzette,* or how many spoonfuls of oil should go into a salad dressing. French cookbooks are full of unusual measurements such as a *pinch* of pepper, a *suspicion* of garlic, or a *generous sprinkling* of brandy. There are constant references to seasoning *to taste,* as if the recipe were merely intended to give a general direction, relying on the experience and art of the cook to make the dish turn out right.
> Raoul de Roussy de Sales, "American and French Cookbooks"

> The rapidity of change and the speed with which new situations are created follow the impetuous and heedless pace of man rather than the deliberate pace of nature. Radiation is no longer merely the background radiation of rocks, the bombardment of cosmic rays, the ultraviolet of the sun that have existed before there was any life on earth; radiation is now the unnatural creation of man's tampering with the atom. The chemicals to which life is asked to make its adjustment are no longer merely the calcium and silica and copper and all the rest of the minerals

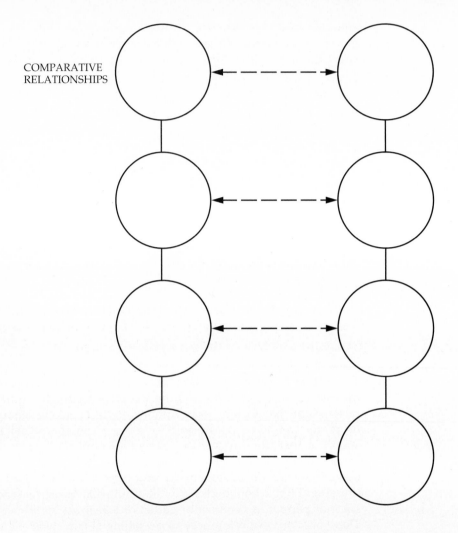

COMPARATIVE
RELATIONSHIPS

washed out of the rocks and carried in rivers to the sea; they are the synthetic creations of man's inventive mind, brewed in his laboratories, and having no counterparts in nature. . . . To adjust to these chemicals would require time on the scale that is nature's; it would require not merely the years of a man's life but the life of generations. And even this, were it by some miracle possible, would be futile, for the new chemicals come from our laboratories in an endless stream; almost five hundred annually find their way into actual use in the United States alone.

Rachel Carson, *Silent Spring*

Physically and psychically women are by far the superior of men. The old chestnut about women being more emotional than men has been forever destroyed by the facts of two great wars. Women under blockade, heavy bombardment, concentration camp confinement, and similar rigors withstand them vastly more successfully than men. The psychiatric casualties of civilian populations under such conditions are mostly masculine, and there are far more men in our mental hospitals than there are women. The steady hand at the helm is the hand that has had the practice at rocking the cradle. Because of their greater size and weight, men are physically more powerful than women — which is not the same thing as saying that they are stronger. A man of the same size and weight as a woman of comparable background and occupational status would probably not be any more powerful than a woman. As far as constitutional strength is concerned, women are stronger than men. Many diseases from which men suffer can be shown to be largely influenced by their relation to the male Y-chromosome. More males die than females. Deaths from almost all causes are more frequent in males of all ages. Though women are more frequently ill than men, they recover from illnesses more easily and more frequently than men.

Ashley Montagu, *The Natural Superiority of Women* ◄

Analogical Relationships

We noted earlier that comparative relationships involve examining the similarities and differences of two items in the same general category, such as items on a menu or methods of birth control. There is another kind of comparison, however, that does *not* focus on things in the same category. Such comparisons are known as *analogies,* and their goal is to clarify or illuminate a concept from one category by saying that it is the same as a concept from a different category.

The purpose of an analogy is not the same as the purpose of the comparison we considered in the last section. At that time, we noted that the goal of comparing similar things is usually to make a choice and that the process of comparing can provide us with information on which we can base an intelligent decision. The main goal of analogies, however, is not to choose or decide; it is to illuminate our understanding. Identifying similarities between very different things can often stimulate us to see these things in a new light, from a different perspective than we are used to. This can result in a clearer and more complete understanding of the things being compared. Consider the following example:

Life's but a walking shadow, a poor player
That struts and frets his hour upon the stage
and then is heard no more.

William Shakespeare, *Macbeth*

In this famous quotation, Shakespeare is comparing two things that at first glance don't seem to have anything in common at all: life and an actor. Yet as we look closer at the comparison, we begin to see that even though these two things are unlike in many ways, there are also some very important similarities between them. What are some of these similarities?

> *Analogy*   A comparison between things that are basically dissimilar made for the purpose of illuminating our understanding of the things being compared.

We ourselves often create and use analogies to get a point across to someone else. Used appropriately, analogies can help us illustrate and explain what we are trying to communicate. This is particularly important when we have difficulty in finding the right words to represent our experiences. Powerful or complex emotions can make us speechless, or make us say things like "words cannot describe what I feel." Imagine that you are trying to describe your feelings of love and caring for another person. To illustrate and clarify the feelings you are trying to communicate, you might compare your feelings of love to "the first rose of spring," noting the following similarities:

- Like the rose, this is the first great love of your life.
- Like the fragile yet supple petals of the rose, your feelings are tender and sensitive.
- Like the beauty of the rose, the beauty of your love should grow with each passing day.

What are some other comparisons of love to a rose?

Like the color of the rose, ⎯⎯⎯⎯⎯⎯⎯⎯⎯⎯⎯⎯⎯⎯⎯⎯⎯⎯⎯⎯.

Like the fragrance of the rose, ⎯⎯⎯⎯⎯⎯⎯⎯⎯⎯⎯⎯⎯⎯⎯⎯⎯⎯.

Like the thorns of the rose, ⎯⎯⎯⎯⎯⎯⎯⎯⎯⎯⎯⎯⎯⎯⎯⎯⎯⎯⎯.

Another favorite subject for analogies is the idea of the meaning or purpose of life, which the simple use of the word *life* does not communicate. We have just seen Shakespeare's comparison of life to an actor. Here are some other popular analogies involving life. What are some points of similarity in each of those comparisons?

1. Life is just a bowl of cherries.

   _____

2. Life is a football game.

   _____

3. "Life is a tale told by an idiot, full of sound and fury, signifying nothing."
   — Shakespeare

   _____

   Create an analogy for life representing some of your feelings, and explain the points of similarity.

4. Life is _____

   _____

In addition to communicating experiences that resist simple characterization, analogies are also useful when we are trying to explain a complicated concept. For instance, we might compare the eye to a camera lens or the immunological system of the body to the National Guard (corpuscles are called to active duty when undesirable elements threaten the well-being of the organism and rush to the scene of danger).

Analogies possess the power to bring things to life by evoking images that illuminate the points of comparison. Consider the following analogies and explain the points of comparison that the author is trying to make.

1. "Laws are like cobwebs, which may catch small flies, but let wasps and hornets break through." — Jonathan Swift

   _____

2. "I am as pure as the driven slush." — Tallulah Bankhead

   _____

3. "He has all the qualities of a dog, except its devotion." — Gore Vidal

   _____

Similes and Metaphors   From the examples discussed so far, we can see that analogies have two parts: an *original subject* and a *compared subject* (what the original is being likened to). In comparing your love to the first rose of spring, the *original subject* is your feelings of love and caring for someone whereas the *compared subject* is what you are comparing those feelings to in order to illuminate and express them — namely, the first rose of spring.

In analogies, the connection between the original subject and the compared subject can be either obvious (explicit) or implied (implicit). For example, we can echo the lament of the great pool hustler, "Minnesota Fats," and say:

A pool player in a tuxedo is like a hotdog with whipped cream on it.

This is an obvious analogy (known as a *simile*) because we have explicitly noted the connection between the original subject (man in tuxedo) and the compared subject (hotdog with whipped cream) by using the comparative term *like*. (Sometimes the structure of the sentence calls for *as* in a similar position.)

> *Simile*   An explicit comparison between basically dissimilar things made for the purpose of illuminating our understanding of the things being compared.

We could also have used other forms of obvious comparison, such as "is similar to," "reminds me of," or "makes me think of."

On the other hand, we could say:

A pool player in a tuxedo *is* a hotdog with whipped cream on it.

In this case, we are making an implied analogy (known as a *metaphor*), because we have not included any words that point out that we are making a comparison. Instead, we are stating that the original subject *is* the compared subject. Naturally, we are assuming that most people will understand that we are making a comparison between two different things and not describing a biological transformation.

> *Metaphor*   An implied comparison between basically dissimilar things made for the purpose of illuminating our understanding of the things being compared.

Create a *simile* (obvious analogy) for a subject of your own choosing, noting at least two points of comparison.

Subject: _____

1. _____

2. _____

Create a *metaphor* (implied analogy) for a subject of your own choosing, noting at least two points of comparison.

Subject: _____

1. _____

2. _____

THINKING ACTIVITY

9.9 ▶ Read the following passage, which uses an analogical pattern of thinking. Identify the major ideas being compared and describe the points of similarity between them. Explain how the analogy helps illuminate the subject being discussed.

> The mountain guide, like the true teacher, has a quiet authority. He or she engenders trust and confidence so that one is willing to join the endeavor. The guide accepts his leadership role, yet recognizes that success (measured by the heights that are scaled) depends upon the close cooperation and active participation of each member of the group. He has crossed the terrain before and is familiar with the landmarks, but each trip is new and generates its own anxiety and excitement. Essential skills must be mastered; if they are lacking, disaster looms. The situation demands keen focus and rapt attention; slackness, misjudgment, or laziness can abort the venture. . . . The teacher is not a pleader, not a performer, not a huckster, but a confident, exuberant guide on expeditions of shared responsibility into the most exciting and least-understood terrain on earth — the mind itself.
>
> Nancy K. Hill, "Scaling the Heights;
> The Teacher as Mountaineer" ◀

Extended Analogies   The analogies considered so far have been of a fairly simple sort, designed for limited purposes and displaying relatively few points of resemblance. We also use analogies for more ambitious purposes, however, such as extended discussions of a subject. In these cases, an analogy can provide the framework for the discussion as we try to explain an idea by comparing it in some detail to something else.

9.10 ▶ The following essay was written by the American logician Irving M. Copi. The thinking structure of the passage is analogical: Copi is using the fictional character of Sherlock Holmes to illuminate and help us understand the scientist's approach to making sense of the world. After reading the essay, answer the questions that follow.

THE DETECTIVE AS SCIENTIST *by Irving M. Copi*

. . . A perennial favorite in this connection is the detective, whose problem is not quite the same as that of the pure scientist, but whose approach and technique illustrate the method of science very clearly. The classical example of the astute detective who can solve even the most baffling mystery is A. Conan Doyle's immortal creation, Sherlock Holmes. Holmes, his stature undiminished by the passage of time, will be our hero in the following account:

1. The Problem

Some of our most vivid pictures of Holmes are those in which he is busy with magnifying glass and tape measure, searching out and finding essential clues which had escaped the attention of those stupid bunglers, the "experts" of Scotland Yard. Or those of us who are by temperament less vigorous may think back more fondly on Holmes the thinker, ". . . who, when he had an unsolved problem upon his mind, would go for days, and even for a week, without rest, turning it over, rearranging his facts, looking at it from every point of view until he had either fathomed it or convinced himself that his data were insufficient."[1] At one such time, according to Dr. Watson:

> He took off his coat and waistcoat, put on a large blue dressing-gown, and then wandered about the room collecting pillows from his bed and cushions from the sofa and armchairs. With these he constructed a sort of Eastern divan, upon which he perched himself cross-legged, with an ounce of shag tobacco and a box of matches laid out in front of him. In the dim light of the lamp I saw him sitting there, an old briar pipe between his lips, his eyes fixed vacantly upon the corner of the ceiling, the blue smoke curling up from him, silent, motionless, with the light shining upon his strong-set aquiline features. So he sat

[1] "The Man with the Twisted Lip."

as I dropped off to sleep, and so he sat when a sudden ejaculation caused me to wake up, and I found the summer sun sinking into the apartment. The pipe was still between his lips, the smoke still curled upward, and the room was full of a dense tobacco haze, but nothing remained of the heap of shag which I had seen upon the previous night.[2]

But such memories are incomplete. Holmes was not always searching for clues or pondering over solutions. We all remember those dark periods — especially in the earlier stories — when, much to the good Watson's annoyance, Holmes would drug himself with morphine or cocaine. That would happen, of course, between cases. For when there is no mystery to be unraveled, no man in his right mind would go out to look for clues. Clues, after all, must be clues for something. Nor could Holmes, or anyone else, for that matter, engage in profound thought unless he had something to think about. Sherlock Holmes was a genius at solving problems, but even a genius must have a problem before he can solve it. All reflective thinking, and this term includes criminal investigation as well as scientific research, is a problem-solving activity, as John Dewey and other pragmatists have rightly insisted. There must be a problem felt before either the detective or the scientist can go to work.

Of course the active mind sees problems where the dullard sees only familiar objects. One Christmas season Dr. Watson visited Holmes to find that the latter had been using a lens and forceps to examine ". . . a very seedy and disreputable hard-felt hat, much the worse for wear, and cracked in several places."[3] After they had greeted each other, Holmes said of it to Watson, "I beg that you will look upon it not as a battered billycock but as an intellectual problem."[4] It so happened that the hat led them into one of their most interesting adventures, but it could not have done so had Holmes not seen a problem in it from the start. A problem may be characterized as a fact or group of facts for which we have no acceptable explanation, which seem unusual, or which fail to fit in with our expectations or preconceptions. It should be obvious that *some* prior beliefs are required if anything is to appear problematic. If there are no expectations, there can be no surprises.

---

[2] Ibid.
[3] "The Adventure of the Blue Carbuncle."
[4] Ibid.

Sometimes, of course, problems came to Holmes already labeled. The very first adventure recounted by Dr. Watson began with the following message from Gregson of Scotland Yard:

> My Dear Mr. Sherlock Holmes:
>   There has been a bad business during the night at 3, Lauriston Gardens, off the Brixton Road. Our man on the beat saw a light there about two in the morning, and as the house was an empty one, suspected that something was amiss. He found the door open, and in the front room, which is bare of furniture, discovered the body of a gentleman, well dressed, and having cards in his pocket bearing the name of 'Enoch J. Drebber, Cleveland, Ohio, U.S.A.' There had been no robbery, nor is there any evidence as to how the man met his death. There are marks of blood in the room, but there is no wound upon his person. We are at a loss as to how he came into the empty house; indeed, the whole affair is a puzzler. If you can come round to the house any time before twelve, you will find me there. I have left everything in status quo until I hear from you. If you are unable to come, I shall give you fuller details, and would esteem it a great kindness if you would favour me with your opinion.
>
>   Yours faithfully
>   TOBIAS GREGSON[5]

Here was a problem indeed. A few minutes after receiving the message, Sherlock Holmes and Dr. Watson "were both in a hansom, driving furiously for the Brixton Road."

2. *Preliminary Hypotheses*

On their ride out Brixton way, Holmes "prattled away about Cremona fiddles and the difference between a Stradivarius and an Amati." Dr. Watson chided Holmes for not giving much thought to the matter at hand, and Holmes replied: "No data yet. . . . It is a capital mistake to theorize before you have all the evidence. It biases the judgment."[6] This point of view was expressed by Holmes again and again. On one occasion he admonished a younger detective that "The temptation to form premature theories upon insufficient data is the bane of our profession."[7] Yet for all of his confidence about the matter, on this one issue Holmes was completely mistaken. Of course one should not reach a *final*

---

[5] *A Study in Scarlet.*
[6] Ibid.
[7] *The Valley of Fear.*

judgment until a great deal of evidence has been considered, but this procedure is quite different from *not theorizing*. As a matter of fact, it is strictly impossible to make any serious attempt to collect evidence unless one *has* theorized beforehand. As Charles Darwin, the great biologist and author of the modern theory of evolution, observed: ". . . all observation must be for or against some view, if it is to be of any service." The point is that there are too many particular facts, too many data in the world, for anyone to try to become acquainted with them all. Everyone, even the most patient and thorough investigator, must pick and choose, deciding which facts to study and which to pass over. He must have some working hypothesis for or against which to collect relevant data. It need not be a *complete* theory, but at least the rough outline must be there. Otherwise how could one decide what facts to select for consideration out of the totality of all facts, which is too vast even to begin to sift?

Holmes' actions were wiser than his words in this connection. After all, the words were spoken in a hansom speeding towards the scene of the crime. If Holmes really had no theory about the matter, why go to Brixton Road? If facts and data were all that he wanted, any old facts and any old data, with no hypotheses to guide him in their selection, why should he have left Baker Street at all? There were plenty of facts in the rooms at 221-B, Baker Street. Holmes might just as well have spent his time counting all the words on the pages of all the books there, or perhaps making very accurate measurements of the distances between each separate pair of articles of furniture in the house. He could have gathered data to his heart's content and saved himself cab fare into the bargain!

It may be objected that the facts to be gathered at Baker Street have nothing to do with the case, whereas those which awaited Holmes at the scene of the crime were valuable clues for solving the problem. It was, of course, just this consideration which led Holmes to ignore the "data" at Baker Street and hurry away to collect those off Brixton Road. It must be insisted, however, that the greater relevance of the latter could not be *known* beforehand but only conjectured on the basis of previous experience with crimes and clues. It was in fact a *hypothesis* which led Holmes to look in one place rather than another for his facts, the hypothesis that there was a murder, that the crime was committed at the place where the body was found, and the murderer had left some trace or clue which could lead to his discovery. Some such hypothesis is always required to guide the investigator in his search for relevant data, for in the absence of any preliminary hypothesis, there are simply too many facts in this world to examine. The preliminary hypothesis ought to be highly tentative, and it must be based on previous knowledge. But a preliminary hypothesis is as necessary as the existence of a problem for any serious inquiry to begin.

It must be emphasized that a preliminary hypothesis, as here conceived, need not be a complete solution to the problem. The hypothesis that the man was murdered by someone who had left some clues to his identity on or near the body of his victim was what led Holmes to Brixton Road. This hypothesis is clearly incomplete: it does not say who committed the crime, or how it was done, or why. Such a preliminary hypothesis may be very different from the final solution to the problem. It will never be complete: it may be a tentative explanation of only part of the problem. But however partial and however tentative, a preliminary hypothesis is required for any investigation to proceed.

3. Collecting Additional Facts

Every serious investigation begins with some fact or group of facts which strike the investigator as problematic and which initiate the whole process of inquiry. The initial facts which constitute the problem are usually too meagre to suggest a wholly satisfactory explanation for themselves, but they will suggest — to the competent investigator — some preliminary hypotheses which lead him to search out additional facts. These additional facts, it is hoped, will serve as clues to the final solution. The inexperienced or bungling investigator will overlook or ignore all but the most obvious of them; but the careful worker will aim at completeness in his examination of the additional facts to which his preliminary hypotheses lead him. Holmes, of course, was the most careful and painstaking of investigators.

Holmes insisted on dismounting from the hansom a hundred yards or so from their destination and approached the house on foot, looking carefully at its surroundings and especially at the pathway leading up to it. When Holmes and Watson entered the house, they were shown the body by the Scotland Yard operatives, Gregson and Lestrade. ("There is no clue," said Gregson. "None at all," chimed in Lestrade.) But Holmes had already started his own search for additional facts, looking first at the body:

> . . . his nimble fingers were flying here, there, and everywhere, feeling, pressing, unbuttoning, examining. . . . So swiftly was examina-

tion made, that one would hardly have guessed the minuteness with which it was conducted. Finally, he sniffed the dead man's lips, and then glanced at the soles of his patent leather boots.[8]

Then turning his attention to the room itself,

> . . . he whipped a tape measure and a large round magnifying glass from his pocket. With these two implements he trotted noiselessly about the room, sometimes stopping, occasionally kneeling, and once lying flat upon his face. So engrossed was he with his occupation that he appeared to have forgotten our presence, for he chattered away to himself under his breath the whole time, keeping up a running fire of exclamations, groans, whistles, and little cries suggestive of encouragement and of hope. As I watched him I was irresistibly reminded of a pure-blooded, well-trained foxhound as it dashes backward and forward through the covert, whining in its eagerness, until it comes across the lost scent. For twenty minutes or more he continued his researches, measuring with the most exact care the distance between marks which were entirely invisible to me, and occasionally applying his tape to the walls in an equally incomprehensible manner. In one place he gathered up very carefully a little pile of gray dust from the floor and packed it away in an envelope. Finally, he examined with his glass the word upon the wall, going over every letter of it with the most minute exactness. This done, he appeared to be satisfied, for he replaced his tape and his glass in his pocket.
>
> "They say that genius is an infinite capacity for taking pains," he remarked with a smile. "It's a very bad definition, but it does apply to detective work."[9]

One matter deserves to be emphasized very strongly. Steps 2 and 3 are not completely separable but are usually very intimately connected and interdependent. True enough, we require a preliminary hypothesis to begin any intelligent examination of facts, but the additional facts may themselves suggest new hypotheses, which may lead to new facts, which suggest still other hypotheses, which lead to still other additional facts, and so on. Thus having made his careful examination of the facts available in the house off Brixton Road, Holmes was led to formulate a further hypothesis which required the taking of testimony from the

---

[8] *A Study in Scarlet.*
[9] Ibid.

constable who found the body. The man was off duty at the moment, and Lestrade gave Holmes the constable's name and address.

> Holmes took a note of the address.
>
> "Come along, Doctor," he said: "we shall go and look him up. I'll tell you one thing which may help you in the case," he continued, turning to the two detectives. "There has been murder done, and the murderer was a man. He was more than six feet high, was in the prime of life, had small feet for his height, wore coarse, square-toed boots and smoked a Trichinopoly cigar. He came here with his victim in a four-wheel cab, which was drawn by a horse with three old shoes and one new one on his off fore-leg. In all probability the murderer had a florid face, and the fingernails of his right hand were remarkably long. These are only a few indications, but they may assist you."
>
> Lestrade and Gregson glanced at each other with an incredulous smile.
>
> "If this man was murdered, how was it done?" asked the former.
>
> "Poison," said Sherlock Holmes curtly, and strode off.[10]

4. *Formulating the Hypothesis*

At some stage or other of his investigation, any man — whether detective, scientist, or ordinary mortal — will get the feeling that he has all the facts needed for his solution. He has his "2 and 2," so to speak, but the task still remains of "putting them together." At such a time Sherlock Holmes might sit up all night, consuming pipe after pipe of tobacco, trying to think things through. The result or end product of such thinking, if it is successful, is a hypothesis which accounts for all the data, both the original set of facts which constituted the problem, and the additional facts to which the preliminary hypotheses pointed. The actual discovery of such an explanatory hypothesis is a process of creation, in which imagination as well as knowledge is involved. Holmes, who was a genius at inventing hypotheses, described the process as reasoning "backward." As he put it,

> Most people if you describe a train of events to them, will tell you what the result would be. They can put those events together in their minds, and argue from them that something will come to pass. There are few people, however, who, if you told them a result, would be

---

[10] *A Study in Scarlet.*

able to evolve from their own inner consciousness what the steps were which led up to that result.[11]

Here is Holmes' description of the process of formulating an explanatory hypothesis. . . . Granted its relevance and testability, and its compatibility with other well-attested beliefs, the ultimate criterion for evaluating a hypothesis is its predictive power.

5. Deducing Further Consequences

A really fruitful hypothesis will not only explain the facts which originally inspired it, but will explain many others in addition. A good hypothesis will point beyond the initial facts in the direction of new ones whose existence might otherwise not have been suspected. And of course the verification of those further consequences will tend to confirm the hypothesis which led to them. Holmes' hypothesis that the murdered man had been poisoned was soon put to such a test. A few days later the murdered man's secretary and traveling companion was also found murdered. Holmes asked Lestrade, who had discovered the second body, whether he had found anything in the room which could furnish a clue to the murderer. Lestrade answered, "Nothing," and went on to mention a few quite ordinary effects. Holmes was not satisfied and pressed him, asking, "And was there nothing else?" Lestrade answered "Nothing of any importance," and named a few more details, the last of which was "a small chip ointment box containing a couple of pills." At this information,

> Sherlock Holmes sprang from his chair with an exclamation of delight. "The last links," he cried, exultantly. "My case is complete."
> The two detectives stared at him in amazement.
> "I have now in my hands," my companion said, confidently, "all the threads which have formed such a tangle. . . . I will give you a proof of my knowledge. Could you lay your hands upon those pills?"
> "I have them," said Lestrade, producing a small white box. . . .[12]

On the basis of his hypothesis about the original crime, Holmes was able to predict that the pills found at the scene of the second crime must contain poison. Here deduction has an essential role in the process of

---

[11] Ibid.
[12] Ibid.

any scientific or inductive inquiry. The ultimate value of any hypothesis lies in its predictive or explanatory power, which means that additional facts must be deducible from an adequate hypothesis. From his theory that the first man was poisoned and that the second victim met his death at the hands of the same murderer, Holmes inferred that the pills found by Lestrade must be poison. His theory, however sure he may have felt about it, was only a theory and needed further confirmation. He obtained that confirmation by testing the consequences deduced from the hypothesis and finding them to be true. Having used deduction to make a prediction, his next step was to test it.

6. Testing the Consequences

The consequences of a hypothesis, that is, the predictions made on the basis of that hypothesis, may require various means for their testing. Some require only observation. In some cases, Holmes needed only to watch and wait — for the bank robbers to break into the vault, in the "Adventure of the Red-headed League," or for Dr. Roylott to slip a venomous snake through a dummy ventilator, in the "Adventure of the Speckled Band." In the present case, however, an experiment had to be performed.

Holmes asked Dr. Watson to fetch the landlady's old and ailing terrier, which she had asked to have put out of its misery the day before. Holmes then cut one of the pills in two, dissolved it in a wineglass of water, added some milk, and

> . . . turned the contents of the wineglass into a saucer and placed it in front of the terrier, who speedily licked it dry. Sherlock Holmes's earnest demeanour had so far convinced us that we all sat in silence, watching the animal intently, and expecting some startling effect. None such appeared, however. The dog continued to lie stretched upon the cushion, breathing in a laboured way, but apparently neither the better nor the worse for its draught.
>
> Holmes had taken out his watch, and as minute followed minute without result, an expression of utmost chagrin and disappointment appeared upon his features. He gnawed his lip, drummed his fingers upon the table, and showed every other symptom of acute impatience. So great was his emotion that I felt sincerely sorry for him, while the two detectives smiled derisively, by no means displeased at this check which he had met.
>
> "It can't be a coincidence," he cried, at last springing from his chair and pacing wildly up and down the room: "it is impossible that it

should be a mere coincidence. The very pills which I suspected in the case of Drebber are actually found after the death of Stangerson. And yet they are inert. What can it mean? Surely my whole chain of reasoning cannot have been false. It is impossible! And yet this wretched dog is none the worse. Ah, I have it! I have it!" With a perfect shriek of delight he rushed to the box, cut the other pill in two, dissolved it, added milk, and presented it to the terrier. The unfortunate creature's tongue seemed hardly to have been moistened in it before it gave a convulsive shiver in every limb, and lay as rigid and lifeless as if it had been struck by lightning.

Sherlock Holmes drew a long breath, and wiped the perspiration from his forehead.[13]

By the favorable outcome of his experiment, Holmes' hypothesis had received dramatic and convincing confirmation.

7. Application

The detective's concern, after all, is a practical one. Given a crime to solve, he has not merely to explain the facts but to apprehend and arrest the criminal. The latter involves making application of his theory, using it to predict where the criminal can be found and how he may be caught. He must deduce still further consequences from the hypothesis, not for the sake of additional confirmation but for practical use. From his general hypothesis Holmes was able to infer that the murderer was acting the role of a cabman. We have already seen that Holmes had formed a pretty clear description of the man's appearance. He sent out his army of "Baker Street Irregulars," street urchins of the neighborhood, to search out and summon the cab driven by just that man. The successful "application" of this hypothesis can be described again in Dr. Watson's words. A few minutes after the terrier's death,

. . . there was a tap at the door, and the spokesman of the street Arabs, young Wiggins, introduced his insignificant and unsavoury person.

"Please, sir," he said touching his forelock, "I have the cab downstairs."

"Good boy," said Holmes, blandly. "Why don't you introduce this pattern at Scotland Yard?" he continued, taking a pair of steel handcuffs from a drawer. "See how beautifully the spring works. They fasten in an instant."

[13] *A Study in Scarlet.*

"The old pattern is good enough," remarked Lestrade, "if we can only find the man to put them on."

"Very good, very good," said Holmes, smiling. "The cabman may as well help me with my boxes. Just ask him to step in, Wiggins."

I was surprised to find my companion speaking as though he were about to set out on a journey, since he had not said anything to me about it. There was a small portmanteau in the room, and this he pulled out and began to strap. He was busily engaged at it when the cabman entered the room.

"Just give me a help with this buckle, cabman," he said, kneeling over his task, and never turning his head.

The fellow came forward with a somewhat sullen, defiant air, and put down his hands to assist. At that instant there was a sharp click, the jangling of metal, and Sherlock Holmes sprang to his feet again.

"Gentlemen," he cried, with flashing eyes, "let me introduce you to Mr. Jefferson Hope, the murderer of Enoch Drebber and of Joseph Stangerson."[14]

Here we have a picture of the detective as scientist, reasoning from observed facts to a testable hypothesis which not only explains the facts but permits of practical application. ■

1. Create a mind map that illustrates the various points of comparison that Copi is making in the essay between the original subject and the compared subject. Elaborate your map by including the points of similarity (and *dis*-similarity) between the original and the compared subject.

2. According to Copi, the starting point of investigation, for detectives like Sherlock Holmes as well as scientists, is identifying a problem to solve, which he defines as "a fact or group of facts for which we have no acceptable explanation, which seem unusual, or which fail to fit in with our expectations or preconceptions."

   Identify and describe some aspect of your experience that illustrates this definition of a "problem." For example, you might identify an undiagnosed problem with your car; unusual, unexplained behavior by someone you know; or a question about how students in your class feel about an important issue.

3. Analyze your problem by using the guidelines Copi identifies that govern the investigations of detectives and scientists. Prepare a written account of your investigation (as Dr. Watson does for Holmes) and then present your findings to the class. ◄

[14] *A Study in Scarlet.*

Causal Relationships

Causal patterns of thinking involve relating events in terms of the influence or effect they have on one another. For example, if you were right now to pinch yourself hard enough to feel it, you would be demonstrating a cause and effect relationship. Stated very simply, a *cause* is anything that is responsible for bringing about something else — usually termed the *effect*. The *cause* (the pinch) brings about the *effect* (the feeling of pain). When we make a causal statement, we are merely stating that a causal relationship exists between two or more things:

> The pinch *caused* the pain in my arm.

Of course, when we make (or think) causal statements, we do not always use the word *cause*. For example, the following statements are all causal statements. In each case, underline the cause and circle the effect.

1. Since I was the last person to leave, I turned off the lights.
2. Taking lots of vitamin C really cured me of that terrible cold I had.
3. I accidentally toasted my hand along with the marshmallows, by getting too close to the fire.

In these statements, the words *turned off*, *cured*, and *toasted* all point to the fact that something has caused something else to take place. Our language contains thousands of these causal "cousins."

Create three statements that express a causal relationship without actually using the word *cause*.

1. _____

_____

2. _____

_____

3. _____

_____

We make causal statements all the time, and we are always thinking in terms of causal relationships. In fact, the goal of much of our thinking is to figure out *why* something happened or *how* something came about. For if we can figure out how and why things occur, we can then try to predict what will happen in the future. These predictions of anticipated results form the basis of many of our decisions. For example, the experience of toasting our hand along with the marshmallows might lead us to choose a longer stick for toasting — simply because we are able to figure out the causal relationships involved and then make predictions based on our understanding (namely, a longer stick will keep my hand further away from the fire, which will prevent it from getting toasted).

Consider the following activities, which you probably performed today. Each activity assumes that certain causal relationships exist, which influenced your decision to perform them. Explain one such causal relationship for each activity.

1. Setting the alarm clock

   Causal relationship: Setting the alarm will cause a noise at a certain time, which will then wake me up.

2. Brushing your teeth

   Causal relationship: _____

   _____

3. Locking the door

   Causal relationship: _____

   _____

Causal Chains

Although we tend to think of causes and effects in isolation — *A* caused *B* — in reality causes and effects rarely appear by themselves. Causes and effects generally appear as parts of more complex patterns, including three that we will examine here:

• Causal chains

• Contributory causes

• Interactive causes

Consider the following scenario:

> Your paper on the topic "Is there life after death?" is due on Monday morning. You have reserved the whole weekend to work on it, and are

just getting started when the phone rings — your best friend from your childhood is in town, and wants to stay with you for the weekend. You say yes. By Sunday night, you've had a great weekend, but have made little progress on your paper. You begin writing, when suddenly you feel stomach cramps — it must have been those raw oysters that you had for lunch! Three hours later, you are ready to continue work. You brew a pot of coffee and get started. At 3:00 A.M. you are too exhausted to continue. You decide to get a few hours of sleep, and set the alarm clock for 6:00 A.M., giving you plenty of time to finish up. When you wake up, you find that it's nine o'clock — the alarm failed to go off! Your class starts in forty minutes, and you have no chance of getting the paper done on time. As you ride to school, you go over the causes for this disaster in your mind. You are no longer worried about life after death — you are now worried about life after this class!

1. What causes in this situation are responsible for your paper not being completed on time?

   a. _____

   b. _____

   c. _____

   d. _____

2. What do you think is the single most important cause?

   _____

3. What do you think your teacher will identify as the most important cause? Why?

   _____

   _____

A *causal chain*, as we can see from these examples, is a situation in which one thing leads to another, which then leads to another, and so on. There is not just *one* cause for the resulting effect; there is a whole string of causes. Which cause in the string is the "real" cause? Our answer often depends on our perspective on the situation. In the example of the unfinished paper on the topic "Is there life after death?" we might see the cause as a faulty alarm clock. The teacher, on the other hand, might see the cause of the problem as an overall lack of planning. Proper planning, he or she might say, does not leave things until the last minute, when unexpected problems can prevent us from reaching our goal. We can illustrate this causal structure with the follow-ing diagram:

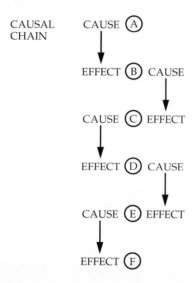

THINKING ACTIVITY

9.11 ▶ 1. Create a similar scenario of your own, detailing a chain of causes that re-sults in being late for class, standing someone up for a date, failing an exam, or an effect of your own choosing.

2. Review the scenario you have just created. Explain how the "real" cause of the final effect could vary depending on your perspective on the situation. ◀

Contributory Causes

In addition to operating in causal chains over a period of time (*A* leads to *B*, which leads to *C*, which leads to *D*, etc.), causes can also act simultaneously to produce an effect. When this happens (as it often does), we have a situa-tion in which a number of different causes are instrumental in bringing some-thing about. Instead of working in isolation, each cause *contributes* to bringing about the final effect. When this situation occurs, each cause serves to sup-port and reinforce the action of the other causes, a structure illustrated in the following diagram.

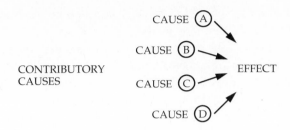

Consider the following situation:

> It is the end of the term, and you have been working incredibly hard at school — writing papers, preparing for exams, finishing up course projects. You haven't been getting enough sleep, and you haven't been eating regular or well-balanced meals. To make matters worse, you have been under intense pressure in your personal life, having serious arguments with your boyfriend or girlfriend. You find that this is constantly on your mind. It is the middle of the flu season and many of the people you know have been sick with various bugs. Walking home from school one evening, you get soaked by an unexpected shower. By the time you get home, you are shivering. You soon find yourself in bed with a thermometer in your mouth — you are sick!

What was the "cause" of your getting sick? In this situation, you can see it probably was not just *one* thing that brought about your illness. It was probably a *combination* of different factors that led to your physical breakdown: low resistance, getting wet and chilled, being exposed to various germs and viruses, physical exhaustion, lack of proper eating, and so on. Taken by itself, no one factor might have been enough to cause your illness. Working together, they all contributed to the final outcome.

THINKING ACTIVITY

9.12 ▶ Create a similar scenario of your own, detailing the contributory causes that led to asking someone for a date, choosing a major, losing or winning a game you played in, or an effect of your own choosing. ◀

Interactive Causes

Our examination of causal relationships has revealed that causes rarely operate in isolation but instead often influence (and are influenced by) other factors. Imagine that you are scheduled to give a speech to a large group of people. As the time for your moment in the spotlight approaches, you become anxious, which results in a dry mouth and throat, making your voice sound more like a croak. The prospect of sounding like a bullfrog increases your anxiety, which in turn dries your mouth and constricts your throat further, reducing your croak to something much worse — silence.

This not uncommon scenario reveals the way different factors can relate to one another through reciprocal influences that flow back and forth from one to the other. This type of causal relationship, which involves an *interactive* thinking pattern, is an extremely important way we have for organizing and making sense of our experience. For example, to understand social relationships, such as families, teams, groups of friends, and so on, we have to understand the complex ways each individual influences — and is influenced by — all the other members of the group.

Understanding biological systems and other systems is similar to understanding social systems. To understand and explain how an organ like your heart, liver, or brain functions, you have to describe its complex, interactive relationships with all the other parts of your biological system. The diagram on page 443 illustrates these dynamic causal relationships.

THINKING ACTIVITY

9.13 ▶ Read the following passages, which illustrate causal patterns of thinking. For each passage:

1. Create mind maps that illustrate cause(s) and effect(s) relationships.

2. Identify the *kind* of causal relationship (direct, chain, contributory, or interactive)

> Nothing posed a more serious threat to the bald eagle's survival than a modern chemical compound called DDT. Around 1940, a retired Canadian banker named Charles L. Broley began keeping track of eagles nesting in Florida. Each breeding season, he climbed into more than 50 nests, counted the eaglets and put metal bands on their legs. In the late 1940's, a sudden drop-off in the number of young produced led him to conclude that 80 percent of his birds were sterile. Broley blamed DDT. Scientists later discovered that DDE, a breakdown product of DDT, causes not sterility, but a fatal thinning of eggshell among birds of prey. Applied on cropland all over the United States, the pesticide was running off into waterways where it concentrated in fish. The bald eagles

INTERACTIVE CAUSES

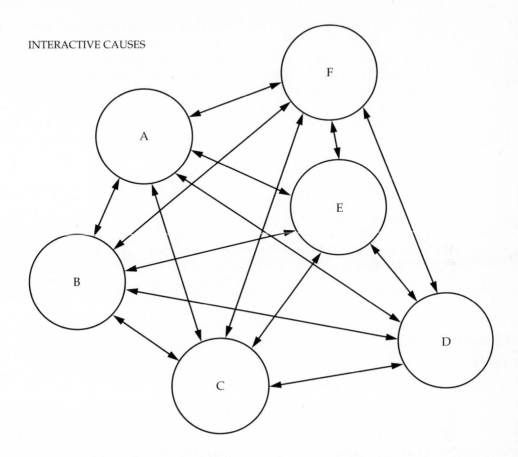

ate the fish and the DDT impaired their ability to reproduce. They were not alone, of course. Ospreys and pelicans suffered similar setbacks.

Jim Doherty, "The Bald Eagle and DDT"

It is popularly accepted that Hitler was the major cause of World War II, but the ultimate causes go much deeper than one personality. First, there were longstanding German grievances against reparations levied on the nation following its defeat in World War I. Second, there were severe economic strains that caused resentment among the German people. Third, there were French and English reluctance to work out a sound disarmament policy and American noninvolvement in the matter. Finally, there was the European fear that communism was a much greater danger than National Socialism. These factors contributed to the outbreak of World War II.

Gilbert Muller, *The American College Handbook*

We crunch and chew our way through vast quantities of snacks and confectionaries and relieve our thirst with multicolored, flavored soft drinks, with and without calories, for two basic reasons. The first is simple; the food tastes good, and we enjoy the sensation of eating it. Second, we associate these foods, often without being aware of it, with the highly pleasurable experiences depicted in the advertisements used to promote their sale. Current television advertisements demonstrate this point: people turn from grumpiness to euphoria after crunching a corn chip. Others water ski into the sunset with their loved ones while drinking a popular soft drink. People entertain on the patio with friends, cook over campfires without mosquitoes, or go to carnivals with granddad munching away at the latest candy or snack food. The people portrayed in these scenarios are all healthy, vigorous, and good looking; one wonders how popular the food they convince us to eat would be if they would crunch or drink away while complaining about low back pain or clogged sinuses.

Judith Wurtman, *Eating Your Way Through Life*
© 1979 Raven Press, New York ◄

THINKING ACTIVITY

9.14 ► Many of the discussions we engage in and the essays we write are based on an extended analysis of a cause-and-effect situation. When this happens, the concept of causality is used both to help us explain our viewpoint and to give us a means of organizing and structuring the topic we are examining. The following article analyzes some of the complex causal relationships that govern the earth's environment. After completing the article, answer the questions that follow.

BIG MAC AND THE TROPICAL FORESTS *by Joseph K. Skinner*

Hello, fast-food chains.

Goodbye, tropical forests.

Sound like an odd connection? The "free-market" economy has led to results even stranger than this, but perhaps none have been as environmentally devastating.

These are the harsh facts: the tropical forests are being leveled for commercial purposes at the rate of 150,000 square kilometers a year, an area the size of England and Wales combined.[1]

At this rate, the world's tropical forests could be entirely destroyed within seventy-three years. Already as much as a fifth or a quarter of the huge Amazon forest, which constitutes a third of the world's total rain forest, has been cut, and the rate of destruction is accelerating. And nearly two thirds of the Central American forests have been cleared or severely degraded since 1950.

Tropical forests, which cover only 7 percent of the Earth's land surface (it used to be 12 percent), support half the species of the world's living things. Due to their destruction, "We are surely losing one or more species a day right now out of the five million (minimum figure) on Earth," says Norman Myers, author of numerous books and articles on the subject and consultant to the World Bank and the World Wildlife Fund. "By the time ecological equilibrium is restored, at least one-quarter of all species will have disappeared, probably a third, and conceivably even more. . . . If this pattern continues, it could mean the demise of two million species by the middle of next century." Myers calls the destruction of the tropical forests "one of the greatest biological debacles to occur on the face of the Earth." Looking at the effects it will have on the course of biological evolution, Myers says:

> The impending upheaval in evolution's course could rank as one of the greatest biological revolutions of paleontological time. It will equal in scale and significance the development of aerobic respiration, the emergence of flowering plants, and the arrival of limbed animals. But of course the prospective degradation of many evolutionary capacities will be an impoverishing, not a creative, phenomenon.[2]

In other words, such rapid destruction will vacate so many niches so suddenly that a "pest and weed" ecology, consisting of a relatively few opportunistic species (rats, roaches, and the like) will be created.

Beyond this — as if it weren't enough — such destruction could well have cataclysmic effects on the Earth's weather patterns, causing, for example, an irreversible desertification of the North American grain belt. Although the scope of the so-called greenhouse effect — in which rising levels of carbon dioxide in the atmosphere heat the planet by preventing infrared radiation from escaping into space — is still being debated within the scientific community, it is not at all extreme to suppose that the fires set to clear tropical forests will contribute greatly to this increase in atmospheric CO_2 and thereby to untold and possibly devastating changes in the world's weather systems.

Big Mac Attack

So what does beef, that staple of the fast-food chains and of the North American diet in general, have to do with it?

It used to be, back in 1960, that the United States imported practically no beef. That was a time when North Americans were consuming a "mere" 85 pounds of beef per person per year. By 1980 this was up to 134 pounds per person per year. Concomitant with this increase in consumption, the United States began to import beef, so that by 1981 some 800,000 tons were coming in from abroad, 17 percent of it from tropical Latin America and three fourths of that from Central America. Since fast-food chains have been steadily expanding and now are a $5-billion-a-year business, accounting for 25 percent of all the beef consumed in the United States, the connections between the fast-food empire and tropical beef are clear.

Cattle ranching is "by far the major factor in forest destruction in tropical Latin America," says Myers. "Large fast-food outlets in the U.S. and Europe foster the clearance of forests to produce cheap beef."[3]

And cheap it is, compared to North American beef: by 1978 the average price of beef imported from Central America was $1.47/kg, while similar North American beef cost $3.30/kg.

Cheap, that is, for North Americans, but not for Central Americans. Central Americans cannot afford their own beef. Whereas beef production in Costa Rica increased twofold between 1959 and 1972, per capita consumption of beef in that country went down from 30 lbs. a year to 19. In Honduras, beef production increased by 300 percent between 1965 and 1975, but consumption decreased from 12 lbs. per capita per year to 10. So, although two thirds of Central America's arable land is in cattle, local consumption of beef is decreasing; the average domestic cat in the United States now consumes more beef than the average Central American.[4]

Brazilian government figures show that 38 percent of all deforestation in the Brazilian Amazon between 1966 and 1975 was attributable to large-scale cattle ranching. Although the presence of hoof-and-mouth disease among Brazilian cattle has forced U.S. lawmakers to prohibit the importation of chilled or frozen Brazilian beef, the United States imports $46 million per year of cooked Brazilian beef, which goes into canned products; over 80 percent of Brazilian beef is still exported, most of it to Western Europe, where no such prohibition exists.

At present rates, all remaining Central American forests will have been eliminated by 1990. The cattle ranching largely responsible for this is in itself highly inefficient: as erosion and nutrient leaching eat away the soil, production drops from an average one head per hectare — measly in any case — to a pitiful one head per five to seven hectares within five to ten years. A typical tropical cattle ranch employs only one person per 2,000 head, and meat production barely reaches 50 lbs./acre/year. In Northern Europe, in farms that do not use imported feed, it is over 500 lbs./acre/year.

This real-term inefficiency does not translate into bad business, however, for although there are some absentee landowners who engage in ranching for the prestige of it and are not particularly interested in turning large profits, others find bank loans for growing beef for export readily forthcoming, and get much help and encouragement from such organizations as the Pan American Health Organization, the Organization of American States, the U.S. Department of Agriculture, and U.S. AID, without whose technical assistance "cattle production in the American tropics would be unprofitable, if not impossible."[5] The ultimate big winner appears to be the United States, where increased imports of Central American beef are said to have done more to stem inflation than any other single government initiative.

"On the good land, which could support a large population, you have the rich cattle owners, and on the steep slopes, which should be left in forest, you have the poor farmers," says Gerardo Budowski, director of the Tropical Agricultural Research and Training Center in Turrialba, Costa Rica. "It is still good business to clear virgin forest in order to fatten cattle for, say, five to eight years and then abandon it."[6]

(Ironically, on a trip I made in 1981 to Morazán, a Salvadoran province largely under control of FMLN guerrillas, I inquired into the guerrilla diet and discovered that beef, expropriated from the cattle ranches, was a popular staple.)

Swift-Armour's Swift Armor

The rain forest ecosystem, the oldest on Earth, is extremely complex and delicate. In spite of all the greenery one sees there, it is a myth that rain forest soil is rich. It is actually quite poor, leached of all nutrients save the most insoluble (such as iron oxides, which give lateritic soil — the most common soil type found there — its red color). Rather, the ecosystem of the rain forest is a "closed" one, in which the nutrients are to be found in the biomass, that is, in the living canopy of plants and in the thin layer of humus on the ground that is formed from the matter shed by the canopy. Hence the shallow-rootedness of most tropical forest plant species. Since the soil itself cannot replenish nutrients, nutrient recycling is what keeps the system going.

Now, what happens when the big cattle ranchers, under the auspices of the Swift-Armour Meat Packing Co., or United Brands, or the King Ranch sling a huge chain between two enormous tractors, level a few tens of thousands of acres of tropical forest, burn the debris, fly a plane over to seed the ash with guinea grass, and then run their cattle on the newly created grasslands?[7]

For the first three years or so the grass grows like crazy, up to an inch a day, thriving on all that former biomass. After that, things go quickly downhill: the ash becomes eroded and leached, the soil becomes exposed and hardens to the consistency of brick, and the area becomes useless to agriculture. Nor does it ever regain anything near its former state. The Amazon is rising perceptibly as a result of the increased run-off due to deforestation.

Tractor-and-chain is only one way of clearing the land. Another common technique involves the use of herbicides such as Tordon, 2,4-D, and 2,4,5-T (Agent Orange). The dioxin found in Agent Orange can be extremely toxic to animal life and is very persistent in the environment.

Tordon, since it leaves a residue deadly to all broad-leaved plants, renders the deforested area poisonous to all plants except grasses; consequently, even if they wanted to, ranchers could not plant soil-enriching legumes in the treated areas, a step which many agronomists recommend for keeping the land productive for at least a little longer.

The scale of such operations is a far cry from the traditional slash-and-burn practiced by native jungle groups, which is done on a scale small enough so that the forest can successfully reclaim the farmed areas. Such groups, incidentally, are also being decimated by cattle interests in Brazil and Paraguay — as missionaries, human rights groups, and cattlemen themselves will attest.

Capital's "manifest destiny" has traditionally shown little concern for the lives of trees or birds or Indians, or anything else which interferes with immediate profitability, but the current carving of holes in the gene pool by big agribusiness seems particularly short-sighted. Since the tropical forests contain two thirds of the world's genetic resources, their destruction will leave an enormous void in the pool of genes necessary for the creation of new agricultural hybrids. This is not to mention the many plants as yet undiscovered — there could be up to 15,000 unknown species in South America alone — which may in themselves contain remarkable properties. (In writing about alkaloids found in the Madagascar periwinkle which have recently revolutionized the treatment of leukemia and Hodgkin's disease, British biochemist John Humphreys said: "If this plant had not been analyzed, not even a chemist's wildest ravings would have hinted that such structures would be pharmacologically active."[8] Ninety percent of Madagascar's forests have been cut.)

But there is no small truth in Indonesian Minister for Environment and Development Emil Salim's complaint that the "South is asked to conserve genes while the other fellow, in the North, is consuming things that force us to destroy the genes in the South."[9]

Where's the Beef?

The marketing of beef imported into the United States is extremely complex, and the beef itself ends up in everything from hot dogs to canned soup. Fresh meat is exported in refrigerated container ships to points of entry, where it is inspected by the U.S. Department of Agriculture. Once inspected, it is no longer required to be labeled "imported."[10] From there it goes into the hands of customhouse brokers and meat packers, often changing hands many times; and from there it goes to the fast-food chains or the food processors. The financial structures behind this empire are even more complex, involving governments and quasipublic agencies, such as the Export-Import Bank and the Overseas Private Investment Corporation, as well as the World Bank and the Inter-American Development Bank, all of which encourage cattle raising in the forest lands. (Brazilian government incentives to cattle ranching in Amazonia include a 50 percent income-tax rebate on ranchers' investments elsewhere in Brazil, tax holidays of up to ten years, loans with negative interest rates in real terms, and exemptions from sales taxes and import duties. Although these incentives were deemed excessive and since 1979 no longer apply to new ranches, they still continue for existing ones. This cost the Brazilian government $63,000 for each ranching job created.)

Beef production in the tropics may be profitable for the few, but it is taking place at enormous cost for the majority and for the planet as a whole. Apart from the environmental destruction, it is a poor converter of energy to protein and provides few benefits for the vast majority of tropical peoples in terms of employment or food. What they require are labor-intensive, multiple-cropping systems.

The world is obviously hostage to an ethic which puts short-term profitability above all else, and such catastrophes as the wholesale destruction of the tropical forests and the continued impoverishment of their peoples are bound to occur as long as this ethic rules.

Notes

[1] Jean-Paul Landley, "Tropical Forest Resources," *FAO Forestry Paper* 30 (Rome: FAO, 1982). This UN statistic is the most accurate to date. For further extrapolations from it, see Nicholas Guppy, "Tropical Deforestation: A Global View," *Foreign Affairs* 62, no. 4 (Spring 1984).

[2] There are amazingly few scientists in the world with broad enough expertise to accurately assess the widest implications of tropical deforestation; Norman Myers is one of them. His books include *The Sinking Ark* (Oxford: Pergamon Press, 1979). See also *Conversion of Moist Tropical Forests* (Washington, D.C.: National Academy of Sciences, 1980), "The End of the Line," *Natural History* 94, no. 2 (February 1985), and "The Hamburger Connection," *Ambio* 10, no. 1 (1981). I have used Myers extensively in the preparation of this article. The quotes in this paragraph are from "The Hamburger Connection," pp. 3, 4, 5.

[3] Myers, "End of the Line," p. 2.

[4] See James Nations and Daniel I. Komer, "Rainforests and the Hamburger Society," *Environment* 25, no. 3 (April 1983).

[5] Ibid., p. 17.

[6] Catherine Caufield, "The Rain Forests," *New Yorker* (January 14, 1985), p. 42. This excellent article was later incorporated in a book, *In the Rainforest* (New York: Knopf, 1985).

[7] Other multinationals with interests in meat packing and cattle ranching in tropical Latin America include Armour-Dial International, Goodyear Tire and Rubber Co., and Gulf and Western Industries, Inc. See Roger Burbach and Patricia Flynn, *Agribusiness in the Americas* (New York: Monthly Review Press, 1980).

[8] Quoted in Caufield, "Rain Forests," p. 60.

[9] Ibid., p. 100.

[10] This is one way McDonald's, for example, can claim not to use foreign beef. For a full treatment of McDonald's, see M. Boas and S. Chain, *Big Mac: The Unauthorized Story of McDonald's* (New York: New American Library, 1976). ■

1. Explain the causal relationships between the following factors (according to Skinner):

   a. Fast-food hamburgers and the tropical rain forests

   b. Deforestation and the agricultural future of South America

   c. Deforestation and the course of biological evolution

   d. Deforestation and weather patterns

2. Explain the human decisions and causal forces that have created this problem.

3. Explain what approaches you think would be most effective in dealing with this problem. Begin by brainstorming a variety of ideas to solve this dilemma: Create a mind map that organizes and elaborates these ideas,

then develop these ideas into a coherent essay with supporting examples and evidence. ◀

Summary

Concepts are the vocabulary of thought, the general ideas that we use to represent our world; thinking patterns are the vehicles we use to relate and organize concepts so that we can make sense of our world. In this chapter we have examined a number of basic thinking patterns that enable us to organize our experience into relationships that have meaning to us:

• Chronological and process relationships
• Comparative and analogical relationships
• Causal relationships

Each of these thinking patterns helps us figure out what has happened in the past, what is occurring in the present, and what will happen in the future. We use these patterns to reveal the way the world is and also to impose our own interpretation on the events of our experience. In this sense we are all scientists and artists, both deciphering the mysteries of the world and composing our own unique perspectives on it. All of us perform these activities in distinctive ways and so construct a view of the world that is uniquely our own. As we refine our abilities to relate and organize the conceptual vocabulary of our minds, we are improving the power and creativity of our thinking processes, while at the same time developing a more complex and accurate understanding of the world.

CHAPTER 10

Reporting, Inferring, Judging

Identify
the basis.

Evaluate
the probability.

Evaluate
the sources.

Identify
the inference.

REPORTING:
Describing information
that can be verified
through investigation.

INFERRING:
Going beyond factual
information to describe
what is not currently
known.

JUDGING:
Expressing an evaluation
based on certain criteria.

Evaluate
supporting
evidence/reasons.

Identify
the criteria.

THE MAIN GOAL of our thinking process is to identify and organize the world in ways that enable us to understand what is going on and then make reasoned decisions based on our understanding. The relationships that we compose and discover express the basic thinking patterns we use to make sense of the world. In the last chapter we critically examined the following basic thinking patterns:

- Chronological and process
- Comparative and analogical
- Causal

In this chapter we will be exploring the way that we use these thinking patterns, and others, to organize our beliefs and knowledge about the world. In Chapter Five, *Believing and Knowing,* we found that beliefs are the main tools we use to make sense of the world and guide our actions. The total collection of our beliefs represent our view of the world, our philosophy of life. More specifically, beliefs are interpretations, evaluations, conclusions, and predictions about the world that we endorse as true.

All beliefs are not equal. In fact, beliefs differ from one another in many kinds of ways. For example, as we saw in Chapter Five, beliefs differ in accuracy. The belief "The earth is surrounded by stars and planets" is considerably more certain than the belief "The positions of the stars and planets determine our personalities and our destinies."

Beliefs differ in other respects besides accuracy. Review the following beliefs and then describe some of their differences in the space provided:

1. I believe that I have hair on my head.
2. I believe that the sun will rise tomorrow.
3. I believe that there is some form of life after death.
4. I believe that dancing is more fun than jogging, and jogging is preferable to going to the dentist.
5. I believe that we should always act toward others in ways that we would like to have them act toward us.

_____

_____

_____

_____

In this chapter we will be thinking critically about three basic types of beliefs we use to make sense of the world:

• Reports

• Inferences

• Judgments

These beliefs are expressed in both our thinking and our use of language, as illustrated in the following sentences:

1. My bus was late today.
   Type of belief: reporting

2. My bus will probably be late tomorrow.
   Type of belief: inferring

3. The bus system is unreliable.
   Type of belief: judging

Now try the activity with a different set of statements.

1. Each modern atomic warhead has over one hundred times the explosive power of the bomb dropped on Hiroshima.

   Type of belief: _____

2. With all of the billions of planets in the universe, the odds are that there are other forms of life in the cosmos.

   Type of belief: _____

3. In the long run, the energy needs of the world will best be met by solar energy technology, rather than nuclear energy or fossil fuels.

   Type of belief: _____

As we examine these various statements, we can see that they provide us with different types of information about the world. For example, the first statements in each list report aspects of the world that we can verify — that is, check for accuracy. By doing the appropriate sort of investigating, we can determine whether the bus was actually late today and whether modern atomic warheads really have the power attributed to them. When we describe the world in ways that can be verified through investigation, we are said to be *reporting* factual information about the world.

> **Reporting Factual Information**   Describing the world in ways that can be verified through investigation.

Looking at the second statements in each list, we can see immediately that they provide a different sort of information from the first ones. These statements cannot be verified. There is no way to investigate and determine with certainty whether the bus will indeed be late tomorrow or whether there is in fact life on other planets. Although these conclusions may be based on factual information, they go beyond factual information to make statements about what is not currently known. When we describe the world in ways based on factual information yet go beyond this information to make statements regarding what is not currently known, we are said to be *inferring* conclusions about the world.

> ***Inferring*** Describing the world in ways that are based on factual information yet going beyond this information to make statements about what is not currently known.

Finally, as we examine the third statements in both lists, it is apparent that they are different from both factual reports and inferences. They describe the world in ways that express the speaker's evaluation — of the bus service and of energy sources. These evaluations are based on certain standards (criteria) that the speaker used to judge the bus service as unreliable and solar energy as more promising than nuclear energy or fossil fuels. When we describe the world in ways that express our evaluation based on certain criteria, we are said to be *judging*.

> ***Judging*** Describing the world in ways that express our evaluation based on certain criteria.

We continually use these various ways of describing and organizing our world — reporting, inferring, judging — to make sense of our experience. In most cases, we are not aware that we are actually performing these activities, nor are we usually aware of the differences among them. Yet these three activities work together to help us see the world as a complete picture.

THINKING ACTIVITY

10.1 ▶ 1. Review the sentences on page 453 and indicate whether they express beliefs that are reports, inferences, or judgments.

2. Compose six sentences that embody these three types of beliefs: two reports, two inferences, and two evaluations.

3. Locate a short article from a newspaper or magazine and identify the reports, inferences, and judgments it contains. ◄

10.2   ► Carefully examine the photograph below. Write five statements based on your observations. Then identify each of your statements as *reporting, inferring,* or *judging,* and explain why you classified them as such. ◄

Reporting Factual Information

The statements that result from the activity of reporting express the most accurate beliefs we have about the world. Factual beliefs have earned this

Courtesy of Frankel Gallery, San Francisco and © The Estate of Gary Winogrand.

distinction because they are verifiable, usually with one or more of our senses. For example, consider the following factual statement:

That young woman is wearing a brown hat in the rain.

This statement about an event in the world is considered to be factual because it can be verified by our immediate sense experience — what we can (in principle or in theory) see, hear, touch, feel, or smell. It is important to say *in principle* or *in theory*, because we often do not use all of our relevant senses to check out what we are experiencing. Look again at our example of a factual statement:

That young woman is wearing a brown hat in the rain.

We would normally be satisfied to *see* this event, without insisting on touching or smelling the hat or giving the person a physical examination. If necessary, however, we could perform these additional actions — in principle or in theory.

We use the same reasoning when we believe factual statements from other people that we are not in a position to check out immediately. For instance:

- The Great Wall of China is more than fifteen hundred miles long.
- There are large mountains and craters on the moon.
- Our skin is covered with germs.

We consider these to be factual statements because, even though we cannot verify them with our senses at the moment, we could in principle or in theory verify them with our senses

- *if* we were flown to China,
- *if* we were rocketed to the moon, or
- *if* we were to examine our skin with a powerful microscope.

The process of verifying factual statements involves *identifying* the sources of information on which they are based, and *evaluating* the reliability of these sources. These are topics that we examined in some detail in Chapter Five, *Believing and Knowing*.

We communicate factual information to each other by means of reports. A *report* is a description of something that has been experienced, communicated in as accurate and complete a way as possible. Through reports we can share our sense experiences with other people, and this mutual sharing enables us to learn much more about the world than if we were confined to knowing only what we experience. The *recording* (making records) of factual reports also makes possible the accumulation of knowledge learned by previous generations.

> ***Reporting Factual Information***   Describing the world in ways that can be verified through investigation.

Because factual reports play such an important role in our exchange and accumulation of information about the world, it is important that they be as accurate and complete as possible. This brings us to a problem. We have already seen in Chapter Four, *Perceiving* and Chapter Five, *Believing and Knowing,* that our perceptions and observations are often *not* accurate or complete. What this means is that often when we think we are making true factual reports, our reports are actually inaccurate or incomplete. For instance, consider our earlier "factual statement":

> That young woman is wearing a brown hat in the rain.

Here are some questions we could ask concerning how accurate our statement really is:

- Is the woman really young, or does she merely look young?
- Is the woman really a woman, or a man disguised as a woman?
- Is that really a hat the woman/man is wearing, or something else (e.g., a paper bag) being used to keep her/his head dry?

Of course, there are methods we could use to clear up these questions with more detailed observations. Can you describe some of these methods?

Besides difficulties with observations, the "facts" that we see in the world actually depend on more general *beliefs* that we have about how the world operates. Consider the question:

> Why did the man's body fall from the top of the building to the sidewalk?

If we have had some general science courses, we might say something like, "The body was simply obeying the law of gravity," and we would consider this to be a "factual statement." But how did people account for this sort of event before Newton formulated the law of gravity? Some popular responses might have included the following:

- Things always fall down, not up.
- The spirit in the body wanted to join with the spirit of the earth.

When people made statements like these and others, such as, "Humans can't fly," they thought that they were making "factual statements." Increased knowledge and understanding have since shown these "factual beliefs" to be inaccurate, and so they have been replaced by "better" beliefs. These "better beliefs" are able to explain the world in a way that is more accurate and predictable. Will many of the beliefs we now consider to be factually accurate also be replaced in the future by beliefs that are *more* accurate and predictable? If history is any indication, this will most certainly happen. (Already Newton's formulations have been replaced by Einstein's, based on the latter's theory of relativity. And Einstein's have been refined and modified as well and may be replaced someday.)

THINKING ACTIVITY

10.3 ▶ From the following list of statements, select the statements that you believe to be "factual." Explain briefly how you might try to verify these statements by identifying the sources of information on which they are based and evaluating the reliability of these sources.

1. Bill has season tickets to see the California Angels.

   How to verify: _____

   _____

2. Many students drop out of college and don't graduate.

   How to verify: _____

   _____

3. Smoking cigarettes will shorten the lives of many people.

   How to verify: _____

   _____

4. British troops fired the first shot at the Battle of Lexington in the American Revolution.

   How to verify: _____

   _____

5. Human beings are descended from other forms of life through a process of evolution.

How to verify: _____

_____ ◀

10.4 ▶ Read the following essay by N. Scott Momaday, which illustrates the way in which reporting factual information can help us understand significant historical events, memorable people, and the spiritual mystery of certain places. After reading the selection, answer the questions that follow.

THE WAY TO RAINY MOUNTAIN *by N. Scott Momaday*

A single knoll rises out of the plain in Oklahoma, north and west of the Wichita range. For my people, the Kiowas, it is an old landmark, and they gave it the name Rainy Mountain. The hardest weather in the world is there. Winter brings blizzards, hot tornadic winds arise in the spring, and in summer the prairie is an anvil's edge. The grass turns brittle and brown, and it cracks beneath your feet. There are green belts along the rivers and creeks, linear groves of hickory and pecan, willow and witch hazel. At a distance in July or August the steaming foliage seems almost to writhe in fire. Great green and yellow grasshoppers are everywhere in the tall grass, popping up like corn to sting the flesh, and tortoises crawl about on the red earth, going nowhere in the plenty of time. Loneliness is an aspect of the land. All things in the plain are isolate; there is no confusion of objects in the eye, but *one* hill or *one* tree or *one* man. To look upon that landscape in the early morning, with the sun at your back, is to lose the sense of proportion. Your imagination comes to life, and this, you think, is where Creation was begun.

I returned to Rainy Mountain in July. My grandmother had died in the spring, and I wanted to be at her grave. She had lived to be very old and at last infirm. Her only living daughter was with her when she died, and I was told that in death her face was that of a child.

I like to think of her as a child. When she was born, the Kiowas were living the last great moment of their history. For more than a hundred years they had controlled the open range from the Smoky Hill River to the Red, from the headwaters of the Canadian to the fork of the Arkansas and Cimarron. In alliance with the Comanches, they had ruled the whole of the Southern Plains. War was their sacred business, and they were the finest horsemen the world has ever known. But warfare for the Kiowas was pre-eminently a matter of disposition rather than of survival, and they never understood the grim, unrelenting advance of the U.S. Cavalry. When at last, divided and ill provisioned, they were driven onto the Staked Plains in the cold of autumn, they fell into panic. In Palo Duro Canyon they abandoned their crucial stores to pillage and had nothing then but their lives. In order to save themselves, they surrendered to the soldiers at Fort Sill and were imprisoned in the old stone corral that now stands as a military museum. My grandmother was spared the humiliation of those high gray walls by eight or ten years, but she must have known from birth the affliction of defeat, the dark brooding of old warriors.

Her name was Aho, and she belonged to the last culture to evolve in North America. Her forebears came down from the high country in western Montana nearly three centuries ago. They were a mountain people, a mysterious tribe of hunters whose language has never been classified in any major group. In the late seventeenth century they began a long migration to the south and east. It was a journey toward the dawn, and it led to a golden age. Along the way the Kiowas were befriended by the Crows, who gave them the culture and religion of the Plains. They acquired horses, and their ancient nomadic spirit was suddenly free of the ground. They acquired Tai-me, the sacred sun-dance doll, from that moment the object and symbol of their worship, and so shared in the divinity of the sun. Not least, they acquired the sense of destiny, therefore courage and pride. When they entered upon the Southern Plains they had been transformed. No longer were they slaves to the simple necessity of survival; they were a lordly and dangerous society of fighters and thieves, hunters and priests of the sun. According to their origin myth, they entered the world through a hollow log. From one point of view, their migration was the fruit of an old prophecy, for indeed they emerged from a sunless world.

Though my grandmother lived out her long life in the shadow of Rainy Mountain, the immense landscape of the continental interior lay like memory in her blood. She could tell of the Crows, whom she had never seen, and of the Black Hills, where she had never been. I wanted to see in reality what she had seen more perfectly in the mind's eye, and drove fifteen hundred miles to begin my pilgrimage.

A dark mist lay over the Black Hills, and the land was like iron. At the top of a ridge I caught sight of Devil's Tower upthrust against the gray sky as if in the birth of time the core of the earth had broken through its crust and the motion of the world was begun. There are things in nature that engender an awful quiet in the heart of man; Devil's Tower is one of them. Two centuries ago, because of their need to explain it, the Kiowas made a legend at the base of the rock. My grandmother said:

"Eight children were there at play, seven sisters and their brother. Suddenly the boy was struck dumb; he trembled and began to run upon his hands and feet. His fingers became claws, and his body was covered with fur. There was a bear where the boy had been. The sisters were terrified; they ran, and the bear after them. They came to the stump of a great tree, and the tree spoke to them. It bade them climb upon it, and as they did so, it began to rise into the air. The bear came to kill them, but they were just beyond its reach. It reared against the tree and scored the bark all around with its claws. The seven sisters were borne into the sky, and they became the stars of the Big Dipper." From that moment, and so long as the legend lives, the Kiowas have kinsmen in the night sky. Whatever they were in the mountains, they could be no more. However tenuous their well-being, however much they had suffered and would suffer again, they had found a way out of the wilderness.

My grandmother had a reverence for the sun, a holy regard that now is all but gone out of mankind. There was a wariness in her, and an ancient awe. She was a Christian in her later years, but she had come a long way about, and she never forgot her birthright. As a child she had been to the sun dances; she had taken part in that annual rite, and by it she had learned the restoration of her people in the presence of Tai-me. She was about seven when the last Kiowa sun dance was held in 1887 on the Washita River above Rainy Mountain Creek. The buffalo were gone. In order to consummate the ancient sacrifice — to impale the head of a buffalo bull upon the Tai-me tree — a delegation of old men journeyed into Texas, there to beg and barter for an animal from the Goodnight herd. She was ten when the Kiowas came together for the last time as a living sun-dance culture. They could find no buffalo; they had to hang an old hide from the sacred tree. Before the dance could begin, a company of soldiers rode out from Fort Sill under orders to disperse the tribe. Forbidden without cause the essential act of their faith, having seen the wild herds slaughtered and left to rot upon the ground, the Kiowas backed away forever from the tree. That was July 20, 1890, at the great bend of the Washita. My grandmother was there. Without bitterness, and for as long as she lived, she bore a vision of deicide.

Now that I can have her only in memory, I see my grandmother in the several postures that were peculiar to her: standing at the wood stove on a winter morning and turning meat in a great iron skillet; sitting at the south window, bent above her beadwork, and afterwards, when her vision failed, looking down for a long time into the fold of her hands; going out upon a cane, very slowly as she did when the weight of age came upon her; praying. I remember her most often at prayer. She made long, rambling prayers out of suffering and hope, having seen many things. I was never sure that I had the right to hear, so exclusive were they of all mere custom and company. The last time I saw her she prayed standing by the side of her bed at night, naked to the waist, the light of a kerosene lamp moving upon her dark skin. Her long black hair, always drawn and braided in the day, lay upon her shoulders and against her breasts like a shawl. I do not speak Kiowa, and I never understood her prayers, but there was something inherently sad in the sound, some merest hesitation upon the syllables of sorrow. She began in a high and descending pitch, exhausting her breath to silence; then again and again — and always the same intensity of effort, of something that is, and is not, like urgency in the human voice. Transported so in the dancing light among the shadows of her room, she seemed beyond the reach of time. But that was illusion; I think I knew then that I should not see her again.

Houses are like sentinels in the plain, old keepers of the weather watch. There, in a very little while, wood takes on the appearance of great age. All colors wear soon away in the wind and rain, and then the wood is burned gray and the grain appears and the nails turn red with rust. The window panes are black and opaque; you imagine there is nothing within, and indeed there are many ghosts, bones given up to the land. They stand here and there against the sky, and you approach them for a longer time than you expect. They belong in the distance; it is their domain.

Once there was a lot of sound in my grandmother's house, a lot of coming and going, feasting and talk. The summers there were full of excitement and reunion. The Kiowas are a summer people; they abide the cold and keep to themselves, but when the season turns and the land becomes warm and vital they cannot hold still; an old love of going returns upon them. The aged visitors who came to my grandmother's house when I was a child were made of lean and leather, and they bore themselves upright. They wore great black hats and bright ample shirts that shook in the wind. They rubbed fat upon their hair and wound their braids with strips of colored cloth. Some of them painted their faces and carried the scars of old and cherished enmities. They were an old council of warlords, come to remind and be reminded of who they were. Their wives and daughters served them well. The women might indulge themselves; gossip was at once the mark and compensation of their servitude. They made loud and elaborate talk among themselves, full of jest and gesture, fright and false alarm. They went abroad in fringed and flowered shawls, bright beadwork and German silver. They were at home in the kitchen, and they prepared meals that were banquets.

There were frequent prayer meetings, and nocturnal feasts. When I was a child I played with my cousins outside, where the lamplight fell upon the ground and the singing of the old people rose up around us and carried away into the darkness. There were a lot of good things to eat, a lot of laughter and surprise. And afterwards, when the quiet returned, I lay down with my grandmother and could hear the frogs away by the river and feel the motion of the air.

Now there is a funereal silence in the rooms, the endless wake of some final word. The walls have closed in upon my grandmother's house. When I returned to it in mourning, I saw for the first time in my life how small it was. It was late at night, and there was a white moon, nearly full. I sat for a long time on the stone steps by the kitchen door. From there I could see out across the land; I could see the long row of trees by the creek, the low light upon the rolling plains, and the stars of the Big Dipper. Once I looked at the moon and caught sight of a strange thing. A cricket had perched upon the handrail, only a few inches away. My line of vision was such that the creature filled the moon like a fossil. It had gone there, I thought, to live and die, for there, of all places, was its small definition made whole and eternal. A warm wind rose up and purled like the longing within me.

The next morning, I awoke at dawn and went out on the dirt road to Rainy Mountain. It was already hot, and the grasshoppers began to fill

the air. Still, it was early in the morning, and birds sang out of the shadows. The long yellow grass on the mountain shone in the bright light,
and a scissortail hied above the land. There, where it ought to be, at the
end of a long and legendary way, was my grandmother's grave. She
had at last succeeded to that holy ground. Here and there on the dark
stones were ancestral names. Looking back once, I saw the mountain
and came away. ■

1. a. The first paragraph of the essay concludes with the statement, "Your
    imagination comes to life, and this, you think, is where Creation was
    begun." Identify Momaday's descriptions of the Oklahoma landscape
    that lead him to this conclusion.

   b. Think of a place that has special meaning for you. Write a passage in
    which you use descriptive reports to create the atmosphere and mean-
    ing that the place has for you.

2. a. Momaday's grandmother, Aho, represents one of the main themes that
    ties this essay together. Identify the key descriptions regarding her life
    that help us understand her personality.

   b. Think about a person with distinctive qualities who occupies a special
    place in your life. Communicate the unique personality of that person
    by providing illuminating descriptions about him or her.

3. a. In many ways the history of the Kiowas mirrored that of the other Na-
    tive American tribes. Describe the key events that shaped their history,
    concluding with the last aborted sun dance in 1890.

   b. Research the history of your own family by interviewing family mem-
    bers and reviewing written records. After collecting your factual infor-
    mation, compose a "brief history" of your family that includes the key
    events that shaped their lives. ◄

THINKING ACTIVITY
10.5 ▶ 1. Locate and carefully read an article that deals with an important social
       issue.

   2. Summarize the main theme and the key points of the article.

   3. Describe the factual statements that are used to support the major theme.

   4. Evaluate the accuracy of the factual information.

   5. Evaluate the reliability of the sources of the factual information. ◄

Inferring

Imagine yourself in the following situations:

1. It is 2 A.M. and your roommate comes crashing through the door into the room. He staggers unsteadily to his bed and falls across it, dropping (and breaking) a nearly empty whiskey bottle. You rush over and ask "What happened?" With alcoholic fumes blasting from his mouth, your roommate mumbles: "I juss wanna hadda widdel drink!" What do you conclude?

2. Your roommate has just learned that she passed a math exam for which she had done absolutely no studying. Humming the song "I did it my way," she comes bouncing over to you with a huge grin on her face and says: "Let me buy you dinner to celebrate!" What do you conclude about how she is feeling?

3. It is midnight and the library is about to close. As you head for the door, you spy your roommate shuffling along in an awkward waddle. His coat is bulged out in front like he's pregnant. When you ask "What's going on?" he gives you a glare and hisses, "Shhh!" Just before he reaches the door, a pile of books slides from under his coat and crashes to the floor. What do you conclude?

In these examples, it would be reasonable to make the following conclusions:

1. Your roommate is drunk.
2. Your roommate is happy.
3. Your roommate is stealing library books.

Although these conclusions are reasonable, they are *not* factual reports; they are *inferences*. You have not directly experienced your roommate's "drunkenness," "happiness," or "stealing." Instead, you have *inferred* it based on your roommate's behavior and the circumstances. What are the clues in these situations that might lead to these conclusions?

One way of understanding the inferential nature of these views is to ask yourself the following questions:

1. Have you ever pretended to be drunk when you weren't? Could other people tell?

2. Have you ever pretended to be happy when you weren't? Could other people tell?

3. Have you ever been accused of stealing something when you were perfectly innocent? How did this happen?

From these examples we can see that whereas factual beliefs can in principle be verified by direct observation, *inferential beliefs* go beyond what can be directly observed.

Inferring   Describing the world in ways that are based on factual information yet going beyond the information to make statements about what is not currently known.

For instance, in the examples given, your observation of certain actions of your roommate led you to infer things that you were *not* observing directly — "He's drunk," "She's happy," "He's stealing books." Making such simple inferences is something we do all the time. It is so automatic that usually we are not even aware that we are going beyond our immediate observations, and we have difficulty in drawing a sharp line between what we *observe* and what we *infer*. Making such inferences enables us to see the world as a complete picture, to fill in the blanks and round out what is actually being presented to our senses. In a sense, we become artists, painting a picture of the world that is consistent, coherent, and predictable. This picture, however, is actually based on observations that are often fragmentary and incomplete.

We do not use inferences just to round out, or complete, the picture of what we are observing. Our picture also includes *predictions* of what will be taking place in the near future. These predictions and expectations are also inferences because we attempt to determine what is currently unknown from what is already known.

Of course, our inferences may be mistaken, and in fact they frequently are. You may infer that the woman sitting next to you is wearing two earrings and then discover that she has only one. Or you may expect the class to end at noon and find that the teacher lets you go early — or late.

In the last section we concluded that not even factual beliefs are ever absolutely certain. Compared with factual beliefs, however, inferential beliefs are a great deal more uncertain. This difference in certainty makes it crucial for us to distinguish factual beliefs from inferential beliefs.

For example, do you ever cross streets with cars heading toward you, expecting them to stop for a red light or because you have the right of way? Is this a factual belief or an inference? Considered objectively, are you running a serious risk when you do this? In evaluating the risk, think of all the motorists who may be in a hurry, not paying attention, drunk, ill, and so on. Or consider these situations, analyzing each situation by asking the questions that follow:

- Placing your hand in a closing elevator door to reopen it.
- Taking an unknown drug at a party.
- Jumping out of an airplane with a parachute on.
- Riding on the back of a motorcycle.
- Taking a drug prescribed by your doctor.

1. Is this action based on a factual belief or an inference?
2. In what ways might the inference be mistaken?
3. What is the degree of risk involved?

Having an accurate picture of the world depends on our being able to evaluate how *certain* our beliefs are. Therefore it is crucial that we

- *Distinguish* inferences from factual beliefs and then
- *Evaluate* how certain or uncertain our inferences are.

This is known as "calculating the risks," and it is one of the key skills in successfully solving problems and deciding what to do.

The distinction between what is observed and what is inferred is paid particular attention in courtroom settings, where defense lawyers usually want witnesses to describe *only what they observed* — not what they *inferred* as part of the observation. When a witness includes an inference such as "I saw him steal it," the lawyer may object that the statement represents a "conclusion of the witness" and move to have the observation stricken from the record. For example, imagine that you are a defense attorney listening to the following testimony. At what points would you make the objection: "This is a conclusion of the witness"?

> I saw Harvey running down the street, right after he knocked the old lady down. He had her purse in his hand and was trying to escape as fast as he could. He was really scared. I wasn't surprised because Harvey has always taken advantage of others. It's not the first time that he's stolen either, I can tell you that. Just last summer he robbed the poor box at St. Anthony's. He was bragging about it for weeks.

Finally, we should be aware that even though *in theory* facts and inferences can be distinguished, *in practice* it is almost impossible to communicate with others by sticking only to factual observations. A reasonable approach is to state our inference *along with* the observable evidence upon which the inference is based (e.g., John *seemed* happy because . . .). Our language has an entire collection of terms (*seems, appears, is likely,* etc.) that signal we are making an inference and not expressing an observable fact.

THINKING ACTIVITY

10.6 ▶ Examine the following list of statements, noting which statements are *factual beliefs* (based on observations) and which are *inferential beliefs* (conclusions that go beyond observations).

For each factual statement, describe how you might go about verifying the information. For each inferential statement, describe a factual observation on which the inference could be based. (*Note:* Some statements may contain *both* factual beliefs and inferential beliefs.)

1. When my leg starts to ache, that means snow is on the way.

   _____

   _____

2. The grass is wet — it must have rained last night.

   _____

   _____

3. I think that it's pretty clear from the length of the skid marks that the accident was caused by that person driving too fast.

   _____

   _____

4. Fifty men lost their lives in the construction of the Queensboro Bridge.

   _____

   _____

5. Nancy said she wasn't feeling well yesterday — I'll bet that she's out sick today.

   _____

   _____ ◀

10.7 ▶ Consider the following situations. What inferences might you be inclined to make based on what you are observing? How could you investigate the accuracy of your inference?

1. A student in your class is consistently late for class.

2. You see a friend of yours driving a new car.

3. A teacher asks the same student to stay after class several times.

4. You don't receive any birthday cards.

5. Driving on the highway, you observe an area of the road containing broken glass and skid marks. ◀

Complicated Inferences

So far we have been exploring relatively simple inferences. Many of the inferences people make, however, are much more complicated. In fact, much of our knowledge about the world rests on the ability to make complicated inferences in a systematic and logical way. Consider the following story and explain what inferences each person is making. Keep in mind, however, that just because an inference is more complicated does not mean that it is more accurate; in fact, the opposite is often the case.

> In a railroad compartment, an American grandmother with her young and attractive granddaughter, a Romanian officer and a Nazi officer were the only occupants. The train was passing through a dark tunnel, and what was heard was a loud kiss and a vigorous slap. After the train emerged from the tunnel nobody spoke, but the grandmother was saying to herself: "I am proud of her." The granddaughter was saying to herself: "Well, grandmother is old enough not to mind a little kiss. Besides, the fellows are nice. I am surprised what a hard wallop grandmother has." The Nazi officer was meditating, "How clever those Romanians are! They steal a kiss and have the other fellow slapped." The Romanian officer was chuckling to himself: "How smart I am! I kissed my own hand and slapped the Nazi!"
>
> Alfred Korzybski, *Perception — An Approach to Personality*

List the observations of each person in the story and describe the inference each makes based on his or her observation.

Individual:	Observation:	Inference:
Grandmother	Loud kiss and vigorous slap	One of the men kissed the granddaughter and she slapped him.
Granddaughter	_____	_____
	_____	_____
Romanian officer	_____	_____
	_____	_____
Nazi officer	_____	_____
	_____	_____

One of the masters of inference is the legendary Sherlock Holmes. In the following passage, Holmes makes an astonishing number of inferences on meeting Dr. Watson. Study carefully the conclusions he comes to. Are they reasonable? Can you explain how he reaches these conclusions?

> "You appeared to be surprised when I told you, on our first meeting, that you had come from Afghanistan."
>
> "You were told, no doubt."
>
> "Nothing of the sort. I *knew* you came from Afghanistan. From long habit the train of thoughts ran so swiftly through my mind that I arrived at the conclusion without being conscious of intermediate steps. There were such steps, however. The train of reasoning ran, 'Here is a gentleman of a medical type, but with the air of a military man. Clearly an army doctor, then. He is just come from the tropics, for his face is dark, and that is not the natural tint of his skin, for his wrists are fair. He has undergone hardship and sickness, as his haggard face says clearly. His left arm has been injured. He holds it in a stiff and unnatural manner. Where in the tropics could an English army doctor have seen much hardship and got his arm wounded? Clearly in Afghanistan.' The whole train of thought did not occupy a second. I then remarked that you came from Afghanistan, and you were astonished."
>
> Sir Arthur Conan Doyle, *A Study in Scarlet*

Describe the observations that led Sherlock Holmes to the following inferences.

Inference: *Observations:*

1. Watson was "an army doctor."   _____

                                   _____

2. Watson "has undergone hardship _____
   and sickness."
                                   _____

3. Watson has come from   _____
   Afghanistan.
                                   _____

THINKING ACTIVITY

10.8 ▶ Describe an experience in which you made an *in*correct inference that resulted in serious consequences. For example, it might have been a situation
in which you mistakenly accused someone, an accident based on a miscal-
culation, a poor decision based on an inaccurate prediction, or some other
event. Analyze that experience by answering the following questions:

1. What was (were) your mistaken inference(s)?
2. What was the factual evidence on which you based your inference?
3. Looking back, what could you have done to avoid the erroneous
   inference? ◀

THINKING ACTIVITY

10.9 ▶ The following essay was written by Stephen Jay Gould, a professor of geology
at Harvard University who also writes widely on scientific themes for non-
scientific audiences. This essay illustrates the ongoing process by which natural scientists use inferences to discover factual information and to construct
theories explaining this factual information. Read the selection carefully and
then answer the questions which follow the selection.

EVOLUTION AS FACT AND THEORY *by Stephen Jay Gould*

Kirtley Mather, who died last year at age 89, was a pillar of both science
and the Christian religion in America and one of my dearest friends.
The difference of half a century in our ages evaporated before our common interests. The most curious thing we shared was a battle we each
fought at the same age. For Kirtley had gone to Tennessee with Clarence

Darrow to testify for evolution at the Scopes trial of 1925. When I think that we are enmeshed again in the same struggle for one of the best documented, most compelling and exciting concepts in all of science, I don't know whether to laugh or cry.

According to idealized principles of scientific discourse, the arousal of dormant issues should reflect fresh data that give renewed life to abandoned notions. Those outside the current debate may therefore be excused for suspecting that creationists have come up with something new, or that evolutionists have generated some serious internal trouble. But nothing has changed; the creationists have not a single new fact or argument. Darrow and Bryan were at least more entertaining than we lesser antagonists today.* The rise of creationism is politics, pure and simple; it represents one issue (and by no means the major concern) of the resurgent evangelical right. Arguments that seemed kooky just a decade ago have re-entered the mainstream.

Creationism Is Not Science

The basic attack of the creationists falls apart on two general counts before we even reach the supposed factual details of their complaints against evolution. First, they play upon a vernacular misunderstanding of the word "theory" to convey the false impression that we evolutionists are covering up the rotten core of our edifice. Second, they misuse a popular philosophy of science to argue that they are behaving scientifically in attacking evolution. Yet the same philosophy demonstrates that their own belief is not science, and that "scientific creationism" is therefore meaningless and self-contradictory, a superb example of what Orwell† called "newspeak."‡

In the American vernacular, "theory" often means "imperfect fact" — part of a hierarchy of confidence running downhill from fact to theory to hypothesis to guess. Thus the power of the creationist argument: evolution is "only" a theory, and intense debate now rages about many aspects of the theory. If evolution is less than a fact, and scientists can't even make up their minds about the theory, then what confidence can

---

* Darrow and Bryan: Clarence Darrow (1857–1938) was the defense attorney in the 1925 trial of John Thomas Scopes for teaching evolution; William Jennings Bryan (1860–1925) was an orator and politician who aided the prosecution in the Scopes trial. [Eds.]

† George Orwell (1903–1950): English journalist and novelist, author of *Animal Farm* and *1984*. [Eds.]

‡ "Newspeak": the official language in Orwell's *1984*, devised to meet the ideological needs of the ruling party and to make all other modes of thought impossible. [Eds.]

we have in it? Indeed, President Reagan echoed this argument before an evangelical group in Dallas when he said (in what I devoutly hope was campaign rhetoric): "Well, it is a theory. It is a scientific theory only, and it has in recent years been challenged in the world of science — that is, not believed in the scientific community to be as infallible as it once was."

Well, evolution *is* a theory. It is also a fact. And facts and theories are different things, not rungs in a hierarchy of increasing certainty. Facts are the world's data. Theories are structures of ideas that explain and interpret facts. Facts do not go away when scientists debate rival theories to explain them. Einstein's theory of gravitation replaced Newton's, but apples did not suspend themselves in mid-air pending the outcome. And human beings evolved from apelike ancestors whether they did so by Darwin's proposed mechanism or by some other, yet to be discovered.

Moreover, "fact" does not mean "absolute certainty." The final proofs of logic and mathematics flow deductively from stated premises and achieve certainty only because they are *not* about the empirical world. Evolutionists make no claim for perpetual truth, though creationists often do (and then attack us for a style of argument that they themselves favor). In science, "fact" can only mean "confirmed to such a degree that it would be perverse to withhold provisional assent." I suppose that apples might start to rise tomorrow, but the possibility does not merit equal time in physics classrooms.

Evolutionists have been clear about this distinction between fact and theory from the very beginning, if only because we have always acknowledged how far we are from completely understanding the mechanisms (theory) by which evolution (fact) occurred. Darwin continually emphasized the difference between his two great and separate accomplishments: establishing the fact of evolution, and proposing a theory — natural selection — to explain the mechanism of evolution. He wrote in *The Descent of Man:* "I had two distinct objects in view; firstly, to show that species had not been separately created, and secondly, that natural selection had been the chief agent of change . . . Hence if I have erred in . . . having exaggerated its [natural selection's] power . . . I have at least, as I hope, done good service in aiding to overthrow the dogma of separate creations."

Thus Darwin acknowledged the provisional nature of natural selection while affirming the fact of evolution. The fruitful theoretical debate that Darwin initiated has never ceased. From the 1940s through the

1960s, Darwin's own theory of natural selection did achieve a temporary hegemony that it never enjoyed in his lifetime. But renewed debate characterizes our decade, and, while no biologist questions the importance of natural selection, many now doubt its ubiquity. In particular, many evolutionists argue that substantial amounts of genetic change may not be subject to natural selection and may spread through populations at random. Others are challenging Darwin's linking of natural selection with gradual, imperceptible change through all intermediary degrees; they are arguing that most evolutionary events may occur far more rapidly than Darwin envisioned.

Scientists regard debates on fundamental issues of theory as a sign of intellectual health and a source of excitement. Science is — and how else can I say it? — most fun when it plays with interesting ideas, examines their implications, and recognizes that old information may be explained in surprisingly new ways. Evolutionary theory is now enjoying this uncommon vigor. Yet amidst all this turmoil no biologist has been led to doubt the fact that evolution occurred; we are debating *how* it happened. We are all trying to explain the same thing: the tree of evolutionary descent linking all organisms by ties of genealogy. Creationists pervert and caricature this debate by conveniently neglecting the common conviction that underlies it, and by falsely suggesting that we now doubt the very phenomenon we are struggling to understand.

Using another invalid argument, creationists claim that "the dogma of separate creations," as Darwin characterized it a century ago, is a scientific theory meriting equal time with evolution in high school biology curricula. But a prevailing viewpoint among philosophers of science belies this creationist argument. Philosopher Karl Popper has argued for decades that the primary criterion of science is the falsifiability of its theories. We can never prove absolutely, but we can falsify. A set of ideas that cannot, in principle, be falsified is not science.

The entire creationist argument involves little more than a rhetorical attempt to falsify evolution by presenting supposed contradictions among its supporters. Their brand of creationism, they claim, is "scientific" because it follows the Popperian model in trying to demolish evolution. Yet Popper's argument must apply in both directions. One does not become a scientist by the simple act of trying to falsify another scientific system; one has to present an alternative system that also meets Popper's criterion — it too must be falsifiable in principle.

"Scientific creationism" is a self-contradictory, nonsense phrase precisely because it cannot be falsified. I can envision observations and experiments that would disprove any evolutionary theory I know, but I cannot imagine what potential data could lead creationists to abandon their beliefs. Unbeatable systems are dogma, not science. Lest I seem harsh or rhetorical, I quote creationism's leading intellectual, Duane Gish, Ph.D., from his recent (1978) book *Evolution? The Fossils Say No!* "By creation we mean the bringing into being by a supernatural Creator of the basic kinds of plants and animals by the process of sudden, or fiat, creation. We do not know how the Creator created, what processes He used, *for He used processes which are not now operating anywhere in the natural universe* [Gish's italics]. This is why we refer to creation as special creation. We cannot discover by scientific investigations anything about the creative processes used by the Creator." Pray tell, Dr. Gish, in the light of your last sentence, what then is "scientific" creationism?

The Fact of Evolution

Our confidence that evolution occurred centers upon three general arguments. First, we have abundant, direct, observational evidence of evolution in action, from both the field and the laboratory. It ranges from countless experiments on change in nearly everything about fruit flies subjected to artificial selection in the laboratory to the famous British moths that turned black when industrial soot darkened the trees upon which they rest. (The moths gain protection from sharp-sighted bird predators by blending into the background.) Creationists do not deny these observations; how could they? Creationists have tightened their act. They now argue that God only created "basic kinds," and allowed for limited evolutionary meandering within them. Thus toy poodles and Great Danes come from the dog kind and moths can change color, but nature cannot convert a dog to a cat or a monkey to a man.

The second and third arguments for evolution — the case for major changes — do not involve direct observation of evolution in action. They rest upon inference, but are no less secure for that reason. Major evolutionary change requires too much time for direct observation on the scale of recorded human history. All historical sciences rest upon inference, and evolution is no different from geology, cosmology, or human history in this respect. In principle, we cannot observe processes that operated in the past. We must infer them from results that still survive: living and fossil organisms for evolution, documents and artifacts for human history, strata and topography for geology.

The second argument — that the imperfection of nature reveals evolution — strikes many people as ironic, for they feel that evolution should be most elegantly displayed in the nearly perfect adaptation expressed by some organisms — the chamber of a gull's wing, or butterflies that cannot be seen in ground litter because they mimic leaves so precisely. But perfection could be imposed by a wise creator or evolved by natural selection. Perfection covers the tracks of past history. And past history — the evidence of descent — is our mark of evolution.

Evolution lies exposed in the *imperfections* that record a history of descent. Why should a rat run, a bat fly, a porpoise swim, and I type this essay with structures built of the same bones unless we all inherited them from a common ancestor? An engineer, starting from scratch, could design better limbs in each case. Why should all the large native mammals of Australia be marsupials, unless they descended from a common ancestor isolated on this island continent? Marsupials are not "better," or ideally suited for Australia; many have been wiped out by placental mammals imported by man from other continents. This principle of imperfection extends to all historical sciences. When we recognize the etymology of September, October, November, and December (seventh, eighth, ninth, and tenth, from the Latin), we know that two additional items (January and February) must have been added to an original calendar of ten months.

The third argument is more direct: transitions are often found in the fossil record. Preserved transitions are not common — and should not be, according to our understanding of evolution . . . — but they are not entirely wanting, as creationists often claim. The lower jaw of reptiles contains several bones, that of mammals only one. The non-mammalian jawbones are reduced, step by step, in mammalian ancestors until they become tiny nubbins located at the back of the jaw. The "hammer" and "anvil" bones of the mammalian ear are descendants of these nubbins. How could such a transition be accomplished? the creationists ask. Surely a bone is either entirely in the jaw or in the ear. Yet paleontologists have discovered two transitional lineages or therapsids (the so-called mammal-like reptiles) with a double jaw joint — one composed of the old quadrate and articular bones (soon to become the hammer and anvil), the other of the squamosal and dentary bones (as in modern mammals). For that matter, what better transitional form could we desire than the oldest human, *Australopithecus afarensis*, with its apelike palate, its human upright stance, and a cranial capacity larger than any ape's of the same body size but a full 1,000 cubic centimeters below ours? If God made each of the half dozen human species discovered in ancient rocks, why did he create an unbroken temporal sequence of

progressively more modern features — increasing cranial capacity, reduced face and teeth, larger body size? Did he create to mimic evolution
and test our faith thereby? . . .

Conclusion

I am both angry at and amused by the creationists; but mostly I am
deeply sad. Sad for many reasons. Sad because so many people who
respond to creationist appeals are troubled for the right reason, but
venting their anger at the wrong target. It is true that scientists have
often been dogmatic and elitist. It is true that we have often allowed the
white-coated, advertising image to represent us — "Scientists say that
Brand X cures bunions ten times faster than . . ." We have not fought it
adequately because we derive benefits from appearing as a new priest-
hood. It is also true that faceless bureaucratic state power intrudes more
and more into our lives and removes choices that should belong to individuals and communities. I can understand that requiring that evolution be taught in the schools might be seen as one more insult on all
these grounds. But the culprit is not, and cannot be, evolution or any
other fact of the natural world. Identify and fight your legitimate enemies by all means, but we are not among them.

I am sad because the practical result of this brouhaha will not be expanded coverage to include creationism (that would also make me sad),
but the reduction or excision of evolution from high school curricula.
Evolution is one of the half dozen "great ideas" developed by science.
It speaks to the profound issues of genealogy that fascinate all of us —
the "roots" phenomenon writ large. Where did we come from? Where
did life arise? How did it develop? How are organisms related? It forces
us to think, ponder, and wonder. Shall we deprive millions of this
knowledge and once again teach biology as a set of dull and uncon-
nected facts, without the thread that weaves diverse material into a supple unity?

But most of all I am saddened by a trend I am just beginning to discern
among my colleagues. I sense that some now wish to mute the healthy
debate about theory that has brought new life to evolutionary biology.
It provides grist for creationist mills, they say, even if only by distortion.
Perhaps we should lie low and rally round the flag of strict Darwinism,
at least for the moment — a kind of old-time religion on our part.

But we should borrow another metaphor and recognize that we too
have to tread a straight and narrow path, surrounded by roads to per-
dition. For if we ever begin to suppress our search to understand nature,

to quench our own intellectual excitement in a misguided effort to present a united front where it does not and should not exist, then we are truly lost. ■

1. According to Gould, evolution is both a scientific "fact" and a scientific "theory" asserting that all life forms are the result of a process of gradual development and differentiation over time, much like the progressive growth of tree branches from the central trunk. In contrast, creationism asserts that all basic forms of life were brought into being in a sudden act by a supernatural creator. Explain what you understand about the theory of evolution and creationism based on your reading of the article.

2. Gould defines "facts" as the "world's data," like observing an apple fall from a tree, as Isaac Newton is alleged to have done. Describe some of the facts Gould gives as evidence to support the theory of evolution.

3. Gould defines "theories" as "structures of ideas that explain and interpret facts," such as Newton's theory of gravitation introduced to explain facts like falling apples. In addition to facts, Gould states that the theory of evolution is supported by reasonable inferences. Describe the inferences he cites as evidence.

4. According to Gould, creationism is neither a scientific fact nor a scientific theory. Describe the reasons he gives to support this belief.

5. At the beginning of the article, Gould gives the example of Kirtley Mather as "a pillar of both science and the Christian religion." Explain how you think it might be possible to believe in both of these viewpoints with respect to the origins of life. ◄

Judging

In the space provided, identify and describe a friend you have, a course you have taken, and the school you attend. Be sure your descriptions are specific and include *what you think* about the friend, the course, and the school.

1. _____ is a friend that I have.

   He/she is _____

   _____

2. _____ is a course I have taken.

It was _____

_____

3. _____ is the school I attend.

It is _____

_____

Now review your responses. Do they include *factual* descriptions? For each response, note any factual information that can be verified.

In addition to factual reports, your descriptions may contain *inferences* about them based on factual information. Can you identify any inferences?

In addition to inferences, your descriptions may also include *judgments* about the person, course, and school.

Judging   Describing the world in ways that express our evaluation based on certain criteria.

Whereas facts and inferences are designed to help us figure out what is actually happening (or will happen), the purpose of judgments is to express our evaluation about what is happening (or will happen). For example:

• My new car has broken down three times in the first six months. (*Factual report*)

• My new car will probably continue to have difficulties. (*Inference*)

• My new car is a lemon. (*Judgment*)

When we pronounce our new car a "lemon," we are making a judgment based on certain criteria we have in mind. For instance, a "lemon" is usually a newly purchased item with which we have repeated problems — generally an automobile.

To take another example of judging, consider the following statements:

• Carla always does her work thoroughly and completes it on time. (*Factual report*)

• Carla will probably continue to do her work in this fashion. (*Inference*)

• Carla is a very responsible person. (*Judgment*)

By judging Carla to be responsible, we are evaluating her on the basis of the criteria or standards that we believe indicate a responsible person. One such criterion is completing assigned work on time. Can you identify additional criteria for judging someone to be responsible?

Review your descriptions of a friend, a course, and your school (on pp. 479–480). Can you identify any judgments in your descriptions? If so, list them here.

1. *Friend:* _____

   Judgment(s): _____

   _____

2. *Course:* _____

   Judgment(s): _____

   _____

3. *School:* _____

   Judgment(s): _____

   _____

For each judgment you have listed, identify the criteria on which the judgment is based.

1. *Judgment:* _____

   Criteria: _____

   a. _____

   b. _____

2. *Judgment:* _____

   Criteria: _____

   a. _____

   b. _____

3. *Judgment:* _____

   Criteria: _____

   a. _____

   b. _____

When we judge, we are often expressing our feelings of approval or disapproval. Sometimes, however, we make judgments that conflict with what we personally approve of. For example:

• I think a woman should be able to have an abortion if she chooses to, although I don't believe it's right.

• I can see why you think that person is very beautiful, even though he or she is not the type that appeals to me.

In fact, at times it is essential to disregard our personal feelings of approval or disapproval when we judge. The judges in our justice system, for instance, should render evaluations based on the law, not on their personal preferences.

Differences in Judgments

Many of our disagreements with other people focus on differences in judgments. As critical thinkers, we need to approach such differences in judgments intelligently. We can do so by following these guidelines:

1. *Making explicit* the criteria or standards used as a basis for the judgment

2. Trying to *establish the reasons* that justify these criteria

For instance, if I make the judgment "That's a beautiful Alaskan malamute," I am basing my judgment on certain criteria of malamute beauty. Once these standards are made explicit, we can discuss whether they make sense and what is the justification for them. If we rely on observing and describing the physical characteristics of the dog — height, weight, shape, coat, and so on — we will never determine whether our judgment ("That's a beautiful malamute") makes sense. Our idea of what makes for a beautiful malamute may be completely different from someone else's idea of malamute beauty. Our only hope for resolving the issue is to:

1. Make explicit the standards we are using to judge malamute beauty.

2. Give reasons that justify these standards. For example, "These are the standards established by the American Kennel Club, and they reflect an overall sense of strength, balance, and proportion. In addition, these criteria evaluate the physical qualities needed for the sled-pulling tasks of the malamute.

In short, not all judgments are equally good or equally poor. The credibility of a judgment depends on the criteria used to make the judgment and the evidence or reasons that support these criteria. For example, there may be legitimate disagreements about judgments on the following points:

- Who was the greatest United States president?
- Which movie deserves the Oscar this year?
- Who should win the Miss America Pageant or the Mr. America Contest?
- Which is the best baseball team this year?
- Which music is best for dancing?

In these and countless other cases, however, the quality of judgments depends on identifying the criteria used for the competing judgments and then demonstrating that our candidate best meets those criteria by providing supporting evidence and reasons. With this approach, we can often engage in intelligent discussion and establish which judgments are best supported by the evidence.

Understanding how judgments function is also important to encourage us to continue thinking critically about a situation. For instance, the judgment "This course is worthless!" does not encourage further exploration and critical analysis. In fact, it may prevent such an analysis by *discouraging* further exploration. Judgments seem to summarize the situation in a final sort of way. And because judgments are sometimes made *before* we have a clear and complete understanding of the situation, they can serve to *prevent* us from seeing the situation as clearly and completely as we might. Of course, if we understand that all judgments are based on criteria that may or may not be adequately justified, we can explore these judgments further by making the criteria explicit and examining the reasons that justify them.

THINKING ACTIVITY

10.10 ▶ Review the following passages, which illustrate various judgments. For each passage:

1. Identify the evaluative criteria on which the judgments are based.
2. Describe the reasons or evidence the author uses to support the criteria.
3. Explain whether you agree or disagree with the judgments, and your rationale.

> One widely held misconception concerning pizza should be laid to rest. Although it may be characterized as fast food, pizza is *not* junk food. Especially when it is made with fresh ingredients, pizza fulfills our basic

nutritional requirements. The crust provides carbohydrates; from the cheese and meat or fish comes protein; and the tomatoes, herbs, onions, and garlic supply vitamins and minerals.

Louis Philip Salamone, "Pizza: Fast Food, Not Junk Food"

Let us return to the question of food. Responsible agronomists report that before the end of the year millions of people if unaided might starve to death. Half a billion deaths by starvation is not an uncommon estimate. Even though the United States has done more than any other nation to feed the hungry, our relative affluence makes us morally vulnerable in the eyes of other nations and in our own eyes. Garrett Hardin, who has argued for a "lifeboat" ethic of survival (if you take all the passengers aboard, everybody drowns), admits that the decision *not* to feed all the hungry requires of us "a very hard psychological adjustment." Indeed it would. It has been estimated that the 3.5 million tons of fertilizer spread on American golf courses and lawns could provide up to 30 million tons of food in overseas agricultural production. The nightmarish thought intrudes itself. If we as a nation allow people to starve while we could, through some sacrifice, make more food available to them, what hope can any person have for the future of international relations? If we cannot agree on this most basic of values — feed the hungry — what hopes for the future can we entertain?

James R. Kelly, "The Limits of Reason" ◀

Many of the judgments we are involved with are *moral* or *ethical* judgments, or judgments that concern the ways we should and should not behave toward other people. These judgments are often based on criteria we have absorbed from our parents. If we have critically examined the ethical beliefs we were raised with, however, we may have found that some of our views diverge from those of our parents. Of course, critical evaluation may also strengthen our endorsement of our parents' beliefs by deepening our understanding of the reasons on which they are based.

THINKING ACTIVITY

10.11 ▶ In the following article, the psychologist Robert Coles examines the moral awareness of children. Coles claims that our society clings to the idea of children as pure innocents and does not see the ethical decisions they make or the complicated moral issues they confront. Through examples of the many children he has met, Coles argues for the need for parents to teach their children moral values. After carefully reading the article, answer the questions that follow.

I LISTEN TO MY PARENTS AND I WONDER WHAT THEY BELIEVE *by Robert Coles*

Not so long ago children were looked upon in a sentimental fashion as "angels" or as "innocents." Today, thanks to Freud and his followers, boys and girls are understood to have complicated inner lives; to feel love, hate, envy and rivalry in various and subtle mixtures; to be eager participants in the sexual and emotional politics of the home, neighborhood and school. Yet some of us parents still cling to the notion of childhood innocence in another way. We do not see that our children also make ethical decisions every day in their own lives, or realize how attuned they may be to moral currents and issues in the larger society.

In Appalachia I heard a girl of eight whose father owns coal fields (and gas stations, a department store and much timberland) wonder about "life" one day: "I'll be walking to the school bus, and I'll ask myself why there's some who are poor and their daddies can't find a job, and there's some who are lucky like me. Last month there was an explosion in a mine my daddy owns, and everyone became upset. Two miners got killed. My daddy said it was their own fault, because they'll be working and they get careless. When my mother asked if there was anything wrong with the safety down in the mine, he told her no and she shouldn't ask questions like that. Then the Government people came and they said it was the owner's fault — Daddy's. But he has a lawyer and the lawyer is fighting the Government and the union. In school, kids ask me what I think, and I sure do feel sorry for the two miners and so does my mother — I know that. She told me it's just not a fair world and you have to remember that. Of course, there's no one who can be sure there won't be trouble; like my daddy says, the rain falls on the just and the unjust. My brother is only six and he asked Daddy awhile back who are the 'just' and the 'unjust,' and Daddy said there are people who work hard and they live good lives, and there are lazy people and they're always trying to sponge off others. But I guess you have to feel sorry for anyone who has a lot of trouble, because it's poured-down, heavy rain."

Listening, one begins to realize that an elementary-school child is no stranger to moral reflection — and to ethical conflict. This girl was torn between her loyalty to her particular background, its values and assumptions, and to a larger affiliation — her membership in the nation, the world. As a human being whose parents were kind and decent to her, she was inclined to be thoughtful and sensitive with respect to others, no matter what their work or position in society. But her father was among other things a mineowner, and she had already learned to shape her concerns to suit that fact of life. The result: a moral oscillation of sorts, first toward nameless others all over the world and then toward her own family. As the girl put it later, when she was a year older: "You should try to have 'good thoughts' about everyone, the minister says, and our teacher says that too. But you should honor your father and mother most of all; that's why you should find out what they think and then sort of copy them. But sometimes you're not sure if you're on the right track."

Sort of copy them. There could be worse descriptions of how children acquire moral values. In fact, the girl understood how girls and boys all over the world "sort of" develop attitudes of what is right and wrong, ideas of who the just and the unjust are. And they also struggle hard and long, and not always with success, to find out where the "right track" starts and ends. Children need encouragement or assistance as they wage that struggle.

In home after home that I have visited, and in many classrooms, I have met children who not only are growing emotionally and intellectually but also are trying to make sense of the world morally. That is to say, they are asking themselves and others about issues of fair play, justice, liberty, equality. Those last words are abstractions, of course — the stuff of college term papers. And there are, one has to repeat, those in psychology and psychiatry who would deny elementary-school children access to that "higher level" of moral reflection. But any parent who has listened closely to his or her child knows that girls and boys are capable of wondering about matters of morality, and knows too that often it is their grown-up protectors (parents, relatives, teachers, neighbors) who are made uncomfortable by the so-called "innocent" nature of the questions children may ask or the statements they may make. Often enough the issue is not the moral capacity of the children but the default of us parents who fail to respond to inquiries put to us by our daughters and sons — and fail to set moral standards for both ourselves and our children.

Do's and don't's are, of course, pressed upon many of our girls and boys. But a moral education is something more than a series of rules handed down, and in our time one cannot assume that every parent feels able — sure enough of her own or his own actual beliefs and values — to make even an initial explanatory and disciplinary effort toward a moral education. Furthermore, for many of us parents these days it is a child's emotional life that preoccupies us.

In 1963, when I was studying school desegregation in the South, I had extended conversations with Black and white elementary-school children caught up in a dramatic moment of historical change. For longer than I care to remember, I concentrated on possible psychiatric troubles, on how a given child was managing under circumstances of extreme stress, on how I could be of help — with "support," with reassurance, with a helpful psychological observation or interpretation. In many instances I was off the mark. These children weren't "patients"; they weren't even complaining. They were worried, all right, and often enough they had things to say that were substantive — that had to do not so much with troubled emotions as with questions of right and wrong in the real-life dramas taking place in their worlds.

Here is a nine-year-old white boy, the son of ardent segregationists, telling me about his sense of what desegregation meant to Louisiana in the 1960s: "They told us it wouldn't happen — never. My daddy said none of us white people would go into schools with the colored. But then it did happen, and when I went to school the first day I didn't know what would go on. Would the school stay open or would it close up? We didn't know what to do; the teacher kept telling us that we should be good and obey the law, but my daddy said the law was wrong. Then my mother said she wanted me in school even if there were some colored kids there. She said if we all stayed home she'd be a 'nervous wreck.' So I went.

"After a while I saw that the colored weren't so bad. I saw that there are different kinds of colored people, just like with us whites. There was one of the colored who was nice, a boy who smiled, and he played real good. There was another one, a boy, who wouldn't talk with anyone. I don't know if it's right that we all be in the same school. Maybe it isn't right. My sister is starting school next year, and she says she doesn't care if there's 'mixing of the races.' She says they told her in Sunday school that everyone is a child of God, and then a kid asked if that goes for the colored too and the teacher said yes, she thought so. My daddy said that it's true, God made everyone — but that doesn't mean we all have to be living together under the same roof in the home or the school.

But my mother said we'll never know what God wants of us but we have to try to read His mind, and that's why we pray. So when I say my prayers I ask God to tell me what's the right thing to do. In school I try to say hello to the colored, because they're kids, and you can't be mean or you'll be 'doing wrong,' like my grandmother says."

Children aren't usually long-winded in the moral discussions they have with one another or with adults, and in quoting this boy I have pulled together comments he made to me in the course of several days. But everything he said was of interest to me. I was interested in the boy's changing racial attitudes. It was clear he was trying to find a coherent, sensible moral position too. It was also borne in on me that if one spends days, weeks in a given home, it is hard to escape a particular moral climate just as significant as the psychological one.

In many homes parents establish moral assumptions, mandates, priorities. They teach children what to believe in, what not to believe in. They teach children what is permissible or not permissible — and why. They may summon up the Bible, the flag, history, novels, aphorisms, philosophical or political sayings, personal memories — all in an effort to teach children how to behave, what and whom to respect and for which reasons. Or they may neglect to do so, and in so doing teach their children *that* — a moral abdication, of sorts — and in this way fail their children. Children need and long for words of moral advice, instruction, warning, as much as they need words of affirmation or criticism from their parents about other matters. They must learn how to dress and what to wear, how to eat and what to eat; and they must also learn how to behave under X or Y or Z conditions, and why.

All the time, in 20 years of working with poor children and rich children, Black children and white children, children from rural areas and urban areas and in every region of this country, I have heard questions — thoroughly intelligent and discerning questions — about social and historical matters, about personal behavior, and so on. But most striking is the fact that almost all those questions, in one way or another, are moral in nature: Why did the Pilgrims leave England? Why didn't they just stay and agree to do what the king wanted them to do? . . . Should you try to share all you've got or should you save a lot for yourself? . . . What do you do when you see others fighting — do you try to break up the fight, do you stand by and watch or do you leave as fast as you can? . . . Is it right that some people haven't got enough to eat? . . . I see other kids cheating and I wish I could copy the answers too; but I won't cheat, though sometimes I feel I'd like to and I get all mixed up. I go home and talk with my parents, and I ask them what should you do if you see kids cheating — pay no attention, or report the kids or do the same thing they are doing?

Those are examples of children's concerns — and surely millions of American parents have heard versions of them. Have the various "experts" on childhood stressed strongly enough the importance of such questions — and the importance of the hunger we all have, no matter what our age or background, to examine what we believe in, are willing to stand up for, and what we are determined to ask, likewise, of our children?

Children not only need our understanding of their complicated emotional lives; they also need a constant regard for the moral issues that come their way as soon as they are old enough to play with others and take part in the politics of the nursery, the back yard and the schoolroom. They need to be told what they must do and what they must not do. They need control over themselves and a sense of what others are entitled to from them — co-operation, thoughtfulness, an attentive ear and eye. They need discipline not only to tame their excesses of emotion but discipline also connected to stated and clarified moral values. They need, in other words, something to believe in that is larger than their own appetites and urges and, yes, bigger than their "psychological drives." They need a larger view of the world, a moral context, as it were — a faith that addresses itself to the meaning of this life we all live and, soon enough, let go of.

Yes, it is time for us parents to begin to look more closely at what ideas our children have about the world; and it would be well to do so before they become teen-agers and young adults and begin to remind us, as often happens, of how little attention we did pay to their moral development. Perhaps a nine-year-old girl from a well-off suburban home in Texas put it better than anyone else I've met:

"I listen to my parents, and I wonder what they believe in more than anything else. I asked my mom and my daddy once: What's the thing that means most to you? They said they didn't know but I shouldn't worry my head too hard with questions like that. So I asked my best friend, and she said she wonders if there's a God and how do you know Him and what does He want you to do — I mean, when you're in school or out playing with your friends. They talk about God in church, but is it only in church that He's there and keeping an eye on you? I saw a kid steal in a store, and I know her father has a lot of money — because I hear my daddy talk. But stealing's wrong. My mother said she's a 'sick girl,' but it's still wrong what she did. Don't you think?"

There was more — much more — in the course of the months I came

to know that child and her parents and their neighbors. But those observations and questions — a "mere child's" — reminded me unforgettably of the aching hunger for firm ethical principles that so many of us
feel. Ought we not begin thinking about this need? Ought we not all be
asking ourselves more intently what standards we live by — and how
we can satisfy our children's hunger for moral values? ■

1. In this article, Coles gives a number of examples of children struggling to
   develop a set of ethical standards that make sense to them.

   a. Identify some of the ethical standards that are illustrated.

   b. Explain how these standards agree and disagree with standards their
      parents believe in.

   c. In those cases where the children's ethical standards diverge from those
      of their parents, describe the reasons that support the children's beliefs.

2. Using this article as a resource, define your own understanding of the
   concept of *moral awareness.*

   a. Describe one or more examples from your own experience that illus-
      trate the concept of *moral awareness.*

   b. Based on these examples, identify the necessary requirements of the
      concept of *moral awareness.*

3. At the end of the article, Coles calls for the need to think about how we
   teach moral awareness:

   > . . . those observations and questions — a "mere child's" — re-
   > minded me unforgettably of the aching hunger for firm ethical prin-
   > ciples that so many of us feel. Ought we not begin thinking about
   > this need? Ought we not all be asking ourselves more intently what
   > standards we live by — and how we can satisfy our children's hunger
   > for moral values?

   Explain what you see as the connections between developing moral awareness and our ability to think critically, as suggested by Coles.

4. a. Identify a moral issue that you feel strongly about, and describe your
      beliefs about this issue.

   b. Describe how you developed your beliefs about this moral issue, based
      on your experience (education, family, friends, critical reflection, etc.).

   c. Explain how you would teach this moral issue to someone else. ◄

Distinguishing Reports, Inferences, and Judgments

Although the activities of reporting, inferring, and judging tend to be woven together in our experience, it is important for us to be able to distinguish them. Each of these activities plays a different role in helping us make sense of our world, and we should be careful not to confuse these roles. For example, although people may appear to be reporting factual information, they may actually be expressing personal evaluations, which are not factual. Consider the statement: "Los Angeles is a smog-ridden city dominated by automobiles." While seeming to be reporting factual information, the speaker is really expressing his or her personal judgment. Of course, speakers can identify their judgments with such phrases as "in my opinion," "my evaluation is," and so forth. Sometimes, however, speakers do not identify their judgments. In some cases they do not do so because the context within which they are speaking or writing (such as a newspaper editorial) makes clear that the information is judgment rather than fact. In other cases, however, they want us to treat their judgments as factual information. Confusing the activities of reporting, inferring, and judging can be misleading and even dangerous.

Confusing factual information with judgments can be personally damaging as well. For example, there is a big difference between the statements:

- I failed my exam today. (*Factual report*)
- I am a failure. (*Judgment*)

Stating the fact "I failed my exam today" describes our situation in a concrete way, enabling us to see it as a problem we can hope to solve through reflection and hard work. On the other hand, if we make the judgment "I am a failure," this sort of general evaluation does not encourage us to explore solutions to the problem or improve our situation.

Finally, another important reason for distinguishing the activities of reporting, inferring, and judging concerns the accuracy of our statements. For instance, we noted that factual statements tend to be reasonably accurate since they are by nature verifiable whereas inferences are usually much less certain. As a result, it is crucial for us to know what type of belief we are dealing with so that we can accurately evaluate the probability of its being true. If we treat an inference — for instance, "I don't think that this exam will be very difficult so I'm not going to bother to study" — as if it had the certainty of a factual statement, we may find ourselves in an unexpected predicament.

THINKING ACTIVITY

10.12 ▶ In the following list of statements, identify the factual reports, the inferences, and the judgments.

- For every *factual report* you identify, describe how you might go about verifying the information.
- For every *inference* you identify, describe a factual report on which it could be based.
- For every *judgment* you identify, list the criteria on which the judgment might be based.

1. He's the best athlete on the team.

   _____

2. Look at the syllabus for this course — it's going to be very difficult.

   _____

3. My mother is a saint.

   _____

4. The tallest building in the world is located in Chicago.

   _____

5. Based on the size of those tracks in the snow, I'd say that there's a very large deer around here.

   _____

6. We all agreed that it was a very exciting movie.

   _____ ◀

THINKING ACTIVITY

10.13 ▶ Carefully read the following description of a neighborhood. After completing your reading, write five statements based on the passage. Identify each of your statements as reporting, inferring, or judging, and explain why you classified them as such.

> The residents of Greenwich Village form a richly diverse parade each morning: young professionals moving purposefully off to work; children in Osh-Kosh overalls and parochial school plaids skipping energetically to a day of education; mothers with strollers mingling with the

self-employed, the unemployed, and the retired, easing into the day at a leisurely pace; and finally, the shopkeepers, hard-working and friendly people from six continents preparing for a day of business.

One of the striking differences between Greenwich Village and other parts of Manhattan is the size of the buildings. Instead of towering structures that blot out the sky and diminish your sense of significance, the architecture of the Village is on a human scale, creating the distinct impression that this is a neighborhood in which people are considered to be more important than the buildings that they occupy.

Many of the small businesses in Greenwich Village — mom-and-pop groceries, tailors, coffee shops with soda fountains — have been replaced with expensive restaurants and exclusive boutiques. Significant increases in commercial rents have driven out the small businesses that can't pay these rents. I think that the trend away from small, privately owned businesses is unfortunate because it reduces the diversity of the neighborhood, it makes residents walk further for needed services, and it decreases our sense of being a member of a social community.

Greenwich Village has a rich history as a unique and creative part of New York City. However, I'm afraid that this creative tradition will be lost in the future as only the wealthy will be able to afford to live there. ◄

THINKING ACTIVITY

10.14 ► Select a neighborhood you are familiar with and write a one-page passage describing it. Your passage should contain the following information:

- A description of the physical appearance of the neighborhood — what it looks like, sounds like, smells like, and so on. Give specific details.

- A description of some of the individuals or types of people who live in the neighborhood and their usual activities.

- Your thoughts and feelings about your neighborhood.

- Your prediction of what will happen to your neighborhood in the future.

After completing your passage, identify (in the margin) each of your statements as reporting, inferring, or judging and explain why you classified it as such. ◄

As you worked through these two exercises, you probably became aware of the way that we continually use the activities of reporting, inferring, and judging to organize and make sense of our world. In addition, you probably experienced some difficulty in distinguishing these different kinds of activities. This is because we rarely make an effort to try to separate them. Instead, the thinking processes we call reporting, inferring, and judging tend to be woven together, organizing our world into a seamless fabric. Only when we make a special effort to reflect and think critically are we able to recognize these activities as being distinct.

Summary

This chapter has explored the thinking processes that create three of the fundamental types of beliefs that we use to make sense of our world. These processes are

Reporting	Describing information that can be verified through investigation
Inferring	Going beyond factual information to describe what is not currently known
Judging	Expressing an evaluation based on certain criteria

Each of these types of beliefs has an important and distinctive role to play in our ongoing efforts to organize and make sense of our world. As critical thinkers, we must learn to recognize each of these different types of beliefs and use them properly. Of course, it is often difficult and confusing to distinguish these types of beliefs because we rarely make an effort to try to separate them. Instead, the thinking activities of reporting, inferring, and judging tend to be woven together, organizing our world into a seamless fabric. Only when we make a special effort to reflect and think critically are we able to recognize these activities as being distinct.

In addition to recognizing and using these types of beliefs appropriately, thinking critically about these beliefs involves evaluating their basis and reliability: What is the reliability of the sources providing information for the *factual reports*? What is the probability that the *inference* is correct? What are the evidence and reasons that support the criteria used in the *judgment*? By distinguishing and critically evaluating these fundamental types of beliefs, we are able to improve their accuracy and effectiveness as we seek to make sense of our world.

Constructing Arguments **11**

**Recognizing
Arguments**
Cue words

**Constructing
Arguments**
Decide
Explain
Predict
Persuade

ARGUMENT:
A form of thinking in which
certain reasons are offered to
support a conclusion.

**Distinguishing Forms
of Arguments**

Deductive: Reasoning from premises
to a conclusion that
follows logically.

Inductive: Reasoning from premises
to a conclusion that does
not follow logically.

**Evaluating
Arguments**
Truth
Validity
Soundness

CONSIDER CAREFULLY the following discussion about whether marijuana should be legalized:

Dennis: Did you hear about the person who was sentenced to fifteen years in prison for possessing marijuana? I think this is one of the most outrageously unjust punishments I've ever heard of! In most states, people who are convicted of armed robbery, rape, or even murder don't receive fifteen-year sentences. And unlike the possession of marijuana, these crimes violate the rights of other people.

Caroline: I agree that this is one case in which the punishment doesn't seem to fit the crime. But you have to realize that drugs pose a serious threat to the young people of our country. Look at all the people who are addicted to drugs, who have their lives ruined, and who often die at an early age of overdoses. And think of all the crimes committed by people to support their drug habits. As a result, sometimes society has to make an example of someone — like the person you mentioned — to convince people of the seriousness of the situation.

Dennis: That's ridiculous. In the first place, it's not right to punish some-one unfairly just to provide an example. At least not in a society that believes in justice. And in the second place, smoking marijuana is noth-ing like using drugs such as heroin or even cocaine. It follows that smoking marijuana should not be against the law.

Caroline: I don't agree. Although marijuana might not be as dangerous as some other drugs, smoking it surely isn't good for you. And I don't think that anything that is a threat to your health should be legal.

Dennis: What about cigarettes and alcohol? We *know* that they are danger-ous. Medical research has linked smoking cigarettes to lung cancer, em-physema, and heart disease, and alcohol damages the liver. No one has proved that marijuana is a threat to our health. And even if it does turn out to be somewhat unhealthy, it's certainly not as dangerous as ciga-rettes and alcohol.

Caroline: That's a good point. But to tell you the truth, I'm not so sure that cigarettes and alcohol should be legal. And in any case, they are already legal. Just because cigarettes and alcohol are bad for your health is no reason to legalize another drug that can cause health problems.

Dennis: Look — life is full of risks. We take chances every time we cross the street or climb into our car. In fact, with all of these loonies on the road, driving is a lot more hazardous to our health than any of the drugs around. And many of the foods we eat can kill. For example, red meat contributes to heart disease, and artificial sweeteners can cause cancer. The point is, if people want to take chances with their health, that's up to them. And many people in our society like to mellow out with marijuana. I read somewhere that over 70 percent of the people in the United States think that marijuana should be legalized.

Caroline: There's a big difference between letting people drive cars and letting them use dangerous drugs. Society has a responsibility to protect people from themselves. People often do things that are foolish if they are encouraged or given the opportunity to. Legalizing something like marijuana encourages people to use it, especially young people. It follows that many more people would use marijuana if it were legalized. It's like society saying "This is all right — go ahead and use it."

Dennis: I still maintain that marijuana isn't dangerous. It's not addictive — like heroin is — and there is no evidence that it harms you. Consequently, anything that is harmless should be legal.

Caroline: Marijuana may not be physically addictive like heroin, but I think that it can be psychologically addictive, because people tend to use more and more of it over time. I know a number of people who spend a lot of their time getting high. What about Carl? All he does is lie around and get high. This shows that smoking it over a period of time definitely affects your mind. Think about the people you know who smoke a lot — don't they seem to be floating in a dream world? How are they ever going to make anything of their lives? As far as I'm concerned, a pothead is like a zombie — living but dead.

Dennis: Since you have had so little experience with marijuana, I don't think that you can offer an informed opinion on the subject. And anyway, if you do too much of anything it can hurt you. Even something as healthy as exercise can cause problems if you do too much of it. But I sure don't see anything wrong with toking up with some friends at a party or even getting into a relaxed state by yourself. In fact, I find that I can even concentrate better on my schoolwork after taking a little smoke.

Caroline: If you believe that, then marijuana really has damaged your brain. You're just trying to rationalize your drug habit. Smoking marijuana doesn't help you concentrate — it takes you away from reality. And I don't think that people can control it. Either you smoke and surrender control of your life, or you don't smoke because you want to retain control. There's nothing in between.

Dennis: Let me point out something to you. Because marijuana is illegal, organized crime controls its distribution and makes all the money out of it. If marijuana were legalized, the government could tax the sale of it — like cigarettes and alcohol — and then use the money for some worthwhile purpose. For example, many states have legalized gambling and use the money to support education. In fact, the major tobacco companies have already copyrighted names for different marijuana brands — like "Acapulco Gold." Obviously they believe that marijuana will soon become legal.

Caroline: Just because the government can make money out of something doesn't mean that they should legalize it. We could also legalize prostitution or muggings, and then tax the proceeds. Also, simply because the cigarette companies are prepared to sell marijuana doesn't mean that it makes sense to. After all, they're the ones who are selling us cigarettes.

Continue this dialogue, incorporating other views on the subject of legalizing marijuana.

Person A: _____

_____

Person B: _____

_____

Person A: _____

_____

Person B: _____

_____

Recognizing Arguments

The preceding discussion is an illustration of two people engaging in *dialogue,* which we have defined (in Chapter Two) as the systematic exchange of ideas. Participating in this sort of dialogue with others is one of the keys to thinking critically because it stimulates us to develop our minds by carefully examining the way we make sense of the world. Discussing issues with others encourages us to be mentally active, to ask questions, to view issues from different perspectives, and to develop reasons to support conclusions. It is this last quality of thinking critically — supporting conclusions with reasons — that we will focus on in this chapter and the next.

When we offer reasons to support a conclusion, we are considered to be presenting an *argument*.

> *Argument*   A form of thinking in which certain statements (reasons) are offered in support of another statement (a conclusion).

At the beginning of the dialogue, Dennis presents the following argument against imposing a fifteen-year sentence for possession of marijuana (argument 1):

Reason: Possessing marijuana is not a serious offense because it hurts no one.

Reason: There are many other more serious offenses in which victims' basic rights are violated — such as armed robbery, rape, and murder — for which the offenders don't receive such stiff sentences.

Conclusion: Therefore a fifteen-year sentence is an unjust punishment for possessing marijuana.

Can you identify an additional reason that supports this conclusion?

Reason: _____

The definition of *argument* given here is somewhat different from the meaning of the concept in our ordinary language. In common speech, "argument" usually refers to a dispute or quarrel between people, often involving intense feelings. (For example: "I got into a terrible argument with the idiot who hit the back of my car.") Very often these quarrels involve people presenting arguments in the sense we have defined the concept, although the arguments are usually not carefully reasoned or clearly stated because the people are so angry. Instead of this common usage, in this chapter we will use its more technical meaning.

Using our definition, we can define the main ideas that make up an argument:

> ***Reasons***   Statements that support another statement (known as a conclusion), justify it, or make it more probable.

> ***Conclusion***   A statement that explains, asserts, or predicts on the basis of statements (known as reasons) that are offered as evidence for it.

The type of thinking that uses argument — reasons in support of conclusions — is known as *reasoning*, and it is a type of thinking we have been doing throughout this book, as well as in much of our lives. We are continually trying to explain, justify, and predict things by the process of reasoning.

Of course, our reasoning — and the reasoning of others — is not always correct. For example, the reasons someone offers may not really support the conclusion they are supposed to. Or the conclusion may not really follow from the reasons stated. These difficulties are illustrated in a number of the arguments contained in the discussion on marijuana. Nevertheless, whenever we accept a conclusion as likely or true based on certain reasons or whenever we offer reasons to support a conclusion, we are using arguments to engage in reasoning — even if our reasoning is weak or faulty and needs to be improved. In these last two chapters we will be carefully exploring both the way we construct effective arguments and the way we evaluate arguments to develop and sharpen our reasoning ability.

Let us return to the discussion about marijuana. After Dennis presents the argument with the conclusion that the fifteen-year prison sentence is an unjust punishment, Caroline considers that argument. Although she acknowledges that in this case "the punishment doesn't seem to fit the crime," she goes on to offer another argument (argument 2), giving reasons that lead to a conclusion that conflicts with the one Dennis made:

Reason: Drugs pose a very serious threat to the young people of our country.

Reason: Many crimes are committed to support drug habits.

Conclusion: As a result, sometimes society has to make an example of someone to convince people of the seriousness of the situation.

Can you identify an additional reason that supports this conclusion?

Reason: _____

Cue Words for Arguments

Our language provides guidance in our efforts to identify reasons and conclusions. Certain key words, known as *cue words,* signal that a reason is being offered in support of a conclusion or that a conclusion is being announced on the basis of certain reasons. For example, in response to Caroline's conclusion that society sometimes has to make an example of someone to convince people of the seriousness of the situation, Dennis gives the following argument (argument 3):

Reason: In the first place, it's not right to punish someone unfairly just to provide an example.

Reason: In the second place, smoking marijuana is nothing like using drugs such as heroin or even cocaine.

Conclusion: It follows that smoking marijuana should not be against the law.

In this argument, the phrases "In the first place" and "In the second place" signal that reasons are being offered in support of a conclusion. Similarly, the phrase "It follows that" signals that a conclusion is being announced on the basis of certain reasons. Here is a list of the most commonly used cue words for reasons and conclusions:

Cue Words Signaling Reasons:

since	in view of
for	first, second
because	in the first (second) place
as shown by	may be inferred from
as indicated by	may be deduced from
given that	may be derived from
assuming that	for the reason that

Cue Words Signaling Conclusions:

therefore	then
thus	it follows that
hence	thereby showing
so	demonstrates that

(which) shows that	allows us to infer that
(which) proves that	suggests very strongly that
implies that	you see that
points to	leads me to believe that
as a result	allows us to deduce that
consequently	

Of course, identifying reasons, conclusions, and arguments involves more than looking for cue words. The words and phrases listed here do not always signal reasons and conclusions, and in many cases arguments are made without the use of cue words. Cue words, however, do help alert us that an argument is being made.

THINKING ACTIVITY

11.1 ▶ 1. Review the discussion on marijuana and underline any cue words signaling that reasons are being offered or that conclusions are being announced.

2. With the aid of cue words, identify the various arguments contained in the discussion on marijuana. For each argument, describe:

a. The *reasons* offered in support of a conclusion.

b. The *conclusion* announced on the basis of the reasons.

Before you start, review the three arguments we have examined so far in this chapter.

3. Go back to the additional arguments you wrote on page 498. Reorganize and add cue words if necessary to clearly identify your reasons as well as the conclusion you draw from those reasons. ◀

Arguments Are Inferences

When we construct arguments, we are composing and relating the world by means of our ability to infer. As we saw in Chapter Ten, *inferring* is a thinking process that we use to reason from what we already know (or believe to be the case) to new knowledge or beliefs. This is usually what we do when we construct arguments. We work from reasons we know or believe in to conclusions based on these reasons.

Just as we can use inferences to make sense of different types of situations, so we can also construct arguments for different purposes. In a variety of situations, we construct arguments to do the following:

- Decide
- Explain
- Predict
- Persuade

An example of each of these different types of arguments is given in the following sections. After each example, construct an argument of the same type.

We Construct Arguments to Decide

Reason: Throughout my life, I've always been interested in all different kinds of electricity.

Reason: There are many attractive job opportunities in the field of electrical engineering.

Conclusion: I will work toward becoming an electrical engineer.

Reason: _____

_____

Reason: _____

_____

Conclusion: _____

_____

We Construct Arguments to Explain

Reason: I was delayed leaving my house because my dog needed an emergency walking.

Reason: There was an unexpected traffic jam caused by motorists slowing down to view an overturned chicken truck.

Conclusion: Therefore I was late for our appointment.

Reason: _____

_____

Reason: _____

_____

Conclusion: _____

_____

We Construct Arguments to Predict

Reason: Some people will always drive faster than the speed limit allows, no matter whether the limit is 55 or 65 mph.

Reason: Car accidents are more likely at higher speeds.

Conclusion: It follows that the newly reinstated 65 mph limit will result in more accidents.

Reason: _____

_____

Reason: _____

_____

Conclusion: _____

_____

We Construct Arguments to Persuade

Reason: Chewing tobacco can lead to cancer of the mouth and throat.

Reason: Boys sometimes are led to begin chewing tobacco by ads for the product that feature sports heroes they admire.

Conclusion: Therefore, ads for chewing tobacco should be banned.

Reason: _____

_____

Reason: _____

_____

Conclusion: _____

_____

Evaluating Arguments

To construct an effective argument, we must be skilled in evaluating the effectiveness, or soundness, of arguments already constructed. We must investigate two aspects of each argument independently to determine the soundness of the argument as a whole:

1. How true are the reasons being offered to support the conclusion?
2. To what extent do the reasons support the conclusion or to what extent does the conclusion follow from the reasons offered?

We will first examine each of these ways of evaluating arguments separately and then see how they work together.

Truth: How True Are the Supporting Reasons?

The first aspect of the argument we must evaluate is the truth of the reasons that are being used to support a conclusion. Does each reason make sense? What evidence is being offered as part of each reason? Do I know each reason to be true based on my experience? Is each reason based on a source that can be trusted? We use these questions and others like them to analyze the reasons offered and to determine how true they are. As we saw in Chapter Five, *Believing and Knowing,* evaluating the sort of beliefs usually found as reasons in arguments is a complex and ongoing challenge. Let us evaluate the truth of the reasons presented in the discussion on pages 496–498.

Argument 1

Reason: Possessing marijuana is not a serious offense.

Evaluation: As it stands, this reason needs further evidence to support it. The major issue of the discussion is whether possessing (and using) marijuana is in fact a serious offense or no offense at all. This reason would be strengthened by stating: "Possessing marijuana is not as serious an offense as armed robbery, rape, and murder, according to the overwhelming majority of legal statutes and judicial decisions."

Reason: There are many other more serious offenses — such as armed robbery, rape, and murder — that don't receive such stiff sentences.

Evaluation: The accuracy of this reason is highly doubtful. It is true that there is wide variation in the sentences handed down for the same offense. The sentences vary from state to state and also vary within states and even within the same court. Nevertheless, on the whole, serious offenses like armed robbery, rape, and murder do receive long prison sentences. The real point here is that a fifteen-year sentence for possessing marijuana is extremely unusual when compared with other sentences for marijuana possession.

Argument 2

Reason: Drugs pose a very serious threat to the young people of our country.

Evaluation: As the later discussion points out, this statement is much too vague. "Drugs" cannot be treated as being all the same. Some drugs (such as aspirin) are beneficial, while other drugs (such as heroin) are highly dangerous. To strengthen this reason, we would have to be more specific, stating "Drugs like heroin, amphetamines, and cocaine pose a very serious threat to the young people of our country." We could increase the accuracy of the reason even more by adding the qualification *"some* of the young people of our country," because many young people are not involved with dangerous drugs.

Reason: Many crimes are committed to support drug habits.

Evaluation: _____

_____

_____

Argument 3

Reason: It's not right to punish someone unfairly just to provide an example.

Evaluation: This reason raises an interesting and complex ethical question that has been debated for centuries. The political theorist Machiavelli stated that "The ends justify the means," which implies that if we bring about desirable results it does not matter how we go about doing it. He would therefore probably disagree with this reason, since using someone as an example might bring about desirable results, even though it might be personally unfair to the person being used as an example. In our society, however, which is based on the idea of fairness under the law, most people would probably agree with this reason.

Reason: Smoking marijuana is nothing like using drugs such as heroin or even cocaine.

Evaluation: _____

_____

_____

_____

THINKING ACTIVITY

11.2 ▶ Review the other arguments from the discussion on marijuana that you identified on page 498. Evaluate the truth of each of the reasons contained in the arguments. ◀

Validity: Do the Reasons Support the Conclusion?

In addition to determining whether the reasons are true, evaluating arguments involves investigating the *relationship* between the reasons and the conclusion. When the reasons support the conclusion, so that the conclusion follows from the reasons being offered, the argument is *valid.** If, however, the reasons do *not* support the conclusion so that the conclusion does *not* follow from the reasons being offered, the argument is *invalid.*

Valid Argument   Argument in which the reasons support the conclusion so that the conclusion follows from the reasons offered.

Invalid Argument   Argument in which the reasons do not support the conclusion so that the conclusion does *not* follow from the reasons offered.

---

*In formal logic, the term *validity* is reserved for deductively valid arguments in which the conclusions follow necessarily from the premises. (See the discussion of deductive arguments later in this chapter.)

One way to focus on the concept of validity is to *assume* that all the reasons in the argument are true and then try to determine how probable they make the conclusion.

The following is an example of one type of valid argument:

Reason: Anything that is a threat to our health should not be legal.

Reason: Marijuana is a threat to our health.

Conclusion: Therefore marijuana should not be legal.

This is a valid argument because, if we assume that the reasons are true, then the conclusion necessarily follows. Of course, we may not agree that either or both of the reasons are true and so not agree with the conclusion. Nevertheless, the *structure* of the argument is valid. This particular form of thinking is known as *deduction*, and we will examine deductive reasoning more closely in the pages ahead.

The following is a different type of argument:

Reason: As part of a project in my social science class, we selected 100 students in the school to be interviewed. We took special steps to ensure that these students were representative of the student body as a whole (total students: 4,386). We asked the selected students whether they thought the United States should actively try to overthrow foreign governments that the United States disapproves of. Of the 100 students interviewed, 88 students said the United States should definitely *not* be involved in such activities.

Conclusion: We can conclude that most students in the school believe the United States should not be engaged in attempts to actively overthrow foreign governments that the United States disapproves of.

This is a good argument because, if we assume that the reason is true, then it provides strong support for the conclusion. In this case, the key part of the reason is the statement that the 100 students selected were representative of the entire 4,386 students at the school. To evaluate the truth of the reason, we might want to investigate the procedure used to select the 100 students to determine whether this sample was in fact representative of all the students. This particular form of thinking is an example of *induction*, and we will explore inductive reasoning more fully in Chapter Twelve, *Reasoning Critically.*

The following argument is an example of an invalid argument.

> *Reason:* George Bush believes that the Stealth Bomber should be built to ensure America's national defense, providing the capability of undetected bombing attacks.
>
> *Reason:* George Bush is the president of the United States.
>
> *Conclusion:* Therefore the Stealth Bomber should be built.

This argument is *not* valid because even if we assume that the reasons are true, the conclusion does not follow. Although George Bush is the president of the United States, the fact does not give him any special expertise on the subject of sophisticated radar designs for weapon systems. Indeed, this is a subject of such complexity and global significance that it should not be based on any one person's opinion, no matter who that person is. This form of invalid thinking is a type of *fallacy*, and we will investigate fallacious reasoning in Chapter Twelve.

The Soundness of Arguments

When an argument includes both true reasons and a valid structure, the argument is considered to be *sound*. When an argument has either false reasons or an invalid structure, however, the argument is considered to be *unsound*.

True reasons Valid structure	⟶ Sound argument
False reasons Valid structure	⟶ Unsound argument
True reasons Invalid structure	⟶ Unsound argument
False reasons Invalid structure	⟶ Unsound argument

From this chart, we can see that, in terms of arguments, "truth" and "validity" are not the same concepts. An argument can have true reasons and an invalid structure or false reasons and a valid structure. In both cases the argument is *unsound*. To be sound, an argument must have *both* true reasons and a valid structure. For example, consider the following argument:

Reason: For a democracy to function most effectively, the citizens should be able to think critically about the important social and political issues.

Reason: Education plays a key role in developing critical thinking abilities.

Conclusion: Therefore education plays a key role in ensuring that a democracy is functioning most effectively.

A good case could be made for the soundness of this argument because the reasons are persuasive and the argument structure is valid. Of course, someone might contend that one or both of the reasons are not completely true, which illustrates an important point about the arguments we construct and evaluate. Many of the arguments we encounter in life fall somewhere between complete soundness and complete unsoundness because we are often not sure if our reasons are completely true. Throughout this book we have found that developing accurate beliefs is an ongoing process and that our beliefs are subject to clarification and revision. As a result, the conclusion of any argument can be only as certain as the reasons supporting the conclusion.

To sum up, evaluating arguments effectively involves both the truth of the reasons and the validity of the argument structure. The degree of soundness an argument has depends on how accurate our reasons turn out to be and how valid the argument's structure is.

THINKING ACTIVITY
_____

11.3 ▶ The AIDS epidemic that has developed in the United States and in many parts of the world is rapidly becoming a public health crisis. Some people believe that in such a crisis situation, protecting the public welfare is most important and that mandatory testing for the disease is a necessary part of this initiative. Other people disagree with this view, insisting that the rights of individuals should not be violated in this way and that any testing should be voluntary.

These complex and important issues are discussed in the following two essays. After carefully reading them, answer the questions that follow.

PROTECT THE PUBLIC HEALTH *by Kirk Kidwell*

According to medical experts meeting in Washington, U.S. public health authorities have failed to control the Aids epidemic because they have refused to implement traditional public health strategies.

The National Conference on HIV was organized by doctors who were concerned with the way the medical knowledge was managed at last

June's [1987] Third International AIDS Conference. It was held November 15th–18th [1987] and was attended by more than 300 medical authorities. Speakers at the National Conference on HIV included Dr. Robert Gallo of the National Cancer Institute, Education Secretary William J. Bennett, White House Domestic Policy Advisor Gary Bauer, presidential AIDS Commission members Cory Servaas and Theresa Crenshaw, and Congressmen William Dannemeyer (R–CA) and Dan Burton (R–IN). . . .

"Public health efforts to date have failed," Colonel Donald S. Burke, a virologist who serves as Chief of the Department of Virus Diseases at the Walter Reed Army Institute of Research, told the conference. Dr. Burke based his assertion on recent findings from the Army's Aids testing program for new recruits. The Army results show a male-to-female ratio among newly infected young adults of less than three to one, compared to the ratio among current Aids patients of 13 to one.

New infections, Burke said, are most common among men in their late teens and early twenties. The Army found that one out of every two hundred men (0.5 percent) aged 25 years was infected with the Aids virus. Among blacks the infection rate was far higher, with nearly two percent of 25-year-old black men testing positive for the Human Immunodeficiency Virus (HIV) that causes Aids.

The number of new infections detected by the Army has increased over the past year [1986–87]. This is especially apparent, Burke said, when new recruits are followed by birth year. For example, of recruits born in 1967 more tested positive for the virus in March 1987 than in October 1985, when the Army's testing program began. Among black men, Burke reported, HIV infections are doubling every three years.

Burke's conclusions conflict with reports that the overall infection rate among military recruits is holding constant. (On May 15, 1987, the federal Centers for Disease Control reported that the HIV infection rate had remained relatively constant at 1.5 per 1,000 individuals over the previous year and a half.) Dr. Burke explained this discrepancy as the result of two factors: First, the CDC did not track the testing data by birth year, thereby giving an appearance of constant rates within age groups. Second, based on anecdotal reports from alternative testing sites, men and women thinking of applying to the military are having themselves tested anonymously before applying. Thus, the data derived from the military recruit testing program is based to some extent upon a prescreened population.

"The incidence of HIV infection is increasing compared to past results," Burke concluded, "particularly in certain segments of the population. These are not in the traditional high-risk groups of the past." The growing number of new infections portends an increasing number of Aids cases in the coming decade, he said, with 100,000 to 200,000 new cases reported each year through the 1990s.

The effort to contain the Aids epidemic has failed, in part, because public health officials have focused on current cases of Aids instead of infection with the Aids virus, Burke explained. The current focus on Aids cases has meant that health authorities are as much as a decade behind the epidemic. Present Aids cases are of only historical interest when it comes to formulating a public health response to the disease, Burke said, since persons infected with the Aids virus remain symptomless for five to ten years after they are infected.

Public health efforts must begin to focus on HIV infection, not Aids cases, Burke and others at the conference urged. "The Aids epidemic of 1997 has already happened," Dr. Robert Redfield, also of the Walter Reed Army Institute of Research, observed, "but we really don't know today how bad it is."

Dr. Vernon Mark, a neurosurgeon from Boston . . . agreed, noting that the current effort to control the Aids epidemic is crippled by "lapses in our scientific knowledge" of the disease. Specifically, Mark pointed out that public health officials do not know how many people are infected, who has it, or how fast it is spreading.

The only way to determine this vital information, he said, is to conduct random, anonymous blood samplings of the American population regularly. In June, President Reagan asked the Public Health Service to initiate this type of survey. Yet PHS officials were reluctant to undertake this project after an initial telephone survey of 2,000 Americans revealed that 30 percent would refuse to be tested. But Dr. Mark argued that the true significance of this survey is that the vast majority of Americans would cooperate. "Think what President Reagan could do on contra aid with 70 percent of the American people backing him," Mark commented.

Instead of conducting a random, anonymous Aids survey, Administration officials now plan to expand secret Aids testing of hospital patients. Currently, the Centers for Disease Control test patients without their knowledge at four midwestern hospitals. According to a November 17, 1987 article in *The Washington Times,* the U.S. Department of Health and Human Services plans to expand the number of hospitals in this "sentinel" program to seven by the end of November [1987] and to 30 by next May [1988].

Beyond the issue of a random blood survey to determine the incidence of Aids infection in the United States, experts at the National Conference on HIV called for increased routine Aids testing. Dr. Redfield and others suggested that an Aids test should become a routine blood test administered whenever a patient visits a physician or hospital for a medical problem. Like other routine blood tests, the Aids tests should not require written informed consent before being performed and could be refused by the patient.

Routine testing is important, Dr. Redfield explained, not only as a public health measure but also as a tool to facilitate optimum health care for HIV carriers. "HIV infection is not a mystery anymore," he said. "Its course is predictable." Redfield emphasized that, while HIV infection is not curable, it is treatable and therefore early diagnosis of HIV disease is crucial. "Medicine has never denied itself the use of tools that science has provided them," he noted. "This is unprecedented."

In addition to routine Aids testing in a clinical setting, conference participants agreed that mandatory Aids testing should be implemented in some circumstances. Mandatory testing of prisoners, especially those convicted of prostitution or drug-related crimes, generated widespread support at the conference, as did premarital testing for Aids. Some participants also urged mandatory testing of women visiting their gynecologist or obstetrician. Others suggested that Aids testing should be mandatory for surgery patients.

Critics of mandatory and/or routine testing have charged that such programs would be costly, inaccurate, and unworkable. For example, an article that appeared in the *Journal of the American Medical Association* (October 2, 1987) concluded that "Mandatory premarital screening in a population with a low prevalence of infection is a relatively ineffective and inefficient use of resources." This study predicted that testing of the estimated 3.8 million persons who married each year would cost more than $23 million and would result in at least 100 infected individuals being told they were not infected and over 350 persons erroneously told they were infected.

Yet, experts attending the National Conference on HIV dismissed such conclusions as blind estimates based upon assumptions. Dr. S. Gerald Sandler, Associate Vice President of the American Red Cross, told conference participants that, based on the experience of the Red Cross, the blood screening tests are "workable, highly reliable and accurate. . . . [The tests] can be recommended as a lab test for low prevalence populations." The Red Cross currently tests an estimated 13 million units of blood each year.

The U.S. military has also found the Aids tests to be accurate and inexpensive. According to Dr. Donald S. Burke, the U.S. Army performs more than 100,000 Aids tests each month at a cost of four dollars per specimen. The entire series of tests takes only 72 hours to perform. The Army has not found any false negative results and the false positive rate has been extremely low — one out of 135,000 persons tested. Based on the Army's experience, premarital testing would cost $15 million per year and would result in virtually no infected persons being told they were uninfected and only 28 persons being falsely informed of a positive test.

Dr. Burke outlined several reasons to implement routine Aids testing. First, rapid, accurate, low-cost Aids screening is available. Second, the national prevalence of HIV is high enough to warrant screening programs. Even using the military data, based essentially upon a prescreened population, at least one in 600 men and one in 1,600 women are infected. Third, voluntary, anonymous testing at VD clinics and elsewhere will not detect the vast majority of infected individuals. Eighty percent of the infected recruits detected by the Army's mass screening program were at the earliest stages of HIV infection — stages at which there are no manifested signs of infection. Finally, Aids has expanded beyond the high-risk groups. Today's Aids cases represent the HIV epidemic of five to ten years ago, Burke reminded the conference. Current data show that HIV infection is spreading among heterosexuals at an increasing rate.

The consensus of opinion among participants at the conference was in favor of widespread routine Aids testing. Education Secretary William J. Bennett, a keynote speaker at the conference, observed:

> There is now substantial agreement . . . on important principles related to testing. Principles like, the more testing we do, the more we will learn about the virus and the more we will be able to do to stop the spread of the virus; and that the more routine — and hence, the more acceptable — Aids testing becomes, the less is the chance that a stigma might be attached to the test itself.

Dr. Burke concluded: "Routine testing can be a powerful public health measure to control the Aids epidemic." Yet, the longer officials responsible for protecting the public's health delay the implementation of routine testing and other public health measures, the longer the Aids epidemic will rage unchecked. ■

WHY MANDATORY TESTING IS A BAD IDEA
by Harvey V. Fineberg and Mary E. Wilson

The acquired immunodeficiency syndrome (AIDS) scares all of us. First recognized in 1981, AIDS has afflicted more than 40,000 Americans and many thousands more worldwide. No one who has developed AIDS has recovered from it. The disease is caused by a virus called the human immunodeficiency virus (HIV), a recalcitrant and subtle pathogen, the HIV renders the body susceptible to other infections and to some forms of cancer; it can also cause dementia. The HIV is known to be spread by sexual intercourse (genital, anal, and oral) and by blood-to-blood transmission as occurs in the sharing of needles and syringes by intravenous drug users. The virus may also be passed from an infected mother to her infant.

One of the more sinister aspects of the AIDS epidemic is the silent nature of the infection. A person who becomes infected with the HIV is then capable of transmitting it to others, yet may have no symptoms of disease for five years or even longer. The number of asymptomatic carriers of the HIV is believed to be many times the number of patients with clinical AIDS, leading to estimates of between one and two million infected persons in the United States. These symptom-free carriers are most likely concentrated in the same groups that comprise most current AIDS patients — men (and in much smaller numbers, women) exposed sexually to infected men, and drug users who share needles. While every state has reported some cases of AIDS, the largest numbers are located in the urban areas of California and New York.

The presence of infection, whether symptomatic or not, may be detected by blood tests for antibodies to the HIV. . . .

At this time, the two most commonly used HIV antibody tests are the enzyme immunoassay (EIA) and the Western blot. The EIA is generally used for initial screening, and the more difficult and expensive Western blot is reserved for retesting the EIA-positive sera. Compared to most medical tests, the HIV antibody tests are very accurate — more than 99 percent accuracy is currently claimed by some EIA manufacturers.

A person who is infected with the HIV is at risk of developing AIDS, a diagnosis based on clinical findings, such as infection with the opportunistic pathogen *Pneumocystis carinii*. Presence of a positive test for HIV antibodies (often imprecisely described as the AIDS test or AIDS antibodies) does not mean that a person has AIDS. It appears that approximately 25 percent of persons infected with the HIV will develop AIDS within five years. What percentage of such persons will ultimately develop AIDS, time alone will tell. Ongoing studies show continued (perhaps even accelerated) risk of clinical disease with the passage of time.

Everyone concerned with the health of the public is eager to take any effective and appropriate measure that could curb the spread of the AIDS epidemic. Testing for an antibody to the HIV can potentially help track the spread of the epidemic and has already helped to contain it. For example, since the spring of 1985, when the HIV antibody tests were first applied to donated blood, the blood supply has become much safer, and the risk of transmission of the HIV to a recipient of blood products is now extremely small. The test is also a critical part of the evaluation of patients who have illnesses or clinical findings that may be the result of HIV infection. Testing for HIV antibody is now part of the evaluation of a prospective organ or semen donor. The antibody tests have also been used to study hundreds of health care workers who have been accidentally exposed by needle-stick to a patient with the HIV, and results have established that the risk of transmission by such exposure is less than 1 percent.

Some people would like to see tests for the HIV applied much more widely and in a compulsory way to try to identify nearly all who are infected. The logic seems straightforward and is deceptively appealing. All responsible persons who know they are infected will of course want to avoid transmitting the virus and will be especially motivated to learn how to do so. Knowing who is infected might enable society to take steps beyond education to protect others, though exactly what might be done on a large scale is not at all clear. Columnist William Buckley once proposed tattooing everyone who has a positive test for the HIV. In Cuba, persons with positive tests are reportedly isolated in special confinement facilities. A recent Gallup Poll reported in the *New York Times* on August 30, 1987, found 60 percent of the public agreed with the statement "People with the AIDS virus should be made to carry a card to this effect," and 33 percent said employers should be able to dismiss employees with the AIDS virus.

In fact, there is no medical or scientific justification for discriminating in employment, housing, or education against persons who carry the HIV. To think otherwise is to ignore the epidemiology of the disease or to react with emotion rather than reason. Studies of family members living in daily contact with patients who are infected with the HIV have found no cases of transmission to those who are not the sexual partners of the patients. A child who carries the HIV poses no risk of infection through everyday contact with teachers and classmates.

One proposal for mandatory AIDS testing that is attracting a good deal of political attention is to require an HIV antibody test before marriage. This sounds similar to the familiar premarital serology screening for syphilis, required in most states since the late 1940s. . . .

Mandatory premarital testing for AIDS today would, in fact, do a lot more harm than good. The problems are serious both in theory and in practice. Key to understanding these problems is a basic principle: Even a highly accurate test sequence for HIV antibodies will produce an unacceptable proportion of falsely positive results when applied to a population with a very low prevalence of HIV infection. This paradoxical effect is an inevitable consequence of applying even very good tests to the wrong population.

Surprising as it may seem, a test can be correctly described as more than 99 percent accurate and still produce a 50 percent or higher rate of error among the positive results. At the present time, the frequency of HIV infection among blood donors is estimated to be approximately 4 per 10,000. This may be a reasonable starting place as an estimate of the current prevalence of infection in the United States among men and women who are about to be married. Suppose that the HIV antibody test sequence were 100 percent accurate in detecting people with infection (a generous assumption, considering that measurable levels of antibody are not present for several weeks to several months following infection). Suppose also that the test sequence is 99.8 percent correct in labeling as negative those people who are truly not infected. Then, if we tested 100,000 men and women before marriage, the test would be correctly positive in all 40 who are infected. Among the 99,960 who are truly not infected, the test would correctly label as negative 99.8 percent or approximately 99,760. This would leave approximately 200 (99,960 minus 99,760) *falsely* labeled as positive. Thus, in this illustration, among the 240 positive results, more than 80 percent would be false-positives.

A more complete and detailed analysis of the sequential use of EIA and Western blot in the low-risk, premarital population might produce a false-positive to true-positive ratio of one to three. But is this proportion of error a price we should be willing to pay? Imagine what such false-positive results would mean to the lives of prospective brides or grooms. A blood bank can well afford to discard needlessly four or five units of blood along with every one truly infected with the HIV if that helps ensure that virtually all remaining blood units are free of the HIV. We should be much more reluctant to discard, wrongly, a lifetime of hopes and dreams in a young couple.

Mandatory premarital screening would also be a relatively ineffective and expensive means of combating the AIDS epidemic. Since most of those infected are men who engage in homosexual behavior and intravenous drug users, looking for the HIV among all premarital couples is a bit like fishing for shrimp in Lake Erie. In the case of syphilis, the incidence of undetected disease by the late 1970s had declined to the point that premarital serologies were producing more false-positive than true-positive results, the costs per detected case were high, and several states ended mandatory premarital screening. If all 3.5 million Americans planning to be married in a year were tested for antibodies to the HIV, less than 1 percent of those currently estimated to be infected with the HIV would be identified. Even among those who are infected, the capacity to reduce sexual transmission of the HIV by premarital screening would be limited, because the majority of young people today report they have had sexual relations prior to the age of marriage. The cost of mounting a proper testing program, including adequate quality control and counseling, would easily exceed $100 million per year. And there are many better ways that money could be spent — in research, in education of the public about AIDS and how to prevent it, and in innovative and compassionate ways of caring for patients with AIDS, to name a few.

Testing is no substitute for education and change in high-risk behavior. In a group at very high risk of infection, such as active homosexuals with multiple partners, application of tests can produce up to several percent of false results among those who test *negative*. This false reassurance in a high-risk group is the flip side of the problem of false-positives in the low-risk premarital population. The false negative results are in part due to the lag of several weeks to months after infection in the development of measurable antibodies. Even a correct negative antibody test is valid only for that moment and not for the future.

If persons who have engaged in high-risk behavior test negative, they must not deceive themselves in thinking that they are somehow magically protected regardless of what they do. The only way they can protect themselves — and others — is by changing their behavior. This message is a truth that needs no adornment by a blood test. Testing will not stop the epidemic; change in behavior will.

Testing for HIV infection will be an essential part of systematic surveillance of the spread of AIDS. Such a surveillance program should be based on scientifically selected samples of the pertinent age, gender, ethnic, and geographic populations. There is no reason why such surveillance testing cannot be conducted in a fully confidential and anonymous fashion. The public purpose of such testing is to gain timely information on the incidence and geographic distribution of infection and to gauge the success of interventions to limit spread. . . .

Testing is, after all, a tool, not a goal. It is a tool that should be used as part of a concerted effort to contend with and contain the AIDS epidemic: compassionate and cost-sensitive care of patients, extensive education to reduce high-risk behavior, and an intensive search for better treatment and an effective vaccine.

Policy decisions about testing for the HIV in the future need to take into account possible changes in the epidemiology of AIDS, possible improvements in the performance or cost of tests, and potential development of treatment that would benefit an asymptomatic HIV carrier. Each of these would alter the balance of benefits, risks, and costs connected with testing for HIV. Judged on this balance, decisions about testing would change in accordance with new knowledge and technology.

A continuing challenge to responsible public officials is to preserve the rights of persons who are believed to carry the AIDS virus or who have clinical disease, while at the same time protecting the legitimate health interests of the community. This requires leadership at national, state, and local levels and education about the HIV, how it is spread, and what it can and cannot do. The recent, tragic experience of the Ray family in Arcadia, Florida, depicts a failure of leadership and of community education.

Since many people whose behavior has put them at risk of HIV infection should be tested, there is a compelling need for strong legislation to protect the confidentiality of test results and to bar discrimination in education, housing, and employment against those who carry the AIDS virus. . . .

A foe as frightening and elusive as AIDS challenges us to rely on rational analysis, sustained commitment of resources, and appropriate use of every means at our disposal, including tests for the HIV. At the present time, mandatory premarital screening or universal testing for HIV is neither sensible nor worthwhile. Rather, a selective, voluntary program of expanded testing is the way to go. ■

1. Identify the key arguments presented by the authors of the two essays and summarize the reasons and conclusion for each argument.

2. Judge the soundness of each of the arguments that you identified by:

   a. Evaluating the truth of the reasons.

   b. Evaluating the validity of the argument, that is, the degree to which the conclusion is supported by the reasons.

3. Construct at least one additional argument for each side of this issue. ◀

Forms of Arguments

We use a number of basic argument forms to organize, relate, and make sense of the world. As we noted, two of the major types of argument forms are *deductive arguments* and *inductive arguments*. In the remainder of this chapter we will explore various types of deductive arguments, reserving our analysis of inductive arguments for Chapter Twelve.

Deductive Arguments

The deductive argument is the one most commonly associated with the study of logic. Though it has a variety of valid forms, they all share one characteristic: If you accept the supporting reasons (also called *premises*) as true, then you must necessarily accept the conclusion as true.

> **Deductive Argument**   Argument form in which one reasons from premises that are known or assumed to be true to a conclusion that follows logically from these premises.

For example, consider the following famous deductive argument:

Reason/Premise: All men are mortal.

Reason/Premise: Socrates is a man.

Conclusion: Therefore Socrates is mortal.

In this example of deductive thinking, accepting the premises of the argument as true means that the conclusion necessarily follows; it cannot be false. Many deductive arguments, like the one just given, are structured as *syllo-*

gisms, an argument form that consists of two supporting premises and a conclusion. There are also, however, a large number of *invalid* deductive forms, one of which is illustrated in Woody Allen's syllogism:

Reason/Premise: All men are mortal.

Reason/Premise: Socrates is a man.

Conclusion: Therefore all men are Socrates.

In the next several pages, we will briefly examine some common valid deductive forms.

Applying a General Rule   Whenever we reason with the form illustrated by the valid Socrates syllogism, we are using the following argument structure:

Premise: All *A* (men) are *B* (mortal).

Premise: *S* is an *A* (Socrates is a man).

Conclusion: Therefore *S* is *B* (Socrates is mortal).

This basic argument form is valid no matter what terms are included. For example:

Premise: All politicians are untrustworthy.

Premise: Bill White is a politician.

Conclusion: Therefore, Bill White is untrustworthy.

Notice again that, with any valid deductive form, *if* we assume that the premises are true, then we must accept the conclusion. Of course, in this case there is considerable doubt that the first premise is actually true.

When we diagram this argument form, it becomes clear why it is a valid way of thinking:

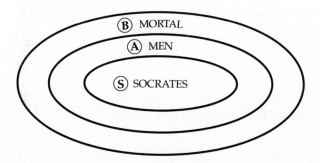

The *first premise* states that classification *A* (men) falls within classification *B* (mortal).

The *second premise* states that *S* (Socrates) is a member of classification *A* (men).

The *conclusion* simply states what has now become obvious — namely, that *S* (Socrates) must fall within classification *B* (mortal).

Although we are usually not aware of it, we use this basic type of reasoning whenever we apply a general rule in the form *All A is B*. For instance:

Premise: All children eight years old should be in bed by 9:30 P.M.

Premise: You are an eight-year-old child.

Conclusion: Therefore you should be in bed by 9:30 P.M.

Review the dialogue at the beginning of this chapter and see if you can identify a deductive argument that uses this form.

Premise: _____

Premise: _____

Conclusion: _____

Describe an example from your own experience in which you use this deductive form.

Premise: _____

Premise: _____

Conclusion: _____

Modus Ponens   Another valid deductive form that we commonly use in our thinking goes by the name *modus ponens* — that is, "affirming the antecedent" — and is illustrated in the following example:

Premise: If I have prepared thoroughly for the final exam, then I will do well.

Premise: I prepared thoroughly for the exam.

Conclusion: Therefore I will do well on the exam.

When we reason like this, we are using the following argument structure:

Premise: If *A* (I have prepared thoroughly), then *B* (I will do well).

Premise: *A* (I have prepared thoroughly).

Conclusion: Therefore *B* (I will do well).

Like all valid deductive forms, this form is valid no matter what specific terms are included. For example:

Premise: If the Democrats are able to register 20 million new voters, then they will win the presidential election.

Premise: The Democrats were able to register more than 20 million new voters.

Conclusion: Therefore the Democrats will win the presidential election.

As with other valid argument forms, the conclusion will be true *if* the reasons are true. Although the second premise in this argument expresses information which can be verified, the first premise would be more difficult to establish.

Review the dialogue at the beginning of this chapter and see if you can identify any deductive arguments that use this form.

Premise: _____

Premise: _____

Conclusion: _____

Modus Tollens   A third commonly used valid deductive form has the name *modus tollens* — that is, "denying the consequence" — and is illustrated in the following example:

Premise: If Michael were a really good friend, he would lend me his car for the weekend.

Premise: Michael refuses to lend me his car for the weekend.

Conclusion: Therefore Michael is not a really good friend.

When we reason in this fashion, we are using the following argument structure:

Premise: If *A* (Michael is a really good friend), then *B* (He will lend me his car).

Premise: Not *B* (He won't lend me his car).

Conclusion: Therefore not *A* (He's not a really good friend).

Again, like other valid reasoning forms, this form is valid no matter what subject is being considered. For instance:

Premise: If Iraq were genuinely interested in world peace, it would not have invaded Kuwait.

Premise: Iraq did invade Kuwait (that is, Iraq did not "not invade" Kuwait).

Conclusion: Therefore Iraq is not genuinely interested in world peace.

This conclusion — and any other conclusion produced by this form of reasoning — can be considered accurate if the reasons are true. In this case, the second premise would probably be easier to verify than the first.

Review the dialogue at the beginning of this chapter and see if you can identify any deductive arguments that use this reasoning form.

Premise: _____

Premise: _____

Conclusion: _____

Disjunctive Syllogism   A fourth common form of a valid deductive argument is known as a *disjunctive syllogism*. The term *disjunctive* means presenting several alternatives. This form is illustrated in the following example:

Premise: Either I left my wallet on my dresser or I have lost it.

Premise: The wallet is not on my dresser.

Conclusion: Therefore I must have lost it.

When we reason in this way, we are using the following argument structure:

Premise: Either *A* (I left my wallet on my dresser) or *B* (I have lost it).

Premise: Not *A* (I didn't leave it on my dresser).

Conclusion: Therefore *B* (I have lost it).

This valid reasoning form can be applied to any number of situations and still yield valid results. For example:

Premise: Either your stomach trouble is caused by what you are eating or it is caused by nervous tension.

Premise: You tell me that you have been taking special care with your diet.

Conclusion: Therefore your stomach trouble is caused by nervous tension.

To determine the accuracy of the conclusion, we must determine the accuracy of the premises. If they are true, then the conclusion must be true.

Review the dialogue at the beginning of this chapter and see if you can identify any deductive arguments that use this reasoning form.

Premise: _____

Premise: _____

Conclusion: _____

All these basic argument forms — applying a general rule, *modus ponens,* *modus tollens,* and disjunctive syllogism — are found not only in informal, everyday conversations but also at more formal levels of thinking. They appear in academic disciplines, in scientific inquiry, in debates on social issues, and so on. Many other argument forms — both deductive and inductive — also constitute human reasoning. By sharpening our understanding of these ways of thinking, we are better able to make sense of the world by constructing and evaluating effective arguments.

THINKING ACTIVITY

11.4 ▶ Read the following arguments and choose one or two of them to analyze. For each argument you have selected:

1. Summarize the reasons and conclusions given.
2. Identify which, if any, of the following deductive argument forms are used.
   - Applying a general rule
   - *Modus ponens* (affirming the antecedent)
   - *Modus tollens* (denying the consequence)
   - Disjunctive syllogism
3. Evaluate the truth of the reasons that support the conclusion.

> For if the brain is a machine of ten billion nerve cells and the mind can somehow be explained as the summed activity of a finite number of

chemical and electrical reactions, [then] boundaries limit the human prospect — we are biological and our souls cannot fly free.

Edward O. Wilson, *On Human Nature*

The state is by nature clearly prior to the family and to the individual, since the whole is of necessity prior to the part.

Aristotle, *Politics*

There now is sophisticated research that strongly suggests a deterrent effect [of capital punishment]. Furthermore, the principal argument against the deterrent effect is weak. The argument is that in most jurisdictions where capital punishment has been abolished there has been no immediate, sharp increase in what had been capital crimes. But in those jurisdictions, the actual act of abolition was an insignificant event because for years the death penalty had been imposed rarely, if at all. Common sense — which deserves deference until it is refuted — suggests that the fear of death can deter some premeditated crimes, including some murders.

George F. Will, *Cleveland Plain-Dealer*, March 13, 1981

If the increased power which science has conferred upon human volitions is to be a boon and not a curse, the ends to which these volitions are directed must grow commensurately with the growth of power to carry them out. Hitherto, although we have been told on Sundays to love our neighbor, we have been told on weekdays to hate him, and there are six times as many weekdays as Sundays. Hitherto, the harm that we could do to our neighbor by hating him was limited by our incompetence, but in the new world upon which we are entering there will be no such limit, and the indulgence of hatred can lead only to ultimate and complete disaster.

Bertrand Russell, "The Expanding Mental Universe"

The extreme vulnerability of a complex industrial society to intelligent, targeted terrorism by a very small number of people may prove the fatal challenge to which Western states have no adequate response. Counterforce alone will never suffice. The real challenge of the true terrorist is to the basic values of a society. If there is no commitment to shared values in Western society — and if none are imparted in our amoral institutions of higher learning — no increase in police and burglar alarms will suffice to preserve our society from the specter that haunts us — not a bomb from above but a gun from within.

James Billington, "The Gun Within"

To fully believe in something, to truly understand something, one must be intimately acquainted with its opposite. One should not adopt a creed by default, because no alternative is known. Education should prepare students for the "real world" not by segregating them from evil but by urging full confrontation to test and modify the validity of the good.

Robert Baron, "In Defense of 'Teaching' Racism, Sexism, and Fascism"

The inescapable conclusion is that society secretly *wants* crime, *needs* crime, and gains definite satisfactions from the present mishandling of it! We condemn crime; we punish offenders for it; but we need it. The crime and punishment ritual is a part of our lives. We need crimes to wonder at, to enjoy vicariously, to discuss and speculate about, and to publicly deplore. We need criminals to identify ourselves with, to envy secretly, and to punish stoutly. They do for us the forbidden, illegal things we *wish* to do and, like scapegoats of old, they bear the burdens of our displaced guilt and punishment — "the iniquities of us all."

Karl Menninger, "The Crime of Punishment" ◀

THINKING ACTIVITY

11.5 ▶ The following articles present two opposing sets of arguments regarding capital punishment. The first article, written by former New York City Mayor Edward I. Koch, gives reasons for supporting capital punishment. The second article, written by South Carolina attorney David Bruck, gives reasons for opposing capital punishment. Read the articles and complete the activities that follow.

DEATH AND JUSTICE:
HOW CAPITAL PUNISHMENT AFFIRMS LIFE *by Edward I. Koch*

Last December a man named Robert Lee Willie, who had been convicted of raping and murdering an 18-year-old woman, was executed in the Louisiana state prison. In a statement issued several minutes before his death, Mr. Willie said: "Killing people is wrong. . . . It makes no difference whether it's citizens, countries, or governments. Killing is wrong." Two weeks later in South Carolina, an admitted killer named Joseph Carl Shaw was put to death for murdering two teenagers. In an appeal to the governor for clemency, Mr. Shaw wrote: "Killing is wrong when

I did it. Killing is wrong when you do it. I hope you have the courage and moral strength to stop the killing."

It is a curiosity of modern life that we find ourselves being lectured on morality by cold-blooded killers. Mr. Willie previously had been convicted of aggravated rape, aggravated kidnapping, and the murders of a Louisiana deputy and a man from Missouri. Mr. Shaw committed another murder a week before the two for which he was executed, and admitted mutilating the body of the 14-year-old girl he killed. I can't help wondering what prompted these murderers to speak out against killing as they entered the deathhouse door. Did their newfound reverence for life stem from the realization that they were about to lose their own?

Life is indeed precious, and I believe the death penalty helps to affirm this fact. Had the death penalty been a real possibility in the minds of these murderers, they might well have stayed their hand. They might have shown moral awareness before their victims died, and not after. Consider the tragic death of Rosa Velez, who happened to be home when a man named Luis Vera burglarized her apartment in Brooklyn. "Yeah, I shot her," Vera admitted. "She knew me, and I knew I wouldn't go to the chair."

During my twenty-two years in public service, I have heard the pros and cons of capital punishment expressed with special intensity. As a district leader, councilman, congressman, and mayor, I have represented constituencies generally thought of as liberal. Because I support the death penalty for heinous crimes of murder, I have sometimes been the subject of emotional and outraged attacks by voters who find my position reprehensible or worse. I have listened to their ideas. I have weighed their objections carefully. I still support the death penalty. The reasons I maintain my position can be best understood by examining the arguments most frequently heard in opposition.

1. *The death penalty is "barbaric."* Sometimes opponents of capital punishment horrify with tales of lingering death on the gallows, of faulty electric chairs, or of agony in the gas chamber. Partly in response to such protests, several states such as North Carolina and Texas switched to execution by lethal injection. The condemned person is put to death painlessly, without ropes, voltage, bullets, or gas. Did this answer the objections of death penalty opponents? Of course not. On June 22, 1984, the *New York Times* published an editorial that sarcastically attacked the new "hygienic" method of death by injection, and stated that "execution can never be made humane through science." So it's not the method

that really troubles opponents. It's the death itself they consider barbaric.

Admittedly, capital punishment is not a pleasant topic. However, one does not have to like the death penalty in order to support it any more than one must like radical surgery, radiation, or chemotherapy in order to find necessary these attempts at curing cancer. Ultimately we may learn how to cure cancer with a simple pill. Unfortunately, that day has not yet arrived. Today we are faced with the choice of letting the cancer spread or trying to cure it with the methods available, methods that one day will almost certainly be considered barbaric. But to give up and do nothing would be far more barbaric and would certainly delay the discovery of an eventual cure. The analogy between cancer and murder is imperfect, because murder is not the "disease" we are trying to cure. The disease is injustice. We may not like the death penalty, but it must be available to punish crimes of cold-blooded murder, cases in which any other form of punishment would be inadequate and, therefore, unjust. If we create a society in which injustice is not tolerated, incidents of murder — the most flagrant form of injustice — will diminish.

2. *No other major democracy uses the death penalty.* No other major democracy — in fact, few other countries of any description — are plagued by a murder rate such as that in the United States. Fewer and fewer Americans can remember the days when unlocked doors were the norm and murder was a rare and terrible offense. In America the murder rate climbed 122 percent between 1963 and 1980. During that same period, the murder rate in New York City increased by almost 400 percent, and the statistics are even worse in many other cities. A study at M.I.T. showed that based on 1970 homicide rates a person who lived in a large American city ran a greater risk of being murdered than an American soldier in World War II ran of being killed in combat. It is not surprising that the laws of each country differ according to differing conditions and traditions. If other countries had our murder problem, the cry for capital punishment would be just as loud as it is here. And I daresay that any other major democracy where 75 percent of the people supported the death penalty would soon enact it into law.

3. *An innocent person might be executed by mistake.* Consider the work of Hugo Adam Bedau, one of the most implacable foes of capital punishment in this country. According to Mr. Bedau, it is "false sentimentality to argue that the death penalty should be abolished because of the abstract possibility that an innocent person might be executed." He cites

a study of the 7,000 executions in this country from 1893 to 1971, and concludes that the record fails to show that such cases occur. The main point, however, is this. If government functioned only when the possibility of error didn't exist, government wouldn't function at all. Human life deserves special protection, and one of the best ways to guarantee that protection is to assure that convicted murderers do not kill again. Only the death penalty can accomplish this end. In a recent case in New Jersey, a man named Richard Biegenwald was freed from prison after serving 18 years for murder; since his release he has been convicted of committing four murders. A prisoner named Lemuel Smith, who, while serving four life sentences for murder (plus two life sentences for kidnapping and robbery) in New York's Green Haven Prison, lured a woman corrections officer into the chaplain's office and strangled her. He then mutilated and dismembered her body. An additional life sentence for Smith is meaningless. Because New York has no death penalty statute, Smith has effectively been given a license to kill.

But the problem of multiple murder is not confined to the nation's penitentiaries. In 1981, 91 police officers were killed in the line of duty in this country. Seven percent of those arrested in the cases that have been solved had a previous arrest for murder. In New York City in 1976 and 1977, 85 persons arrested for homicide had a previous arrest for murder. Six of these individuals had two previous arrests for murder, and one had four previous murder arrests. During those two years the New York police were arresting for murder persons with a previous arrest for murder on the average of one every 8.5 days. This is not surprising when we learn that in 1975, for example, the median time served in Massachusetts for homicide was less than two and a half years. In 1976 a study sponsored by the Twentieth Century Fund found that the average time served in the United States for first-degree murder is ten years. The median time served may be considerably lower.

4. *Capital punishment cheapens the value of human life.* On the contrary, it can be easily demonstrated that the death penalty strengthens the value of human life. If the penalty for rape were lowered, clearly it would signal a lessened regard for the victims' suffering, humiliation, and personal integrity. It would cheapen their horrible experience, and expose them to an increased danger of recurrence. When we lower the penalty for murder, it signals a lessened regard for the value of the victim's life. Some critics of capital punishment, such as columnist Jimmy Breslin, have suggested that a life sentence is actually a harsher penalty for mur-

der than death. This is sophistic nonsense. A few killers may decide not to appeal a death sentence, but the overwhelming majority make every effort to stay alive. It is by exacting the highest penalty for the taking of human life that we affirm the highest value of human life.

5. *The death penalty is applied in a discriminatory manner.* This factor no longer seems to be the problem it once was. The appeals process for a condemned prisoner is lengthy and painstaking. Every effort is made to see that the verdict and sentence were fairly arrived at. However, assertions of discrimination are not an argument for ending the death penalty but for extending it. It is not justice to exclude everyone from the penalty of the law if a few are found to be so favored. Justice requires that the law be applied equally to all.

6. *Thou Shalt Not Kill.* The Bible is our greatest source of moral inspiration. Opponents of the death penalty frequently cite the sixth of the Ten Commandments in an attempt to prove that capital punishment is divinely proscribed. In the original Hebrew, however, the Sixth Commandment reads "Thou Shalt Not Commit Murder," and the Torah specifies capital punishment for a variety of offenses. The biblical viewpoint has been upheld by philosophers throughout history. The greatest thinkers of the 19th century — Kant, Locke, Hobbes, Rousseau, Montesquieu, and Mill — agreed that natural law properly authorizes the sovereign to take life in order to vindicate justice. Only Jeremy Bentham was ambivalent. Washington, Jefferson, and Franklin endorsed it. Abraham Lincoln authorized executions for deserters in wartime. Alexis de Tocqueville, who expressed profound respect for American institutions, believed that the death penalty was indispensable to the support of social order. The United States Constitution, widely admired as one of the seminal achievements in the history of humanity, condemns cruel and inhuman punishment, but does not condemn capital punishment.

7. *The death penalty is state-sanctioned murder.* This is the defense with which Messrs. Willie and Shaw hoped to soften the resolve of those who sentenced them to death. By saying in effect, "You're no better than I am," the murderer seeks to bring his accusers down to his own level. It is also a popular argument among opponents of capital punishment, but a transparently false one. Simply put, the state has rights that the private individual does not. In a democracy, those rights are given to the

state by the electorate. The execution of a lawfully condemned killer is no more an act of murder than is legal imprisonment an act of kidnapping. If an individual forces a neighbor to pay him money under threat of punishment, it's called extortion. If the state does it, it's called taxation. Rights and responsibilities surrendered by the individual are what give the state its power to govern. This contract is the foundation of civilization itself.

Everyone wants his or her rights, and will defend them jealously. Not everyone, however, wants responsibilities, especially the painful responsibilities that come with law enforcement. Twenty-one years ago a woman named Kitty Genovese was assaulted and murdered on a street in New York. Dozens of neighbors heard her cries for help but did nothing to assist her. They didn't even call the police. In such a climate the criminal understandably grows bolder. In the presence of moral cowardice, he lectures us on our supposed failings and tries to equate his crimes with our quest for justice.

The death of anyone — even a convicted killer — diminishes us all. But we are diminished even more by a justice system that fails to function. It is an illusion to let ourselves believe that doing away with capital punishment removes the murderer's deed from our conscience. The rights of society are paramount. When we protect guilty lives, we give up innocent lives in exchange. When opponents of capital punishment say to the state, "I will not let you kill in my name," they are also saying to murderers: "You can kill in your *own* name as long as I have an excuse for not getting involved."

It is hard to imagine anything worse than being murdered while neighbors do nothing. But something worse exists. When those same neighbors shrink back from justly punishing the murderer, the victim dies twice. ■

THE DEATH PENALTY *by David Bruck*

Mayor Ed Koch contends that the death penalty "affirms life." By failing to execute murderers, he says, we "signal a lessened regard for the value of the victim's life." Koch suggests that people who oppose the death penalty are like Kitty Genovese's neighbors, who heard her cries for help but did nothing while an attacker stabbed her to death.

This is the standard "moral" defense of death as punishment: even if executions don't deter violent crime any more effectively than imprisonment, they are still required as the only means we have of doing justice in response to the worst of crimes.

Until recently, this "moral" argument had to be considered in the abstract, since no one was being executed in the United States. But the death penalty is back now, at least in the southern states, where every one of the more than 30 executions carried out over the last two years has taken place. Those of us who live in those states are getting to see the difference between the death penalty in theory, and what happens when you actually try to use it.

South Carolina resumed executing prisoners in January with the electrocution of Joseph Carl Shaw. Shaw was condemned to death for helping to murder two teenagers while he was serving as a military policeman at Fort Jackson, South Carolina. His crime, propelled by mental illness and PCP, was one of terrible brutality. It is Shaw's last words ("Killing was wrong when I did it. It is wrong when you do it. . . .") that so outraged Mayor Koch: he finds it "a curiosity of modern life that we are being lectured on morality by cold-blooded killers." And so it is.

But it was not "modern life" that brought this curiosity into being. It was capital punishment. The electric chair was J. C. Shaw's platform. (The mayor mistakenly writes that Shaw's statement came in the form of a plea to the governor for clemency: actually Shaw made it only seconds before his death, as he waited, shaved and strapped into the chair, for the switch to be thrown.) It was the chair that provided Shaw with celebrity and an opportunity to lecture us on right and wrong. What made this weird moral reversal even worse is that J. C. Shaw faced his own death with undeniable dignity and courage. And while Shaw died, the TV crews recorded another "curiosity" of the death penalty — the crowd gathered outside the deathhouse to cheer on the executioner. Whoops of elation greeted the announcement of Shaw's death. Waiting at the penitentiary gates for the appearance of the hearse bearing Shaw's remains, one demonstrator started yelling, "Where's the beef?"

For those who had to see the execution of J. C. Shaw, it wasn't easy to keep in mind that the purpose of the whole spectacle was to affirm life. It will be harder still when Florida executes a cop-killer named Alvin Ford. Ford has lost his mind during his years of death-row confinement, and now spends his days trembling, rocking back and forth, and muttering unintelligible prayers. This has led to litigation over whether Ford meets a centuries-old legal standard for mental competency. Since the Middle Ages, the Anglo-American legal system has generally prohibited the execution of anyone who is too mentally ill to understand what is about to be done to him and why. If Florida wins its case, it will have earned the right to electrocute Ford in his present condition. If it loses, he will not be executed until the state has first nursed him back to some semblance of mental health.

We can at least be thankful that this demoralizing spectacle involves a prisoner who is actually guilty of murder. But this may not always be so. The ordeal of Lenell Jeter — the young black engineer who recently served more than a year of a life sentence for a Texas armed robbery that he didn't commit — should remind us that the system is quite capable of making the very worst sort of mistake. That Jeter was eventually cleared is a fluke. If the robbery had occurred at 7 P.M. rather than 3 P.M., he'd have had no alibi, and would still be in prison today. And if someone had been killed in that robbery, Jeter probably would have been sentenced to death. We'd have seen the usual execution-day interviews with state officials and the victim's relatives, all complaining that Jeter's appeals took too long. And Jeter's last words from the gurney would have taken their place among the growing literature of death-house oration that so irritates the mayor.

Koch quotes Hugo Adam Bedau, a prominent abolitionist, to the effect that the record fails to establish that innocent defendants have been executed in the past. But this doesn't mean, as Koch implies, that it hasn't happened. All Bedau was saying was that doubts concerning executed prisoners' guilt are almost never resolved. Bedau is at work now on an effort to determine how many wrongful death sentences may have been imposed: his list of murder convictions since 1900 in which the state eventually *admitted* error is some 400 cases long. Of course, very few of these cases involved actual executions: the mistakes that Bedau documents were uncovered precisely because the prisoner was alive and able to fight for his vindication. The cases where someone is executed are the very cases in which we're least likely to learn that we got the wrong man.

I don't claim that executions of entirely innocent people will occur very often. But they will occur. And other sorts of mistakes already have. Roosevelt Green was executed in Georgia two days before J. C. Shaw. Green and an accomplice kidnapped a young woman. Green swore that his companion shot her to death after Green had left, and that he knew nothing about the murder. Green's claim was supported by a statement that his accomplice made to a witness after the crime. The jury never resolved whether Green was telling the truth, and when he tried to take a polygraph examination a few days before his scheduled execution, the state of Georgia refused to allow the examiner into the prison. As the pressure for symbolic retribution mounts, the courts, like the public, are losing patience with such details. Green was electrocuted on January 9, while members of the Ku Klux Klan rallied outside the prison.

Then there is another sort of arbitrariness that happens all the time. Last October, Louisiana executed a man named Ernest Knighton. Knighton had killed a gas station owner during a robbery. Like any murder, this was a terrible crime. But it was not premeditated, and is the sort of crime that very rarely results in a death sentence. Why was Knighton electrocuted when almost everyone else who committed the same offense was not? Was it because he was black? Was it because his victim and all 12 members of the jury that sentenced him were white? Was it because Knighton's court-appointed lawyer presented no evidence on his behalf at his sentencing hearing? Or maybe there's no reason except bad luck. One thing is clear: Ernest Knighton was picked out to die the way a fisherman takes a cricket out of a bait jar. No one cares which cricket gets impaled on the hook.

Not every prisoner executed recently was chosen that randomly. But many were. And having selected these men so casually, so blindly, the death penalty system asks us to accept that the purpose of killing each of them is to affirm the sanctity of human life.

The death penalty states are also learning that the death penalty is easier to advocate than it is to administer. In Florida, where executions have become almost routine, the governor reports that nearly a third of his time is spent reviewing the clemency requests of condemned prisoners. The Florida Supreme Court is hopelessly backlogged with death cases. Some have taken five years to decide, and the rest of the Court's work waits in line behind the death appeals. Florida's death row currently holds more than 230 prisoners. State officials are reportedly considering building a special "death prison" devoted entirely to the isolation and electrocution of the condemned. The state is also considering the creation of a special public defender unit that will do nothing else but handle death penalty appeals. The death penalty, in short, is spawning death agencies.

And what is Florida getting for all of this? The state went through almost all of 1983 without executing anyone: its rate of intentional homicide declined by 17 percent. Last year Florida executed eight people — the most of any state, and the sixth highest total for any year since

Florida started electrocuting people back in 1924. Elsewhere in the U.S. last year, the homicide rate continued to decline. But in Florida, it actually rose by 5.1 percent.

But these are just the tiresome facts. The electric chair has been a centerpiece of each of Koch's recent political campaigns, and he knows better than anyone how little the facts have to do with the public's support for capital punishment. What really fuels the death penalty is the justifiable frustration and rage of people who see that the government is not coping with violent crime. So what if the death penalty doesn't work? At least it gives us the satisfaction of knowing that we got one or two of the sons of bitches.

Perhaps we want retribution on the flesh and bone of a handful of convicted murderers so badly that we're willing to close our eyes to all of the demoralization and danger that come with it. A lot of politicians think so, and they may be right. But if they are, then let's at least look honestly at what we're doing. This lottery of death both comes from and encourages an attitude toward human life that is not reverent, but reckless.

And that is why the mayor is dead wrong when he confuses such fury with justice. He suggests that we trivialize murder unless we kill murderers. By that logic, we also trivialize rape unless we sodomize rapists. The sin of Kitty Genovese's neighbors wasn't that they failed to stab her attacker to death. Justice does demand that murderers be punished. And common sense demands that society be protected from them. But neither justice nor self-preservation demands that we kill men whom we have already imprisoned.

The electric chair in which J. C. Shaw died earlier this year was built in 1912 at the suggestion of South Carolina's governor at the time, Cole Blease. Governor Blease's other criminal justice initiative was an impassioned crusade in favor of lynch law. Any lesser response, the governor insisted, trivialized the loathsome crimes of interracial rape and murder. In 1912 a lot of people agreed with Governor Blease that a proper regard for justice required both lynching and the electric chair. Eventually we are going to learn that justice requires neither. ■

For each article on capital punishment:

1. Identify the arguments that were used and summarize the reasons and conclusion for each.

2. Describe the types of argument forms that you identified.

3. Evaluate the truth of the reasons that support the conclusion for each of the arguments that you identified.

4. Construct additional arguments on both sides of this issue, using the argument forms described in this chapter. ◄

11.6 ► Select a current issue of interest to you. (Possible choices are animal rights, helmet laws for motorcyclists, mandatory AIDS testing, drug testing for athletes, and so on.) Following these guidelines, construct an argumentative essay that explores the issue.

1. Locate two articles about the issue you have selected, and use them as resources. (It would be helpful to find articles with opposing points of view.)

2. List arguments on both sides of the issue, organizing them into premises and conclusions.

3. Make notes evaluating the strengths and weaknesses of each argument.

4. Identify the most important arguments and make an outline including the arguments you plan to use in the essay.

5. Using the outline and notes as a guide, write your essay. The essay should begin with a paragraph that introduces the issue and should end with a paragraph that sums up and concludes it. ◄

Summary

In this chapter we have focused mainly on deductive arguments, an argument form in which it is claimed that the premises constitute conclusive evidence for the truth of the conclusion. In a correct deductive argument, which is organized into a valid deductive form, if the premises are true, the conclusion must be true; it cannot be false.

Although *deductive* forms of reasoning are crucial to our understanding the world and making informed decisions, much of our reasoning is nondeductive. The various nondeductive argument forms are typically included under the general category of *inductive* reasoning. In contrast to deductive arguments, inductive arguments rarely provide conclusions that are totally certain. The premises merely offer some evidence in support of the conclusion.

> **Inductive Argument**   Argument form in which one reasons from premises that are known or assumed to be true to a conclusion that is supported by the premises but does not follow logically from them.

We will explore the area of inductive reasoning more fully in the next chapter, *Reasoning Critically*.

CHAPTER 12

Reasoning Critically

INDUCTIVE REASONING:
Reasoning from premises assumed to be true to a conclusion supported (but not logically) by the premises.

Empirical Generalization:
Drawing conclusions about a target population based on observing a sample population.

Is the sample known?
Is the sample sufficient?
Is the sample representative?

Causal Reasoning:
Concluding that an event is the result of another event.

Scientific Method

1. Identify an event for investigation.
2. Gather information.
3. Develop a theory/hypothesis.
4. Test/experiment.
5. Evaluate results.

FALLACIES:
Unsound arguments that can appear logical.

Fallacies of Generalization:
Hasty generalization
Sweeping generalization
False dilemma

Causal Fallacies:
Misidentification of cause
Post Hoc Ergo Propter Hoc
Slippery slope

Fallacies of Relevance:
Appeal to authority
Appeal to pity
Appeal to fear
Appeal to ignorance

539

IN THIS BOOK we have been engaged in a systematic exploration of the thinking process, which we defined in the first chapter as the active, purposeful, organized process we use to make sense of the world. Our assumption has been that by improving our understanding of the way our minds operate, we can learn to think more effectively, an achievement that will aid us in every area of our lives. We have described this project of carefully examining our thinking (and the thinking of others) as *critical thinking.* It is one of the most important kinds of thinking that we can practice because it allows us to clarify and improve our understanding of the world.

Chapter Eleven, *Constructing Arguments,* introduced the concept of reasoning, the type of thinking that uses arguments — reasons in support of conclusions — to decide, explain, predict, and persuade. Effective reasoning involves using all of the intellectual skills and critical attitudes we have been developing in this book, and in this chapter we will further explore various dimensions of our reasoning process.

Chapter Eleven focused on *deductive reasoning,* an argument form in which one reasons from premises that are known or assumed to be true to a conclusion that follows logically from the premises. In this chapter we will examine *inductive reasoning,* an argument form in which one reasons from premises that are known or assumed to be true to a conclusion which is supported by the premises but does not follow logically from them.

> *Inductive Reasoning*   An argument form in which one reasons from premises that are known or assumed to be true to a conclusion that is supported by the premises but does not follow logically from them.

When we reason inductively, our premises provide evidence that makes it more or less probable (but not certain) that the conclusion is true. The following statements are examples of conclusions reached through inductive reasoning.

1. A recent Gallup poll reported that 74 percent of the American public believe that abortion should remain legalized.

2. On the average, a person with a college degree will earn over $300,000 more in his or her lifetime than a person with just a high school diploma.

3. In a recent survey, twice as many doctors interviewed stated that if they were stranded on a desert island they would prefer Bayer Aspirin to Extra Strength Tylenol.

4. The outbreak of food poisoning at the end-of-year school party was probably caused by the squid salad.

5. The devastating disease AIDS is caused by a particularly complex virus that may not be curable.

6. The solar system is probably the result of an enormous explosion — a "big bang" — that occurred billions of years ago.

The first three statements are forms of inductive reasoning known as *empirical generalization,* a general statement about an entire group made on the basis of observing some members of the group. The final three statements are examples of *causal reasoning,* a form of inductive reasoning in which it is claimed that an event (or events) is the result of the occurrence of another event (or events). We will be exploring the ways each of these forms of inductive reasoning function in our lives and in various fields of study.

In addition to examining various ways of reasoning logically and effectively, we will also explore certain forms of reasoning that are not logical and, as a result, usually not effective. These ways of pseudoreasoning (false reasoning) are often termed *fallacies:* arguments that are not sound because of various errors in reasoning. Fallacious reasoning is typically used to influence others. It seeks to persuade not on the basis of sound arguments and critical thinking but rather on the basis of emotional and illogical factors.

Fallacies Unsound arguments that are often persuasive because they can appear to be logical, because they usually appeal to our emotions and prejudices, and because they often support conclusions that we want to believe are accurate.

Empirical Generalization

One of the most important tools used by both natural and social scientists is empirical generalization. Have you ever wondered how the major television and radio networks can accurately predict election results hours before the polls close? These predictions are made possible by the power of empirical generalization, which is defined as reasoning from a limited sample to a general conclusion based on this sample.

> *Empirical Generalization*   A form of inductive reasoning in which a general statement is made about an entire group (the "target population") based on observing some members of the group (the "sample population").

Network election predictions, as well as public opinion polls that occur throughout a political campaign, are based on interviews with a select number of people. Ideally, pollsters would interview everyone in the *target population* (in this case, voters), but this, of course, is hardly practical. Instead, they select a relatively small group of individuals from the target population, known as a *sample,* who they have determined will adequately represent the group as a whole. Pollsters believe that they can then generalize the opinions of this smaller group to the target population. And with a few notable exceptions (such as in the 1948 presidential election, when New York Governor Thomas Dewey went to bed believing he had been elected president and woke up a loser to Harry Truman), these results are highly accurate. (Polling techniques are much more sophisticated today than they were in 1948.)

There are three key criteria for evaluating inductive arguments:

• Is the sample known?
• Is the sample sufficient?
• Is the sample representative?

Is the Sample Known?

An inductive argument is only as strong as the sample on which it is based. For example, sample populations described in vague and unclear terms — "highly placed sources" or "many young people interviewed," for example — provide a treacherously weak foundation for generalizing to larger populations. In order for an inductive argument to be persuasive, the sample population should be explicitly *known* and clearly identified. Natural and social scientists take great care in selecting the members in the sample groups, and this is an important part of the data which is available to outside investigators who may wish to evaluate and verify the results.

Is the Sample Sufficient?

The second criterion for evaluating inductive reasoning is to consider the *size* of the sample. It should be sufficiently large to give an accurate sense of the group as a whole. In the polling example discussed earlier, we would be concerned if only a few registered voters were interviewed and the results of these interviews were generalized to a much larger population. Overall, the larger the sample, the more reliable the inductive conclusions. Natural and social scientists have developed precise guidelines for determining the size of the sample needed to achieve reliable results. For example, poll results are often accompanied by a qualification such as "These results are subject to an error factor of ± 3 percentage points." This means that if the sample reveals that 47 percent of those interviewed prefer candidate X, then we can reliably state that 44 to 50 percent of the target population prefer candidate X. Because a sample is usually a small portion of the target population, we can rarely state that the two match each other exactly — there must always be some room for variation. The exceptions to this are situations in which the target population is completely homogeneous. For example, tasting one cookie from a bag of cookies is usually enough to tell us whether or not the entire bag is stale.

Is the Sample Representative?

The third crucial element in effective inductive reasoning is the *representativeness* of the sample. If we are to generalize with confidence from the sample to the target population, then we have to be sure the sample is similar to the larger group from which it is drawn in all relevant aspects. For instance, in the polling example, the sample population should reflect the same percentage of men and women, of Democrats and Republicans, of young and old, and so on, as the target population. It is obvious that many characteristics, such as hair color, favorite food, and shoe size, are not relevant to the comparison. The better the sample reflects the target population in terms of *relevant* qualities, however, then the better the accuracy of the generalizations. On the other hand, when the sample is *not* representative of the target population — for example, if the election pollsters interviewed only females between the ages of thirty and thirty-five — then the sample is termed *biased*, and any generalizations made about the target population will be highly suspect.

How do we ensure that the sample is representative of the target population? One important device is *random selection,* a selection strategy in which every member of the target population has an equal chance of being included in the sample. For example, the various techniques used to select winning lottery tickets are supposed to be random — each ticket is supposed to have an equal chance of winning. In complex cases of inductive reasoning — such as polling — random selection is often combined with the confirmation that all of the important categories in the population are adequately represented. For example, an election pollster would want to be certain that all significant geographical areas are included, and then would randomly select individuals from within those areas to compose the sample.

Understanding the principles of inductive reasoning is of crucial importance to effective thinking because we are continually challenged to construct and evaluate inductive arguments in our lives.

THINKING ACTIVITY

12.1 ▶ Review the following examples of inductive arguments. For each argument, evaluate the quality of the thinking by answering the following questions:

1. Is the sample known?

2. Is the sample sufficient?

3. Is the sample representative?

4. Do you believe the conclusions are likely to be accurate? Why or why not?

> In a study of a possible relationship between pornography and antisocial behavior, questionnaires went out to 7,500 psychiatrists and psychoanalysts, whose listing in the directory of the American Psychological Association indicated clinical experience. Over 3,400 of these professionals responded. The result: 7.4 percent of the psychiatrists and psychologists had cases in which they were convinced that pornography was a causal factor in antisocial behavior; an additional 9.4 percent were suspicious; 3.2 percent did not commit themselves; and 80 percent said they had no cases in which a causal connection was suspected.

> A survey by the Sleep Disorder Clinic of the VA hospital in La Jolla, California (involving more than one million people), revealed that people who sleep more than ten hours a night have a death rate 80 percent higher than those who sleep only seven or eight hours. Men who sleep less than four hours a night have a death rate 180 percent higher, and women with less [than four hours] sleep have a rate 40 percent higher. This might be taken as indicating that too much and too little sleep cause death.

> "U.S. Wastes Food Worth Millions." Americans in the economic middle waste more food than their rich and poor counterparts, according to a study published Saturday. Carried out in Tucson, Arizona, by Univer-

sity of Arizona students under the direction of Dr. William L. Rathje, the study analyzed 600 bags of garbage each week for three years from lower-, middle-, and upper-income neighborhoods. They found that city residents throw out around 10 percent of the food they brought home — about 9,500 tons of food each year. The figure amounts to $9 to $11 million worth of food. Most of the waste occurred in middle-class neighborhoods. Both the poor and the wealthy were significantly more frugal.

Being a general practitioner in a rural area has tremendous drawbacks — being on virtually 24-hour call 365 days a year; patients without financial means or insurance; low fees in the first place; inadequate facilities and assistance. Nevertheless, America's small town G.P.s seem fairly content with their lot. According to a survey taken by *Country Doctor*, fully 50 percent wrote back that they "basically like being a rural G.P." Only 1 in 15 regretted that he or she had not specialized. Only 2 out of 20 rural general practitioners would trade places with their urban counterparts, given the chance. And only 1 in 30 would "choose some other line of work altogether." ◄

THINKING ACTIVITY

12.2 ► Select an issue that you would like to poll a group of people about — for example, the population of your school or your neighborhood. Describe in specific terms how you would go about constructing a sample both large and representative enough for you to generalize the results to the target population accurately. ◄

Fallacies of False Generalization

In Chapter Eight, *Forming and Applying Concepts,* we explored the way that we form concepts through the interactive process of generalizing (identifying the common qualities that define the boundaries of the concept) and interpreting (identifying examples of the concept). This generalizing and interpreting process is similar to the process involved in constructing empirical generalizations, as we seek to reach a general conclusion based on a limited number of examples and then apply this conclusion to other examples.

Although generalizing and interpreting are useful in forming concepts, they also can give rise to fallacious ways of thinking, including the following:

- Hasty generalization
- Sweeping generalization
- False dilemma

Hasty Generalization

Consider the following examples of reasoning. Do you think that the arguments are sound? Why or why not?

> My boyfriends have never shown any real concern for my feelings. My conclusion is that men are insensitive, selfish, and emotionally superficial.

> My mother always gets upset over insignificant things. This leads me to believe that women are very emotional.

In both of these cases, a general conclusion has been reached that is based on a very small sample. As a result, the reasons provide very weak support for the conclusions that are being developed. It just does not make good sense to generalize from a few individuals to all men or all women. Our conclusion is *hasty* because our sample is not large enough and/or not representative enough to provide adequate justification for our generalization.

Of course, many generalizations are more warranted than the two given here because the conclusion is based on a sample that is larger and more representative of the group as a whole. For example:

> I have done a lot of research in a variety of automotive publications on the relationship between the size of cars and the gas mileage they get. In general, I think it makes sense to conclude that large cars tend to get fewer miles per gallon than smaller cars.

In this case, the conclusion is generalized from a larger and more representative sample than those in the preceding two arguments. As a result, the reason for the last argument provides much stronger support for the conclusion.

Unfortunately, many of the general conclusions we reach about the world are not legitimate because they are based on samples that are too small or are not representative. In these cases, the generalization is a distortion because it creates a false impression of the group that is being represented. These illegitimate generalizations are sometimes called *stereotypes*. Stereotypes affect our perception of the world because they encourage us to form an inaccurate idea of an entire group based on insufficient evidence ("Men are insensitive and selfish"). Even if we have experiences that conflict with our stereotype ("This man is not insensitive and selfish"), we tend to overlook the conflicting information in favor of the stereotype ("All men are insensitive and selfish — except for this one").

THINKING ACTIVITY

12.3 ► Have you ever been the victim of a stereotyped generalization? Describe the experience and explain why you believe that you were subjected to this kind of generalization. ◄

THINKING ACTIVITY

12.4 ► There are many stereotypes in our culture — in advertising, in the movies, on television, in literature, and so on.

1. Describe one such stereotype.
2. Identify some specific examples of places where this stereotype is found.
3. Explain the reasons why you think this stereotype developed. ◄

Sweeping Generalization

Whereas the fallacy of hasty generalization deals with errors in the process of generalizing, the fallacy of *sweeping generalization* focuses on difficulties in the process of interpreting. Consider the following examples of reasoning. Do you think that the arguments are sound? Why or why not?

> Vigorous exercise contributes to overall good health. Therefore vigorous exercise should be practiced by recent heart attack victims, people who are out of shape, and women who are about to give birth.

> People should be allowed to make their own decisions, providing that their actions do not harm other people. Therefore people who are trying to commit suicide should be left alone to do what they want.

In both of these cases, generalizations that are true in most cases have been deliberately applied to instances that are clearly intended to be exceptions to the generalizations because of special features that the exceptions possess. Of course, the use of sweeping generalizations stimulates us to clarify the generalization, rephrasing it to exclude instances, like those given here, that have special features. For example, the first generalization could be reformulated as "Vigorous exercise contributes to overall good health, *except for* recent heart attack victims, people out of shape, and women who are about to give birth." Sweeping generalizations become dangerous only when they are accepted without critical analysis and reformulation.

THINKING ACTIVITY

12.5   ▶ Review the following examples of sweeping generalizations, and in each case (a) explain *why* it is a sweeping generalization and (b) reformulate the statement so that it becomes a legitimate generalization.

1. A college education stimulates you to develop as a person and prepares you for many professions. Therefore, all persons should attend college, no matter what career they are interested in.

2. Drugs such as heroin and morphine are addictive and therefore qualify as dangerous drugs. This means that they should never be used, even as pain killers in medical situations.

3. Once criminals have served time for the crimes they have committed, they have paid their debt to society and should be permitted to work at any job they choose. ◀

False Dilemma

The fallacy of the false dilemma — also known as the either/or fallacy or the black-or-white fallacy — occurs when we are asked to choose between two extreme alternatives without being able to consider additional options. For example, we may say, "Either you're for me or against me," meaning that a choice has to be made between these alternatives. Sometimes giving people only two choices on an issue makes sense ("If you decide to swim the English Channel, you'll either make it or you won't"). At other times, however, viewing situations in such extreme terms may be a serious oversimplification — for it would mean viewing a complicated situation in terms that are too simple.

12.6 ▶ The following statements are examples of false dilemmas. After analyzing the fallacy in each case, suggest different alternatives than those being presented.

> *Example:* "Everyone in Germany is a National Socialist — the few outside the party are either lunatics or idiots." (Adolf Hitler, quoted by the *New York Times,* April 5, 1938.)

> *Analysis:* This is an oversimplification. Hitler is saying that if you are not a Nazi, then you are a lunatic or an idiot. By limiting the population to these groups, Hitler was simply ignoring all the people who did not qualify as Nazis, lunatics, or idiots.

1. "America — love it or leave it!"

2. "She loves me; she loves me not."

3. "Live free or die."

4. "If you're not part of the solution, then you're part of the problem." (Eldridge Cleaver)

5. "If you know about BMW, you either own one or you want to." ◀

Causal Reasoning

A second major type of inductive reasoning is causal reasoning, in which an event (or events) is claimed to be the result of the occurrence of another event (or events).

> **Causal Reasoning**   A form of inductive reasoning in which an event (or events) is claimed to be the result of another event (or events).

As we use our thinking abilities to try to understand the world we live in, we often ask the question, "Why did that happen?" For example, if the engine of our car is running roughly, our natural question is, "What's wrong?" If we wake up one morning with an upset stomach, we usually want to figure out, "What's the cause?" Or maybe the softball team we belong to has been losing recently. We typically wonder, "What's going on?" In each of these cases we assume that there is some factor (or factors) responsible for what is occurring, some *cause* (or causes) that results in the *effect* (or effects) we are observing (the rough engine, the upset stomach).

As we saw in Chapter Nine, *Relating and Organizing*, causality is one of the basic patterns of thinking we use to organize and make sense of our experience. For instance, imagine how bewildered we would feel if a mechanic looked at our car engine and told us there was no explanation for our poorly running engine. Or suppose we take our upset stomach to the doctor, who examines us and then concludes that there is no possible causal explanation for the malady. In each case we would be understandably skeptical of the diagnosis and would probably seek another opinion.

The Scientific Method

Causal reasoning is also the backbone of the natural and social sciences; it is responsible for the remarkable understanding of our world that has been achieved. The *scientific method* works on the assumption that the world is constructed in a complex web of causal relationships that can be discovered through systematic investigation. Scientists have devised an organized approach for discovering causal relationships and testing the accuracy of conclusions, an approach explored in Irving M. Copi's essay, "The Detective as Scientist" (pp. 426–436). The sequence of steps is as follows:

1. Identify an event or relationship between events to be investigated.

2. Gather information about the event (or events).

3. Develop a theory or hypothesis to explain what is happening.

4. Test the theory or hypothesis through experimentation.

5. Evaluate the theory or hypothesis.

How does this sequence work when applied to the situation of the rough-running engine we mentioned earlier?

1. *Identify an event to be investigated.* In this case, the event is obvious — our car engine is running poorly and we want to discover the cause of the problem so we can fix it.

2. *Gather information about the event.* This step involves locating any relevant information about the situation that will help us solve the problem. We initiate this step by asking and trying to answer a variety of questions: When did

the engine begin running poorly? Was it abrupt or gradual? When did we last have a tune-up? Are there other mechanical difficulties that might be related? Has anything unusual occurred with the car recently?

3. *Develop a theory or hypothesis to explain what is happening.* After reviewing the relevant information, we want to identify the most likely explanation of what has happened. This possible explanation is known as a *hypothesis.* (A *theory* is normally a more complex model that involves a number of interconnected hypotheses, such as the theory of quantum mechanics in physics.)

> **Hypothesis** A possible explanation that is introduced to account for a set of facts and that can be used as a basis for further investigation.

Although our hypothesis may be suggested by the information we have, it goes beyond the information as well and so must be tested before we commit ourselves to it. In this case the hypothesis we might settle on is "water in the gas." This hypothesis was suggested by our recollection that the engine troubles began right after we bought gas in the pouring rain. This hypothesis may be correct or it may be incorrect — we have to test it to find out.

When we devise a plausible hypothesis to be tested, we should keep three general guidelines in mind:

- *Explanatory power:* The hypothesis should effectively explain the event we are investigating. The hypothesis that damaged windshield wipers are causing the engine problems doesn't seem to provide an adequate explanation of the difficulties.

- *Economy:* The hypothesis should not be unnecessarily complex. The explanation that our engine difficulty is the result of sabotage by an unfriendly neighbor is possible but unlikely. There are simpler and more direct explanations we should test first.

- *Predictive power:* The hypothesis should allow us to make various predictions to test its accuracy. If the "water in the gas" hypothesis is accurate, we can predict that removing the water from the gas tank and gas line should clear up the difficulty.

4. *Test the theory or hypothesis through experimentation.* Once we identify a hypothesis that meets these three guidelines, the next task is to devise an experiment to test its accuracy. In the case of our troubled car, we would test our hypothesis by pouring several containers of "dry-gas" into the tank, blowing out the gas line, and cleaning the carburetor. By removing the

moisture in the gas system, we should be able to determine whether our hypothesis is correct.

5. *Evaluate the theory or hypothesis.* After reviewing the results of our experience, we usually can assess the accuracy of our hypothesis. If our engine runs smoothly after we remove moisture from the gas line, then this strong evidence supports our hypothesis. On the other hand, if our engine does *not* run smoothly after our efforts, then this persuasive evidence suggests that our hypothesis was not correct. There is, however, a third possibility. Removing the moisture from the gas system might improve the engine's performance somewhat but not entirely. In that case, we might want to construct a *revised* hypothesis along the lines of "Water in the gas system is partially responsible for our rough-running engine, but another cause (or causes) might be involved as well."

If the evidence does not support our hypothesis or supports a revised version of it, we then begin the entire process again by identifying and testing a new hypothesis. The natural and social sciences engage in an ongoing process of developing theories and hypotheses and testing them through experimental design. Many theories and hypotheses are much more complex than our "moisture in the gas" and take years of generating, revising, and testing. Determining the subatomic structure of the universe and finding cures for various kinds of cancers, for example, have been the subjects of countless theories and hypotheses, as well as experiments to test their accuracy. We might diagram this operation of the scientific process as follows:

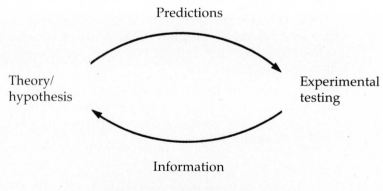

Predictions

Theory/
hypothesis

Experimental
testing

Information

(Acceptance, rejection, or revision
of the theory/hypothesis)

THINKING ACTIVITY

12.7 ▶ Select one of the following situations or describe a situation of your own choosing. Then analyze the situation by working through the various steps of the scientific method listed directly after.

• Situation 1: You wake up in the morning with an upset stomach.

• Situation 2: Your grades have been declining all semester.

• Situation 3: (Your own choosing)

1. *Identify an event or a relationship between events to be investigated.* Describe the situation you have selected.

2. *Gather information about the event.* Elaborate the situation by providing additional details. Be sure to include a variety of possible causes for the event. (For example, an upset stomach might be the result of food poisoning, the flu, anxiety, etc.).

3. *Develop a theory or hypothesis to explain what is happening.* Based on the information you have described, identify a plausible hypothesis that (a) explains what occurred, (b) is clear and direct, and (c) leads to predictions that can be tested.

4. *Test the theory or hypothesis through experimentation.* Design a way of testing your hypothesis that results in evidence proving or disproving it.

5. *Evaluate the theory or hypothesis.* Describe the results of your experiment and explain whether the results lead you to accept, reject, or revise your hypothesis. ◀

In designing the experiment in Thinking Activity 12.7, you may have used one of two common reasoning patterns.

Reasoning pattern 1: A caused *B* because *A* is the only relevant common element shared by more than one occurrence of *B*.

For example, imagine you are investigating your upset stomach and you decide to call two friends who had dinner with you the previous evening to see if they have similar symptoms. You discover they also have upset stomachs. Because dining at "Sam's Seafood" was the only experience shared by the three of you that might explain the three stomach problems, you conclude that food poisoning may in fact be the cause. Further, although each of you ordered a different entrée, you all shared an appetizer, "Sam's Special Squid," which suggests that you may have identified the cause. As we can see, this pattern of reasoning looks for the common thread linking different occurrences of the same event to identify the cause; stated more simply, "The cause is the common thread."

> *Reasoning pattern 2: A* caused *B* because *A* is the only relevant difference between this situation and other situations in which *B* did not take place.

For example, imagine that you are investigating the reasons that your team, which has been winning all year, has suddenly begun to lose. One way of approaching this situation is to look for circumstances that might have changed at the time your team's fortunes began to decline. Your investigation yields two possible explanations. First, your team started wearing new uniforms about the time they started losing. Second, one of your regular players was sidelined with a foot injury. You decide to test the first hypothesis by having the team begin wearing the old uniforms again. When this doesn't change your fortunes, you conclude that the missing player may be the cause of the difficulties, and you anxiously await the player's return to see if your reasoning is accurate. As we can see, this pattern of reasoning looks for relevant differences linked to the situation we are trying to explain; stated more simply, "The cause is the difference."

Controlled Experiments

Although our analysis of causal reasoning has focused on causal relationships between specific events, much of scientific research concerns causal factors influencing populations composed of many individuals. In these cases, the causal relationships tend to be much more complex than the simple formulation *A* causes *B*. For example, on every package of cigarettes sold in the United States appears a message such as: "Surgeon General's Warning: Smoking Causes Lung Cancer, Heart Disease, Emphysema, And May Complicate Pregnancy." This does not mean that every cigarette smoked has a direct impact on one's health, nor does it mean that everyone who smokes moderately, or even heavily, will die prematurely of cancer, heart disease, or emphysema. Instead, the statement means that if you habitually smoke, your chances of developing one of the diseases normally associated with smoking are significantly higher than are those of someone who does not smoke or who smokes only occasionally. How were scientists able to arrive at this conclusion?

The reasoning strategy scientists use to reach conclusions like this one is

the *controlled experiment,* and it is one of the most powerful reasoning strategies ever developed. There are three different kinds of controlled experiment
designs:

1. Cause-to-effect experiments (with intervention)

2. Cause-to-effect experiments (without intervention)

3. Effect-to-cause experiments

Cause-to-Effect Experiments (With Intervention)   The first of these forms of reasoning is illustrated by the following example. Imagine that you have developed a new cream you believe will help cure baldness in men and women
and you want to evaluate its effectiveness. What do you do? To begin with,
you have to identify a group of people who accurately represent all of the
balding men and women in the United States, because testing it on all balding
people simply isn't feasible. This involves following the guidelines for inductive reasoning we explored in the last section. It is important that the group
you select to test be *representative* of all balding people (known as the *target
population*), because you hope your product will grow hair on all types of
heads. For example, if you selected only men between the ages of twenty and
thirty to test, the experiment would only establish whether the product works
for men of these ages. Additional experiments would have to be conducted
for women and other age groups. This representative group is known as a
sample. Scientists have developed strategies for selecting sample groups to
ensure that they mirror fairly the larger group from which they are drawn.

Once you have selected your sample of balding men and women — say
you have identified 200 people — the next step is to divide the sample into
two groups of 100 people that are alike in all relevant respects. The best way
to ensure that the groups are essentially alike is through the technique we
examined earlier called *random selection,* which means that each individual
selected has the same chance of being chosen as everyone else. You then
designate one group as the *experimental group* and the other group as the *control group.* You next give the individuals in the experimental group treatments
of your hair-growing cream, and you give either no treatments or a harmless,
non–hair-growing cream to the control group. At the conclusion of the testing
period, you compare the experimental group with the control group to evaluate hair gain and hair loss.

Suppose that a number of individuals in the experimental group do indeed
show evidence of more new hair growth than the control group. How can we
be sure this is because of the cream and not simply a chance occurrence?
Scientists have developed a statistical formula based on the size of the sample

and the frequency of the observed effects. For example, imagine that 13 persons in your experimental group show evidence of new hair growth, whereas no one in the control group shows any such evidence. Statisticians have determined that we can say with 95 percent certainty that the new hair growth was caused by your new cream; that the results were not merely the result of chance. This type of experimental result is usually expressed by saying that the experimental results were significant at the 0.05 level, a standard criterion in experimental research. The following diagram shows the cause-to-effect experiment (with intervention).

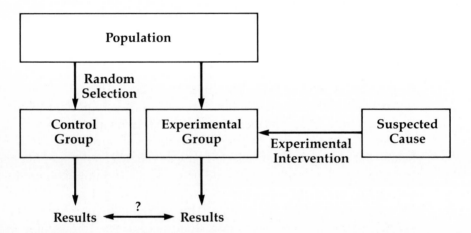

Cause-to-Effect Experiments (Without Intervention)   The second form of controlled experiment is known as the *cause-to-effect experiment (without intervention)*. This form of experimental design is similar to the one we just examined except that the experimenter does not intervene to expose the experimental group to a proposed cause (like the hair-growing cream). Instead, the experimenter identifies a cause that a population is already exposed to and then constructs the experiment. For example, suppose you suspect that the asbestos panels and insulation in some old buildings cause cancer. Because it would not be ethical to expose people intentionally to something that might damage their health, you would search for already existing conditions in which people are being exposed to the asbestos. Once located, these individuals (or a representative sample) could be used as the experimental group. You could then form a control group of individuals who are not exposed to asbestos but who match the experimental group in all other relevant respects. You could then investigate the health experiences of both groups over time, thereby evaluating the possible relationship between asbestos and cancer.

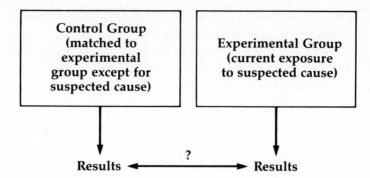

The diagram on the top of page 557 illustrates the procedure used in cause-to-effect experiments (without intervention).

Effect-to-Cause Experiments   A final form of reasoning employing the controlled experimental design is known as the *effect-to-cause experiment*. In this case the experimenter works backward from an existing effect to a suspected cause. For example, imagine that you are investigating the claim by many Vietnam veterans that exposure to the chemical defoliant Agent Orange has resulted in significant health problems for them and for children born to them. Once again, you would not want to expose people to a potentially harmful substance just to test the hypothesis. And unlike the asbestos case we just examined, people are no longer being exposed to Agent Orange as they were during the war. As a result, investigating the claim involves beginning with the effect (health problems) and working back to the suspected cause (Agent Orange). In this case the target population would be Vietnam veterans who were exposed to Agent Orange, so you would draw a representative sample from this group. You would form a matching control group

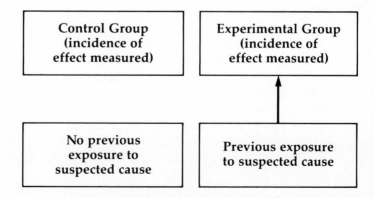

from the population of Vietnam veterans who were *not* exposed to Agent Orange. Next, you would compare the incidence of illnesses claimed to have been caused by Agent Orange in the two groups and evaluate the proposed causal relation. The diagram at bottom of page 557 illustrates the procedure used in effect-to-cause experiments.

THINKING ACTIVITY

12.8   ▶ Read the following experimental situations. For each situation:

1. Describe the proposed causal relationship (the theory or hypothesis).
2. Identify which kind of experimental design was used.
3. Evaluate:
   a. The representativeness of the sample.
   b. The randomness of the division into experimental and control groups.
4. Explain how well the experimental results support the proposed theory or hypothesis.

> New studies reported in the *Journal of the American Medical Association* indicate that vasectomy is safe. A group headed by Frank Massey of UCLA paired 10,500 vasectomized men with a like number of men who had not had the operation. The average follow-up time was 7.9 years, and 2,300 pairs were followed for more than a decade. The researchers reported that, aside from inflammation in the testes, the incidence of diseases for vasectomized men was similar to that in their paired controls.
>
> Edward Edelson, *New York Daily News*

> Canadian reseachers led by D. G. Perrin of the department of pathology at the Hospital for Sick Children in Toronto have found an important biochemical difference in the bodies of children who died from sudden infant death syndrome (SIDS), compared with infants who died from other causes. According to the scientists, the research suggests that infants at high risk for SIDS may manufacture the brain chemical transmitter dopamine at abnormally high levels. Theoretically, if the results of the investigation are borne out, a child at risk might be treated with dopamine-blocking drugs as a preventive measure, but the scientists caution it is too early to consider doing that. "Just because (dopamine)

is abnormal does not necessarily mean it's a primary cause," says Perrin. "It may be a secondary cause."

Perrin and his colleagues examined the carotid bodies of 13 SIDS babies and five infants who died from other causes. All but two of the SIDS babies had dopamine levels far in excess of those in the controls.

SIDS claims about ten thousand infants between two months and four months of age each year in the United States. All SIDS deaths involve the mysterious cessation of breathing during sleep.

J. Greenberg, *Science News*, September 15, 1984

A study released last week indicates that Type A individuals, who are characteristically impatient, competitive, insecure and short-tempered, can halve their chances of having a heart attack by changing their behavior with the help of psychological counseling.

In 1978, scientists at Mt. Zion Hospital and Medical Center in San Francisco and Stanford University School of Education began their study of 862 predominantly male heart attack victims. Of this number, 592 received group counseling to ease their Type A behavior and improve their self-esteem. After three years, only 7 percent had another heart attack, compared with 13 percent of a matched group of 270 subjects who received only cardiological advice. Among 328 men who continued with the counseling for the full three years, 79 percent reduced their Type A behavior. About half of the comparison group was similarly able to slow down and cope better with stress.

This is the first evidence "that a modification program aimed at Type A behavior actually helps to reduce coronary disease," says Redford Williams of Duke University, an investigator of Type A behavior.

Science News, August 18, 1984, p. 109 ◀

THINKING ACTIVITY

12.9 ▶ Construct an experimental design to investigate a potential causal relationship of your own choosing. Be sure that your experimental design follows the guidelines we have established:

- A clearly defined theory or hypothesis expressing a proposed relationship between a cause and an effect in a population of individuals.

- Representative samples.

- Selection into experimental and control groups.

- A clear standard for evaluating the evidence for or against the theory or hypothesis. ◀

12.10 ▶ Human history is filled with examples of misguided causal thinking — bleeding people's veins and applying leeches to reduce fever; beating and torturing emotionally disturbed people to drive out the devils thought to possess them; sacrificing young women to ensure the goodwill of the gods, and so on. When the bubonic plague ravaged Europe in the fourteenth century, the lack of scientific understanding led to causal explanations like "God's punishment of the unholy" and "the astrological position of the planets."

Contrast this fourteenth-century plague with what some people have termed the plague of the twentieth century — acquired immune deficiency syndrome (AIDS). We now have the knowledge, reasoning, and technical capabilities to investigate the disease in an effective fashion, though no cure or preventative inoculation has yet been developed. Read the following article describing the scientific battle against AIDS and then answer the questions that follow.

FOR A NATIONAL EFFORT TO DEVELOP A VACCINE TO COUNTERACT AIDS *by Robert E. Pollack*

The time has come for the Government to underwrite a nationwide effort to produce an effective vaccine against HTLV III, the virus that causes AIDS. Though a frightening new disease, AIDS is no longer so novel that such an effort would be premature.

Samples of the virus have been isolated and their entire sets of genes decoded. The human populations for testing and eventual inoculation with a vaccine exist and are ready to volunteer. Yet the communities of physicians, and of public and corporate researchers, seem unable to organize the process. Why is the nation unwilling or unable to expend the effort and money to launch an applied-biology and bio-engineering effort to develop and test a vaccine?

Let's examine what is known about viruses. Most viruses cannot "find" just any human cell; they have to attach to a cell's surface, and the attachment has to be a specific match between a portion of the cell's surface membrane and a portion of the virus's coat. HTLV III is ordinary in its habits much like other viruses. It is remarkable only for the fastidious way in which it chooses the cell it will attach to, enter and take over.

HTLV III must find and attach to a particular kind of white blood cell.

This sort of cell is the very one everyone's body needs in order to recognize and reject a multiplicity of micro-organisms, fungi, parasites, yeasts and bacteria. That is the reason AIDS patients suffer from so many different diseases. As the virus takes over these cells, the body loses its defenses and eventually succumbs to one or many of a host of infectious agents.

Two scientific reasons are given for the reluctance to begin a national effort to develop a vaccine. One is that AIDS might be caused by a family of closely related variants of the same virus and that therefore no vaccine could be effective. The other is that there are no animals suitable for initial testing of a vaccine and thus no way to be sure a vaccine is safe for testing in people.

It seems to me and to some colleagues that these objections, though sound, are not conclusive. The exquisite specificity of HTLV III's recognition of certain white blood cells suggests that all variants of the virus will have in common at least one part of their outer coat — the region that finds and binds to this specific kind of cell.

Gene-splicing is the answer to the second objection and the key to making a vaccine. HTLV III is a new virus, but its known properties so far suggest that it is not so exotic as to be beyond the grasp of recombinant DNA techniques. All the genes of more than one AIDS virus have been isolated and chemically identified. This knowledge should permit scientists to put genes from an AIDS virus into a bacterium. Once they are there, the bacterium, grown in large quantities, can be the source of material for testing as a vaccine. And vaccines produced this way would be totally incapable of causing AIDS.

In the absence of an animal model for AIDS, such vaccines could not now be tested in volunteers, because Government regulations require that new vaccines be first tested in an animal. These rules no longer make sense for vaccines produced by recombinant techniques.

There is at least one other reason for our nation's inability to act: irrational fear and hostility directed at a minority. The population at risk and ready to volunteer for testing is largely homosexual. Our political leaders apparently do not wish to be involved with this minority. As a result, the clock runs out on thousands of victims without even the beginning of an effort to develop the vaccine that might prevent new cases from occurring. This is a social disaster.

Consider what we could be doing. We have a population of homosexuals available for prospective study of such vaccines. These men, like the estimated million or so Americans who already have antibodies to HTLV III, are highly motivated to participate in the large-scale studies necessary to develop an optimal vaccine.

We have as well a population of perhaps 100,000* people with what is known medically as "AIDS-related complex" — a syndrome in which a person has an AIDS virus in his blood but does not show the full set of symptoms characteristic of AIDS. In addition, there are perhaps 10,000 people with AIDS whose white cells are drastically reduced. These 10,000 have a currently irreversible disease, and many have repeatedly offered themselves for any experimental treatments.

A vaccine for any virus-caused cancer will have to be made by recombinant techniques in order to separate the gene for the vaccine from all cancer-causing genes in the virus. Therefore, if we proceed immediately to organize biotechnology for the production and testing of recombinant AIDS vaccines, we gain time on the eventual production of vaccines for leukemias, lymphomas and other human tumors that are likely to be caused by viruses.

All physicians have taken an oath to do no harm. But in fact they do harm by sitting quietly by, or referring AIDS victims to another physician or hoping the disease will quietly go away after it destroys a few thousand homosexual men and narcotics addicts. It is not enough to offer succor and solace. Physicians and scientists should lobby actively for a nationwide effort to develop an AIDS vaccine. ■

1. Explain the process by which the HTLV III virus causes the AIDS syndrome.

2. Construct an experimental design that would test the AIDS vaccine which Dr. Pollack thinks should be developed. Be sure that your experimental design follows the guidelines detailed in Thinking Activity 12.9 on page 559.

3. Dr. Pollack believes that a national effort to develop a vaccine to deal with the AIDS epidemic is overdue, and states: "All physicians have taken an oath to do no harm. But in fact they do harm by sitting quietly by . . ." Explain whether you agree with this view or not and state the reasons that support your position. ◄

---

* This figure represents the estimate in 1985. In 1990, estimates of persons with AIDS-related complex in the United States ranged as high as 1 million (Editor's note).

Causal Fallacies

Because causality plays such a dominant role in the way we make sense of the world, it is not surprising that people make many mistakes and errors in judgment in trying to determine causal relationships. The following are some of the most common fallacies associated with causality:

- Questionable cause
- Misidentification of the cause
- *Post hoc ergo propter hoc*
- Slippery slope

Questionable Cause

The fallacy of *questionable cause* occurs when someone presents a causal relationship for which no real evidence exists. Superstitious beliefs, such as "If you break a mirror you will have seven years of bad luck," usually fall into this category. Some people feel that astrology, a system of beliefs tying one's personality and fortunes in life to the position of the planets at the moment of birth, also falls into this category.

Consider the following passage from St. Augustine's *Confessions*. Does it seem to support or deny the causal assertions of astrology? Why or why not?

> Firminus had heard from his father that when his mother had been pregnant with him, a slave belonging to a friend of his father's was also about to bear. . . . It happened that since the two women had their babies at the same instant, the men were forced to cast exactly the same horoscope for each newborn child down to the last detail, one for his son, the other for the little slave. . . . Yet Firminus, born to wealth in his parents' house, had one of the more illustrious careers in life . . . whereas the slave had no alleviation of his life's burden.

Other examples of this fallacy include explanations like those given by fourteenth-century sufferers of the bubonic plague who claimed that "the Jews are poisoning the Christians' wells." This was particularly nonsensical since an equal percentage of Jews were dying of the plague as well. The evidence did not support the explanation.

Misidentification of the Cause

In causal situations we are not always certain about what is causing what — in other words, what is the cause and what is the effect. *Misidentifying the cause* is easy to do. For example, which are the causes and which are the effects in the following pairs of items? Why?

- Poverty and alcoholism
- Headaches and tension
- Failure in school and personal problems
- Shyness and lack of confidence
- Drug dependency and emotional difficulties

Of course, sometimes a third factor is responsible for both of the effects we are examining. For example, the headaches and tension we are experiencing may both be the result of a third element — such as some new medication we are taking. When this occurs, we are said to commit the fallacy of *ignoring a common cause*. On the other hand, there also exists the fallacy of *assuming a common cause* — for example, assuming that both our sore toe and our earache stem from the same cause.

Post Hoc Ergo Propter Hoc

The translation of the Latin phrase *post hoc ergo propter hoc* is "After it, there-fore because of it." It refers to those situations in which, because two things occur close together in time, we assume that one caused the other. For example, if your team wins the game each time you wear your favorite shirt, you might be tempted to conclude that the one event (wearing your favorite shirt) has some influence on the other event (winning the game). As a result, you might continue to wear this shirt "for good luck." It is easy to see how this sort of mistaken thinking can lead to all sorts of superstitious beliefs.

Consider the following causal conclusion arrived at by Mark Twain's fic-tional character Huckleberry Finn in the following passage. How would you analyze the conclusion that he comes to?

> I've always reckoned that looking at the new moon over your left shoul-der is one of the carelessest and foolishest things a body can do. Old Hank Bunker done it once, and bragged about it; and in less than two years he got drunk and fell off a shot tower and spread himself out so that he was just a kind of layer. . . . But anyway, it all come of looking at the moon that way, like a fool.

Can you identify any of your own superstitious beliefs or practices that might have been the result of *post hoc* thinking?

Slippery Slope

The causal fallacy of *slippery slope* is illustrated in the following advice:

> Don't smoke that first marijuana cigarette. If you do, it won't be long before you are smoking hashish. Then you will soon be popping pills and snorting cocaine. Before you know it, you will be hooked on heroin and you will end your life with a drug overdose in some rat-infested hotel room.

Slippery slope thinking asserts that one undesirable action will lead to a worse action, which will lead to a worse one still, all the way down the "slippery slope" to some terrible disaster at the bottom. Although this progression may indeed happen, there is certainly no causal guarantee that it will.

Create slippery slope scenarios for one of the following warnings:

1. If you get behind on one credit card payment . . .
2. If you fail that first test . . .
3. If the United States lets El Salvador go to the Communists . . .

THINKING ACTIVITY

12.11 ▶ Identify and explain the causal pitfalls illustrated in the following examples:

1. The person who won the lottery says that she dreamt the winning number. I'm going to start writing down the numbers in my dreams.
2. Yesterday I forgot to take my vitamins and I immediately got sick. That mistake won't happen again!
3. I'm warning you — if you start missing classes, it won't be long before you flunk out of school and ruin your future.
4. I always take the first seat in the bus. Today I took another seat, and the bus broke down. And you accuse me of being superstitious!
5. I think the reason I'm not doing well in school is because I'm just not interested. Also, I simply don't have enough time to study. ◀

THINKING ACTIVITY

12.12 ▶ Many people want us to see the cause-and-effect relationships that they believe exist, and they often utilize questionable or outright fallacious reasoning. Consider the following examples:

1. Politicians assure us that a vote for them will result in "a chicken in every pot and a car in every garage."

2. Advertisers tell us that using this detergent will leave our wash "cleaner than clean, whiter than white."

3. Doctors tell us that eating a balanced diet will result in better health.

4. Educators tell us that a college degree is worth an average of $300,000 additional income over an individual's life.

5. Scientists inform us that nuclear energy will result in a better life for all of us.

In each of these examples, certain causal claims are being made about how the world operates in an effort to persuade us to adopt a certain point of view. As critical thinkers, it is our duty to evaluate these various causal claims in an effort to figure out whether they are sensible ways of organizing the world.

Explain how you might go about evaluating whether each of the following causal claims makes sense.

- *Example:* Taking the right vitamins will improve health.
- *Evaluation:* Review the medical research that examines the effect of taking vitamins on health; speak to a nutritionist; speak to a doctor.

1. Sweet Smell deodorant will keep you drier all day long.

2. Allure perfume will cause men to be attracted to you.

3. Natural childbirth will result in a more fulfilling birth experience.

4. Aspirin Plus will give you faster, longer-lasting relief from headaches.

5. Radial tires will improve the gas mileage of your car. ◀

THINKING ACTIVITY

12.13 ▶ Many of the discussions in which we engage and the essays that we write are based on an extended analysis of a cause-and-effect situation. When this happens, the concept of causality is used both to help us explain our viewpoint and to give us a means of organizing and structuring the topic we are examining. Read the following essay on the topic of teenage pregnancies and answer the questions that follow.

TEEN PREGNANCIES INVOLVE MORE THAN SEX
by Caryl Rivers

A virtual epidemic of pregnancies is under way in this nation's teen-age population; in 1979 alone, 262,700 babies were born to unwed teens. Predictably, educators, parent groups and editorial writers have responded to this news with a clamor for more and better sex education. Indeed, that is urgently necessary, but sex education alone is not the answer. We need to take a clear-eyed look at how we are bringing up young girls in this culture; otherwise, we won't come anywhere near understanding the psychological dynamics that lead little girls into unwed teen-age motherhood.

We tend to see teen-age pregnancy in terms of sexuality, which we start worrying about when girls reach puberty. In fact, that is a dozen years too late. The lessons that little girls learn when they are 2 or 5 or 7 have a direct bearing on the issues they will confront when they reach adolescence. The girl who receives early training in independence and assertiveness has a good chance of not falling into the trap of premature motherhood.

Why is this so? If you examine the sexual behavior of teen-agers, you find that, for girls, the driving force is not libido but the need for love and acceptance. When you read the letters that teen-agers send to advice columnists, one theme emerges with great frequency: "I don't want to have sex, but I'm afraid I'll lose my boyfriend."

It is very hard for a teen, at an age when peer pressure and the desire for male attention is intense, to insist that she will set her own timetable for when she will engage in sex. And, if she decides that she is ready for sex, she probably has to take the initiative in insisting on contraception. To do this requires a sense that she can and must control her own destiny. The ability to make demands, handle conflict, plan ahead — these are not qualities that a girl can develop overnight at puberty. Yet too often we do not train our girls early in these traits.

When psychologists Grace Baruch and Rosalind Barnett of the Wellesley Center for Research on Women and I surveyed the scientific literature on women and young girls, we found a number of troublesome currents. We found that girls tend to underestimate their own ability, and that they do so in pre-school and when they are seniors in college. We also found that the closer they got to adulthood, the less they valued their own sex.

Psychologist Lois Hoffman of the University of Michigan, a specialist in this field, says that girls' undeveloped self-confidence causes them to cling to an infantile fear of abandonment and a belief that their safety lies only in their dependence on others.

I saw a demonstration of this when I was a chaperone on a Girl Scout camping trip. The girls, age 9 to 12, repeatedly ran to the troop leader, seeking her approval before deciding where to put a sleeping bag or whether to put on bug spray. They needed far more help and approval in making even simple decisions than would a group of boys the same age — even though many girls of that age are bigger and stronger than boys.

One reason for this behavior is that girls get more approval when they ask for help than boys do. When psychologist Beverly Fagot studied parents of 2-year-olds, she found more expressions of approval given to girls seeking help than to boys. This was true even when the parents said they believed in treating both sexes alike.

Girls receiving such messages are less likely to take risks, to test their own abilities. Instead, they try to figure out what it is that adults want from them and concentrate on being "good little girls." They never learn to handle conflict or even temporary lack of approval.

At adolescence, too often they transfer this dependency from parents to boyfriends. They get pregnant "by accident," not really understanding that they have any responsibility for or control over what happens in their lives.

If we care, not only about teen-age pregnancy but also about the psychological health of girls, we must be on guard against the viruses of self-devaluation and dependence. We must be sure that girls are not given permission to fail because of "those little eyes so helpless and appealing."

Unfortunately, many of the school programs designed to enhance the development of girls' skills — encouraging them to try science and math, sharpening their athletic abilities — are falling by the wayside in an era of budget-cutting. It may not be easy to see how a girl's ability to do calculus or sink a free throw relates to the pregnancy statistics, but the link is there. If we help girls develop confidence and self-esteem, then perhaps they can deal with issues of sexuality as strong individuals, not merely as victims.

All the sex education in the world will not put a real dent in the pregnancy rate if we can't persuade young girls that they can — and must — control their future, not merely collide with it. ■

1. What is the basic cause-and-effect relationship the author is presenting?
2. What evidence does the author offer to support her belief in this cause-and-effect relationship?
3. Can you think of other causes of teenage pregnancy that the author has overlooked?
4. Do you think that the author has fallen into any of the causal pitfalls that we explored? Explain why or why not. ◄

Fallacies of Relevance

Many fallacious arguments appeal for support to factors that have little or nothing to do with the argument being offered. In these cases, false appeals substitute for sound reasoning and a critical examination of the issues. Such appeals, known as *fallacies of relevance,* include the following kinds of fallacious thinking:

• Appeal to authority
• Appeal to pity
• Appeal to fear
• Appeal to ignorance
• Appeal to personal attack

Appeal to Authority

In Chapter Five, *Believing and Knowing,* we explored the ways in which we sometimes appeal to various authorities to establish our beliefs or prove our points. At that time, we noted that to serve as a basis for beliefs, authorities must have legitimate expertise in the area in which they are advising — like an experienced mechanic diagnosing a problem with our car. People, however, often appeal to authorities who are not qualified to give an expert opinion. Consider the reasoning in the following advertisements. Do you think the arguments are sound? Why or why not?

> Hi. You've probably seen me out on the football field. After a hard day's work crushing halfbacks and sacking quarterbacks, I like to settle down with a cold, smooth Maltz beer.

> SONY. Ask anyone.

> Over 11 million women will read this ad. Only 16 will own the coat.

Each of these arguments is intended to persuade us of the value of a product through the appeal to various authorities. In the first case, the authority is a well-known sports figure; in the second, the authority is large numbers of people; and in the third, the authority is a select few, appealing to our desire to be exclusive ("snob appeal"). Unfortunately, none of these authorities offers legitimate expertise about the product. Football players are not beer experts; large numbers of people are often misled; and exclusive groups of people are frequently mistaken in their beliefs. To evaluate authorities properly, we have to ask:

- What are the professional credentials on which the authorities' expertise is based?
- Is their expertise in the area they are commenting on?

Appeal to Pity

Consider the reasoning in the following arguments. Do you think that the arguments are sound? Why or why not?

> I know that I haven't completed my term paper, but I really think that I should be excused. This has been a very difficult semester for me. I caught every kind of flu that came around. In addition, my brother has a drinking problem, and this has been very upsetting to me. Also, my dog died.

> I admit that my client embezzled money from the company, your honor. However, I would like to bring several facts to your attention. He is a family man, with a wonderful wife and two terrific children. He is an important member of the community. He is active in the church, coaches a little league baseball team, and has worked very hard to be a

good person who cares about people. I think that you should take these things into consideration in handing down your sentence.

In each of these arguments, the reasons offered to support the conclusions may indeed be true. They are not, however, relevant to the conclusion. Instead of providing evidence that supports the conclusion, the reasons are designed to make us feel sorry for the person involved and so agree with the conclusion out of sympathy. Although these appeals are often effective, the arguments are not sound. The probability of a conclusion can only be established by reasons that support and are relevant to the conclusion.

Appeal to Fear

Consider the reasoning in the following arguments. Do you think that the arguments are sound? Why or why not?

> I'm afraid I don't think you deserve a raise. After all, there are many people who would be happy to have your job at the salary you are currently receiving. I would be happy to interview some of these people if you really think that you are underpaid.

> If you continue to disagree with my interpretation of *The Catcher in the Rye,* I'm afraid you won't get a very good grade on your term paper.

In both of these arguments, the conclusions being suggested are supported by an appeal to fear, not by reasons that provide evidence for the conclusions. In the first case, the threat is that if you do not forgo your salary demands, your job may be in jeopardy. In the second case, the threat is that if you do not agree with the teacher's interpretation, then you will fail the course. In neither instance are the real issues — Is a salary increase deserved? Is the student's interpretation legitimate? — being discussed.

People who appeal to fear to support their conclusions are interested only in prevailing, regardless of which position might be more justified.

Appeal to Ignorance

Consider the reasoning in the following arguments. Do you think that the arguments are sound? Why or why not?

You say that you don't believe in God. But can you prove that He doesn't exist? If not, then you have to accept the conclusion that He does in fact exist.

Greco Tires are the best. No others have been proved better.

"With me, abortion is not a problem of religion. It's a problem of the Constitution. I believe that until and unless someone can establish that the unborn child is not a living human being, then that child is already protected by the Constitution, which guarantees life, liberty, and the pursuit of happiness to all of us."

Ronald Reagan, October 8, 1984

When this argument form is used, the person offering the conclusion is asking his or her opponent to *disprove* the conclusion. If the opponent is unable to do so, then the conclusion is asserted to be true. This argument form is not valid because it is the job of the person proposing the argument to prove the conclusion. Simply because an opponent cannot *dis*prove the conclusion offers no evidence that the conclusion is in fact justified. In the first example, for instance, the fact that someone cannot prove that God does not exist provides no persuasive reason for believing that he does.

Appeal to Personal Attack

Consider the reasoning in the following arguments. Do you think that the arguments are valid? Why or why not?

Your opinion on this issue is false. It's impossible to believe anything you say.

How can you have an intelligent opinion about abortion? You're not a woman, so this is a decision that you'll never have to make.

"Well, I guess I'm reminded a little bit of what Will Rogers once said about Hoover. He said it's not what he doesn't know that bothers me, it's what he knows for sure just ain't so."

Walter Mondale characterizing Ronald Reagan, October 8, 1984

This argument form has been one of the most frequently used fallacies through the ages. Its effectiveness results from ignoring the issues of the argument and focusing instead on the personal qualities of the person making the argument. By trying to discredit the other person, the effort is being made to discredit the argument — no matter what reasons are offered. This fallacy is also referred to as the *ad hominem* argument, which means "to the man" rather than to the issue, and *poisoning the well*, because we are trying to ensure that any water drawn from our opponent's well will be treated as undrinkable.

The effort to discredit can take two forms, as illustrated in the examples above. The fallacy can be *abusive* in the sense that we are directly attacking the credibility of our opponent (as in the third example). In addition, the fallacy can also be *circumstantial* in the sense that we are claiming that the person's circumstances, not character, render his or her opinion so biased or uninformed that it cannot be treated seriously (as in the second example). Other examples of the circumstantial form of the fallacy would include disregarding the views on nuclear plant safety given by an owner of one of the plants, or ignoring the views of a company comparing a product it manufactures with competing products.

THINKING ACTIVITY

12.14 ▶ Locate (or develop) an example of each of the following kinds of false appeals. For each example, explain why you think that the appeal is not warranted.

1. Appeal to authority
2. Appeal to pity
3. Appeal to fear
4. Appeal to ignorance
5. Appeal to personal attack ◀

Thinking Critically as a Way of Life

The purpose of this text has been to introduce the fundamental thinking and language abilities needed to understand the world and make informed decisions. The development of our intellectual abilities and critical attitudes is a lifelong project that requires continual study and practice, and it must be tied to our personal growth as mature and socially responsible individuals. Being a critical thinker involves not simply accumulating an arsenal of thinking skills; it also involves using these abilities to make intelligent decisions, to empathize genuinely with viewpoints other than our own, and to behave responsibly.

The following reading selection by John Sabini and Maury Silver is a fitting close to this text because it demonstrates so graphically the destructive effects of *failing* to think critically as well as suggesting ways to avoid these failures. After reading this provocative selection, answer the questions that follow.

CRITICAL THINKING AND OBEDIENCE TO AUTHORITY
by John Sabini and Maury Silver

In his 1974 book, *Obedience to Authority*, Stanley Milgram reports experiments on destructive obedience. In these experiments the subjects are faced with a dramatic choice, one apparently involving extreme pain and perhaps injury to someone else. When the subject arrives at the laboratory, the experimenter tells him (or her) and another subject — a pleasant, avuncular, middle-aged gentleman (actually an actor) — that the study concerns the effects of punishment on learning. Through a rigged drawing, the lucky subject wins the role of teacher and the experimenter's confederate becomes the "learner."

In the next stage of the experiment, the teacher and learner are taken to an adjacent room; the learner is strapped into a chair and electrodes are attached to his arm. It appears impossible for the learner to escape. While strapped in the chair, the learner diffidently mentions that he has a heart condition. The experimenter replies that while the shocks may be painful, they cause no permanent tissue damage. The teacher is instructed to read to the learner a list of word pairs, to test him on the list, and to administer punishment — an electric shock — whenever the learner errs. The teacher is given a sample shock of 45 volts (the only real shock administered in the course of the experiment). The experimenter instructs the teacher to increase the level of shock one step on the shock generator for each mistake. The generator has thirty switches labeled from 15 to 450 volts. Beneath these voltage readings are labels ranging from "SLIGHT SHOCK" to "DANGER: SEVERE SHOCK," and finally "XX."

The experiment starts routinely. At the fifth shock level, however, the confederate grunts in annoyance, and by the time the eighth shock level is reached, he shouts that the shocks are becoming painful. Upon reaching the tenth level (150 volts), he cries out, "Experimenter get me out of here! I won't be in the experiment any more! I refuse to go on!" This response makes plain the intensity of the pain and underscores the learner's right to be released. At the 270-volt level, the learner's response becomes an agonized scream, and at 300 volts the learner refuses to answer further. When the voltage is increased from 300 volts to 330 volts, the confederate shrieks in pain at each shock and gives no answer. From 330 volts on, the learner is heard from no more, and the teacher has no way of knowing whether the learner is still conscious or, for that matter, alive (the teacher also knows that the experimenter cannot tell the condition of the victim since the experimenter is in the same room as the teacher).

Typically the teacher attempts to break off the experiment many times during the session. When he tries to do so, the experimenter instructs him to continue. If he refuses, the experimenter insists, finally telling him, "You must continue. You have no other choice." If the subject still refuses, the experimenter ends the experiment.

We would expect that at most only a small minority of the subjects, a cross section of New Haven residents, would continue to shock beyond the point where the victim screams in pain and demands to be released. We certainly would expect that very, very few people would continue to the point of administering shocks of 450 volts. Indeed, Milgram asked a sample of psychiatrists and a sample of adults with various occupations to predict whether they would obey the orders of the experimenter. All of the people asked claimed that they would disobey at some point. Aware that people would be unwilling to admit that they themselves would obey such an unreasonable and unconscionable order, Milgram asked another sample of middle-class adults to predict how far other people would go in such a procedure. The average prediction was that perhaps one person in a thousand would continue to the end. The prediction was wrong. In fact, 65 percent (26/40) of the subjects obeyed to the end.

It is clear to people who are not in the experiment what they should do. The question is, *What features of the experimental situation make this clear issue opaque to subjects?* Our aim is to suggest some reasons for such a failure of thinking and action and to suggest ways that people might be trained to avoid such failures — not only in the experiment, of course, but in our practical, moral lives as well. What are some of the sources of the failure?

The experimental conditions involve entrapment, and gradual entrapment affects critical thought. One important feature inducing obedience is the gradual escalation of the shock. Although subjects in the end administered 450-volt shocks, which is clearly beyond the limits of common morality and, indeed, common sense, they began by administering 15-volt shocks, which is neither. Not only did they begin with an innocuous shock, but it increased in innocuous steps of 15 volts. This gradualness clouds clear thinking: we are prepared by our moral training to expect moral problems to present themselves categorically, with good and evil clearly distinguished. But here they were not. By administering the first shock, subjects did two things at once — one salient, the other implicit. They administered a trivial shock, a morally untroublesome act, and they in that same act committed themselves to a policy and procedure which ended in clear evil.

Surely in everyday life, becoming entrapped by gradual increases in commitment is among the most common ways for us to find ourselves engaging in immoral acts, not to mention simple folly. The corrective cannot be, of course, refusing to begin on any path which *might* lead to immorality, but rather to foresee where paths are likely to lead, and to arrange for ourselves points beyond which we will not go. One suspects that had the subjects committed themselves — publicly — to some shock level they would not exceed, they would not have found themselves pushing the 450-volt lever. We cannot expect to lead, or expect our young to lead, lives without walking on slopes: our only hope is to reduce their slipperiness.

Distance makes obedience easier. Another force sustaining obedience was the *distance* between the victim and the subject. Indeed, in one condition of the experiment, subjects were moved physically closer to the victim; in one condition they had to hold his hand on the shock plate (through Mylar insulation to protect the teachers from shock). Here twelve out of forty subjects continued to the end, roughly half the number that did so when the subjects were farther from their victim.

Being closer to the victim did not have its effect by making subjects think more critically or by giving them more information. Rather it intensified their *discomfort* at the victim's pain. Still, being face to face with someone they were hurting probably caused them at least to focus on their victim, which might well be a first step in their taking seriously the pain they were causing him.

Both the experimenter's presence and the objective requirements of the situation influenced decisions to obey authority. The experimenter's *presence* is crucial to the subjects' obedience. In one version of the experiment he issued his commands at a distance, over the phone, and obedience was significantly reduced — to nine out of forty cases. The experimenter, then, exerts powerful *social influence* over the subjects.

One way to think about the experimenter's influence is to suppose that subjects uncritically cede control of their behavior to him. But this is too simple. We suggest that if the experimenter were to have told the subjects, for example, to shine his shoes, every subject would have refused. They would have refused because shining shoes is not a sensible command within the experimental context. Thus, the experimenter's ability to confuse and control subjects follows from his issuing commands which make sense given the ostensible purpose of the experiment; he was a guide, for them, to the experiment's objective requirements.

This interpretation of the experimenter's *role* is reinforced by details of his behavior. For example, his language and demeanor were cold — bureaucratic rather than emotional or personal. The subjects were led to see his commands to them as his dispassionate interpretations of something beyond them all: the requirements of the experiment.

Embarrassment plays a key role in decisions to obey authority. The experimenter entrapped subjects in another way. Subjects could not get out of the experiment without having to explain and justify their abandoning their duty to the experiment and to him. And how were they to do this?

Some subjects attempted to justify their leaving by claiming that they could not bear to go on, but such appeals to "personal reasons" were rebutted by the experimenter's reminding them of their duty to stay. If the subjects could not escape the experiment by such claims, then how could they escape? *They could fully escape his power only by confronting him on moral grounds.* It is worth noting that this is something that virtually none of the hundreds of subjects who took part in one condition or another fully did. Failing to address the experimenter in moral terms, even "disobedient" subjects just passively resisted; they stayed in their seats refusing to continue until the experimenter declared the experiment over. They did *not* do things we might expect them to: leave, tell the experimenter off, release the victim from his seat, and so on. Why did even the disobedient subjects not confront the experimenter?

One reason seems too trivial to mention: confronting the experimenter would be embarrassing. This trivial fact may have much to do with the subjects' obedience. To confront the experimenter directly, on moral grounds, would be to disrupt in a profound way implicit expectations that grounded this particular, and indeed most, social interaction: namely, that the subject and experimenter would behave as competent moral actors. Questioning these expectations is on some accounts, at least, the source of embarrassment.

Subjects in Milgram's experiment probably did not realize that it was in part embarrassment that was keeping them in line. Had they realized that — had they realized that they were torturing someone to spare themselves embarrassment — they might well have chosen to withstand the embarrassment to secure the victim's release. But rather we suspect that subjects experience their anticipation of embarrassment as a nameless force, a distressing emotion they were not able to articulate. Thus the subjects found themselves unable to confront the experimenter on moral grounds and unable to comprehend why they could not confront the experimenter.

Emotional states affect critical thought. Obviously the emotions the subjects experienced because of the embarrassment they were avoiding and the discomfort produced by hearing the cries of the victim affected their ability to reason critically. We do not know much about the effects of emotion on cognition, but it is plausible that it has at least one effect — a focusing of attention. Subjects seem to suffer from what Milgram has called "Tunnel Vision": they restricted their focus to the technical requirements of the experimental task, for these, at least, were clear. This restriction of attention is both a consequence of being in an emotional state more generally, and it is a strategy subjects used to avoid unwanted emotional intrusions. This response to emotion is, no doubt, a formidable obstacle to critical thought. To reject the experimenter's commands, subjects had to view their situation in a perspective different from the technical one the experimenter offered them. But their immediate emotional state made it particularly difficult for them to do just that: to look at their own situation from a broader, moral perspective.

How can we train individuals to avoid destructive obedience? Our analysis leads to the view that obedience in the Milgram experiment is *not* primarily a result of a failure of knowledge, or, at least knowledge of the crucial issue of what is right or wrong to do in this circumstance. People do not need to be told that torturing an innocent person is something they should not do — even in the context of the experiment. Indeed, when the experimenter turns his back, most subjects are able to apply their moral principles and disobey. The subjects' problem instead is not knowing *how* to break off, how to make the moral response without social stickiness. If the subjects' defect is not primarily one of thinking correctly, then how is education, even education in critical thinking, to repair the defect? We have three suggestions.

First, we must teach people how to confront authority. We should note as a corollary to this effort that teaching has a wide compass: we teach people how to ride bikes, how to play the piano, how to make a sauce. Some teaching of how to do things we call education: we teach students how to do long division, how to parse sentences, how to solve physics problems. We inculcate these skills in students not by, or not only by, giving them facts or even strategies to remember, but also by giving them certain sorts of experiences, by correcting them when they err, and so on. An analogy would be useful here. Subjects in the Milgram experiment suffered not so much from a failure to remember that as center fielders they should catch fly balls as they did from an inability to do so playing under lights at night, with a great deal of wind, and when there is ambiguity about whether time-out has been called. To improve the players' ability to shag fly balls, in game conditions, we recommend practice rather than lectures, and the closer the circumstances of practice to the conditions of the actual game, the more effective the practice is likely to be.

Good teachers from Socrates on have known that the intellect must be trained; one kind of training is in criticizing authority. We teachers are authorities and hence can provide practice. Of course, we can only do that if we *remain* authorities. Practice at criticizing us if we do not respect our own authority is of little use. We do not have a recipe for being an authority who at the same time encourages criticism, but we do know that is what is important. And sometimes we can tell when we are either not encouraging criticism or when we have ceased being an authority. Both are equally damaging.

Practice with the Milgram situation might help too; it might help for students to "role play" the subjects' plight. If nothing else, doing this might bring home in a forcible way the embarrassment that subjects faced in confronting authority. It might help them develop ways of dealing with this embarrassment. Certainly, it would at least teach them that doing the morally right thing does not always "feel" right, comfortable, natural. There is no evidence about whether such experiences generalize, but perhaps they do.

If they are to confront authority assertively individuals must also be taught to use social pressure in the service of personal values. Much of current psychology and education sees thought, even critical thought, as something that goes on within individuals. But we know better than this. Whether it be in science, law, or the humanities, scholarship is and must be a public, social process. To train subjects to think critically is to train them to expose their thinking to others, to open *themselves* to criticism, from their peers as well as from authority. We insist on this in scholarship because we know that individual thinking, even the best of it, is prey to distortions of all kinds, from mere ignorance to "bad faith."

Further, the support of others is important in another way. We know that subjects who saw what they took to be two other naive subjects disobey, and thus implicitly criticize the action of continuing, were very likely to do so themselves. A subject's sense that the experimenter had the correct reading was undermined by the counter reading offered by the "other subjects." Public reinforcement of our beliefs can liberate us from illegitimate pressure. The reason for this is twofold.

Agreement with others clarifies the cognitive issue and helps us see the morally or empirically right answer to questions. But it also can have another effect — a nonrational one.

We have claimed that part of the pressure subjects faced in disobeying was produced by having to deal with the embarrassment that might emerge from confrontation. Social support provides a counterpressure. Had the subjects committed themselves publicly to disobedience before entering the experiment then they could have countered pressures produced by disobedience (during the experiment) by considering the embarrassment of admitting to others (after the experiment) that they had obeyed. Various self-help groups like Alcoholics Anonymous and Weight Watchers teach individuals to manage social pressures to serve good ends.

Social pressures are forces in our lives whether we concede them or not. The rational person, the person who would keep his action in accord with his values, must learn to face or avoid those pressures when they act to degrade his action, but equally important he ought to learn to *employ* the pressure of public commitment, the pressure implicit in making clear to others what he values, in the service of his values.

Students should know about the social pressures that operate on them. They should also learn how to use those pressures to support their own values. One reason we teach people to think critically is so that they may take charge of their own creations. We do not withhold from engineers who would create buildings knowledge about gravity or vectors or stresses. Rather we teach them to enlist this knowledge in their support.

A second area requires our attention. We need to eliminate intellectual illusions fostering nonintellectual obedience. These are illusions about human nature which the Milgram experiment renders transparent.

None of these illusions is newly discovered; others have noticed them before. But the Milgram experiment casts them in sharp relief.

The most pernicious of these illusions is the belief, perhaps implicit, that only evil people do evil things and that evil announces itself. This belief, in different guises, bewildered the subjects in several ways.

First, the experimenter looks and acts like the most reasonable and rational of people: a person of authority in an important institution. All of this is, of course, irrelevant to the question of whether his commands are evil, but it does not seem so to subjects. The experimenter had no personally corrupt motive in ordering subjects to continue, for he wanted nothing more of them than to fulfill the requirements of the experiment. So the experimenter was not seen as an evil man, as a man with corrupt desires. He was a man, like Karl Adolf Eichmann, who ordered them to do evil because he saw that evil as something required of him (and of them) by the requirements of the situation they faced together. Because we expect our morality plays to have temptation and illicit desire arrayed against conscience, our ability to criticize morally is subverted when we find evil instructions issued by someone moved by, of all things, duty. [For a fuller discussion of this point, see Hannah Arendt's *Eichmann in Jerusalem* (1965), where the issue is placed in the context of the Holocaust.]

And just as the experimenter escaped the subjects' moral criticism because he was innocent of evil desire, the subjects escaped their own moral criticism because *they too* were free of evil intent: they did not *want* to hurt the victim; they really did not. Further, some subjects, at least, took action to relieve the victim's plight — many protested the experimenter's commands, many tried to give the victim hints about the right answers — thus further dramatizing their purity of heart. And because they acted out of duty rather than desire, the force of their conscience against their own actions was reduced. But, of course, none of this matters in the face of the evil done.

The "good-heartedness" of people, their general moral quality, is something very important to us, something to which we, perhaps rightly, typically pay attention. But if we are to think critically about the morality of our own and others' acts, we must see through this general fact about people to assess the real moral quality of the acts they do or are considering doing.

A second illusion from which the subjects suffered was a confusion about the notion of responsibility. Some subjects asked the experimenter who was responsible for the victim's plight. And the experimenter replied that he was. We, and people asked to predict what they would do in the experiment, see that this is nonsense. We see that the experimenter cannot discharge the subjects' responsibility — no more than the leader of a bank-robbing gang can tell his cohorts, "Don't worry. If we're caught, I'll take full responsibility." We are all conspirators when we participate in planning and executing crimes.

Those in charge have the right to assign *technical* responsibility to others, responsibility for executing parts of a plan, but moral responsibility cannot be given, taken away, or transferred. Still, these words — mere words — on the part of the experimenter eased subjects' "sense of responsibility." So long as the institutions of which we are a part are moral, the need to distinguish technical from moral responsibility need not arise. When those institutions involve wanton torture, we are obliged to think critically about this distinction.

There is a third illusion illustrated in the Milgram experiment. When subjects threatened to disobey, the experimenter kept them in line with prods, the last of which was, "You have no choice; you must go on." Some subjects fell for this, believed that they had no choice. But this is also nonsense. There may be cases in life when we *feel* that we have no choice, but we know we always do. Often feeling we have no choice is really a matter of believing that the cost of moral action is greater than we are willing to bear — in the extreme we may not be willing to offer our lives, and sometimes properly so. Sometimes we use what others have done to support the claim that we have no choice; indeed, some students interpret the levels of obedience in the Milgram experiment as proof that the subjects had no choice. But we all know they did. Even in extreme situations, we have a choice, whether we choose to exercise it or not. The belief that our role, our desires, our past, or the actions of others preclude our acting morally is a convenient but illusory way of distancing ourselves from the evil that surrounds us. It is an illusion from which we should choose to disabuse our students. ■

1. The authors of this article describe the reasons they believe that the majority of subjects in the Stanley Milgram experiment were willing to inflict apparent pain and injury on an innocent person. Explain what you believe were the most significant reasons responsible for this disturbing absence of critical thinking and moral responsibility.

2. The authors argue that the ability to think critically must be developed within a social context, that we must expose our thinking to the criticism of others because "individual thinking, even the best of it, is prey to distortions of all kinds, from mere ignorance to 'bad faith.'" Evaluate this claim, supporting your answer with examples and reasons.

3. The authors contend that in order to act with critical thinking and moral courage, people must be taught to confront authority. Explain how you think people could be taught and encouraged to confront authority in a constructive way.

4. "Even in extreme situations, we have a choice, whether we choose to exercise it or not. The belief that our role, our desires, our past, or the actions of others preclude our acting morally is a convenient but illusory way of distancing ourselves from the evil that surrounds us." Evaluate this claim and give examples and reasons to support your view. ◄

ILLUSTRATION ACKNOWLEDGMENTS

Pages 143, 144: Photo by Ronald C. James.

Page 145: bird/rabbit: From *Psychology*, third edition, by Camille B. Wortman and Elizabeth F. Loftus, copyright © 1988, Alfred A. Knopf, Inc. Reproduced with permission of McGraw-Hill, Inc.

Page 149: "The Investigation" cartoon: © John Jonik. Reproduced with permission. This cartoon first appeared in*Psychology Today*, February 1984.

Page 155: Illustration from "Long-Term Memory for a Common Object" by Raymond S. Nickerson and Marilyn J. Adams in *Cognitive Psychology 11*, 287–307. Copyright © 1979 by Academic Press. Used by permission of Academic Press, and the authors.

Page 159: From *Psychology and Life,* 12/e by Philip G. Zimbardo. Copyright © 1985, 1979 by Scott, Foresman and Company. Reprinted by permission of Harper Collins Publishers.

Page 297: Drawing by M. Stevens; © 1985 The New Yorker Magazine, Inc.

Page 371: Map of the Western hemisphere © 1982, 1990 by JesseLevine, 7040 Via Valverde, San Jose, CA 95135. Used by permission.

Page 373: Tree used by permission of the author.

ACKNOWLEDGMENTS

Page 6: "Scientists Pinpoint Brain Irregularities in Drug Addicts" by Daniel Goleman: Copyright © 1990 The New York Times Company. Reprinted by permission.

Page 20: From *The Autobiography of Malcolm X* by Malcolm X, with the assistance of Alex Haley. Copyright © 1964 by Alex Haley and Malcolm X. Copyright © 1965 by Alex Haley and Betty Shabazz. Reprinted by permission of Random House Inc.

Page 57: Material by Peter Rondinone used by permission of the author.

Page 79: "Life Sentence: Individual Autonomy, Medical Technology, and the 'Common Good'" by Howard Moody: Reprinted with permission. Copyright Oct. 12, 1987, *Christianity & Crisis,* 537 West 121st St., New York, N.Y. 10027.

Page 84: "Court's Hideous Decision Makes Life the Ultimate Absurdity" by Frank Morriss: Reprinted with permission from *The Wanderer,* 201 Ohio Street, St. Paul, MN 55107–2096; February 5,1987, p. 4.

Page 86: From *Mortal Choices* by Ruth Macklin. Copyright © 1987 by Ruth Macklin. Reprinted by permission of Pantheon Books, a division of Random House, Inc

Page 121: "Young Hate," by David Shenk, *CV Magazine.* Reprinted by permission.

Page 126: "A Month in the Life of Campus Bigotry": Excerpted with permission from National Institute Against Prejudice and Violence, 31 South Greene Street, Baltimore, MD 21201.

Page 128: "Profiles of Today's Youth: They Couldn't Care Less" by Michael Oreskes: Copyright © 1990 by The New York Times Company. Reprinted by permission.

Page 133: "Looking Ahead: More Mouths, Less Food": From *The Washington Spectator,* Vol. 16, No. 10, May 15, 1990. © 1990, The Public Concern Foundation, Inc.

Page 162: Material from the February 22, 1965, *New York Times:* Copyright © 1965 by The New York Times Company. Reprinted by permission.

Page 163: Extract from *Life Magazine* © TIME WARNER. REPRINTED WITH PERMISSION.

Page 163: Extract from *The New York Post,* February 22, 1965, reprinted by permission.

Page 558: Reprinted with permission from *Science News*, the weekly newsmagazine of science, copyright 1984 by Science Service, Inc.:

Page 559: Reprinted with permission from *Science News*, the weekly newsmagazine of science, copyright 1984 by Science Service, Inc.

Page 560: "For a National Effort to Develop a Vaccine to Counteract AIDS" by Robert E. Pollack: Copyright © 1985 by The New York Times Company. Reprinted by permission.

Page 567: Article by Caryl Rivers reprinted by permission of *The Los Angeles Times*, and the author.

Page 574: Article by John Sabini and Maury Silver reprinted from *National Forum: The Phi Kappa Phi Journal*, Winter 1985, pp. 13–17, by permission.

Index